# Meeting the Standards

## Social Studies Readings for K-6 Educators

▼ ▼ ▼ ▼ ▼

edited by

**Mary E. Haas** and
**Margaret A. Laughlin**

National Council for the Social Studies
www.socialstudies.org

National Council for the Social Studies
3501 Newark Street, NW
Washington, DC 20016
202 966-7840
www.socialstudies.org

Editorial staff on this publication: Michael Simpson, Terri S. Ackerman, Rich Hancuff, Beth Hatch, Melissa Spead
Art Director/Production: Gene Cowan
Cover Design: Paul Wolski

Library of Congress Catalog Card Number: 96-071672
ISBN: 0-87986-072-3

Printed in the United States of America
Second printing, October 1999

9 8 7 6 5 4 3 2

# TABLE OF CONTENTS

# CREDITS

National Council for the Social Studies expresses appreciation to the following organizations and institutions for granting permission to reprint articles from their publications.

American Bar Association

Association For Childhood Education International

Association for Supervision and Curriculum Development

Center for Civic Education

Educators for Social Responsibility

Helen Dwight Reid Educational Foundation

Massachusetts Global Education Program

National Council for Geographic Education

National Council on Economic Education

National Education Association

National Science Teachers Association

New Jersey Council for the Social Studies

Southern Poverty Law Center

STS Press

Texas A&M

Webster University

Minor editorial changes have been made in a number of articles to prevent confusion arising from time-specific references (e.g., the words "next year").

Figures and tables not considered essential to articles have often been dropped, and references in the original articles to these figures and tables have been amended to avoid confusion.

# PREFACE

The fundamental goals of most social studies programs are developing citizenship responsibilities and handing on the cultural heritage of a nation to the next generation. Democratic citizenship not only bestows certain fundamental rights but also places the burden of numerous responsibilities on our citizens. In our democratic republic, the duties related to the office of citizen are among our most important tasks. The schools—along with other important social institutions such as the family; church, temple, synagogue, or mosque; community; and the media—all have important roles to assume in the development of citizenship responsibilities. With a rapidly changing interdependent world, educators need to prepare young learners for their citizenship responsibilities as the world moves forward to the twenty-first century. Social studies is the curriculum content area best equipped to help young learners prepare to become active citizens.

Recognizing the changing educational climate, the demands for effective teaching of strong content and basic skills, and the need to develop nationally recognized social studies standards, a task force of members of National Council for the Social Studies (NCSS)—along with the advice and suggestions from members of the larger social studies community—prepared a set of curriculum standards for use by social studies educators. In 1994, NCSS approved and published *Expectations of Excellence: Curriculum Standards for Social Studies*. Ten thematic strands were identified:

- ❶ CULTURE
- ❷ TIME, CONTINUITY, AND CHANGE
- ❸ PEOPLE, PLACES, AND ENVIRONMENTS
- ❹ INDIVIDUAL DEVELOPMENT AND IDENTITY
- ❺ INDIVIDUALS, GROUPS, AND INSTITUTIONS
- ❻ POWER, AUTHORITY, AND GOVERNANCE
- ❼ PRODUCTION, DISTRIBUTION, & CONSUMPTION
- ❽ SCIENCE, TECHNOLOGY, AND SOCIETY
- ❾ GLOBAL CONNECTIONS
- ❿ CIVIC IDEALS AND PRACTICES

The first seven strands are social science discipline oriented, while the remaining three are multidisciplinary. Each interconnected strand offers appropriate content for teachers to draw upon to enhance student learning in grades K-12. For the most part, there is agreement among leaders in social studies education and the social science disciplines that the ten strands represent key concepts that form an important base for teaching and learning social studies. The NCSS standards document should be viewed as an overarching umbrella under which other social science disciplines standards are viewed. No single discipline provides a sufficiently broad perspective of the social studies.

State and local adoption of the ten strands allows students, parents, community members, and educators at all grade levels, and in several disciplines, to engage in discussions that are substantive and meaningful. The strands build on the NCSS definition of social studies as being the "Integrated study of the social sciences and humanities to promote civic competence" whose primary purpose "is to help young people develop the ability to make informed and reasoned decisions for the public good as citizens of a culturally diverse, democratic society in an interdependent world" (1992). The NCSS Curriculum Standards are in keeping with the national movement to develop rigorous educational standards to ensure that the United States, as a nation, will remain competitive in the marketplace of a global economy.

The NCSS publication *Meeting the Standards: Readings for K-6 Educators* is the first of several forthcoming publications that focus on the ten social studies strands. This publication, along with others in the series, is intended to help social studies educators design, implement, and assess social studies teaching and learning practices. This first publication consists of a series of articles reprinted from a variety of sources and includes practical lessons, thoughtful reflections, and discussions related to several social studies curriculum issues.

In deciding which articles to include in this publication, the editors solicited nominations of articles for possible inclusion from more than three hundred elementary teachers, administrators, university faculty members, editors of social studies or social studies-related professional journals, and others who have a strong interest in social studies. We thank all of our colleagues who took time from their busy schedules to offer valuable suggestions concerning articles considered for inclusion in this publication.

A number of articles selected were nominated by one or more persons, and we, the editors, reached a consensus on the final selection of articles. The criteria used to select particular articles included the following. The articles presented

- a range of authors representing a variety of perspectives and learning activities;
- include both theory and research, as well as practical examples of teaching and learning practices at both the primary and intermediate grade levels;
- address important content and concepts inherent in the standards;

- promote active student learning both in classroom settings and in the larger community; and
- include the creative use of textbooks, instructional materials, and teaching strategies.

The first ten chapters of this publication consist of reprinted articles that address one or more of the ten strands identified in the social studies standards. In reviewing several hundred articles, it soon became evident that important issues related to curriculum development and teaching social studies extended well beyond the thematic focus of the ten strands. Therefore, the book also includes five chapters that pay particular attention to issues in social studies curriculum, social studies and integrated studies, relating literature to social studies instruction, cooperative learning, and student assessment in social studies. The inclusion of these articles provides a broader and richer context for planning the social studies curriculum and selecting instructional activities.

In making the final selection of articles, the editors included a number of articles written by scholars and teachers who had an expertise in fields other than social studies. Their contributions to our field are likely to stimulate new thinking about the social studies standards and related issues. Effective teaching and learning practices are often cross-cultural and worthy of being shared across international borders. Therefore, as editors, we were pleased to find that several of the authors teach and live beyond the borders of the United States. Their perspectives on social studies are valuable assets to social studies educators in the United States.

The editors have included an already published article, "Social Studies Standards: A Pathway to Professional Development" as an introduction to this publication. The article provides an overview of the standards and discusses their role in curriculum and professional development. It establishes a tone for the other readings that have been included in the publication. Each of the chapters has an introduction that elaborates on the individual standards, or issues, and provides an overview of the articles. The chapters may be read in any sequence that makes sense to the reader and best meets his or her needs. Readers are reminded of the overarching nature of the strands and that a number of the articles could well have been placed in one of several chapters.

The editors would like to thank Michael Simpson, NCSS publications director, and other NCSS staff members who worked on this publication and its distribution. We also express our appreciation to the authors and publishers who allowed us to reprint their articles. A listing of credits follows the table of contents.

Finally, the editors welcome comments from readers about the content of this publication. It is designed to help elementary teachers by providing information and suggestions for effective social studies planning, teaching, and learning. Social studies educators are faced with the challenge of preparing a curriculum designed to pass on cultural heritage, and to prepare young learners for the responsibility of citizenship in an increasingly interdependent world.

**MARY E. HAAS**
Professor of Curriculum and Instruction
West Virginia University, Morgantown

**MARGARET A. LAUGHLIN**
Professor of Education
University of Wisconsin-Green Bay

# INTRODUCTION

## Social Studies Standards:
## A Pathway to Professional Development

**H. Michael Hartoonian**
**Margaret A. Laughlin**

*"One must not always think so much about what one should do, but, rather what one should be. Our works do not ennoble us; but we must ennoble our work."*

*Meister Eckhart*

The traditional role of standards within the elementary school curriculum is that of asking important questions regarding the construction of quality curriculum and instructional programs. The NCSS curriculum standards, *Expectations of Excellence: Curriculum Standards for Social Studies* (1994) serves such a role, as well as establishes a framework or umbrella under which the other social studies discipline standards can find a home. The NCSS standards were designed to establish the scope of the social studies program. That is, they help to determine how single social studies disciplines, such as, anthropology and political science; and integrated content, such as, globgD connections, will be structured using sophisticated knowledge drawn from the several social science disciplines, the arts and humanities, and the natural sciences and mathematics. The scope of such social studies programs can be pictured in the chart.

These interrelated themes offer a broad framework for curriculum planning, design, and assessment.

In addition to establishing a curriculum framework, another and even more important role for the NCSS standards is to have them serve as a discussion paper or script which allows educators to better communicate with one another as well as with the several fields of inquiry that make up the content of our craft. This script provides the common grammar and logic that will inform professional development designs, and foster understanding of the fundamental knowledge of social studies.

The standards enable teachers to communicate across grade levels and subject specializations with one another and with others (i.e., students, parents, colleagues, and the larger community) by using a common vocabulary. For example, the curriculum standards have identified the knowledge, skills, and essential understandings students should gain as they study and work their way through school. To this end, teachers need to plan meaningful instructional activities to help students achieve important social studies content, skills, and attitudes.

| SCOPE (Themes) | SEQUENCE |
|---|---|
| | K 1 2 3 4 5 6 7 8 9 10 11 12 |
| | I CULTURE |
| | II TIME, CONTINUITY, AND CHANGE |
| | III PEOPLE, PLACES, AND ENVIRONMENT |
| | IV INDIVIDUAL DEVELOPMENT AND IDENTITY |
| | V INDIVIDUALS, GROUPS, AND INSTITUTIONS |
| | VI POWER, AUTHORITY, AND GOVERNANCE |
| | VII PRODUCTION, DISTRIBUTION, AND CONSUMPTION |
| | VIII SCIENCE, TECHNOLOGY, AND SOCIETY |
| | IX GLOBAL CONNECTIONS |
| | X CIVIC IDEALS AND PRACTICES |

As teachers reflect on the ten social studies themes they should grapple with such questions as:

- Why teach social studies?
- What information, knowledge, and wisdom constitute a quality social studies program for our school?
- What do our students need to know to confront major issues affecting them and their world?
- What instructional activities will allow students to be active learners? What does this mean in my classroom?
- How can our students meet the performance expectations inherent in strong social studies programs?
- What new information do I as a teacher need to know within my content field (the several social science disciplines) to be an effective teacher of social studies? How will I update my information base?
- How will I apply new findings from research concerning the social science disciplines, effective teaching, student learning, student assessment, and so forth in my classroom?

The social studies standards can help teachers address all of these questions and more, when they are used as a dialogue to engage us and to help us create a community of scholars.

There is no more exciting field of study than that of human individuals and society, both women and men, in different settings and cultures, in different time periods, engaging in the ordinary and extraordinary events of daily life. We should make learning social studies irresistible for students. What drama is more exciting than studying about people who make a difference in our lives past and present? To get us to this point, we must also use the standards to construct and implement professional development programs.

Let us start with a truism: a teacher can only teach two things — what he or she knows, and who he or she is (character). In their broadest sense, knowledge means an understanding of the content fields we teach, our instructional practices, human growth and development, and the larger social context for learning known as the community. Broadly speaking, character means integrity, a commitment to excellence, achievement, and justice.

All of us need to address these factors of knowledge and character. We know, for example, that the half-life of a baccalaureate degree is about 3 years or less. That is, one-half of what we have learned is obsolete or irrelevant within 2 or 3 years after graduation.

What does this indicate to those of us who have been teaching for 10 or 25 years, or even longer? How do we confront new information as it becomes available to us? How do we conceptualize an ever-changing world? On the other hand, our character is challenged every day by a society that seems to have misplaced many of its values. Yet, the community expects educators, and rightly so, to be ethical pillars of society and role models for students. Meeting these challenges, we believe, will help to ensure the survival of our republic.

How can the NCSS standards help with all of this?

With regard to knowledge, the standards provide a curriculum design that is comprehensive. It is a design that will allow teachers to construct a discipline-oriented and integrated contemporary curriculum that addresses both theory and instruction "best practices." But, especially important, when it comes to knowledge, the 10 themes provide an excellent blueprint for quality professional development programs. Each of the themes establishes a framework within which K-12 teachers can learn and work together.

All of the standards have a K-12 content component which becomes more sophisticated as young learners progress grade by grade through school. For example, the content standard "civic ideals and practices" may require young learners to help construct rules for their classroom which they will practice within their school. Older children may engage in community service by volunteering to tutor younger children in their school or they may gather, analyze, and apply information about a policy issue facing their local community, such as, the location of a new highway or shopping center.

High school students might examine the role of the media in shaping public opinion to support or defeat a political candidate or an issue facing the community or state, e.g., to extend the school day by an hour and/or the school year to 240 days. Activities such as these allow students to understand aspects of civic participation with increasing degrees of active involvement in shaping policies which affect them. Such activities lay the foundation for later civic action in their adult lives.

Numerous staff development opportunities enable teachers to work together to develop the themes of the standards. For example, colleagues or outside resource people (discipline content specialists) could be invited to help teachers gain content information on each theme, to become aware of additional resources for teaching the content, and to plan effective learning activities. Other consultants who have expertise in assessing student performance, and so forth could also be invited to provide needed staff development. Teachers could also take advantage of nearby conferences and workshops which offer content and methodology for implementing the NCSS standards. Such programs should include attendance at the annual NCSS national, regional, and state social studies meetings.

While the NCSS curriculum standards were designed to serve as a K-12 framework within which all other social studies discipline standards can and should find a home, perhaps their most important role will be in the establishment and design of professional development programs that help all of us enhance our understanding of who we are, what we know, and what we want our students to learn.

Copies of *Expectations of Excellence: Curriculum Standards for Social Studies* (1994) may be obtained from National Task Force for Standards in Social Studies, Bulletin #89, BU890094 for $15.00 ($12.75 for NCSS members) plus $2.50 for postage and handling. Call 1 800 683-0812.

## ABOUT THE AUTHORS

H. Michael Hartoonian is Past President of NCSS. Margaret A. Laughlin is a Professor of Education at the University of Wisconsin-Green Bay, where she teaches both elementary and secondary social studies methods courses concurrently, as well as courses in curriculum and foundations. Dr. Laughlin is an active member in NCSS and has published in *Social Education*. She is also active in the Wisconsin statewide social studies curriculum and assessment committees and is a vice-president of the Wisconsin Council for the Social Studies.

# PART 1

## ● CULTURE

Humans create, learn, and adapt culture. Culture has an impact on our lives by giving unique individuals a common set of beliefs, knowledge, values, and traditions. The United States is multicultural, democratic, capitalistic, and increasingly more technological. Throughout their lives, students must learn to function as participants with others in various settings. Children need to realize that all people, even those in a single setting, have perspectives influenced by the cultures of their heritage and region. Because cultures are created by people, students need to recognize that there are various aspects of culture that allow people to live and work together, and that cultural differences are expressions of an individual's unique cultural heritage.

When studying cultures, students seek answers to such questions as, What are the common characteristics of different cultures? How are people alike? What are the important differences in people? How do belief systems, such as religion or political ideals of a culture, influence the other parts of the culture? How do cultures change to accommodate different ideas and beliefs? The study of culture typically appears across the social studies curriculum in lessons, units, and courses dealing with geography, history, anthropology, and multicultural issues.

The selected articles address the rationale and issues related to teaching culture to elementary students as well as suggesting how and what to teach. All of the authors advocate active learning by the students as they seek similarities, differences, and explanations. Soldier discusses several important concepts and generalizations of anthropology for children and suggests ways to incorporate these into the school curriculum beginning in the earliest grades. Gloria Ladson-Billings explains why it is necessary for teachers to confront stereotyping and prejudice in the classroom and suggests ways to accomplish this goal.

Sesow et al. recognize that all classrooms have students of various cultures. They suggest concrete ways to approach the study of culture by investigating diversity in each classroom. Laney and Moseley provide a sample lesson, "Who Packed the Suitcase?", in which students assume the roles of anthropologists.

Because the study of Native Americans has long been an important part of the elementary curriculum, several articles about Native Americans are included. Harvey suggests concepts to use in the study of Native Americans across the curriculum. Weatherford illustrates the advanced nature of Native American culture by pointing out its worldwide impact — particularly its impact on American political institutions with origins in Native American cultures. Important links between weather, climate, soil, and cultural geography are examined in an extensive, interdisciplinary unit on Native American food by Marturano titled "Horticulture and Human Culture." Each article is intended both to inform the reader and stimulate thinking about the impact of culture on a society. The lessons serve as models that can be used with any number of different cultural and ethnic groups.

# 1

# Making Anthropology a Part of the Elementary Social Studies Curriculum

## Lee Little Soldier

Anthropology is a discipline about which much of the general public knows little. It is a mystery to many educators as well. The lack of awareness results in part from not teaching anthropology as a discipline in its own right in our schools. Inasmuch as anthropology is a social science, however, certain topics and themes that overlap with such other social science disciplines as sociology, economics, and the like are taught both at elementary and secondary levels. Since anthropology is rarely taught as a separate subject below the college level, students find it difficult to discuss it apart from other social sciences. Teachers have consequently overlooked anthropology as an important discipline for developing integrated social science experiences for children. It can, moreover, provide opportunities for language enhancement and activities in the fine arts.

People within any given culture tend to be ethnocentric and believe their way of living the natural or logical way. Children are naturally egocentric and ethnocentric. Inasmuch as anthropology is built upon the very broad concept of culture, it offers promise for providing a realistic focus for the social studies curriculum in the elementary grades. To understand their world and their place in it, children first need an awareness of their own culture. This understanding can later be enhanced by comparison and contrast with other cultures.

## CULTURE BASIC TO ANTHROPOLOGY

Culture as a basic concept is the sum total of a group's survival response in a particular locale or environment. It is a way of explaining non-biological human variation. Study of a particular culture attempts to look at how and why people of that culture have interpreted their world and given meaning to their existence. People belong to societies but they have cultures within which social organizations or institutions exist. These organizations or institutions regulate the social behavior of their members. Children should be exposed to the concept of culture because it is the only means by which they can organize data concerning human behavior in contextual settings and develop understanding of how and why groups of people differ from one another in their customs, habits, and traditions.

Generally it is upon entering school that young children initially encounter persons of other races and cultures. They are required to interact with children and adults whose physical characteristics, language, and ways of reacting in social situations may differ from those to which they are accustomed. They may laugh, cry, or otherwise react to these differences on an emotional level. In culturally diverse schools, the need for developing the notion of cultural relativity must hold high priority; however, in all classrooms it is necessary to promote the understanding that the behavior of all people must be judged within the context in which it occurs. Cross-cultural comparisons are legitimate; cross-cultural exclusion of a different social behavior as invalid is not.

## CONCEPTS AND GENERALIZATIONS

What concepts and generalizations from anthropology are appropriate for elementary students? First we should develop the understanding that people are more similar than dissimilar because all persons have the same basic needs for such tangible items as food, clothing, and shelter. Less obvious but equally important are the needs for such less tangible things as safety, recreation, and a sense of belonging. With examples from the lives of children in the classroom, teachers can begin to develop a sense of the unity of humankind. Looking at the cultural and individual variations among families represented in class and helping pupils become aware of these differences, teachers can move to the important generalization that these needs are met in many ways by different families and cultures. We begin at the children's level of thinking and ways of doing things and expand their understanding as they move toward acceptance of how others do these things. By understanding themselves, children begin to understand others.

In addition, children need to acquire a sense of the relationship between the environment and the ways in which people have met their needs. By comparing the material cultures of different groups of people in diverse locations, pupils may, for example, perceive rice as a diet staple of Asian groups not as an idiosyncratic choice, but as due rather to climate, soil, and water availability in parts of Asia. Children should be encouraged to appreciate differences in food, clothing, and shelter as wondrous ways in which human beings have adapted for survival within a range of environmental differences around the globe.

Because we are social beings, it is necessary to develop the concept of interdependence. People depend on one another to satisfy their needs. At the present time, societies are so highly specialized and technical that our survival is contingent upon getting along with others whose goals and values are not identical with and may run contrary to ours.

Reprinted from *Social Education*, January 1990, Volume 54, Number 1. Copyright 1990 by National Council for the Social Studies.

Children can begin to understand the interdependence of the roles of various members within the family, school, and community and how each person's contribution helps make each social group function.

After developing an understanding of likenesses, the teacher can focus on the generalization that, although people are physically different from one another, these differences are superficial. The usual comparisons are skin coloration, hair, facial features, height, weight, and so on. The positive nature of diversity is a theme that should run throughout the year and permeate the curriculum. When children grasp that people are basically the same the world over, despite differences in physical characteristics, they can begin to deal with the idea that cultural variations are normal, expected, and positive.

Children can learn something about a people by studying how they meet their needs for food, clothing, and shelter, their family patterns, holidays and other special days, their fine arts, recreation, religion, and traditions. Although material culture is emphasized, even young children can gain some understanding of a people's worldview by interrelating these aspects of the culture over time and understanding the concept of values. Thus units dealing with an isolated aspect of culture or what is superficial may promote more misunderstanding than understanding. Black History Week and American Indian Day, unless part of a larger context, become mere excursions into ways of life that may be foreign to children and be perceived as quaint or archaic.

Studies of a culture or part of a culture must be placed in space and time. Both of these concepts are difficult for young children to grasp but are critical to understanding any group of people. Where are the people under study to be found? If environment affects the culture, maps and globes must be used. What era are we going to study? Are we going to study present-day Native Americans, pre-Columbian, or that period in our history of westward expansion that became the focus of the cowboys and Indians films? A sense of chronology must be developed as well. Time lines that begin with the child's own life span and expand to include wider and wider social circles can help pupils gain some sense of how and why cultures change.

We should also help children acquire several concepts about culture. Some obvious examples are the borrowing from other cultures that has transpired, making Mexican food standard fare, cowboy boots the dress code of the day in certain parts of the country, and territorial-style homes the fashion in the Southwest. Help children examine their own lives for examples that show how this borrowing has taken place and affected their own lives.

Cultures are learned. Children recognize and learn acceptable behavior by watching and listening to their own family members, practicing that behavior, being rewarded for certain kinds of behavior, and punished perhaps for others. What is acceptable behavior in one family but not in another may represent a basic cultural difference or merely an individual family difference. (This is an important thing for teachers to understand too, particularly when diverse culture groups are represented in the classroom.)

Family members and larger social groups share cultures. Sharing and borrowing are means by which cultures change. We learn from one another by borrowing and sharing and thus acquire new ways of doing things that enhance our lives. When we add to our own culture, we enrich it.

Anthropology can be incorporated into the curriculum in various ways. A particular facet of life, such as the arts, may organize experiences for children that embody diversity. Focusing upon the basic needs of human beings for food, clothing, and shelter makes clear the comparisons and contrasts across cultures. More typically, we can deal with topics traditionally found in the social studies curriculum, such as celebrations of certain holidays and special days, the study of ancient civilizations and dinosaurs, and American Indians and Eskimos, all of which draw heavily on anthropological content. The latter approach may appear least valuable unless emphasis is shifted from particular facts to basic understanding and generalizations about human beings.

## ACTIVITIES

If teachers wish, for example, to incorporate a study of "Indians" into the curriculum, it is important to begin not by selecting books, materials, and activities, but by determining the goals and objectives for the units in terms of desired changes in pupil behavior. In addition, the unit should be planned to articulate with other aspects of the curriculum, to provide a variety of materials and activities that cut across subject matter lines, and to reinforce and enrich the new learning beyond what is done in the unit.

Many activities used in elementary classrooms can help build basic anthropological understanding. It should be reiterated, however, that activities should be selected on the basis of goals and objectives to be accomplished within a particular strand of the curriculum. The activities that follow are highlighted only to show how they might be used to reinforce or enrich basic concepts and generalizations from anthropology that are appropriate for elementary grades.

1. *Generalization: Relationship of the environment and the ways people meet their needs.* When children pop popcorn, study the origin of corn—where it grows and how and why it has become a cultural focus for many Native American groups. *Corn Is Maize* by Aliki might be an appropriate book to introduce to children.
2. *Generalization: Different cultures use symbols to communicate with each other.* Show pupils symbols such as a flag, stop sign, or cross. Discuss what these symbols mean and help pupils discuss other symbols in our culture. Emphasize that these symbols are examples of culture because they represent ideas that people within our culture agree upon and use to communicate with one another.

3. *Generalization: Artifacts identify how a culture has developed.* Place a collection of diverse objects in a bag that you might call your time capsule. Have the children look at each object and speculate about how people from another planet or a future era might view these artifacts and how they might use the items. You may include such things as paper clips, toothpicks, a sponge, plastic cups, etc.

4. *Generalization: Cultures change over time as a consequence of industrialization, technology, and borrowing from other cultures.* Obtain reprints from the library or commercial sources of outdated mail order catalogs. Have the pupils compare items in different catalogs with items in a current catalog. Ask them to locate items in the older catalogs that are no longer available and consider why these things are not featured in current catalogs. Have them trace the development of electronic equipment and locate items that are relatively new in the catalog. The concept of cultural change is difficult to grasp unless it can be brought into focus by using items that are significant to the learner.

The above generalizations represent a small sample of the possibilities that exist for teaching basic concepts and generalizations from the social sciences with an emphasis on anthropology, after goals and objectives for units and lessons have been clearly defined.

## SUMMARY

Anthropology can provide cohesion for the elementary social studies curriculum and help provide direction for determining what should be taught. Because of our shrinking world and the multicultural nature of society, it is imperative that teachers help children develop an awareness of their social world and their important place in it.

## SUGGESTED RESOURCES

Aliki. *Corn Is Maize: The Gift of the Indians*. New York: Crowell, 1982.

Farmer, Rod, and lane Schisgall. "The Culture Box: Teaching with Artifacts." *Southern Social Studies Quarterly* (Spring 1982): 5-9.

Messick, Rosemary. "Implementing the Anthropology Strand in Elementary Programs." *Social Studies Review* (Fall 1983): 45-50.

Olson, Tazuko. "Child's Cultural Awareness." *Social Studies* (January/February 1982): 25-31.

Pang, Valerie. "Teaching about Ethnic Heritage: More than Costumes and Unusual Food." *Learning* 88 (January 1988): 56-57.

Lee Little Soldier is Professor and Chair of Elementary, Bilingual, Reading, and Early Childhood Education at Texas Tech University, Lubbock. [1990 note]

# 2

# I Don't See Color, I Just See Children
## *Dealing with Stereotyping and Prejudice in Young Children*

**Gloria Ladson-Billings**

*Red-headed, freckled-faced Marco was completing an art project when he looked up at the African-American parent helper and then looked across at the preschool's only two African-American children playing at the puzzle table. "Which one is yours," asked Marco. The parent smiled and said, "The little girl, Jessica, is my daughter." Marco replied, "I knew one of those black ones was yours." The [W]hite teachers at the preschool were noticeably uncomfortable with Marco's comment. On another day, Marco proudly displayed a beautiful hand-knitted sweater his grandmother sent him from Italy. The African-American parent helper admired his sweater and jokingly suggested that maybe she should live at Marco's house so that she, too, could receive such lovely gifts. "You can't live at my house," Marco laughed. "Only [W]hite people live at my house, no black ones." The [W]hite teachers seemed embarrassed and one reprimanded Marco for not displaying a sharing attitude.*

## THE MYTH OF COLOR BLINDNESS

The vignette related above is a true story. Marco, the child of recent Italian immigrants, spoke openly and honestly about the reality he observed. His teachers, however, who never discussed student racial and/or ethnic background were playing a dangerous game of ignoring reality. Perhaps they were doing so because they thought that by ignoring it, the problem would disappear. Perhaps they were doing it because they wanted to appear "fair" or "neutral" toward all of their students. Most likely, they were doing it because discussions regarding racial and ethnic differences are difficult for adults to handle and they believed they are even more difficult for young children.

During the presentation of the landmark Brown vs. Board of Education case that declared that separate education was inherently unequal education, the NAACP legal team used the social science research of Kenneth and Mamie Clark to demonstrate that children were aware of racial differences at a very early age (Clark, 1955). Unfortunately, children's awareness of racial difference often is dismissed or ignored by the adults around them, particularly their teachers.

In the highly acclaimed book *White Teacher*, Vivian Paley (1979) confronts her own battle with the pretense

Reprinted from *Social Studies and the Young Learner*, November/December 1992, Volume 5, Number 2. Copyright 1992 by National Council for the Social Studies.

of color blindness. Until she is confronted by an African-American parent, Ms. Paley continued to do those things that marginalized and stereotyped children of diverse racial and ethnic backgrounds. The parent told Paley:

My children are [B]lack They don't look like your children. They know they're [B]lack and we want it recognized. It's a positive difference, an interesting difference, and a comfortable natural difference. At least it could be more so, if you teachers learned to value difference more. What you value you talk about (p. 138).

In my own teaching of White student teachers, it became apparent how uncomfortable the students were discussing their own ethnicity (King & Ladson-Billings, 1990). Because their "whiteness" had gone unexamined, the students were nervous about discussing what it meant to be white and how their white skins privileged them (McIntosh, 1988). To them the huge disparities between the economic and social status of Whites and African-Americans are the result of slavery. Almost none of them understood the dynamics of racism and how it contributed to unequal access to power and opportunities. These novice teachers did not understand that with a backdrop of racism and social inequity, prejudice and stereotypes would persist. They could not merely dismiss student racial and ethnic differences by pretending to ignore students' skin color.

## RECOGNIZING PREJUDICE AND STEREOTYPING IN THE CLASSROOM

The literature on stereotyping, prejudice, and cultural diversity is growing at a rapid pace (for examples see C. Grant, 1992: Nieto, 1992: Banks & Banks, 1989; Bennett, 1990). One force driving this expansion is the rapidly changing demographics of both the society in general and the school population in specific (Hodgkinson, 1989). Around the year 2000 almost one out of three persons in the U.S. will be of color. African-American, Latino, and Asian-American birth rates are higher than that of Whites. While the student population is becoming increasingly diverse, the teaching population is becoming increasingly monocultural (Whitaker, 1989). These demographic changes coupled with economic hard times make for a volatile and sometimes hostile environment in which to address issues of prejudice and stereotyping. Students are not immune to these societal and cultural changes.

Another reason for the need to pay attention to issues like prejudice and stereotype reduction is the need for students to be equipped to build community. The transience of the American population, the rise in immigration, and increased economic disparity underscore our need to organize ourselves as members of a civic community. We need opportunities to exploit our differences as a way to develop unity. We need to understand that the strength of our communities and the nation is that we bring these differences to bear on common civic goals of freedom, justice, and equality.

A related reason for increased attention on issues of race, ethnicity, prejudice and stereotyping is that of national unity. At the same time we build our specific local communities, we must reclaim our national inheritance-that of building one nation out of many. The entire history of this nation is multicultural. Even before Columbus arrived in the Americas, the land was populated by many diverse nations of Native Americans. Students must understand that if we do not live together, we will surely destroy ourselves individually.

Children do not come into the classroom as empty vessels. They come with knowledge, skills, attitudes, and values. Much of the knowledge, skills, attitudes, and values that students bring with them has been shaped and informed by their parents and other relatives, friends and playmates, books and television. Schools can either reinforce what children bring with them or counter it. When that knowledge is prejudicial and/or stereotypical, teachers have a moral and ethical obligation to correct it.

> Jackie was a student teacher. She was excited about working in the second-grade class to which she was assigned. The class was racially and linguistically diverse with African American, Latino, Asian, and [W]hite students. As Martin Luther King, Jr. Day approached, Jackie prepared several activities to help increase the students' knowledge about the famed civil rights leader. As she walked around the class, while her students were completing a reading worksheet on Martin Luther King she noticed one [W]hite boy had drawn a huge black x over the entire worksheet. When she questioned him as to why he did that he replied, "I don't believe in Martin Luther King. My dad says I don't have to do nothin' that has to do with Martin Luther King."

What should Jackie have done? What do most teachers do when students express hostility and prejudice toward information about people who are different from them? In this case, Jackie reported the incident to her cooperating teacher. The cooperating teacher chose to ignore it but Jackie felt a moral obligation to do something. She mentioned it in passing to the school principal (although she sounded casual. this was a deliberate move on her part) and the principal was concerned enough to contact the parents and explained to them the principles upon which the school was based. The principal informed the parents that the school was no place for the displaying and cultivation of prejudicial or racist attitudes.

Jackie's case was obvious and had a reasonably simple resolution. How do we handle more subtle (and sometimes more insidious) examples of stereotypical and prejudicial behavior and practices in the classroom? Not many teachers have the opportunity to get feedback from colleagues and supervisors concerning the possibility of their reinforcing prejudice and stereotypes. Not many teachers want that kind of feedback. What if colleagues were to observe your practice for prejudicial and stereotypical behaviors? Would they see differential discipline practices for minority children who were engaging in the same behaviors as their White classmates? What would seating arrangements suggest? Which children are regarded as the smartest? The slowest? Who does the teacher call on during lessons? What does the room environment reveal? Are photographs, pictures, and books representative of the diversity of the society? If there is a toy corner, are there multiracial dolls? Are both boys and girls encouraged to participate in all games and activities? Is the question of racial, ethnic, and linguistic differences ever brought up as a part of curricular discussions? Are linguistically different children integrated into classroom lessons and activities or are they ignored until the teacher or classroom aide has time to attend to their needs? Are parents of culturally diverse students encouraged to participate in classroom activities? Does the teacher stop trying to get participation of diverse parents after one or two unsuccessful attempts? How often does the teacher telephone the parents of diverse students with good news about the students' progress? How many home visits does the teacher make during the course of a year? How much does the teacher know about students' background and home culture? What does the teacher say to his or her colleagues about the culturally diverse students? What attempts has the teacher made to learn about effective teaching strategies for diverse learners?

Teachers need opportunities to analyze their own and their colleagues' practice in order to discuss ways in which prejudicial and stereotypical behaviors are reinforced or counteracted. They need open forums for discussion of ideas and strategies for uncovering their own and their students' misperceptions and ignorance about race, ethnicity, gender and disability.

## CLASSROOM STRATEGIES FOR COMBATING PREJUDICE AND STEREOTYPING

Despite what some educators may think. the classroom is not a neutral place (McLaren, 1989). Some students are privileged in the classroom while others are disadvantaged. Teachers need to be able to recognize conditions both overt and covert that contribute to inequality in the classroom. Two areas in which teachers can begin to combat prejudice and stereotypes are curriculum and instruction.

Curriculum scholars have long recognized the fact that school curricula and the textbooks used to facilitate them are not neutral (Apple, 1990: Apple & Christian-Smith. 1991). However, teachers are not often asked to examine the political and cultural messages that are transmitted via the curriculum and texts. I am suggesting here that teachers must begin to uncover the messages, both explicit and implicit, that reside in the pages of curriculum guides and textbooks. They must ask themselves what is this content advocating? Should I use this with my students? How can I counteract negative and erroneous information so that students' prejudicial and/or stereotypical thinking is not reinforced.

They must also ask themselves in what ways they can improve the teaching-learning environment to oppose stereotypes and prejudice. What pictures and representations should they bring to the classroom, i.e., is a picture of Michael Jordan one of role modeling or stereotyping regarding African American male athletic prowess? They must be prepared to respond to images and messages that inadvertently come into the classroom through student or adult comments, media, and texts. When students read "classics" (or adaptations of such books) that reflect the prevailing stereotypes of the time,[1] teachers need ways to address these stereotypes so that students will not misread these stereotypes as teacher endorsement.

Another strategy being employed by many school districts is one of curriculum infusion (Shujaa & Ballard, 1991). This strategy involves bringing multicultural content into the classroom within the existing structure of the curriculum to correct errors in historical and social knowledge. Banks (1991) suggests a four-level model of integration of ethnic content. The first level is the contributions approach which involves a focus on discrete cultural elements such as heroes and holidays. The second level is the additive approach which, like many curriculum infusion models, leaves the basic structure of the curriculum intact and adds content, concepts, themes, and perspectives of various groups. The third level is the transformation approach which envisions a change of the curriculum structure to ensure that students have the opportunity to examine and understand concepts, issues, and events from the perspective of various groups. Finally, the fourth level is the social action approach which suggests that students not only receive new knowledge and information, but they are prepared to act on important social issues. This curriculum cannot transform students by itself. Educators serious about these issues must also examine instruction—the ways in which we teach—in order to combat stereotypic and prejudicial thinking.

There is a need for what I have termed a "culturally relevant pedagogy" (Ladson-Billings. 1990; Ladson-Billings, 1991). This is the kind of pedagogy that empowers students, through the use of their home and community culture, to make connections and critique dominant culture knowledge and ideology. The assertion here is that how you teach children is equally as important as what you teach children. Indeed. culturally relevant pedagogy can serve as an important counter-strategy to biased and inaccurate curriculum because the culturally relevant teacher naturally takes a critical perspective on the content. At the same time, these teachers are able to respond to stereotypic and prejudiced student and adult comments in ways that inform and correct.

## EPILOGUE

Although this discussion has focused on prejudice and stereotypes, it is important to understand them in the larger context of racism and discrimination. Prejudice is a disposition or judgment (either positive or negative) beforehand without knowledge of the facts. It is an attitude while discrimination is an action. However, they do not operate solely on a personal level. Weinberg (1990) asserts that "racism is always collective. Prejudiced individuals may join the large movement but they do not cause it. The point, sometimes difficult to grasp, is fundamental."

This means that while classroom teachers must work to combat the individual attitudes of prejudice and the individual actions of discrimination among their students, they must not be blind to the collective racism that exists in the school, community, and nation. Issues of school personnel staffing patterns, parental and community relations, and school and district-wide policies must be examined for evidence of racist and discriminatory practices. Teachers who are willing to embrace a pluralistic, multicultural society must also be willing to work to change existing conditions where they live and work to bring about such a society.

## NOTE

[1] I refer here to books like *Huckleberry Finn* or *Robinson Crusoe* that have obvious literary merit but present stereotypic depictions of African Americans.

## REFERENCES

Apple, M. (1990). *Ideology and Curriculum*, 2nd ed. New York: Routledge.

Apple, M. & Christian-Smith, L. (1991). *The Politics of the Textbook*. New York: Routledge.

Banks, J. (1991). *Teaching Ethnic Studies*, 5th ed. Boston: Allyn & Bacon.

Banks, J. & Banks, C. (Eds.). (1989). *Multicultural Education: Issues and Perspectives*. Boston: Allyn & Bacon.

Bennett, C. ( 1990). *Comprehensive Multicultural Education: Theory and Practice*, 2nd ed. Boston: Allyn & Bacon.

Clark, K. (1955). *Prejudice and Your Child*. Boston: Beacon Press.

Grant, C. (1992). "Culture and Teaching: What Do Teachers Need to Know?" In Kennedy, M. (Ed.). *Teaching Academic Subjects to Diverse Learners*, 231-256. New York: Teachers College Press.

Hodgkinson, H. (1989). "The Schools We Need For the Kids We've Got." Paper included in a colloquium collection of the Tenth Anniversary Meeting of the College Board's Council on Academic Affairs, May 4-5.

King, J. & Ladson-Billings. G. (1990). "The Teacher Education Challenge in Elite University Settings: Developing Critical Perspectives For Teaching in Democratic and Multicultural Societies." *European Journal of Intercultural Education*, 1 (2), 15-30.

Ladson-Billings, G. (1990). "Cultural Relevant Teaching: Effective Instruction for Black Students." *The College Board Review*, No. 155, Spring, 20-25.

——. (1991). "Culturally Relevant Teaching: The Key to Making Multicultural Education Work." In Grant. C. (Ed.). *Research and Multicultural Education: From the Margins to the Mainstream*. London: Palmer Press.

McIntosh, P. ( 1988). "White Privilege and Male Privilege: A Personal Account of Coming to See Correspondences Through Work in Women's Studies." Working Paper No. 189. Wellesley College Center for Research on Women. Wellesley, MA.

McLaren, P. (1989). *Life in Schools*. White Plains, NY: Longman.

Nieto, S. (1992). *Affirming Diversity: The Sociopolitical Content of Multicultural Education*. White Plains, NY: Longman.

Paley, V. (1979). *White Teacher*. Cambridge, MA: Harvard University Press.

Shujaa, M. & Ballard, K. (1991). "Teachers Perceptions of a New Policy to Infuse African and African-American Content into the School Curriculum." Paper presented at the Twelfth Annual Ethnography in Education Research Forum. University of Pennsylvania, PA, Feb. 22-24.

Weinberg, M. (1990). Introduction. In Weinberg, M. (Ed.). *Racism in the United States: A Comprehensive Classified Bibliography*. New York: Greenwood Press. pp. xii-xiii.

Whitaker, L. (January 1989). *The Disappearing Black Teacher*. Ebony, 122-126.

Readers interested in a list of books for teachers and children, please contact Dr. Ladson-Billings, University of Wisconsin-Madison, Department of Curriculum and Instruction, 225 North Mills St., Madison. WI 53711.

Gloria Ladson-Billings is an Assistant Professor in the Department of Curriculum and Instruction at the University of Wisconsin-Madison, where she teaches courses in social studies methods, multicultural foundations of education, and culturally relevant pedagogy. She is a 1988-89 recipient of the National Academy of Education's Spencer postdoctoral fellowships, which allowed her to pursue her interest in teachers who are successful with African American students. She has participated in the Stanford Teacher Assessment Project and has consulted with the National Board for Professional Teaching Standards. She was selected to be a community leadership fellow in Palo Alto, California, and was named one of the San Francisco Bay Area's outstanding Black women (1985). She has published several articles on multicultural education and culturally relevant pedagogy. She is currently writing a book related to her research with successful teachers of African American students. She was formerly both an administrator and Assistant Professor at Santa Clara University (Santa Clara, California). [1992 note]

**F. William Sesow**
**David Van Cleaf**
**Bob Chadwick**

Culture includes "all of the human-made components in a society and their symbolic meanings, such as tools, language, values and institutions" (Banks & Clegg, 1985, p. 205). The aspects of culture are often abstract, making it a challenging concept to teach. Typical textbook lessons do not provide concrete activities that enable elementary students to develop an understanding of the concept. However, teachers and students form a classroom culture that is in some ways similar to other cultures. A concrete way to teach students about culture is to engage them in an investigation into their classroom culture. Thus, by examining activities and artifacts representative of their class, students begin developing a concrete understanding of culture that will then enable them to explore other cultures.

This article describes a series of instructional activities designed to help students develop the conceptual foundation necessary for later lessons about other cultures. The instructional activities are also designed to engage students in the critical thinking skills of observing, grouping-labeling, and generalizing (Winocur, 1986). While these activities are appropriate for grades three through twelve, they have also been used successfully with undergraduate and graduate college students.

To start the examination of the classroom's culture, the teacher conducts a class discussion of what is meant by culture. For the purposes of this activity, culture is an expression of the lifestyles of a group of people and includes how they behave and what they believe. Anthropologists examine artifacts as they attempt to describe the behaviors and beliefs of a culture. In the following activities, students act like anthropologists and form generalizations about the classroom's culture by examining artifacts of individuals within their classroom.

## CULTURE ARTIFACTS BOX

Begin by instructing class members to bring several items to school that represent things they like, believe in, value, or use. Two items per student are sufficient, but if a class consists of fewer than twenty students, each student should bring three or four items. In order to compile a varied collection of artifacts, caution students not to tell each other what objects they plan to bring. The teacher and

Reprinted from *Social Studies and the Young Learner*, January/February 1992, Volume 4, Number 3. Copyright 1992 by National Council for the Social Studies.

other adults who are a part of the classroom environment are expected to contribute items too. Inform students that fragile or valuable items may be represented with photos or pictures students have drawn.

Students secretly place their artifacts in a covered artifact box. The size of the box will depend on the number of artifacts anticipated. Decorate the artifact box with pictures and symbols, and label it the "Cultural Artifacts Box." The decorations could include pictures cut from magazines representing individuals and groups of people engaged in various activities as well as a variety of objects used and enjoyed by people.

## OBSERVATION OF ARTIFACTS

The first critical thinking skill used in investigating the culture of the classroom is observation. Divide students into cooperative learning groups and remind them that observations are made by using as many of our senses as possible.

Depending on the number of cooperative learning groups, subdivide the artifacts that had been placed in the box evenly and distribute them to the groups. For ease of exchanging the artifacts among groups, the items are placed in grocery sacks and each sack is numbered. This way sacks are rotated to each of the groups, thus ensuring that each group has access to all of the artifacts.

As each group observes the artifacts, group members record their observations using a standard form. [Note: Cooperative learning typically calls for roles assigned to each participant. For this activity you need an observation leader, an observation recorder, a grouping and labeling leader, a grouping and labeling recorder, a generalization leader, and a generalization recorder.]

In most cases, students will not taste or smell the artifacts. However, such headings should be included on the form to remind students that they should observe objects by using as many senses as possible. Also, these headings will be useful with other observation activities where taste and smell are appropriate.

## GROUPING AND LABELING

This activity is a variation of Hilda Taba's (1967) concept formation strategy and requires students to engage in the processes of grouping and labeling. First, students examine their artifacts list and arrange the artifacts into groups. Instruct students to look for common characteristics (attributes) among the artifacts. Students' categories usually relate to family, religion, sports and hobbies, pets, and foods. Caution students to try to limit the number of groups. Six to ten labels are appropriate. Each label is then assigned a number or letter and written beside the corresponding item on the observation list. Some items may have more than one letter or number assigned because their attributes fit more than one group. However, it is desirable to have younger students limit each artifact to only one group.

## MAKING GENERALIZATIONS

After the artifact has been grouped and labeled, the cooperative learning groups develop generalizations about their culture. These generalizations arrived at may be similar to the following:

▮ Our class likes fast foods
▮ Our class is religious
▮ Our class participates in sports
▮ Our class enjoys reading
▮ Our class uses computer technology
▮ Our class has pet animals

Once generalizations have been developed, each of the cooperative learning groups gives a report to the entire class about observations made, groups and labels given to the artifacts, and generalizations about the class culture. The teacher then displays each artifact and asks who placed it in the box and why. At this time the artifacts can be returned to their owners.

## SUBCULTURES

If students are developing a sound understanding of the concept of culture, it is appropriate to consider the concept of subculture. All major cultures have subcultures, which may be based on religious, racial, ethnic, regional, or gender differences. Depending on the make-up of a particular group of students, distinctive subcultures may be obvious. The most obvious basis of subcultures in most classrooms is gender. Male and female students often bring different artifacts to represent their subcultures.

To explore the classroom's subcultures, students should reexamine the artifacts and be asked to place them into subgroups based on gender differences. Some items may be clearly appropriate for one gender or the other. Other items may be difficult to classify because the items are appropriate for both subcultures. If using gender as the basis for studying subcultures, care should be taken to avoid sexist attitudes.

The teacher should then lead the class in a discussion that requires students to explain how subcultures can have unique artifacts and still be part of a larger culture. This will require students to explain how subcultures contribute to the primary culture. It will also require students to consider differences existing within their primary culture.

## CULTURAL SIMILARITIES

Social groups develop artifacts, symbols, and rituals to help them and their members respond to major events in life as well as to respond successfully to challenges imposed by the environment. Although cultures have unique ways of expressing these responses, cultures have many

similarities. David Elkind (1981) encouraged teachers to focus on these cultural similarities rather than on differences because "understanding based on similarities requires logic and reasoning . . ." (p. 437). During this activity, students should look through textbooks, magazines, newspapers, and reference materials and identify items two other cultures use that are related to the labels and generalizations developed earlier by the cooperative learning groups. A chart listing these labels and generalizations should be given to students to guide their efforts.

This activity will help students discover that although cultures may appear quite different, many of the differences are merely unique ways to demonstrate similar needs. For example, various cultures have different ways of expressing relationships with the spiritual world. Similarly, while mode of dress and expressions may differ, many cultural groups dance to celebrate milestones in their members' lives. As a means of extending this activity, students could select one of the labels from their chart and make a collage of various ways other cultures respond to a similar cultural phenomenon.

## CONCLUSION

In all cases, the authors have found that when students explored the culture of the class, social bonding occurred. At the conclusion of the observing, grouping and labeling, and forming generalizations activities, students have requested that the authors provide similar activities. In the case of sixth graders at Blessed Sacrament School, a greater appreciation and caring for each other developed as a result of examining the cultural artifacts of their class.

Culture is a nebulous concept and therefore challenging to teach. The activities presented in this article provide a concrete means of teaching about culture. It is also a way to help students develop more positive attitudes about people from different cultures, and subcultures, as well as within their own culture.

## REFERENCES

Banks, J. A., & Clegg, A. A. (1985). *Teaching Strategies for the Social Studies*. White Plains, NY: Longman.

Elkind, D. (1981). Child development and the social studies curriculum. *Social Education*, 45, 43 5-437.

Taba, H. (1967). *Teachers Handbook for Elementary Social Studies*. Palo Alto, CA: Addison-Wesley.

Winocur, S. Lee. (1986). IMPACT - Improve Minimal Proficiencies by Activating Critical Thinking. *Phi Delta Kappan*.

F. William Sesow is an Associate Professor in the Center for Curriculum and Instruction at the University of Nebraska-Lincoln. He teaches both graduate and undergraduate professional social studies courses. David Van Cleaf is a Professor at Washburn University, Topeka, Kansas. He teaches courses in social studies education and provides staff development for teachers in area school districts. Bob Chadwick was a sixth grade teacher at Blessed Sacrament School in Lincoln, Nebraska. [1992 note]

# Who Packed the Suitcase?
## *Playing the Role of an Archaeologist/Anthropologist*

**James D. Laney**
**Patricia A. Moseley**

Are there any among us who have not enjoyed looking at the contents of a box or trunk long forgotten but newly discovered in the attic or rescued from the back of the closet? As we examine each article, if the contents are the remnants of an earlier time in our lives, we may recall an emotion or activity, associate pleasantly or unpleasantly, or connect our present activities with past ones. If, however, the contents represent the life of an ancestor, we carefully examine each article in great detail as if the object could speak, thus providing some insight into the behavior and character of the unknown person. We become, in fact, an archaeologist/anthropologist.

The archaeologist/anthropologist approach motivates students because of its relevance and encourages students to look at their surroundings in a context of cultural continuity and adaptation. Simulating the work of the archaeologist/anthropologist activates the students' skills of observing, hypothesizing, and inferring. In a sense, they become detectives using clues to interpret within their personal frames of reference. In addition to using skills they already possess, they expand their knowledge and skills because, through use, additional perceptions of the world and innovative applications of skills are acquired. These new perceptions and skills can then be applied to current issues as they arise. The following lesson simulates the work of the archaeologist/anthropologist, allowing students to apply the methodologies of professional social scientists to the study of people and their culture.

In implementing the lesson, the teacher should encourage students to observe, listen, and apply their knowledge of the world in order to make valid inferences. Initially, the teacher should discourage wildly deviant inferences, but at some time students should be helped to understand the consistently inconsistent nature of people. For example, while the most logical inference about the book used in the lesson, *Birds of North America: A Field Guide to Identification*, is that the person is a bird watcher, it could be that the book was borrowed from or given by a friend. Therefore, it is important to view the artifacts and clues derived from them as a whole in order to insure the generation of consistent, reasonable inferences. This approach will assist the students in learning why there are inconsistencies sometimes in what archaeologists and anthropologists report.

It is highly desirable that students work together as excavators, catalogers, and interpreters. Students will learn from each other as observations and inferences are made; they will benefit from drawing upon their collective store of past experiences. This lesson will be entertaining and challenging, showing students that learning involves making sense of the world around them.

The lesson design is consistent with contemporary models of inquiry problem solving and cooperative learning activities. With its step-by-step use of the processes of problem question posing, data gathering processing, and inference making, the design can be easily adapted to other content. Teachers are encouraged to use this design because of its emphasis upon process as well as knowledge acquisition.

## LESSON TITLE/TOPIC
**Who Packed the Suitcase?**
**Playing the Role of an Archaeologist/Anthropologist**
*Grade Level:* Intermediate Elementary
*Objectives:* Presented with artifacts from a suitcase, the students will be able to make accurate observations about the items found in the suitcase.

Based on their observations, the students will be able to make reasonable inferences about the contents of the suitcase and the person who packed the suitcase.

After playing the role of archaeologists/anthropologists, the students will be able to describe the work done by these social scientists.
*Materials:*

- Suitcase.
- Tissue paper to be placed between items in the suitcase, thus forming layers analogous to layers of soil.
- Various items to be packed in the suitcase. These things should be borrowed from an adult whom the students all know: Some sample items are as follows:
  *Layer 1:* A book (e.g. *Birds of North America: A Field Guide to Identification*).
  *Layer 2:* A sewing kit.
  *Layer 3:* A jewelry box with assorted pieces of jewelry indicating religious affiliation, organizational memberships, honors, hobbies, etc.
  *Layer 4:* A hair curler bag containing an old-fashioned hair curler, old-fashioned hair-wave clip, and a broken barrette.

*Procedure:* Activity Description
State the objectives of the lesson.

Define the following terms for students: *prehistory* (prior to the invention of writing) and *history* (after the invention of writing).

Explain that human-made objects from the past help us learn about human life and culture in past ages. These objects are especially important with respect to prehistory, for they are our only source of information about humankind during that time period.

Define the following four terms for students: *artifact, archaeologist, anthropologist,* and *excavate.*

Explain that, with the passage of time, human tools and other objects are covered by layers of soil. Archaeologists dig in the earth to uncover these items. The deeper they dig, the older are the objects that they find.

Place the packed suitcase before the students. Ask the students to pretend that they are archaeologists/anthropologists. Tell them that their goal is to answer the question, "Who packed the suitcase?" They must do this by making appropriate observations and inferences as they unpack (or excavate) the suitcase.

Have students take turns as the excavator. The excavator's job is to remove objects (or artifacts) from the suitcase, layer by layer. As each object is removed, the excavator briefly describes it. Meanwhile the rest of the students keep a written record of these observations.

Also have students take turns as the cataloger. The cataloger's job is to draw a large cross-sectional illustration of the suitcase showing the layers of tissue paper and the position of each object as it is uncovered by the excavator.

Divide the class into groups of four and appoint a recorder/spokesperson within each group. Ask each group to generate a list of inferences, based on their previous observations about the person who packed the suitcase. These inferences may be recorded in a three column table with the column headings Object, Description, and Inference. Write the following cues on the chalkboard to guide students in their inference making:

1. Sex?
2. Age?
3. Education?
4. Physical characteristics?
5. Personality characteristics?
6. Interests or hobbies?
7. Organizational memberships?
8. Honors?
9. Education?
10. Religion?
11. Place of residence?
12. First item packed?
13. Last item packed?

After sufficient time has been provided for making inferences. direct the groups to look at their list of inferences. Ask: (1) "Are your inferences consistent With each other?" ( 2 ) "Do any of your early inferences need to be revised in light of objects and observations that were found/made at a later time?"

Direct the groups to look at the objects and observations derived from them as a whole. Ask: "Are there any additional inferences you can make?"

Ask each recorder/spokesperson to share and justify that group's conclusions.

In order to check the accuracy of the students' conclusions, have the person who packed the suitcase visit the class and answer questions as needed.

Ask students to summarize what they have learned about the work of archaeologists/anthropologists.

## SOURCES OF ADDITIONAL ACTIVITIES RELATED TO ARCHAEOLOGY/ANTHROPOLOGY

Allen, R. E, and R. G. Felston. (Winter 1980). What in the World? Artifact Analysis in Social Education. *Georgia Social Science Journal*, 11 (1), 1-3, 16.

Aanes, L. M. J. (September 1981). Archeology in the Classroom. *Science and Children*, 19 (1), 40-41.

Carroll, R. F. (March, April 1987). Schoolyard Archaeology. *The Social Studies*, 78 (2), 69-75.

Carter, E. (November, December 1981). An Archeological Dig: Activity Outline. *Social Activities*, 18 (4), 3-5.

Danley, A. G. (May 1982). Flax, Greece, and Relevance in the Social Studies. *Social Education*, 46 (5) 353-56.

Diers, R.. and James Lo Giudice. (March, April 1982). Archaeology: A Means of Challenging the Gifted Student. *G/C/T*, 22, 2-7.

MATCH. (1966). *House of Ancient Greece. Teacher's Guide.* Nashua, N.H.: Delta Education.

Plants, R. W. (February 1984). Projectile Point Classification. *Science and Children*, 21 (5) 6-9.

Smith, M. R. (Winter 1982). Hands-On History: Techniques Derived from Archaeology. *History and Social Science Teacher*, 17 (2), 115-18.

Van Tilburg, J. A. (November. December 1981). Creating Your Own Archaeological Dig. *The Social Studies*, 72 (6) 261-64.

Watts, L. .E. (September 1985). They Dig Archaeology. *Science and Children*, 23 (1) 5-9.

James D. Laney and Patricia A. Moseley are members of the Department of Elementary Education at North Texas State University, Denton. Dr. Laney has authored articles on geographic education, economic education, and inquiry-oriented social studies. Dr. Moseley writes in the area of elementary social studies, particularly in economics and Texas studies. [1990 note]

**Karen Harvey**

Perhaps now is the long awaited "teachable moment"—the point in time when we, as a nation, are eager, willing, and receptive to learning about our Native people. It certainly is time that we teach our children about America's indigenous people. Consider the following:

▌ In 1992 we commemorated Christopher Columbus' arrival in the "new world" and taught about this historical event. This arrival has been described variously as discovery, encounter, or invasion.

▌ Americans are beginning to consider the health of the earth and ways to protect and preserve our natural environment from destruction. The Native American concept of "Mother Earth" has new and urgent meaning.

▌ As a nation, a recognizable trend has indicated that people are weary of the notion that more is better and are returning to voluntary simplicity and more humane values. Models of less complex lifeways, simple and enduring values, and cooperative cultures are needed.

New ways of expressing human spiritual needs are becoming increasingly acceptable. There has been, at least in some sectors of the country, a renewed interest in Native American spirituality.

Holistic ways of becoming healthy and of healing have become more acceptable—the awareness of mind, body, spirit connection is creating interest in Native lifestyles and traditional healing practices.

▌ There is a pressing social and moral imperative to teach all students about the treaty rights and trust responsibilities the nation has with Native American people.

▌ Native people are not going to assimilate; they have no desire to become part of the "melting pot." Their place in this country and their relationship to it is different than those who have immigrated here. They have a unique and special place in the past, present, and future of the United States.

This list would indicate that we have practical and personal, as well as political and moral reasons, for teaching about Native Americans.

For teachers, the "teachable moment" or the willingness or eagerness to learn means only that learners are ready to learn. However, it does not necessarily mean that the teacher is adequately prepared to teach. As teachers, our obligation and our challenge when teaching about

Native Americans is to provide sound educational experiences that are authentic, accurate, unbiased, and sensitive. Further, appropriate instruction should help young people learn powerful ideas that will help them understand their own world. Consider the following challenge to social studies teachers.

". . .[T]eachers need to be historically accurate and fair, as well as sensitive to the contemporary needs and concerns of a dominated, often displaced, and threatened people. They need to be acutely aware of the moral and ethical values inherent in the study of the historical and contemporary lives of Native Americans. Curriculum materials and instructional aids should be free of racism and ethnocentrism. Teachers must recognize the contributions of Native Americans throughout the curriculum and each and every teacher must be cognizant of the negative effects of stereotypes, and the prejudice and discrimination rampant in our treaties, policies, and government and public practices in the treatment of and interaction with Native peoples" (Harvey, Harjo & Jackson, 1990).

This statement asks teachers to confront the fundamental questions, "What do I need to know to be adequately informed about Native Americans and professionally prepared to teach?" and "What learning objectives and experiences are appropriate for my students?" For many teachers, the answers lie not only in examining their own knowledge, experiences, and perspectives, but also in sorting through the many materials about Native Americans to discover the concepts and generalizations that give meaning to the cultural, political, economic, and historical and contemporary myths and realities about our Native peoples.

First, let's look briefly at how teachers can become more knowledgeable about the history, culture, contemporary lives, and pressing concerns of Native Americans. The following approaches seem reasonable for teachers at any level and in most geographical areas.

*Study:* Develop authoritative information by taking classes offered by colleges, universities, museums, and historical societies.

*Read:* Obtain a variety of perspectives on any given tribe, incident, policy, or period of time. Make every effort to read works by Native authors including novels in order to hear Indian voices. Native newspapers are appropriate resources on contemporary culture and issues. Some general books are recommended at the conclusion of this article.

Reprinted from *Social Studies and the Young Learner*, March/April 1992, Volume 4, Number 4. Copyright 1992 by National Council for the Social Studies.

| CONCEPTS | ORGANIZING GENERALIZATIONS |
|---|---|
| ENVIRONMENT/ RESOURCES | The physical environment and natural resources of a region affect how people meet their basic needs of food, clothing, and shelter. Culture is related to geographic location and to the particular time in which people live. |
| CULTURE/DIVERSITY | Cultures are comprised of a human-made system of artifacts, beliefs, and patterns of behavior that enables people to meet their needs in their physical and social environment. Cultures use a diversity of means to attain similar goals and to satisfy human needs. Individuals become human by learning the culture of their group. There are many ways of being human. An individual's culture strongly influences his or her behavior and values. |
| ADAPTATION/CHANGE | Culture change takes place when diverse cultures come in contact. Every culture consists of a variety of borrowed cultural elements. Culture is an integrated whole. Changes in one part are reflected in all its components. Conflict sometimes leads to social change. |
| CONFLICT/ DISCRIMINATION | Conflict usually results when people from different cultures and subcultures interact. Groups are often the victims of discrimination and prejudice because of age, gender, racial, religious, or cultural differences. |

Harvey, D. K., Harjo, L. D. & Jackson, J. K. *Teaching About Native Americans*. Washington, DC: National Council for the Social Studies, 1990.

*Consult:* Seek the views and opinions of Native American elders, historians, artists, and tribal members to obtain their perspective.

*Understand:* Recognize the effects of historical bias, the presence of racism, and the existence of varying perspectives and worldviews.

*Participate:* Enjoy cultural events such as powwows, rodeos, and art shows in your community, whenever possible.

It seems reasonable to conclude that teachers initially must assume responsibility for their own professional knowledge. The kind of teaching and learning that is so urgently needed will only happen when teachers are cognizant of the diversity and similarity of Native people (in the past and the present), aware of their own biases and cultural perspectives, sensitive to the damaging legacies of conquest, appreciative of the pervasive power and importance of culture, and able to teach about the treaty rights and trust responsibilities of the United States government in regard to Native Americans. Only then is it possible to teach responsibly.

Before answering the second question about how to organize learning experiences and plan for sound instruction, let's first look at the practical world of most teachers. Throughout the nation and at elementary, middle, and high school levels, each teacher usually has a specific teaching assignment and a mandated or recommended curriculum for which he or she is responsible. Although there are some monocultural ethnic studies that specifically teach about Native cultures, most frequently teaching units about Native Americans are sprinkled throughout and integrated into the curriculum. Grade levels, subject areas, or courses that tend to have places for the study of Native people are:

- Holidays (specifically Thanksgiving, Columbus Day, and Native American or American Indian Day)—all elementary levels.
- Regions of the world—usually third- or fourth-grade social studies.
- State history—usually third- or fourth grade social studies and sometimes in middle or junior high school.
- American history—usually fifth grade, eighth grade, and throughout high school.
- United States government—middle school and high school.
- Contemporary issues—high school.
- Literature/English/Language Arts/ Reading—all grade levels.

Consequently, many teachers teach something about Native Americans—but only occasionally is the subject a major focus of study. The possibility for disorganization and fragmentation of this important topic is not only possible, but is highly likely. Unlike areas of the curriculum such as social studies, science, language arts, or American literature, which have recognized and accepted structures and designated knowledge objectives to be taught and learned, the study of Native Americans has not had a structure nor identified objectives which articulate a scope or sequence of instruction. As a consequence, we tend to teach bits and pieces, old favorite lessons, or depend on our personal experiences, preferences or biases to determine what is worthy of teaching. The end result can be a hodge-podge curriculum with unclear outcomes.

The identification of powerful organizing concepts and generalizations renders it possible to make informed decisions as to what should be taught. Using four major concept clusters such as Environment/Resources, Culture/Diversity, Adaptation/Change, and Conflict/Discrimination can provide a solid and useful structure for all teachers, K-12, and can be used to develop curriculum and create learning activities in a variety of content areas.

A question that is certain to be asked is related to the simplicity of the model. Is it possible to focus an entire curriculum around the study of four concept clusters? The answer to this significant question is reassuring. Concepts with great power and with a hierarchical nature can be developed at increasingly higher levels and in greater depth as students engage in new experiences and develop deeper understanding. The intent is to help them gain increasingly complex knowledge and sophistication about these identified concepts. Every concept may not be taught at each grade level, or in all instructional units, but should recur throughout the entire K-12 curriculum in an organized and coherent way.

Focusing on these four concept clusters has great potential to assist students to develop greater understanding from the curriculum than they would obtain from presenting a collection of interesting facts. Clearly, the understanding of major concepts and generalizations is a developmental process. It does not occur after one lesson, one unit, or one year—it occurs over time in ever increasing complexity. A developmentally appropriate curriculum designates learning outcomes and provides learning activities that help students construct meaning from their school experiences throughout their school years beginning in the earliest grades.

## ILLUSTRATIVE LESSON PLAN

The following lesson plan is to illustrate how this concept-based model for teaching about Native Americans can be used at elementary grade levels and can be expanded into a comprehensive multidisciplinary unit. It also demonstrates that teachers who are knowledgeable about and sensitive to the beauty and the struggles of Native American cultures can, through their selection of instructional materials and techniques, teach children important ideas about our indigenous people.

*Grade Level:* Intermediate (grades 2-4).
*Basic Concepts:* Change, adaptation, and culture.
*Organizing Generalizations:* The book *Pueblo Storyteller* is rich in possibilities for teaching three major generalizations: (1) new technologies stimulate cultural change, (2) culture change takes place when diverse cultures come in contact, and (3) all cultures have traditions and rituals that help to maintain group solidarity and identification. The focus for a lesson or unit can be on any one or more of these three generalizations.
*Culture Area:* Southwest.
*Time Period:* Contemporary.

*Background:* This book describes, in a young girl's words, how she lives in a contemporary Pueblo world, learning Cochiti history, traditions, and ways of life. Students will be able to see how contemporary technology and the ways of the dominant society have changed the lives of the Native people and how the children still learn "to take what I need from the earth to live, but also how to leave something behind for future generations . . . to live in harmony with the world, and [to] collect memories of life to share one day with children and grandchildren."
*Objectives:*
Knowledge (Content)
Students will:
1. Locate Cochiti Pueblo on a map of New Mexico (see Mays, 1985).
2. Describe how a pueblo is built and discuss its features.
3. Recognize that the pueblo people speak four native languages including Tanoan, Zuni, Shoshonean, and Keresan (the language of Cochiti Pueblo).
4. Describe some of the traditional values of the Cochiti people.
5. List at least five ways Cochiti people of today have adapted to new technology.
6. Discuss or illustrate how April is learning traditional pueblo ways and how these traditions and rituals help her to be a Cochiti.
7. Identify ways the Cochiti have adopted aspects of the dominant culture such as basketball and golf.
*Skills:*
Students will:
1. Compare traditional ways of Cochiti Pueblo with contemporary ways.
2. Use classification skills.
3. Practice interviewing strategies by interviewing their grandparents or other older adults.
*Values:*
Students will:
1. Appreciate the traditional lifeways of the Cochiti.
2. Value the need for traditions in all cultures.
3. Respect the importance of maintaining Indian cultures.
*Activities:*
1. Introduce the term pueblo and talk about the pueblos located in the Southwest. It would be helpful to show a film or video about southwestern pueblos and life in the desert Southwest.
2. Read the story aloud to the children. Time should be spent on discussing the illustrations.
3. Label two large sheets of butcher paper with the words Traditional Pueblo Ways and New Pueblo Ways. As you reread the story, ask children to identify traditional ways of the Cochiti and new ways and begin to write them on the charts. If multiple copies of the book were available, children could easily do this in cooperative groups.
4. A discussion should then focus on technology—what is technology and how do new technological inventions change our lives. Bread would be a good example. How

was bread made long ago? How did people obtain the ingredients? Who made it? How was it baked? How is bread made now? How did the Cochiti make bread long ago? How do they make it now? Why is bread made in traditional ways for special occasions? Why do the people choose to use old methods and old technologies? Are there examples of other contemporary people making bread in old or special ways (Challah bread for the Sabbath in Jewish homes; holiday breads). Are there other kinds of breads that are traditional for other cultures (tortillas, bagels, croissants)? Ask students to code the items on the New Pueblos Ways chart as to whether the change is a result of coming in contact with another culture or it if is a result of new technology, or both. An example of both influences would be television which has had a powerful effect on traditional cultures by bringing the world of the dominant society to them.

5. Now, add two other charts labeled Traditional Pueblo Ways Used Today and Our Traditions. As the lesson progresses, complete the charts with the students. Discussion should center around the idea that although technology has made it possible to do things easier, faster, and, in many cases, cheaper, people choose to maintain some traditions and rituals as part of being who they are—as part of their culture and identity. The Cochiti teach their children traditional ways of being a Cochiti and our families do this also in different ways in order to maintain some of our diverse cultures or as a way to develop group or family solidarity.

6. Ask children to interview their parents, grandparents, or other older adults about family or cultural traditions that they maintain. Take time to teach the children about good interview questions and strategies. Add to the charts.

7. Try to arrange for a Native American speaker to come to the classroom or arrange for the children to visit a museum to explore other traditional ways. The focus should be on how traditional ways are kept alive in contemporary times.

*Extensions:* This particular book could well lead to a more in-depth study of pueblo Indians (past and/or present) or other Southwestern Native cultures. As well as learning about contemporary lifeways, the continuing archeological work in the area offers many possibilities for engaging study about America's earliest people and about archeologists and their work. Some possibilities for enrichment activities include:

1. Making models of pueblos and/or adobe bricks.
2. Reading pueblo stories and legends.
3. Making clay storytellers or drums.
4. Researching traditional Indian games for children.
5. Planting corn, beans, and squash in the traditional manner.
6. Making bread and sharing a traditional pueblo meal.

7. Writing to: Mary and Leonard Trujillo, P.O. Box 147, Cochiti Pueblo, NM 87041, about storytellers; Gabriel "Yellowbird" Trujillo, P.O. Box 72, Cochiti Pueblo, NM 87041, about Cochiti drums; Andy Garcia, P.O. Box 1055, San Juan Pueblo, NM 87566, about Pueblo dance group.
8. Inviting a Native storyteller to tell traditional stories.
9. Learning to tell stories.
10. Visiting an area powwow or Indian Center.
11. Touring an art museum, focusing on the work of pueblo artists or learning about various kinds of Native American pottery through time.
12. Finding out why *pueblo* is a Spanish word and why the names in the book (Trujillo and Garcia) are Spanish names.
13. Reading *The Hopi* and listing how Hopi people have adapted to technology and how they continue to learn traditional ways.
14. Researching how drums of various tribal groups are made and used.
15. Listening to authentic Native American music.
16. Learning some traditional social dances (take care to distinguish between social dancing, powwow dancing, and ceremonial dancing which is religious in nature and not appropriate to imitate).
17. Watching the newspaper and television news for cultural events that help to maintain culture identify or solidarity for groups of people. A bulletin board can feature these newspaper clippings. It would be appropriate to review school traditions.
18. Writing about one of their cultural or family traditions. After completing the writing and editing process, a class book or display can be created.

*Evaluation:* In discussion or in writing, students should be able to give a personal or Cochiti example of a tradition or ritual that is used to maintain cultural identity or solidarity and explain how young people learn that tradition.

*Materials and Resources:*

Bahti, M. (1988). *Pueblo Stories and Storytellers*. Tucson, AZ: Treasure Chest.

Hoyt-Goldsmith, D. (1991). *Pueblo Storyteller*. New York, NY: Holiday House.

Mays, B. (1985). *Indian Villages of the Southwest*. San Francisco, CA: Chronicle Books.

Tomchek, A.H. (1987). *The Hopi*. Chicago, IL: Children's Press.

It is time to extend our professional knowledge about the history of Native people in America and about the complicated contemporary issues facing Native Americans, to review both old and new instructional materials, and to renew and revise lesson plans to insure that social studies instruction focuses on significant, not trivial, facts and concepts. The lessons taught will be more accurate, more sensitive and thoughtful, and more respectful of the first people to inhabit this land.

## REFERENCES

Harvey, K. D., Harjo, L. D., & Jackson, J. K. (1990). *Teaching About Native Americans*. Washington, DC: National Council for the Social Studies.

Hoyt-Goldsmith, D. (1991). *Pueblo Storyteller*. New York, NY: Holiday House.

## RECOMMENDED RESOURCES
### BASIC REFERENCE BOOKS

Billard, J. G. (1989). *The World of the American Indian*. Washington, DC: National Geographic.

Carter, F. ( 1976). *The Education of Little Tree*. Albuquerque, NM: University of New Mexico Press.

Deloria, V., Jr. (1988). *Custer Died for Your Sins*. Norman, OK: University of Oklahoma Press.

Josephy, A. M. R. & Brandon, W. (Eds.) (1988). *The American Heritage Book of Indians*. New York, NY: American Heritage Books.

Kopper, P. (Ed.) (1986). *The Smithsonian Book of North American Indians*. Washington, DC: Smithsonian Institute.

Lame Deer, J. & Erdoes, R. (1972). *Lame Deer: Seeker of Visions*. New York, NY: Pocket Books.

Maxwell, J.A. (1978). *America's Fascinating Indian Heritage*. Pleasantville, NY: Reader's Digest.

Sale, Kirkpatrick. (1990). *The Conquest of Paradise*. New York, NY: Alfred A. Knopf.

Standing Bear, L. (1933/1978). *Land of the Spotted Eagle*. Lincoln, NE: University of Nebraska.

Waldman, C. (1985). *Atlas of the North American Indian*. New York, NY: Facts on File.

Waldman, C. (1988). *Encyclopedia of Native American Tribes*. New York, NY: Facts on File.

Viola, H. J. (1990). *After Columbus, the Smithsonian Chronicle*. New York, NY: Smithsonian Oriole.

## MAGAZINES/JOURNALS [1992 INFORMATION]

*Native Peoples*
P.O. Box 3620
Phoenix, AZ 85067-6820
(602) 277-7852

*Native Monthly Reader*
P.O. Box 217
Crestone, CO 81131
(719) 256-4848

*American Indian Art*
7314 East Osborn Drive
Scottsdale, AZ 85251
(602) 994-5445

*Daybreak Star Reader*
United Indians of all Tribes
Daybreak Star Arts Center - Discovery Park
P.O. Box 99100
Seattle, WA 98199
(206) 285-4425

*American Indian Culture and Research Journal**
American Indian Studies Center
3220 Campbell Hall
University of California, Los Angeles
405 Hilgard Avenue
Los Angeles, CA 90024-1548

*Journal of Indian Education**
Center for Indian Education
College of Education
Arizona State University
Tempe, AZ 85287-1311

\* *These two journals are scholarly in content and are excellent resources for those who teach Native American students or teach Native Studies courses.*

## NEWSPAPERS

*Akwasasne Notes*
Rooseveltown, NY 13683-0196
(518) 358-9531

*Lakota Times*
1920 Lombardi Drive
Rapid City, SD 57701
(605) 341-0011

*Navajo Times*
P.O. Box 310
Window Rock, AZ 86515

*News From Indian Country*
RT. Box 2900-A
Hayward, WI 54843

*United Tribes News*
3315 University Drive
Bismark, ND 58504
(701) 255-3285

## ACKNOWLEDGMENT

The author wishes to acknowledge the children, faculty, staff, and school board at Rough Rock Community School in Rough Rock, Arizona, for their friendship and support. They are her teachers.

Karen Harvey is the Assistant Dean for Academic Affairs in the University College at the University of Denver, Colorado. She has taught social studies and multicultural education throughout her career. [1992 note]

# Horticulture and Human Culture
## *Connect Natural Sciences and Cultural Geography through Gardening*

**Arlene Marturano**

Last year, the fourth-grade students at my school participated in an activity that links science and geography—gardening. Through planting gardens similar to those of four regional native American tribes, the children created a concrete example of native culture, a "snapshot in time." How did the project turn out? It was wonderful, a truly memorable learning experience for students and teachers.

### THE PLOT BEGINS

We teachers began our research on several fronts. We contacted archaeologists in the state who had reconstructed ancient gardens, and we visited a museum that had replicated a Catawba garden. We also attended a native foods festival to see how garden yield and wild foods were prepared. We read avidly everything available on the regional tribes, including books, journals, and seed catalogs.

When we felt secure enough in our background knowledge to put our ideas into action, we assigned each of the four fourth-grade classes to research, design, plant, maintain, and harvest a garden typical of one of four native American tribes—the Iroquois of the Northeast, the Sioux of the Midwest, the Hopi of the Southwest, and the Cherokee of the Southeast. The children did library research to learn more about these gardens, especially what crops were grown, how the gardens were plotted, and where native seeds could be found today.

Through reading archaeological and historical records, the children discovered that evidence gathered from plant and seed remains, gardening tools, food production artifacts, and analysis of human bones provides clues to the crops grown. Historical accounts from early settlers, explorers, and naturalists are intriguing resources for students since they often describe native farming practices and foods. For example, a man named William Bartram, who wrote of his travels throughout the Southeast in the 1700s, reported that the native Americans made the hickory nut into a cream and added it to hominy and corn cakes (Van Dorn, 1924, p. 57). Interviews of native peoples made by anthropologists yield detailed accounts of gardening practices. Three of the most readable and delightful accounts for children were transcribed by Gilbert L. Wilson: *Goodbird the Indian: His Story; Waheenee: An Indian Girl's Story;* and *Buffalo Bird Woman's Garden.* Such interviews can also suggest a format for students to follow if they have the opportunity to talk with contemporary native Americans. One of my students, whose heritage is Choctaw, told us that she had planted a Choctaw garden of sunflowers, corn, beans, squash, and watermelon at home while studying her family genealogy.

By contacting the archaeology department at our state university, we found an archaeologist, Gail Wagner, to help us with our project. She had already done one native American garden reconstruction and she became an enthusiastic advisor to us, opening our eyes to the wild plants on the school—peppergrass, goosefoot, sumac, and barley—that were food sources for native Americans.

### SEEDS OF SCIENCE

Since we wanted the garden to present an authentic portrait of the past, we decided to plant native, or heirloom, seeds, which we found through seed catalogs and seed-saver exchanges. Seed-saver exchanges are sources of heirloom varieties collected by home gardeners who are dedicated to conserving the crop heritage of our country. After a harvest, exchange members return a portion of the resulting seeds to the exchange. Students can participate as seed guardians while growing heirloom gardens. (See Appendix A.)

Seed catalogs are treasures of historical and scientific information. Searching for seeds can become a mysterious and competitive quest for students. As seed explorers, our students charted the catalogs for native American varieties, finding Hopi blue flint corn and tepary beans, dipper and bottle gourds, scarlet runner beans, Cherokee blue and white dent corn, and purple tepee beans. Ordering seeds from catalogs added to the children's excitement and anticipation. Because deliveries can take up to eight weeks, you should place your order at least three months before planting time.

Once the seeds arrived, students examined them with hand lenses, noting the variety of seed shapes, sizes, colors, and textures. Our archaeologist advisor obtained electron microphotographs for us, which we showed students through the slide projector.

### A SUNFLOWER FENCE

The space available for our garden plots was behind and adjacent to the fourth-grade portable classrooms. When planning this type of project, it is best to do a soil test six months ahead. (Contact your local Department of Agriculture extension service for instructions; in most cases, that agency will analyze the soil sample for you.) Our garden site, located in the sandhills of South Carolina, required the addition of several pickup truckloads of organic compost that we obtained from the county compost (not sludge) site. Along with the compost, lime and a 5-10-10 starter fertilizer were tilled into the soil prior to planting. We discussed with students the fact that the sandy soil available to us would not have been a site chosen by native Americans for a garden. Rather, they would have preferred riverbanks rich in humus. Although we were adding chemical fertilizer to begin the garden, we hoped that eventually our plot would become fertile through composting and interplanting. (See Appendix C)

Seeking advice and assistance on soil preparation from the county extension agent and/or master gardeners will help to ensure proper procedures and schedules for planting in a given region of the country. Students can compare the native American planting legends to contemporary recommendations. For example, the Iroquois planted corn when the leaves of the dogwood tree were as big as a squirrel's ear (Eames-Sheavly, 1993, p. 18); today, horticulturists recommend that corn be sown in a warm soil, approximately 15-18° C.

Influenced by Buffalo Bird Woman's narrative on garden design, the children decided that each of the four rectangular plots would measure 6m long by 3m wide and have a sunflower fence (we found similar plot designs in the literature on the Iroquois [Eames-Sheavly, 1993, pp. 18-19] ). For the fence, we sowed three sunflower seeds per hole and spaced the holes about 30cm apart. Native American tribes valued the sunflower stalk for its fibers and used the seed to make oil and to eat.

Within the sunflower fence, the children made hills 30cm high and 45cm in diameter, spaced about 1m apart. Then, because the literature continually named corn and beans as staple native American crops, the students planted five to seven corn seeds on each hilltop and four to five bean seeds on each surrounding slope. The one-meter spaces between hills were planted in pumpkins, squashes, gourds, and other crops unique to a tribe; the Hopi plot, for example, also contained amaranth, chia, and watermelon (see Appendix B).

Once the garden was planted, maintenance began. A calendar that included reminders about watering, weeding, fertilizing, and scouting for problems was mounted in the classroom. It scheduled pairs of students to handle the tasks on a rotating, weekly basis. The calendar also noted the dates predicted by the seed packets for germination (which we later compared to actual germination dates). For the summer break, we recruited parent-and-student pairs to devote one week each to water and weed the garden. The school custodial staff, anxious to share in the harvest and extremely helpful throughout the project, assisted with the garden tasks as well.

## HARVEST BOUNTY

We planted the seeds in April and by late June beans, gourds, and pumpkins were appearing. Over the summer, teachers, parents, and students visited the gardens on both an impromptu and scheduled basis to water, weed, fertilize, scout for signs of disease, and observe the developing harvest. The following autumn, the same students, now in fifth grade, gathered the yield and welcomed the new fourth-grade students to the gardening experience by sharing seeds, recipes, and success stories. We experimented with historic native American recipes like Iroquois succotash, Hopi tepary beans, Sioux sunflower seed balls, and Cherokee corn cakes. Searching for such recipes can be just as exciting as preparing and sampling these delicious dishes. For example, Buffalo Bird Woman gives a detailed description of how to make a breakfast mush, mapi nakapa, from hard white flint corn (Wilson, 1987, p. 60).

For a class treat, we adapted this succotash recipe from *Heritage Gardening—Vegetables* by Jane Taylor (see Resources).

*Ingredients:*
   4 strips bacon
   4 chopped onions
   2 L lima beans
   I L water
   2 L frozen corn
   120 mL margarine

*Directions:*
   Place the bacon, beans, and onions in water and bring to a boil. Simmer 20 minutes. Add corn and margarine and simmer another 10 minutes. This serves 24 students.

Reenacting harvest rituals can be enjoyable for students, who especially relish making and eating the "mess." Tasting the harvest enhances memory and retention of native contributions to our lives. The children can also do such crafts as cornhusk dolls, gourd bowls and ladles, and seed necklaces.

By practicing specific seed-saving techniques, we can maintain our seed reserves for years to come; in fact, we will even have a surplus of seeds available for trading, selling, and returning to seed exchanges. To preserve seeds, students will need to air-dry them (try setting the seeds on a screen) for seven to 10 days. Then the seeds should be placed in a glass jar with a tight-fitting lid. Add 30ml silica gel or powdered milk to the inside of the jar to absorb excess moisture. Label each container as to contents and date placed in storage. Store in a cool, dry location (a refrigerator will work) and check periodically for evidence of mold.

For an exchange, students can design their own seed envelopes, complete with planting instructions and historical information.

## PLANTING A FUTURE

The seeds of excitement that grew among the children and parents involved in this project have encouraged us to continue and expand student involvement "in the field." Everyone seemed to enjoy the experience. As one child remarked, "All the kids paid attention perfectly and were interested. They loved gardening." In a relatively short time, our garden project provided tangible evidence to all the children that they could succeed in school. When students heard, "Look what you've grown! I'm really proud of you," their self-esteem blossomed, too.

## RESOURCES

Cox, B., and Jacobs, M. (1991). *Spirit of the Harvest: North American Indian Cooking*. New York: Stewart, Tabori, and Chang.

Eames-Sheavly, M. (1993). *The Three Sisters: Exploring an Iroquois Garden*. Ithaca, NY: Cornell University Extension Service.

Kavena, J.T. (1980). *Hopi Cookery*. Tucson: University of Arizona.

Nabhan, G. (1989). *Enduring Seeds: Native American Agriculture and Wild Plant Conservation*. San Francisco: North Point Press.

Parker, A.C. (1968). "Iroquois Uses of Maize and Other Food Plants." In *New York State Museum Bulletin* 144. Syracuse, NY: Syracuse University Press.

Swanton, J.R. (1987). "The Indians of the Southeastern United States." In *Bureau of American Ethnology Bulletin* 137. Washington, DC: Bureau of American Ethnology.

Taylor, J.L., and Taylor, J.L. (1985). "Heritage Gardening — Vegetables." In *Bulletin 4-H* 1279. East Lansing, MI: Cooperative Extension Service, Michigan State University.

Van Dorn, M. (Ed.). (1924). *The Travels of William Bartram*. New York: Dover.

Wagner, G. (1990). "Charcoal, Isotopes, and Shell Hoes: Reconstructing a 12th Century Native American Garden." *Expedition*, 32(2), 34-43.

Williamson, D., and Railsback, L. (1987). *Cooking with Spirit - North American Indian Food and Fact*. Bend, OR: Maverick.

Wilson, G.L. (Ed.). (1981). *Waheenee: An Indian Girl's Story Told by Herself to Gilbert L. Wilson*. Lincoln, NE: University of Nebraska.

____. (1985). *Goodbird the Indian: His Story by Edward Goodbird*. St. Paul, MN: Minnesota Historical Society.

____. (1987). *Buffalo Bird Woman's Garden*. St. Paul, MN: Minnesota Historical Society.

## APPENDIX A: HEIRLOOM SEED SOURCES AND SEED-SAVER EXCHANGES [1995 INFORMATION]

Heirloom Seed Sources
American Indian Agriculture Project c/o Jane Pleasant
Cornell University
152 Emerson Hall
Ithaca, NY 14853

Fox Hollow Herb and Heirloom Seed Co.
P.O. Box 148
McGrann, PA 16236

Harris Seeds
Moreton Farm
3670 Buffalo Rd.
Rochester, NY 14624

J.L. Hudson, Seedsman
P.O. Box 1058
Redwood City, CA 94064

Johnny's Selected Seeds
Foss Hill Rd.
Albion, ME 04910

Kids in Bloom
P.O. Box 344
Zionsville, IN 46077

Pinetree Garden Seeds
Box 300
New Gloucester, ME 04260

Seeds Blum
Idaho City Stage
Boise, ID 83706

Seeds of Change
P.O. Box 157-10
Santa Fe, NM 87506

Shepherd's Garden Seeds
30 Irene St.
Torrington, CT 06790

R.H. Shumway's
P.O. Bog 1
Graniteville, SC 29829

## SEED-SAVER EXCHANGES

*For information on joining an exchange, send a stamped, self-addressed envelope to one of the groups listed below.*
AHS Seed Exchange Program
7931 East Boulevard Dr.
Alexandria, VA 22308

Blue Ridge Seed Savers
P.O. Box 106
Batesville, VA 22924

CORNS
Carl and Karen Barnes
Rte. 1, Box 32
Turpin, OK 73950

KUSA Research Foundation
P.O. Box 761
Ojai, CA 93023

Native Seed/SEARCH
Number 325
2509 N. Campbell Ave.
Tucson, AZ 85719

Seed Savers Exchange
Kent Wheatly
R.R.3, Box239
Decorah, IA 52101

Southern Exposure Seed Exchange
P.O. Box 158
North Garden, VA 22959

## APPENDIX B: NATIVE AMERICAN GARDEN VARIETIES
What Does Your Garden Grow?

*The following list shows the varieties we planted for each type of garden.*

Iroquois: Iroquois white flour corn, Seneca red stalk corn, large bottle gourds, scarlet runner beans, purple tepee beans, yellow crookneck squash, Connecticut field pumpkin

Hopi: Hopi blue flint corn, Anasazi beans, black turtle bush beans, Cushaw squash, Hopi pumpkin, Hopi white tepary beans, Santa Domingo melon, Navajo watermelon, Hopi red dye amaranth, Tarahumara chia

Cherokee: Cherokee yellow wax bean, Cherokee yellow corn, Cherokee blue and white dent corn, large bottle gourds, sugar baby watermelon, yellow crookneck squash, striped popcorn, sugar pie pumpkin

Sioux: white half runner beans, ornamental Indian corn, black sweet corn, Hubbard squash, sugar pie pumpkin, lamb's quarters, ornamental gourds

## APPENDIX C: THE THREE SISTERS MYTH
An Iroquois myth presents corn, beans, and squash as three loving sisters that must live together in order to be happy. The tall and graceful older sister, corn, supports her younger sister, the bean, who twines around her. Squash, the youngest sister, spreads at the feet of the others and protects them from harm.

As our plantings of corn, beans, and squash grew, we encouraged the students to interpret the ancient myth in contemporary scientific terms. First, we pointed out that the practice of planting more than one crop together is referred to as interplanting and is still done today. The advantages of this method include conserving soil moisture (squash, for example, acts as a mulch, preventing soil erosion and evaporation from the soil surface) and reducing damage from pests that target only one specific crop. Also, as crops use nutrients from the soil, interplanted companions resupply nutrients needed by each other. For example, the bacteria within the bean plant's root nodules fix nitrogen gas in the atmosphere into a form that the other plants can use. Moreover, these three crops supplied a variety of dietary nutrients that sustained generations of natives. Beans and corn eaten together, for example, are complementary protein sources, because each is low in different essential amino acids.

Nevertheless, the ancient myth of the "three sisters" has a decidedly unscientific, anthropomorphic flavor. Through further discussion and observation, the students began to realize that the plants were not protecting each other with sisterly devotion, rather they were competing for light and water and for mineral nutrients in the soil without regard to their neighbors' fate. (If the beans are vigorous enough, they will climb up the corn stalks and shade them so much that no ears of corn will develop.) It is important that students conclude on their own that it is incorrect and misleading for us to think of plants as having emotions. Rather, it is phototropism and hydrotropism that explain the plants' movements.

Arlene Marturano teaches science at summit Parkway Middle School in Columbia, South Carolina. [1995 note]

## Jack Weatherford

In the fall of each year, just after school is back into full swing, Indian Season opens throughout the nation's schools. Between Columbus Day on October 12 and Thanksgiving Day at the end of November, teachers and students color pictures of little Spanish ships sailing the ocean blue, make Pilgrim hats and Indian feather bonnets out of construction paper for a quick class play, and perhaps stack up a few ears of corn and pumpkins in a corner of the class. Teachers repeat once again the stories about Squanto, who taught the Pilgrims to plant corn and use fish as fertilizer, or retell the dramatic episode in which Pocahontas saved the life of Captain John Smith.

Indian season retains something of an arts-and-crafts theme, and as the students get older, this season becomes less important. Indian season is a colorful time for younger students, but the topics seem to lose importance as students move toward the bigger issue in later grades.

As teachers, whether in kindergarten or college, all of us face a problem during Indian season. We have anecdotes and stories, graphic images and lists of famous Indians or their crops, but we do not have a way of integrating Indians into the social history of our world. They seem to be just a passing phase in early colonial history, a mere preamble to the important history that happened later, after the arrival of the European settlers and immigrants. The American Indians constitute a colorful aside, but hardly a major part, of the great drama of world history.

Contrary to these stereotypes, Indians did play a major role in shaping our modern world. In many regards, we might say that the Indians "Americanized" us. Even though the Indians did not make the European settlers into Indians, they did change their lives dramatically from what they had been in Europe (Poatgierter 1981). Two areas in which they most changed the settlers were in their diets and in their forms of government. In both of these domains, much of what we think of today as so typically American is, in fact, something that comes to us from the American Indians.

## NATIVE FOOD AND AGRICULTURE

It is the Indian foods that make our cuisine American. Many of the dishes that we eat not only have Indian ingredients but also still have their Indian names. These include succotash, chili, hominy, barbecue, tamale, and also jerky.

---

### GUIDELINES FOR TEACHING ABOUT AMERICAN INDIAN HISTORY
#### CHECKLIST

*A sample checklist for evaluating books about American Indian history continues in development. As a first approximation, the following questions are proposed, based on criteria provided by Center advisor Cheryl Metoyer-Duran, Assistant Professor at the UCLA School of Library and Information Sciences. Discussions with Center staff and Fellows also added qualifications. As other questions occur to those using this checklist, the editor would appreciate suggestions and refinements. Rather than promote censorship, these questions are intended to specify the criteria used to judge a fair representation of Indian-related subjects and to assist readers in selecting materials for the classroom.*

1. Is the image of Indians being presented that of real human beings with strengths and weaknesses, joys and sadness?
2. Do Indians initiate actions based on their own values and judgments, rather than react to outside factors?
3. Are stereotypes and cliches avoided or are references made to "obstacles to progress" or "noble savages" who are "blood thirsty" or "child like" or "spiritual" or "stoic"?
4. If fiction, are characters appropriate to situations and interactions rooted in a particular time and place?
5. Does the presentation avoid loaded words (savage, buck, chief, squaw) and tone that is offensive, insensitive, and inappropriate?
6. Do Indians appear to have coherent motivations of their own comparable to those attributed to non-Indians?
7. Are regional, cultural, and tribal differences recognized when appropriate?
8. Are communities presented as dynamic, evolving entities that can adapt to new conditions, migrate to new areas, and keep control of their own destinies? (Are traditions viewed as rigid, fixed, and fragile?)
9. Are gross generalizations avoided? (No reference to THE Indian, or THE Indian language, or THE Indian word for X.)
10. Are historical anachronisms present? (No prehistoric horses, glass beads, wheat, or wagons.)
11. Are encounters between Indians and others regarded as exchanges? (Are Indian sources of food, medicine, and technology acknowledged?)
12. Are captions and illustrations specific and appropriate for a time and place? (No wrapped skirts in the Arctic, or feather bonnets in the North Pacific, or totem poles in the Plains.) Are individuals identified by name when possible?
13. Are Indians viewed as heirs of a dynamic historical tradition extending back before contact with Europeans?
14. Are Indian/Indian relations expressed as part of native life, both within and outside of individual communities?
15. Can this book contribute to an understanding and appreciation of American–and human–history?

*These guidelines are reprinted with permission and first appeared in Meeting Ground, No. 23, Summer 1990. Meeting Ground is published biannually at the Newsletter of the D'Arcy McNickle Center for the History of the American Indian. The Newberry Library, 60 W. Walton, Chicago, IL 60610-3380; (312) 943-9090.*

The Indians may not have been technologically sophisticated warriors who knew how to make steel swords or concoct the gunpowder necessary for muskets or cannons, and they may not have been great sailors who roamed the world conquering other people's homes. Without question, however, the Indians of the Americas were the world's greatest farmers (Driver 1969). Approximately 60 percent of all the food crops grown in the world today originated with the native farmers of North and South America.

It is now difficult to imagine how bland the diets of the Old World would be without these foods. We would live on cabbages, beets, carrots, and a variety of grains stewed into gruel or porridge and, for those who could afford it, baked into breads. The American Indian tomato made Italian pastas and pizzas come alive, just as American Indian paprika added zest to the stews of central Europe. Chili peppers made Szechwan food into an international cuisine, and together with cashews and peanuts, they helped make for livelier curries in India. The Swiss found a thousand ways to eat the Indian treat of chocolate, and the whole world found new taste sensations in vanilla (Farb and Armelagos 1980).

The new foods from the American Indians not only added spice and variety to the world's larder but also made possible the greatest agricultural and demographic revolution since the discovery of farming ten thousand years ago. Europe first benefited from the American largess when the white potato spread from its home in Bolivia and Peru through Ireland and on across the European continent to Russia (Rogers 1982). This new miracle tuber produced more calories and nutrition per acre than any form of grain, and it did so on land so poor that even oats would not grow (Crosby 1972; Salaman 1949). Even though the Europeans never learned to eat maize, it improved their diet when they fed it to chickens and pigs, and it thereby greatly increased their supply of protein through eggs and meat.

The agricultural gifts of the Indians have spread from the settler farmers of North America to farmers around the world. Through thousands of years of careful breeding, Indian farmers adapted corn to some of the coldest hottest, wettest, and driest places in America. Today, corn has a larger growing area than any other cultivated food in the world. Whereas the Old World grains grow only in temperate climates and rice grows only in tropical, wet climates, corn grows virtually anywhere that farmers can cultivate crops. In my research, I have seen corn growing on the plains of frigid Russia, in steamy jungle clearings in the Amazon, on arid oases around Timbuktu, on the slopes of the Andes, and in high valleys of Tibet.

In Asia, the American sweet potato and maize grew in soils where rice would not, and their wide adoption by Chinese farmers allowed for the settlement of whole new areas of that continent. The oils from sunflowers and peanuts, as well as the protein from a wide variety of beans, helped to feed the growing population and to supply them with better animal foods.

Even today, when the United States has an astronomical trade imbalance, crops of Indian origin still supply some of our most desired exports. While we consume a seemingly endless flow of European and Asian automobiles, textiles, and electronic gewgaws, the world is not buying our industrial products in return. Foreign markets want our farm produce and its byproducts: corn, corn oil, corn syrup, cotton, cotton oil, cotton seed, sunflower seeds and oil, tobacco, potatoes, peanuts, and dozens of other crops given to us by the American Indians.

The economies of many nations now depend on these American Indian crops. Just as the United States leads the world in maize production and cotton production (a major source of oil and of animal food), the Soviet Union is the world's largest producer of potatoes and sunflowers. China leads in the production of sweet potatoes, India leads in peanut production, and the Ivory Coast is the largest producer of cacao.

In the five hundred years since the first Europeans came to America, many American Indian foods have spread around the world, but the impact of these foods may have only just begun. Indians in remote areas of the Americas still cultivate crops that have barely made their debut onto the world stage. The desert maize of the Hopis may one day help feed the drought plagued Sahel of Africa or help Iowa and Minnesota farmers withstand severe drought. The super-nutritious quinoa grain of the Incas of the Andes may one day increase life expectancy in the harsh environment of the Himalayas. Amaranth of the Aztecs in Mexico may have the potential of feeding millions on the harsh steppes of Mongolia, and who knows what potential Ojibwa wild rice may have to make the tundra of Siberia into farmland.

Corn, potatoes, pumpkins, and cranberries are all easy to visualize because they are material objects. It becomes much more difficult to see the impact of native Americans in nonmaterial domains—in the world of ideas. Even here, however, their impact has been great, particularly in their influence on modern ideas of democracy and federalism.

## OUR DEMOCRATIC DEBT TO THE AMERICAN INDIANS

The first person to call publicly for a union of the thirteen American colonies was Chief Canassatego. speaking in 1744 to a Pennsylvania assembly negotiating the Treaty of Lancaster. Canassatego spoke for the Haudenosaunee, the Iroquois League, which had grown weary of negotiating one agreement with New York and then another with Pennsylvania and yet another with New Jersey and with Massachusetts. Canassatego urged the colonies to follow the example of the Haudenosaunee and unite in a single government with one voice. Pennsylvania's Indian agent, Benjamin Franklin, took Canassatego's words seriously at the Albany Congress in 1754 by repeating the call for union (Johanien 1982).

Before signing the Declaration of Independence, John Hancock penned a long speech to the Iroquois in which he quoted the advice of Canassatego. A delegation of colonial officials carried this speech to the Iroquois nations in 1775 to plead for Iroquois help in the coming struggle against the British. As the largest Indian government in America, the Iroquois held the potential balance of power between the feuding colonists and King George.

When the delegates of all the colonies finally met in July 1776 in Philadelphia to proclaim independence, Iroquois representatives attended the meetings as friends and official observers from the Haudenosaunee. The presence of these Indian delegates marked the first recognition of the newly formed United States by any other government.

After the American colonists won their freedom, Franklin urged the Constitutional Convention to adopt many governmental features directly from the Indians. Franklin and some of the delegates had intimate acquaintance with the Iroquois constitution called the Kayanesha'Kowah, or the Great Law of Peace (Morgan 1851). One provision of the Haudenosaunee system allowed the impeachment of any one of the fifty elected sachems by a vote of the women. No counterpart to this existed in European law, but the Founding Fathers included the principle of impeachment in the American Constitution without, however, the Haudenosaunee practice of female suffrage.

The Founding Fathers also adopted aspects of Iroquois federalism. In the League, the five (later six) member nations exercised equal voices irrespective of size; this became the founding principle for the Continental Congress and eventually for the United States Senate. The league also accepted new members on an equal status with the old. The Americans copied this tradition, allowing admission of potential new states rather than exploiting new territories as subject colonies (Barreiro 1987; Burton 1986; Wilson 1959).

The Indians of the eastern United States coast met frequently with the European settlers in meetings at which each person had an equal voice in decisions. The colonists had so little experience with democratic institutions that when they started using such meetings themselves, they had to adopt the Algonquin word caucus to designate this new decision-making procedure. Eventually, this grew into a major organizing factor in the Congress and, even more important, in local town meetings. The caucus still operates today in the American convention system to nominate political candidates, and the influence of the caucus system has spread to institutions as diverse as student councils, city governments, and the annual stockholders meetings of public corporations.

Thomas Jefferson, Charles Thomson, Thomas Paine, and John Adams boasted with pride of the ideas and institutions that they borrowed from the American Indians. In recognition of the uniqueness of American democracy, the architects of the United States capitol building fashioned the columns to resemble stalks of Indian corn and covered the ceiling with tobacco leaves and flowers.

As the United States moved toward civil war in the nineteenth century, this pride in Indian heritage was obscured. Southern politicians recognized that the practices of Indian liberty were incompatible with the bizarre concept of a slave democracy as practiced in Greece. Rejecting notions of Indian liberty, the slaveholders emphasized instead a mythological American connection to Athens and the ancient city states of Greece where democracy was practiced by an elite few while the majority of the population worked in slavery.

These new politicians covered over the original architecture of the Capitol with Greek columns, and they replaced the tobacco leaves with the Greek acanthus leaves. To dramatize the tie to the classical world, slaveowners gave their horses, hunting dogs and even their slaves Greek and Roman names such as Cicero, Pericles, Homer, or Cato. The slaveholders made a fetish of Greek style, as they built courthouses, churches, and even their own plantations and gazebos in a mock classical style.

If visitors to the U.S. Capitol today look closely in some of the oldest parts of the building, they can still see the original sandstone carvings of Indian images and plants showing through the overlay of classical marble. The Indian heritage of America is not lost; it is only ignored.

Food and politics represent only two areas in which the native Americans have had a major influence on world history. The native people of the Americas influenced medicine by providing approximately two hundred important drugs, from quinine and curare to the first treatment for scurvy. About a thousand English words — from hurricane and canoe to barbecue and husky—come to us from native American languages; these words helped make English into a richer and more international language. In the realm of technology, Indians first developed the vulcanization of rubber, the bulb syringe, snowshoes, etching with acid, and an air furnace for melting ore at high altitudes. In science, Indian astronomers in Mexico calculated a calendar more accurate than that of the Europeans, and they developed a sophisticated mathematical system that used the zero.

These Indian cultures did not disappear; instead they became a part of the rich cultural fabric of the modern world. Today in our daily lives, we use native American foods, fabrics, dyes, technology, science, and ideas. We have incorporated parts of these ancient cultures, but we have often failed to acknowledge the origins of these things.

The Indian era before the arrival of European settlers in America was more than a colorful prelude to the modern era. It was the time when the roots of the modern world began. The contributions of the American Indians far surpass the traditional stories and anecdotes of Indian Season; their contributions form an integral part of the modern world.

## REFERENCES

Barreiro, J., ed. 1987. "Indian roots of American democracy." *Northeast Indian Quarterly* (Winter).

Burton, B. 1986. "Iroquois Confederate law and the origins of the U.S. Constitution." *Northeast Indian Quarterly* (Fall).

Crosby, A. W. 1972. *The Columbian Exchange*. Westport, Conn.: Greenwood Press.

Driver, H. E. 1969. *Indians of North America*. 2d ed. Chicago: University of Chicago Press.

Farb, P., and G. Armelagos. 1980. *Consuming Passions: The Anthropology of Eating*. New York: Washington Square Books.

Johansen, B. 1982. *Forgotten Founders*. Ipswich, Mass.: Gambit.

Morgan, L. H. 1851. *League of the Iroquois*. Rochester, N.Y.: Sage.

Poatgierter, H. 1981. *Indian Legacy*. New York: Julian Messner.

Rogers, R. E. 1982. *The Incredible Potato*. National Geographic (May): 668-940.

Salaman, R. 1949. *The History and Social Influence of the Potato*. Cambridge, England: Cambridge University Press.

Weatherford, J. 1988. *Indian Givers*. New York: Crown Publications.

——. 1991. *Native Roots*. New York: Crown Publications.

Wilson, E. 1959. *Apologies to the Iroquois*. New York: Farrar, Straus & Giroux.

## RESOURCES FOR TEACHERS AND STUDENTS

Libraries Unlimited of Englewood, Colorado, has published another book in their data book series: *American Indian Reference Books for Children and Young Adults*. This reference book, compiled by Barbara J. Kuipers, provides a carefully selected annotated list of American Indian nonfiction works. For more information about the book, write to Libraries Unlimited, Inc., P.O. Box 3988, Englewood, CO 80155-3988.

Jack Weatherford is an Associate Professor in the Anthropology Department of Macalester College in Saint Paul, Minnesota. [1991 note]

# PART 2

## ⚈ TIME, CONTINUITY, AND CHANGE

People need to know their historical roots so that they can develop a personal identity and see themselves as members of families, communities, nations, and humanity. Studying about what things were like in the past, what has changed, and what remains the same are the basis of historical knowledge. Determining what and why things happened is the motivation for a careful search for, and analysis of, the data obtained. Young learners enjoy hearing stories about the lives and views of other people and solving puzzles to give meaning to documents and events. Important questions approached in studying this theme include the following: How has the world changed, and how might it change in the future? How can the perspectives we have about our own experiences be viewed as a part of the larger human story? How do personal stories of our families reflect varying points of view and affect contemporary ideas and actions?

Young students must begin early to develop the skills of the historian if they are to understand the reality of past events and separate them from fantasy. Articles in this section actively engage students in studying history through a variety of topics while serving as model lessons, with emphasis on developing the skills and attitudes of the historian. In Part 2, several articles are devoted to teaching historical content through reading and other related skills. Many articles in this section suggest using local resources and topics that can be applied to units on the local community and state. Kirman provides detailed instructions on preparing sets of customized photographs for studying local history. Hatcher explains how the local neighborhood or home is a source of a wide variety of historical information. She suggests five strategies to help children understand the past. Rule and Sunal describe a lesson that illustrates how specialized collections of historical items can be used to illustrate and explain historical changes. Historians regularly seek documents from various governmental records and archives. "Petition for a Fair Representation of African Americans at the World's Columbia Exposition" not only provides the reader with an 1890's perspective of African Americans concerning their role in U.S. history but also illustrates procedures for analyzing a written document.

All elementary students encounter Columbus's voyage of 1492 many times during their school years. Nash encourages looking beyond the event of the discovery itself to the consequences this event had on people throughout the world. Among the consequences of this voyage were demographic changes, cultural interchanges, political and economic transformations, and agricultural diffusions.

Many historians consider World War II the greatest single event of the twentieth century, yet American students at all grades study little about World War II. Haas and Tipton discuss the need to teach about World War II in elementary classes and provide a variety of lessons to help children grasp the war's impact on the world, while Totten offers concrete guidelines on how to approach the teaching of the Holocaust with children.

When emphasizing the Time, Continuity, and Change strand, the teacher can choose to focus on one of literally hundreds of different events and topics, as illustrated in the range of articles provided here. Teachers will want to select those events and topics that they and their students find interesting. Therefore, the facts learned may change from year to year, although the emphasis on the skills and attitudes necessary to determine the truth concerning historical events will remain the same.

# 8

# Teaching about Local History Using Customized Photographs

## Joseph M. Kirman

The value of pictures and photographs as teaching aids is firmly established. Teachers are well aware of the now trite statement that one picture is worth a thousand words. Apropos of this, point-and-shoot cameras can provide the most novice photographer with near perfect photographs. With modern automatic 35mm cameras, you can become the producer of customized study prints and slides, and develop mini-units based on them. Automation is virtually total-from focusing to flash photography. In fact, it has been said that the only thing the camera can't do for us is tell us whether the picture is worth taking in the first place.

### CURRICULUM OBJECTIVES

One interesting technique for teaching about local areas is re-photographing scenes in pictures of earlier times. Such old pictures provide interesting information about the history, geography, and social life of the past. They lend themselves to units found in the elementary, ever-widening circle curriculum such as My Family, My Community, My Province or State, secondary units dealing with local history and geography, and reflective thinking. When these old pictures are compared with photographic updates, the following objectives can be explored:
1. Perceiving change over time
2. Examining the impact of technology
3. Proposing city or area planning ideas
4. Determining environmental impact
5. Suggesting alternate land use

You must have the answers to two questions to use this technique. First, where can these old photos and pictures be found? Second, how are the scenes re-photographed?

Photos from earlier eras can be found at government archives, museums, historical societies, and in the collections of local unofficial historians, old newspapers and magazines, and family albums. Sometimes local libraries and places of historical interest sell sets of old photographs.

### RE-PHOTOGRAPHING A SCENE

To re-photograph a scene, the following are of importance:
1. Where is the location from which the photograph was taken? Here you have to determine where the original photographer was standing when he or she took the picture. This can sometimes be a problem if the area is

Reprinted from *Social Education*, January 1995, Volume 59, Number 1. Copyright 1995 by National Council for the Social Studies.

no longer accessible to the public, or the scene from the original location is now blocked by a re-growth of vegetation or buildings. You may have to compromise and take the next best location to re-photograph the scene. A good technique is to match the center of your photograph with that of the original photograph's. In one case, in re-photographing the location of old Fort Edmonton, I found that the original view from the top of a river valley was blocked by vegetation. However, the manager of a nearby high rise building allowed me to shoot from the building's roof.

2. What is the photograph's perspective, i.e., ground level, oblique downward or upward, or overhead aerial? This is often resolved by finding the original shooting location.

3. What is covered from edge to edge and top to bottom in the photograph? This can be a problem when the angle covered by your lens does not match that of the original one. For example, your lens may provide wide angle coverage compared with the original photo, so that the subject matter looks too far away in your view-finder. There are two options in this case. If you have a zoom lens or can change lenses, zoom in or change to a telephoto lens. If you have a fixed lens camera, try to change your position by moving closer to the subject area.

4. What is the format of the photograph's edges, e.g., square, rectangle, round? If the original photo's format is different from that of your camera, there are two options. The first is to ignore the format and concentrate on getting the best area coverage. In this case, you will probably sacrifice some of the area shown in the original photograph. The second is to make a wider angle photograph by moving further back, zooming, or changing lenses. When the print is made, hand draw the format lines of the original photo directly on the print. Because of the wide angle of the new photograph, it may be necessary to enlarge the photograph to bring out the details shown in the original photograph. Enlarged photographs can also be custom cropped to eliminate extraneous detail and concentrate on the desired subject matter.

Even if you try to follow all of the above suggestions, at times it is not possible to get the exact area in the old photograph. This happens when you must shoot from a different compass point or angle than the original, or when the old photograph has been dramatically cropped and enlarged by the original photographer. This latter element may make it impossible to get the identical area unless you have a super length telephoto lens. These were problems I faced in re-photographing the original Fort Edmonton picture.

Sometimes you may not want the exact original scene. Perhaps you may wish to show the area around the scene for dramatic changes. Or perhaps newer structures or vegetation are blocking interesting items, and you need a different angle to show these items. Whether or not your photograph captures the exact scene, the key requirement is that the resulting photograph will meet your educational objectives.

## COMPARATIVE PHOTOGRAPHS-TEACHING PROCEDURES
Once a set of comparative photographs has been made, the photographs can be used for motivations, discussion stimulators, and creative activities. The latter include essays and student drawings about how the area will appear in the future, and what the area could have looked like now if certain historical events had not happened or if other events had happened. Students could be encouraged to examine photos of their relatives and home, and write family histories illustrating them with current photographs comparing then and now. They can also speculate on their own and their families' futures with essays and drawings. Another use of the comparative photographs is to allow classroom guest speakers such as senior citizens and local historians to comment on them.

## GENERAL QUESTIONS
The following general questions can be used to help guide discussion and inquiry:
1. How has the scene changed?
2. Is the change for the better or the worse?
3. What is in the modern photograph that is in the earlier photograph?
4. What is in the modern photograph that could never be in the earlier photograph?
5. If you were in charge of developing this area from the date of the earlier photograph, would you have done anything different than what is shown in the modern photograph? Why?
6. What type of life-style does the earlier photograph represent? How do you know?
7. What type of life-style does the modern photograph represent? How do you know?
8. What type of environmental impact do the older and newer photographs show?
9. Is anything being done in the old photograph that would not be permitted today, or in the modern photograph that would not be permitted in earlier times?

Take your camera with you when you travel. This allows you to photograph interesting subject matter for later use, e.g., the national parks and points of historical or geographic interest. It also provides a personal archive of photographs that can be used after the fact for comparisons with old photographs. This is especially valuable if you are familiar with the availability of earlier photographs on various subjects. For example, pictures of boats taken while visiting a fishing village can be compared with pictures of fishing boats from the turn of the century. A visit to a farm during harvest can provide you with pictures to compare with harvesting in an earlier era. Such thematic photographs do not have to be of the same places, but only of the same genre. You could even photograph your own class to compare with a photograph of an earlier classroom.

## A SAMPLE UNIT OUTLINE
One example of what can be done is to compare an old school classroom photograph to your current classroom. The result of a comparison could be a mini-unit on education, examining subjects taught in the past, school behavior and rules of the past, the people who went to school then and for how long, educational changes, the scientific and technological impact on education, the changing duties of teachers, and the responsibilities of students over the years.

## UNIT DISCUSSION QUESTIONS
Discussion questions that can be based on the class photographs are the following:
1. How does this classroom of the past differ from our classroom today?
2. If a student from that old picture could visit our classroom, what questions would that person ask?
3. How do the people in the old picture differ from us? How are they the same?
4. Did the students in the old photograph study the same things we do? How did their curriculums differ from ours? Why?
5. Do teachers today do the same things that teachers did years ago?
6. How do you think the community has changed since those students went to school?

## UNIT ACTIVITIES
Activities based on the pictures include the following:
1. Running the class for a short time using teaching methods from an earlier era.
2. Examining scientific and technological developments that have occurred since the old picture was taken. Decide what changes have been made in schools because of them.
3. Comparing old and new schools for safety features.
4. Comparing school textbooks from the past to modern school textbooks. Discuss why changes have occurred. Determine if any content has remained the same, and discuss your findings.
5. List the school's equipment that was not invented when the earlier picture was taken.
6. Invite a retired teacher to discuss how schools have changed.

7. Compare our community school taxes today with school taxes in 1910. Discuss why they are so different.
8. Discuss what future schools may be like? Do you think that changing technologies may eliminate schools as we now know them?

## UNIT REFLECTIVE QUESTIONS
Reflective questions for discussion at the end of the unit are the following:
1. What would you prefer to be, a student today, or one in 1910?
2. Some people say "School days are the happiest days of your life." Do you agree with this? Would the students in the old picture agree with it?
3. What kind of a world were the students in the old picture being trained to live in? What kind of a world are we being trained to live in? Is our education meeting this need? Can our education be improved? If so, what can we do about it?

With fewer dollars available for instructional items, producing your own customized classroom teaching materials with a camera is an excellent value for the money. The photographs are good reusable teaching aids and can even be used years from now for updated comparisons.

Joseph M. Kirman is a Professor in the social studies subject area in the Department of Elementary Education at the University of Alberta, Edmonton, Alberta, Canada. Dr. Kirman is also Editor of the magazine *Canadian Social Studies*. [1995 note]

# 9

# Children's Homes and Neighborhoods: Untapped Treasures from the Past

**Barbara Hatcher**

*The attic seemed to hold all the answers to my questions about the past. Anything I wanted to know about was to be found there, hidden under a dust cover or wrapped in some shoebox. There were stacks of yellow letters bound in faded ribbons, a handstitched bear with tattered whiskers, wire rim glasses, and delicate, flowered handkerchiefs with a musty smell. There were lamps with cockeyed shades, an old victrola, and roller skates. The room was silent with forgotten dreams. Oh, the wonder and delight in uncrating those mementos and memories!*

Teachers have the rare privilege of helping children to understand the past by investigating the "treasures" most closely identified with their daily lives — their homes and neighborhoods. In the process, educators will stimulate an interest in the lives and contributions of men and women of the past. Children will develop an appreciation for the continuity of life from one generation to another. Students will discover that individuals of all ages have similar needs and interests. And, finally, children will observe first hand the impact of technological innovation on lifestyles, past and present.

## CHILDREN'S UNDERSTANDING OF THE PAST

"Concepts of time are slow to develop in a child's mind. It is not until about age nine that anything more than a very shallow time perspective begins to develop."[1] As Schlereth suggests, children are only beginning to realize that time did not begin with them and that events happened and items were created before they were born, many times, long before.

How then can teachers help children develop a historical perspective? First, they can capitalize on children's propensity to question and examine. Second, they need to plan experiences which encourage pupils to investigate the past in relation to their own homes and neighborhoods.

Piaget viewed children as being naturally curious about their surroundings and thus motivated toward exploration. Exploration, in turn, results in the construction of knowledge by the child.[2] The following strategies are designed to stimulate students' curiosity and to promote their relevant, personal inquiry into the environment of their own homes and communities. In the process, these activities hold the

promise of nurturing a feeling of continuity with the past and of deepening children's sense of personal history.

## STRATEGIES TO STRENGTHEN CHILDREN'S PERCEPTIONS OF THE PAST

*Strategy 1: Conduct a Personal Home Furnishings Inventory*
Have pupils study a room in their home that contains a variety of furniture. Use an inventory form which classifies furniture according to type, description, original owner, authenticity, and date of manufacture. Do not include decorative items such as pictures or ornamental figurines, vases, etc.

After the inventory, children should be able to determine the periods most represented in the room. The following time spans may serve as guides: 1620-1720, 1720-1825, 1825-1875, 1875-1925, 1925-1940, 1940-1960, and 1960 to the present.

The room inventory activity is valuable because it encourages children to discuss the origin and personal history of home furnishings with family members. This experience enables children to discover that, generally, homes have a variety of furnishings, many with a history and previous owner. This reinforces the concept that much of what they enjoy today has come from others, i.e., the present is a composite of the past. For example, "This coffee table was once a library table, but Aunt Juanita had the legs shortened to make it more useful. She gave it to your Dad when we married so we could have it in our home." In addition, the object from a loved one becomes a bridge to something personally shared with the past.

Family traditions and values are also "passed down" to the next generation. Teachers may wish to extend this activity with a discussion of family values and customs. This is a beginning of an understanding of the continuity of life from one generation to the next.

*Strategy 2: Create a "Then" and "Now" Class Museum*
A class museum allows children to observe the influence of technology and social change on family lifestyles past and present. Pupils prepare for this experience by contrasting items from an 1897 Sears catalogue with current Sears merchandise. This will provide pupils with visual clues for items to bring for the museum. Categories in the museum might include: home/family care products, clothing, toys, home appliances and utensils, communications, transportation. In the grouping entitled "home appliances and utensils," for example, students may bring early examples of cookware, such as, cast iron kettles, or wooden spoons as well as more recent cooking items such as

crockpots and electric skillets. Flat irons from the past will provide a sharp contrast with modern electric, steam irons. In the "toys" category, students should include wooden wagons, wire hoops, and china dolls to highlight the change to today's toys, cabbage patch kids and electronic video games. Objects should be chronologically arranged on a continuum from the oldest to the most recent. Students should label the exhibit item with the name and approximate date of use.

If objects are too large to display or are not available, photographs may be substituted. However, a "hands on" display is preferred. The class museum illustrates how technology has changed ways of living and playing. In addition, children can observe how production has changed from simple, hand-crafted items to machine, mass-produced goods. Pupils can also note the change in materials used to produce the products, from wood, metal, and natural fibers to durable plastics and synthetics. This experience encourages children to observe the "evolution" of items and to develop an insight into the daily lives of grandparents and forefathers. The "then" and "now" museum visually communicates to young people that people in the past had similar needs and interests and were "much like me and my family today."

*Strategy 3: Plan an "Old Objects" With "New Uses" Survey*
This experience enables children to observe how outmoded objects from the past can have value. Plan an "old objects" survey and encourage students to identify items for their house and yard that are used for a purpose different from their original intent.

With such a survey, children will discover that when more efficient or convenient ways of doing something are invented, the earlier way becomes obsolete. This does not mean that an item has no value but rather that the object is outmoded as far as the original function is concerned. Many times, however, a new use has been found. This activity highlights the creative ways individuals use items from the past to meet present needs and illustrates technological innovation. The survey emphasizes to children that objects have beauty, function, and sentimental value regardless of their age.

*Strategy 4: Organize a Grandpa's Garage and Granny's Attic Day*
Garages, attics, and trunks are often filled with enchanting mementos that make the past plainly visible to children. Teachers can capitalize on this fact and plan a special day for students to bring to class an item that is meaningful to grandma, grandpa, or their great grandparents. Pupils should know that history behind the item and why the object is treasured. For example, items might include grandma's first pair of high heel shoes or her favorite baby doll. Grandpa might share a boyhood collection of wooden toys, an athletic letter from a sporting event, or military memorabilia. Teachers need to warn students that items that are irreplaceable or priceless should not be selected. Children develop insight into the personal

## TREASURE HUNT LIST

1. Identify a structure that has been changed from its original use; for example, a home into a business or a warehouse into a restaurant, etc. (5 points)

_____

*Location and brief description.*

2. Identify a structure that has been modified from its original appearance; for example, a room has been added; remodeling has occurred or is in process to the inside or outside. (3 points)

_____

*Location and brief description.*

3. Identify a structure that has been restored to its original appearance with attention to historical accuracy. (3 points)

_____

*Location and brief description.*

4. Identify a structure that is over 100 years old. It may be designated by a medallion or seal. Buildings often have the date posted on the edifice. (5 points)

_____

*Location and brief description.*

5. Identify a structure that is an example of a pure architectural style; for example, "Spanish Colonial," "Gothic Revival," etc. Use Blumenson's book as a reference. (4 points)

_____

*Location and brief description.*

6. Identify a building or house of interest to you. Interview someone knowledgeable about the construction or history of the structure. Be prepared to share what you have learned with the class so take notes. What did you discover that surprised you? (3 points)

_____

*Location and interesting information.*

7. Identify a structure that has housed the same family for several generations. You may need to talk with your parents, neighbors, or friends for ideas. Be prepared to support your findings with a diagram illustrating residency in the house. (5 points) If you can interview a family member currently living in the house about the history of the structure, you will receive 2 bonus points.

_____

*Location and interesting information.*

memories, beliefs, and past lifestyle of their grandparents and will begin to empathize and understand that grandparents were young once, too. Students will also begin to understand that, regardless of their age, all individuals have cherished dreams, memories, and mementos. As an extending activity, pupils should be encouraged to identify and discuss a personal item they treasure.

*Strategy 5: Neighborhood Architectural Treasure Hunt*
A neighborhood architectural treasure hunt heightens pupil awareness of the past. This activity will increase student's sensitivity to the space in which people live today and have lived in the past.

Danzer suggests that social function, technological development, aesthetic taste, and economic factors are all revealed in buildings and neighborhoods.[3] Examining homes and communities with this in mind makes an earlier way of life understandable and interesting to students.

As an introductory step to the activity, teachers can lead students on a walking tour of the treasure hunt neighborhood and can discuss differences in architectural style and building use. After the walk, pupils should be able to identify the predominate architectural mode of the homes and buildings in their neighborhood. *Blumenson's Identifying American Architecture: A Pictorial Guide to Styles and Terms, 1600-1945*, and Lester Walker's *American Shelter: An Illustrated Encyclopedia of the American Home* are excellent and easy-to-use references for both students and teacher.

Students then form into teams for the hunt with a suggested "treasure hunt" list in hand. The list should reflect the neighborhood and community of the students. Pupils should document the location of the home or building with an address and include a brief description of the structure before treasure hunt points are accepted. The teacher should post a map in the classroom which identifies the homes and buildings students have discovered. This will highlight interesting patterns of development in the neighborhood and community and serve as a impetus for further investigations.

An architectural treasure hunt provides pupils with an opportunity to identify the styles of homes and buildings in their neighborhood, to note technological innovation in construction, to observe change in the form and function of structures, and to recognize that over time homes can serve as residences for several generations or families. In addition, students might look for signs of immigration, industrialization, urbanization, economic growth and decline, social mobility, and land use in their locale. An architectural treasure hunt illustrates historical change and makes lifestyles of the past comprehensible to children.

> My neighborhood changed as I learned more about the homes. I used to think all houses were the same. Now I like to think of them as enchanting storybooks filled with history.

## NURTURING A FEELING OF CONTINUITY

When exploring neighborhoods, teachers have a marvelous opportunity to strengthen children's perceptions of the past. They can provide pupils with a personal understanding of history, nurture a feeling of continuity with the past, and expand student concepts of the impact of technology on lifestyles past and present. In the process, children will uncover "acres of diamonds" as they explore the "treasures" most closely identified with their daily lives—their own homes and neighborhoods!

## NOTES
[1] Thomas J. Schlereth, *Artifacts and the American Past*. (Nashville: American Association for State and Local History, 1980), p. 220.
[2] Jean Piaget. *The Origins of Intelligence in Children*. (New York: International University Press, 1952).
[3] Gerald A. Danzer, "Buildings as Sources: Architecture and the Social Studies," *The High School Journal* 57, No. 5 (February 1974), p. 206.

## REFERENCES
Burke, Mary C. "The Object, the Past, and the Social Studies Classroom," *The Social Studies* 74 (September/October 1983): 193-197.

Cohen, Lizabeth. "How to Teach Family History by Using an Historic House," *Social Education* 41 (November/December): 466-469.

Ellsworth, Linda. *The History of a House: How to Trace It*. Nashville: American Association for State and Local History (Technical Leaflet no. 89): 1978.

Kavett, Hyman. "Architectural Awareness An Important Aspect of Historical Study," *The Social Studies* 75 (January/February 1984): 42-45.

Levstik, Linda S. "A Child's Approach to History," *The Social Studies* 74 (November/December 1983): 232-236.

Patton, Thomas W. "Studied a Building Lately?" *The Social Studies* 72 (January/February): 26-29.

Schlereth, Thomas J. *Historic Houses as Learning Laboratories: Seven Teaching Strategies*. Nashville: American Association for State and Local History (Technical Leaflet no. 105): 1978.

## SUGGESTED RESOURCES FOR TEACHERS
### ARCHITECTURAL
*Blumenson, John J. G. *Identifying American Architecture: A Pictorial Guide to Styles and Terms, 1600-1945*. Nashville: American Association for State and Local History, 1977.

Devlin, Harry. *What Kind of House is That?* New York: Parents, 1977.

Harrison, Henry S. *Houses*. Chicago: National Association of Realtors, 1978.

Hiller, Carl E. *From Tepees to Towers: A Photographic History of American Architecture*. Boston: Little, Brown and Company, 1967.

Moore, Lamont. *The First Book of Architecture*. New York: Franklin Watts, Inc., 1961.

Rifkind, Carole. *A Field Guide to American Architecture*. New York: New American Library, 1980.

*Walker, Lester. *American Shelter: An Illustrated Encyclopedia of The American Home*. Woodstock, New York: The Overlook Press, 1981.

Whiffen, Marcus. *American Architecture Since 1780: A Guide to the Styles*. Cambridge, Massachusetts: The M.I.T. Press, 1969.

## HOME FURNISHINGS

Aaronson, Joseph. *The Encyclopedia of Furniture*. New York: Crown Publishers, Inc. 1965.

Filbee, Marjorie. *Dictionary of Country Furniture*. New York: Hearst Books, 1977.

Kane, Patricia E. *Three Hundred Years of American Seating Furniture*. Boston: New York Graphics Society, 1976.

McKlinton, Katherine Morrison. *An Outline of Period Furniture*. New York: Clarkson N. Potter, Inc. 1972.

*Naeve, Milo. *Identifying American Furniture: A Pictorial Guide to Styles and Terms Colonial to Contemporary*. Nashville: American Association for State and Local History, 1981.

Nutting, Wallace. *Furniture Treasury: All Periods of American Furniture with some Foreign Examples in America also American Hardware and Household Utensils*. New York: Macmillan Publishing Co., Inc. 1928.

## GENERAL MERCHANDISE

*Israel, Fred L. Editor. *1897 Sears Roebuck Catalogue*. New York: Chelsea House Publishers, 1976.

\* *most useful resources*

Barbara Hatcher teaches elementary and early childhood education in the Department of Education at Southwest Texas State University in San Marcos. [1985 note]

# 10

# Buttoning Up a Hands-On History Lesson
## *Using Everyday Objects to Teach About Historical Change*

**Audrey C. Rule**
**Cynthia Szymanski Sunal**

Introducing elementary school students to history concepts is difficult because, due to their age, they have few reference points for comprehending change over time (Thornton & Vukelich, 1988). A historical collection of everyday items can provide concrete examples to help students construct a concept of change.

Artifacts of the past are all around us. Items found in the home, school, and community have a history and have undergone change. Even something as common as a button can be surprisingly useful in revealing how technology, fashion, and the physical materials for creating clothing have evolved over time. Likewise, the consistent patterns of socioeconomic and other differences across history can be identified.

Student interest might guide the selection of items for study. Dolls, toys, comic books, cameras, tools, quilts, clocks, jewelry, keys, shoes, etc. all reflect a history and could lead to meaningful investigations. Collections of a particular item might be discovered among family members, located through collector's clubs (see your local history society for referral), or developed in the classroom (by soliciting the donation of particular items or securing them at garage sales or rummage sales). Any small, inexpensive, easily stored item that has undergone style, material, or technological changes will work well as a basis for lessons of this type. The investigation of a collection, particularly one that students have contributed to or one containing familiar items, can help students recognize their own relationship to the past. This article will concentrate on using a button collection to illustrate historical change.

## DEVELOPING PROCESS SKILLS

■ *First, the lesson concentrates on the important process skills of making observations and inferences and classifying real objects* (Taba, 1967). Begin the lesson by dividing students into small groups. Give each group a representative set of eight to ten buttons to explore. Students will be surprised at the tremendous variety of buttons. Allow them ample time to discuss and record their observations and inferences. What different characteristics do buttons have? How are individual buttons different? What can you infer about the age of a button from these characteristics?

After they've had some time to make observations and inferences, ask students to arrange their buttons in a timeline from most recent to oldest, based upon the information they've gathered. While their information is limited, this activity will help students consider differences they have noted and utilize any prior knowledge they have that relates to changes in button design or materials. For example, one student may remember reading that plastic did not come into wide use until the late 1950s. Another student might note a previously popular rock star or commercial logo on a button. The utilization of prior knowledge builds connections between the new learning and existing information. Students' timelines may be inaccurate but they represent their current knowledge and enable the teacher to informally assess that knowledge. Have them think about how buttons have changed through time. Why are buttons from one time period different from those of another? Each small group should record its ideas on a list and then share their findings.

■ *Next, the whole class brainstorms different characteristics of button design and draws them as a web or concept map.* As characteristics are identified, have students show buttons which demonstrate these characteristics.

■ *Then the class considers factors that affect button design and webs them.* Identify as many examples of these as you can. Then ask the students if they can think of examples that will link the two webs together. After they've done so, choose a few button examples and call on students to classify the characteristics of each button to see where it would be located on the web.

## UNDERSTANDING FACTORS FOR CHANGE

■ *At this point the expert (collector or teacher) steps in to broaden and deepen students' knowledge* (Lawson, Abraham, & Renner, 1989). The expert shows students new examples from the button collection, demonstrates how button design has changed over time, and makes connections between economic, political, and cultural characteristics of the past and button design. For example, in the late 19th century manufacturers sought a substitute for ivory, which was becoming increasingly rare, and celluloid, originally developed as a substitute for billiard balls, became a popular medium for buttons.

Also at this time, "vegetable ivory," made from nuts of the South American tagua palm was used extensively. Some men's suits sold today still have old stock vegetable ivory buttons.

## EXAMPLES OF EVENTS THAT HAVE AFFECTED BUTTON DESIGN

| EVENT | EFFECT ON BUTTON DESIGN |
|---|---|
| **1870s**<br>John Wesley Hyatt develops celluloid as a substitute for ivory billiard balls. | Celluloid becomes a popular medium for buttons; transparent celluloid replaces glass, "ivoroid" replaces ivory. |
| **1861**<br>Prince Albert dies. Queen Victoria wears black mourning clothing with jet buttons. | Black is the fashion, even wedding gowns are often black. An inexpensive substitute for jet, black glass, becomes popular for buttons. |
| **Post Civil War to early 1900s**<br>Industrial growth and labor organizations. | Brass uniform buttons are numerous and fashionable. |
| **"Gay 1890s" period of rising prosperity**<br>Many millionaires are made in the banking, mining, manufacturing, trade, and transportation businesses. | Large buttons with a gaudy central jewel are popular. |
| **1902**<br>Teddy Roosevelt refuses to shoot a bear cub encountered on a hunting expedition. Toy bears are used as party favors for the President's daughter Alice's birthday. They become known as "Teddy Bears." | Sew-on political buttons featuring Teddy Bears become popular. |

■ *Students should compare their timeline arrangement of buttons with the new information they have received.* The expert should answer questions and discuss the examples.

■ *Then a chart of events affecting button design is completed.*

## LINKING PERSONAL LIVES WITH "THE BIG PICTURE"

■ *Personal significance of artifacts such as buttons is connected to larger historical realities and can be related to modern trends as well.*

Discuss for example:

1. Why are most buttons now sold in stores plastic?

2. What motifs (patterns) do we find today on buttons? Snoopy, Ninja Turtles, and dinosaur buttons have recently been sold in stores. How are these related to popular television shows and movies? What other motifs are common today?

3. Why are the beautiful glass buttons of the 1950s no longer popular? Could this be related to the popularity of spin washers and tumble dryers?

4. What about the recent trend of selling ornate removable button covers for plain blouse buttons? Does this save buttons from the rigors of automatic washers and dryers?

■ *Close the lesson by having each student choose one button, describe it, and explain how it is consistent with its current or historical circumstances.*

■ *Teacher's goals are achieved as adequate background research and high level student thinking leads to significant generalizations.* Depending on the grade level of the students and the particular goals of the lesson, students may learn to connect resource concepts with business and marketing realities, and they may even evaluate the material and political culture in which they find themselves.

The depth and significance of the lessons will depend on the depth and significance of the teacher's own research and historical, social, and political goals.

## BUTTON COLLECTING REFERENCES AND RESOURCES

Albert, A. H. (1976). *Record of American Uniform and Historical Buttons*. Boyertown, PA: Boyertown Pub.

Albert, L. S., & Adams, J. F. (1970). *Essential Data Concerning China Buttons*. Akron, OH: The National Button Society of America.

Ertell, V. B. (1973). *The Colorful World of Buttons*. Princeton, NJ: Pyne Press.

Houart, V. (1977). *Buttons: A Collector's Guide*. London: Souvenir Press Ltd.

Hughes, E., & Lester, M. (1981). *The Big Book of Buttons*. Boyertown, PA: Boyertown Pub.

Lamm, R., Lorah, B., Lorah, L., & Schuler, H. W. (1970). *Guidelines for Collecting China Buttons*. Akron, OH: The National Button Society of America. From the same volume as Albert & Adams (1970) above.

Luscomb, S. C. (1967). *The Collector's Encyclopedia of Buttons*. New York: Crown.

Schiff, S. O. (1979). *Buttons: Art in Miniature*. Berkeley, CA: Lancaster-Miller Pub.

Button collecting is the third largest organized hobby in the U.S. There is a national society for button collectors: The National Button Society, Ms. Lois K. Pool, Secretary, 2733 Juno Place, Akron, OH 44313. Contact the National Button Society and ask for the name of the button collector's group nearest you.

## REFERENCES

Lawson, A., Abraham, M., & Renner, J. (1989). *A Theory of Instruction: Using the Learning Cycle to Teach Concepts and Thinking Skills*. Atlanta: National Association for Research in Science Teaching Monograph #1.

Sunal, C. S., & Haas, M. (1993). *Social Studies and the Elementary/Middle School Student*. Ft. Worth, TX: Harcourt Brace Jovanovich, 120-121.

Taba, H. (1967). *Teacher's Handbook for Elementary Social Studies (Introductory Edition)*. Menlo Park, CA: Addison-Wesley.

Thornton, S., & Vukelich, R. (1988). "Effects of children's understanding of time concepts on historical understanding." *Theory and Research in Social Education*, 16(1), 69-82.

Audrey C. Rule teaches in a multiage classroom at the Capitol School in Tuscaloosa, Alabama. She holds a doctorate in geology and is an artist. Cynthia Szymanski Sunal is Professor of Social Studies Education at The University of Alabama, Tuscaloosa. She has authored two methods texts in social studies education including *Social Studies for the Elementary/Middle School Student*. [1994 note]

# Petition for a Fair Representation of African Americans at the World's Columbian Exposition

# 11

**Wynell Burroughs Schamel**
**Richard A. Blondo**

The study of an exposition or fair can provide a microcosmic glimpse of the culture and society of its day, giving teachers an opportunity to focus on social studies issues in a rich and unusual context. World's fairs, the generic term for such events, showcase the technological and cultural advancements of a society through the exhibition of the latest inventions, the finest examples of cultural achievement, and items that typify the society. Fairs usually include amusement rides and attractions that add to the festive atmosphere.

The modern World's Fair movement began with the 1851 Crystal Palace Exhibition in London and extends through Expo '92 held in Seville, Spain, to commemorate the quincentenary of the first Columbian exploration of North America. The World's Columbian Exposition held in Chicago almost one hundred years ago marked the quadricentennial of Columbus's first voyage to the continent. That exposition, belatedly held in 1893, clearly mirrored the racial climate of the United States in the late nineteenth century, and a study of it presents opportunities to discuss race relations then and today.

Twenty-one million people attended the 1893 World's Columbian Exposition. They observed the noble achievements and technological and industrial progress made during the four hundred years since Columbus's first voyage; they walked amid the splendid buildings and statuary of the ethereal White City, with its grandiose architecture electrically illuminated; they rode the wondrous new Ferris wheel and enjoyed a breathtaking view of the fairgrounds and the city of Chicago: they also saw an array of exhibits that included a copy of the Declaration of Independence, the sixteenth-century map first bearing the notation "America," a full-sized seaworthy replica of the caravel Santa Maria, and a detailed model of the Brooklyn Bridge constructed of Ivory soap bars.

The World's Columbian Exposition included some 220 buildings and "interesting places" situated in Jackson Park, a 1.3-mile-long tract bordered on the east by Lake Michigan. The main fairgrounds included buildings representing thirty-nine states and theme structures such as the children's, women's, transportation, U.S. government, and electricity buildings. The fairgrounds also contained special areas for open-air activities such as the mile-long Midway Plaisance, a narrow rectangular tract that adjoined the western edge of the main fairgrounds and contained many novel amusements including the world's first Ferris wheel. In his study of the World's Columbian Exposition, *The Great American Fair*, historian R. Reid Badger noted that for many visitors the Midway experience was their most cherished fair memory (1979, 109). The term "midway," used today to refer to any area where sideshows and other amusements are offered, has its origins in this area of the World's Columbian Exposition.

Originally conceived as a "dignified and decorous" ethnological display, the Midway featured outdoor ethnological exhibits that sought to portray the lifestyles and cultures of a variety of peoples. Small groups of Laplanders, Egyptians, Arabs, Sudanese, Chinese, Algerians, and Africans appeared on display in re-creations of their habitats. Exhibits such as the Yucatan Ruins, Samoan Village, South Sea Islanders Village, and Native American exhibits featuring artifacts taken from mounds in the Southwest and the Ohio Valley presented a cultural diversity unfamiliar to most fairgoers.

As fairgoers walked about the grounds in Victorian garb, what they did not see were many exhibits depicting the progress made by eight million African Americans in the thirty years since the Emancipation Proclamation. Well-educated African Americans initially viewed the fair as a potential showcase for African American achievement, but their enthusiasm dampened when the white fair officials required that application for special exhibits be made through all-white state boards, effectively eliminating the possibility African Americans had to independently present their own version of African American achievement.

Fair officials deflected efforts to mount more African American exhibits. They allegedly did not wish to become enmeshed in a disagreement within the African American intellectual community over whether an African American achievement exhibit should be housed in its own building or whether evidence of their progress should be integrated into existing exhibits throughout the fair. Ferdinand L. Barnett, a prominent African American lawyer, urged fair officials to make a special effort to encourage African American exhibits and to display them in appropriate departments throughout the fair.

Although white officials did not respond to Barnett's pleas, a few small African American displays were allowed. Deemed acceptable were vocational and industrial education displays such as the Hampton Institute exhibit submitted as part of the U.S. Department of Education display in the manufacturers and liberal arts building. Booths

Reprinted from *Social Education*, October 1992, Volume 56, Number 6. Copyright 1992 by National Council for the Social Studies.

elsewhere on the grounds represented Wilberforce University, Tennessee Central College, and Atlanta University. Needlework and drawings from several African Americans from New York and Philadelphia were on display in the women's building. On the whole, evidence of the role of African Americans in U.S. history and contemporary society was not sufficient to garner much public attention at the fair, and the lack of broad representation of African American life probably reinforced conventional stereotypes regarding supposed intellectual limitations.

What did gain attention at the fair was the Dahomey Village, where one hundred native Africans lived in an artificial community purportedly demonstrating their domestic, religious, and marital customs. According to the venerable Frederick Douglass, the weekly Dahomey "tribal dance" further reinforced racist notions that Africans were "primitive savages" and suggested that African Americans were equally "barbaric." Indeed, most fair exhibits proclaimed the achievements of a Eurocentric white America, thus reflecting a commonly held western European and U.S. conviction that as their societies prospered in a material, cultural, and technological sense, they stood higher on an evolutionary scale of nations and peoples.

As a concession to those protesting the lack of adequate representation, the fair directors designated August 25, 1893, "Colored People's Day." Having previously scheduled numerous similar celebrations for nationalities and groups such as Germans, Swedes, the Irish, and people from Brooklyn, the officials thought such an approach appropriate for African Americans. Antilynching firebrand Ida B. Wells viewed the notion of a Colored People's Day as patronizing mockery. Contrarily, Frederick Douglass, otherwise a Wells ally on major civil rights issues, argued that having this separate occasion afforded an opportunity to display African American culture and "the real position" of their race.

Douglass delivered the day's major address and proclaimed a belief that members of his race were "outside of the World's Fair [which was] consistent with the fact that we are excluded from every respectable calling" (1965, 361). Wells's expressed antagonism toward the special day proposal, combined with overwhelming support of her position in the African American press, apparently affected African American popular response—fewer than five thousand African Americans attended. After Wells read newspaper reports of Douglass's speech, she conceded his effectiveness in articulating African Americans' pervasive sense of alienation from and disillusionment with the United States. He had made it clear that the fair not only symbolized the nation's technological and material progress but also had inadvertently spotlighted its moral failure to treat its largest racial minority equitably.

For foreign visitors, who might otherwise fail to realize the considerable role African Americans had played in U.S. history, particularly in the years since slavery was abolished, Ida B. Wells compiled and edited a collection of essays entitled *The Reason Why the Colored American Is Not in the World's Columbian Exposition* (1991). As originally conceived, the free booklet was to be distributed in French, German, Spanish, and English. Because of a lack of funds, only the twenty thousand English-language copies were printed. As one of its contributors, Frederick Douglass wrote, "The exhibit of the progress made by a race in 25 years of freedom as against 250 years of slavery, would have been the greatest tribute to the greatness and progressiveness of American institutions which could have been shown the world" ( 1991, 49). He submitted that instead the exposition and its White City "to the colored people of America, morally speaking, . . . is a 'whited sepulcher'" (1991,52).

When it became clear that fair authorities would not acquiesce to the call for wider and better balanced African American representation, African Americans, according to Ferdinand Barnett, "hoped that the Nation would take enough interest in its former slaves to spend a few thousand dollars making an exhibit which would tell to the world what they as freedmen had done" (1991, 135). They believed their last, best hope for recognition at the fair lay with the U.S. government and its enormous 1.25 million dollar exhibit building. A nationwide petition drive urged Congress to fund and authorize "the Board of Management and Control of the United States Government Exhibit to collect, compile for publication, and publish certain facts and statistics, pertaining to the labor-products, the moral, industrial and intellectual development of the colored people of African descent residing in the United States, from January, 1863, to January 1893...and to form a part of the published report of the United States Government Exhibit."

Congress did not respond to the petitions. Barnett, in *The Reason Why*, ended his essay by remarking that "The World's Columbian Exposition draws to a close and that which has been done is without remedy. . . . Our failure to be represented is not of our own working and we can only hope that the spirit of freedom and fair play of which some Americans so loudly boast, will so inspire the Nation that in another great National endeavor the Colored American shall not plead for a place in vain" (1991, 136-37).

The petition, dated November 21, 1892, addressed to the U.S. Senate and House of Representatives and signed by fifty-nine citizens of New York, may be found at the National Archives in Record Group 46, Records of the U.S. Senate, Select Committee on the Quadro-Centennial World's Columbian Exposition, Petitions, Memorials, Resolutions of State Legislatures and Related Documents (SEN52A-J27.1), Box 138, folder 7 of 7. For copies of the petition, contact the National Archives Education Branch.

*New York, Nov 21st 1892*

To the Honorable the Senate and House of Representatives of
The United States, in Congress assembled:

The undersigned citizens of the State of *N. Y.* very
respectfully represent to your Honorable Body that we are native born
citizens of the United States of America, and under the Constitution and
Laws thereof are declared entitled to equal rights, privileges and
opportunities as are granted to other American citizens; notwithstanding
this National declaration of our rights we are (by the force of an
unjust American prejudice directed against us, because of our descent
and complexion) kept apart as a separate and distinct class of American
citizens, and therefore are deprived of equal opportunities in making
that progress in the pursuit of moral, educational and industrial
advancement as are enjoyed by our white fellow-citizens.

We further respectfully represent that under the system and rules
established by the Board of Directors of the World's Columbian Exposition for the display of Exhibits, your petitioners, because of this
ENFORCED separation as a distinct class of American citizens, are
entirely deprived from showing in any DISCERNIBLE MANNER their relation
to, or participation in, our Country's wonderful progress in the development of its resources, and the advancement of its civilization; and
therefore there will not be found in this grand International Exposition
the slightest evidence of the value of, or any credit to, the American
Negro's labor during the last 200 years in the development of his
Country's resources, of his patriotic services in defending and maintaining the glory and perpetuity of his Country, or of his worth as a
peaceful, law-abiding and industrious citizen.

We further respectfully represent that because of this conspicuous
absence at this Exposition of the American Negro as an important factor
in the production of our Country's material prosperity and intellectual
grandeur, the millions of American and European visitors to this Exposition will naturally reach the conclusion, and render a verdict, that
the 7,000,000 of American Negroes are unfit for freedom, and incapable
of improvement by the influences of American civilization. From this
unjust verdict against us and all other American citizens, your
petitioners most earnestly protest, and appeal to your Honorable Body
for partial redress from this great injustice.

We therefore very respectfully petition your Honorable Body to pass a
Bill authorizing the Board of Management and Control of the United
States Government Exhibit to collect, compile for publication, and pub-
lish certain facts and statistics, pertaining to the labor-products, the
moral, industrial and intellectual development of the colored people of
African descent residing in the United States, from January, 1863, to
January, 1893, the same to illustrate the growth of liberty, morality
and humanity of the United States, and to form a part of the published
report of the United States Government Exhibit at the World's Columbian
Exposition. And your petitioners will ever pray.

Very respectfully,

| NAME. | ADDRESS. |
|---|---|
| *Thos B McNeil* | *24 Butler St Bklyn N.Y.* |
| *WH Sissemi* | *514 Broadway* |
| *Daniel Marland* | *680 Lexington av* |
| *Thos Jackson* | *680 " "* |

## TEACHING SUGGESTIONS
### DOCUMENT ANALYSIS

Distribute copies of the document to your students and ask them the following questions:
1. What type of document is this?
2. What is the date of the document?
3. Who created the document?
4. Who received the document?

### CLASS DISCUSSION

1. Review the First Amendment to the U.S. Constitution with your students, emphasizing the right to petition the government for a redress of grievances.
2. Divide the class into four groups, assigning each group to read and analyze one paragraph of the petition based on, for example, the following prompts:
   a. Paragraph 1: On what basis are the petitioners presenting their grievance to Congress? What grievances are expressed in this paragraph?
   b. Paragraph 2: What grievances are expressed in this paragraph? What topics are presented to demonstrate what could be highlighted in an exhibit about African Americans?
   c. Paragraph 3: What do the petitioners perceive to be the harm in not providing a representation of African Americans at the fair?
   d. Paragraph 4: What do the petitioners request that Congress do in response to their concern? Why use January 1863 through January 1893 as the time period?

   Upon completion, a representative of each group should present the group's ideas to the class.
3. Discuss the concept of "separate but equal" embedded in the argument about an African American exhibit at the World's Columbian Exposition. See the February 1989 *Social Education* for information on the *Plessey v. Ferguson* decision.
4. Discuss the changes in acceptable terms used over time to refer to Americans of African descent such as *negro, colored, Afro-American, Negro, black, Black, black American, Black American, person of color,* and *African American.*

### WRITING ACTIVITIES

Identify a grievance about which your students feel strongly. You may wish to guide their thinking by focusing on an issue of local importance or by choosing a topic of national or global importance. Designate or elect a committee to draft a petition for consideration by the class to send to an appropriate individual or organization. Discuss with your students who or what groups should receive the petition.

### RESEARCH ACTIVITIES

1. Ask your students to research and present reports on topics reflected in the petition such as:
   a. In the context of equal rights, how did the U.S. Constitution treat slaves as originally stated in Article 1, section 2, and as modified under the Fourteenth Amendment?
   b. What provisions are made in U.S. society today to compensate for the deprivation of "equal opportunities in making . . . progress in the pursuit of moral, educational and industrial advancement." Consider programs such as affirmative action and educational loans for minority groups. How are these programs threatened today?
   c. What national "resources" were developed by slaves during their more than two hundred years of labor?
   d. What "patriotic services" were rendered by African Americans not just in the Civil War, as alluded to in the petition, but in World Wars I and II, and the Korean, Vietnam, and Persian Gulf wars?
   e. There was a conspicuous absence of an African American presence at the World's Columbian Exposition, which commemorated the 400th anniversary of Columbus's first voyage to North America. How were African Americans represented at Expo '92 in Seville, Spain, which commemorated the 500th anniversary of the voyage?
   f. In 1895, two years after the World's Columbian Exposition, a separate exhibit devoted to African Americans was erected at the Cotton States and International Exposition held in Atlanta, Georgia. Ask your students to research that exhibit and present a report on how it represented African Americans. Include in the study Ida B. Wells's and Ferdinand Barnett's reactions to that exhibit.
   g. Review some of the components of the 1893 World's Columbian Exposition with your students and ask them to research buildings, exhibits, or attractions of interest and to present reports or prepare an exhibit commemorating the 1993 centennial of the fair.

### REFERENCES

Badger. R. Reid. *The Great American Fair: The World's Columbian Exposition and American Culture*. Chicago: Nelson Hall, 1979.

Harris, Trudier, comp. *Selected Works of Ida B. Wells*. New York: Oxford University Press, 1991.

Rudwick, Elliott M., and August Meier. "Black Man in the 'White City': Negroes and the Columbian Exposition, 1893." *Phylon* 26, no. 4 (1965): 361.

Wynell Burroughs Schamel and Richard A. Blondo, Educational Specialists at the Education Branch of the National Archives and Records Administration, serve as editors for "Teaching with Documents," a regular department of *Social Education*. [1992 note]

# 12

# The Consequences of 1492
## *Teaching about the Columbian Voyages*

**Gary B. Nash**

Generations of children have read about the voyages of Columbus that opened the ancient Americas to European exploration, conquest, and settlement. Until very recently, the voyages have been regarded in history texts as the heroic beginning of an overseas expansion of European peoples that brought "civilization" to an "uncivilized" part of the world. In this country, our history texts have been written mostly in terms of how the Columbian voyages set in motion the forces that would eventually lead to the origins of the United States. Columbus thus stands at the beginning of a long line of heroes who brought freedom to the Americas. This is history at its ethnocentric worst.

All teachers know these days that it is Eurocentric to teach about the "discovery" of the Americas by Europeans because native peoples have been living in the hemisphere for millennia. But we are still in the early stages of developing a multidimensional approach to the significance of Columbus's exploits. This essay argues that while we are viewing the coming of Europeans to North and South America as the history of society building and institution building, we ought to recognize explicitly that this is history from the European point of view. From there we must also read the Columbian voyages from the American Indian and African-American points of view. For Native Americans, it was the beginning of a long and tragic history of exploitation and oppression—a long-term crisis of survival. From the African-American point of view it was the beginning of a bitter diaspora of the many peoples of Africa under the harshest form of slavery ever invented by human beings.

Teaching about the Columbian voyages from more than one point of view allows teachers to show students how history is an ongoing dialogue about the past among people whose experiences—and thus their reading of history—differs. Columbus's voyages led to the largest movement of human populations in the annals of history. They initiated the convergence of huge numbers of Native American, African, and European peoples who had not previously been in contact with each other. The history of that historic tri-racial encounter can be read in many ways, and whether we regard the story as triumphant or tragic (or some combination of the two) will depend on whose history after 1492 we are considering. If students can see

Reprinted from *Social Studies and the Young Learner*, March/April 1992, Volume 4, Number 4. Copyright 1992 by National Council for the Social Studies.

this, they are on their way to understanding that history is not truly scientifically derived but is many-sided and, at root, interpretive.

Columbus's voyages also provide an opportunity to get students to put aside names, facts, and dates in order to focus on big ideas, cause and effect relationships, and the long-term versus short-term consequences of particular events. In escaping history which, as one wit put it, is "one damned thing after another," the relevance of history to our own lives becomes more obvious. Most students do not know why they are studying history and fail to find value in it precisely because it seems so remote, so unconnected to their own lives. This is the fault of a names-dates-facts approach to history. A wider framework and a multi-perspective and interpretive approach can infect students with a passion for history.

Let us look at some of the long-range consequences of 1492 and how they explain much of the world—with all its problems and possibilities—as we know it today.

*Demographic Revolutions:* When Columbus reached the Caribbean, and when Spanish soldiers and settlers soon reached parts of Central America and Mexico, an epoch began that produced some of the most gigantic population changes the world has ever known. During the first century of Spanish colonization, the transfer of human beings from Spain to the Americas was relatively slight. But several thousand Spaniards touched off a biological holocaust that catastrophically depopulated the Caribbean islands and much of Central America. European arrivers had one extraordinary advantage over American Indians because the former had been exposed for centuries to killer parasites that infect humans on an epidemic scale in the temperate zone and had built up immunities to smallpox, measles, diphtheria, and other diseases. Native peoples, geographically sealed off from such diseases, were without immunities and thus utterly defenseless against the "domesticated" microbial infections carried inside the bodies of the invaders.

The results were horrendous. Probably 90 percent of the huge native population of Central America and the Caribbean (perhaps 25 million in 1492) died within the first 100 years of contact. Wherever Europeans intruded in the hemisphere in the next three centuries, the catastrophe repeated itself. Whether Protestant or Catholic, whether French, English, or Spanish, whether male or female, every newcomer from the Old World participated in the collective germ warfare that typically eliminated at least two-thirds of the native peoples within a few generations. Millions of Native Americans who never saw a

European died of their diseases. For example, if we think in terms of the total number of people living in Mexico, it was not until about 1940 that the population regained its level of 1519, the year of Cortez's conquest of the Aztecs.

The second enormous population shift came as a result of the African slave trade. Slave traders probably carried no less than 12 million people from Africa to the European colonies in the western hemisphere. This greatly depopulated Africa in ways that would affect its development for centuries. Though the history of the Americas since Columbus's voyages has been told primarily as the story of Europeans who went there to build institutions and societies, the startling fact is that of every six people who crossed the Atlantic to settle in North and South America in the 350 years after 1492, five were African.

*Cultural Interchange:* Along with population shifts of immense magnitude came genetic and cultural intermingling of a kind and extent that the world had never seen. Even though Africans were brought in chains and Native Americans suffered horrendous population losses, the mixing of genetic pools that occurred when Europeans, Africans, and Native Americans converged was extraordinary. The intermingling was far more extensive in Latin America than North America for a variety of reasons, but in both areas extensive race mixture occurred. It is obvious today in the variety of complexions of people in all parts of the hemisphere. In the historic encounter of American Indian, African, and European peoples, the Americas were not only a battleground but a meeting ground and a mating ground as well.

Along with genetic intermingling came cultural borrowing. Historians, predominately white, have usually written as if the flow of culture went from superior Europeans to inferior Africans and Native Americans. We are overcoming this Eurocentric view and recognizing that while European political institutions, economic systems, and laws prevail, African and Indian pharmacopoeia, foodways, language, dress, music, rituals, religious beliefs, and many other components of culture affected the way Europeans lived, thought, and behaved. Evidence of this profound interpenetration of cultures is everywhere around us today.

*Political Transformations:* Columbus's voyages also gave rise to the first worldwide empires in the history of humankind and, in the process, a tremendous enlargement of the arena of conflict between European nations. The impulse to expand overseas was itself partially the result of ambitious monarchs in France, England, Aragon, and Castile coming to power in the second half of the 1400s. The New World, once its possibilities unfolded, became an area where Europeans fought each other for centuries for possession of land, minerals, and control over native and enslaved populations. Warfare itself expanded geographically as a result of 1492 as the move to colonize in North and South America led to the rise of merchant fleets, armed navies, and enlarged armies on an unprecedented scale.

Teachers should encourage students to think expansively about how 1492 triggered a 450-year period during which Europeans conquered and colonized around the world as they built their global empires. The history of the last half-century, since the end of World War II, can then be seen as a remarkable period when indigenous peoples reversed the long epoch of European colonization. In Africa, Asia, Oceania, the Middle East, and the Caribbean, colonized peoples in English, French, German Dutch, Spanish, Belgian, and Portuguese colonies have thrown off their colonial masters.

*Economic Transformations:* The European discovery of huge deposits of gold and silver in Mexico and Peru, extracted from the earth primarily with Indian and African labor, expanded the supply of money in Europe eightfold by 1600. That expansion led to the quickening of trade, both in luxury items like silks and spices from the Far East and in bulk commodities grown on plantations in the Americas such as rice, sugar, coffee. and tobacco. The expansion of commercial networks and the rise of large-scale risk taking would turn the Atlantic basin into a fertile field of capitalist development in the seventeenth and eighteenth centuries. Hence we can say that capitalism itself as an economic system was immensely spurred by 1492 and its aftermath.

*A Revolution in Diet:* Within a few generations after 1492 Europeans began to grow a large number of crops indigenous to the Americas that they had never known before. Among the most important were potatoes, cocoa, tomatoes, sweet potatoes, peanuts, maize, and green beans. Within 200 years highly nutritious maize (corn) and potatoes had become the main sources of protein in some parts of Europe, as farmers converted their fields from wheat, barley, and oats. One extraordinary long-term effect of this crop conversion was an increase in Europe's food supply because farmers could produce far more food, acre for acre, when they replaced their cereal crops with Indian maize and potatoes. Ironically, the increase in Europe's food supply led to population increase that, in the nineteenth century, when potato crops failed, impelled millions of Europeans to immigrate to the Americas. That, in turn, placed great pressure on lands held by American Indian peoples, both in North and South America.

A second revolution in what Europeans ingested came through the development of three cash crops that came to dominate agricultural production in the Americas. Sugar, a luxury item until the 1600s, became available to even poor families, and Europeans embarked on a craze for sweetness that has never abated. Coffee was the second cash crop and it, too, gradually came within the reach of masses of Europeans. The third substance was tobacco, cheap enough by the 1600s to turn most Europeans into smokers. These three substances were all stimulants—addictive and unhealthy—and all three became what one historian has called "proletarian drug foods" that killed hunger while giving momentary rushes of energy.

Some sense of how these crops affected Africans and Native Americans can be gathered from the comment of one French observer about three centuries after Columbus's voyages: "I do not know," wrote J. H. Bernardin de St. Pierre in *Voyage to Isle de France* . . . in 1773, if coffee and sugar are essential to the happiness of Europe, but I know well that these two products have accounted for the unhappiness of two great regions of the world; America has been depopulated so as to have land on which to plant them; Africa has been depopulated so as to have the people to cultivate them."

*Redividing the World's Labor:* A final change of great magnitude that resulted from 1492 was a new division of the world's laboring people and an awful increase in the use of slave labor. In Europe where serfdom decreased rapidly from the fifteenth to the seventeenth century, free labor came to predominate. However, in the areas where Europeans colonized, they enslaved American Indians whenever they could and transported Africans in chains in huge numbers. Columbus himself eagerly enslaved Arawaks and carried them back to Europe, thus initiating the Atlantic slave trade, though in the reverse direction that would come to characterize it. The "new world" for Africans and American Indians who found themselves in perpetual servitude was no place of renewal, but rather a place of new sorrow and travail.

Europeans would celebrate their conquest of the Americas (and so have most white historians) as a giant leap forward—as progress. Particularly in the United States, historians have portrayed the initial European settlements as the first step in the construction of free institutions and systems of self-government. But for far larger numbers of people, American Indian and African, this extension of freedom involved mass enslavement and exploitation; it was, in their lives, a grotesque retrogression in human history.

## REFERENCES

Crosley, Alfred W., Jr. (1972). *The Columbian Exchange.* Westport, CT: Gordon Press.

Nash, Gary B. (1991). *Red, White, and Black: The Peoples of Early North America.* 3rd Ed. Englewood Cliffs, NJ: Prentice Hall.

Gary B. Nash is Professor of History at the University of California, Los Angeles, and Associate Director of the National Center for History in the Schools. [1992 note]

# Studying World War II in the Elementary School

# 13

**Mary E. Haas**
**Janet K. Tipton**

A variety of activities are suggested here which reflect "real world" content and provide for meaningful learning. Local resources might also be integrated throughout, using pictures and information about your own community and its citizens, from local and regional historical societies, museums, and newspapers.

## I. THE SIGNIFICANCE OF THE WAR
## MEMORIALS AND HEROES

View a picture or visit a local memorial or cemetery where World War II is commemorated and allow the children to respectfully examine the site, ask questions, and speculate on the answers. Prompt the students if necessary with such questions as:

1. Why was a memorial created to this war and not to another war or to a more pleasant event?
2. Why do you think people selected this type of a memorial?
3. What is the first impression the memorial gives?
4. Do you think the people being honored would like to be honored in this way?
5. Are there others who could or should be honored? Who are they?
6. What makes a person a hero or heroine?
7. Are any of these people still living today?
8. What would you want to ask these people or say to them if you had the chance?

Follow-up this discussion by investigating the details concerning the memorial's establishment and maintenance. Seek answers to the students' questions and hypotheses through research.

### INTERVIEWING FOR DATA

Interview grandparents, other relatives, or neighbors of elementary school students who were children or youth during World War II. Ask about how the war affected their lives, families, schools, and communities. Prepare a questionnaire after some study of the home front, and send it to the interviewees or use it during the interview. Record interview responses and analyze them in a class; draw conclusions by summarizing answers to questions and noting exceptions. In the lower grades, an appropriate guest speaker might be interviewed by the class. Teachers should be conscious of gaining responses from representative ethnic groups and both females and males. Students should be encouraged to ask questions which gather facts, express feelings, and draw conclusions or make evaluations.

Questions might include:

1. How did you learn about the events that were taking place in the war?
2. What did you do to contribute to the war effort? (How does recycling during World War II compare with recycling today? — a follow-up question.)
3. What did other members of your family do to contribute to the war effort?
4. Who do you know who was in military service? (See also questions below.)
5. When you and your friends discussed the war, what did you talk about? What didn't you talk about?
6. What things did you do in school to learn about the war?
7. How did the war affect your everyday life?
8. What did you do for fun or entertainment during the war years?
9. Do you remember what you did when you heard that the war was over?
10. What feelings or fears did you have during the war?
11. What do you think are the two or three most important things for young people to know about World War II?

Men and women who served in the military had a wide variety of experiences, very different from those of children and civilians. Special questions that might be asked of or about veterans include:

1. Where did you (they) serve and with whom did you (they) serve during the war?
2. What kind of training did you (they) receive?
3. Why did you (they) join the military?
4. How did the war change your (their) life? Describe your experience.
5. What do you think are the two or three things young people should know about World War II?
6. Who in the war did you (they) know that you (they) would consider a hero?
7. How has serving in the military affected the rest of your (their) life?

Interview people in your community who lived through the war in other nations to further enrich the students' understanding of World War II.

### BIOGRAPHIES AND NOVELS

Compare similarities and differences in the war experiences of those in the local community, other parts of the

Reprinted from *Social Studies and the Young Learner*, November/December 1994, Volume 7, Number 2. Copyright 1994 by National Council for the Social Studies.

state, the nation, and the world. There are a number of books for young readers that reveal the impact of the war on the lives of children: Ken Mochizuki's *Baseball Saved Us* (1993), a story of Japanese Americans in an internment camp; Mischling, *Second Degree* (1990), C. I. Cain's trying childhood in Nazi Germany; *The Hidden Children* (Greenfield, 1993) stories of 13 Jewish children hidden during the war; *Pearl Harbor Child* (Nicholson, 1993), the story of a civilian girl living at Pearl Harbor on the day the bombs fell and through the remaining events of World War II. Historical fiction can also be used: The American Girls Collection books about Molly and her family and friends, reviewed in the Teacher's Resources column; and *Daniel's Story* (Matisse, 1993), a composite story of the experiences of Jewish children in Germany and the concentration camps—also available in a video from the U.S. Holocaust Memorial Museum.

Ask students to:

1. Relate two or three things the characters in the book say about World War II. Where or from whom have you heard similar statements about the war?
2. Explain if and why you think the main character loved his/her country.
3. Identify one or two characters whom you admire the most and explain the characters' admirable traits and behaviors.
4. Identify examples of unjust acts. Explain what actions you believe should have been taken and explain your choices.

Comparing and contrasting the lives of children in the books and the lives of children in their local community during the war on such characteristics as safety, happiness, scarcity, and sacrifices will reveal some of the immediate consequences of the war and also provide opportunities to examine prejudice and stereotypes and their consequences.

## II. LIFE ON THE HOME FRONT DURING WORLD WAR II

Primary sources in the form of radio excerpts, music, posters, magazines, and newspapers from the 1940s can change the appearance of the classroom and simulate life during World War II. Television was not as widely used as it is today; radio and posters were the important media. Experiential simulations which affect our use of energy, gasoline, and various foods can also lead to enriched understandings of life on the home front.

### TURN THE RADIO ON

Play "turn the radio on" with the students several times a day and ask students to comment on the mood of the music or the message they hear. Have copies of song lyrics available for reference. Compare the radio broadcasts:

1. What is the intended meaning of the message (in the music, news broadcast, or public service announcement)?
2. How do you think people living during World War II responded?
3. Would Americans respond the same way today? Which of the songs do you like the best?

4. "God Bless America" was a particular favorite of many Americans including General Eisenhower. Why might this have been the case?
5. Why do you think that some of the music, particularly the military's songs, are so happy?

### SAY IT WITH POSTERS

Examine the posters or postcard reproductions in small groups and follow with a discussion of the groups' conclusions. Provide students with suggestions of things to consider in analyzing the posters:

1. Locate symbols used on the poster and tell what you think they mean.
2. Decide on the meaning of words or phrases on the poster.
3. Toward whom is the poster addressed? Who produced the poster?
4. If people follow the request of the poster, what are the potential consequences of their behavior toward themselves, their family, the nation, and the war effort?
5. Why was it necessary for the government to put out so many posters?

Ask students to examine the Home Front poster in the starter kit prepared by the 20th Anniversary of World War II Commemoration Committee to determine the ways people and the community are involved in the war effort. Reach a consensus and write a short statement comparing and contrasting life during World War II and life today.

### LIVING WITH RATIONING

Simulate the sacrifices that families and children made during the war because of rationing. This can be done in the classroom and the school or with the cooperation of parents, both at home and at school. Foods containing sugar, fats, dairy products, and meat; food in metal containers; and electrical energy, batteries, or gasoline must be limited during the simulation. After several days, ask students to respond to the experience individually in a short statement or by answering a set of questions in which they describe what they gave up and how they felt about the experience. Ask students to share their individual responses and as a class discuss two or three items that students missed the most during the simulation.

1. Why might there be some disagreement among the students on what they missed the most?
2. What did you do to occupy your time when you would have been watching TV, playing video games, or talking on the telephone?
3. What do you think the children did during World War II?
4. What would be your response if you would have to continue the simulation for another month? Are there any conditions under which you would be willing to continue giving up these things?
5. Americans generally let the free market and prices solve problems of scarcity. Why do you think rationing replaced supply and demand influence on prices during the war?

## BUY AND INVEST IN AMERICA

Using issues in the local newspaper from 1941-1945, determine how people in your community spent their money. Consider:

1. What was advertised for sale and what was not for sale?
2. What recreational activities were shown in the paper?
3. What did corporations and the government encourage people to buy and save?
4. Given a specific resource allowance, select items you might have needed and valued at that time.

## III. THE PEOPLE & PLACES OF THE WAR
### GEOGRAPHY OF THE EVENTS OF WORLD WAR II

Because World War II involved so many of the nations of the world, students will need to study the locations of these nations and nearby bodies of water. The more emphasis the teacher places on the fighting and battles, the greater the need to locate places and plot data on maps. Most people do not know the names and locations of the small islands in the Pacific Ocean where many Americans died, but in the study of World War II these islands become important to learn. The use of a globe, rather than a map, clearly shows the geographic locations of the Pacific nations and islands in relation to each other and to the U.S.

1. Compare the size of the Atlantic and Pacific Oceans and the relative isolation and closeness of nations involved in the war. Discuss how these differences might impact the fighting, rescuing, and supplying of soldiers and civilians.
2. Describe Hawaii's location in relationship to the U.S. and Japan. Viewing Hawaii as the protector of the west coast of the U.S. and as a threat to the expansion of Japan and Japan's ability to dominate east and southeastern Asia helps students to see why Japan thought it necessary to attack Pearl Harbor and why regaining captured territory took so many years.
3. Show the closeness of Africa to southern Europe, the location and extent of the world occupied by the Axis and the location of the Allies on a globe. The great distance of Western Europe and the U.S.S.R. from the U.S. suggests the importance of the oceans as supply routes and the opposition of the German U-boats to the U.S. as a supplier for the Allied nations.

### ALL-AMERICAN MATCHING EXERCISE

Winning the war required interdependent actions among Americans from all racial, ethnic, and social groups. It also was an exercise in interdependence among the Allies which continued into the post war years. Combining the All-American Matching Exercise with a textbook and library search for the answers is one way students can become acquainted with the roles of diverse groups in World War II. It also allows them to discover that written history books are often incomplete and biased or prejudiced in their interpretations of events. Correct the exercise and discuss answers to such questions as:

1. Why do you think your textbook didn't provide you with enough information to make all of the matches?
2. How did gaining additional facts through a variety of books change your view of who fought in World War II?
3. How do you think people whose ancestor's stories are left out of the history book might feel?
4. What evidence of patriotism, prejudice, and heroism is there in the statements about these diverse groups?

## STUDYING WORLD WAR II IN THE ELEMENTARY SCHOOL

One of America's greatest celebrations marked the end of World War II. Yet, the war lingers on through its consequences and touches the lives of everyone everyday. The historian, Paul Gagnon (1989), suggests that the first thing this generation of students should learn, to nurture their political sophistication, is the impact of World War II on their lives. He recommends not only a close examination of the consequences of the Allies' Victory, but the probable consequences for the world had the Axis Powers not been completely defeated.

Unfortunately, teachers, facing a scarcity of time, often fail to teach about World War II. World War II is near the end of a few very thick textbooks and missing from most elementary textbooks. Many educators doubt that the study would be appropriate for young students. War is violent, and violence is something people want to reduce in our society. Since teaching about World War II holds potential for the glorification of or fascination with violence, it may be neglected, although the American Revolution and the Civil War are commonly taught. Deciding what, when, and how to teach about World War II are curriculum concerns especially as the commemoration of the war's end is upon us.

## WORLD WAR II CURRICULUM CONCERNS

Some view World War II as the best of times while others see it as the worst of times. To many it was the best of times because Americans pulled together and accomplished an important goal by defeating dictators and preserving democracy. Others saw the war as opening the door to better, more interesting, and self-fulfilling lives and jobs. The crimes of the Holocaust, the great number of deaths, the destruction of property, and the prejudice and unfair treatment of women and minorities in employment, salary, loss of property, and forced internment reflect the worst of times.

Many historical accounts fail to recognize the efforts of minority groups of loyal Americans whose work and sacrifice to support the democratic ideal did much toward winning the war. And texts seldom recognize that choices of all leaders resulted in violence toward people and nations. It is important for teachers to deal with the negative consequences of American leaders' decisions and to see that everyone examines the participation and hardships of all Americans when studying World War II.

# ALL-AMERICAN MATCHING EXERCISE

DIRECTIONS: Match the statements at the right with the correct group label on the left. First search for the answers in your textbook, and then use the resources of the library to help you find the answers. You may need to consult books devoted to information about special groups of Americans rather than only books about World War II. Use the index to help you in locating information in such books.

**a**   Navajo

**b**   African American Women

**c**   Native Americans

**d**   Japanese Americans

**e**   Chinese Americans

**f**   American farmers

**g**   Women factory workers

**h**   African Americans

**i**   Army & Navy nurses

**j**   Filipino Americans

**k**   Hispanic Americans

**l**   Rosie the Riveter

**m**   Mexican Americans

**n**   WASP

**o**   Statue of Liberty

**p**   WAVE

**1**   This group of Americans had the highest rate of volunteering for miltary service.

**2**   Thirty-eight of these women died while flying planes from the factories to military bases across the U.S. It was not until 1979 that they were officially admitted into the U.S. Air Force.

**3**   About 850 _____ members of the 6888th worked 24 hours a day to deliver mail and packages to American soldiers fighting in Europe.

**4**   These 67 are called "Angels of Bataan and Corregidor" and spent most of the war in a prison camp in the Philippine Islands.

**5**   Public Law 100-383 made an official apology for the injustice done to them and grants of $20,000 financial reparation to those interned.

**6**   These Americans served in integrated units but were a particularly large percent of reserve units from the southwestern states.

**7**   This popular song praised the efforts of women working in the defense plants producing ammunition, tanks, planes, and ships.

**8**   Large naturalization ceremonies were held specifically so that these Asians could become citizens and join the military services.

**9**   After December 7, 1941, members of this group wore buttons telling their ethnic heritage so people wouldn't think they were Japanese.

**10**  The 442nd Regimental Combat Team was the "most decorated unit in U.S. military history." They were all members of this ethnic group.

**11**  Almost all of the women trained at The Military Intelligence Service Language School to be translators and interpreters were _____.

**12**  The "Lonely Eagles" were fighter pilots who trained at the Tuskegee Institute and all were _____.

**13**  The lights on this famous American landmark endeared to so many European Americans were turned off for the duration of the war.

**14**  In New York City 40% of this population was inducted into military service.

One approach is to use the spiral curriculum model and assign certain sub-topics and interpretations of World War II to various grade levels. The least controversial information would be used for the primary children, and that with the greatest variety of interpretations and the most negative and violent aspects of the war would be examined by students in the upper grades. This model is too simple and has a number of problems.

It assumes that all students at a given grade level approach a study with the same background knowledge and experiences, which they do not. Even the youngest children know that war involves deaths. Children from various ethnic groups may recognize stereotypes and prejudices in the study of World War II and bring these out in the classroom, and they may withdraw or become outraged because the information presented is incomplete and misleading.

Another way to approach this topic is through an analysis of its key concepts and the conflicting values which emerge during their study. This model requires an in-depth examination because it includes several interpretations, many factual accounts from specialized studies of various groups of people, and comparisons and interpretations of various historical truths. Some criticize this model for sacrificing the complete coverage of a topic and for potential bias in the selection of concepts to be examined.

The study of World War II requires the analysis of important organizing concepts and values such as interdependence, scarcity, heroism, stereotype, prejudice, propaganda, freedom, security, social responsibility, justice, and human dignity. With younger students the concept model builds vocabulary and asks the students to form simple relationships between a few concepts, revise the concept definitions and test the generalizability of the conclusions (Sunal and Haas, 1993; Cousteau, 1991). The study of World War II need not be the study of long ago and far away. Students can discover that history is a dynamic process of seeking the truth which requires hard work, thoughtful problem solving, and analysis.

Because Americans of all races and ages contributed to the World War II efforts, there is a wealth of information in every community with which students can become actively involved. Local resources while meaningful and stimulating will not provide the entire story, but the 50-year commemoration is stimulating the publishing of many additional books, films, personal memories, and commemorative reprints which provide helpful background instructional material. Additionally, to gain perspectives on the war from other parts of the U.S., the world, and ethnic groups not represented in their own community, teachers can use computer networks and bulletin boards to contact other interested teachers and classes to gain and compare knowledge. This commemoration provides a particularly appropriate time to begin to teach students at all ages about World War II and to involve them in both gathering and recording the complex stories of this most important event which continues to impact our lives and about which young people have learned so little in the past.

## CONCLUSION

Studying history helps students understand change, gain perspectives on life, and practice making critical judgments. The activities in the companion piece to this article illustrate how to actively involve elementary students in critically studying World War II and how to link history to personal knowledge, interests, and experiences. Only by combining instructional strategies that require students to be researchers, producers of knowledge, and consumers of other's research, can students learn to respect the hard work involved in seeking historical truth and develop a critical perspective toward the presentation of history.

## REFERENCES

Cousteau, A. L. (1991). "Teaching For, Of, and About Thinking." In *Developing Minds: A Resource Book for Teaching Thinking*. Alexandria, VA: Association for Curriculum Development, 24-31.

Gagnon, P. (1989). *Democracy's Half Told Story*. Washington, DC: American Federation of Teachers.

Sunal, C. S., & Haas, M. E. (1993). *Social Studies for the Elementary/Middle School Student*. Fort Worth: Harcourt Brace Jovanovich.

## TEACHING RESOURCES [1994 INFORMATION]

*Art to Zoo*
Office of Elementary and Secondary Education
Smithsonian Institute
Washington, D.C. 20560
202-357-2404
(Issue on World War II, January 1988.)

*Cobblestone Magazine*
Cobblestone Publishing
7 School Street
Peterborough, NH 03458-1454
603-924-7209 or 800-821-0115
(Issues titled WW II: The Home Front, WWII: Americans in Europe, and WWII: Americans of the Pacific.)

National Archives Resources
National Archives Trust Fund
NEP - Department 1941
P.O. Box 100793
Atlanta, GA 30384
(A source of inexpensive documents, related music, etc.)

Bredhoff, S. (1994). *Powers of persuasion: Poster art from World War II*. Washington, DC: National Archives Records Administration.

Gregory, G. H. (Ed.). (1993). *Posters of WWII*. New York: Gramercy Book.

National Archives. (1993). *Internment of Japanese Americans*. Dubuque, IA: Kendall/Hunt.

National Archives. (1993). *Women in industry: World War II*. Dubuque, IA: Kendall/Hunt.

National Archives and SIRS, Inc. (n.d.). *World War II: The home front* (A supplementary teaching unit). Boca Raton, FL: Author.

National Archives - Central Plains Region. (n.d.). *Through my eyes, A child's view of WW II*. Kansas City, MO: Author.

50th Anniversary of WW II Commemoration Committee
1213 Jefferson Davis Highway
Crystal Gateway 4, Suite 702
Arlington, VA 22202
(A free starter kit is available to teachers. It includes the Home Front poster.)

## REFERENCES TO CHILDREN'S LITERATURE

Cain, G. I. (1990). *Mischling, Second Degree: My Childhood in Nazi Germany*. New York: Puffin Books.

Greenfield, H. (1993). *The Hidden Children*. New York: Ticnor & Fields.

Drucker, M., & Halperin, M. (1993). *Jacob's Rescue: A Holocaust Story*. New York: Bantam.

Leitner, I., & Leitner, I. A. (1993). *The Big Lie: A True Story*. New York: Scholastic.

Matisse, C. (1993). *Daniel's Story*. New York: Scholastic.

Mochizuki, K. (1993). *Baseball Saved Us*. New York: Lee & Low.

Nicholson, D. M. (1993). *Pearl Harbor Child*. Kansas City, MO: Woodson House.

Ransom, C. F. (1993). *So Young to Die: The Story of Hannah Senesh*. New York: Scholastic.

Toll, N. S. (1993). *Behind the Secret Window: A Memoir of a Hidden Childhood During World War II*. New York: Dial.

van der Rol, R., & Rian, V. (1993). *Anne Frank: Beyond the Diary*. New York: Viking.

Whitman, S. (1992). *"V" is for Victory: The American Home Front During World War II*. Minneapolis: Learner.

Pleasant Co. American Girl Series:
Tripp, V. (1989). *Meet Molly; Molly Learns a Lesson; Molly's Surprise; Happy Birthday, Molly; Molly Saves the Day;* and *Chances for Molly*. Middleton, WI: Pleasant Co. Reviewed in Teacher's Resources column.

Thomson Learning World War II Series:
Cross, R. (1993). *Victims of War*. New York: Thomson Learning.

Cross, R. (1994). *Aftermath of War; Children and War; Technology and War*. New York: Thomson Learning.

Reynoldson, F. (1993). *Women and War*. New York: Thomson Learning.

Ross, S. (1993). *Propaganda; World Leaders*. New York: Thomson Learning.

Mary E. Haas is Associate Professor of Curriculum and Instruction at West Virginia University, Morgantown. Dr. Haas is also President of the Early Childhood/Elementary SIG of NCSS and coauthor of *Social Studies for the Elementary/ Middle School Student* published by Harcourt, Brace, and Jovanovich College Publishers. Janet K. Tipton is a sixth grade teacher at Bursfield Elementary School, West La Fayette, Indiana. Ms. Tipton is also a master teacher in social studies at Purdue University, where she is currently a doctoral student and visiting instructor. [1994 note]

**Samuel Totten**

*How do you teach events that defy knowledge, experiences that go beyond imagination? How do you tell children, big and small, that society could lose its mind and start murdering its own soul and its own future? How do you unveil horrors without offering at the same time some measure of hope? Hope in what? In whom? In progress, in science and literature and God. (Wiesel, 1978, p. 270)*

These heartrending words, thoughts, and interrogatives go to the very core of the difficulty that teachers—especially upper elementary and middle school teachers—face when teaching about the Holocaust. What took place during the Nazi reign of terror is horrifying, ghastly, and yes, almost unbelievable. But it did happen, and there is a moral imperative to teach young students about certain aspects of that watershed event.

The story of the Holocaust becomes even more horrifying when one realizes that "up to one and a half million children were murdered by the Nazis and their collaborators between 1933 and 1945" (United States Holocaust Museum, 1993, p. 1). While "the overwhelming majority of them were Jewish, thousands of Roma (Gypsy) children, disabled children, and Polish children were also among the victims" (United States Holocaust, 1993, p. 1).

In this piece some general guidelines, teaching strategies, and resources for teaching the Holocaust at the upper elementary and middle level will be briefly discussed. It is written in the spirit that children need to know about this event but they need not and, indeed, should not be barraged with one horrifying story or image after another.

## GUIDELINES FOR TEACHING AND LEARNING ABOUT THE HOLOCAUST

The first thing that teachers need to ask themselves is the question: "Why teach elementary and middle school children about the Holocaust?" Without clearly delineated goals and objectives, it is not wise to teach about the Holocaust or any subject for that matter. Indeed, to not raise such questions with a topic as overwhelming as the Holocaust leaves the study bereft of focus and in danger of degenerating into a barrage of horrifying stories and photographs which numb the students. Such teaching not only constitutes poor pedagogy but is morally unconscionable.

Reprinted from *Social Studies and the Young Learner,* November/December 1994, Volume 7, Number 2. Copyright 1994 by National Council for the Social Studies.

In addition to the issue of why students should learn this history, teachers should identify the most significant lessons students can learn about the Holocaust and how a particular reading, image, document, or film is an appropriate medium for conveying the selected Holocaust lesson (Parsons & Totten, 1993).

In *Guidelines for Teaching About the Holocaust,* Parsons and Totten (1993) suggest that teachers:

- decide how the term "Holocaust" will be defined before teaching about the subject;
- avoid comparisons of pain between and amongst various people and situations;
- avoid simple answers to complex historical questions;
- strive for precision when discussing facts, different types of sources of information (e.g., fact, opinion, fiction and/or types of sources—primary or secondary), and the use of terminology/language (e.g., there was a distinct difference between concentration camps and killing centers just as there was between armed and spiritual resistance);
- avoid stereotypical descriptions;
- do not romanticize the history or various situations for the purpose of reaching the students;
- contextualize the history, put it into a historical perspective;
- translate statistics into real people (the point is, millions of anything, let alone peoples' deaths, are meaningless to most people, so focus on the human story);
- select appropriate content and resources (don't use something that is too complex or too horrifying);
- and select developmentally appropriate and sensitive learning activities (pp. 1-8).

Pre and post assessment of learning is critical to the study of the Holocaust. One outstanding way of beginning a lesson or unit on the Holocaust is simply to ask the students to brainstorm all that they know about the Holocaust.

As they do so the teacher can write their answers and comments on the board. In this way, the teacher will immediately be able to assess the depth of their understanding, the amount of factual material they actually know, and what myths and misconceptions are held regarding the event. Teachers can accomplish the same goal by having every student create a cluster or mindmap around the target word Holocaust. The students are then directed to develop as detailed and accurate a cluster as they possibly can. Such clusters are collected by the teacher and/or discussed with the class. At the end of the lesson or unit, the students could be asked to do a new cluster, this time based on their new knowledge, and then they could compare and contrast, orally or in writing, the differences between their original and their second clusters.

The appreciation of the Holocaust victims as individuals is also a key concern for student learning. Mothers, fathers, grandfathers, grandmothers, brothers, sisters, uncles and aunts were the victims of the Nazis. This is generally not conveyed in a discussion about the millions who perished. In order to avail the students of these individual stories, both first-person accounts of those who experienced the Holocaust and/or fictional accounts (short stories, novellas, and novels) of individuals who faced its trials and tribulations in different ways and met different ends should be included. The use of first-person accounts in the classroom can transform the study from "a welter of statistics, remote places and events, to one that is immersed in the 'personal' and 'particular' " (Totten, 1987, p. 63).

When using videotapes (e.g., documentaries, first-person accounts, fictional dramas), a solid method of moving the students from passive to active is to have them address the following three questions *in writing* (either while watching the video or at the conclusion of it):

1. Name the most important thing you learned about the Holocaust from this video, and state why you consider it to be so important; 2. Briefly describe the most interesting thing you learned from the video, and state why you consider it so interesting; and 3. Name one thing you learned from the video that you may never forget, and state why that is so. Another interesting question that teachers may wish to substitute for one of the above questions is: Name one new aspect of the Holocaust that you learned from the video, and briefly state why you found it so interesting or important. These are not the only questions, of course, that teachers could ask. Teachers, in fact, may wish to design their own questions and use them in place of any and/or all of the aforementioned questions. No matter what, though, teachers should require that the students (all of them) write down their responses. Why? Because, this will engage all of the students in thinking—not just one or two of them. It will also provide the students with notes to speak from during the subsequent discussion. This activity, of course, could also serve as an outstanding prewriting activity from which the students could be asked to write a more detailed piece (essay, poem, short story, etc.)

## RESOURCES FOR ELEMENTARY AND MIDDLE LEVEL TEACHERS

For many years there were only a small number of outstanding resources about the Holocaust for upper elementary and middle level teachers. In fact, more often than not many teachers relied solely on the classic story of Anne Frank. The diary that Anne Frank wrote is outstanding and many students find it extremely engaging. However, it only tells part of the Holocaust story. That is, it relates the ever-increasing discriminatory actions of the Nazis, a family's life in hiding, and a young girl's perspicuous insights, but it concludes prior to the deportation of Jews and others to the death camps.

So, when teachers use only Anne Frank's story, the study remains incomplete. Some teachers have also noted that their female students find the story more engaging than the males.

Fortunately, there are an increasing number of outstanding, historically accurate, and highly engaging works (personal accounts, novels and nonfiction pieces) written especially for an upper elementary and middle school audience. Some of the better written, most accurate, and most engaging pieces will be mentioned and succinctly commented upon here.

## GUIDELINES FOR TEACHING ABOUT THE HOLOCAUST

Darsa, J. (1992). "Educating about the Holocaust: A Case Study in the Teaching of Genocide." In I. Chamy (Ed.). *Genocide: A Critical Bibliographic Review*, 2, (pp. 175-193). New York: Facts on File.

Parsons, W. S., & Totten, S. (1993). *Guidelines for Teaching About the Holocaust*. Washington, DC: United States Holocaust Memorial Museum. Available from the U.S. Holocaust Memorial Museum, 100 Raoul Wallenberg Place SW, Washington, DC 20024.

Totten, S. (1987). "The Personal Face of Genocide: Words of Witnesses in the Classroom." *Social Science Record*, 24(2), 63-67. Discusses the strategy of personalizing the statistics of the Holocaust. See this entire special issue of the *Social Science Record* ("Genocide: Issues, Approaches, Resources").

## GENERAL HISTORY OF THE HOLOCAUST

Altshuler, D. (1978). *Hitler's War Against the Jews*. New York: Behrman House.

Meltzer, M. (Ed.). (1976). *Never to Forget: The Jews of the Holocaust*. New York: Harper & Row.

Rogasky, B. (1988). *Smoke and Ashes: The Story of the Holocaust*. New York: Holiday House.

## FIRST-PERSON ACCOUNTS

Frank, A. (1969). *Anne Frank: The Diary of a Young Girl*. New York: Washington Square Press. The Perfection Form Company (Logan, IA) provides a teacher's guide to this book containing extensive resource material. Another teacher aid is: Shawn, K. (1989). *The End of Innocence: Anne Frank and the Holocaust*. New York: Anti-Defamation League of B'nai B'rith.

Friedman, I. R. (1990). *The Other Victims: First-person Stories of Non-Jews Persecuted by the Nazis*. Boston: Houghton Mifflin. A set of first-person stories about the Holocaust which includes the experiences of Gypsies, certain Christians, Blacks, Jehovah's witnesses, and homosexuals, also targeted by the Nazis.

Totten, S. (1991). *First-Person Accounts of Genocidal Acts Committed in the Twentieth Century: An Annotated Bibliography*. Westport, CT: Greenwood Press. A wide range of first-person accounts, some of which would be useful at the upper elementary and middle school level.

Wiesel, E. (1960). *Night*. New York: Hill & Wang. One of the most powerful first-person accounts of the Holocaust. It provides a harrowing report of the round-ups, deportations, and life and death in the camps. This volume should primarily be read by older and/or mature middle level students because of its graphic images.

## FICTION

Lowry, L. (1968). *Number the Stars*. New York: A Yearling Book.*

Matas, C. (1993). *Daniel's Story*. New York: Scholastic Inc.

Reiss, J. (1972). *The Upstairs Room*. New York: Harper Trophy.*

Siegal, A. (1981). *Upon the Head of the Goat: A Childhood in Hungary 1939-1944*. New York: Puffin Books.*

\* *These books are among the works of fiction about the Holocaust which are either a Newbery Award Winner or a Newbery Honor Book.*

## RESOURCES FROM THE
## U.S. HOLOCAUST MEMORIAL MUSEUM

United States Holocaust Memorial Museum. (1993). *Annotated Bibliography*. Washington, DC: Author.

———. (1993). *Annotated Videography*. Washington, DC: Author.

———. (1992). *Children in the Holocaust (An Information Sheet)*. Washington, DC: Author.

———. (1992). Artifact poster series. Washington, DC: Author. This series is comprised of photographs on 3' x 2' color posters of artifacts that are found in the Museum in Washington, D.C. Each artifact serves to highlight a theme/topic that is critical to understanding various aspects of the Holocaust years. Among the artifacts that are highlighted are: a Hollerith machine, which was the precursor of the modern computer and was used for census taking; a pile of prisoner shoes; and stars and armbands the Nazis forced different groups of people to wear.

## CONCLUSION

Teaching young people about the Holocaust is never an easy task. How could it be? However, it is one that is vitally significant and one that must be undertaken with considerable thought and sensitivity.

As for the educator's role, philosopher Hannah Arendt had this to say:

> "Education is the point at which we decide whether we love the world enough to assume responsibility for it and by the same token save it from ruin which, except for renewal, except for the coming of the new and young, would be inevitable" (Greene, 1982).

## REFERENCES

Greene, M. (1982). *Wide Awakeness in Dark Times*. Paper presented at Teacher's College, Columbia University, New York.

Volavkova, H. (Ed.). (1993). *I Never Saw Another Butterfly: Children's Drawings and Poems from Terezin Concentration Camp, 1942-1944*. New York: Schocken Books.

Wiesel, E. (1978). "Then and Now: The Experiences of a Teacher." *Social Education*, 42(4), pp. 266-271.

Samuel Totten is an Associate Professor at the University of Arkansas, Fayetteville. Dr. Totten is also an educational consultant to the U.S. Holocaust Memorial Museum Education Department in Washington, D.C., a member of the Council of the Institute on Holocaust and Genocide, Jerusalem, and an advisory board member for the Center for Comparative Genocide Studies, Sydney, Australia. [1994 note]

# PART 3
## ◉ PEOPLE, PLACES, AND ENVIRONMENTS

People change the places in which they live, thereby changing their environment. At the same time, the physical and cultural environments in which people live may limit the actions and decisions that people make. Television and computer technology bring distant people and places into the everyday life of today's students. Examining the interactions between people, places, and environments raises questions such as, Where are things located? Why are they located where they are? Do people in similar environments make similar decisions about how to use their resources? Are environmental changes in one place limited only to that place and the people living there? How have humans altered their environments?

Elementary students enjoy learning not only about their own area but also about the places and people living great distances from them. Young learners are also concerned with preserving the natural environment for future generations. This strand is present in studies of global issues, and is basic to geography and integral to all time periods. Peters argues that there is a need to nurture in young children an environmental and social ethic as an integrated part of their global citizenship responsibilities. McKeown-Ice offers specific examples, demonstrating how cultural and geographical perspectives play an important role in environmental education. Kronholm and Ramsey present a unit of study in which fifth graders examined the perceptions and issues related to the Timber Wolf Recovery Plan in Wisconsin.

Another approach to teaching aspects of this geography-oriented strand is presented through the use of the five themes of geography. Murphey defines these themes and provides examples of how teachers can tailor each theme to the study of their individual school sites. Gutierrez and Sanchez describe how their school developed an outdoor laboratory and over a year's time involved young children in learning key geographic concepts and mapping skills. Mulloy and Collins present an activity in which students practice map skills and discover Spanish names and terms on the American landscape. The Muir and Cheek article is devoted entirely to identifying the necessary skills for understanding maps. It provides teachers with examples of how to assess students' levels of understanding in relation to their developmental abilities. In using the assessment tasks presented in the article, teachers and curriculum developers will be able to identify the difficulties children have in mastering each skill, and thereby obtain assistance in teaching developmentally appropriate map skills that are more likely to be understood and mastered by the student.

The twenty-first century will bring great challenges and greater interdependence among people throughout the world. Students will be called on to help formulate and implement policies concerning the environment. Studying this strand during the elementary grades prepares students to critically examine both the roles of geography and their own behavior, and the impact they have on the environment. This strand also helps children learn of the physical and cultural diversity of the world.

**Richard Peters**

A little over a decade ago, the International Activities Committee of National Council for the Social Studies declared that technological advances, increased trade, tourism and cultural exchanges, environmental concerns, market competition and scarce resources will draw nations into increasingly complex relationships. The day-to-day lives of people in all nations will be influenced by increased cross-cultural links, as well. Individuals will be required to understand and interact with peoples, cultures, languages, lifestyles and value systems that differ from their own.

Because we live in a global age, existing simultaneously within the context of several interrelated and interactive real world environments, today's children must begin to comprehend the character and complexity of the global community. They will need this knowledge in order to become effective citizens of the 21st century.

Because humans and nature are inextricable entities sharing a common global lifespace, natural and social (human-made) environments are interactive and interdependent. This interconnection is necessary for the prosperity of the various species. Environmental phenomena (e.g., people, places, things and events) exist in a perpetual state of interlocking dependency.

Humans constantly intrude upon nature. In order to successfully live in natural and social worlds, humans must understand the origins, composition, characteristics and life-sustaining processes of these worlds.

Children's attention should be focused on the diversity of natural and social settings, those close to home as well as far-removed. During the course of a typical school day, they should be provided ample opportunities to interact with, and learn from, natural and social phenomena. To isolate children from the lifespace environment of the local community, and the world-at-large, is to diminish the relevance of formal education in their daily lives.

Children need to acquire a social ethic that:

- develops their awareness of the natural and social worlds around them
- informs them about past and present conflicts, issues and situations related to natural and social environments, cultures and ethnic groups
- allows them to have empathy for the plights of nature and diverse cultures and ethnic groups

- helps them to understand the character of diverse natural and social environments both close to home and far-removed
- enables them to exhibit, through proactive involvement, attitudes and opinions about ecology-related and social environment-related issues in contemporary life
- helps them to perceive and understand relationships between humans and nature
- helps them understand relationships among cultures and ethnic groups
- allows them to recognize the differences and similarities among diverse cultures.

Today, as in the past, the place of humans in the world is to coexist with nature and other peoples. Action must be taken in our schools today to help tomorrow's global citizens think and act in responsible ways to 1) clean-up natural and social environments, 2) establish and enforce policies and programs that guarantee the maintenance of a quality global lifespace and 3) educate a *nature sensitive and culture literate* citizenry.

A natural/physical and social science-fused curriculum that is continuous (K-12) integrated (interdisciplinary) and sequential (developmental) can be designed to introduce students to:

- the effect(s) that personal/ group decisions and actions have on others and themselves
- the need to take responsibility for protecting living things that are dependent upon humans for their survival
- the creation of an environmental ethic
- the character of natural and social environments
- an understanding of the impact humans have had/are having upon the total lifespace environment
- an understanding of the impact nature has had/is having upon human lifestyles, cultures and value systems
- an awareness of community service activities that will promote participatory citizenship and decision-making
- the need for a stewardship attitude regarding the conservation and management of natural and human/social resources
- the development of social attitudes, behavior patterns and values
- the concept of perceptual self-denial through everyday living
- the problems and situations affecting natural and social environments—and related phenomena
- the differing personal styles of working actively for conflict-resolution and problem-solving.

Humans and nature lead a common existence on earth. What is the role of humans in nature? How do we, as individuals, fit into established culture patterns and social schemes? Each generation of the human species must ask these questions. Each generation of the human species must find its place in the global biosphere. How we answer these questions, and how we choose to act upon those answers, will determine the inevitable fate of humans and nature on earth—in the 21st century and beyond.

Richard Peters is an Assistant Professor of Education at Texas A&M University, Corpus Christi. [1993 note]

**Rosalyn McKeown-Ice**

Geographers and geography educators have been interested in environmental research, issues, and education for decades. This interest stems from geographers' attempts to understand spatial patterns. Geographers study both natural and cultural landscapes, thus forming a disciplinary bridge between the natural and social sciences. Non-geographers are rarely aware of this interest or the vast geographic literature about environmental topics. The purposes of this article are 1) to describe common geographic approaches to the study of the environment, 2) to describe major contributions of geography education to environmental education, and 3) to note four educational activities which will shape the role of geography in environmental education.

## INQUIRY INTO THE ENVIRONMENT

Geographers study the environment through four avenues of inquiry. First, geographers study the natural environment using scientific methods and techniques. Second, geographers study how human behaviors affect the environment. Third, geographers study how the environment influences human behaviors. Fourth, geographers study how populations perceive their surrounding environments and how those perceptions are expressed in the landscape. Within these avenues of inquiry, geographers examine spatial patterns of environmentally related topics at different scales—local, regional, and global. Some of these avenues of study are unique to geography while others are common with other disciplines in the natural and social sciences.

## STUDY OF THE NATURAL ENVIRONMENT

Like biologists, ecologists. geologists, chemists, and geophysicists, geographers study the natural environment. Geography encompasses the study of both biotic and abiotic elements of the natural landscape, the distribution of those elements, and how they change over space and time. Geographers also inquire into the processes that affect the surface of the Earth. They study why the wind blows and what it brings with it, where different types of trees grow and why; they map the migration paths of different animals and ponder the pressure those animals put on migration routes. They also study the frequency of floods and droughts. Geographers study the changing patterns

Reprinted with permission from Texas A & M, from *Journal of Geography*, January/February 1994, Volume 93, Number 1. Copyright 1994 by Texas A & M.

of vegetation in the tropics since the last glaciation. Geographers also study the distribution of streamflow in various physiographic regions, searching for explanations of why some rivers flow year round while others flow only after rainfall. In this line of inquiry geographers often ask, What is the distribution of a natural phenomenon in nature? What do we know about this phenomenon? What causes or influences the distribution of this phenomenon?

Geographers also study the processes that change natural landscapes. These geomorphic natural processes include erosion and deposition by streams, wind, and ice. For example, geographers study erosional processes which change the shapes of mountains and beaches.

## STUDY OF HUMAN IMPACT ON THE ENVIRONMENT

Geographers study the impact of humans on the environment. In the study of human influence and alteration of the environment, geography is a bridge between the natural and social sciences, uniting the study of the natural environment and the study of human behavior. Geographers look at how human behaviors affect the environment. For example, biogeographers study how forest fire suppression affects succession, and how pollution such as acid rain affects plant and animal communities. Physical geographers study how damming rivers affects the flood frequency and how soil compaction affects erosion. Geographers also study how human-induced environmental degradation affects the economy.

Geographers also study the cultural processes that affect landscapes. Some cultural processes are settlement, urbanization, land-use change, and the diffusion of ideas around the world and tangible items (such as food stuffs). For example, geographers study the diffusion of the potato from the New World to the Old World and how it changed agricultural and dietary patterns.

## STUDY OF ENVIRONMENTAL INFLUENCES ON HUMAN BEHAVIORS

Geographers look at how the environment affects human behavior. That is not to say that the environment dictates human behavior (environmental determinism), but that the environment influences human behavior. For example, repeated flooding and subsequent governmental regulations often lead to prohibitions against building permanent residential and/or industrial structures on floodplains. People also tend to build houses with characteristics that reflect their adaptation to regional climates. For example, houses in Florida have less insulation than those in Alaska. Geographers are currently looking at environmental pressures, such as the availability of water, which could limit industrial, agricultural, and population growth in the arid American Southwest during the next decades.

## STUDY OF CULTURAL PERCEPTIONS OF THE ENVIRONMENT

Geographers study how different peoples and cultures perceive their surroundings and how those perceptions affect the way people use the environment. In the aerial photography of Gerster, the presence of roads on the American landscape is striking. The American people have used acres of farmland and millions of cubic meters of gravel and asphalt to create an intricate system of freeways, highways, and roads. The roads branch into streets and eventually into individual driveways. We consume millions of gallons of petroleum to fuel our use of these roadways. We as a society have decided to dedicate a vast quantity of our resources to make convenient, individual use of automobile transport possible. This pattern of roadways and use of resources is not apparent in South America or on some of the other continents. A population's perception of the value of resources affects more than road patterns; it influences a society's awareness, use, and/or conservation of energy, water, and other natural resources.

## USE OF SCALE IN THE STUDY OF THE ENVIRONMENT

Geographers study resource use and environmental change on three scales: local, regional, and global. Maps which display the spatial distribution of phenomena often move geographers to inquiry. Geographers frequently map a phenomenon and try to explain the pattern of the spatial distribution.

These four avenues of inquiry and the consideration of different scales form the foundation for a geographic perspective for teaching about the environment.

## MAJOR THEMES OF ENVIRONMENTAL EDUCATION

Environmental education has its roots in nature education, geographic education, conservation education, outdoor education, and science education; however, environmental education is emerging as a discipline of its own. In spite of many different disciplinary approaches and little agreement on the definition of environmental education, several major themes can be identified. They are: 1) the interrelationship between natural and social systems, 2) the unity of humankind with nature, 3) the impacts of a society's technology and decision making, and 4) the continuation of learning throughout the human life cycle (Roth 1991).

Parallels in geographic education are found for each of the themes of environmental education. 1) Geography also bridges natural and social science, revealing interrelationships between natural and social systems. 2) Geographers view humans as agents of landscape change, effecting and affecting processes that modify their surroundings. Geographers rarely seek places for research that are unaffected by humans, rather they include humans as part of the study.

3) For years, geographers have been examining the effects of technology and the impact of the choice of technologies on the land and the people. 4) Geography educators, like environmental educators, mathematics educators, science educators, etc., strive to motivate students to be life-long learners. Given the parallel nature of environmental and geographic education, many educators see geography as the ideal disciplinary vehicle for environmental education.

## CONTRIBUTIONS OF GEOGRAPHY TO ENVIRONMENTAL EDUCATION

A common and widely adopted approach to geographic education in the United States is to organize geography content using the five themes. The five themes are: location, place, human-environment interactions, movement, and regions. The commonalities between geographic education and environmental education are perhaps the most obvious through the theme of human-environmental interactions. Examples of human-environmental interactions have been described previously. The other four themes— location, place, movement, and region—can have strong environmental components as well. For example, residents of the Love Canal neighborhood became very concerned about the *location* of their homes in relation to the toxic dump, and the physical presence of the toxic wastes became part of the description of the cultural and physical components of the *place*. The *movement* of the Islip garbage barge was watched by millions of Americans on the evening news as its captain tried to find a port that would accept the garbage. *Regions* are also being defined by environmental parameters, such as the region of increasing desertification south of the Sahara in Africa. Environmental concerns can be studied using all of the five themes.

Some educators hold the opinion that geography's greatest contributions to environmental studies and environmental education are use of scale and emphasis of global interconnections. The use of three scales (local, regional, and global) is essential for students to understand the global implications of local environmental degradation. For example, the draining and filling of wetlands for development may appear to have few global impacts; however, the environmental alteration can destroy nesting and feeding grounds of waterfowl, thereby affecting hemispheric patterns of waterfowl migration and population. Through environmental education, students must realize that local actions can positively or negatively affect global environmental health. The use of geographic scale and interconnections are essential to the process of local learning leading to global understanding of environmental issues.

Maps also illustrate that local problems are often an important component of global problems. Maps in atlases such as *Gaia: An Atlas of Planet Management* (Myers 1984) or *World Resources, 1993* (World Resources Institute 1992) help students visualize the magnitude of local environmental degradation repeated around the world. For example, a map of global production, exports, and imports of oil compared to a map of visible oil slicks rapidly illustrates the magnitude of marine pollution. Cartography and map interpretation offer a strong analytic component to environmental education.

## MULTICULTURAL PERSPECTIVE

A current educational trend that is reflected in environmental education is to create curricula which include multicultural perspectives. Geography inherently uses a multicultural approach, because of its international focus and its study of the different cultural perceptions and uses of the environment. Geography provides the opportunity for students to study other cultures and compare them to their own. This comparison leads to the realization that cultures around the world use their resources in different ways resulting in different patterns on the landscape. It also leads to the understanding that cultural norms are not the same around the world and it fosters greater tolerance of other peoples and cultures.

## THE FUTURE OF ENVIRONMENTAL AND GEOGRAPHIC EDUCATION

Four major events have the potential to shape the future of environmental and geographic education in the United States well into the 21st century. First, environmental literacy standards are currently being drafted by the American Society for Testing and Measurement (ASTM). The lack of environmental education standards, either written or commonly accepted, has led to confusion among groups such as grant making agencies, school boards, curriculum developers, business and industry participating in and supporting environmental education, and the general public promoting quality basic education (Roth 1991). Creation of the environmental literacy standards is a consensus process. Fortunately, the current draft of the standards has a distinctly geographic nature.

Second, teacher certification standards are being written for environmental education. These certification standards are also being created through an ASTM committee process.

Third, many states are creating comprehensive environmental education initiatives. The movement to create these initiatives is supported by the North American Association for Environmental Education, which is sponsoring workshops and publishing a handbook to assist state environmental education organizations with the process. Representation of geography in these initiatives will depend on geographers in each state identifying the beginning of the process and working to include geography as an integral part of the initiative.

Fourth, national assessment standards and learning outcomes are being written for science and geography. Geographers have included a major section on environment called "Environment and Society" in the Geography Assessment Framework. Geographers also have an environmental education advisory committee that assists the writing committee to produce learning outcomes and assessment standards related to the environment for grades 4, 8, and 12.

## RECOMMENDATIONS FOR ACTION

The National Council of Governors endorsed a national educational plan that calls for five core subjects—English, history, math, science, and geography. Environmental education has two points of entry into the K-12 curriculum, science and geography. Despite sentiments to exclude Earth science, and thus physical geography, from the national science standards, science and geography educators need to share the responsibility of teaching about the environment. Geography and science educators should work together to define roles and responsibilities in teaching environmental education in the K-12 curriculum. They should not battle for turf or ignore each other's efforts, as they have so frequently in the past.

Geographers and geography educators can become involved in the process of teaching science educators and environmental educators about the geographic knowledge base, the geographic skills, and the wealth of geographic resources related to the environment. We can present papers and workshops at national and regional conferences of the National Science Teachers Association and the North American Association of Environmental Educators. We can review working papers and drafts of the National Science Education Standards, the Environmental Literacy Standards, the Environmental Education Teacher Certification Standards, etc. We can become involved in the creation of state environmental education initiatives. We can assist local schools to integrate geography into their curriculums. In essence, geographers must move outside comfortable and familiar circles of professional communication and talk with professionals of other disciplines and associations on national and local levels. A few geographers have been doing this for years. They will tell you it is not easy, but it is necessary.

## CONCLUSION

Geography has a rich knowledge base pertaining to environmental research and education. It is our responsibility as geographers and geography educators to work with environmental and science educators to assure that geography has a meaningful role in the assessment frameworks, learning outcomes, curriculums, statewide environmental education initiatives, literacy standards, and other educational projects which will shape the future of environmental education.

## REFERENCES

Gerster, G. 1976. *Granddesign: The Earth from Above*. New York: Paddington Press.

Roth, C. 1991. "Toward Shaping Environmental Literacy for a Sustainable Future." *ASTM Standardization News*, April.

Rosalyn McKeown-Ice works with the Center for Geography and Environmental Education at the University of Tennessee, Knoxville. [1994 note]

# 17

# Issues and Analysis
## *A Teaching Strategy for the Real World*

**Martha Kronholm**
**John Ramsey**

Today science-related social issues abound, but many teachers don't know how to approach a real-life, controversial topic in the classroom. Most prefer to stick with traditional science content and "play it safe." Some may use current events as lecture topics; others might choose to base lessons on episodic methods. But if you'd like to take youngsters a step beyond simple awareness into active issue involvement, try out the extended case study (ECS) strategy. I took the ECS tack with my fifth graders—the results may be just the inspiration you need.

My students have a keen interest in wild animals, particularly those that live in the area, so we chose to follow a regional environmental issue, the Timber Wolf Recovery Plan. Advocated by the Wisconsin Department of Natural Resources, the plan proposes to make the timber wolf population in northern Wisconsin more viable by introducing additional wolves into the environment.

I began the ECS strategy by having the students write an essay describing what they already knew about the timber wolf. The essays produced some exceptional excerpts.

> Whenever I think of wolves, I think of bats, snakes, and spiders. They are mean!

> I think of bats, Frankenstein, mummies, and all the other wolves' monster buddies.

> When I think of wolves I think of stories like "Little Red Riding Hood" and movies like Teen Wolf. The words I think of are sharp teeth, scary, hairy, forest, claws, blood, full moon, and howl!

Obviously, my students didn't know much about the natural history of wolves. To provide a solid knowledge base, I then assigned students a variety of readings from secondary sources and taught lessons about predator-and-prey relationships, forest ecosystems, the niche concept, and population dynamics. Students soon understood that their initial negative feelings had been based on misconceptions.

In the ECS approach, once students have been properly informed, they can fully explore the issue—processing information, generating better research questions,

collecting primary data, and deciding what actions, if any, should be taken.

The next part of our timber wolf ECS focused on identifying the positions, beliefs, and values of the various players involved in the issue. Through guest speakers and secondary source information, students learned much about the timber wolf. For example, some hunters kill wolves in an effort to increase the size of the deer herd. People interested in snowshoeing, skiing, and snowmobiling sometimes worry that an increased number of wolves might lead to restricted traffic on wilderness trails. Lumber industry personnel believe that the recovery plan could mean future restrictions and lost revenue. Farmers are concerned about wolves preying on their livestock.

Ramsey, Hungerford, and Volk (1989a) call a comprehensive analysis such as this one "issue analysis." My students summarized their issue analysis by constructing a Timber Wolf Recovery Plan Issue Web, a type of concept map. We displayed a picture of a timber wolf on the bulletin board and connected it with strings to various issue players and their beliefs and values. Looking at the completed web, students were able to see the issue's "big picture." The web then became a springboard for identifying and communicating a number of questions about wolves and the proposed plan.

## ON TO INVESTIGATE

Students decided that determining local residents' beliefs and attitudes about the Timber Wolf Recovery Plan was the most important goal of their investigation.

After much discussion and planning, students decided to send a 10-question survey to 350 residents of northern Wisconsin selected at random from telephone directories. With each survey, students included a hand-written cover letter and a self-addressed stamped envelope; they even enclosed pictures of themselves as a personal touch.

Within a matter of days, responses began to pour in. The class was thrilled. Amazingly, 211 surveys (60 percent) were returned. Evidently, the handwritten cover letters helped a great deal. Not only were the surveys returned, but many were accompanied by personal letters, newspaper clippings, drawings, magazine articles, and photographs. Some people even sent us envelopes, asking that we mail them back our findings. Respondents' letters also contained some provocative comments.

> It is ridiculous to introduce wolves into an area where they do not now reside and pay a ton of money to replace the livestock and deer they kill.

I personally will shoot any wolf, coyote, or domestic dog I see running a deer trail-legal or illegal-in or out of season.

I became acquainted with the timber wolf in 1929, when as a Forest Service employee, I was transferred from Colorado to assist in the establishment of the Nicolet National Forest. I have admired the timber wolf since he kills for food and not for sport. He is now an endangered species. I have not heard of one killing a human.

I do not support translocating wolves. The money spent on wolf restoration could be better spent. How about feeding the homeless in Wisconsin?

Although the data revealed many different beliefs and values, the results indicated that almost three-fourths of the respondents supported the Timber Wolf Recovery Plan. Because of this, the class inferred that the majority of local residents would be in favor of the plan.

It is difficult to describe how excited and interested the students became in this project. They invested a lot of thinking and a lot of effort. Collecting data about an interesting animal, getting involved in a real-life issue, communicating with real people, trying to answer an important question-all of these tasks contributed to students' developing a sense of issue ownership.

## NOW, MAKE A DECISION

Once students had analyzed and investigated the issue, it was time to decide on appropriate actions. Taking into consideration their newly acquired scientific knowledge as well as the evidence collected from the investigation, the students identified the positive and negative consequences of possible actions. Together they decided to support the Timber Wolf Recovery Plan by raising money to donate to the Timber Wolf Alliance, a group working for

the plan. Students raised more than $100 by selling buttons, pencils, and Plaster of Paris wolf footprints. The students' actions were not superficial; they acted on knowledge they had gained and the evidence they had acquired through a process of thoughtful consideration.

You can imagine the unlimited interdisciplinary opportunities afforded by any ECS. My students wrote poems and songs, prepared skits and role-played drew pictures constructed life-sized papier maché wolf, did library research, wrote reports, prepared graphs, and calculated averages.

So take the ECS approach with your class. Your students will become more knowledgeable, learn new skills, and perhaps even do some tangible good as citizens of their community.

## RESOURCES

Hungerford, H.R., Litherland, R.A., Peyton, R.B., Ramsey, J.M., and Volk, T.L. (1988). *Investigating and Evaluating Environmental Issues and Actions: Skill Development Modules*. Champaign, IL: Stipes.

Ramsey, J.M. (1989). "A Curricular Framework for Community-Based STS Issue Instruction." *Education and Urban Society*, 22( I ), 40-53.

Ramsey, J.M., and Hungerford, H.R. (1989). "So . . . You Want to Teach Issues?" *Contemporary Education*, 60(3), 137-142.

Ramsey, J.M., Hungerford, H.R., and Volk, T.L. (1989a). *A Science-Technology-Society Case Study: Municipal Solid Waste*. Champaign, IL: Stipes.

———. (1989b). "Analyzing the Issues of STS." *The Science Teacher*, 57(3), 60-63.

Martha Kronholm teaches fifth grade at Mead Elementary School in Wisconsin Rapids, Wisconsin. John Ramsey is an Assistant Professor of Curriculum and Instruction at the University of Houston, University Park, Texas. [1991 note]

# Using the Five Themes of Geography to Explore a School Site

# 18

## Carol E. Murphey

The State of California's new *History-Social Science Framework* for grades kindergarten through 12 organizes the teaching of geography into five overlapping themes, *location, place, region, movement,* and *human-environment interactions,* which were originally outlined in the *Guidelines for Geographic Education* (Joint Committee for Geographic Education, 1984). *Location* can be absolute and relative. By definition it tells where, or answers the question "where?". *Place* is the unique physical and human characteristics that give an area its recognizable character. *Regions* are defined by the characteristics that make them a unique functioning area and delineate them from other large areas. *Human environment interactions* are those relationships man has with the space around him, specifically change and its consequences. *Movement* is the exchange of goods and services, ideas, and people from one place to another. A school is an ideal site to illustrate these themes.

The five themes can be easily illustrated for students through the exploration of their own school site and its surrounding environment. The school can be found at an exact location on a map. It has describable characteristics. The area from which a school draws its population constitutes a region. Schools interact with people and the landscape. Schools are constantly changing—trees are planted, trash is scattered, portable buildings come and go. These changes involve human-environment interactions. There is constant movement of people and goods in and around, as well as to and from a school site. The following lesson involves students in actively discovering the geography of their school while working cooperatively in groups. It has been successfully used by adults and elementary and secondary students to help them develop a geographic perspective that addresses more than location and place. This lesson can be implemented at sites other than schools. It has been conducted in the Oakland Convention Center, a woman's clubhouse, a Catholic retreat house, and on the campuses of Sacramento State University and the University of Hawaii.

### PREPARATION

Task one requires a compass, a United States map, and a local area map. Chart paper, graph paper, writing paper, pens, pencils, and crayons are necessary for the other tasks. Parents or other school personnel should be utilized to

supervise the students in their explorations of the surrounding area. The five routes the student groups will follow must be pre-scouted by the teacher in order to choose the one that best illustrates the geographic theme being examined. A packet of materials for each theme with instruction sheets for each student in the group are necessary. The time necessary to complete the task depends on the age of the participants and the depth of exploration a teacher wants. Young children can spend part of each day for a week, exploring each theme individually; older students will need two or three class periods to do the jigsaw-like format. An adult group should be able to complete the lesson in one and a half hours.

### ACTIVITY

▮ Begin the activity by discussing the various things students read: books, magazines, signs, newspapers, advertisements, etc. Explain that they are going to learn to read something new, the landscape which involves looking beyond the beauty or ugliness of a place, and noting the details.

▮ Divide the participants into five groups, making them as heterogeneous as possible. Each member of the group is given a specific job such as recorder, reporter, map or direction reader, instruction reader, and time keeper. Everyone is also a gatherer of information. The objective is to gather as much data as possible utilizing everyone's skills.

▮ Ask each group to read its instructions, record its findings, complete its task, and return to the starting point in 30 minutes.

▮ After the group returns, ask the reporter in each group to share the group's observations, findings, and final product with the other groups, while the teacher records the findings on chart paper, under the appropriate heading (i.e., *location, place, region, human-environment interactions,* and *movement*). Discuss the areas where these categories overlap. It may be necessary to point out examples if the students have not already discovered them. It is important that these categories not be viewed as absolute, but simply as a tool for reading the landscape.

▮ Using the information from the charts and the discussion, instruct the students to write a geographic description of their school, encouraging them to use all of the themes.

▮ Compare their descriptions with that of the school handbook or any other document that describes the school.

■ Invite the employee that has been at the site the longest to talk about the changes that have occurred during the time he or she has worked at the school.

## GROUP INSTRUCTIONS

*Location:* Location can be absolute and relative. It tells where, or answers the question "where?".

*absolute* (handwritten in margin)

1. Pinpoint the location of the site on a United States map.
   ■ What is the latitude? What is the longitude?
   ■ What major cities are north of, south of, east of, and west of the site on the United States map?
   ■ What major landmarks are nearby?
2. Use your compass to determine what direction the front door faces. Record that direction.
3. Walk to the first intersection. Record all street signs, note the intersection of streets, and look for landmarks such as parks, drainage ditches, fire stations, student homes, stores, etc. Use the compass to determine in what directions the intersecting streets run.
4. Continue walking and recording until you have enough information to find your location on a local map. The compass reader should tell the group if it is walking north, south, east, or west.
5. Return to the front door. Use the information you have just collected to find your site on a local area map. Use the map index to locate streets. Use the compass to orient your map correctly.
6. Draw a detailed map of the immediate area of the school site. Mark the route you walked.
7. When all the groups have completed their task, share your information with them.

*Place:* Place is the unique physical and human characteristics that give an area its recognizable character. How does it look?

1. Walk to the front of the site and record what the place looks like.
   ■ What is the shape of the land?
   ■ Describe the surface (paved, planted, natural setting, etc.).
   ■ What colors do you see?
   ■ What objects do you see?
   ■ What buildings do you see? What is their approximate age?
   ■ Do you see any people? What are they doing?
   ■ Describe the traffic patterns. How does the air smell?
   ■ Describe the plants and animals.
2. Walk to the back of the site. Use the directions above to record your observations.
3. Follow the same plan in describing any part of the site.
4. Using all of the information you have gathered, draw, as a group, a picture of this place. Discuss together what you will draw, then assign each person a space on the paper. Use descriptive words to label the drawing.
5. When all the groups have finished, share your information and drawing with them.

*Regions:* Regions are defined by the characteristics that make them a unique functioning area and delineate them from other large areas.

1. Go to the front door of the site and walk to the nearest intersection. From that intersection walk in two directions as far as your time allows. Look for evidence of the following regional types:

| REGION | EXAMPLES OF EVIDENCE |
|---|---|
| Economic | *residential, agricultural, recreational* |
| Cultural | *religion, language, education, food sources* |
| Political | *car stickers, signs, mail, police, sanitation* |
| Environmental | *climate, living things, landforms* |

2. Return to the site. List the regions you can identify. Determine if any of them overlap. Make a map or pictorial chart of the regions you found.
3. When all the groups have finished share your information with them.

*Human-Environment Interactions:* Human-environment interactions are those relationships humans have with the space around him. They deal with change and its consequences.

1. Walk around the site. Identify and record.
   ■ boundaries, barriers, and open space
   ■ hazards and safety features
   ■ litter, vandalism, and beautification
   ■ natural sounds and man-made sounds
   ■ evidence of change to the site and its effects
   ■ quality of the air
   ■ land use
   ■ economic and cultural use of the area
   ■ buildings, type and use
   ■ types of plants and animals and their effects on the environment
2. Enter the building. Observe and record your impressions of this environment. Does this interior have positive or negative effects on humans? Why?
3. As a group, write a short essay to share with the other groups. Discuss with each other what you want to include, such as: how people interact with the environment at this site; how humans are changing this environment and the consequences of this change. Dictate to your recorder exactly what you wish to say.
4. When all the groups have finished, share your information with them.

*Movement:* Movement is the exchange of goods and services, ideas, and people from one place to another.

1. Find an area at the site that has a lot of activity (parking lot, intersection, playground, etc.).
2. List the kinds of movement that you see, and then select a movement for each person to observe and tally for five minutes. Make a graph illustrating the types and amount of movement at your chosen observation point.

3. Go inside the building and interview at least two key people at the site. Select questions from the <u>list below</u> that are appropriate to the person being interviewed.

- How do people and their belongings get to the site?
- Where do the people come from? (farthest-nearest)
- Are there more or less people at this site than in previous years?
- What goods are used at the site? How are goods and services brought to the site?
- Where did the goods and services originate? How are the goods and services paid for and by whom?
- Does the site produce any goods or services? How are these moved from the site?
- Does this site exchange ideas with the outside world? What ideas? How are the ideas shared?

4. Write a summary of your findings. When all the groups have finished, share your graph and summary of findings with them.

## SUGGESTED FOLLOW-UP ACTIVITIES

1. Design a map of the school to be used by visitors and new pupils.
2. Interview neighbors and others who can talk about the site and what it was like before the school was built Videotape the interviews to share with other classes. Make the tape a "then and now" production.
3. Using photographs, paintings, and written descriptions, explore a historical site such as Gettysburg, the Forbidden City, Mount Vernon, The Parthenon, the Tower of London, Machu Picchu, etc.
4. Kindergarten children can map the route between their home and school.
5. Explore a local shopping mall using the same procedure outlined here noting regions, the movement patterns, and the human-environment interactions that are occurring.

Carol E. Murphey teaches at Whitehead Elementary School in Woodland, California. [1991 note].

# Hilltop Geography for Young Children: Creating an Outdoor Learning Laboratory

**Esta Diamond Gutierrez**
**Yvette Sanchez**

*"It is through the power of observation, the gifts of eye and ear, of tongue and nose and finger, that a place first rises up in our mind. Afterward it is memory that carries the place, that allows it to grow in depth and complexity. For as long as our records go back, we have held these two things dear: Landscape and Memory. The one feeds us figuratively and literally, the other protects us from lies and tyranny"* (Lopez 1989).

Sombrillo Elementary School is located in the semi-arid foothills of the Sangre de Cristo range of the Southern Rockies in New Mexico. Water is scarce; overgrazing in past years has caused extensive erosion. Four-wheelers have carved paths through the grasslands and up the steep hills. At the same time, local Pueblo Indian potters still come here, as they have for hundreds of years, to dig up the "white sand" formed from ancient volcanic ash deposits, to provide the proper consistency for their clay.

Recognizing the richness of this environment, several teachers began bringing their students out to the hills recently for nature walks, mapping activities, and cross-country runs, etc. In the spring of 1991, as part of an Earth Day contest, a committee of Sombrillo teachers wrote a proposal to formalize an idea based on these activities in the nearby hills for an outdoor learning laboratory. Our goal was to involve school and community in a project that would promote appreciation for and understanding of our local environment. We also wanted to collect successful curriculum ideas and lesson plans which could be shared with other teachers. The activities described here were carried out by the two authors of this article with our first and second grade classes.

Our geography adventure began when we took our young children on a short walk out the back door of our school, across the playground. and up the hill. Twenty-two first and second graders, a teacher, a foster grandparent, and sometimes a mom or a dad were out to explore a local landscape rich in the wonders of the earth.

On top of the mesa, we began with the very basic idea of "near and far," painting and sketching distant mountain ranges and the cactus fruit right in front of our eyes. Looking in the four directions, we noted our location on the surface of the earth—mountain ranges to the east and to the west, the highway moving south toward Santa Fe, and the village of Santa Cruz to the north. Later we constructed a landscape compass to mark our sense of direction with greater accuracy.

From our hilltop classroom, the students observed the subtle changes that occur in a landscape as the seasons change. They noted the lengthening of shadows, the comings and goings of birds and insects, and the stages of the yucca plant as it flowered in spring and bore fruit in autumn.

Hiking up and down these hills, the children developed a sense of the local topography. Back inside the classroom the students' landscape observations became the basis for the creation of models formed out of clay, including mountains, hills, valleys, and mesas.

During the latter part of the school year, the focus of our field geography activities progressed from the physical environment to the impact of humans on the landscape. The class undertook a study of ancient cliff-dwelling Native Americans who lived in our region. Returning to our hilltop, we explored how the earth might have sustained these people with its plants, rocks, clay, and wildlife. After watching a film about the history and life style of the Anasazi, we visited the Puye Cliff ruins. The children then dug up clay from the earth, mixed it with the volcanic ash found on one of our hilltops, and made their own small pots. They also tried their hand at making cord and weaving with the stringy leaves of the Yucca plant that grows so abundantly around the school.

These weekly or semi-weekly forays into the hills were integrated into our reading, literature, and writing. One book in particular, *The Other Way to Listen*, helped the children to focus on detail, and to observe by looking and listening with both ears and heart to what might be passed over as insignificant. "All I know is suddenly I wasn't the only one singing. The hills were singing too. I stopped. I didn't move for maybe an hour; I never listened so hard in my life" (Baylor and Parnell 1978). Two first graders found a rock and after looking at it hard I wrote: "I found a diamond rock and it is pretty. It has two colors and it has some dirt in it. It has water and it has holes in it. It has black spots. There are lines on it. It has white spots on the other colors. It looks like a 'D.' It looks like a diamond."

Writing and drawing sessions sometimes took place outdoors or in the classroom as an immediate followup to a walk. Stories and poems were collected throughout the year in writing folders.

Reprinted with permission from Texas A & M, from *Journal of Geography*, July/August 1993, Volume 92, Number 4. Copyright 1993 by Texas A&M.

## MAPPING ACTIVITIES: DO YOU KNOW WHERE YOU ARE ON THE PLANET?

The following activities will take weeks of work with primary students. Ease of access to an outdoor area and previous mapping experiences of the students will affect the time needed for a class to complete these projects. Since we integrated these activities into our overall curriculum, the projects continued all year long.

Developmentally, first and second grade students are just realizing their own bodies' place in space. Two children moving a desk to a new location will more often result in a funny dance as they push and pull each other about, trying to discover how to take the desk to its final destination.

Outside of the classroom, we want these same children to be able to find their way around their immediate local environment. their community, and eventually their planet. How can teachers help children achieve this, when the young child's world is self-centered and strongly oriented to what the body can see, feel, manipulate, and care about? The following progression describes how Yvette Sanchez helped second graders to connect their immediate observations and physical manipulation of the environment to more abstract symbols, maps, and geographical concepts.

We began by building a compass on the highest of the nearby small mesas. With the help of one child's Grandma, a magnetic compass, and a six foot rope (handmade by two Mexican cowboys), the first and second graders found a center spot and then stretched the rope as far as it would go to the north. Using a pickaxe, they dug a hole, planted one post on the spot, and secured the post with rocks and dirt. They then painted a big "N" on the pole. A sixth grade student had taught us the saying "Never Eat Soggy Worms" so that the children could remember an order for the four directions, north (never), east (eat), south (soggy), west (worms), as we constructed the compass. From the center spot, using the rope and hand compass, additional posts labeled "East," "South," and "West" were erected. We now had a student-made landscape compass for our outdoor classroom.

Each week we hiked up to our compass to see what we could observe in each direction. Taking paints, pencils, and journals. with us, we recorded plants, rocks, insects, and animals seen near each post. Then we looked farther away to record roads and buildings, and even farther to include the familiar mountain ranges, noting the directions in which the sun rises and sets.

Finally we recorded the names of familiar cities and towns that we could not see, but knew existed in each direction. The children began to use direction as they described a location: "My Grandma's house is over there, to the west" or, "My house is in Chimayo, that's north."

Back in the classroom, the children's desks were set in groups of four or five. Each group was given a paper circle two feet in diameter, along with clay. paint, and crayons. The children worked cooperatively to make a map of the Outdoor Laboratory, using a cross and compass rose as the center. The map and materials were left in the center of each group for the duration of this project, approximately one week. In this way the children were able to add geographic features that came to mind during the course of the day.

The results were both creative and geographically sound. One group had a rising sun in the east. and a setting sun in the west. Others included animals seen in each direction. All depicted the road going north to south. with the school correctly positioned to the north. One group placed a volcano in the west, symbolizing Black Mesa, the remains of an extinct volcano.

A small but wonderful measure of our success came one day when a second grader named Edgar missed the school bus. When the teacher taking him home asked for directions, he replied, "Go to the end of this road and turn east."

## MOVING TOWARD A PERMANENT OUTDOOR LABORATORY

These fieldwalks and mapping projects gradually began to evolve into the establishment of more permanent learning tools. First came the directional markers (our landscape compass), with the center pole that would later become part of a sundial. Fifth graders worked together with the younger children, mixing cement to make a more stable base for the poles. A local lumberyard donated wooden poles to build a simple shelter to provide some shade from the sun on the barren hilltop.

Future plans include the creation of a nature trail. with identifying markers for the native vegetation. The county Soil Conservation Office is teaching the students about the various grasses and flowers that can help reclaim eroded land, without benefit of irrigation. Most recently, the New Mexico State Highway Department has made monies available for creating trails on school lands. For schools with no suitable land for an Outdoor Laboratory, the State Land Commissioner offers tracts of land ranging from one to ten acres. They also provide transportation and grass seed to interested schools.

Our school is located in a school district where fieldtrips are not a priority and minimal funds are available for transportation. Thus, taking advantage of this rich, accessible resource that lies just beyond our school's doorstep is practical, as well as educationally enriching.

In our effort to get support from the school administration, several teachers presented our work in the Outdoor Laboratory to the Espanola Board of Education, showing pictures, and taking board members on an imaginary trip back in geological time. Response was very positive, and we are presently applying for grant monies to enable us to move ahead with our plans.

There is no dearth of ideas for the future. We envision the creation of a community nature park with nature trails that are well-signed and wheelchair accessible. We would like to erect a simple outdoor amphitheater for our classes. We plan to invite experts from the community who will educate teachers, parents, and students as to how we can each become better stewards for this unique piece of earth.

## CONCLUSION

Trips and fieldwalks have provided the basis for our "Hill-top Geography" curriculum. First and second graders need these immediate experiences with the here and now to facilitate the development of thinking skills that will allow them to make the transition to more abstract explorations of the far away and long ago. The Outdoor Laboratory has also provided an ideal meeting ground for involving parents, community members, and school administrators. Parents initially questioned the purpose of our outdoor studies; but once they understood, they became frequent participants on walks and later helped out in the classroom as volunteers. They have also begun to help out in the fundraising process.

The outdoor laboratory has provided us with a rich resource for exploring location. Moving from the direct experiences on our hilltops to the hands-on mapping activities, and learning in a manner appropriate to their developmental age, the children were able to grasp fundamental geographical concepts.

The teachers at Sombrillo Elementary School are especially fortunate in the accessibility of a beautiful local mesa, but we would argue that wherever a school may be located—urban or rural, flat or hilly, coastal or inland—there is a landscape nearby with the potential to become an outdoor laboratory for young children.

## REFERENCES

Lopez, B. 1989. *The American Geographies*. Harpers, 279:19-21.

Baylor, B., and P. Parnell. 1978. *The Other Way to Listen*. New York: Charles Scribner and Sons.

**Paul Mulloy**
**Tom Collins**

This activity not only provides students with practice using locational skills, it also develops understandings related to the themes of place (physical characteristics) and movement. In order to complete all aspects of the activity, students need some experience working with latitude and longitude.

*Objectives:* Students will be able to:

1. Locate places in the United States that have Spanish terms in their names.
2. Understand why Spanish terms have been used as place names in the United States.
3. Give the absolute location of places having Spanish names.

*Time Required:* 1-2 class periods

*Materials and Preparation:* You will need a copy of the vocabulary handout which follows and a student atlas for each class member.

*Procedure:*

1. Write the following Spanish terms on the chalkboard: *mesa, boca, costa, laguna.* Ask students if they know what these terms mean. The answers are: *mesa* (high table), *boca* (mouth), *costa* (coast), and *laguna* (lagoon). Explain that each term has a geographic meaning and is also used to name a place in the United States.
2. Tell students that in some areas of the United States, especially in the West and Southwest, there is a strong connection to Spanish language and culture. One way to determine the extent of this connection is to see how many places have Spanish terms in their names.
3. Distribute the vocabulary handout and, with the atlases as a reference, ask the students to find a place in the United States that incorporates each term in its name. That place name should be written in the blank next to the term.
4. In the space next to each place name, students should write in the correct latitude and longitude for the center of that particular place. An example is presented on the handout.
5. Conclude by discussing with students' reasons why these names were chosen and how they reflect the geographical features of the location.

*Follow-up:*

1. Have teams of students use their atlases to identify other places in the United States where non-English terms are included in the names. Each team should give the absolute locations (latitude and longitude) of each place found; teams could then trade lists and find the locations described by the other team.
2. Ask students to locate places in the United States that have been named after places in other countries. Students should give the absolute locations for the U.S. site and the place for which it was named.

## VOCABULARY HANDOUT
*Spanish Terms in U.S. Place Names*

1. *amarillo* (yellow): <u>Amarillo. Texas 101°W 35°N</u>
2. *arroyo* (brook, dry stream bed): _____
3. *blanco* (white): _____
4. *boca* (mouth, estuary): _____
5. *cerro, morro* (hill): _____
6. *colorado* (reddish): _____
7. *costa* (coast): _____
8. *de, del* (of): _____
9. *este* (east): _____
10. *grand(e)* (big): _____
11. *laguna* (lagoon): _____
12. *los, las* (the): _____
13. *mesa* (high table): _____
14. *nevada* (snowfall): _____
15. *norte* (north): _____
16. *occidental* (western): _____
17. *oriente* (east): _____
18. *paso* (pass): _____
19. *pueblo* (town, village): _____
20. *rio* (river): _____
21. *sierra* (mountain): _____
22. *sur* (south): _____
23. *valle* (valley): _____
24. *vegas* (fertile lowland, plain): _____

Paul Mulloy and Tom Collins developed this activity as part of the Global Links Project, Washington, D.C.

# Assessing Spatial Development: Implications for Map Skill Instruction

**Sharon Pray Muir**
**Helen Neely Cheek**

Map reading and mapmaking constitute one of the broadest skill applications in the elementary school curriculum. Maps are found in reading programs; orienteering skills appear in science curricula; recent mathematics curricula include mapping; and making maps is sometimes included in art education. Primarily, mapping constitutes a recurring skill in that part of the social studies program that derives from geographic education.

Mapping skills derive from the ability to imagine relationships between and among places. Spatial ability helps an individual to answer the question, Where? That development in children chronicles their acquisition of related spatial concepts and skills, helping youngsters visualize viewpoints, locate places, find their way, and represent directions (horizontal and vertical) and spaces. Because that relationship exists between spatial development and map skills, it is important for teachers to understand the mental development typical of most schoolchildren.

According to Muir and Frazee (1986), eight skills make up the elementary map curriculum: interpreting symbols, viewing perspective, finding location, determining direction, calculating distance, computing elevation, imagining relief, and understanding scale. Those authors have also described ways of teaching these skills in a developmentally appropriate manner in an earlier issue of this journal; Muir and Cheek (1986) have also suggested a relationship between map skills and the mathematics curriculum. The first skill—interpreting symbols—is visual, or graphic, rather than spatial. The remaining seven skills, however, depend on spatial ability.

Research describes behaviors common among children who complete tasks that provide insight into children's spatial development. Researchers and curriculum developers can use these tasks to determine when teachers should introduce new skills and concepts. Teachers can informally diagnose problems children encounter in spatial reasoning by modifying the complicated exercises and administering them in classrooms.

Jean Piaget and interpreters of his work created the tasks described in this article. Five traits characterize the tasks: (1) they are administered individually; (2) they involve active manipulation; (3) they have game-like qualities; (4) they elicit a verbal explanation from the children;

Reprinted from *Social Education* September 1991, Volume 55, Number 5. Copyright 1991 by National Council for the Social Studies.

and (5) administrators often try to talk the youngsters out of a correct explanation to determine if the explanation is fixed or random.

This article describes briefly some common problems encountered by elementary schoolchildren with the seven spatial map skills. It describes at least one task for each skill and suggests ways of adapting the more complex exercises to the classroom. Typical responses that illustrate the children's progression of development are described in three phases. The steps do not conform with Piaget's preoperational, concrete, or formal stages; some phases constitute Piagetian substages. Administration and analysis of Piaget's tasks are described further by Copeland (1979) and by Voyat (1982).

We have deliberately omitted the age at which a phase reportedly appears. Most studies follow Piaget's procedure of reporting the age level when 75 percent of students in an age group perform a given task successfully. That tradition often conceals the fact that as many as a quarter of the children at a reported age level are unsuccessful. Furthermore, comparison to norms is less useful diagnostically than is the observation of an individual child's performance.

## PERSPECTIVE

Perspective is the ability to imagine or recognize an object from the aerial, or "bird's-eye" view. Mapping literature refers to this skill as "orientation," "viewpoint," or "orthogonal perspective." Most children lack opportunities to view geographic areas from above. As Vanselow (1974, 11) points out, "Direct experience with the environment usually occurs at the ground level, giving the individual a horizontal perspective." Perspective is fundamental to understanding the concept of a map, yet formal instruction in the skill's relationship to maps is absent in many mathematics and social studies programs.

Pedde (1966) asked children to draw a map of a three-dimensional village that contains buildings and trees. Drawings by younger children portrayed each object from the horizontal perspective on a single baseline. To solve the problem of an object that was behind another, children normally placed the background object on top of the one in the foreground. At a higher cognitive level, drawings combined both aerial and horizontal perspectives. Buildings, for example, often were drawn from the aerial perspective, trees and chimneys from the side. In the final stage, children began, without prompting, to depict each object from an aerial perspective.

Performance on Piaget's coordination of perspectives,

## FIGURE 1: DEVELOPMENTAL PROGRESS ON SELECTED SPATIAL TASKS

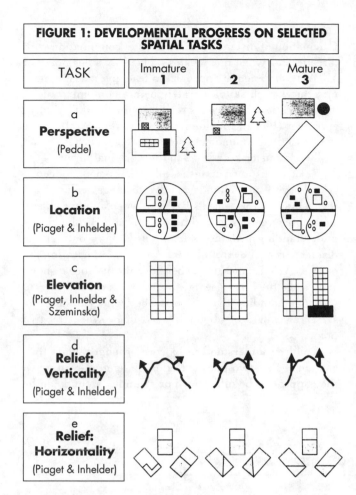

| TASK | Immature 1 | 2 | Mature 3 |
|---|---|---|---|
| a **Perspective** (Pedde) | | | |
| b **Location** (Piaget & Inhelder) | | | |
| c **Elevation** (Piaget, Inhelder & Szeminska) | | | |
| d **Relief: Verticality** (Piaget & Inhelder) | | | |
| e **Relief: Horizontality** (Piaget & Inhelder) | | | |

or "three-mountain," task also reveals the emergence of perspective ability (Piaget and Inhelder 1948). In this exercise, the child views three model mountains of different colors and strikingly different shapes. Approximately twenty photographs of the mountains seen from different angles are shown to the pupil. While the child remains seated in one position, a doll is moved to various viewpoints (opposite the child, to the left, to the right, and in several aerial positions). The child selects the photograph that shows what the doll "sees."

Children at first egocentrically imagine that their personal viewpoint constitutes all possible perspectives. No matter where the doll is moved, the child selects the view that he or she sees. Next, when they realize that other perspectives exist, they select views other than their own, but are unable to select correctly. Finally, they recognize and accurately describe other points of view. You can replicate this task in the classroom by using three boxes, painted different colors. Teachers can take photographs or prepare drawings from which children select the predicted points of view.

## LOCATION

Two grid systems can be used to locate places on maps: simple alphanumeric coordinates and latitude-longitude. Most educators agree that simple alpha-numeric coordinates (e.g., A-3, H-7) are appropriate for use with elementary schoolchildren, and a growing number of advocates (e.g., Bartz 1970, Brown et al. 1970, Welton and Mallan 1988) recommend delaying instruction in latitude and longitude until students are capable of formal, abstract reasoning.

Children who perform Piaget and Inhelder's (1948) diagrammatic layouts task demonstrate the ability to locate. The child views a three-dimensional model of an area that is divided into quadrants by an intersecting road and a stream. Different numbers of trees, barns, and sheds are arranged within each quadrant. The child reproduces the model having been given only the stream and the road as baselines. A young child's reproduction often bears no resemblance to the model; sometimes all of the trees, barns, and sheds are placed in the same quadrant. As spatial ability increases, the child places the correct number of objects in each quadrant, but location within the quadrant is inaccurate. Eventually, the child uses several different reference points simultaneously to reproduce the model successfully. This exercise can be modified by distributing common classroom materials—pencils, erasers, paper clips—on a paper divided into quadrants by different colored lines.

## DIRECTION

Although pupils in elementary schools may understand directions on flat maps, they find it more difficult to apply global directions to the real world. Labeling the sides of a

## FIGURE 2: PERSPECTIVES TASK

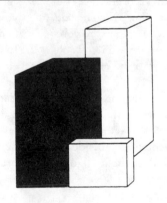

## FIGURE 3: LOCATION TASK

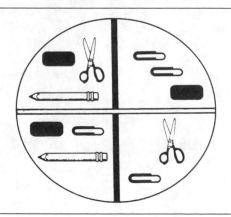

flat piece of paper—as on outline maps, wall maps, or in textbooks—is an insufficient method of verifying children's understanding of global direction.

Pattison (1967) found that three categories of directional concepts emerge in childhood. Youngsters first understand environmental directions, described by prepositions such as *in*, *under*, and *behind*. Next, children accurately use terms that express personal directions (i.e., *front*, *forward*, *left*, *clockwise*, and their antonyms). Children understand global directions (e.g.. *north*, *southeast*) only after they learn environmental and personal directions. The directional categories correspond to three stages: (1) an egocentric understanding of direction only in relation to oneself; (2) inconsistent understanding of other persons' (or objects') points of view; and (3) a coordinated system that correctly imagines other persons' (or objects') points of view. A child's developmental category or stage becomes clear as he or she answers questions in order to describe the location of objects or points using environmental, personal, and global vocabulary. Interview questions for environmental, personal, and global directions, developed by Muir and patterned after Piaget's Right and Left exercise (Piaget and Inhelder 1948), are shown below.

## DISTANCE

Calculation of distance is often used in combination with direction, as when one locates a place "X miles north of Y." A developmental approach to teaching measurement introduces each skill separately before combining them. Two Piagetian tasks assess readiness for the skill of measurement (Piaget, Inhelder, and Szeminska 1960). Since these tasks use common classroom materials, teachers can easily administer both tasks in their original forms.

Relative distance underlies all measurement concepts. A child who understands relative distance realizes that the distance is the same as BA even when another object, such as a screen, is placed between A and B. The child's understanding progresses from (1) looking only at the distance from A or from B to the screen, but ignoring the overall (AB) distance, to (2) believing the distance is shortened since the screen seems to absorb space, and then to (3) understanding that the distance from A to B is the same regardless of objects placed in between the two points.

Children understand properties of length when they can agree that two lines are equal in length, even when they appear to be different. For example, a child can be

---

| TABLE 1: DIRECTION INTERVIEWS |
|---|

*Environmental*

1. Give the child a box of crayons: "Put the crayons over you, . . . behind you, . . . in front of you, . . . next to you."

2. "Put the crayons over me, . . . behind me, . . . in front of me, . . . next to me."

3. Prepare a box that contains a stapler and scissors, with a shoe on top, and a box of crayons behind it: "Show me something inside the box, . . . behind the box, . . . over the box."

4. "Move the crayons into the box, . . . under the box, . . . in front of the box."

5. "What does it mean to go *up* to the store, . . . *over* to a friend's house, . . . *in* to town, . . . *down* to the river?"

*Personal*

1. Sitting next to the child: "Show me your right hand, . . . your left hand, . . . my right hand, . . .my left hand."

2. Lay a pencil and a penny next to each other: "Is the pencil to the right or to the left of the penny?"

3. Facing the child, the interviewer has a coin in one hand and a bracelet on the opposite arm: "Is the penny in my left or right hand? Is the bracelet on my left or right arm?"

4. Lay a coin, a key, and a pencil in a row: "Is the pencil to the left or to the right of the key? . . . of the penny? Is the key to the left or to the right of the penny? . . . of the pencil? Is the penny to the left or to the right of the pencil? . . . of the key?"

5. Lay a key, a card, and a pencil in a row. The child views them for 15 seconds before they are covered: "Tell me from memory how the items were arranged." If correct: "Was the pencil to the left or to the right of the key?" Follow with the remaining questions from 1 (above)

*Global*

1. "Point to your north, . . . south, . . . east, . . . west. Point to my north, . . . south, . . . east, . . . west."

2. Lay a pencil and a penny next to each other: "Is the pencil to the north, south, east, or west of the penny?"

3. Lay a map flat with north pointing north and with five cities circled: "Is (City A) north, south, east, or west of (City B)?" (Repeat with at least two other combinations.)

4. Turn the map so north points south: "Is (City C) north, south, east, or west of (City D)?" (Repeat with at least two other combinations.)

5. Turn the map so north points east or west: "Is (City E) north, south, east, or west of (City A)?" (Repeat with at least two other combinations.)

asked to compare a straight line to a zigzag line of the same overall length. In the earliest stage, the child focuses on the end points and, therefore, believes the straight line is longer. The child makes inconsistent responses during the next stage, but eventually the child realizes that both lines are equal in length.

## ELEVATION

The concept of elevation can be defined as "vertical distance." In contrast to horizontal distance, elevation is represented (1) in intervals rather than exact measurements, (2) in feet or meters rather than miles or kilometers, and (3) in color rather than by shape symbols.

A measurement task (Piaget, Inhelder, and Szeminska 1960) determines if a child understands the relationship between vertical distance and a base level. In this task, children are instructed to duplicate a model building using materials that vary in size (e.g., different size blocks) and on bases (e.g., tables) that vary in height. At first, children construct the new building using the same number of blocks as the model, regardless of their size. Next, they use measurement, but they fail to take into account the difference in base levels. Finally, they spontaneously select standard or nonstandard measuring tools and apply them solely to the building, irrespective of its base.

## RELIEF

The concept of relief involves topography or contour. Understanding relief when reading a one-dimensional map involves distinguishing between horizontal and vertical space in concave and convex areas. Two tasks assess that distinction (Piaget and Inhelder 1948). A verticality task determines if a child understands the vertical plane. The original task asked the child to draw a plumb line in a bottle that is tilted to the left and then to the right. The exercise is easily adapted by observing a child draw trees on a mountain. In the first stage, the child believes the trees tilt with the mountain's slope. Later, the child visualizes inconsistent relationships. Finally, the child consistently places trees perpendicular to an unseen baseline. The horizontality task requires a child to hypothesize how the water level would change if a glass that sits upright were tilted to the left or to the right. At first, the child imagines the water line to be parallel either to the bottom or to the sides of the bottle. Next, the imagined view is independent of the bottle's perimeters, but the lines are diagonal. Finally, the child correctly imagines the water as perpendicular to ground level.

## SCALE

Scale refers to the size of a map's reproduction. A child who comprehends the concept of ratio, or the relationship between two units, recognizes the difference between an area's actual size in space and its reduced size on a map. Towler and Nelson (1968) devised a task involving scale that used a three-dimensional model and a small map of the model's area. Given symbols of various size, the child selects those that are most appropriate to use on the map.

Maps that contain insets at different scales require an understanding of proportion. In this case, children must understand the relationship between an area's actual and reduced, or map, size when compared to the actual and reduced size of the second scale. Karplus and Peterson's (1970) Mr. Short-Mr. Tall activity analyzes the understanding of proportion. The child uses small and large paper clips to measure the height of a stick figure. Later, the task administrator provides only one measurement in small paper clip lengths; and asks the student to determine the height of an unseen figure if he or she used large paper clips. In the first stage, the child is unable to predict the figure's height. In the second stage, they apply addition. Only in the final stage does the child multiply by the correct factor.

## SUMMARY

Assessment of spatial abilities is integral to designing instruction for children in making or reading maps. Total success on the tasks described in this article is not a prerequisite for instruction; moreover, it is unrealistic to expect teachers to administer each task to every child. It is realistic, however, to use these tasks to analyze the difficulties certain children have with maps to determine if the activities are appropriate to their spatial development. Both teachers and curriculum developers can gain insight into the learning process by interviewing children as they perform these manipulative exercises. As teachers become increasingly aware of children's misunderstandings and difficulties, they are relieved of the guilt that their teaching method is to blame for those problems, and they become aware of the extent to which an existing curriculum is or is not developmentally appropriate. In turn, curriculum developers can implement the findings from teachers' observations, resulting in more effective instruction.

## REFERENCES

Bartz, Barbara S. "Maps in the Classroom." *Journal of Geography* 69 (1970): 18-24.

Brown, T. W., et al. *An Investigation into the Optimum Age at Which Different Types of Map Questions May Best Be Set to Pupils in the Teaching of Geography*. ERIC Document No. 064191 (1970).

Copeland, Richard W. *How Children Learn Mathematics*. 4th ed. New York: Macmillan, 1979.

Karplus. R., and R. W. Peterson. "Intellectual Development Beyond Elementary School, II: Ratio, a Survey." *School Science and Mathematics* 70 (1970): 813-820.

Muir, Sharon R. and Helen N. Cheek. "Mathematics and the Map Skill Curriculum." *School Science and Mathematics* 86 (1986): 284-291.

Muir, Sharon R. and Bruce Frazee. "Teaching Map Reading Skills: A Developmental Perspective." *Social Education* 50 (March 1986): 199-203.

Pattison, William D. "Territory, Learner and Map." *The Elementary School Journal* 67 (1967): 146-153.

Pedde, M. L. "Children's Concepts of Base Area Symbols." Masters thesis, University of Alberta, Canada. 1966.

Piaget, Jean. and Barbel Inhelder. *The Child's Conception of Space*. London: W. W. Norton, 1948.

Piaget, Jean, Barbel Inhelder, and Alina Szeminska. *The Child's Conception of Geometry*. London: Routledge and Kegan Paul, 1960.

Towler, John O., and L. D. Nelson. "The Elementary School Child's Concept of Scale." *Journal of Geography* 67 ( 1968): 24-28.

Vanselow, G. W. "On the Nature of Spatial Images." Proceedings of the Association of American Geographers 6 (1974): 11-14.

Voyat, Gilbert E. *Piaget Systematized*. Hillsdale, N.J.: Lawrence Erlbaum, 1982.

Welton, David A., and John T. Mallan. *Children and Their World*. 3d ed. Boston: Houghton Mifflin, 1988.

Sharon Pray Muir is Professor and Chairperson of the Department of Curriculum, Instruction, and Leadership at Oakland University, Rochester, Michigan. [1991 note]

# PART 4

## Ⅳ INDIVIDUAL DEVELOPMENT AND IDENTITY

Personal identity is shaped by many factors, including culture, groups, friends, knowledge, and institutions. Examining human behavior helps students form norms and values as they learn how to deal with other people. An understanding of how one has grown and changed and how one is likely to develop and change in the future helps students accept their increasing abilities and ethical citizenship responsibilities. Questions examined in the study of individual development and identity include the following: How do people learn? What influences learning and growth? How do individuals relate to one another? Content for this strand comes from disciplines such as psychology, sociology, and anthropology and is applied to individuals, societies, and cultures. Elementary teachers often deal with this strand when counseling students on a one-to-one basis concerning their class behaviors, learning progress, and individual social needs. Units of study that address this strand assist students in learning about the commonality of people across time and space and in gaining greater understanding of the individual life span, building a self-concept, and interacting in social situations. In a society where technology, financial considerations, and fear often isolate individuals and generations, stressing this theme may help teachers create and maintain a positive learning environment in their classrooms where all students learn and come to enjoy learning.

In their article, Dynneson and Gross provide a theoretical basis for citizenship education by linking human development with appropriate topics of study and learning activities for students. They explain their six stages of citizenship development and illustrate the role and importance of the teacher and school in helping students grow socially, so that they can deal with multiple and diverse groups of people living in a democracy. Pate reviews the research on how to reduce prejudice in children. He stresses the importance of human-relations training, which is both cognitive and affective, and describes multiple approaches, materials, and activities that are most helpful in reducing prejudice and promoting a positive self-concept. Closely related is the article by Aronson, who also describes how friends, schools, and teachers can help children build self-esteem and counter prejudice, thereby teaching tolerance. By helping children make sense of the world around them, teachers and counselors can assist children in accepting others who have different personal characteristics. He identifies resources and activities for teachers and parents to use. Walsh identifies the dispositions for critical thinking and offers examples of how schools and teachers can use critical thinking to help reduce prejudice.

Prejudice can arise over gender, racial, ethnic, physical, linguistic, or religious differences. McClain and Nielsen provide descriptions of classroom-tested ways to address concerns about religion with elementary students throughout the school year. Gallagher addresses the all too common situation in which inappropriate language is being used to hurt others. She presents lessons that require students to use honest discussion skills to develop sensitivity to what they say, how they say it, and how other students are likely to respond to the ways they believe others treat them.

Schools have a socializing function, which is to help children learn to get along with others and to grow and mature. Social studies is the subject that most appropriately addresses this general goal. In the past, units devoted to this strand have often been limited to very young children and their adjustment to school. Clearly, the authors of the articles presented here see that the strand plays an important role for all elementary school students as they seek to be accepted and learn to accept others as friends and citizens of the same community.

# An Eclectic Approach to Citizenship: Developmental Stages

# 22

**Thomas L. Dynneson**
**Richard E. Gross**

Citizenship education has evolved into so many approaches that teachers are confused by the different content, skills, and attitudes that are being promoted under the banner of citizenship education. Students are receiving different orientations to citizenship and the end result may be that we are producing a citizenry that is confused, fragmented, and disunited about various aspects of American life and the rights and responsibilities associated with American citizenship. We are in danger of losing sight of the fact that the purpose of citizenship education is to help adults face their responsibilities with confidence and determination and to help them realize a degree of national unity and purpose in light of democratic principles.

The challenge facing educators today in regard to citizenship education is to produce a unified and synthesized approach to citizenship, an approach that will select and combine the best elements of currently existing approaches to citizenship education and to reassemble them into a unified (or eclectic) approach that is correlated to the growth and development of children and that meets the appropriate needs and expectations of society. Through this effort we may be able to generate an integrated and balanced citizenship education program that will be adopted throughout the nation. The imperatives of such a proposed program would include the following considerations:

▮ Essential human activities and processes.
▮ Social goals, needs, and problems.
▮ Tasks and concerns of children and youth.
▮ Fundamental understanding and skills from history and the social sciences.
▮ Relevant learning from other curricular events.
▮ Contemporary developments and issues.
▮ The ideals and foundations of the government and economy of the United States.

We have decided to shoulder this burden by proposing an eclectic citizenship program that can be used by teachers for the grades kindergarten through twelve. In addition, we have attempted to key this proposal to a theoretical model that explains the sequence of events that occurs in children's lives as they evolve an internalized schema of citizenship. It is our belief that this model can become the basis for structuring and developing a sound citizenship

Reprinted with permission from the Helen Dwight Reid Educational Foundation, from *The Social Studies*, January/February 1985. Published by Heldref Publications, 1319 Eighteenth Street, NW, Washington, D.C. 20036-1802. Copyright 1985.

education program of the eclectic type. While an extensive amount of field research will be required to establish our contentions, we have made some preliminary inquiries into the behavior of children and these inquiries have given us a degree of confidence in the model.

Before proceeding, it may be helpful to review briefly the eight citizenship approaches before presenting our theoretical developmental model. [1]

## REVIEW OF EIGHT APPROACHES TO CITIZENSHIP EDUCATION

1. *Citizenship as Persuasion, Socialization, and Indoctrination.* These approaches are all based on the belief that children need to be taught the perceived norms and values of their society and culture.
2. *Citizenship as Contemporary Issues and Current Events.* This approach is based on the belief that students must participate in the study of contemporary events in order to execute their duties as American citizens.
3. *Citizenship as the Study of American History, Civics, and Geography and the Related Social Sciences.* This approach is based on the belief that students need to be knowledgeable about American heritage, the process of American government, the lands, peoples, and regions of America, as well as other social, economic, and political institutions.
4. *Citizenship as Civic Participation and Civic Action.* This approach is based on the belief that students should participate directly in the affairs and activities of adult society including issues, debates, movements, and causes.
5. *Citizenship as Scientific Thinking.* This approach is based on the belief that students should be trained in intellectual or cognitive processes that prepare them to make decisions choose between alternatives, and find solutions for the social, economic, and political problems.
6. *Citizenship as a Jurisprudence Process.* This approach is based on the belief that the student must become familiar with constitutional and legalistic processes that help to determine the outcomes associated with societal conflicts and controversial issues.
7. *Citizenship as Humanistic Development.* This approach is based on the belief that in order to become a "good" citizen a child must be cared for wholistically. Wholistic care includes tending to the physical, emotional, and intellectual needs of the child.
8. *Citizenship as Preparation for Global Interdependence.* This approach is based on the belief that future generations will have to deal with international issues that affect all of the peoples of the earth. Modern technology has spanned the distances that traditionally have separated

peoples, cultures, and nations.

While all of the above described approaches to citizenship education are useful and provide guidelines needed by the teacher as a means for promoting student citizenship, each approach tends to require certain levels of attainment. These levels of attainment involve both cognitive and emotional aspects of development. In other words, they involve a hierarchical order that is appropriate or inappropriate according to the attained intellectual and emotional development of the student. While individual students are unique in the realms of intellectual and emotional attainment, they tend to share some regularities of development that can be used for educational purposes in the development of citizenship. Therefore, we must attempt to identify the regularities of development that help indicate which citizenship training approach or combinations of approaches would be most effective with students at a given age. As a result of this need, we have put forth the following developmental structure as our framework for sorting, combining, and assigning the approaches of citizenship as the basis for our eclectic citizenship curriculum.

## DEVELOPMENTAL CITIZENSHIP
According to our theoretical model, the child proceeds through six stages of citizenship development. The first stage begins at birth when the child forms an intimate relationship with his mother. The final stage begins after the years when the adolescent makes the transition to adulthood and assumes the privileges and duties of the adult.

## SIX STAGES OF CITIZENSHIP DEVELOPMENT
### 1. *Biological Citizenship: The Needs Dependent Infant (birth to three years).*
During the first three years of life, the child begins his first social relationship by being totally dependent on his mother. It is a period of time in which an almost exclusive biological dependency is the basis for the infant's first social relationship. The behavior of the child is the result of this relationship and is established when the mother interacts with the child. This is accomplished as routines and patterns of behavior are established. The infant is shaped and manipulated by the mother and the child learns to manipulate and interact with this restricted world. The infant must satisfy the basic biological needs that dominate this period of time; therefore, the baby learns to experiment and manipulate his surroundings and also learns about the reliable features and patterns of his world.

Citizenship during the period of biological dependency is a basic and critical episode in the future development of the child. A good social relationship with the mother will lead to positive future relationships that are of a supportive nature. On the other hand, a poor social relationship may hamper the future social development of the child and the child may develop a warped view of himself and his world. He will either come to expect good treatment from others and be willing to extend that treatment to others or he will come to distrust others. When the latter is

the case, these children will be unwilling to extend trust or help to others. This then becomes the basis of a "poor" citizenship. The period of biological dependency will determine not only future social relationships of the child but also future behaviors associated with his citizenship.

### 2. *Family Citizenship: A Reference for Social Citizenship (four to five years).*
As the child grows and matures, he expands his social world, especially within the family. By the age of three the child has developed basic linguistic skills which are used to develop new social relationships within the family. Other family members, including the father and siblings, will affect the infant's behaviors through these relationships. While these new relationships have a fundamental kinship in nature, social familiarity becomes the source of influence. The father may become an important influence in the life and development of the child depending on the quantity and quality of interaction that takes place during this period of time. The same is true of older siblings.

It is during this phase of expanding dependencies that the child becomes aware of the meaning of family membership. Family membership and the concomitant development of family loyalty becomes the source of citizenship within the family. Family citizenship will set in motion the internalized and subconscious development of citizenship that will serve as a model of behavior for the child. Later on, this internalized model will serve as a sort of definitional reference and as a framework for assessing and valuing social relationships. The quality of social relationships determines the quality of one's citizenship. Family rules and expectations are used to measure and define family citizenship and families vary greatly in regard to rules and expectations. Peer relationships test both the infant's ability to form nonkinship relationships and to measure the influence of the family in terms of its success in establishing acceptable behaviors. Positive family relationships tend to support the retention of family values, while poor family relationships tend to diminish the retention of family values, especially when they are challenged by influences outside the family.

Family citizenship establishes the important subconscious values that will guide the individual as he expands his social relationships. This citizenship establishes the notion of proper and improper behavior and it establishes the individual's concept of himself in terms of relationships with others. The citizenship foundations established at this time will be very difficult to modify or change. When a child experiences problems with social relationships and poor citizenship, it may be due to inadequate or inappropriate family experiences that will be very difficult to overcome.

### 3. *Formative Social Citizenship: The Initiation of Nonbiological Dependencies (five to nine years).*
The beginning of nonbiological citizenship occurs when the infant comes into contact with peers outside the family;

however, the formative phase of nonbiological dependencies begins in earnest when the child enters the classroom. This is an extremely critical phase in the life of the child because he must learn a whole new set of relationships and behavior. These relationships may be considered secondary social relationships. Instead of being based on family or biological associations, they are based on social associations. The classroom environment becomes a sociological challenge for the child. It is an ordeal in which the student must learn new behavior, form new relationships, establish himself within an unfamiliar social environment, learn the difference between appropriate and inappropriate behavior, in varying situations, and learn to differentiate between reliable expectancies and unpredictable (or inconsistent) future events. It is an experience in which the student will have to come to grips with himself and his classmates. This is a time in which the child will be required to rely upon his internalized resources and to extend them. Internalized resources are resources that have been stored away from past experiences. They can be used by the child to establish his membership in this new, nonbiologically determined society. Social citizenship will take time to develop and the most critical years are the early years of the elementary school.

As time passes, social citizenship becomes more important to the child, but it never replaces family citizenship. Family or biological citizenship serves as both a retreat for the child and as a source of security and assurance during these often troubled years.

The teacher is normally the first adult outside the home that contributes directly and consistently to the child's understanding of social citizenship. As a mediator of social citizenship, the teacher directs and corrects student conduct associated with appropriate and inappropriate behavior. The teacher also should serve as a civic model. In other words, the teacher is the student's source of information pertaining to citizenship behavior vis-á-vis the adult world. While the student generally is concerned about social relationships within peer groups, he is greatly influenced by the communicated view of the teacher regarding his status in the classroom. The teacher/student relationship tends to transcend all other relationships during the first four years of school and this relationship is critical to the future development of citizenship. Therefore, school officials must be diligent to see that teachers are aware of their influence and responsibilities in citizenship. The monitoring of teacher/student relationships should play an important role in the evaluation and retention of all teachers, especially primary elementary teachers. School administrators also need to establish a school environment that promotes civic competency on the part of teachers and pupils.

Large and small group activities should be used to help students learn to work together. These activities should be used as a media for working out all kinds of issues and problems associated with social relationships. Roles and responsibilities should be rotated so that each child learns to lead, support, and follow others. In addition, the teacher should emphasize mutual respect as the rightful expectation of every student in the classroom. These activities should include the rotation of offices, tasks, and chores that contribute to the overall welfare of the classroom. Children need to experience inquiry and decision-making processes which provide a foundation for fundamental civic qualities essential for individuals who participate effectively in a free society.

## 4. Stratified Social Citizenship: The Development of Social Categories and Membership Behavior (ten to twelve years).

The intermediate elementary school years correspond with the years of social development that are characterized by multiple group memberships that require specialized behavior and loyalties. During this phase of development, most children can identify readily the groups to which they can claim membership. Most of these groups can be classified as either groups affiliated with the conjugal family or as formal and informal sociological groups. Formal sociological groups include organizations such as the scouts, Sunday school classes, football teams, drill squads, choirs, etc. Informal sociological groups include cliques, friends, classmates, neighborhood pals, etc. Both formal and informal groups require certain expected behavior from individual group members, including values and loyalties that are taught and enforced through a variety of group social methods including ostracism. The study of these group affiliations are important to the individual's understanding of citizenship within and between groups. Lessons learned at this age will teach the student stratagems of behavior that can be used successfully within groups and within society in general.

At this age, the student begins to perceive society in terms of multiple group relationships and he can identify and categorize these groups into hierarchies of importance. He also can deal with social groups in terms of sociological distance. By sociological distance we mean the amount of contact that exists between the individual and the group and the amount of influence that the group or organization exerts on the daily life of the child. Citizenship and citizenship participation often are determined by the individual's priorities (hierarchy of importance) and by the constancy of contact that the individual has with groups within society. Therefore, the child must be in touch with others, be aware of the events that affect his life and the lives of group members, and be able to work cooperatively and constructively for the common good of the group. These years are critical to the development of values and attitudes associated with the individual's responsibilities to others.

Curricula programs that emphasize the development of appropriate social relationships within a class or group setting will be very effective with students in the intermediate years. Models of appropriate behavior will help the student modify and adjust his self interests in order to achieve status within groups. In addition, the teacher can provide opportunities that will encourage the examination and evaluation of groups and group behavior. It is important that the student realize that group associations are also a source of self identification and affect the individual's status within society as a whole.

This is an age when teachers should emphasize current events. Current events can be used as a source of raw materials for evaluating human and social behavior. Students in this age category are concerned especially about ethical questions such as justice and fair play. They can begin to deal with controversial social issues that relate to group behavior. The building of healthy value bases for responsible action as well as growth in humane attitudes would seem to be essential goals for this developmental stage of civic competency.

5. *Horizontal Social Relationships: A Period of Expanded Citizenship within Groups (thirteen to fifteen years)*.

This is a time in which the peer group relationships exert an extraordinary amount of influence on the behavior of the students; biological factors re-emerge in importance. While other relationships remain influential for the adolescent, peer relationships are dominant. Peer relationships are based upon shared value norms. Value norms are expressed in terms of fashion and dress, the use of unique phrases and colorful language, and a willingness to defer to others who are commonly accepted as "elites" or important persons. Traditional family values are not swept away by peer values, but they are often sublimated to emerging elements of adolescent culture and serve as the mechanism through which the youth seeks important peer associations. This is also the age when the adolescent seriously reflects on the personal values that have guided his social behavior in the past. He willingly uses self-examination as a means of reflection. During this age, students should continue to be taught to value the processes associated with logic, objectivity, and the process of scientific thinking.

Teachers should provide opportunities for the examination of social relationships and various aspects of human behavior from an objective and rational perspective. The historic actions of important public personalities and the effect of their behavior on American society would help students evaluate the consequences of ethic and value norms. Students should examine exemplary behavior under stressful and threatening conditions. In addition, students should be given every opportunity to examine and to express their ideologies in light of actions and consequences.

6. *Vertical Social Relationships: A Search for Stability within and between Stratified Groups (sixteen to twenty-one years)*.

This age is characterized by a search for personal order and structure within and between social groups. During these years, the individual is attempting to establish a sense of belonging and a sense of harmony. The individual's identity may become relatively "fixed" for life during this period and this identity will be reinforced throughout life by his behavior. Personal perspective will guide the behavior of the individual in relation to others including societal institutions. Individuals in this phase of development are ready to aban-

don many of the horizontal relationships and values that characterized the previous period. These relationships will be replaced by vertical relationships that span age, sex, occupational, racial, religious, and cultural affiliations. All of these new relationships will have to be kept in balance in order to maintain the harmony that the individual is seeking; therefore, the individual will have to accommodate a broader value perspective than what existed at an earlier time. He will have to justify his actions to others in order to maintain order and structure within and between the social groups that are his source of support and identity.

The strategies for maintaining order and structure are highly individualized and come close to approaching our definitions of personality. Strategies for maintaining harmony in light of controversial issues, for instance, differ greatly among individuals. While one person seeks to maintain relationships at the expense of personal values, another will prefer the reverse. By this time individuals have developed these strategies to perfection and they become known for these personal qualities. Democratic societies are made up of individuals with many different types of personal qualities. These qualities have been developed and shaped by their families, friends, adult leaders, and community members as well as by biological factors and, of course, their accumulated experiences.

Democratic societies tolerate more variations within society than the arbitrary societies. This tolerance needs to be balanced with established understandings, beliefs, and loyalties that characterize youth who are willing to fulfill their obligations associated with citizenship. In order for democracies to survive the challenges that arise from internal and external sources, ethical values must become the individual's mechanism for maintaining relationships within and between vertical groups.

The last years of formal education should emphasize the enforcement of ethical judgment and ethical behavior. This can be accomplished through the study of issues that contain controversies that require ethical solutions. Students should be taught about personal sacrifice and the role that it plays as a necessary component of society and about cooperation and compromise, the essentials of democratic life. In addition, students need to experience the strategies that can successfully resolve human conflict in order to maintain harmony and stability within society. Classroom instruction should center on these issues and methods during the final years of instruction.

## NOTE

[1] Thomas L. Dynneson and Richard E. Gross, "Citizenship Education and the Social Studies: Which is Which?" *The Social Studies*, 73(Sept./Oct. 1982), pp. 229-234.

Thomas L. Dynneson is an Associate Professor of Education and Anthropology at the University of Texas. Richard E. Gross is Chairperson of the Department of Curriculum and Teacher Education at Stanford University, Stanford, California. [1985 note]

# Research on Reducing Prejudice

# 23

**Glenn S. Pate**

In spite of gains made by the civil rights movement and by affirmative action programs, the belief of millions of Americans that our society has effectively eradicated racism is false and therefore one to which we are not entitled.

In January 1987, the nation's attention was focused on all-white Forsyth County, Georgia. During the previous month, a black-white confrontation in Howard Beach, New York, had escalated into a major crisis. Some members of virtually every minority group are victims of racism. For example:

▋ A number of farmers in the Midwest in 1986 blamed their economic problems on Jews.

▋ Violent acts against Asian Americans increased from 50 in 1982 to 195 in 1984.

▋ In 1984, the Alamo Christian Foundation, a fundamentalist religious sect, distributed a pamphlet which claimed that the Roman Catholic Church had ordered the assassination of Abraham Lincoln and John Kennedy.

▋ Groups of whites and Hispanics in Lawrence, Massachusetts, battled each other with rocks, bottles, and Molotov cocktails in 1984.

Of course, thousands of incidents of racism that occur each year are not publicized. If the tip of the iceberg looks bleak, we must wonder how fraught with prejudice our society really is. Despite these dismal notes, we are still closer to a prejudice-free society than we have ever been in the past. Part of our progress may be attributable to efforts to use knowledge for reducing prejudice. Over the years, wide-ranging research projects have sought to increase knowledge of how to lessen the prejudice in individuals. Some of these projects have been successful: others have not. This report compiles relevant research findings and presents them in a manner that may help educators increase their prejudice-reduction efforts. The report is organized according to the approach used, with each approach crossing age levels.

## AUDIOVISUAL APPROACHES

For years, teachers have made use of films that may affect students' attitudes. A large number of films designed to lessen student prejudice have become available only in relatively recent years. The research conducted yields several helpful generalizations. The major finding is that films

can indeed reduce prejudice. Films that are realistic, have a plot, and portray believable characters are more effective than message films.

When students are able to identify with human emotions, dreams, fears, and problems, they are drawn into the drama and have a clearer picture of the effects of prejudice than they had before. If may be that we possess some innate sense of justice and react to discrimination, especially when vicariously and emotionally involved with the victim. Dramas are more realistic and effective with an integrated cast than with a cast made up entirely of a single ethnic group. Films or television shows with only one ethnic group present may even create or promote negative stereotypes and make the situation worse.

Modeling is another factor that enhances the power of films. Films should depict characters who model desired attitudes or, even better, who model a positive change in attitude. The least effective films are the ones perceived as message films. These films are unrealistic and homiletic and may produce resistance in viewers who perceive them as propaganda.

## APPROACHES USING SPECIAL MATERIALS

Several studies have focused on materials specifically selected for their prejudice-reducing potential. As with films, the materials that drew students emotionally into the lives of particular people or characters affected the students positively. Approaches that were academic with less vicarious identification were less successful.

A project with 2d graders used reading books selected for having multiethnic characters. The books portrayed characters of several ethnic groups as decent, hardworking people with estimable values. A comparison group read the same books with the characters showing the same qualities, except they were all white Anglo people. Students who had read the multiethnic books developed more positive attitudes toward other ethnic groups than did the comparison students (Litcher 1969).

Another study with elementary students also provided an opportunity for students to identify with particular individuals. It used a series of dramatic plays based on the lives of real and fictional people. The situation was such that students could empathize and identify with certain individuals and resulted in positive attitude changes (Gimmestad and De Chiara 1982).

High school students read nine books dealing with blacks, six of which were fiction, two nonfiction, and one a photographic essay. Although we may not know the relative power of the fiction and nonfiction books, the exercise

Reprinted from *Social Education*, April/May 1988, Volume 52, Number 4. Copyright 1988 by National Council for the Social Studies.

presented an opportunity for students to identify emotionally with individual characters and the results indicated positive attitude changes (Hayes 1969).

The power of emotion and identification may also be seen in a study that did not yield positive results. Junior high students were required to read nonfiction books about certain target ethnic groups and give oral and written reports on their reading. The students were also exposed to a series of guest speakers (Lessing and Clarke 1976). Lack of positive results may have resulted from racial tensions in the community at the time of the study or students may have perceived the study as too academic, abstract, and as a propaganda effort. What appear to be different in this study compared with the previously reviewed ones are the elements of emotion and vicarious experience.

## COGNITIVE APPROACHES

It seems reasonable that the more we know about other groups, the less likely we are to hold negative attitudes. It also seems reasonable that good thinking processes will guard against our becoming prejudiced. Research has tested these assumptions and they have generally proven true, with qualifications.

The cognitive approaches do not mean simply collecting factual information, but rather thinking on a higher and more complex level than before. The cognitive training must equip students with the mental skills to avoid thinking in oversimple terms and in overgeneralizations. Overgeneralization is the base of all stereotypes. Studies, such as Handler (1966), demonstrate that students, trained when to differentiate between relevant and irrelevant characteristics of people, display less prejudice than before the training. Gardiner (1972) reinforces this point in a study which gave students cognitive complexity training and reduced their level of prejudice.

In addition to increasing cognitive complexity, we can reduce students' prejudice by providing a framework or different conceptual lens for viewing phenomena. For example, students who studied semantics had less prejudice after such study, even though prejudice was not the focus of the study. A detailed study of the tools and concepts of anthropology at the high school level gave students a new mental framework and resulted in reducing their prejudices.

We have learned to increase the power of cognitive approaches by adding the element of empathy. Studies at the 5th grade level and the high school level demonstrate that level of prejudice is reduced considerably by empathic role-playing or other vicarious experiences in teaching activities. These findings imply that prejudice is not a single phenomenon but is comprised of three dimensions: cognition, affection, and behavior. If we can change one of the dimensions, the other two do not necessarily change. It also does not follow that better results are obtained if an effort to reduce prejudice is targeted at more than one dimension.

Cognitive approaches do work, but we must remember that they need to include more than factual information.

"We need to realize that, although sound knowledge is necessary to combat false information, it is not sufficient to change attitude. Facts do not speak for themselves; rather they are interpreted through the experience and biases of those hearing them" (Moreland 1963, 125).

## COOPERATIVE LEARNING APPROACHES

Most of us have been in situations where we work with others to solve a common problem and are aware that the experience affects our attitudes toward and relations with the other people. Researchers have used analogs of these situations to reduce prejudice. The essence of the idea is that, when we share common problems, tasks, goals, and success with people of another ethnic group, we develop positive feelings toward them. Educators have worked with a variety of cooperative learning arrangements that have resulted in lessening prejudice and increasing cognitive learning.

One experiment has students grouped with ethnically heterogeneous teams. Each student receives a portion of the learning task, then teaches it to teammates. This jigsaw method has been effective with a wide range of ages. Another cooperative approach has teammates help one another study for a test or prepare for a competitive game. Although there are a variety of the cooperative learning approaches, they all share the same essential elements and have proven effective. Using cooperative learning teams is one of the most promising approaches for reducing prejudice today.

## HUMAN RELATIONS TRAINING

Human relations training is one of the most common approaches for fostering positive intergroup relations. The military, private companies, and schools have used this approach with mixed success and have identified some problems.

A key problem is that people do not like to be manipulated. When they perceive that they are required to attend a workshop or series of meetings that have the stated intent of changing the participants' thinking, they resist the message. For this reason, many required human relations workshops have made little, if any, positive attitude change in the participants, and some training has resulted in increased prejudice.

Another problem is that many of the training sessions have been too brief and too superficial. A Saturday workshop or a meeting after school may not provide participants with a sufficient number of meaningful experiences to produce change. Participants need to become emotionally involved and have a stake in the situation. Too often, people in a human relations training session are influenced by the atmosphere in the session and consciously or unconsciously say the "right" thing. Types of activities are key elements in human relations training. Participants need to be involved, and lectures are demonstrably not effective. Although some studies have yielded positive findings, human relations training requires great care and planning; otherwise, the sessions offer little more than lip service to reducing prejudice.

## DIRECT APPROACHES

In our efforts to reduce student prejudice, one of the most obvious approaches is to offer direct, anti-prejudice lessons or units. Many of the problems noted above with human relations training are present here. There are the overt or covert pressures to do and say the "right" thing; the feeling of being manipulated; the too brief, too superficial experiences without real involvement. If students are to study prejudice, the approaches should be scholarly and cognitive. The study may be part of a sociology, history, anthropology, or psychology teaching unit. The idea is for students to study the subject and people's behavior from an objective outsider's viewpoint and not be threatened personally; otherwise, the threat to one's own beliefs and attitudes and the feeling of being manipulated may be too great to overcome.

## SCHOOLWIDE CONDITIONS

There are circumstances and conditions over which teachers and principals have control that can lead to reducing or increasing prejudice. A simple and obvious condition is to avoid the practice of segregated seating in the classroom. On a school level, scheduling should avoid homogeneous grouping or classes that are ethnically or racially unbalanced, especially if the grouping is based on culturally biased tests.

By example and practice, teachers and principals can emphasize the value of worthwhile social goals such as good student-to-student interaction and teacher-to-student interaction. Not only can teachers and principals deliberately provide opportunities for students to practice socially desirable behavior but their own modeling can have a powerful influence. School administrators should also manage the school so that students of different ethnic groups work and play together. Clearly they should avoid practices that divide students along ethnic lines.

The school should have multicultural curricula and materials. The multicultural aspects should permeate the curricula and not be treated as peripheral to the real curricula. Although it is good to teach minority culture and history, the teaching should be an integral part of the curricula. It is of questionable value to feature a particular ethnic group for a week or a day. This approach has been referred to as the "zoo" approach.

The principal is the key person, and she or he must have teachers and staff who are knowledgeable and sincere in their efforts to reduce prejudice. Giving lip service to a prejudice reduction campaign can be counterproductive.

## OTHER APPROACHES

Several other studies are different from the above approaches and some of their findings are quite powerful and have great promise.

One of the closest correlatives of prejudice is self-esteem. Studies not only show a high correlation between prejudice and self-esteem but come close to demonstrating a cause-and-effect relationship. When we improve persons' self-concept and increase their self-esteem, we see a reduction in prejudice. If a teacher or school were limited to affecting only one aspect of students, the greatest good would come from increasing students' self-esteem.

Another idea that appeals to common sense and is supported by research is the need for perceiving members of another group, an outgroup, as different from each other. When we perceive all members as alike in important characteristics, we tend to overgeneralize and stereotype, usually in a negative way. Members of a given ethnic group obviously have different strengths, dreams, problems, ideas, and appearances from one another. Research has shown that learning this diminishes students' negative attitudes toward members of the group.

A new approach that has had positive effects is counterstereotyping. A teacher must deliberately choose sample individuals of a given ethnic group who are counter to the popular stereotype. Examples of this could be Jewish athletes, black intellectuals, Hispanic white-collar workers. Characteristics of groups as a whole should also be included, such as that the majority of Puerto Ricans in New York are gainfully employed. The approach is subtle and probably slow, but it shows good promise.

## TEACHER EDUCATION

A degree of logic tells us that, if we educate present and future teachers to lessen their level of prejudice and if we equip them with skills to reduce prejudice, the effects can be extremely positive.

Education students in college who were exposed to a comprehensive multicultural education program became less prejudiced than comparable students who had been exposed to a workshop approach. Based on results noted earlier, this finding is not surprising. It is also not surprising that a study that had guest speakers address future teachers was not effective.

An approach that had positive results involved university students' selecting target ethnic groups to study. Each student took a particular group, studied its history and culture, prepared materials to teach about it, and then taught a lesson on the group to local precollege students. This involvement resulted in lessening prejudice of the university students.

If we are to make a serious attack upon prejudice, surely teacher education has the potential to produce positive results.

Several facts stand out. Knowledge available about prejudice reduction is already adequate to yield great positive results. Although the concept of prejudice is extremely complex and there is much we do not understand, we do know some principles and approaches that work. Perhaps equally important, we know some approaches that are frequently ineffective. Because the knowledge of the tools of reducing prejudice is available and awaits our use, we can make significant inroads on the problem by acting on it.

## REFERENCES

Gardiner, Garth S. "Complexity Training and Prejudice Reduction." *Journal of Applied Social Psychology* 2, no. 4 (1972): 326-42.

Gimmestad, Beverly J., and Edith DeChiara "Dramatic Plays: A Vehicle for Prejudice Reduction in the Elementary School." *Journal of Education Research* 76, no. 1, (September/ October 1982): 45-49.

Handler, June Moss. "An Attempt to Change Kindergarten Children's Attitudes of Prejudice toward the Negro." Ed.D. Diss. Columbia University. 1966.

Hayes, Marie Therese. "An Investigation of the Impact of Reading on Attitudes of Racial Prejudice." ERIC ED 123-319. 1969.

Lessing, Elise E, and Chester C. Clarke. "An Attempt to Reduce Ethnic Prejudice and Assess Its Correlates in a Junior High School Sample." *Educational Research Quarterly* 1, no. 2 (Summer 1976).

Litcher, J.W., and D.W. Johnson. "Changes in Attitudes toward Negroes of White Elementary School Students after Use of Multiethnic Readers." *Journal of Educational Psychology* 60 (1969): 148-52.

Moreland, J. Kenneth. "The Development of Racial Bias in Young Children." *Theory into Practice* 2, no. 3: 125.

Glenn S. Pate is an Associate Professor of Education at the University of Arizona, Tempe. [1988 note]

# The Inside Story

*Counseling for Tolerance in the Early Years Means Paying Attention to the Way Children Think and Feel about the World and Themselves*

**David Aronson**

*"Hey, what is this, One Flew Over the Cuckoo's Nest?"*

It was Meredith Kimber's first meeting with a 6th grade class she would be counseling as part of her year-long internship with Inventing the Future, a racism-prevention project, and Kimber was encountering more than the usual dose of suspicion. The students were from predominantly Irish families in a blue-collar Massachusetts town with a reputation for insularity and xenophobia. Kimber's project was to help children address the inner source of the violence and racism that seem to surge in the middle school years.

A graduate of Harvard Divinity School, Kimber was shocked by the attitudes she encountered among many of the children. "These kids had derogatory names for everyone," she recalls. "They used to ride the subway searching for black kids to pick fights with. They'd come in punching each other, calling each other 'fag.'" They initially had little interest in pursuing an inner exploration of their own biases.

Still, Kimber persisted "We didn't ever tell the children what was right or wrong. Instead, we asked them how they felt about things, trying to get them to change. If someone said 'fag,' we said, 'OK, here's the homosexuality issue again.'" Kimber's hope was that by getting the children to disclose their beliefs, values and fears, she and the other counselors on her team could help the children overcome the irrational thinking underlying their prejudice.

"By the end of the year, a lot of the kids had come to accept us and were relying on us to help them think through a lot of issues about racism, sex and violence."

Increasingly, for school counselors and psychologists, helping students become more tolerant and accepting means starting at the very earliest ages. Even then, however, racism may already have sprouted its first insidious roots. Debra Van Ausdale, a doctoral student in sociology at the University of Florida, witnessed a disturbing number of racial incidents when she worked as a teacher's aide at Gainesville Day Care Center in Gainesville, Fla.

"When a white girl became weary pulling an Asian girl in a wagon one day, the Asian girl hopped out and offered to pull," Van Ausdale recalls. "The white girl said, 'You can't pull the wagon. Only white people can pull the wagon.'" It was, says Van Ausdale, an incident that crystallized for her just how well her students understood the power of racial identity.

"We often think of the early years as an age of innocence," says Dr. Kevin Dwyer, assistant executive director of the National Association of School Psychologists. "In fact, prejudice is probably developed before children enter school—as is a predisposition to violence. School forces children together who might not have had the chance to exhibit that sort of anti-social behavior before they arrive."

The psychological development of prejudice in children was brilliantly illuminated 40 years ago in the work of Gordon Allport. Today, school counselors have developed an effective approach to reducing prejudice in the crucial early years, when the direction of the child's emotional and psychological growth can be set for life. This approach relies less on proselytizing than on changing the way young children make sense of the world—and themselves.

Because of their training, counselors have a better understanding than most about how young children form opinions, feelings and personalities around what they see and experience. And because of their position—their 'beat" is typically an entire school—counselors can intervene at every level, from advising the troubled child who may have violently expressed his or her prejudice, to developing teacher training programs, to working with parents on addressing racial tensions in the community.

Successful early intervention efforts are based on the premise that hatred and prejudice are tools of the subconscious that ease the feeling of insecurity by offering the illusion of superiority. Counselors try to offer more responsible ways to achieve emotional security.

"Giving children a positive experience of themselves, teaching them to recognize the validity of human differences, and providing them with the tools to express their emotions—all these are ways that intolerance can be counteracted," says Pat Schwallie-Giddis, associate director for the American Counseling Association.

Like strands in a rope, the various elements that Schwallie-Giddis speaks about—self-awareness, self-expression and self-esteem—are all widely recognized as intertwined aspects of the tolerant person. Children cannot freely express their emotions or feel secure with others unless they feel secure with themselves. And they can't feel good about themselves without having some understanding of who they are. Though any effort to separate these elements is necessarily artificial, they do build on and strengthen each other and can he thought of sequentially.

## SELF-AWARENESS AND SELF-EXPRESSION

School counselors can help foster children's self-awareness through exercises designed to help children see themselves and others for who they are, apart from the expectations and stereotypes that can easily color their thinking.

In one activity, called "The Me Bag," children are each given a plain brown grocery bag that they may decorate any way they choose. Then they are encouraged to fill the bag at home with things they value, things that represent what they love and feel proudest of. The next day, children get to show off what they've brought in. A recent immigrant from Bolivia may come in with an embroidered doll, for example, and another student may bring an LA Lakers cap.

Although each bag looks different, they all contain precious items. Children learn that the things that make them unique are as valuable as the things that they have in common. They learn to appreciate differences rather than fear them. And they learn to see themselves as others might see them: as individuals with their own enthusiasms and cultural traditions, neither better nor worse than others.

With an awareness of themselves as distinct individuals, children can better learn how to express their emotions in responsible and appropriate ways. The ability to articulate feelings is one of the most difficult things for children to learn, says Kevin Dwyer of the National Association of School Psychologists—yet it is absolutely critical. "So much depends on it: how well you're able to work as a team member, how well you resist acting on impulse, how you deal with the problems you're having."

Because it is often easier to make sense of other people s feelings than of one's own. educators have found that one of the best ways to develop children's emotional expressiveness is by asking them to think about the experiences of fictional characters. Through specially designed reading programs children learn how failing to identify and express feelings can lead to increasing frustration and self-defeating behavior. Consider the following scenarios, taken from two popular reading programs in schools today *PUMSY: In Pursuit of Excellence* and *Kids Have Feelings, Too.*

In the first, Pumsy the dragon is having a terrible day. While her friends are out picnicking on the beach, having the best times of their lives, Pumsy is moping under a tree. Usually, her best friend Steve would come tell her to stop feeling sorry for herself. But today, he's decided to let her make her own decisions.

In the second, a little girl from the picture book *Sometimes I Feel Awful* is also having a pretty rotten time. She has invited her best friend, David, over to play. But David just sits around playing with a puzzle, while she wants to go outside and climb a tree. Maybe a good swift punch will bring him around—but, of course, that only makes David want to leave. Now the little girl—who is never given a name, and who might, therefore, be any child—is lonelier than ever.

Children listening to these stories are encouraged to think about the consequences of the characters' actions and to offer alternatives. The little girl in *Sometimes I Feel Awful* explodes in anger because she isn't able to express to David how frustrated she is feeling. One group of children in Florida had very definite ideas about how she should behave.

"She should tell him!" called out one tousle-headed boy.

"Tell him what?" the boy was asked.

"That she wants to go play in the tree!" he shouted, with the certainty of a 4-year-old.

The goal of these programs is for the children to take the insights they've learned from others and apply them to their own lives. Programs that develop children's powers of self-expression give them a feeling of control over their environment and make them less likely to lash out in violence and anger.

In Hillsboro County, Fla., an early childhood program has as its guiding image a stop sign. Bright red stop sign stickers, plastered everywhere in the classroom, emphasize children's power as decision-makers. By teaching children to stop and think before they act, the "stop sign" program encourages "smart behavior."

"So much in our society encourages children to act on impulse," Dwyer notes. "Get out a watch and time how long any single camera angle lasts in a TV show. There's rarely more than three or four seconds between cuts. Teaching kids to slow down, not to go after the immediate gratification, is essential to reducing violent outbursts, which express the very worst kind of intolerance."

## SELF ESTEEM

Self-awareness and self-expression are steppingstones for self-esteem. "Those persons with high self-esteem have fewer inhibitions and can relate to and accept others far more easily than those who do not," says Schwallie-Giddis. "By contrast, vengeful, intolerant behavior reflects poor self-esteem."

Self-esteem is a complicated subject that is easy to parody: "I'm OK and you're OK, but you got an 'F' on the test." And some self-esteem programs can focus so much on affirming the child's self-identity that they seem to ignore the child's own perceptions and experiences. It takes more than simply asserting the child's worth for the child to feel worthy.

True self-esteem develops out of a variety of experiences. A vital ingredient is the attention, acceptance, approval, acknowledgment and affection that a child receives from parents, primarily, but also from teachers, friends and counselors.

From these "Five A's" come feelings of competence, security, social responsibility and self-discipline, as well as strongly held values. Positive self-esteem, in other words, isn't just "feeling good about yourself." Rather, it's feeling that your life matters to others and to yourself. With that feeling comes the capacity to get along with others and the desire to conform to the rules of society.

An effective self-esteem program gives children the opportunity to learn about themselves in an environment that nurtures their growth and validates their feelings. Activities that promote self-esteem begin by teaching children to recognize the thought patterns and emotional habits that have a negative impact on their self-concept. As an alternative. such programs offer affirmations of the child as a unique being whose perceptions and feelings are valuable and appreciated. Eventually, it is hoped, the child internalizes that affirmation. No longer insecure or dissatisfied, the child is able to recognize his or her own worth and respond to the worth of others.

Some counselors have used self-portraits as a way to bring out the best in children. They ask the children to draw portraits of themselves. Then, without discussing the pictures, they have each child personally compliment the others in his or her group of six to eight fellow students ("I like your smile," "I like your shoes," etc.). Then they have the children draw their self-portraits once again, and ask them what was different this time around. Did they draw happier, prettier pictures? How did it make them feel to receive compliments from others? Did receiving compliments affect their self-portraits?

"Learning to respect yourself as an individual is, in an odd sort of way, one of the best ways to learn to respect other people and other cultures," says Jackie Allen, a school counselor who works in two trilingual elementary schools in California. "That's what it's about, ultimately, respecting individuals not because they are from another race or culture but because they are individuals."

## COUNSELING FOR THE FUTURE

School counselors, therapists and psychologists already have an extraordinary range to cover. With their many other responsibilities and involvements, it's no wonder that most feel stretched too thin. They have been lobbying for greater funding to place more counselors and psychologists in the schools.

They're needed because many of the same intervention techniques that promote tolerance can help children avoid other problems, as well: violence, drug abuse, suicide, teenage pregnancy. The whole raft of social ills that manifest themselves with such virulence in today's schools, and that speak to the existence of so much pain and emotional distress, are to varying degrees addressed by focusing on psychological issues in early childhood.

Forty years ago, at the end of his analysis of prejudice, Gordon Allport arrived at a penetrating insight: Those who hate, he told us, are hurting. By giving children the tools to overcome the pain they feel, by listening to, caring for and comforting them, by helping to build healthier and stronger psyches, counselors can play a crucial role in arresting the dismaying rise in hatred and violence.

Like a sport that requires the coordination of various skills and muscle groups, tolerance is by its nature a complex undertaking. By isolating and strengthening the fundamental psychological components of self-esteem, self-awareness and self-expression, counselors and

psychologists hope to encourage children to become healthier, more tolerant human beings.

## COMMENTARY
### THE AGES OF INTOLERANCE

In *The Nature of Prejudice*, first published in 1954, social scientist Gordon Allport developed a powerful explanation of the psychological roots of prejudice.

Allport says that from a startlingly young age children begin learning the lessons of tolerance or intolerance—recognizing certain differences, for example, while still in diapers. There's nothing intrinsically worrisome about this. The 10 or 12-month-old baby who cries at the approach of a stranger is doing exactly what he or she is biologically programmed to do: alert Mom or Dad to the presence of a potential source of danger.

But if the parents are themselves prejudiced, the infant's reaction to a stranger of a different skin color or different physical features may be subtly reinforced, generating an apparently seamless education in bigotry that justifies itself as "natural." "My baby just doesn't like people of such and such a color," some parents may report, oblivious of their own role in shaping the child's perceptions.

By age 3 or 4, children begin to pick up on more explicit clues about in-groups and out-groups from their own family, the media and their peers. Children at this age are at the cusp of racial awareness and may be extremely curious about physical differences. Although they may use derogatory remarks, they often have little idea what they mean. And while they may utter racist sentiments, and even use race and gender to exclude others, their opinions and attitudes haven't yet gelled.

Of all influences on the child's ideas at this age, the family is clearly the most important. "The family," wrote Allport port, "supplies a constant undertone of acceptance or rejection, anxiety or security." Even parents who avoid making overt racist comments may teach their kids negative racial values. The parent's tightening grip around the child's hand or the sound of the car doors being locked shut when a group of teenage males of a different race or ethnicity passes by—these communicate the parent's attitudes about others as clearly as words do.

By age 6 or 7, children have begun to recognize that there are distinct categories of people—that the janitor belongs to a different social class from the doctor, for example. And they've also begun to understand that many of these identities, such as race, gender and ethnicity, are fixed. They recognize that social status and positive or negative qualities can be ascribed to people based on their affiliation within these groups. And they've begun to make the connections between their individual identity and their group identity.

Often the lessons children learn at this age are as much about societal hypocrisy as they are about race. Parents who mutter something about the "wrong section of town" and then deflect their child's questions about what they meant aren't teaching their child that racism is bad; they are teaching the child to be cautious about speaking his or her mind on issues of race.

By age 10 or so children may start consistently excluding others who belong to an out-group, or, if they are themselves members of a minority, to develop a complex of attitudes that include defiance, self-doubt and hostility. Children this age are an excellent barometer of societal attitudes, for, in contrast to their elders, they tend to voice racial stereotypes quite freely.

A final stage comes in the teenage years, when the child learns those subtler rules of etiquette that govern relations between people. They've learned that "prejudiced talk and democratic talk are reserved for the appropriate occasions," Allport writes. What is said between friends in the mall may never be voiced in an official forum like a classroom. "It takes the entire period of childhood and much of adolescence to master the art of ethnocentrism," Allport concludes.

## RESOURCES [1995 INFORMATION]

The World of Difference Institute of the Anti-Defamation League sponsors workshops promoting diversity awareness in the classroom. The Institute's *Elementary Study Guide* is an outstanding resource packed with activities and insights to address diversity.

Anti-Defamation League
1100 Connecticut Ave.,
Suite 1020
Washington, DC 20036
(202) 452-8310

The two volumes of *Thinking, Feeling, Behaving: An Emotional Education Curriculum for Children* ($25.95 each) are compendiums of classroom activities based on the principle that thinking things through rationally is one of the best ways to overcome problems. The activities focus on developing the children's emotional intelligence. (Grades 1-6 and 7-12)

Research Press
2612 N. Mattis Ave.
Champaign, IL 61821
(217) 352-3273

*The Best Self-Esteem Activities for the Elementary Grades* offers an excellent overview of the theory behind self-esteem and emotion management for children, as well as strategies for promoting children's sense of personal agency and self-fulfillment.

Innerchoice Publishing
P.O. Box 2476
Spring Valley, CA 91979
(619) 698-2437

*Counselor in the Classroom* ($19.95) gives counselors the keys to integrating the fundamental lessons of people-skills into enjoyable learning activities designed for all children.

Innerchoice Publishing
P.O. Box 2476
Spring Valley, CA 91979
(619) 698-2437

*PUMSY: In Pursuit of Excellence* ($210) is an 8-week self-esteem program featuring a cuddly dragon puppet and a variety of workbooks, posters and other supporting material. This structured program develops children's emotional skills by involving them in the trials and tribulations of Pumsy, the dragon who sometimes acts up. (Ages 6-9)

Timberline Press
P.O. Box 70187
Eugene, OR 97401
(503) 345-1771

*Sometimes I Feel Awful* ($8.95) is an affecting book about a young girl who's having a lousy day. The accompanying teacher's guide ($8.95) gives practical suggestions for helping children identify and express their emotions. (Ages 48)

Fearon Teacher Aids
P.O. Box 280
Carthage, IL 62321
(800) 242-7272

**Debbie Walsh**

*"Ask a child to question and he'll question for a day. Teach a child to question and he'll question for a life-time." (Wolf 1987)*

Much of our thinking is subconscious and automatic—based on habit and conditioning. We tend to see what we want to see, hear what we want to hear. We tend to accept without question what is compatible with our beliefs and to reject out of hand what conflicts with them. This kind of thinking is dangerous. It makes us susceptible to emotional appeals rather than rational ones; it makes us susceptible to manipulation. It makes us suspicious, fearful, and even hostile to anyone or anything different. It can make us prejudiced.

What does it mean to be prejudiced? It means "to have prejudged," to have formed a judgment or opinion without full and sufficient examination, without just grounds or sufficient knowledge. Webster defines prejudice as "an irrational attitude of hostility directed against an individual, a group, a race, or their supposed characteristics." The opposite of prejudicial thinking is judging with full and sufficient examination and forming opinions with just grounds and sufficient knowledge. We can teach children how to look at their world this way. If we expect to survive as a rich pluralistic nation, that is what we must do.

## THE ROLE OF THE SCHOOL

How do we teach students anti-prejudicial thinking? We infuse a child's school experience with an emphasis on thinking critically about knowledge and life. Thinking critically is the antithesis of prejudicial thinking. It is, as Robert Ennis (1983) defines it, "reasonably going about deciding what to do or believe." This means that one's beliefs—and consequently one's actions—are grounded in reasoned judgment, in thorough examination, in solid evidence.

Critical thinking is a way of looking at the world, a filter which qualifies our experiences. If our worldview is inaccurate, it is because the beliefs that constitute it are inaccurate. Intelligent people may arrive at vastly different conclusions from the same evidence. It is their use of the evidence to fit their worldview that makes the difference. A critical thinker strives for as accurate a worldview as possible so as to make informed judgments.

This view of teaching for thinking involves more than simply teaching students discrete little subskills on someone's list of critical thinking skills. Thinking critically begins with being disposed to question, to examine, to suspend judgment until the available evidence is weighed.

Young children come to us with an incredible sense of wonder about the world. Any primary teacher has noticed how this natural wonder, this urgent desire to know *why*, diminishes as years go by in our "one-size-fits-all" factory model of schooling, in which *what* is the priority. Only in classrooms where *why* remains critically important—where asking the right question is as important as giving the right answer—can we nurture that natural wonder and foster dispositions of the critical spirit.

## CRITICAL THINKING DISPOSITIONS

An attitude is a mental posture, a disposition, a natural tendency. D'Angelo (1971) has described the attitudes or dispositions essential to the development of critical thinking:

1. *Intellectual curiosity*—seeking answers to various kinds of questions and problems; investigating the causes and explanations of events; asking why, how, who, when, where.
2. *Objectivity*—using objective factors in the process of making decisions; relying on evidence and valid arguments and not being influenced by emotive and subjective factors in reaching conclusions (in deciding what to do or believe).
3. *Open-mindedness*—willingness to consider a wide variety of beliefs as possibly being true; making judgments without bias or prejudice.
4. *Flexibility*—willingness to change one's beliefs or methods of inquiry; avoiding steadfastness of belief, dogmatic attitude, and rigidity; realizing that we do not know all the answers.
5. *Intellectual skepticism*—postponing acceptance of a hypothesis as true until adequate evidence is available.
6. *Intellectual honesty*—accepting a statement as true when there is sufficient evidence, even though it conflicts with cherished beliefs; avoiding slanting facts to support a particular position.
7. *Being systematic*—following a line of reasoning consistently to a particular conclusion; avoiding irrelevancies that stray from the issue being argued.
8. *Persistence*—supporting points of view without giving up the task of finding evidence and arguments.
9. *Decisiveness*—reaching certain conclusions when the evidence warrants.
10. *Respect for other viewpoints*—listening carefully to other

points of view and responding relevantly to what was said; willingness to admit that one may be wrong and that other ideas one does not accept may be correct.

## OBSTACLES TO TEACHING FOR THINKING

Are schools, as they are presently structured, designed to develop and nurture these attitudes? We currently operate on a one-size-fits-all factory model of schooling with many obstacles to teaching for thinking. Large classes, bland textbook pabulum, pressure to cover unrealistic amounts of content, accountability on standardized tests that do not measure critical thinking skills and dispositions, and a one-right-answer mentality are just a few of the hindrances that face teachers committed to helping students learn how to think for themselves.

This structure has been described as obedience training. In other words, students rarely learn to trust their own thinking, to view themselves as authorities, when in fact, teaching them to think for themselves is the most valuable gift we can give them. It is also the most valuable antidote to prejudice.

## TEACHING FOR THINKING DESPITE THE OBSTACLES

In an ideal world, schools would be restructured so that fitting the system to students would be the goal rather than vice versa as we do today. This vision of schools includes restructuring the governance of schools so that those closest to the students will make the decisions on instruction (textbooks, class size, student groupings), and it includes restructuring instruction with an emphasis not on content coverage and lower-level thinking skills, but on content depth and higher-level thinking skills.

Research tells us that this emphasis equips students with the mental skills to avoid thinking in simplistic terms and overgeneralizing. Evidence suggests that we can reduce students' prejudice by giving them a framework or different conceptual lens through which to view the world (Pate, forthcoming). Establishing a worldview that is grounded in reasoned judgment, where one's beliefs—and consequently one's actions—are based on thoughtful examination of the evidence, is the rationale of teaching for thinking.

In a less-than-ideal school system, there are still some things that can be done to bring the dream of a prejudice-free society closer to reality. Schools should play a vital role in helping students develop as fair-minded a worldview as possible so that they may assess information thoughtfully and fairly, whether it be a history lesson or an incident in their daily lives, thereby becoming more aware of and reducing the effects of bias, prejudice, and self-deception in their thinking.

Schools need to begin to explode the myth of the one-right-answer. This myth simply misrepresents the real world in which many questions do not have right—or even good—answers. We may also need to reexamine an environment where mistakes are equated with "sins," the impact of this kind of environment on risk taking with one's thoughts and ideas, and the role that competition plays in fostering or inhibiting critical thinking. In some experimental studies designed to reduce competitiveness and increase cooperation in learning (Johnson and Johnson 1975), cognitive outcomes included retention, application and transfer of information, concepts, and principles; problem-solving ability and success; and divergent and risk-taking thinking. Affective outcomes included acceptance and appreciation of cultural, ethnic, and individual differences, reduction of bias and prejudice; pluralistic and democratic values; valuing education; and positive attitudes toward school and self.

## CLASSROOM ESSENTIALS AND STRATEGIES

Let us return to the dispositions of a critical thinker and examine ways they can be modeled, encouraged, fostered, "taught," reinforced, and rewarded in the classroom.

■ *A climate of trust and respect*—Students will not take risks with their thinking in an atmosphere of fear and ridicule. Taking chances with one's ideas must be valued and safeguarded by classroom rules that demand respect for the ideas and opinions of others.

■ *A "community of inquiry"* (Lipman 1980)—An environment where asking right questions is as important as giving right answers. An environment where there is a balance between questions that have right answers and those for which there may be more answers than one.

■ *A balance between teacher talk and student talk*—In classrooms where teachers do most of the talking, students get the idea that what they have to say is not important. Students need to discuss, entertain, and grapple with ideas, problems, and concepts, and it is through discussion that we can deepen students' understanding and depth of knowledge.

■ *Success and self esteem*—One of the best-established correlations with prejudice reduction is self-esteem—a correlation so close as almost to demonstrate a cause-and-effect relationship (Pate, forthcoming). The significance of an encouraging and success-oriented environment is crucial to the development of confidence in one's reasoning and consequently to one's level of prejudice.

■ *An emphasis on thinking about thinking*—Getting students to think about their thinking is extremely important; asking questions about logic in addition to questions about content: "How did you arrive at that conclusion?" "What evidence supports that?" "Can you explain how you worked that out?" The expectation should prevail in the classroom that students need to justify what they say with reasons, evidence, and support.

Research suggests that direct teaching of prejudice-reduction techniques may be ineffective, whereas indirect teaching of the skills and dispositions needed to combat prejudice is effective. This simply means that merely telling students they should not be prejudiced is ineffectual. Historical events and literature relevant to issues of prejudice (e.g., *To Kill a Mockingbird, The Diary of Anne Frank*), used with sensitivity and care, are essential. The teaching and valuing of the contributions of the great writers, scientists, and leaders of all races, creeds, and ethnic groups is imperative. In addition, an emphasis on the dispositions for critical thinking can and should be incorporated into every aspect of school life. Some examples of classroom lessons and activities that emphasize both critical-thinking skills (for example, inferring, making assumptions, drawing conclusions, evaluating evidence, supporting positions with evidence, etc.) and dispositions are:

■ *Intellectual curiosity and being systematic.* Frances Hunkins (1985) devised a strategy for helping students ask their own questions. After identifying an issue or topic, have the students plan the investigation of the topic—brainstorming possible guiding questions, identifying (together or in small groups) the most important questions, and assessing the reasoning embedded in their sequence of questions.

■ *Objectivity and respect for other viewpoints.* One cooperative learning activity developed by Johnson and Johnson (1975) involves organizing students into groups of four, with two students assigned the pro side of an issue and two the con. Each pair of pros and cons finds another pair of the same side and spends an allotted amount of time in this group identifying arguments for their respective sides. The original groups then reconvene and debate the issue, with each person in the group of four having three minutes to lay out the arguments or rebut. After each person in the group has taken a turn, the sides then change positions, with the pros arguing the con side and vice versa. After each person has argued the opposite position, the group then drops its advocacy roles, comes to a group consensus on a position, and identifies the best arguments for that position.

■ *Open-mindedness and flexibility.* Hazel Hertzberg of Teachers College, Columbia University, uses this activity in her social studies classes, but it has also been used successfully with elementary and high school students. The "Penny Lesson" involves students in small groups who are asked to look at pennies and, pretending they know nothing about the culture that made a given penny, identify as many inferences as they can about the culture that made it (for example, they had an advanced technology, this was a religious society, this was a bilingual society). Each group shares its inferences, supporting them with evidence provided by the penny. The lesson can be extended by examining the inferences—which are true or false, what would have to be done to test some of the inferences (e.g., a "male-dominated" society?), written assignments (e.g., a day in the life of a penny). This exercise illustrates how difficult it is to suspend one's bias in an enjoyable, nonthreatening manner.

■ *Decisiveness.* Edys Quellmaltz (1984), formerly of Stanford University, worked with classroom teachers in developing lessons for 2d and 3d grade students that required them to take a position on an issue and sup-

port it. For example, before reading "Jack and the Beanstalk," the students are asked to read and decide whether Jack is a greedy boy or a curious boy. The class discusses some of the characteristics of greedy and curious people. After the students read the story, the teacher elicits examples from the students and places them under headings "Jack was greedy" and "Jack was curious" on the board. Finally, after much groundwork, the students write a composition in which they take a position, supporting their position with two good reasons from the story. This is a powerful lesson for 3d graders. They get the message that what they think is important, that they must support their positions with good reasons, that one's use of evidence affects the conclusions drawn.

■ *Intellectual honesty.* A hallmark of a critical thinker is ability to distinguish between appeals to reason and appeals to emotion, recognizing that a tendency exists to seek out only evidence that supports one's viewpoints. We often accept without question what agrees with our views and automatically reject what does not. Kevin O'Reilly, of the Critical and Creative Thinking Program at the University of Massachusetts-Boston, developed a history lesson on the Battle of Lexington to give students an opportunity to evaluate critically conflicting sources of information on "who fired the first shot on Lexington Green." Students are given excerpts from an American history textbook, a book written by Winston Churchill, and two eyewitness accounts of the battle. Through discussion and examination, students are asked to analyze each passage in terms of the use of language (emotionally loaded terms, such as 'patriot' and 'rebel'), the quality of the reasoning, the use of rhetorical devices to slant, and so on. The essence of the lesson is the questions students ask in assessing the credibility of the sources.

## TOWARD A PREJUDICE-FREE SOCIETY

If we teach our children to (1) ask questions, (2) go beyond the superficial to the substance, (3) take positions on issues and explain and defend those positions, (4) be aware of multiple perspectives on important issues and the importance of knowing all sides of an issue before taking a position, and (5) assess information carefully and fairly, they will increase their awareness of their own biases, heighten their openness to rethinking their positions in the face of conflicting evidence, and take time to reflect rather than merely react.

## REFERENCES

D'Angelo, Edward. *The Teaching of Critical Thinking* Amsterdam: B.R Gruner, 1971.

Ennis, Robert H. "Goals for a Critical Thinking Curriculum" Illinois Thinking Project, University of Illinois, Champaign-Urbana, 1983.

Hunkins, Frances P. "Helping Students Ask Their Own Questions." *Social Education* 49, April 1985.

Johnson, David, and Roger Johnson. *Learning Together and Alone*. Englewood Cliffs: Prentice-Hall, 1975.

Lipman, Matthew, et al. *Philosophy in the Classroom*. Philadelphia: Temple University Press, 1980.

O'Reilly, Kevin. "Teaching Critical Thinking in High School U.S. History." *Social Education* 49, April 1985.

Quellmaltz, Edys, Higher Order Thinking (H.O.T.) Program Stanford University, personal correspondence, 1984.

Pate, Glenn S. "What Does Research Tell Us about the Reduction of Prejudice?" Presentation at the December 1987 Anti-Defamation League (ADL) Conference in Chicago, Illinois, on "American Citizenship in the Twenty First Century Education for a Pluralistic, Democratic America".

Walsh, Debbie, and Richard Paul. *The Goal of Critical Thinking: From Educational Ideal to Educational Reality*. American Federation of Teachers, Washington, DC, 1986.

Wolf, Dennis Palmer. "The Art of Questioning." *Academic Connections*, Winter 1987.

Debbie Walsh is the Associate Director in the Educational Issues Department at the American Federation of Teachers, Washington, D.C. [1988 note]

# Religion in the Elementary Classroom — A Laboratory Approach

26

**Janet E. McClain**
**Lynn E. Nielsen**

Recently, textbook publishers and curriculum specialists have come under fire for grossly underplaying the role of religion when reporting the history of the United States and the world. While the exclusion of religion from textbooks may not be excusable, it is somewhat understandable given the social climate of the last two decades.

Throughout the sixties and seventies traditional social beliefs, roles, and values were regularly scrutinized and challenged. Many Americans questioned the government's role in Southeast Asia. Women challenged institutionally established patterns of sexual discrimination by demanding greater autonomy in politics and the work place. Minority groups sought equal representation in government, business, and education while raising America's consciousness of an overlooked underrepresented multi-ethnic segment of society. Public nativity scenes and crosses were questioned along with traditional social roles as civil libertarians challenged generations of Protestant majority rule.

While these time-honored values and roles were being redefined on the street and in the courts, classroom teachers grew increasingly uneasy about "religion in the classroom" for fear of transgressing the uncertain wall of "separation of church and state." As one elementary teacher put it, "Most classroom teachers only needed to be reprimanded once by a militant parent for teaching about religion before they learned to avoid the topic completely."

The issue is not whether religion should be dealt with in the schools but how. The problem confronting classroom teachers lies not in distinguishing between the sacred and the secular but rather in distinguishing between the devotional and the informational. For over 25 years the courts have been striking down prayer and devotional Bible reading in the schools while encouraging schools to teach about religion. The National Council for the Social Studies' position statement on religion in the schools (R&PE, Vol. 11: 4, 40) echoes the Supreme Court's position.

Applying these principles in the classroom requires teachers to deal with religion in a natural, objective, and straightforward manner regardless of the setting. The particular level, however, ranging from the kindergarten classroom to the high school world history course, will dictate a particular approach that matches the developmental needs of students. The court decisions and the NCSS position statement make fairly obvious how the secondary school teacher should deal with religion in a history or literature course. But how does the primary grade teacher, who offers neither history or literature courses, deal objectively with religion in the classroom? The rest of this article outlines how primary teachers at Malcolm Price Laboratory School used seasonal celebrations to sensitize students to diversity within the religious fabric of the classroom, community, nation, and world.

"Celebrations" is a social studies unit taught at the second- and third-grade levels at Malcolm Price Laboratory School during a three week period in November-December. The main objective is to develop pupils' awareness and understanding that celebrations are a natural part of American heritage and reflect our religious and multicultural diversity. Although this teaching unit was not initially designed to teach students about specific religions, information about religious beliefs and practices was included in some lessons to provide a more comprehensive understanding of the nature of celebrations as a dimension of our culture. Through creative lessons and activities students are afforded the opportunity to:

- develop an appreciation for their own family celebrations and traditions
- become aware that some people choose not to participate in the observance of various celebrations because of personal, political, or religious beliefs, and that this choice is a constitutional privilege that should be respected by others
- realize that celebrations are observed in a variety of ways
- learn about various American celebrations whose customs and traditions originated in other countries
- study five winter celebrations that are set aside to honor a holy person or an event.

The focus of the first three lessons is on the family unit and celebrations observed by the family.

## LESSON I: CELEBRATE

Students formulate a group definition of the term "celebration" by generating a list of the many celebrations they know. Personal choices of a favorite celebration are written about and voluntarily shared. Teachers are sensitive to the fact that some children observe certain celebrations because of religious beliefs held by their families. It is important that teachers use this opportunity to increase student awareness and understanding of religious practices that may be different from their own in order to better demonstrate a respect and tolerance for the beliefs of others in a diverse nation and world.

*Reprinted with permission from Webster University, from Religion & Public Education, Spring 1988, Volume 15, Number 2. Copyright 1988 by Webster University.*

*102*

## LESSON II: A FAMILY AFFAIR

Students become interviewers and ask two important questions of family members: 1) What is our family's favorite celebration? 2) How does our family celebrate this special time? A special form with these questions is sent home with each student to be completed and returned the following day.

Collected information is shared during class time. The teacher facilitates the discussion by helping students realize that not every family identifies the same celebration as its favorite, and that those who do may or may not observe the celebration in exactly the same way. The concept of "traditions" is introduced and explored. Students identify the ways in which they observe a favorite celebration (sing songs, have special foods, exchange gifts, religious ceremonies) and categorize their list. With this basic information, the teacher can emphasize that these differences are okay and can lead students toward developing an awareness and acceptance of the diversity within the classroom. Through discussions, literature, additional surveys, or assigned group projects and reports, students can further investigate the diversity within their own community, state, nation, and the world.

## LESSON III: FAMILY DAYS AND WAYS

Each student enjoys special celebrations unique to his/her own family. A calendar is one way a family can note important family dates during the year. A discussion of the history of our calendar and seasons of the year provides students with background information concerning this common measurement of time. Students are also made aware that other types of calendars are used by people in America and other parts of the world: i.e., Chinese calendar, Jewish calendar, Western Christian church calendar.

Students are provided with a blank calendar pre-printed on white paper and bound. Family celebrations are entered first, then names of religious and non-religious celebrations for each month. Historical information relating to the significance of each celebration is discussed with students. Calendars are completed during several class periods and presented to families as gifts.

## LESSONS IV-IX: WINTER CELEBRATIONS

Students learn that the late fall and winter months of November through February have many holidays and special events that are observed by people of various ethnic and religious origins.

To develop young students' awareness of the religious history and multicultural nature of many American celebrations and to develop their ability to view celebrations through a more global perspective, information about Christmas, Hanukkah, Kwanzaa, Three Kings' Day/Epiphany/Twelfth Night, and the Chinese New Year is presented. Customs and beliefs associated with each observance are also shared as students become involved in many of the following projects related to each celebration. Guest speakers, films, children's literature, songs,

games, art work, and service projects are also incorporated into the study to enrich students' learning.

## CHRISTMAS (DECEMBER 25)

No one knows exactly when Jesus Christ was born, but December 25 is the date many Christians observe as the birthday of Jesus. The story of His birth is found in the chapters of Luke 2 and Matthew 1-2 in the Bible. Students are read or told the story of Jesus' birth and encouraged to share what they already know about Christmas. They are made aware that Christmas was initially observed as a religious festival by Christians in various parts of the world with prayer and religious ceremonies. Gradually Christmas became integrated with customs from many lands. In America, Santa Claus, hanging stockings, and Christmas trees reflect the traditions borrowed from other cultures. Students learn about some of the customs and symbols associated with Christmas and discuss their own family traditions. How Christmas is celebrated elsewhere, such as Germany, Mexico, or Africa, is also discussed. Various projects involving students in developing Christmas decorations, making specific food, or gifts that could be used by the students' families are supervised by the teacher.

## KWANZAA (DECEMBER 26-JANUARY 1)

Kwanzaa is a black American celebration that originated in the 1960s under the inspiration of M. Ron Karenga and other black Americans. This holiday is a celebration of the African heritage commonly shared by black Americans.

Beginning December 26, children in many black families learn about their African heritage and seven principles with names taken from the Swahili language:

1. *Umoja* (oo-moh'jah): unity
2. *Kugichagulia* (koo-jee-chah-goo-lee'ah): self-determination
3. *Ujima* (oo-jee'mah): collective work and responsibility
4. *Ujaama* (oojah'mah): cooperative economies
5. *Nia* (nee-ah): purpose
6. *Kuumba* (koo-um'bah): creativity
7. *Imani* (ee-mah'nee): faith

Each night the family gathers around the kinara, a seven-holed candleholder, to light one of the seven candles, (three red, three green, and one black). The black candle, which signifies unity, is lit by one of the children on the first night. The parents then talk about what unity means Each consecutive night another candle is lit and one of the seven principles is discussed. Handmade gifts are given each night, and a feast on the final night culminates this seven-day celebration.

Information about Kwanzaa is shared and the significance of giving gifts to others is discussed. Students are involved in making a gift that can be given to a family member.

## EPIPHANY/THREE KINGS' DAY/TWELFTH NIGHT (JANUARY 6)

January 6 is a holy festival observed by Eastern Christian churches to celebrate the baptism of Christ. Western Christian churches recognize January 6 as the date the Three Kings (Magi) brought gifts to the Christ Child in Bethlehem.

The story about the Magi is found in the Bible in Matthew Chapter 2. The Bible refers to an unspecified number of wise men who followed a "star in the East" to Bethlehem where they found the Christ Child. These wise men gave Christ gifts of frankincense, myrrh, and gold.

In Central and South America, children look forward to a visit from the Three Kings. On January 5, they fill their shoes or small boxes with grass or straw and leave a small cup of water for the Kings' camels. The shoes or boxes are placed under their beds. The next morning children find small gifts left by the Three Kings inside their shoes or boxes, in place of the straw and water.

In Italy, on January 5, children wait for Befana, an old witch, who was too busy cleaning to go with the Three Kings to Bethlehem. Later she regretted her decision not to go and hurriedly gathered a bundle of gifts for the Christ Child. She was unable to catch up with the Three Kings, and it is said that she has rushed from house to house each year with presents, still searching for the Christ Child the Three Kings spoke of.

In England, January 6 is known as Twelfth Night, the twelfth day after Christmas. It is customary that a bean cake be served on this night. One large bean, or similar object, is baked into the batter. Whoever finds the bean in his/her piece of cake is the lucky person. There are many variations on this tradition. In many homes, January 6 is also the time to pack away Christmas decorations.

Students are made aware that January 6 is observed as a religious holiday in the United States and other countries and has many different associated traditions. To increase student knowledge about one tradition associated with January 6, students make paper boxes and fill them with straw. They take their boxes home and share information with the parents about Three Kings' Day. One family observed Three Kings' Day by filling their child's box with a gift and a note from the Three Kings. Another student, whose birthday was January 6, brought individual bean cakes as a birthday treat. Each cake had either a marble to represent world travel, a penny to represent wealth, or a star to represent fame baked inside, as predictions of each student's future.

## CHANAKAH/HANUKKAH

Hanukkah is an eight-day Jewish festival that begins on the 25th day of the lunar month of Kislev (November-December). This holiday, sometimes called The Feast of Dedication or The Festival of Lights, commemorates the day the Temple of Jerusalem was rededicated to God and the miracle that happened over 2000 years ago. When Judah Macabee and his followers searched for oil to light the menorah, they found enough oil to last only one day. Through a miracle the oil lasted eight days. Judah proclaimed that an eight-day holiday be observed each year on the 25th day of the Hebrew month of Kislev to celebrate the miracle God performed.

On the first night of Hanukkah, one candle is used to light the first of eight candles on a special candelabrum, or menorah. Each night another candle is lit and songs are sung. Latkes, or potato pancakes cooked in oil, are one of the traditional foods served. Children are given gifts and Hanukkah "gelt" or money. The dreidel (spinning top) games are played during this celebration. Hebrew letters printed on the dreidel stand for the words "A great miracle happened there."

Students are provided the opportunity to learn this historical information firsthand from a Jewish parent or teacher when possible. Dreidels are made by the children and traditional Hanukkah treats are shared.

## CHINESE NEW YEAR

Students are asked to share information about how they celebrate January 1, New Year's Day. Discussion focuses on student responses, as well as such traditions as the New Year's parade, attending "watch" services at church, watching football games on TV, and making New Year's resolutions.

In contrast, facts about China, the Chinese New Year celebration, and the ancient Chinese lunar calendar are shared. Students are made aware of the fact that our 12-month calendar is one of many calendars used by people in the United States and elsewhere in the world. It is important that students be able to view and discuss other calendars, such as a Jewish calendar, a Western Christian church calendar, or a Chinese calendar.

The Chinese New Year occurs between mid January and mid February. Lengths of months are determined by the cycles of the moon. Each year is given the name of one of the twelve animals included in the Chinese Zodiac: Rat, Rabbit, Ox, Dragon, Tiger, Snakes, Horse, Rooster, Ram, Dog, Monkey, and Boar.

Traditionally in China, New Year's Day is the day when everyone celebrates his/her birthday. It is a family holiday. Decorations symbolizing good luck, long life, happiness, and wealth are displayed, and special meals are prepared. In many homes, household gods are presented offerings. It is appropriate to share information about Buddhism so that children better understand the customs associated with the celebration of Chinese New Year. Children receive "lad see," or good luck gifts of money wrapped in red paper.

Firecrackers, traditional dancing contests, exhibits, and the Dragon Parade are part of the community festivities enjoyed by many Chinese, as well as Chinese-Americans in the United States.

Students are involved in a variety of activities to prepare for the celebration of the Chinese New Year. Banners are made, with Chinese characters that say "Happy New Year." Fortune cookie treats, red envelopes with shiny, new pennies for the students, and a dragon parade to the accompaniment of percussion instruments are just a few ways second- and third-grade students become involved in learning about the Chinese New Year.

## CULMINATION

As a culminating activity, students participate in a winter festival that provides an opportunity to apply information about the celebrations they studied. During the festival, students sing songs appropriate to the holidays they studied, play the dreidel game, and sample traditional holiday foods.

## CONCLUSIONS

The study of celebrations does not end when the treats are gone, the last song sung, or the game won. The calendar is full of opportunities for students to continue celebrating cultural diversity and ethnic heritage. Children's literature can be used to highlight other important days, national, religious, or personal. Taking advantage of these periodic celebrations provides many incidental opportunities to teach about cultural diversity and religious heritage.

Young children receive much instruction via their families about celebrations and religion prior to entering school. Upon entering school, they find celebrations as ordinary as singing "Happy Birthday," exchanging valentines, and putting up classroom decorations. Celebrations should be a viable part of the school curriculum and it is only logical that students learn about the religions and religious beliefs and practices associated with these celebrations.

As educators, we must strive to help students develop the basic knowledge, attitudes, and abilities to prepare them for a world in which religion and religious expression will continue to have a major social impact. The accomplishment of this task is in itself a celebration.

## REFERENCES FOR TEACHERS

American Association of School Administrators. *Religion in the Public Schools*. Arlington, VA, 1986.

Bauer, Caroline Feller. *Celebrations*. Bronx, New York: The H.W. Wilson Company, 1985.

Cordello, Becky Stevens. *Celebrations*. New York: Butterick Publishing, 1977.

Durkin, Lisa Lyons (Editor). *Celebrate Every Day*. Bridgeport, CN: First Teacher Press, 1987.

Haynes, Charles. "Religious Literacy in the Social Studies," *Social Education*, November/December 1987, 488-490.

Hopkins, Lee Bennett, and Arenstein, Misha. *Do You Know What Day Tomorrow Is?* New York: Citation Press, 1975.

Ickis, Marguerite. *The Book of Religious Holidays and Celebrations*. New York: Dodd, Mead & Company, 1966.

Kniker, Charles R. "How Teachers Treat Religion in Their Classes," *Religion and Public Education*, The Journal of the National Council on Religion and Public Education, 14(1), 1987, 101-103.

———. Teaching About Religion in the Public Schools, *Phi Delta Kappa*, Eighth and Union, Box 789, Bloomington, IN 47402, 1985.

National Council for the Social Studies. "Including the Study About Religions in the Social Studies Curriculum: A Position Statement and Guidelines," *Social Education*, May 1986, 413-414.

Polon, Linda, and Cantwell, Aileen. *The Whole Earth Holiday Book*. Glenview, IL: Scott, Foresman & Co., 1983.

## REFERENCES FOR CHILDREN

Adler, David. *A Picture Book Of Hanukkah*. New York: Holiday House, 1982.

Behrens, June. *Gung Hay Fat Choy, Happy New Year*. Chicago: Children's Press, 1982.

Brown, Tricia. *Chinese New Year*. New York: Henry Holt & Company, 1987.

Cashman, Greer Fay. *Jewish Days and Holidays*. New York: Adama Books, 1986.

De Paola, Tomie. *The Legend of Old Befana*. New York: Harcount Brace Jovanovich, 1980.

Kalman, Bobbie. *We Celebrate Winter*. New York: Crabtree Publishing Company, 1986.

Livingston, Myra Cohn. *Celebrations*. New York: Holiday House, 1985.

Pienkowski, Jan. *Christmas, The King James Version*. New York: Alfred A. Knopf, 1984.

Van Woerkom, Dorthy. *The Rat, The Ox, and The Zodiac, A Chinese Legend*. New York: Crown Publishers, 1976.

Winthrop, Elizabeth. *A Child is Born: The Christmas Story*. New York: Holiday House, 1983.

Janet E. McClain and Lynn E. Nielsen work in the Malcolm Price Laboratory School at the University of Northern Iowa, Cedar Falls. [1988 note]

### Arlene F. Gallagher

A victim is someone who has suffered either by intentional or accidental action. A child tends to see suffering and action in terms of extremes: good and bad, or right and wrong. Viewing victimization on a continuum from severe to minor, with many shades of grey between, is more realistic and more useful. A broader perspective on suffering and the action that causes it enables the child to assess incidents through classification, comparison and contrast.

Children can be victimized by adults or by each other. Regardless of the source or the severity of the action, there are common results. The child feels alone, disconnected, and powerless. The books and activities described here are intended to empower children by helping them to view incidents on a continuum and by encouraging them to act and react appropriately.

## THE POWER OF NAMES ACTIVITY
Your name is on the first and last legal documents of your life: birth certificates and death certificates. There are laws to protect the illegal use of your name by you and by anyone else. Forgery is a crime. The law also protects, defines, and awards privileges to you, with labels such as minor, senior citizen, landlord and tenant.

''You are what you eat'' proclaims a sign in a health food store. You are also what you are named, called or labeled. The law protects individuals and groups of individuals from the damages that result from naming and labeling, but names can be used to achieve positive results as well as negative ones.

## STICKS AND STONES
"Sticks and stones can break my bones but names can never hurt me" is still chanted on playgrounds today, and it is as untrue now as it ever was. Names do hurt. Labeling can be used to create a self-fulfilling prophecy, to disenfranchise, or to dehumanize. This first activity focuses students' attention on how names influence people, while the second one suggests a way to use this knowledge to improve self-concepts.

Here is a list of names we might be called:

Have the class be creative and suggest both positive and negative labels. Have the class as a whole or have students independently sort the list into two categories: names they would like to be called and names they would not like to be called.

Discuss the possible origins of the labels. A good dictionary will help with some of the names. More detailed information for the last eight items on this list can be found in Susan Kelz Sperling, *Tenderfeet and Lady Fingers: A Visceral Approach to Words and Their Origins*. New York: The Viking Press. 1981.

## EXTENDING THE ACTIVITY
Find situations in history where names and labels have played a significant role. For example, during slavery slaves' last names were ignored. and children of slaves were often given the last name of their owner. Read Mildred Taylor's *The Friendship* out loud and discuss how using a person's first name was a measure of status.

Discuss the arrival of immigrants in our country. Often people whose names were difficult for immigration officers to pronounce or spell had them changed without their permission. This was sometimes justified as an attempt to "Americanize" new arrivals.

## "ALSO KNOWN AS" ACTIVITY
It is entirely legal to use more than one name unless you are attempting to defraud in some way. If more than one name is used. the letters A.K.A. (for "also known as") follow the first name.

Students find this a satisfying and exciting challenge. They can interview parents and relatives about the meaning of their names and find out how their particular name was chosen.

In this activity students have a chance to create new names for themselves and each other.

---

| | | | | |
|---|---|---|---|---|
| honey | dumbo | strong | short | leatherneck |
| sweetheart | smart | nasty | four-eyes | hippie |
| handsome | clever | nerd | foreigner | rubbernecker |
| ugly | honest | awesome | highbrow | redneck |
| fatso | mean | purple | tenderfoot | skinflint |
| skinny | cruel | tall | lazybones | |

## PROCEDURE

Explain to the class that many Native American names were symbolic. They may have told of some behavior, event or accomplishment by the person, or the names might have been related to nature, the climate or the seasons.

First, brainstorm and list words on the chalkboard that come to mind when you think about seasons, animals, and behavior. The class may be divided into small groups for this activity, or it can be done as a whole class activity. Each person in the group or in the class creates a name for every other person. The only rules are that the name must be a positive one and that it must somehow relate to the individual.

The teacher should participate fully in this activity. receiving and giving names. Names are written on slips of paper and may be handed to the person or placed in anonymous envelopes tacked to a bulletin board. The activity can be done in one class period or it can last as long as a week. Every day students will look forward to seeing what new names appear in their envelopes. At the end of the activity each student chooses the name by which he or she wishes to be called.

## MOUNTAINS FROM MOLEHILLS ACTIVITY

We sometimes make victims of ourselves by the way we perceive others' actions. We make "mountains out of molehills," claiming someone has caused us great harm when the incident was really a minor one. Everyone experiences times when he or she feels cheated or victimized by others. but clearly some experiences are worse than others. This activity will help you classify items according to whether or not they are examples of being a victim or being mistreated but not necessarily victimized.

## PROCEDURE

Reproduce the following examples on cards and distribute them to the class. Place two labels on the chalkboard: MOUNTAIN and MOLEHILL. Have each student read the incident out loud and then discuss with the class whether it is a mountain. an act that victimizes someone. or a molehill, a minor accident or small act of mistreatment.

LIST:

- A Poke in the Eye with a Sharp Stick
- Pulling Someone's Chair out When They Are About to Sit Down
- Borrowing Someone's Pen or Pencil
- Taking Someone's Lunch
- Taking the Dessert from Someone's Lunch
- Putting Your Foot in the Aisle So That Someone Will Trip
- Holding Your Thumb on the Water Fountain and Squirting the Next Person Who Tries to Get a Drink
- Copying Someone's Answers on a Test

Add others that have happened in your class or ones that the students suggest.

Use the following questions to focus the discussion:

1. What are the potential consequences of the act? What damage could result? How serious an injury could result from this act? Is the damage something that can not be repaired?
2. Do the consequences of the act determine its severity?
3. What was the intent of the act? Does the motive make a difference? Was the act an accidental one?

## TATTLING OR RESPONSIBLE REPORTING ACTIVITY

Too often children do not report when they are being tormented. victimized or abused because they fear reprisals or have been admonished about tattling. This activity encourages discussion of when it is appropriate to inform an adult about something and when it is not.

## PROCEDURE

Write the following categories on the chalkboard: TATTLING and RESPONSIBLE REPORTING. Discuss the meaning of these terms. With younger children it might be helpful to use the book *The Berenstain Bears Learn About Strangers*, which gives concrete examples. For older children use the novel *Chernowitz*, in which a boy is being tormented by a bully but doesn't want to tell his parents or teachers.

Go back through the list of actions from Mountains and Molehills. and identify those incidents which should be reported to an adult, discussing who would be the most logical person to tell—parent,. teacher, police officer or other persons.

## CHILDREN'S LITERATURE: CHILDREN AS VICTIMS

Stories are excellent vehicles for opening discussion about victims and abuse. Too often the abused child feels guilty and somehow responsible, which prevents communication and increases a sense of alienation. Stories about children with similar experiences, even if they do not give the child the courage to talk about his or her experience, do reduce the feelings of isolation. The use of books to help children confront and solve their personal problems has become an accepted and useful teaching method.

This list is only a sampling of what is available for and intermediate grade students. Many of the books can be read independently or they can be read aloud in conjunction with the activities.

The following levels are suggested but should not be viewed restrictive since many books are appropriate for all ages:

P = primary grades: 1, 2, and 3
I = intermediate grades: 4, 5, and 6
YA = young adult grades: 7, 8, and 9

## TEASING

Caple, Kathy. *The Biggest Nose*. Boston: Houghton Mifflin, 1985. P. An elephant child named Eleanor is teased by classmates who claim she has the biggest nose in the whole school. They keep threatening to measure it until Eleanor figures out a way to give them a poignant lesson why we shouldn't criticize others.

Berenstain, Stan and Jan. *The Berenstain Bears Learn About Strangers*. New York: Random House, 1985.

P. The popular Berenstain Bears deal with two very important issues for the younger child: knowing when to be cautious with strangers and knowing the difference between tattling and responsible informing. Warned by her parents to beware of strangers, at first Sister Bear sees everyone and everything as scary, even the frogs and butterflies. until she learns how to decide whether a person is a stranger. Sister Bear is accused of tattling by Brother Bear until their mother explains that tattling is "telling just to be mean" but that reporting something to an adult is not always tattling.

Irma. Joyce. *Never Talk to Strangers: A Book About Personal Safety*. New York: Western Publishing Company, 1967. P. This light-hearted rhyming book reinforces the rule about strangers in a way that doesn't frighten yet helps children to identify potential danger.

## LEARNING TO SAY NO

Cosgrove, Stephen. *Squeakers*. Los Angeles, CA: Price Stern Sloan. Inc., 1987. P. Squeakers, a young squirrel, is victimized by an elder mole who takes fur from her silver tail. Squeakers is afraid to refuse this adult until her parents teach her that all she has to do is say "no."

Wachter, Oralee. *No More Secrets for Me*. Boston: Little, Brown and Company. 1983.I First published in 1983. This book has had many reprintings because it has served a real need for parents and teachers. Four different stories illustrate that there are times when a child should say no to an adult. Each story involves an adult that is known to the child, not a stranger. This familiar relationship makes it much harder for the child to say "no."

## THE CHILD AND SEXUAL ABUSE

Howard, Ellen. *Gillyflower*. New York: Atheneum, 1986. I and YA. The "bad thing" that affects Gillian's life at home is incest. Typical of sexual abuse victims, Gilly feels ashamed and guilty until she learns from a friend that some secrets are not for keeping.

Irmin. Hadley. *Abby, My Love*. New York: McElderry/Atheneum, 1985. YA. Written in journal style, this first person account of sexual abuse is told by a fourteen-year-old girl.

## PHYSICAL ABUSE

Byars, Betsy. *Cracker Jackson*. New York: Viking. 1985. I and YA. Cracker wants to save his "second mother," his babysitter, and her children from an abusing husband. The story brings out the vicious cycle of abuse and how victims can permit themselves to be abused.

Roberts, Willo Davis. *Don't Hurt Laurie*. New York: Atheneum, 1977. I. Reprinted often since published, this is the story of a young girl physically abused by her mother. Laurie is afraid to tell because she doesn't think people will believe that her endless injuries were not accidents but the result of attacks by her mother.

Peet, Bill. *Big Bad Bruce*. Boston: Houghton Mifflin, 1977. P. Bruce, a great big bully of a bear. torments the partridges and rabbits who are smaller than him until a crafty witch magically shrinks his size. Little Bruce then becomes the victim. Bruce seems to change until on the final page he starts tormenting bugs and insects that are still smaller than him. The story raises questions about the validity of forcing the bully into the victim's shoes. The role switch story is excellent for reading aloud and generates good discussion on how to handle a bully.

Arrick, Fran. *Chernowitz*. New York: Bradbury, 1981. I and YA. Bobby Cherno is tormented by an anti-Semitic bully in his class. Bobby has to wrestle with the problems of telling his parents, protecting himself, and his own desire for revenge. The theme of revenge as an unsatisfying and ineffective response to a bully is similar to the one in *Big Bad Bruce*.

Sleator, William. *Among the Dolls*. New York: E.P. Dutton. 1975. I. A young girl who abuses the dolls in her dollhouse is "drawn into" the dolls' lives and is treated with the same cruelty she formerly imposed on the dolls. She learns that the "rough and violent things she had made them do had become their personalities." The author is a master at evoking a sense of horror and entrapment, and in this story the main character learns a better way to be from her experience.

## NEGLECT AS ABUSE

Byars, Betsy. *The Pinballs*. New York: Harper, 1977. I. Four children who are victims of different kinds of abuse meet at a foster home. Strangely, but realistically, they would all rather be back in their own homes no matter how bad it was. Bounced around they feel like "pinballs" until they learn to become a family.

Voigt, Cynthia. *Homecoming*. New York: Random House, 1981 YA. A mother abandons four children in a shopping center. They survive by ducking authorities, sleeping in cemeteries and doing anything they have to to stay together as a family. The story of the Tillerman family continues in *Dicey's Song*, winner of the 1983 Newberry Medal.

Arlene F. Gallagher is an Adjunct Faculty member at the Boston University School of Education, Boston, Massachusetts. [1988 note]

# PART 5

## ⓥ INDIVIDUALS, GROUPS, AND INSTITUTIONS

Institutions are created to help carry out the social values and goals of the community. As people mature, their needs change, as do the groups and institutions they encounter. Institutions such as schools, churches, families, courts, and other governmental agencies therefore play an integral role in our lives. Students need to learn how institutions are formed, maintained, and changed, as well as how institutions control and influence the lives of people. The impact and role of an individual within groups and institutions are studied through questions such as the following: How am I influenced by institutions? What are the roles of groups and institutions in our society? Can I help or change institutions to better serve people? Why do the goals or actions of groups and institutions frequently conflict with one another? Because of its link to practical application and public policies, aspects of this theme are present in other curriculum strands focusing on history, government, sociology, psychology, anthropology, and culture.

The school provides students with a long and intimate involvement with one institution. Therefore, the school plays an important role in teaching about democratic governance. Becoming an active, effective member of the school community is good training for adulthood. Helping children function as part of the class and school in positive ways is the focus of four of the articles in this chapter. Schools reflect the cultures of the populations they serve and the society in which they live. Violence has had an impact on schools, and teaching children to deal with violence has become a major concern for many schools. Derman-Sparks provides a research base that indicates the need to begin empowering children at a young age so that they can live in a caring world. She describes what educators personally need to learn and do to accomplish this goal through teacher education and staff development programs. Nakagawa and Pang tell of the need to teach cooperative pluralism in American schools and provide two sample lessons that teach key concepts of interdependence, cooperation, and group identity. Levin discusses the impact of violence in society on young children and presents dialogues between children and teachers that illustrate ways of dealing with the problems of societal violence and its consequences. Stomfay-Stitz describes how teaching conflict resolution and peer mediation helps schools to reduce conflicts between students and identifies several school, state, and national conflict resolution programs being used today.

Schools also cooperate with and teach about other institutions. Procter and Haas provide a rationale for the social studies program to involve children systematically at all ages while serving the community individually or through societal institutions. Braun and Sabin describe how celebrating a school's heritage helps to create a sense of community and respect as students learn about the past. The article from *Teaching Tolerance* looks at the rights of children and identifies resources for teaching about human rights. Greenawald provides activities for teaching the concept of justice, which is an important component in our legal system. In encountering this standard, children who are learning to be active citizens of a democracy learn how the society in which they live influences the lives of citizens and how they can both obtain services and serve the society.

# Empowering Children to Create a Caring Culture in a World of Differences

**Louise Derman-Sparks**

The following poem by Bill Martin, Jr.
(1987) captures the essence of what I think it means to empower children to create a caring culture in a world of differences.

> I like me, no doubt about it,
> I like me, can't live without it,
> I like me, let's shout about it,
> I am Freedom's Child.
> You like you, no doubt about it,
> You like you, can't live without it,
> You like you, let's shout about it,
> You are Freedom's Child.
> We need all the different kinds of people we can find,
> To make freedom's dream come true,
> So as I learn to like the differences in me,
> I learn to like the differences in you.
> I like you, no doubt about it,
> You like me, can't live without it,
> We are free, let's shout about it,
> Hooray for Freedom's Child!

Reprinted by permission of
SRA/Macmillan/McGraw-Hill School Publishing Co.

Racism, sexism, classism, heterosexism and ableism are still deeply entrenched and pervasive in society, making it very difficult for millions of children to be "Freedom's Child." What must we do as educators to ensure that all children can develop to their fullest potential—can truly become "Freedom's Child"?

## CHILDREN'S DEVELOPMENT OF IDENTITY AND ATTITUDES

Take a moment to listen to the voices of children. Members of the Anti-Bias Curriculum Task Force developed the anti-bias approach after a year spent collecting and analyzing children's thinking and trying out activities. They collected the following anecdotes:

- Steven is busy being a whale on the climbing structure in the 2-year-old's yard. Susie tries to join him. "Girls can't do that!" he shouts.
- Robby, 3 years old, refuses to hold the hand of a dark-skinned classmate. At home, he insists, after bathing, that his black hair is now "white because it is clean."
- "You aren't really an Indian," 4-year-old Rebecca tells one of her child care teachers. "Where are your feathers?"

Reprinted with permission from Louise Derman-Sparks and the Association for Childhood Education International, from *Childhood Education*, Winter 1993/94, Volume 70. Copyright 1993 by the Association for Childhood Education International, 11501 Georgia Avenue, Suite 315, Wheaton, Maryland.

- "Malcolm can't play with us. He's a baby," Linda tells their teacher. Malcolm, another 4-year-old, uses a wheelchair.

Those voices reflect the impact of societal bias on children. Now, listen to voices of children in programs that practice anti-bias curriculum:

- Maria, 4 years old, sees a stereotypical "Indian warrior" figure in the toy store. "That toy hurts Indian people's feelings," she tells her grandmother.
- Rebecca's kindergarten teacher asks the children to draw a picture of what they would like to be when they grow up. Rebecca draws herself as a surgeon—in a pink ball gown and tiara.
- After hearing the story of Rosa Parks and the Montgomery bus boycott, 5-year-old Tiffany, whose skin is light brown, ponders whether she would have had to sit in the back of the bus. Finally, she firmly asserts, "I'm Black and, anyway, all this is stupid. I would just get off and tell them to keep their old bus."
- In the school playground, 5-year-old Casey and another white friend, Tommy, are playing. Casey calls two other boys to join them. "You can't play with them. They're Chinese eyes," Tommy says to him. Casey replies, "That's not right. All kinds of kids play together. I know. My teacher tells me civil rights stories."

Children do not come to preschool, child care centers or elementary school as "blank slates" on the topic of diversity. Facing and understanding what underlies their thoughts and feelings are key to empowering children to resist bias. The following is a brief summary of research about how children develop racial identity and attitudes:

- As early as 6 months, infants notice skin color differences. (Katz, 1993)
- By 2 years of age, children not only notice, they also ask questions about differences and similarities among people. They soon begin forming their own hypotheses to explain the diversity they are seeing and hearing. When my daughter was 3, she commented one day, "I am thinking about skin color. How do we get it?" I launched into an explanation about melanin, which was clearly above her level of understanding. Finally, I asked her, "How do you think we get skin color?" "Magic markers!" she replied. (Derman-Sparks, Tanaka Higa & Sparks, 1980)

At my family's 1991 Passover Seder (the Seder honors the ancient Jewish Exodus from slavery in Egypt), my niece announced, "I'm half Jewish." "Uh huh," I replied (one parent is Jewish). She continued, "The Jewish people went through the water and they didn't get wet. They got to the other side. The people who weren't Jewish got drowned."

"That is what the Passover story tells us, that the Egyptian soldiers drowned," I affirmed, but her expression remained quizzical. So, I decided to ask her, "What do you think happened to the people who were half Jewish?"

"They got to the other side, too," she replied, paused and then concluded, "but they got a little bit wet." Afterward, a cousin wondered, "How did you ever think of that question?" (The Passover story does not mention people being "half Jewish").

I don't know if my question was "right" in any absolute sense, but trying to follow my niece's line of thinking, I sensed that the issue was important to her. She seemed emotionally satisfied with her solution. Moreover, it was a cognitively clever one — she got to the other side safely AND she acknowledged her identity as she understood it.

■ How we answer children's questions and respond to their ideas is crucial to their level of comfort when learning about diversity. Statements such as, "It's not polite to ask," "I'll tell you later" or "It doesn't matter," do not help children form positive ideas about themselves or pro-diversity dispositions toward others. (Derman-Sparks & ABC Task Force, 1989)

■ Between 2½ to 3½ years of age, children also become aware of and begin to absorb socially prevailing negative stereotypes, feelings and ideas about people, including themselves. All children are exposed to these attitudes in one form or another, usually through a combination of sources (parents, extended family, neighbors, teachers, friends, TV, children's books, movies). (Derman-Sparks & ABC Task Force, 1989)

■ Throughout the early childhood period, children continue to construct and elaborate on their ideas about their own and others' identities and their feelings about human differences. In the primary years, children's development goes beyond the individual to include a group identity. Some researchers believe that after age 9, racial attitudes tend to stay constant unless the child experiences a life-changing event. (Aboud, 1988)

The research literature also points to the great damage racism, sexism and classism have on all children's development. Young children are harmed by a psychologically toxic environment. How they are harmed depends on how they are affected by the various "isms" — whether they receive messages of superiority or inferiority. (Clark, 1955; Dennis, 1981)

For children of color, the wounds can be overt. Often, however, they are quite subtle. Chester Pierce calls these subtle forms of racism "micro-contaminants" (Pierce, 1980). Kenyon Chan notes that these micro-contaminants "are carried by children like grains of sand, added one by one, eventually weighing children down beyond their capacity to carry the sand and to grow emotionally and intellectually to their fullest" (Chan, 1993).

Racism attacks young children's growing sense of group, as well as individual, identity. Thus, the children are even less able to resist racism's harm. Chan cites an example: A Chinese American girl enrolled in a suburban kindergarten in Los Angeles. Her European American teacher claimed that her name was too difficult to pronounce and promptly renamed her "Mary," calling it an "American" name. This young child is forced to wonder what is wrong with her name and what is wrong with her parents for giving her such a "bad" name. And her doubts originated with the very person who is responsible for supporting and cultivating her development.

Moreover, as Lily Wong-Fillmore's research documents, young children who come from homes where a language other than English is spoken pay a terrible price if they experience a too-early loss of continued development in their home language. The price includes the gradual impoverishment of communication between the child and parents (and other family members) and the potentially serious weakening of the "family's continued role in the socialization of its children" (Wong-Fillmore, 1991).

White, English-speaking children also experience psychological damage. Although this issue has been less studied, the research we do have suggests some disturbing problems:

■ First, racism teaches white children moral double standards for treating people of racial/ethnic groups other than their own. This leads to the possibility of general ethical erosion (Clark, 1955) and to a form of hypocrisy that results in primary school-age children saying words that sound like acceptance of diversity, while acting in ways that demonstrate the opposite (Miel, 1976).

■ Second, children may be constructing identity on a false sense of superiority based on skin color. White children's self-esteem will be rather vulnerable if/when they come to realize that skin color does not determine a person's value.

■ Third, racism results in white children developing fears about people different from themselves They do not gain the life skills they need for effectively interacting with the increasing range of human diversity in society and the world.

Racial stereotyping is not the only danger. Children's absorption of gender stereotypes limits their development. As young as 3 and 4, children begin to self-limit their choices of learning experiences because of the gender norms they are already absorbing. One of the negative consequences of this process is a pattern of uneven cognitive development, or "practice deficits," related to the types of activities boys and girls choose (Serbin, 1980 p.. 60). Girls tend to function below potential in math and boys in expression of their feelings.

Furthermore, research on children's development of ideas and feelings about disabilities indicates that by 2 and 3, they notice, are curious about and sometimes fear people with a disability and their equipment (Froschl, Colon, Rubin & Sprung, 1984; Sapon-Shevin, 1983). Children's fears appear to come from developmental misconceptions that they might "catch" the disability, as well as from adults' indirect and direct communication of discomfort. Moreover, the impact of stereotypes and biases about people with disabilities affects primary age children's treatment of any child who does not fit the physical "norms" of attractiveness, weight and height.

Research also suggests that young children who learn about people with disabilities through a variety of concrete activities are much more likely to see the whole person, rather than just focusing on the person's disability.

## WHAT EMPOWERING CHILDREN TO CREATE A CARING CULTURE REQUIRES OF US

*Clarity About Goals.* The following goals are for all children. The specific issues and tasks necessary for working toward these goals will vary for children, depending on their backgrounds, ages and life experiences.

■ *Nurture each child's construction of a knowledgeable, confident self-concept and group identity.* To achieve this goal, we must create education conditions in which all children are able to like who they are without needing to feel superior to anyone else. Children must also be able to develop biculturally where that is appropriate.

■ *Promote each child's comfortable, empathic interaction with people from diverse backgrounds.* This goal requires educators to guide children's development of the cognitive awareness, emotional disposition and behavioral skills needed to respectfully and effectively learn about differences, comfortably negotiate and adapt to differences, and cognitively understand and emotionally accept the common humanity that all people share.

■ *Foster each child's critical thinking about bias.* Children need to develop the cognitive skills to identify "unfair" and "untrue" images (stereotypes), comments (teasing, name-calling) and behaviors (discrimination) directed at one's own or others' identities. They also need the emotional empathy to know that bias hurts.

■ *Cultivate each child's ability to stand up for her/himself and for others in the face of bias.* This "activism" goal requires educators to help every child learn and practice a variety of ways to act: a) when another child acts in a biased manner toward her/him, b) when a child acts in a biased manner toward another child, c) when an adult acts in a biased manner. Goal 4 builds on goal 3 as critical thinking and empathy are necessary components of acting for oneself or others in the face of bias.

These four goals interact with and build on each other. We cannot accomplish any one goal without the other three. *Their combined intent is to empower children to resist the negative impact of racism and other "isms" on their development and to grow into adults who will want and be able to work with others to eliminate all forms of oppression.* In other words, the underlying intent is not to end racism (and other "isms") in one generation by changing children's attitudes and behaviors, but rather to promote critical thinkers and activists who can work for social change and participate in creating a caring culture in a world of differences.

*Preparing ourselves.* Effective anti-bias education requires every teacher to look inward and commit to a life-long journey of understanding her/his own cultural beliefs, while changing the prejudices and behaviors that interfere with the nurturing of all children. Teachers need to know:

■ how to see their own culture in relationship to society's history and current power realities

■ how to effectively adapt their teaching style and curriculum content to their children's needs

■ how to engage in cultural conflict resolution with people from cultural backgrounds other than their own

■ how to be critical thinkers about bias in their practice

■ how to be activists—engaging people in dialogue about bias, intervening, working with others to create change.

Achieving these goals takes commitment and time, and is a developmental process for adults as well as for children. One must be emotionally as well as cognitively involved and ready to face periods of disequilibrium and then reconstruction and transformation.

## IMPLEMENTATION PRINCIPLES AND STRATEGIES

To create a caring culture in which children can be empowered, teachers must be "reflective practitioners" who can think critically about their own teaching practice and adapt curriculum goals and general strategies to the needs of their children.

*Critical thinking.* Be aware of "tourist multicultural curriculum" and find ways to eliminate tourism from your program. Tourist multicultural curriculum is the most commonly practiced approach in early childhood education and elementary school today. The majority of commercial curriculum materials currently available on the market and many published curriculum guides reflect a tourist version of multicultural education. Unfortunately, tourist multicultural curriculum is a simplistic, inadequate version of multicultural education.

In a classroom practicing a tourist approach, the daily "regular" curriculum reflects mainstream European American perspectives, rules of behavior, images, learning and teaching styles. Activities about "other" cultures often exhibit the following problems:

■ *Disconnection:* Activities are added on to the curriculum as special times, rather than integrated into all aspects of the daily environment and curriculum.

■ *Patronization:* "Other" cultures are treated as "quaint" or "exotic." This form of tourism does not teach children to appreciate what all humans share in common.

■ *Trivialization:* Cultural activities that are disconnected from the daily life of the people trivialize the culture. A typical example is multicultural curriculum that focuses on holidays—days that are different from "normal" days. Children do not learn about how people live their lives, how they work, who does what in the family—all of which is the essence of a culture. Other forms of trivialization include: turning cultural practices that have deep, ritual meaning into "arts and crafts" or dance activities, or asking parents to cook special foods without any further lessons about the parents' cultures.

▪ *Misrepresentation:* Too few images of a group oversimplifies the variety within the group. Use of images and activities based on traditional, past practices of an ethnic group rather than images of contemporary life confuse children. Misusing activities and images that reflect the culture-of-origin of a group to teach about *the life of cultures in the U.S.* conveys misconceptions about people with whom children have little or no face-to-face experience.

In sum, tourist multicultural curriculum does not give children the tools they need to comfortably, empathetically and fairly interact with diversity. Instead, it teaches simplistic generalizations about other people that lead to stereotyping, rather than to understanding of differences. Moreover, tourist curriculum, because it focuses on the unusual and special times of a culture and neglects how people live their daily lives, does not foster children's understanding and empathy for our common humanity. Moving beyond tourist multicultural curriculum is key to our profession's more effective nurturing of diversity.

*Incorporate multicultural and anti-bias activities into daily curriculum planning.* Diversity and anti-bias topics are integral to the entire curriculum at any education level. One practical brainstorming technique for identifying the numerous topic possibilities is "webbing."

*Step one* is determining the center of the "web." This can be: 1) an issue raised by the children (e.g., a person who is visually impaired cannot work); 2) any number of traditional preschool "units" (e.g., my body, families, work); 3) High/Scope's (Weikart, 1975) "key experiences" (e.g., classification or seriation); 4) any of the traditional content areas of the primary curriculum (science, math, language arts, physical and health curriculum).

*Step two* involves brainstorming the many possible anti-bias, multicultural issues that stem from the subject at the web's center. *Step three* involves identifying specific content for a particular classroom based on contextual/developmental analysis. *Step four* involves listing possible activities that are developmentally and culturally appropriate for your particular class.

## CULTURAL APPROPRIATENESS: ADULT/CHILD INTERACTIONS

Effective teaching about diversity, as in all other areas, *is a continuous interaction between adults and children.* On the one hand, teachers are responsible for brainstorming, planning and initiating diversity topics, based on their analyses of children's needs and life experiences. On the other hand, careful attention to children's thinking and behavior, and to "teachable moments," leads educators to modify initial plans.

*Find ways to engage children in critical thinking and the planning and carrying out of "activism" activities appropriate to their developmental levels, cultural backgrounds and interests.*

Critical thinking and activism activities should rise out of real life situations that are of interest to children. The purpose of such activities is to provide opportunities for children, 4 years old and up, to build their empathy, skills and confidence and to encourage their sense of responsibility for both themselves and for others. Consequently, activities should reflect *their* ideas and issues, not the teacher's. The following two examples are appropriate activism activities.

In the first situation, the children's school did not have a "handicapped" parking space in their parking lot. After a parent was unable to attend open school night because of this lack, the teacher told the class of 4- and 5-year-olds what had happened and why. They then visited other places in their neighborhood that had "handicapped" parking and decided to make one in their school lot. After they did so, they then noticed that teachers were inappropriately parking in the "handicapped" spot (their classroom overlooked the parking lot), so they decided to make tickets. The children dictated their messages, which their teacher faithfully took down, and drew pictures to accompany their words. They then ticketed those cars that did not have "handicapped parking" plaques in their windows.

In the second example, a class of 1st- through 3rd-graders visited a homeless shelter and talked to the director to find out what people needed. They started a toy and blanket collection drive, which they promoted using posters and flyers. They visited several classrooms to talk about what they were doing. They also wrote to the Mayor and the City Council to say that homeless people needed more houses and jobs.

## PARENTS AND FAMILY INVOLVEMENT

*Find ways to involve parents and other adult family members in all aspects of anti-bias education.* Education and collaboration with parents is *essential*. Educators have to be creative and ingenious to make this happen. Parents can help plan, implement and evaluate environmental adaptations and curricular activities. They can serve on advisory/planning committees with staff, provide information about their lifestyles and beliefs, participate in classroom activities and serve as community liaisons. Teachers can send home regular short newsletters to share ongoing plans and classroom activities, and elicit parent advice and resources. Parent meetings on child-rearing and education issues should also incorporate relevant diversity topics.

When a family member disagrees with an aspect of the curriculum, it is essential that the teachers listen carefully and sensitively to the issues underlying the disagreement. Objections may include: 1) family's belief that learning about differences will "make the children prejudiced" ("colorblind" view), 2) parent's belief that teaching about stereotyping and such values belongs in the home, not at school, 3) family members' strong prejudices against specific groups.

Staff need to find out all they can about the cultural and other issues that influence the family's concerns, and then work with family members to find ways to meet their needs while also maintaining the goals of anti-bias education. The techniques for working with parents on anti-bias issues are generally the same as those used for other child development and education topics. The difference, however, lies in the teachers' level of comfort about addressing such topics with other adults.

## TEACHER EDUCATION AND PROFESSIONAL DEVELOPMENT

Teacher training must incorporate liberating pedagogical techniques that:

- engage students on cognitive, emotional and behavioral levels
- use storytelling to enable students to both name and identify the ways that various identity contexts and bias have affected their lives
- use experiential activities that engage learners in discovering the dynamics of cultural differences and the various "isms"
- provide new information and analysis that give deeper meaning to what is learned through storytelling and experiential activities
- create a balance between supporting and challenging students in an environment of safety, not necessarily comfort.

The most useful way to work on our own development is to join with others (staff, or staff and parents) in support groups that meet regularly over a long period of time. By collaborating, sharing resources and providing encouragement, we can work on our self-awareness issues, build and improve our practices, strengthen our courage and determination and maintain the joy and excitement of education.

In sum, children of the 21st century will not be able to function if they are psychologically bound by outdated and narrow assumptions about their neighbors. To thrive, even to survive, in this more complicated world, children need to learn how to function in many different cultural contexts, to recognize and respect different histories and perspectives, and to know how to work together to create a more just world that can take care of all its people, its living creatures, its land.

Let's remember the African American novelist Alice Walker's call to "Keep in mind always the present you are constructing. It should be the future you want" (Walker, 1989, p. 238).

## REFERENCES

Aboud, F. (1988). *Children and Prejudice*. London: Basil Blackwell.

Chan, K. S. (1993). "Sociocultural Aspects of Anger: Impact on Minority Children." In M. Furlong & D. Smith (Eds.), *Anger, Hostility, and Aggression in Children and Adolescents: Assessment, Prevention, and Intervention Strategies in Schools*. Brandon, VT: Clinical Psychology Publishing.

Clark, K. (1955). *Prejudice and Your Child*. Boston: Bacon.

Dennis, R. (1981). "Socialization and Racism: The White Experience." In B. Bowser & R. Hunt (Eds.), *Impacts of Racism on White Americans* (pp. 71-85). Beverly Hills, CA: Sage.

Derman-Sparks, L., Tanaka Higa, C., & Sparks, B. (1980). *Children, Race, and Racism: How Race Awareness Develops*. Bulletin, 11(3 & 4), 3-9.

Derman-Sparks, L., & ABC Task Force (1989). *Anti-Bias Curriculum: Tools for Empowering Young Children*. Washington, DC: National Association for the Education of Young Children.

Froschl, M., Colon, L., Rubin, E., & Sprung, B. (1984). *Including All of Us: An Early Childhood Curriculum about Disability*. New York Educational Equity Concepts.

Katz, P. (May, 1993). "Development of Racial Attitudes in Children." Presentation given to the University of Delaware.

Martin, B., Jr. (1987). *I am Freedom's Child*. Allen, TX: DLM Teaching Resources.

Miel, A. (1976). *The Short-Changed Children of Suburbia*. New York: Institute of Human Relations Press.

Pierce, C. (1980). "Social Trace Contaminants: Subtle Indicators of Racism in TV." In Withey & Abelis (Eds.), *Television and Social Behavior*. New Jersey: Lawrence & Erlbaum.

Sapon-Shevin, M. (1983). "Teaching Young Children about Differences." *Young Children*, 38(2), 24-32.

Serbin, L. (1980). "Play Activities and the Development of Visual-Spatial Skills." *Equal Play*, 1(4), 5.

Walker, A. (1989). *The Temple of my Familiar*. New York: Pocket Books.

Weikart, D. (1975). *Young Children in Action*. Ypsilanti, MI: High Scope Press.

Wong-Fillmore, L. (1991). "Language and Cultural Issues in Early Education." In S. L. Kagan (Ed.), *The Care and Education of America's Young Children: Obstacles and Opportunities*. The 90th yearbook of the National Society for the Study of Education (pp. 3-49). Chicago: University of Chicago Press.

Louise Derman-Sparks is the Director of the Anti-Bias Leadership Project at Pacific Oaks College, Pasadena, California. [1993 note]

**Mako Nakagawa**
**Valerie Ooka Pang**

As a democratic society it is less important for our students to learn to appreciate ethnic foods than it is for students to understand equal rights. Yet, much of what we have taught under the label of "multicultural education" has fallen into the trap of "Tacos on Tuesdays." That is the pitfall of teaching about cultures and about cultural differences without teaching an understanding of how cultural gender, class, religious, ethnic racial handicapped and age differences contribute to the unified whole of our democratic nation.

## COOPERATIVE PLURALISM AS AN EDUCATIONAL PHILOSOPHY

As a nation of interdependent individuals and groups whose survival demands a cooperative effort, Cooperative Pluralism is an educational philosophy that complements and strengthens traditional multicultural educational approaches while blending them with cooperative learning and democratic education. Three beliefs guide Cooperative Pluralism:

1. The powerful recognition of the interdependence of all people.
2. The importance of cross-cultural relationships and communications between individuals and groups that enhance and complement effective cooperation[1] rather than the studies of the manifestations of the culture of specific ethnic groups.
3. The significance of teaching active participation skills which are crucial to the development of responsible citizens in a functional democracy.[2]

Cooperative Pluralism promotes student skill building in working with others and acceptance of social responsibility nurturing equitable relationships that are the essential foundations of a democracy

Cooperative Pluralism also focuses on interdependence at the personal community national and international levels. Helping students understand how all of us are interdependent can guide our young people in exploring fresh and creative avenues in building solid bridges of trust between people. Students should understand how the welfare of the individual is integrally linked with the welfare of the collective.

Reprinted from *Social Studies and the Young Learner*, March/April 1990, Volume 2, Number 4. Copyright 1990 by National Council for the Social Studies.

## COOPERATIVE PLURALISM AS AN EDUCATIONAL PROGRAM

The focus of most multicultural education programs has been the discussion primarily of ethnicity, and an "ethnic studies" approach to teaching about ethnic and cultural differences. This can emphasize a "they" orientation rather than "we" perspective. The approach often involves the study of the four major categories of collective minorities in the United States: African Americans, Asian Americans, Chicano/Latino Americans, and Native Americans. While this approach is a big advance over the earlier tokenism or total neglect it has often consisted of over-simplified presentations of outward manifestations that serve to extend rather than to reduce stereotypes. In addition. there has been little attention placed upon the issues of gender, class, or handicappism. Studying groups in isolation from each other has the potential of misleading young students into thinking of cultural groups as wholly separate from each other, self-contained, and unchanging. This orientation fails to address the dynamic relations between cultural groups while disregarding the complexity of and diversity within minority and majority cultures. A student may be Hispanic, middle-class, and male. This youngster is a member of several cultural groups and these various memberships impact on the way he behaves and what he values.

Cooperative Pluralism directs students and teachers to focus upon the interaction between the various elements to build bridges of positive communications. This stresses looking at an issue from a holistic perspective while examining aspects of cross-cultural group commonalities and focusing upon interrelational skills.

One example of this approach is in teaching the concept of justice. The phenomena of shifting the attention from the source of the problem and placing the justification of a misdeed onto the victim represents "blaming the victim" syndrome. There is a commonality of experiences among various individuals from different groups, i.e., the common experience of oppression. Native Americans are blamed for standing in the way of progress because others covet their land. African American parents are often told their children fail in school because of poor quality parenting and lack of academic commitment. Qualified Asian American students are denied equal access into higher education because of ceiling quotas on admissions. Elder Americans are told they are not suitable for various positions because they are too old to think quickly and efficiently. Teenagers are held responsible for lack of morality in America because they are young and perceived as undisciplined. These are examples of misconceptions from the present which can be utilized in teaching about justice. Martin Luther King, Jr. Succinctly stated, "Injustice anywhere is a threat to justice everywhere." Students might be asked what issue they think is most important and what could they do to impact the understanding of others. It could be a letter to the editor, or it could be in the form of a play given to another class.

When students have the opportunity to view issues from a variety of group experiences, they can develop a better understanding of the complexity of society and the need for cooperative solutions. The focus is upon "unity amidst diversity" and in this way the goals of harmony coupled with the understanding of interdependency provide the foundation for preparing our students to keep the issue of equal rights at the forefront.

## DEVELOPING INSTRUCTIONAL ACTIVITIES FOR ELEMENTARY STUDENTS

The following are a few examples of learning objectives which guide the curriculum for Cooperative Pluralism. They are:

1. Culture consists of shared human experiences and yet within a given collective group each person has his her own unique profile of that culture.
2. We draw from many cultural groupings to form our own unique patterns, like spiders developing highly individual webs.
3. There is diversity within any group, including a cultural group.
4. People in the world need one another and depend on one another in many ways.
5. Individuals and groups can interact cooperatively for the benefit of all.
6. People from diverse groups can learn how to communicate and work effectively with each other to their mutual benefit.
7. As members of a democracy, each citizen in the United States has the responsibility to preserve and protect the rights of liberty, equality, and justice for all.

## EXAMPLE LESSONS
### ORGANIZING CONCEPT-SELF IDENTITY: INDIVIDUAL AND COLLECTIVE
### LESSON 1. WHAT IS A GROUP?

Objectives:

■ To develop and write an operational definition of a "group."

■ To identify groups in the development of the awareness that people belong to many groups.

■ To compare similarities and differences *within* as well as *between* groups.

■ To work cooperatively in groups.

Procedure:

Teacher: "Let's define the term *group* in a people setting." Using verbal responses and dictionary definitions, the class establishes a working definition. It may be "A group is two or more people with something in common." (A group can be a unit with a shared purpose, but there are ethnic groups which may not have the same goals but have common physical or cultural ties. Sometimes groups have involuntary parameters.)

The teacher writes the consensus definition on the board.

Teacher: "To what groups do you belong?"

The teacher encourages identification of groups beyond gender, ethnicity, and student role, trying to elicit less frequent groups. e.g., ping-pong players, chocolate ice cream lovers, and those who can curl their tongues.

After the students have suggested many possibilities, the teacher divides the class into teams of four to six students representing diversity in gender and ethnicity.

Each team is to identify and list the maximum number of groups to which at least one team member belongs. The teacher encourages each member to contribute at least two ideas.

The teacher pairs students and asks them to identify two groups in which they hold memberships in common, and two groups in which they belong that are different. Then, students are asked to list commonalities and differences among the four groups.

## LESSON 2. WE ARE ALL CONNECTED

Objectives:

■ To define the terms *interdependent* and *independent*.

■ To speculate on how he/she is interconnected with others they do not know.

■ To write a paragraph about being interconnected.

Procedure:

Teacher: "What does it mean to be interdependent?" "What does it mean to be independent?"

The teacher lists on the board those things done independently and interdependently.

Examples: *Interdependent:* Play Baseball, Follow Traffic Rules

*Independent:* Brush Teeth, Eat Lunch

Teacher: "Many times we are interconnected though we don't realize it. If a driver of a car does not stop at a stop sign, that person could hit us if we were in the crosswalk. We are interconnected. Though there are many things that we do independently, many of our activities are dependent upon cooperation. For the baseball team to win, the team members must work together as a cohesive group.

"Our actions often affect others. The world we live in is an interconnected system Look in your social studies book. Write a story describing how someone you see in the text, but who you do not know, may be interconnected with you. (For example, the farmer grows food which we might be eating. The factory worker is making a car that your parents buy and you depend on to get you to school.)

Teacher: "What does it mean to be interdependent? Interconnected?"

Teacher: Is there something we can do as a school which helps us show how we feel about participating in our community?"

Students may say: "Have a food drive every month and not just during Thanksgiving."

Write a class letter to the editor of the local newspaper expressing their views about the homeless, threat of a nuclear war, need for sidewalks, installation of a traffic light at a dangerous intersection, or a similar vital issue.

## SUMMARY

Cooperative Pluralism is a synthesis of multicultural education, democratic education, and cooperative learning. It affirms the importance of a responsible citizenry and emphasizes the magnitude of interdependence of all people.

## NOTES

[1] David W. Johnson, Roger T. Johnson, Edythe Johnson Holubec, and Patricia Roy (1984). *Circles of Learning: Cooperation in the Classroom*. Alexandria, VA: Association for Supervision and Curriculum Development.

[2] Amy Gutmann. (1987). *Democratic Education*. Princeton, NJ: Princeton University Press.

Mako Nakagawa is the Equity Specialist for the Washington State Office of the Superintendent of Public Instruction. Valerie Ooka Pang is an Assistant Professor at San Diego State University, San Diego, California. [1990 note]

Eleanor Roosevelt convinced the United Nations to adopt its first statement on human rights in December of 1948. The Universal Declaration of Human Rights has now been translated into the native languages of all countries. It begins with the assertion that "all human beings are born free and equal in dignity and rights. They are endowed with reason and conscience and should act towards one another in a spirit of brotherhood."

The Declaration of Human Rights, like all UN declarations, is simply a statement of shared beliefs. It is not a law. In the years since the declaration was adopted, the UN has sought to establish international laws through its conventions on the rights of women, children and minorities around the world. These conventions become law only in the countries that choose to ratify them.

The oldest and most widely ratified human rights convention is the International Convention on the Elimination of All Forms of Racial Discrimination. By 1990, it was accepted as international law by 128 nations. In that document, the United Nations says discrimination is a threat to world peace. It reminds us that racial discrimination harms not only those who are its victims but also those who practice it.

Other human rights conventions include the Convention on the Elimination of Discrimination Against Women and the Convention on the Rights of the Child. The United States has signed these three major human rights conventions to indicate our country's agreement with their principles, but the U.S. has not yet ratified, or accepted as law, the provisions of these conventions.

## CHILDREN'S RIGHTS HIGHLIGHTS

The United Nations Convention on the Rights of the Child says, in part, that:

- All children have the right to life, to a name and a nationality.
- All children's opinions shall be given careful consideration, and their best interests shall be protected.
- All children shall be educated in a spirit of understanding, peace and tolerance.
- Disabled children shall have the right to special treatment, education and care.
- All children have a right to health care.
- All children shall be cared for, by their parents if at all possible, by others if necessary.

- Children shall be protected from forced labor, drug trafficking, kidnapping and abuse.
- Children exposed to war should receive special protection. No child under 15 shall go to war.
- Children of minority populations shall freely enjoy their own culture.
- All children have the right to rest and play and the right to equal opportunities for cultural and artistic activities.

*Adapted from* Convention on the Rights of the Child, *a UN publication.*

## ACTIVITY

- As a group, develop a list of rules for your school or classroom that would help students follow the first principle of the Universal Declaration of Human Rights, which says: "All human beings are born free and equal in dignify and rights. They are endowed with reason and conscience and should act towards one another in a spirit of [sisterhood and] brotherhood."
- Examine the rules set forth in one of the three major human rights conventions mentioned above. (They can be found in libraries or ordered from United Nations Publications, 800-253-9646.) Investigate the reasons why the United States has not ratified that UN human rights convention. Do you agree with those reasons? Hold a cross debate on these issues and take a vote to determine whether your classmates would ratify the convention. Write to your U.S. senators and representatives offering your opinions and suggestions.
- Investigate violations of one of the UN human rights conventions in your neighborhood, city or state. Prepare a report to send to your governor, mayor and the appropriate United Nations agency.
- Outline the actions that young people con take in your community to protect the rights of children as described in the UN Convention on the Rights of the Child.

## RESOURCES [1994 INFORMATION]

\* Texts of the Universal Declaration of Human Rights and the Convention on the Rights of the Child, as well as a variety of posters, books and lesson plans, are available from the UN.

UN Publications
2 United Nations Plaza
Room DC2-853
New York NY 10017
(800) 253-9646

\* *Human Rights for Children* ($10.95) helps children ages 3 to 12 develop an awareness of their own rights and the rights of others. The Universal Declaration of Human Rights ($20), a 20-minute video, portrays the 30 articles of the Declaration in innovative animated form. Other resources are available for all age levels.

> Amnesty International
> 322 Eighth Ave.
> New York, NY 10001
> (212) 807-8400

\* *In the Spirit of Peace* ($7.95) was produced to help teenagers and adults think, write and take action on the key issues outlined in the UN Convention on the Rights of the Child. Further materials, including a newsletter on children's rights, are available.

> Defense for Children International-USA
> 30 Irving Place, 9th Floor
> New York, NY 10003
> (212) 228-4773

\* *Hate and Destruction* is a free 5-minute music video by the British group Soul II Soul for the United Nations High Commissioner for Refugees. The video and teaching guide are designed to help motivate students in grades 6 and up to understand and take action against xenophobia and racism.

> UNHCR
> Public Information
> 1718 Connecticut Ave. NW, Suite 200
> Washington, DC 20009

\* *A Child's Right: A Safe and Secure World*, an eight-lesson curriculum for grades 5-10, helps children understand key UN concepts of world peace and human rights.

> UNA-USA
> 485 Fifth Ave.
> New York, NY 10017
> (212) 697-3232

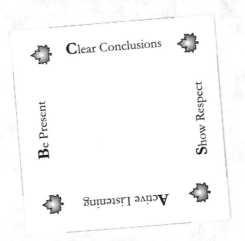

# 31

# Building a Peaceable Classroom
*Helping Young Children Feel Safe in Violent Times*

**Diane E. Levin**

## Imagine these scenarios:

▮ A 5-year-old child is on an airplane. After running the pre-flight airplane safety video, the flight attendant announces a special video feature "for our passengers' viewing pleasure." Suddenly, the child's mother is horrified to see a rebroadcast of a TV news program that summarizes recent mass murders, complete with detailed film footage of the victims. The mother is especially distraught because she has made every effort in her home to protect her child from such graphic depictions of violence.

▮ A 9-year-old begins having nightmares following a "sleep-over" at a good friend's house. When his parents discuss the nightmares with him, they discover that the boy watched his first "R-rated" violent suspense movie with his friend and his friend's father.

▮ A child care class is on a field trip. As the children are about to cross a busy street, a police officer offers to stop traffic so the children may cross safely. One child runs screaming to the teacher. Later, the teacher finds out that the police arrested the child's father the previous weekend when the child was present.

Children growing up today are regularly confronted by violence. Their sense of safety is repeatedly undermined as they see—in the home, school, community and media—that the world is a violent and dangerous place, and that people regularly hurt each other and use fighting to solve their problems. And parents and teachers are often powerless to protect children from this violence (Carlsson-Paige & Levin, 1990).

While the amount and severity of the violence to which children are exposed and the degree to which they are affected varies across society, few children are exempt (Garbarino, Dubrow, Kostelny & Pardo, 1992). Children's exposure to violence fits along a continuum of severity—from entertainment violence (which touches most children's lives) to chronic and direct exposure to violence within their immediate environment (which affects fewer children but which builds on the more prevalent violence). The degree to which children are affected is likely to increase as they move up the continuum.

## HOW CHILDREN ARE AFFECTED BY VIOLENCE

▮ Recently, a talented 7-year-old tennis player suddenly refused to play anymore. Gradually, she opened up enough to explain that she would not compete because she "didn't want to get stabbed [like Monica Seles]."

▮ During the Persian Gulf war, a 5-year-old burst into tears because he was worried about his grandparents' safety. In an effort to reassure him about his own safety, adults had told him that "the war was far away" from his home. Unfortunately, because his grandparents lived "far away" he thought they were in danger.

The children in the above scenarios are struggling to construct meaning out of the violence they see (Carlsson-Paige & Levin, 1985, 1990 & 1992). Children construct meaning from their experiences through play, art and discussions with others. The meaning depends on their individual characteristics, current level of development, family background and prior experiences.

Adults need to understand children's perspectives in order to successfully counteract the effects of violence. Similarly, the more a child has been exposed to violence, the more important it will be for adults to help them make meaning of that violence.

Children's development can be profoundly affected by their experiences with violence (Craig, 1992; Garbarino, et al., 1992; Levin, 1994; Wallach, 1993). For instance, a sense of trust and safety—the deep belief that the world is a safe place and that "I can count on being cared for and being kept safe"—is at the heart of early development (Erikson, 1950). Today, children regularly see that they are not safe and that adults are often powerless to keep them safe. They see that they have to fight and that weapons will help them keep themselves safe (Levin & Carlsson-Paige, in press). Children who feel mistrustful and unsafe devote much of their energy, thoughts and feelings into avoiding danger and many aspects of their development and learning are undermined.

Children extrapolate from their experiences to build ideas about how the world works, their role in society, how people treat each other and how one can participate effectively (Carlsson-Paige & Levin, 1992). These ideas affect how they interpret experience, how they act with others and how they view themselves as actors, learners and contributors to their world. The ideas they are developing now will serve as the foundation upon which they will gradually build more mature ideas.

Today, many children are being socialized into a culture of violence. Violence is a central part of children's experience. The violence becomes a lens that children use to

| TABLE 1 | |
|---|---|
| **TEXT** | **COMMENTARY ON PEACEABLE CLASSROOMS** |

**TEXT**

**Teacher:** I have been noticing something that doesn't feel safe. There are several children who make weapons when they go to the scrounge area. When they're done they start running around the room, pointing their weapons at other children and making shooting noises. When they do that it makes me feel like the other children aren't safe. How do you all feel about it?

**Henry:** I never do that. I always make cars.

**T:** Yes, Henry. There are a lot of other things children can make at scrounge besides weapons. But I don't think we should talk about which children make what now. Remember, we all agreed that it feels safer for everyone not to mention the names of specific children when we talk about problems? Right now, I want to hear how children feel when the guns are pointed at them.

**William:** I hit 'em when they do it. That stops 'em.

**T:** It sounds like you don't feel safe when they point the gun at you. So, then you want to hit them to try to keep yourself safe. How have other children felt when the guns were pointed at them?

**Matilda:** I ran away when they came after me.

**T:** That's something else we sometimes do when we don't feel safe: try to get away. Anyone else?

**Charlotte:** I don't like it, like how would they like it if I yelled in their face?

**T:** So you don't like the noises they make either. How do they make you feel?

**Charlotte:** I'm scared and mad.

**T:** So it sounds like children don't like having the guns pointed at them or the noise. And some of you have felt like you needed to fight back and hit, or run away to feel safe. That sure doesn't feel safe to me. Everyone knows our number one class rule: Everyone needs to feel safe here. So we need to find something to do about the guns that helps everyone feel safe. When you have to hit back to feel safe, then someone can get hurt. Then they are not safe. We've talked about that a lot before. What are some of the ideas we came up with before about keeping safe that could help us now—some things we could do to make sure children aren't scared by weapons? I'll write your ideas down so we can remember them all. Then we'll decide which ones we think we should try.

**Jules:** Use your words.

**T:** Okay. Any ideas about what words you could use?

**James:** Say, "Don't hit."

**Melissa:** I would say, "Go away. I don't like that."

**Matilda:** You could say, "I'll tell the teacher."

**William:** Say, "Go away or I'll hit you."

**T:** You have come up with a lot of things to say using words. *(She reads the list to the children.)* What other ideas do you have about what we could do besides using words.

**Juanda:** No guns at school. That's what we did at my Head Start.

**T:** Yes, we could have a rule that says no guns made in school. Any other ideas?

**Manny:** There could be no noises. I hate that.

**Nick:** Real guns are really, really, really loud!

**T:** Yes, real guns make a terribly loud noise. No one can feel safe with a sound like that. And, in here I've noticed that loud gun noises seem to stop the activities other kids are doing—that's kind of like their work time isn't safe. Any other ideas?

**Jose:** You could only make noises outside.

**T:** That's another possibility.

**Henry:** You could shoot only your friends.

**Tanaka:** I don't want my friends shooting at me.

**Larry:** Only if the friend says it's okay.

**T:** So you could ask your friends if it's okay to pretend to shoot them? Well, you have come up with a really good list of things to try. It's taken a long time. So, let's come back to this tomorrow—come back to our list and decide which ones to try. You can even try using them during the day and report back so we can hear how they worked. And those of you who make pretend weapons and use them in here, see what you think about how the rules work for you, too. I'll leave our list up so you can come look at it when you need to.

**COMMENTARY ON PEACEABLE CLASSROOMS**

- Shows the children that creating a safe environment for them is a priority and that she will help to ensure their safety.
- Asks the children to express their own thoughts and feelings about the situation, rather than casting blame or solving the problem.

- Acknowledges and validates Henry's egocentric response.
- Sets a limit by repeating the class rule about using names at meeting, demonstrating that she will make sure the meeting stays safe for everyone.
- Brings the discussion back on-task by repeating her request for children's ideas.

- Focuses on the reason for his actions, helping the group see that hitting is one response to feeling unsafe.
- Helps children see that diverse ideas are valued.

- Validates a different response.
- Connects it to the safety issue.
- Repeats it so everyone in the group hears and understands it.

- Conveys value of an idea by asking for elaboration.

- Helps children make logical connections between their ideas and safety issues.
- Helps children see their interconnectedness - how their actions affect others.
- Relies on rules created earlier with the class and helps children see how to apply them to the current situation.
- Helps children work on devising new rules for the class through a "democratic" process.
- Creates a structure for helping children feel their contributions to the community are important.
- Writes down the children's ideas to foster and model the reading process, although the children cannot yet read.

- Helps children think about how to put their ideas into action.

- Helps the children learn to "read" the options so they can use it themselves.
- Tries to expand children's thinking to new possibilities.

- Validates and makes clear the idea without stating a position about it.

- Brings the discussion back to safety issues and additional ways some individuals' actions affect others.

- Helps children see how the rule just suggested might work.
- Acknowledges children's contribution to the group.
- Helps children see what comes next in their democratic rule-making process.
- Promotes autonomy by empowering them to take responsibility for trying out each other's suggestions and collecting data to contribute at the next meeting.

*\* Text is reprinted with permission from:* Teaching Young Children in Violent Times: Building a Peaceable Classroom. *Cambridge, MA: Educators for Social Responsibility.*

interpret new experiences and even guide their behavior. Such an atmosphere only serves to undermine children's ability to become responsible and nonviolent adults.

## BUILDING A PEACEABLE CLASSROOM

Adults who care for children must be vigilant in counteracting the profoundly negative effects that exposure to violence can have on children's thoughts, feelings and development as adults (American Psychological Association, 1993; National Association for the Education of Young Children, 1993; Zero to Three, 1994). Educational settings cannot possibly solve all of the problems of a violent society. They can, however, play a vital role when specifically designed to help children cope with violence in developmentally, culturally and individually appropriate and meaningful ways.

In such a peaceable classroom, adults help children work through their experiences with violence. Children are taught about nonviolence, conflict resolution and feeling safe. A peaceable classroom emphasizes both violence intervention and violence prevention. Effective intervention helps children to experience a sense of safety and trust while surrounded by violence. They learn to work through and make meaning of that violence in order to put their energy into healthier and more productive activities. Prevention offers children alternative, nonviolent experiences that they can incorporate into their developing ideas, attitudes, behaviors and feelings.

A discussion with kindergartners (see Table 1) illustrates the central features of a peaceable classroom. The principles and techniques it exemplifies can be adapted to a wide range of settings. The discussion took place at a class meeting after three boys had created a stressful classroom situation. Before beginning the meeting, the teacher talked to the three boys to make sure they felt comfortable having the whole class talk about the problem.

## THE SAFETY RULE

The teacher leading the dialogue organized her classroom around the notion that "we all need to feel safe here—our bodies are safe, our feelings are safe, our ideas and words are safe, our possessions and work are safe." This safety rule provides a simple and developmentally appropriate way to guide children's classroom behavior. Furthermore, the rule can easily be generalized to fit a wide range of classroom situations. Throughout the year, the teacher helps her students learn how to apply the safety rule in increasingly complex ways.

As seen in the give-and-take dialogue, one of many that occur throughout the week, the teacher chooses topics that are highly relevant and meaningful to the children—experiences they will utilize and build onto their ideas and experiences. The teacher structures and guides the discussion, but she does not impose her own ideas on the children or tell them how they should think. She conveys a sense of trust in the children's ability to work out their problems and also lets them know that how they think and feel is

important. By so doing, they are learning how to be active and contributing members of a peaceful community.

In addition, she is expanding the children's understanding of positive ways people can treat each other, even when conflicts arise (Carlsson-Paige & Levin, 1992). Such efforts not only help children feel safe and respected, they also teach them how to treat others that way. By regularly using the safety rule as the standard for evaluating and planning appropriate behavior, the children experience the security that can come from living in a predictable and appropriately structured nonviolent environment.

This teacher infuses "the safety rule" into her curriculum and the school day in many other ways. Whenever a child behaves in a way that suggests he or she is not feeling safe (remember that aggression is a common response to feeling unsafe), she uses the rule as a vehicle for helping that child work through the problem.

In addition to "the safety rule," the teacher uses many strategies to convey to children that they are safe in her classroom. Because children are more likely to feel safe at school when meaningful connections are made between the home and school (Balaban, 19c85), she also builds many opportunities for children to use outside experiences in the classroom curriculum, and works closely with their parents. She tries to help children learn to rely on her as a trusted adult who will do everything possible to ensure their safety. She plans activities that will help the children develop a sense of connection and community—where they learn to rely on each other and work cooperatively. Finally, when conflicts do occur among children or between herself and a child, she uses an approach similar to that in the sample dialogue (see Table 1). The children learn to solve their problems without violence, and in a mutually satisfactory way (Carlsson-Paige & Levin, 1992).

## CONCLUSION

Children are increasingly experiencing the same violence that permeates society and thus often feel unsafe and out of control. They need our help to feel safe and keep themselves safe without violence. At the same time, teachers everywhere are struggling to cope with the effect of violence.

This milieu of violence puts an unfair and demoralizing burden on children and adults. We still have a great deal more to learn about how to foster healthy development and learning in the midst of violence. No amount of effort on our parts could ever fully counteract the devastating effects violence is having on children and society. But we cannot close our eyes.

Children should not have to carry the burden of keeping themselves safe from the dangers that surround them; this should be the job of adults. We must do everything in our power to help children feel safe in violent times and thus ensure greater safety for future generations.

## REFERENCES

American Psychological Association. (1993). *Violence and Youth: Psychology's Response. Volume 1: Summary Report.*

Washington, DC: Author.

Balaban, N. (1985). *Starting School: From Separation to Independence*. New York: Teachers College Press.

Carlsson-Paige, N., & Levin, D. E. (1985). *Helping Young Children Understand Peace, War and the Nuclear Threat*. Washington, DC: National Association for the Education of Young Children.

———. (1990). *Who's Calling the Shots? How to Respond Effectively to Children's Fascination with War Play and War Toys*. Philadelphia, PA: New Society Publishers.

———. (1992). "Making Peace in Violent Times: A Constructivist Approach to Conflict Resolution." *Young Children*, 48(1), 4-13.

Craig, S. (1992). "The Educational Needs of Children Living with Violence." *Phi Delta Kappan*, 74(1), 67-71.

Erikson, E. (1950). *Childhood and Society*. New York: W.W. Norton.

Garbarino, J., Dubrow, N., Kostelny, K., & Pardo, C. (1992). *Children in Danger: Coping with the Effects of Community Violence*. San Francisco: Jossey-Bass.

Levin, D. (1994). *Teaching Young Children in Violent Times: Building a Peaceable Classroom*. Cambridge, MA: Educators for Social Responsibility.

Levin, D., & Carlsson-Paige, N. "Television For (Not Against) Children: Developmentally Appropriate Programming." *Young Children*.

National Association for the Education of Young Children. (1993). NAEYC position statement on violence in the lives of children. *Young Children*, 46(6), 80-84.

Wallach, L. (1993). "Helping Children Cope with Violence." *Young Children*, 48(4), 4-11.

Zero to Three. (1994). *Caring for Infants and Toddlers in Violent Environments: Hurt, Healing and Hope*. Arlington, VA: National Center for Clinical Infant Programs.

Diane E. Levin is a Professor of Education at Wheelock College, Boston, Massachusetts. [1994 note]

# 32

# Conflict Resolution and Peer Mediation
*Pathways to Safer Schools*

**Aline M. Stomfay-Stitz**

Most educators will agree that finding ways to resolve conflict peaceably in America's schools may be our primary challenge. As waves of violence and incidents of racial and societal unrest spill over into our classrooms, we must take a closer look at the process for building safer, more harmonious schools.

## CONFLICT RESOLUTION AND PEER MEDIATION DEFINED
Conflict resolution is a method or strategy that enables people to interact with each other in positive ways in order to resolve their differences. Peer mediation programs are based on a foundation of applied conflict resolution. Such programs empower students to share responsibility for creating a safe, secure school environment. Mediators help their peers to summarize the main points of their dispute and puzzle out possible solutions. Schoolchildren learn essential skills, such as intervention and conflict prevention.

Those who study conflict resolution generally identify its origin with Mary Parker Follett's research in the 1920s. Follett concentrated on "problem solving as integration of the needs of the bargainers" (Follett, 1941; Fogg, 1985). Since that time, the field of conflict resolution has expanded as a tool for business management, intergroup and community mediation, divorce, juvenile justice, civil courts and international negotiations.

## A THEORETICAL OR RESEARCH BASE
The research base for conflict resolution and peer mediation includes the theories of Jean Piaget, Lev Vygotsky, Albert Bandura and Kurt Lewin. Morton Deutsch, David and Roger Johnson and others conducted research on the effects of cooperative and competitive classroom settings.

During middle childhood, children continually assess, weigh and judge their experiences in school, absorbing new behaviors into their existing knowledge. Piaget's cognitive development theory states that children will assimilate and accommodate new experiences into ones previously learned. The added context of social interaction, especially with one's peers, enhances the cognitive development process. Essentially, children need to watch adults think through problems so that they can practice those newly observed skills themselves (Seifert, 1993). Students hone these skills when they verbally and mentally work their way through the problem-solving process.

Vygotsky's theories on children's thinking emphasized a process in which children shared problem-solving experiences with a teacher, parent or peer. As a result, children's own language and thought intermingled and served as the vehicle for their own development (Vygotsky, 1962).

Social learning theorists, particularly Albert Bandura and Kurt Lewin, contributed to the research base. Bandura emphasized that children are essential actors and agents in their own learning and behavior as they model, observe and duplicate responses to a social situation (Seifert, 1993; Catron & Allen, 1993). Furthermore, those who observe conflict resolution or peer mediation confirm that an intellectual and emotional impact results when a potentially dangerous conflict is resolved and disputants "save face" and continue with their school lives.

Kurt Lewin's field theory is of special interest. Specifically, Lewin warned that "one has to face the education situation with all its social and cultural implications as one concrete dynamic whole . . . analysis must be a 'gestalt-theoretical' one" (Maruyama, 1992). Lewin believed that the individual in a school setting is affected by personal and environmental variables that have an impact on student behavioral outcomes (Maruyama, 1992). Equally important is the way that authority figures structure the environment and reward the system—what Lewin calls the "social climate" (Maruyama, 1992). Accordingly, Lewin delineated the concept of conflict as a situation in which forces acting on the individual move in opposite directions.

For several decades, Morton Deutsch (Deutsch, 1949, 1973, 1991) and David and Roger Johnson (Johnson & Johnson, 1979, 1989, 1991) have emphasized that cooperative, rather than competitive, relationships within the classroom's social milieu create the constructive, positive environment that fosters true learning and conflict resolution. The Johnsons believe that students can learn to respect others' viewpoints through controversy experiences. The structured controversy approach can enhance and open students' minds to differing or opposing views (Johnson & Johnson, 1991).

Used as a corequisite with conflict resolution, cooperative learning permits students to practice skills, communicate and solve problems. Their social/emotional skills are likewise enhanced as they learn to listen to the ideas of others and to clarify, summarize, gather and analyze data. Such skills encourage reflective listening, compromise and an honest expression of feelings (Nattiv, Render, Lemire & Render, 1989).

One current education model has been described as a peace education curriculum; that is, it helps children understand and learn to resolve conflicts in peaceful ways. A multi-disciplinary group of researchers (Spodek & Brown, 1993) recommends that peace education curriculum teach children skills in negotiating, conflict resolution and problem-solving. An interrelated focus would include cooperative learning, conflict resolution and education for peace (Deutsch, 1991). The concept of peace education is multifaceted and cross-disciplinary, including peace and social justice, economic well-being, political participation, nonviolence, conflict resolution and concern for the environment (Stomfay-Stitz, 1993).

## OBJECTIVES FOR PEER MEDIATION

A peer mediation program's first objective is to ensure that all students have learned the basic skills required to resolve conflicts. Usually, a guidance counselor or teacher supervises 15-20 hours of training. Peer mediators may be nominated by teachers or chosen by peers. Johnson and Johnson suggest that all students serve as peer mediators after mastering the basic skills. Peer mediators are assigned specific days and hours during which they are "on call" to handle conflicts that arise throughout the school (Johnson & Johnson, 1991).

Complementary goals would include teaching respect for the differences of others and encouraging attitudes and values required for a harmonious classroom. In Montgomery County, Maryland, the basic program emphasizes sensitivity to cultural diversity and provides mediation services for students fluent in Spanish and Vietnamese. A federal court order to desegregate schools in Westchester County, New York, sparked interest in peer mediation in that community. Their middle schools and high schools instituted such programs in 1987 (National Peace Foundation, 1991).

## BASIC SKILLS FOR PEER MEDIATION

One model program, Peace Works, developed by the Peace Education Foundation, provides a student mediation manual that carefully explains the basic skills for peer mediation. The program urges students to listen carefully, be fair, ask how each disputant feels, keep what they are told confidential and mediate in private. At the same time, they should not try to place blame, ask who started it, take sides or give advice (Schmidt, Friedman & Marvel, 1991).

## BENEFITS OF PEER MEDIATION

Strategies to prevent conflicts and identify situations that could provoke violence often include students, parents and school personnel- truly the entire school community. New York City's Project SMART teaches alternatives to violence, focusing on student/teacher conflicts. The program resulted in fewer incidents of vandalism and calls to police (National Peace Foundation, 1991).

Peer mediation may also include intervention strategies for situations with the potential for conflict, such as play behavior and playground disputes. Researchers criticized school staffs' lack of concern in fully addressing bullying as a widespread problem (Hazier, Hoover & Oliver, 1992). An older study revealed that victimization by bullies reaches its highest level during the middle school years (Hazier, Hoover & Oliver, 1991). In a videotape describing the Conflict Manager Program, a former bully describes how, as a peer mediator, he slowly came to understand his victims' viewpoints and how his behavior harmed the weaker and smaller students (Community Board of San Francisco, 1992). Bullying should receive wider attention in school peer mediation programs.

Students, faculty and administrators who participated in a detailed program at Greer Elementary School in Charlottesville, Virginia, reported positive results. Teachers reported that "pressure on teachers to serve as disciplinarians" decreased as a result of the program. The 5th-grade students themselves reported using "creative solutions when given the opportunity." They came to show greater respect for each other as they grew more adept at using their communication and problem-solving skills. The researcher recommended that peer mediation and conflict resolution skills be infused or "embedded in the entire curriculum and philosophy of a school." In cases where "the decision-making in the class is teacher-dictated, the program would be ineffective" (Stuart, 1991).

In a second study at a rural elementary school in West Virginia, the school counselor taught conflict resolution and peer mediation skills to 80 5th-graders. Results showed a decrease in behavior problems in the classroom, on the playground and in referrals to the principal's office (Messing, 1992).

Schools continue to report their success with conflict resolution and individual peer mediation programs. While many results are based on anecdotal evidence, several are based on data collected from students, faculty and administrators. A pilot program in Minnesota that was based on the Peacemaker Program reported that the "frequency of student-student conflicts . . . dropped 80 percent" while conflicts referred to the principal were reduced to zero (Johnson, Johnson, Dudley & Burnett, 1992). A Wisconsin middle school reported that 189 successful student disputes were mediated during the first six months of its program (Koch & Miller, 1987).

One researcher described a "ripple effect" from the programs. Parents and students indicated that they were resolving their home conflicts "in new and more productive ways" (Lane & McWhirter, 1991) and with noticeable benefits to sibling relationships (Gentry & Benenson, 1993).

Peer relationships are powerful ones, based on social interactions that can help others to learn, share and help each other. Each year of development makes the process more complex and inclusive. Peer relationships will eventually supplant the influence of family for children. Thus, autonomy, achievement and social skills are all influenced by peer relationships (Benard, 1990).

## SUCCESS OF SYSTEM-WIDE
## AND STATE-WIDE PROGRAMS

In recent years, entire school systems have adopted detailed plans for conflict resolution and peer mediation. The school system in Ann Arbor, Michigan, has included the Conflict Manager Program in all schools and summer neighborhood community centers (National Peace Foundation, 1991).

Several national organizations are helping to disseminate instructional and training materials, and also are serving as clearinghouses and networks for those interested in conflict resolution and peer mediation. Educators for Social Responsibility (ESR) reported greater demand for training in their Resolving Conflict Creatively Program (RCCP). Education organizations have also joined the effort. Phi Delta Kappa and the Association for Supervision and Curriculum Development have planned professional development institutes. The National Association for Mediation in Education (NAME), the Consortium for Peace, Research, Education and Development (COPPED), the National Institute for Dispute Resolution (NIDR) and the Children's Creative Response to Conflict (CCRC) all work to enhance knowledge and research on conflict resolution and peer mediation.

Ohio deserves attention as a leader in the creation of community and school-based projects under a model known as the Ohio Commission on Dispute Resolution and Conflict Management (OCDRCM). A three-year data collection and evaluation project is currently underway to assess the effect of pilot programs in mediation and conflict resolution in 17 schools throughout the state (OCDRCM, 1993). In New Mexico, a state-wide model included over 60 schools (K-12), in addition to juvenile justice, family and victim offender mediation programs (New Mexico Center for Dispute Resolution, 1993).

## CONCLUSION

Peer mediation programs in the schools offer alternatives to violence. Instead of physical fights, threats and verbal abuse, students are taught specific communications and conflict resolution skills. These skills lead students and their peer mediators through a process of critical thinking and problem-solving in order to arrive at a mutually beneficial solution. Susan Schultz of the Ann Arbor Public Schools assessed the benefits that accrued from their system-wide initiative:

> Teaching conflict management skills is good. For the children to see adults around them using conflict management skills is better. For both the children and the adults to use these skills at school, at home, at work, and at play is best. (National Peace Foundation, 1991)

Clearly, conflict resolution and peer mediation offer viable opportunities for an entire school community to create a safer, more harmonious world. At the same time, growing numbers of educators have recognized that, through such programs, students are learning skills that have wider applications. These skills have the potential to create safer and more peaceful homes, schools and communities.

## REFERENCES

Benard, B. (1990). *The Case For Peers*. Portland, OR: Northwest Regional Educational Laboratory. Ed 327-755.

Catron, C. E., & Allen, J. (1993). *Early Childhood Curriculum*. Columbus, OH: Merrill.

Community Board Of San Francisco. (1992). *Conflict Manager Program*, Videotape.

Deutsch, M. (1949). *A Theory Of Cooperation And Competition. Human Relations*, 2, 129-152.

———. (1973). *The Resolution Of Conflict*. New Haven, CT: Yale University Press.

———. (1991). "Educating Beyond Hate." *Peace, Environment, And Education*, 2(4), 3-19.

Fogg, R. W. (1985). Dealing With Conflict: A Repertoire Of Creative, Peaceful Approaches. *Journal Of Conflict Resolution*, 29(2), 330-358.

Follett, M. P. (1941). *The Collected Papers Of Mary Parker Follett*. London: Pittman.

Gentry, D. B., & Benenson, W. A. (1993). "School-to-home Transfer Of Conflict Management Skills Among School-age Children." *Families In Society: The Journal Of Contemporary Human Services*, 4(2), 67-73.

Hazler, R., Hoover, J. H., & Oliver, R. (1991). "Student Perceptions Of Victimization By Bullies In School." *Journal Of Humanistic Education And Development*, 29, 143-150.

———. (November, 1992). "What Kids Say About Bullying." *Executive Educator*, 14(11), 20-22.

Johnson, D., & Johnson, R. (1979). *Circles Of Learning*. Edina, MN: Interaction Book.

———. (1989). *Cooperation And Competition: Theory And Research*. Edina, MN: Interaction Book.

———. (1991). *Teaching Students To Be Peacemakers*. Edina, MN: Interaction Book.

Johnson, D. W., Johnson, R. T., Dudley, B., & Burnett, R. (1992). "Teaching Students To Be Peer Mediators." *Educational Leadership*, 50(1),10-13.

Koch, M. S., & Miller, S. (1987). "Resolving Student Conflicts With Student Mediators." *Principal*, 66, 59-61.1

Lane, P. S., & Mcwhirter, J. J. (1992). "A Peer Mediation Model: Conflict Resolution For Elementary And Middle School Children." *Elementary School Guidance And Counseling*, 27, 15-23.3

Maruyama, G. (1992). "Lewin's Impact On Education: Instilling Cooperation And Conflict Management Skills In School Children." *Journal Of Social Issues*, 48(2), 155-159.

Messing, J. K. (1992). *Impact Of Conflict Resolution Curriculum On Elementary School Students' Perception Of Conflict And Problem Solving*. Charleston, Wv: Appalachia Educational Laboratory.

National Peace Foundation (1991, Fall). "Where Does Peace Education Stand Today?" *Peace Reporter*, 1-12.

Nattiv, A., Render, G. F., Lemire, D., & Render, K. R. (1989). "Conflict Resolution And Interpersonal Skill Building Through The Use Of Cooperative Learning." *Journal Of Humanistic Education And Development*, 28, 96-10

New Mexico Center For Dispute Resolution. (1993). Brochure And Publications. Albuquerque, NM: Author.

Ohio Commission On Dispute Resolution And Conflict Management. (1993). *Model School Program In Conflict Resolution And Peer Mediation*. Columbus, Oh: Author

Schmidt, F., Friedman, A., & Marvel, J. (1992). *Mediation For Kids: Kids In Dispute Settlement*. Miami, FL: Peace Education Foundation.

Seifert, K. L. (1993). "Cognitive Development And Early Childhood Education." In B. Spodek (Ed.), *Handbook Of Research On The Education Of Young Children* (Pp. 9-23). New York: Macmillan.

Spodek, B., & Brown, P. C. (1993). "Curriculum Alternatives In Early Childhood Education." In B. Spodek (Ed.), *Handbook Of Research On The Education Of Young Children* (Pp. 91-104). New York: Macmillan

Stomfay-Stitz, A. (1993). *Peace Education In America 1828-1990. Sourcebook For Education And Research*. Metuchen, NJ: Scarecrow Press

Stuart, L. A. (1991). *Conflict Resolution Using Mediation Skills In The Elementary Schools*. Charlottesville, Va: University Of Virginia. Ed 333 258.

Vygotsky, L. (1962). *Thought And Language*. Cambridge, MA: MIT Press

## ORGANIZATIONS AND RESOURCES FOR TEACHING CONFLICT RESOLUTION AND PEER MEDIATION [1994 INFORMATION]

Ann Arbor Public Schools, 2555 South State St., Ann Arbor, MI 48106.

Educators for Social Responsibility, 11 Garden St., Cambridge, MA 02138

Friends Conflict Resolution Programs, 1515 Cherry St., Philadelphia, PA 19102.

Interaction Book Company, 7208 Cornelia Dr., Edina, MN 55435, 612-831-9500.

Concerned Educators Allied for a Safe Environment (CEASE), 17 Gerry St., Cambridge, MA 02138, 617-864 0999.

Peace Education Committee of the Jane Addams Peace Association, Women's International League for Peace and Freedom, 1213 Race St., Philadelphia, PA 19107.

Ohio Commission on Dispute Resolution and Conflict Management, 77 S. High St., Columbus, OH 43266-0124,

National Association for Mediation in Education (NAME), 425 Amity St., Amherst, MA 01002.

National Peace Foundation, 1835 K St., NW, Suite 610, Washington, DC 20006.

Center for Peace and Conflict Studies, Wayne State Univ., 3049 Faculty Admin. Bldg., Detroit, MI 48202.

Consortium on Peace Research, Education, and Development (COPPED), George Mason University, 4400 University Dr., Fairfax, VA 22030.

Aline M. Stomfay-Stitz is an Associate Professor in the Education Department at Christopher Newport University, Newport News, Virginia. [1994 note]

# 33

# Social Studies and School-Based Community Service Programs: Teaching the Role of Cooperation and Legitimate Power

**David R. Procter**
**Mary E. Haas**

In an inner-city ghetto, three teenaged men confront 12-year-old Mark and demand that he give them his new tennis shoes. Throughout the world, international charities and governments work together to provide famine relief in Somalia. Every Thursday afternoon in a mid-Western city John puts on a clown's costume and makeup to entertain children in the local hospital. Elsewhere, a young woman is shot and her infant child thrown from the car when a man hijacks the car she is driving. All four of these actions have a common denominator. All describe the exercise of power, but only some are examples of legitimate power. One of the most important tasks for social studies is to help students discriminate between the uses of power.

## ROLE OF COOPERATION IN EXERCISING LEGITIMATE POWER AND AUTHORITY

The NCSS Curriculum Guidelines (1979) recommend activities that stimulate students to investigate and respond to the human condition in the contemporary world. Theodore Kaltsounis (1990) elaborates by saying that the knowledge, values, and skills learned in school need to be blended into a demonstration of democratic citizenship through action. We agree and suggest that the essence of democracy is cooperation that can only be realized through the use of legitimate power and authority. We would like to discuss the role of cooperation through the exercise of power and authority in school-based community service projects. Such projects serve as a link between the theory and practice of democratic education and citizenship and appropriate volunteer service activities for all grade levels.

Social studies educators, community leaders, administrators, and politicians are considering community service as a focus for middle school and high school students. Some even advocate that students complete voluntary service in order to graduate from high school. Although this idea has some merit, it seems ironic to require voluntarism which, in reality, denies individuals the opportunity of free choice. In at least one community, compulsory community service is being challenged in the courts (Carpenter 1992). However, citizenship is awarded to individuals at birth and nurturing students in active, successful, and meaningful democratic participation begins early in life.

Reprinted from *Social Education*, November/December 1993, Volume 57, Number 7. Copyright 1993 by National Council for the Social Studies.

It should also be a part of formal education beginning in the primary grades and continuing through graduation. The responsibilities and opportunities for community and social behaviors are present and need to begin at an early age. Indeed, those who drop out of secondary schools still have the rights and responsibilities of citizenship. Waiting until high school to offer students school-based community service is too late for many, particularly those who have not had positive role models and whose adult family members have grown up in a society without a democratic tradition.

Such situations present a challenge to education and particularly to social studies because of its unique and important role of helping students understand how individuals contribute to solving community problems within the democratic tradition in the United States. Most curriculums overlook voluntary service to the community. The tradition of voluntarism can develop only if individuals have become aware of social problems, consider their serious consequences, and decide to act to prevent unacceptable consequences.

Experiencing the practices and the outcomes of cooperation is necessary if students are to understand the concept of democracy. Furthermore, the failure to include a strong emphasis on cooperation in the social studies leaves a huge gap in students' understanding of the important role of the individual in the community. Presently filling that gap is an excessive emphasis on individualism and competition that has contributed to isolationism and economic and social deterioration.

We must cease to see the primary goal of schooling as the ideological indoctrination and preparation for competing in the job market. Rather, we must view schooling with the high goal of preparing students for active citizenship in the community where employment is only one of the many ways an individual exhibits a responsible civic attitude. Not only must students learn how to cooperate with one another and in groups, they must also learn to study social issues. They must learn to channel their personal power and authority toward legitimate social goals through compassion and cooperation that recognize human dignity rather than competition that is destructive because it accepts bias and prejudice. The social studies curriculum with its emphasis on the examination of social issues and problems requires the development of attitudes and skills that enable citizens to exercise their power and authority for legitimate social goals (Engle and Ochoa 1988). Social studies teachers (non-citizenship educators) have a responsibility to talk with students as early as possible about the conflict between the values of individualism and cooperation in the community. The classroom, then, becomes the ideal forum for controlled and responsible disagreement and dissent under the guidance of caring, sensitive, and knowledgeable teachers, who are in essence, community leaders.

## LEGITIMATE POWER AND AUTHORITY

Only a few people exert political power on a daily basis whereas many more use their power and authority informally and infrequently. People learn the informal use of power and exercise it within less formal social institutions such as the family, neighborhood, and local clubs. Organized and formal uses of power and influence begin with political institutions at the community level. Today's geographical boundaries do not limit many of the issues and concerns of people throughout the world. Such issues become political because they are more likely to involve legal and political mandates in their solutions. Although political activism tends to receive a large share of publicity and historical recognition, social activism historically has responded more quickly to the needs of people, has improved their lives, and has stimulated much of the social legislation we take for granted. Therefore, citizens perform an important role when they take part in social activism particularly in a large, diverse democracy such as the United States (Sunal and Haas 1993).

Participation within the community is the final step in problem solving and decision making and the logical extension of classroom preparation for active citizenship. Students should undertake social or political action only after careful study and preparation so they might understand their involvement in a project and discover how to complete it. School-based community service, therefore, is the only true test of active citizenship, and it provides the opportunity for students to begin exercising their legitimate power with the encouragement, support, and guidance of adults (NCSS 1979, 262).

Although all teachers may not feel comfortable in guiding students to participate politically in elections and legislation, others feel comfortable in helping their students to participate in forms of personal and social caring within their community. Teachers often encourage their students to participate in short-term activities such as food drives, clean-up campaigns, or making posters for local activities. Tradition has often driven these activities. They may have been extracurricular activities without clearly-defined links to the curriculum or the consideration of why such activities are needed or desirable.

As a result, students often develop misconceptions that some problems are important only at certain times of the year or can be solved quickly through simple actions. This not only minimizes the problem, but it also trivializes the role of the citizen in a democracy.

## DEVELOPING PARTICIPATION THROUGH THE SOCIAL STUDIES

Because schools teach theories of society, they should also teach students to apply these theories to the real world. Well-designed and operated school-based community service programs serve as catalysts for community-based political and social activism carried out throughout one's lifetime. Using community study, interviews, and simulations teachers can help students develop the knowledge, values, and skills and make the emotional investment to motivate and assist youth in performing community service.

The incorporation of school-based community service programs allows young people to enter into political and social activism through voluntary service, projects, and internships. For such programs the greatest opportunities can occur only in an environment of cooperation among the members of the community beyond the classroom including students, teachers, administrators, parents, and social and political agencies. During the development of a citizen, the social studies curriculum serves as the foundation for the formative stage of citizenship preparation. It should include school-based community service as a means to implement, monitor, and evaluate students' active participation. In a detailed examination of four community-based school service programs those programs that included advance preparation with regular opportunities for monitoring and evaluating student experiences provided students with the confidence and ability needed to handle the responsibilities and tensions of community service (Procter 1992).

Introducing cooperative learning techniques into the curriculum, although a step in the right direction, is not enough. Cooperative learning breaks down barriers within a classroom, but it does not guarantee that students will voluntarily transfer these behaviors into actions outside the classroom. In addition, students must experience the presence of conflicts that arise in everyday situations because people differ from one another in the ways they understand and interpret one another's actions. Community participation has great potential for producing skills and attitudes to confront such conflicts and can enhance cooperation among a variety of social, ethnic, and age groups. Because people encounter and cope with these conflicts throughout life, we should not limit the social studies curriculum from studying these conflicts until the secondary grades. In fact, omitting experiences that include conflict creates harmful misconceptions and fails to help students to use their legitimate power and authority and may tend to encourage youth to use their power in selfish and destructive ways.

## VARIETY IN SERVICE PROJECTS

Table 1 gives an overview and summarizes the kinds of school-based community service programs currently operating in U.S. schools and the corresponding relationships of the inherent skills, values, and citizenship concepts that students can derive from them. It should help

## TABLE 1
## HIERARCHY OF SCHOOL-BASED COMMUNITY SERVICE PROJECTS AND THEIR LEARNING OUTCOMES

| KIND OF PROJECT | SKILLS | VALUES | CITIZENSHIP CONCEPTS | GRADE LEVELS | *BASIC* |
|---|---|---|---|---|---|
| 1. School Service Project | Identifying Needs, Organizing Group Dynamics | Cooperation, Self-esteem, Pride in Accomplishment | Participation, Activism | K-12+ | |
| 2. Community Service Project | Communication Critical Thinking Decision Making | Respect, Brotherhood, Empathy | Community and Democratic Values | 3-12+ | |
| 3. Individual Service Project | Time Management, Problem Solving, Adaptability, Self Direction | Human Dignity, Justice, Responsibility | Appreciation of Cultural Diversity, Social Justice | 7-12+ | |

Teacher's Role: Evaluating Student Feedback and Guiding Reflection            *COMPLEX*

to establish a scope and sequence for community-based service programs. The activities are arranged in a hierarchy with the highest level, the Individual Service Project, including the skills, values, and concepts of the two previous levels. The first level, school service projects is a one-time activity of short duration that provides a service for the school community such as planting trees or a spring clean-up of the grounds.

The Community Service Project is also a one-time effort, but is designed to serve the neighborhood or the entire community and may include cooperating with other groups and usually requires more time and demands a greater variety of skills and talents from the students than the short activities. Converting a vacant lot into a playground for young children or collecting and distributing clothing to help the homeless are examples of such projects. With community service projects students are likely to encounter challenges to their efforts including social and political obstacles such as vested interests and legal procedures.

Individual Service Projects are continuing commitments of several hours of service per week over an extended period of time: students perform one of a variety of different activities including delivering meals-on-wheels, tutoring children, volunteering in a nursing home, or serving as emergency medical volunteers on a regular basis. These types of projects present a wide variety of unique challenges that individuals must solve.

The suggested grade levels in table 1 are generalized for school class projects as a result of examining current practices. Exceptions to this may be special family or neighborhood projects. Likewise, exceptionally motivated students or even entire classes might perform service on higher levels.

The teacher's role at all levels is similar; it always aims to nurture student success and help students to understand the role of cooperation and legitimate power in a democracy. Inherent within the teacher's role is the primary emphasis on education by examining knowledge about the problems and decisions of society.

## POTENTIAL PROBLEMS

A school should not undertake a school-based community service program without a great deal of thought and planning. Although service programs generally reward the students with great personal satisfaction and the community with services and products from their labors, many potential individual, legal, and economic problems may arise. These problems increase in both number and complexity as the activities move to the higher levels of the hierarchy (table 1). Just as life does not protect youth from encountering problems, a program that leaves the exclusive bounds of the school exposes students to life's problems that are beyond the control of schools and families. Schools must provide for continuous monitoring of students, in part to assist students who encounter any of a wide range of individual problems. For example, not all neighborhoods are safe, and working in hospitals or nursing homes can create stress and depression as students encounter illness and death. Students may become disappointed if they do not realize their anticipations by their efforts, or with the slow pace of democracy, or legal requirements. The school and all participating organizations need to examine legal implications and insurance liability. For example, in Pennsylvania a compulsory service requirement for graduation is currently being challenged in the courts on the grounds that it is a violation of the ban on involuntary servitude in the Thirteenth Amendment (*Asheville Citizen-Times* 1992). Likewise, if the schools, volunteers, and agencies are legally liable during community service all parties must be insured. The most important factor for the success of community service programs appears to be the quality of leadership. Consistent, sensitive, and caring leaders must be capable of working with a wide variety of people and with a schedule of working hours that is very different from those of classroom teachers (Procter 1992).

## CONCLUSION

Opportunities are available for students in all grades to perform service in their community and schools have good reasons to involve all students in such activities. Young people in the past have been asked to perform activities such as war bond drives, walk-a-thons, and collections for donations of food or clothing from their families and friends. Students have responded to these calls, but they have provided only their physical strength and have not been asked to apply their thinking and problem-solving abilities. When school-based community service is an integral part of the social studies curriculum, students receive far more than a fleeting good feeling. They grow and develop intellectually and socially. They learn to respect the legitimate power and authority of people and realize their roles in the success of democracy.

As the debate for community service in the schools continues, it is unfortunate that the scope extends only to the higher grades. In so doing the major concerns of teachers in elementary schools and those teaching many minority groups are largely missing. Indeed, even the youngest students and those who drop out of secondary schools still have the rights and responsibilities of citizenship. The need, therefore, is not so much for a capstone course as it is for all students to receive repeated opportunities and experiences for growth in understanding, valuing, and using legitimate power in the community. Although rioting is one form of activism, it is not a legitimate or constructive expression of power. Parents, media, government, and schools must help students discriminate between legitimate and illegitimate expressions of power and encourage use of the former. The social studies curriculum is the natural place to provide the means for students to investigate and review opportunities to participate in expressing the legitimate uses of personal power. When properly used throughout the curriculum, community-based school service can be an effective vehicle for using legitimate power and preparing students for active and responsible citizenship.

## REFERENCES

Carpenter, Paul. "The Lesson for Today Is about Logic." *Allentown Morning Call* (27 September 1992): section B, 1.

Dewey, John. *Democracy in Education: An Introduction to the Philosophy of Education*. New York: The Free Press, 1966.

Engle, Shirley H., and Anna S. Ochoa. *Education for Democratic Citizenship*. New York: Teachers College Press, 1988.

Kaltsounis, Theodore. Letter to the Editor. *Social Education* 54 (February 1990): 65.

National Council for the Social Studies. "Revision of the NCSS Social Studies Curriculum Guidelines." *Social Education* 43 (April 1979): 262.

Procter, David R. "School-based Community Service: A Descriptive Analysis of Four High School Programs." Ph.D. diss., West Virginia University, 1992.

Procter, David R., and Mary E. Haas. *Handbook of School-Based Community Projects for Student Participation*. ED 326 467. ERIC/ChESS, 1990.

"Students Serve Their Community to Meet Graduation Requirements." *Asheville Citizen-Times* (19 December 1992): section C, 2.

Sunal, Cynthia S., and Mary E. Haas. *Social Studies and the Elementary/Middle School Student*. Fort Worth, Texas: Harcourt Brace Jovanovich, 1993.

David R. Procter earned a doctorate in curriculum and instruction from West Virginia University in 1992 and is currently an educational consultant. Mary E. Haas is an Associate Professor of Curriculum and Instruction at West Virginia University in Morgantown. [1993 note]

**Joseph A. Braun, Jr.**
**Kent Sabin**

*Tis an old maxim in the schools,*
*That flattery's the food of fools;*
*Yet now and then your men of wit,*
*Will condescend to take a bit.*

In a 1713 verse, Jonathan Swift wrote the above stanza during a period of his life marked by a miscellany of prose and poetry. Condescending to take some flattery, however, may be a wise decision on the part of a school. Schools can avoid the condition that Swift describes—having flattery become the food of fools—with a coordinated effort by a committed faculty. This paper will describe such an effort by one elementary school that used the occasion of the seventy-fifth anniversary of its founding to promote social studies instruction, integrated with other areas, and at the same time call community attention to the school's heritage. In addition, strategies for developing a heritage study and an anniversary celebration for other schools will be given.

Heritage includes property as well as tradition or legacy. A school is an excellent example of the concept of heritage. Because one of the goals of public education is to instill in students a sense of national heritage, there are two solid reasons why the anniversary of the founding of the school should be studied and celebrated. First, before students develop an appreciation of national heritage, the study of a local institution such as the school provides the necessary concreteness and immediacy that is more meaningful to the lives of elementary-age children. By discovering the values, aspirations, and changes at the school in their own community, the students can later expand their understanding of heritage to include legacy at a national level. A second reason for celebrating the founding of the school is the benefit from encouraging the community to focus its attention on the positive accomplishments of the local school and its students. How did one school go about organizing a study of its heritage? In what ways was the community involved in the celebration of the school's legacy?

## CELEBRATING A SCHOOL'S HERITAGE

For months the local newspaper featured articles, photographs, and letters to the editor promoting the upcoming seventy-fifth anniversary of Lincoln School. The publicity generated a great deal of pride and fostered a sense of heritage in this rural community about 70 miles west of Chicago. Being featured in the paper, however, was only one noteworthy aspect of the celebration honoring the years of education that took place at Lincoln School. The teachers used the occasion to develop units of study that promoted inquiry into the origins and heritage of their school. After these units were completed, students planned an open house for parents and alumni. At this open house, called "A Reunion for the Class of 1910," students displayed products of their investigations into the history of the school and gave parents and alumni an opportunity to visit and reflect upon the changes that had taken place.

## A SCHOOL SONG

To initiate the units of study and heighten interest in learning about the heritage of their school, students attended an assembly four months before the actual date of the open house. At this time a school song written by some students with assistance from the music teacher was performed and taught to the student body. At the assembly the music teacher explained that music is one way people commemorate important events. The students learned that most colleges and high schools have a school song, and the music teacher elaborated by noting how an anthropologist would explain that songs are a common symbol for honoring a school in our culture. The music teacher extended this concept after the assembly by teaching several college fight songs during regularly scheduled music lessons. The assembly concluded with teachers from the various grade levels describing some of the learning activities they were planning as part of the units of study on the heritage of Lincoln Elementary. Students and teachers left the assembly feeling highly motivated to begin their investigations and activities.

Art activities proved immensely popular and reinforced social studies instruction. Teachers encouraged students to design buttons depicting the anniversary, and a school-wide contest was held to select a button design to be printed and distributed to the students and the community. Teachers also encouraged students to design posters or murals commemorating the anniversary. These posters and murals were displayed in the school and in local businesses throughout the course of the celebration. Under the direction of a teacher who had an instructional media background, students developed a slide and tape presentation that premiered at the open house. The students incorporated pictures of current students

Reprinted with permission from the Helen Dwight Reid Educational Foundation, from *The Social Studies*, November/December 1986. Published by Heldref Publications, 1319 Eighteenth Street, NW, Washington, D.C. 20036-1802. Copyright 1986.

and their work, along with old photographs and documents, into this presentation.

## FOCUSING ON THE FACTS

In language arts classes, teachers encouraged students to write reports focusing on important facts about the school. Assignments included writing themes on subjects such as what it would have been like to go to school seventy-five years ago. Some teachers helped students write and produce skits depicting how Lincoln School teachers and students had changed over the years. Other teachers broadened spelling instruction to include the names of local points of interest as bonus words. Students composed letters inviting alumni and various dignitaries to the open house, as well as thanking all those who helped in the project. An invitation was sent to then-President Reagan, who replied with a special congratulatory message on White House stationery but declined to attend because of his busy schedule.

The fifth grade teachers taught social studies by assigning their classes a research project in which they investigated the origin of the school. Old documents and newspaper reports were used to gather information about the reasons for building Lincoln School. This included information about those who suggested and approved building it, how the property was acquired, how long it took to build, and what it looked like upon completion. Public library personnel used microfiche to provide guidance throughout this assignment, which proved an excellent hands on experience, giving children an opportunity to use primary sources to answer their questions.

Primary students, with the assistance of their teachers, invited senior residents of the community into their classrooms to provide an oral history describing these older citizens' remembrances of Lincoln School. The teachers also helped the students develop interview questions, which they posed to their guests. As a follow up activity, language experience charts were composed to extend the students' understanding of the information presented and reinforce comprehension and vocabulary skills.

Other activities included a day when students dressed as they might have if they were going to school in 1910. Students looked toward the future as they brainstormed what should be included in a time capsule that was buried on be day of the open house. The students formed a committee to help decide what suggestions should be incorporated into this capsule.

## THE REUNION

The culmination of the units of study about the heritage of Lincoln School was "A Reunion for the Class of 1910" — the open house. On the big day, guest registers were located in the lobby. Traditional reunion prizes were awarded for categories such as: oldest alumni in attendance, former student who had traveled the farthest to attend, and alumni with the largest family. An assembly was part of the open house. The students had learned the

school song, which they sang for those attending. The principal gave a welcoming address and described some of the learning activities students had carried out in conjunction with the units of heritage study. Distinguished alumni and retired faculty gave speeches about their fond remembrances and the special events that had occurred at Lincoln. Balloons and candy were distributed by volunteers dressed as clowns and the parent-teacher organization served an anniversary cake. The open house ceremonies ended with the burial of a time capsule that will be recovered and added to every five years.

A five-year time span for the recovery of the time capsule seemed appropriate because it corresponded to the passage of another generation of students from the school. Thus, every five years a study of events that had transpired could be undertaken on a school-wide basis.

At Lincoln, teachers are looking forward to adding new ideas to the various units developed for the seventy-fifth anniversary. But before the staff at Lincoln School begins a heritage study and celebration with its next cycle of students, they will examine their previous strategies.

## INITIATING A HERITAGE STUDY FOR YOUR SCHOOL

In addition to the lesson ideas mentioned previously, the following suggestions can be organized into units and incorporated into the existing curriculum. Students could inquire into the many family arrangements that exist within their school. Has the makeup of families changed over the years; if so, how? How did the pioneer settlers in the community provide education to their youngsters? Do residents of the community work nearby or do they commute? How far do they travel; what means of transportation do they use? If a celebration such as the reunion at Lincoln School is to be held, the following basic steps should be taken to promote the event:

1. Solicit input and commitment from a variety of sources, including staff, students, and the parent-teacher organization. Appoint a special committee to help coordinate activities.
2. Notify the local newspaper and other media such as radio and television to publicize the event.
3. Invite community organizations to become involved. If there is a local historical society, work with them since their participation can be mutually beneficial.
4. Inform school board members and other elected officials, including the mayor or city council members.
5. Have students be responsible for writing and distributing invitations and thank you notes.

A characteristic unique to the American educational system is the autonomy and respect for the local school as a focal point of community interest and attention. A number of schools were built at the height of the baby-boom and have been a part of their communities for a decade or more. Since they were built, many changes in demographic patterns and school construction have taken place. Whatever their nature, these changes constitute the heritage of a school. Organizing a study and celebration of this heritage, the authors found, provided concrete learning experiences for children, rekindled community attention, and fostered positive interest in the local school.

The experience at Lincoln School shows how studying the heritage of a school sells itself. Teachers had numerous creative ideas for meaningful activities. Parents and other community members were eager to get involved. In addition to the positive attention and interest that develops, studying the heritage of their school helps students gain a sense of group identity and connectedness to the school. Studying the life of a school can be of great interest to children; it can serve as a vehicle for learning essential social studies skills and other content area objectives such as language arts. Most important, the local school, when used as a source of heritage study, provides for a collective understanding to help students recognize the purpose and legacy of the institution that dominates so much of their lives. Finally, if carefully planned, an elementary school reunion can be flattering to a community and avoid becoming the "food for fools" that Swift warns us to avoid.

Joseph A. Braun, Jr., is an Assistant Professor of Elementary Social Studies Education at California State University, Chico. Kent Sabin is the Principal of the Lincoln School in Rochelle, Illinois. [1986 note]

**Dale Greenawald**

This activity is designed to help primary students to analyze situations where a wrong has occurred and offer recommendations for corrective justice.

## OBJECTIVES

To apply the concept of corrective justice and develop critical thinking and problem solving skills. To emphasize that courts are to help those who were wronged, not just punish people.

## PROCEDURES

The teaching time is approximately 30 minutes for grades K-3 and approximately 45 minutes for grades 4-6. This lesson is a natural for a community resource person from the justice community (e.g., a lawyer or judge).

Explain that after a case is decided and a person is found guilty a court has several functions. It wants to protect society so that the person can't hurt anyone else. It also wants to help the guilty person improve himself/herself. It also wants to punish the guilty person so that he/she won't break the law again. Finally, the court wants to help the person who was hurt.

Read each case. Ask students to explain what happened. Ask what might be done by those involved to correct the situation. Why do they think that their solution is a good one? The resource person will critique responses.

## K-3 READINGS

1. Mike wrote on the bathroom walls. When he admitted that he had been the person responsible, the principal asked him how he might make things right.

    Ask the class for suggestions about what would be fair. What might Mike do and why should he do that? Why is this a good suggestion and how will it help? Critique answers in a positive manner—"what about?" "did you think of . . .?"
2. Sarah was shopping with a friend and she took and ate some candy without paying for it. When she tried to leave the store the manager asked why she hadn't paid for the candy she ate. Sarah did not have any money to pay for the candy. She doesn't have any money anywhere. What can Sarah do to make this wrong right?
    A. Have the class brainstorm solutions and how they might make things better. What would be fair?
    B. What can the manager do if he wishes to stop this kind of behavior?

3. Three children are playing with matches at the picnic grounds, Blue Bell Shelter. A strong wind comes up and a spark sets the grass on fire. The shelter and many acres of land are burned, and several animals kept in a small zoo nearby are killed or injured. Before trying to make this wrong right, think about:
    ▌ Some animals are gone forever.
    ▌ The children are too small to rebuild the shelter.
    ▌ The community cannot use the picnic grounds.
    ▌ It cost a lot of money to put out the fire.
    ▌ It costs a lot of money to rebuild the shelter.
    A. How can this wrong be made right? What would be fair?
    B. What can the children do even though they cannot make things the way they were?

## FOR USE WITH GRADES 4-6

Several students at Westmeadow Elementary School see a television ad for the Whiz-Bang Mighty Automobile toys. It looks like a really neat set of toys. In the ad it looks like the toys are several feet long and have motors. The set costs $45.00. Each of the children work very hard cutting grass, doing chores and helping neighbors for several months to earn money. They stop going to movies and buying candy so that they can save all of their money for the Whiz-Bang Mighty Automobile toys. When the toys arrive, they are about six inches long, made of plastic, and powered by a rubber band. All of the toys are broken within a few days of use. They simply fell apart. It is clear that the advertisement was misleading.

## CLASS DISCUSSION

1. What is fair?
2. What are the legal rights of the children?
3. How can this wrong be righted?
4. If you were a judge and this case came to your court, how would you right the wrong?

The resource person should explain the rights of the children in this case and what would probably happen if they complained to the county consumer affairs office. Also, if the students took their case to small claims court what might happen?

The lawyer or judge should tell about different programs and ways the courts can right wrongs. For example:
1. work release programs
2. community service sentences
3. paying back the cost of the damages (restitution)
4. repairing what can be fixed.

Dale Greenawald is an educator in Boulder, Colorado. [1987 note]

# PART 6

## Ⓥ POWER, AUTHORITY, AND GOVERNANCE

The study of power, authority, and governance enables young people to learn about fundamental concepts and practices that are basic to our democratic government. In a democracy, the ultimate power and authority to govern rest with the people. All individuals need to develop an ability to use their power effectively for the common good. In our democracy, young learners have a strong interest in justice (fairness) and order (responsibility). Starting at a young age, children need to begin learning about their rights and power (responsibilities) as citizens and how they can fairly and justly share that power with others.

Although ongoing changes in American society require adjustments in governmental processes, change does not alter the underlying principles and values fundamental to our democracy. Our political system involves the use of public decision making to solve problems that cannot be resolved by individuals. Fundamental questions asked in the study of power, authority, and governance include the following: What is legitimate power? How is power gained and used? How are governments created, structured, maintained, and changed? How are individual rights protected within the context of majority rule? What are the major forms of government that people have created throughout history? Who are our elected officials? What limits the power of government? In seeking answers to these and other questions, problem-solving and decision-making skills are developed.

Passe argues that citizenship skills are learned through interactions and problem solving. He also suggests teaching students appropriate classroom behaviors necessary for developing citizenship responsibilities. He recommends linking events and problems at school with the real world so that important civic concepts and practices can be experienced first hand by students. One important real world civic concept is freedom of speech. Anderson offers teachers several guideposts and examples of teaching and learning processes related to freedom of speech. The expression of our fundamental rights requires responsible individual and collective behaviors from all citizens. McBee advocates confronting, rather than avoiding, controversial topics with young children. She explains how law-related education and its methods involve children in understanding how the legal system addresses controversial questions.

The learning activities suggested in *Law in a Free Society* are adapted from activities developed by the Center for Civic Education. These activities offer instructional ideas for teaching about rights and responsibilities related to the ownership of property. Bloom's activity uses a mini mock trial to help students learn about due process. Because children are already familiar with many fairy tales, lessons like that presented by Norton which bring the Big Bad Wolf to trial allow for student engagement in discussions about the justice system and related legal concepts. She has also included an excellent list of resources to help teachers prepare lessons related to understanding the law. Finally, Haas, Hatcher, and Sunal help teachers organize lessons and activities to teach about the president and presidential elections. These learning activities will help students experience citizenship responsibilities related to elections and voting at an early age.

Each of these teaching strategies provides excellent examples of instructional activities that help young learners gain valuable information about our fundamental rights and responsibilities as citizens. Each encourages students to use their personal, political power within our democratic tradition.

# Citizenship Education:
## Its Role in Improving Classroom Behavior

**Jeff Passe**

The nature of citizenship education is misunderstood. It is not boring. It is not flow charts of "How a Bill Becomes a Law." It is not reading a textbook chapter on the "separation of powers."

An essential point of social studies instruction is being missed. Citizenship is not learned by studying flow charts or textbooks; it is learned from our daily interactions! Studying the behavior of other people in other places is not as relevant as the study of ourselves. Teachers of young children have an ideal opportunity to develop citizenship awareness because few arenas provide as much data for citizenship education than the elementary classroom. The constant interaction of rules, authority, groups, individuals, and circumstance creates an endless resource for learning about group behavior.

Another misconception concerning citizenship education is the emphasis on the future. Much of the content included in the citizenship portion of the elementary curriculum attempts to prepare children to be active citizens once they reach voting age. Yet, John Dewey (1963) reminded us many years ago that learning is a present-oriented endeavor. Children are active citizens in a number of groups—family, classroom, neighborhood friends, athletic teams, etc. As important as voting is, children do not have to wait for adulthood to practice the skills of citizenship. Developing and enforcing rules, resolving conflicts, and carrying out the goals of a group are important skills at any age. Citizenship education could provide immediate benefits, not just future ones.

A problem in the teaching of citizenship concerns the use of fear tactics in promoting classroom behavior. Anyone who has visited a typical elementary classroom recently has probably noticed large signs listing rules and punishments for violating those rules. This emphasis is partially a result of Canter's Assertive Discipline (1976) which promotes teacher authority as a central tenet of behavior management.

For many teachers, some aspects of the assertive discipline approach have helped to systematize their approach to classroom citizenship. By providing specific standards and punishments, their students are better able to conform to teacher expectations. Unfortunately, the use of fear as a motivator tends to be ineffective (Bandura 1969). It only works temporarily; it seldom carries over to other

Reprinted from *Social Studies and the Young Learner*, September/October 1988, Volume 1, Number 1. Copyright 1988 by National Council for the Social Studies.

situations; it is harmful to children's psyches; and, it harms the learning process. Think of the handful of students in every classroom who shudder at the thought of breaking a rule. Those children are victims of the traditional approach to classroom citizenship. Then there are the students who do not respond to the fear tactics, the ones who are always misbehaving. They, too are victims because the discipline methods are not helping them learn.

Instead of scaring children, we can develop an understanding of the rights and responsibilities of citizenship. For when students understand rules, they are likely to follow them (Good & Brophy, 1987). Not because they are afraid of the teacher and the consequences, but because the rules make sense, because they value the security that comes from a cooperative atmosphere, and because they feel a sense of responsibility for the success of the group.

Too often, when students violate standards of behavior, it is because they do not recognize the need for the rule. This is especially common in the early grades. Some of our youngest students have never been taught about the need for such rules as being quiet in the hallways or not calling out. The effects of those misbehaviors had never occurred to them. The cure is simple: We must teach them about behavior. We must teach them how the world works. That is basic citizenship education. It is the primary emphasis of social studies education.

## STRATEGIES TO CONNECT SOCIAL STUDIES AND CLASSROOM BEHAVIOR

The connection between social studies and content and classroom behavior can be achieved in a variety of ways. One approach is to teach the appropriate concepts for each grade level, but then relate them to classroom issues. For instance, in a third-grade social studies classroom, teachers would normally teach lessons on community law enforcement. Those concepts could then be related to events at school. The teacher could initiate discussion of classroom rule enforcement. The children might identify how better enforcement of certain rules could improve the atmosphere for learning. By making that connection, social studies instruction is reinforced as classroom problems are attacked.

A second approach is to identify problems and then relate them to the social studies curriculum. For instance, students frequently argue over who gets to use the swings or other playground equipment. Teachers can use those arguments to introduce the concept of scarcity and the need to develop systems for sharing valuable resources.

Then, in social studies, students can analyze similar problems in their areas of study. First graders can discuss how families control access to the television set. Fourth graders may look at the allocation of state highway funds. Sixth graders can study the distribution of oil resources around the world. Relating the school problem to social studies allows the students to place their quarrels in perspective. Doing so may decrease tensions. It may also promote social studies learning.

## OTHER SOCIAL STUDIES CONCEPTS RELATED TO CLASSROOM SITUATIONS

*Multiple Causation*. When classroom problems occur, children and teachers are often quick to blame someone or something. Identifying a simple cause or culprit is appealing because problems are then easily settled. Yet, by doing so, we tend to overlook other contributing causes, some of which may be more influential than our first choice of blame. The same is true in historical analyses, such as the causes of the Civil War or the reasons why a shopping mall is located where it is. Instruction in the concept of multiple causation can enable students to look beyond simple explanations and develop a more mature perspective, whether it is applied to history or classroom events.

*Interdependence and Responsibility*. An anathema for teachers is the child who constantly calls out answers, thus decreasing participation opportunities for other members of the class. Instead of punishing the child, it may be more effective to discuss the concepts of interdependence and responsibility. Children are often unaware of how their behavior affects others. If we show how students depend on each other to follow classroom rules, call-outs may be decreased. This concept can be applied to other classroom problems in which the group is hurt by the behavior of individuals. Then, the children can be shown examples of interdependence and responsibility in our society, such as family chores, traffic laws, and tax collection.

*Justice*. The issue of tattling is a tough one for teachers. They are annoyed by reports of minor misbehavior but need to know about serious problems. How does one eliminate the former without discouraging the latter? It may help to teach children about the allocation of justice. Young children have an intense need to see justice done, with little regard for the seriousness of a crime (Damon, 1983). They believe so strongly in rules that, in their egocentrism, they assume the teacher shares their values. Teachers must give students guidelines in the allocation of justice. They must differentiate between minor and major problems, just as our society must. As children learn that not all rules are enforced with equal fervor, whether in the classroom or the government, they can modify their insistence on the allocation of justice in all circumstances.

*Power*. Children who refuse to obey or who talk back are often amazed at the fury in the teacher's response. The issue is power. Teachers have it and some students are willing to struggle for it. Those incidents may be avoided with calm explanations of the powers that are given to teachers in managing their classrooms. Rather than raise one's voice in a display of power (which can frighten even innocent children to the point of nightmares!), a teacher can remind students of the class rules and the teacher's role in enforcing them. Then the students can be shown how power works in other situations, for the parent or the policemen or the Supreme Court.

*Laws*. Fist fighting is a common occurrence in elementary schools. When teachers break them up, children are quick to explain their actions by citing parental advice to "hit back" when someone hits them. It is helpful in these situations to discuss laws concerning assault. In our society, citizens can have the police intervene if assaulted. Successful prosecution can result in financial damages being paid to the victim. Fighting back may only tend to confuse the case. It may be unclear to the authorities who assaulted whom. If the teacher can serve as an officer of the law and zealously prosecute the one who hit first, students would be more likely to refrain from fighting. Students would not only learn about the law, but they would be safer in the school environment.

*History*. When teachers are forced to break up a fight, they usually ask about immediate causes. They might be better off investigating the history of the relationship between the combatants. Just as in local, national, and world problems, there are circumstances that occurred in the past that contributed to the present situation. Teachers often discover that student quarrels have their origins at the bus stop, in the neighborhood, or from previous antagonisms between other family members. If students are taught to consider the historical antecedents of problems that they confront, they may be able to solve them more effectively. They can relate that awareness to our societal problems too.

*Tolerance*. Children are capable of ugly behavior. They may tease a handicapped child or ridicule someone with unpopular religious beliefs. In their efforts to put a stop to cruelty, teachers are apt to severely punish the guilty parties. It may be more effective to introduce the concept of tolerance, especially as it relates to our national heritage. By reminding the students of the broad range of cultures in America and our forefathers' insistence on the freedom to be different, the children may learn to value and respect the differences among us. It may be appropriate to discuss the horrors of persecution, be it of Christians in Rome, blacks in South Africa, or Jews in Nazi Germany. It is never too early to learn of the dangers of intolerance.

*Cooperation*. Classrooms cannot be managed without the cooperation of the students. When students are willing to work with the teacher in achieving classroom goals, they are likely to be met. A first step in gaining cooperation is convincing the students of the need for it. For instance, teachers must make it clear to the students that special activities like games, skits, and art projects are dependent on the students' behavior. When they can demonstrate their willingness to cooperate by such behaviors as following rules and cleaning up materials, the students get to do more enjoyable activities. By the same token, if the students fail to cooperate, the activity should be suspended. Most children will gladly assist the teacher under those terms. Their cooperation can be likened to other examples of cooperation such as family members organizing an outing, community members maintaining recreational areas, and soldiers preparing for battle.

*Conflict Resolution.* In the interests of peace and harmony, teachers prefer to avoid conflict. Yet, whenever children congregate, quarrels are likely to occur. Rather than view conflict as an unfortunate circumstance, we may view it as an opportunity to teach about conflict resolution. Children have a great interest in how disagreements are settled. We can show them how mediators are used in labor disputes, how judges settle arguments and how compromises are made when purchasing a car. The arbitrator role that the teacher is often called on to play can be contrasted with those strategies. The students may develop alternatives to fist fighting and tattling by learning about conflict resolution in our everyday world.

## SUMMARY

For many years, elementary teachers and students have indicated their dislike for social studies (Goodlad, 1984). Ironically, two frequently cited reasons for the subject's unpopularity are a lack of relevance and little time in the school day. If teachers can form a relationship between classroom behavior problems and the social studies curriculum, the relevance of the content will become apparent. By doing so, they may find a decrease in the amount of time spent on disciplinary matters. That would provide additional time in the school day for the teaching of citizenship education, which may be the most relevant topic in the elementary school.

## REFERENCES

Bandura, A. (1969) *Principles of Behavior Modification*. New York: Holt, Rinehart & Winston.

Canter, L. (1976) *Assertive Discipline*.

Damon, W. (1983) *Social and Personality Development*. Toronto: W.W. Norton & Co.

Dewey, J. (1963) *Experience and Education*. New York: Collier.

Good, T. L. & Brophy, J. E. (1987) *Looking in Classrooms*. New York: Harper & Row.

Goodlad, J. (1984) *A Place Called School*. New York: McGraw-Hill.

Jeff Passe is an Assistant Professor at the University of North Carolina at Charlotte. As a member of the faculty of Curriculum and Instruction in the College of Education, Dr. Passe teaches courses in social studies methods. He taught elementary school for five years before earning a doctorate at the University of Florida. [1988 note]

**Charlotte C. Anderson**

*"Freedom of expression is the well-spring of our civilization..."*

                    *Justice Felix Frankfurter, 1951.*

Justice Frankfurter's potent analogy characterizing freedom of speech as the well-spring of our civilization—our democracy—is a good place to begin in teaching the First Amendment. Webster defines well-spring as "a source of continual supply," as a "fountainhead...a source of a stream, a principle source." If free speech/ freedom of expression is the well-spring, the First Amendment seeks nothing less than to guarantee that this vital well-spring keeps flowing—that our democracy receives the essential life-sustaining nourishment that flows from that well-spring. To put it simply, with free speech democracy grows. Without free speech democracy dies. (Children who live in arid areas where irrigation water is so evidently the life-source of the plants in the fields will find this analogy especially meaningful.)

Free speech as a democratic principle is, of course, not the mere uttering of sounds into the air. Rather, the principle of free speech is wrapped in a full complement of values, meanings, and legislative and judicial processes that have emerged over time and been incorporated into our institutions and our collective civic conscience as citizens of this particular democratic society, the United States of America. Free speech is the fundamental right of each and every citizen as well as our individual and collective responsibility. It is up to us to both nourish ourselves from the well-spring and to keep the well-spring flowing.

Free speech is central to democracy, and it is multidimensional. The centrality and complexity of the principle of free speech compels schools of a democratic society to give it a fundamental place in citizenship education. This means starting this educational focus early and continuing it throughout the school years.

Teachers of young children have a special responsibility to provide children with foundational understandings and underlying competencies and commitments related to the principle of free speech. In carrying out such instruction, teachers may seldom use the words "the First Amendment" or "freedom of speech" while they are, nevertheless, preparing children to be stewards of this critical right and responsibility as democratic citizens. While the specifics of this educational base will shift according

Reprinted from *Social Studies and the Young Learner*, September/October 1991, Volume 4, Number 1. Copyright 1991 by National Council for the Social Studies.

to the children one teaches and the context in which they are taught, certain guideposts will keep this critical instructional responsibility on course. The following discussion highlights a few key guide posts.

## WHAT TEACHERS SHOULD BE AWARE OF IN TEACHING RELATED TO FREEDOM OF SPEECH.

Quality instruction relating to freedom of speech rests on the development of underlying competencies that promote the exercise of and commitment to free speech. There are certain competencies that facilitate children's capacities to understand, to consider and to act in the interest of others—all of which are critical to reciprocal free speech. Among these are the development of perspective consciousness, decreasing egocentrism and ethnocentrism, avoidance of stereotypic perceptions, and intercultural communication skills. Each of these competencies is a complex mix of knowledge, skills, and affective orientations. Age and developmental level must, of course, be taken into consideration in approaching instruction related to each of these tasks. However, as Vygotsky's zone of proximal development theory informs us, instruction must not wait upon development but, rather, we must engage children in tasks that challenge and stretch them. As Vygotsky (1978) observes, "children grow into the intellectual life of those around them."

Of the competencies listed here, perspective consciousness is the most fundamental, undergirding each of the others. Perspective consciousness, according to Hanvey, is "the recognition or awareness on the part of the individual that he or she has a view of the world that is not universally shared, that this view of the world has been and continues to be shaped by influences that often escape conscious detection, and that others have views of the world that are profoundly different from one's own." Our perspective shapes our values and our actions and, thus, can have a profound impact on how we relate to others. While it is essential that children become conscious of perspective, teachers will undoubtedly want to move beyond developing consciousness to developing the capacity to project oneself into alternative perspectives. Children need to be able to imagine themselves in the other's position and "experience" the world from that perspective. Hanvey cautions that perspective consciousness is very difficult to achieve and must be distinguished from opinion which "is the surface layer, the conscious outcropping of perspective." (The question "What is your perspective on that?" is using perspective as a synonym for opinion.)

Perspective consciousness is a good touchstone for teachers and provides another reason for probing children to tell "What do you see in this picture?" "What did the story tell us about that dog?" Differences in perspective, rather than misreading of cues, may be at the basis of "wrong" answers. Probing for reasons behind responses will help distinguish errors from alternative perspectives. Such probing is especially critical in heterogeneous, culturally diverse classrooms where a broad range of perspectives growing out of alternative heritages and life experiences can be expected.

Intercultural communication skills call into play each of the other competencies—perspective consciousness, decreased egocentric and ethnocentric perspectives, and avoidance of stereotyping—and are essential tools for all children growing up in this nation that is fast becoming a microcosm of the world's people. The maintenance of the well-spring of freedom of expression becomes an ever more complicated task when voices speak from such diverse heritages as those now coming into the polity.

Cultural and gender differences must be considered when exploring and applying free speech issues. While teachers in multicultural classrooms have special opportunities to foster free speech competencies for a pluralistic society, all teachers in this increasingly pluralistic society must be cognizant of the differences in cultural mores surrounding issues of free speech. Complicating the teaching task is gender differences. Instruction that encourages children to critically examine issues, to express their own opinions, and to challenge others—even authority figures—may be in diametric opposition to the values of the homes and cultural heritages of some children. While core American values encourage children to express themselves to and with adults, such is not the case in some of the traditional cultures represented in many of our communities and schools.

Classroom activities that call upon children to vigorously exchange ideas and express alternative opinions are weighted in favor of the aggressively verbal child and may leave others out of the process. Spending time in working on listening and reinforcing/responding skills will sensitize children to differences and to their dual responsibility for self-expression and supporting other's rights to expression. Just imagine the rich democratic discourse that is being incubated in such classrooms! With the changing demographic profile of our population, these early and continuing learning experiences will be critical to the inclusion of all citizens in the maintenance and enhancement of our democratic society.

The principle of free speech will be internalized and actualized to the extent that children have practice in applying the principle and in managing conflict. Children need many and varied opportunities to explore free speech in application and action. When free speech is exercised, especially in a pluralistic society, conflict is inevitable. This means that teaching related to free speech must entail teaching conflict management. Children who are skilled conflict managers will come to free speech situations confident in their own capacities to work through the conflict to achieve mutually supportive, community-sustaining resolutions.

A study conducted with fifth through ninth graders twenty years ago provides insights into the instructional task (Zellman and Sears, 1971). These researchers found that most students mirrored the adult norms of our democratic society and said they "believed in free speech for all, no matter what their views might be." However, when these same students were asked to respond to specific cases where free speech was being exercised they denied the right and retreated to positions of bias—denying free speech to those whom they disliked (in these cases, supporters of communists, Vietcong, and Nazis).

In discussing their results, Zellman and Sears note that "teaching a more sophisticated view of conflict can produce more accepting attitudes toward conflict and greater tolerance for civil liberties. Nevertheless our data show that the main "message" that young children normally get about nonconforming minorities is that they should be repressed . . . They are taught free speech only in slogan form, not how to apply it to concrete situations; and clearly they are not taught any larger view of society that would convey why such extensions must be made" (p. 134). That "larger view" is being conveyed by teachers who address free speech as the well-spring of our civilization!

Good citizenship is taking responsibility for the civic life of the community. Effective exercising of free speech rights and responsibilities are critical elements of citizenship development. Some of the most effective teaching occurring in this area is often not recognized as "teaching" at all. It is teaching by example and through action. Take, as a case in point, the teacher that begins each school year by engaging children in discussing and developing the rules by which they will live out their year together. Or, the school that develops a true representative form of government in which child-focused and child-sized issues—such as the rules of behavior in the cafeteria and the playground—are discussed in each classroom and problems are resolved in the student council. Or, the class that identifies a problem in the community, initiates discussion with adults in the community, and works to find a solution to the problem. Such participatory democratic experiences develop both children's competencies and their expectations for their evolving role as citizens in the larger civic community.

Teachers' must recognize their own ethical and moral responsibilities in developing children's own "voices" and providing them opportunities to express themselves in taking responsible social action. As authoritarian regimes have too often demonstrated, indoctrinating young minds into given thought and value patterns is a relatively simple matter. These extreme cases alert us to the awesome power teachers have and to the potential for slipping into indoctrination while in the pursuit of education. Opinions expressed by teachers often carry considerable weight among their charges. However, repressing such overt expression doesn't mean that the teacher's particular values and opinions won't "color"

## EXAMPLES OF TEACHING AND LEARNING RELATING TO FREE SPEECH

| Teachers would be teaching — | Children would be learning — |
| --- | --- |
| self-esteem and efficacy | "My ideas are important."<br>"People will listen to me if I have sound reason for my ideas and can communicate them effectively." |
| respect for others | "Sharing ideas and cooperatively exploring ideas is an important way to build and maintain a community, a society." |
| criteria for evaluating ideas and speech | "We need to be able to make choices about what ideas to express and when and how to express them." |
| conflict management skills | "Conflict is OK and can be productive when ideas are openly shared." |
| that freedom of speech is a pan-human value and struggle—pointing to such universal documents as the Declaration of Human Rights and the Convention of the Rights of the Child | "Human beings around the world want and have an inherent right to free speech." |
| that free speech, although central to democracy, is a fragile commodity | "Guarding free speech rights is a central civic responsibility of all citizens." |

instruction. They will. Probably the best teachers can do is to strive to develop their own perspective consciousness, expose children to a range of opinions on any issue under examination, help children develop sound criteria based on democratic principles for making choices among such alternatives, and do all this with open access to parents and the community. In other words, let the well-spring flow.

## UNDERSTANDINGS, COMMITMENTS, AND ORIENTATIONS THAT CHILDREN SHOULD DEVELOP RELATING TO FREE SPEECH

Imagine classrooms where successful teaching relating to freedom of speech is occurring. Imagine that those children are able to articulate what they are learning. What would be happening? What would the children be saying/knowing/learning?

## SOME EFFECTIVE INSTRUCTIONAL PRACTICES AND STRATEGIES

Here in very abbreviated form are some suggested instructional practices and strategies.

Effective classroom management strategies include bringing children into the process of classroom rule making, engaging them in discussing alternative resolutions for playground disputes, and providing opportunities for group decision making relating to any of the many class activities pursued throughout the school year.

Potent "generic" instructional strategies that can be used in classroom management processes and throughout the curriculum include the use of decision trees, case studies, role playing, simulations, and debates. A decision tree is a graphic device that compels children to identify several al-

ternatives in solving a problem, note both the negative and positive aspects of each alternative, and make a choice in light of their values. Case studies can be as simple as an incomplete story in which a dilemma occurs or as complex as a restating of a court case. Teachers' and children's daily lives provide fodder for the former. Write your own. They spring from the dilemmas children face when overhearing a child called a bad name or when the lunch money comes up short. What should I/we say? What should I/we do? Role-playing and simulations are, of course, time honored means for helping students try on different roles and experience a situation from different perspectives.

## REFERENCES

Hanvey, R. (no date given) *An Attainable Global Perspective*. The American Forum for Global Education.

Vygotsky, L.S. Edited by Michael Cole, et al. (1978). *Mind in Society: The Development of Higher Psychological Processes*. Cambridge, Massachusetts: Harvard University Press.

Zellman, G. L., & Sears, D.O. (1971). "Childhood Origins of Tolerance for Dissent." *Journal of Social Issues*, Vol. 27, No. 2, 109-136.

Charlotte C. Anderson is President of Education for Global Involvement, Inc., and a Research Associate with the Chicago Teacher's Center, College of Education, Northeastern Illinois University. Dr. Anderson has published and worked extensively in law-related social studies. She is coeditor, with Linda Falkenstein, of *Daring to Dream: Law and Humanities for Elementary Schools*, published in 1980 by the American Bar Association, and is President-Elect of NCSS. [1991 note]

## Law in a Free Society

The purpose of government as stated in the Declaration of Independence is the protection of the individual's right to life, liberty, and property. The Constitution of the United States protects property by limiting government. But what should happen when one individual's reckless use of private property endangers the life, liberty, or property interests of others in the community?

In this lesson young children focus upon the question of what should be the scope and limits of ownership. Students begin by reading a story about a boy who owns a brand new bike and then discuss whether owning something gives the person the right to use that property any way he or she wishes. They discuss some of the rights they think should accompany ownership of a bicycle, and what responsibilities, if any, the owner of a bicycle should have. Students then gather information on rules and laws within their own community which help determine the scope and limits of ownership. Students work in small groups to develop policies regarding the scope and limits of the use of property. The class then meets as a whole to discuss the policies developed by each group.

## PROCEDURES

Begin the lesson by reading the following hypothetical story to students. After they have listened to the story, discuss its content in terms of the questions that follow.

*George's New Bike*

George had a brand new bike. Did he feel great! This was HIS bike. He could do anything he wanted with it. Now he wouldn't have to borrow his sister's bike anymore. He wouldn't have to listen to her saying, "Take care of my bike!" "Don't go over curbs or you'll ruin the tires!" "Get off, you've ridden long enough!"

George pedaled down the street. He practiced going up and down curbs for a while. Then he tried a few wheelies. Next he worked on his hand signals—signal for right turn . . . signal for left turn. Things were getting dull. Just then he saw a group of children crossing at the corner. "Hah, I think I'll give 'em a scare," he thought. Straight toward the children he rode—faster and faster. "Better get out of the way," he yelled, "cause I'm coming through!" The children ran in all directions.

"George, you can't just ride at people and scare them half to death!" yelled one of the boys who had just reached the curb.

"It's my bike so I can ride it anywhere I want. You should've stayed out of my way!" George answered.

George rode on—past the corner and into the intersection. A woman driving a car slammed on her brakes and came to a screeching halt.

"Young man," she called, "that's a very good way to get hurt. Don't you know any better than to ride right into an intersection?"

George was a little frightened. After all, he had almost gotten hit by a car. Even so, he gathered up his courage and said, "You can't tell me what to do. It's my bike and I can ride it any way and anywhere I want to."

The woman shook her head and drove off. George looked around. It was getting dark. Time to start for home. George decided to ride on the sidewalk since he didn't have a light on his bike. Just then he saw his next-door neighbors, Jerry and Lisa. "Hey, want a ride?" George called.

"Sure," they both answered.

Lisa climbed on the handlebars and Jerry sat behind George. Off they went, laughing and singing. As they rounded the last corner on the way home, they saw an old woman with a shopping cart in their path.

"Look out!" shouted Lisa and Jerry. But it was too late.

The bicycle missed the woman but it hit the shopping cart. Cartons of milk and cans of vegetables flew every which way. The three children hopped off the bike to pick up the cart and reload the groceries.

"Don't you children know any better than to ride three on a bicycle in the dark on the sidewalk?"

George muttered to himself, "Who do you think you are to tell me what to do with my own bike? If I want to ride three people, I will. And if I want to ride it on the sidewalk, that's my business. You don't own the sidewalk."

"What did you say, young man?" asked the old woman sharply.

"Nothin'," George said quietly.

"You go on home now, do you hear, or I'm going to speak to your parents," the old woman said.

The three children walked the rest of the way to their homes. George said goodbye to Lisa and Jerry and leaned his bike on the lawn up against his house.

"Better put that new bike in the garage, Georgie," teased his sister who was standing on the porch. "It's going to get wet and all rusted if you leave it outside."

Reprinted with permission from the Center for Civic Education, from *Update on Law-Related Education*, Spring 1987, Volume 11, Number 2. Adapted from materials developed by the Center for Civic Education/Law in a Free Society. Copyright 1987 by the Center for Civic Education.

"So what!" shouted George. "It's my bike. I'll put it wherever I please. If it gets wet and rusty that's my business."

## DISCUSSION QUESTIONS

1. What are some of the ways George used his bicycle in the story?
2. Which of these do you think are ways George should be allowed to use his bicycle? Can you explain why?
3. Do you think there are any ways in which George should not be allowed to use his bicycle? Can you explain why?
4. What are some rights you think the owner of a bicycle should have?
5. Are there responsibilities you think the owner of a bicycle should have? If so, what are they?

## GATHERING INFORMATION

At this point, students might be asked to suggest ways of gathering information on rules and laws within their own community which help determine the scope and limits of ownership in regard to the use of bicycles. For example, students might want to invite to the classroom:

1. A police officer or other city official to discuss community laws dealing with the ownership and use of bicycles.
2. A school administrator or member of the school safety patrol to discuss school rules and regulations covering the use of bicycles owned by students.
3. Representatives of different families to discuss rules they have made to cover the use of bicycles by family members.

After students have gathered data related to the rights and responsibilities of ownership and use of bicycles, they might discuss what they have learned in terms of the following questions:

1. If George lived in your community, what laws would affect the ways he might use his bicycle? Why do you think your community has these laws? Do you think these laws should be followed? Why? Are there any laws you would add? Change? Remove? Why?
2. If George went to your school, what rules would he have to follow if he wanted to use his bicycle? Why do you think your school has these rules? Do you think these rules should be followed? Why? Are there any rules you would add? Change? Remove? Why?
3. If George were your brother, what rules would he have to follow if he wanted to use his bicycle? Why do you think your family has these rules? Do you think these rules should be followed? Why? Are there any rules you would add? Change? Remove? Why?

## DECIDING WHAT TO DO

Next, the class should make a list of its policies for determining the scope and limits of bicycle use. In so doing, students should take into account the additions, deletions and changes made in response to the three questions above as well as any further suggestions they may have. When the policies have been completed, students might attempt to apply them to George's case. For example, students might role-play a situation in which a parent, teacher, or police officer explains bicycle-use policies to George. Students might then discuss the following questions:

1. Should these policies be applied to the use of bicycles by all owners?
2. Should age be a factor in determining which policies should apply?
3. Are there other factors which might be taken into account?

As a final activity, divide the class into small groups of five to eight students each to develop policies regarding the scope and limits of the use of property other than bicycles. For example, all students who own pets might form one group, students who own books another, students who own a particular toy another group. Each group will then discuss the rights and responsibilities of ownership of the particular example of property and the scope and limits of use which should attend such ownership. After each group has finished, the class might meet as a whole to discuss the policies developed by each group. For more advanced and upper elementary children, it is suggested you use portions of the Constitution (Article I, Section 9; and Amendments 3, 4, and 5) to investigate how the individual's right to property can be regulated and protected.

**Jennifer Bloom**

Mock trials conducted within one or two class periods help students learn about courts and trials in an interesting and enjoyable way. Although students obviously will not be as polished as they are in more lengthy mock trial programs, their abilities to quickly become familiar with trial process, to learn their roles, and to discuss rules of evidence and constitutional protections will surprise even the most seasoned observer.

In addition to the value of the learning experience for students, mini mock trials are an excellent activity for lawyers who want a "guaranteed" success. With only little advance preparation, a lawyer can guide the students through the mock trial experience, helping them develop appropriate questions and then serving as the judge for the trial. Most lawyers are so comfortable with this activity, and find the positive student response so rewarding, that they are usually willing to schedule return engagements.

Use the procedure in this lesson with the situation included in this article, or use it with a more complex situation for older students.

The time needed for conducting a trial is only 1-½ to 2 hours. (If time is short, omit or greatly shorten the discussion in the next section.)

## BEGINNING

Begin the class session by discussing trials. Because most students have seen television programs such as "People's Court" and "Divorce Court," they already have some basic information. Ask them if they watch these programs. Then ask them to list the people who are present in the courtroom. This list will include:

- lawyers
- judge
- jurors
- bailiff
- police officers
- clerk
- witnesses
- defendant
- plaintiff
- court reporter
- public
- sketch artist

Discuss what these people do in the courtroom. Depending upon the sophistication of the audience and the time available, short discussions of the following topics can be conducted: trial by judge or jury; civil v. criminal trials; the need for a court reporter and court record; the constitutional right to a public trial; the controversy surrounding cameras in the courtroom; the reason for courtroom decorum.

## PREPARING

Read the one paragraph summary of the facts of the case with the students (see below). Ask the students to volunteer for the parts in the mock trial. Four students should be assigned to be the lawyers for each side of the case. One student may present the opening statement, one the direct examination, one the cross examination, and the other the closing argument. Reserve discussion of objections for later.

Students are also assigned to roleplay the witnesses, bailiff, court reporter, media representatives and sketch artists (these students can write articles and prepare drawings for the articles), and members of the jury and audience.

Before the start of actual trial preparation, briefly describe the steps of a trial. Remind students that they will be helped through the process by the judge and that confusion at this point is expected. If students have sufficient background and understanding of the trial process, explain the reasons and grounds for objections. (I recommend using only a limited number of objections.) If they lack knowledge, reserve discussion of objections until one occurs during the trial. (No matter what age the students are, one will object to a question during the trial. The objection might be made in the form of "She can't do that, can she?" or "This isn't fair!" Regardless of the language used, the students usually have made the objections at appropriate times. They are now ready to learn about objections.)

## ROLE-PLAYING

Students are given approximately 15 minutes to review their statements and develop questions and opening and closing statements. Although this is a short period of time, the facts of the cases are simple and a longer period of time would result in a restless jury and audience. Quickly review the parts with the other "actors."

*Begin the trial.* The trial will take 45 minutes to 1 hour. Remember the goal of this activity is to increase the students' knowledge of courts and trials. Do not expect them to sound like experienced trial lawyers. You will enjoy watching them develop their questions and arguments on

---

objections and listen to the answers with great care.

*Instruct the jury at the end of the trial.* Juries usually require only a few minutes to reach a verdict. After they have announced the verdict, ask them to explain how they decided on it.

*Debrief the trial.* Encourage all students to participate in the discussion of the trial. Questions that facilitate discussion include: Who was the most important person? Could the trial take place without the judge? (Yes, another judge could be used.) Without the lawyers? (Yes, other lawyers could be used.) Without the witnesses? (No.) Did any of the students change their minds during the trial? When and why? Who was the most believable witness? Why? Are there other ways that the problem could have been settled? What would have been the advantages or disadvantages?

Complete the activity with a short discussion of the need for citizens to participate in the process. Ask them what they will remember to do if they witness an action or are asked to serve on a jury.

## OBJECTIONS

Either the prosecutor or the defense counsel may object to a question or the admission of an exhibit. The judge will usually ask the person objecting "on what rule of evidence are you relying?" Then the judge either allows the objection, preventing the evidence from being introduced, or overrules the objection, allowing the question or exhibit to be admitted as evidence.

Reasons for objections (also known as grounds for objections or the rule of evidence being relied upon) include:

1. *Leading question.* Prosecutors must allow their witnesses to tell their own story; they must not lead their witnesses through the story. Defense attorneys must follow the same rule when questioning their witnesses.
2. *Hearsay.* The questions must limit witnesses to facts they know from personal knowledge. Other information they have is hearsay evidence.
3. *Immaterial and irrelevant.* The information is not closely related to the case, and is therefore not important.
4. *Opinions and conclusions.* Unless the witness is an expert, he or she should not give opinions or conclusions.
5. *Nonresponsive answer.* The witness is not answering the question asked.

These are only a few objections. They are probably the most common ones used. They will adequately serve your needs.

## MOCK TRIAL PROCEDURES

*Participants*
- Judge
- Prosecution (in criminal cases), or plaintiff's attorney (in civil cases)
- Defense attorney
- Witnesses for prosecution or plaintiff's attorney
- Witnesses for defendant
- Bailiff
- Jury

*Opening of Trial.* Bailiff enters and says: "Please rise. The Court of ____ is now in session, the Honorable ____ presiding." Everyone remains standing until judge is seated. The judge asks that the calendar be called and the bailiff says, "Your honor, today's case is ____ v. ____." Judge asks if both attorneys are ready.

## TRIAL

*Opening statement:* prosecution or plaintiff's attorney introduces himself or herself and states what their side hopes to prove. State what facts on your side will show and ask for the verdict that you want.

Defendant's attorney then introduces herself or himself and explains the evidence on her or his side that will deny what the prosecution is attempting to prove. State the decision you hope the jury will reach.

*Direct examination:* prosecution calls its first witness.

Witnesses should have reviewed their statements. Witnesses may testify to additional facts that logically follow from their statements but should not contradict the given facts. Prosecutor asks clear and simple questions that allow the witness to tell his or her side of the story in his or her own words.

*Cross examination:* defense attorney questions witnesses for the prosecution to try to discredit their testimony. Ask leading questions and emphasize portions of testimony that favor your side.

After all of the prosecution witnesses have been questioned and cross-examined, the defense calls its witnesses and questions them under direct examination. Then the prosecutor cross examines.

*Closing statement:* prosecutor speaks to the jury and tries to convince them that the evidence presented during the trial has proved his or her side of the case. Then the defense attorney does the same.

*Jury instructions:* judge instructs the jury as to the law that applies to the case and then directs them to retire and decide upon a verdict.

*End of trial:* jury deliberates and reaches a verdict. They report the verdict to the judge after returning to the courtroom.

## SAMPLE TRIAL CASE

Here is the fact pattern for a mock trial that works well with elementary youngsters.

*Facts:* Tony and several of his friends were riding their bikes around the neighborhood on Friday, March 15, 1985. At about 6:00 p.m. a few kids from a different neighborhood rode by Tony and his friends. They teased Tony and his friends and dared them to throw stones at Mr. Wiley's windows. Mr. Wiley is an old man who often tells the children to stay off his property. Several windows were broken, and when Mr. Wiley ran out of his house to stop the children, he recognized Tony. The State has now charged Tony with the crime of vandalism.

*Issue:* Did Tony throw the stones that broke Mr. Wiley's windows?

*Witnesses:* For the prosecution, Mr. Wiley, Leslie the paper carrier; for the defense, Tony, Sandy.

*Witness Statements*

Mr. Wiley: I have lived in this neighborhood for 47 years. My wife and I built our little house when we were married. My wife died five years ago. Since then, I have been a victim of many attacks of vandalism. On Friday evening, March 15, 1985, I was watching the 6:00 p.m. news when I heard glass breaking in my front porch. I ran out my back door and around the house to see what was going on. I saw lots of kids. I recognized Tony because he lives down the block and often rides his bike past my house. It was clear to me that this group of kids was responsible for breaking my windows. In fact, Tony had a rock in his hand and was getting ready to throw it.

Leslie, the Paper Carrier: I have delivered newspapers in Mr. Wiley's neighborhood for three years. On Friday, March 15, 1985. I was delivering a newspaper to Ms. Crowley who lives three houses away from Mr. Wiley when I heard kids screaming and then I heard breaking glass. I ran over to Mr. Wiley's house. I saw about 10 children on the front yard. Tony and another kid were pushing each other. It looked to me like the other kid was trying to stop Tony from throwing a stone. I did not see anyone throw stones.

Sandy: Tony and I were out riding our bikes with some other friends on Friday. March 15, 1985. We were riding up and down Tony's block when a bunch of kids we didn't know rode up to us and started teasing. They dared us to throw stones at grouchy old Mr. Wiley's windows. We tried to ignore them. They threw a stone and hit a front porch window. Then they threw some more stones. I think a couple of windows were broken. Tony and I and our friends stood and watched. When one of the other kids picked up a stone to throw, Tony tried to stop him. Then Mr. Wiley came around the house. The other kids said they didn't throw the stones, they said that Tony did. I think they were mad at Tony because he tried to stop them. Tony is a real nice friend, he wouldn't try to break Mr. Wiley's windows.

Tony: I was riding bikes with my friends on Friday, March 15, 1985. It was almost getting dark when a bunch of kids we didn't know rode up to us and started bugging us. They wanted us to throw rocks with them. They were going to try to break some of Mr. Wiley's front porch windows. Even though I don't like Mr. Wiley very much, we said we wouldn't do that. I saw one kid standing next to me pick up a rock. I tried to take it out of his hand so he wouldn't throw it. That's when Mr. Wiley came around the corner. Leslie the newspaper carrier also showed up. I did not throw any stones.

*Instructions.* The prosecution must set out such a convincing case against the defendant that the jury believes "beyond a reasonable doubt" that the defendant is guilty.

*Sub-issues*

1. Was it too dark to see clearly?
2. Was Tony throwing stones or stopping someone else from throwing stones?
3. Was Mr. Wiley "out to get Tony" because he rides his bike around his house?
4. Did Tony dislike Mr. Wiley enough to break his windows; was there motive?
5. Which witnesses should be believed?

## CONCEPTS

1. Circumstantial evidence vs. direct proof,
2. Credibility of witnesses,
3. Burden of proof: beyond a reasonable doubt.

## LAW

Whoever intentionally causes damage to physical property of another without his or her consent is guilty of a misdemeanor and will be sentenced to imprisonment for not more than 90 days or payment of a fine of not more than $500 or both.

Jennifer Bloom is a lawyer and Director of the Minnesota Center for Community Legal Education at Hamline University School of Law in St. Paul, Minnesota. [1986 note]

# The State vs. the Big Bad Wolf
## A Study of the Justice System in the Elementary School

**Judith Norton**

When I returned to the classroom after practicing law for several years, I was eager to try to share with my fifth-grade students a glimpse of the "real world" of courts and the justice system. As I remembered my own childhood experiences in school with topics such as law and government, I realized that my challenge would be to spark interest in the judicial process.

I therefore went about designing a curriculum in which there would be a high level of student participation through role playing and dramatization of the trial experience along with the use of outside resources in the real-life legal community. The main objectives of the program were to (1) focus student interest on and provide an understanding of the justice system and due process; and (2) provide a challenging format to encourage students to use critical thinking and problem-solving skills.

To accomplish my goals, I revised the popular fairytale "Little Red Riding Hood" to present the facts of a criminal case in which the defendant wolf is accused of several crimes. The students then carefully analyzed the case and took on the roles of lawyers, witnesses, judges, jurors, and defendants, and the classroom became a courtroom. The justice system concepts presented through the mock trial experience were integrated into all themes and subject areas throughout the curriculum.

## THE FACTS OF THE CASE

On her way to grandmother's house Little Red Riding Hood is stopped by the wolf who finds out where she is going. The wolf convinces her to pick flowers and hurries ahead to Granny's cottage. The wolf tricks Granny by impersonating Little Red Riding Hood and is welcomed inside. After beating Granny, the wolf locks her in the closet and then takes one of Granny's nightgowns out of her drawer, puts it on, and jumps in bed. When Little Red Riding Hood arrives, the door to the cottage is open. She enters and goes into the bedroom to see Granny. After a short conversation, Little Red Riding Hood discovers that it is the wolf in Granny's bed. The wolf threatens to eat Little Red Riding Hood, but she runs out of the cottage and all the way home. Little Red Riding Hood calls the police. The police officers chase a suspicious acting wolf through the forest near Granny's cottage. After punching one of the officers, the wolf is arrested. A body search

Reprinted from *Social Studies and the Young Learner*, September/October 1992, Volume 5, Number 1. Copyright 1992 by National Council for the Social Studies.

reveals that in the wolf's gown pocket is some marijuana. Before questioning the wolf, the officers read the wolf the Miranda rights (i.e., right to remain silent, etc.). The wolf elects not to answer any questions before talking to an attorney.

## ANALYZING THE FACTS OF THE CASE

The case is introduced by asking the students what they remember about the story "Little Red Riding Hood." After several versions of the story have been discussed, the teacher explains that they are about to hear another version of the story, different from any version they have heard before. The student's purpose in listening to "The Case of Little Red Riding Hood" is to determine what crimes have been committed.

After the story is read, the students summarize the events and the case is carefully analyzed. First the perpetrator and victims are identified and the students discuss and list the crimes committed. The students are then asked which laws they think were violated.

## CHARGING THE DEFENDANT

The teacher distributes the Criminal Code which sets forth the elements of these crimes: assault, battery, felonious restraint, resisting arrest, disorderly conduct, possession of marijuana and theft. The elements of each crime are read and discussed, and the students determine the criminal charges to bring against the wolf.

## THE MOCK TRIAL: THE STATE VS. THE BIG BAD WOLF

In preparing for the trial of the Big Bad Wolf, students can be introduced to the criminal court system through a variety of audio-visual materials as well as classroom visitors who are experts in this area (see Resources).

---

### FIGURE 1
### CRIMINAL CODE

1. **Battery:** Unlawful touching of another person (such as hitting, beating, or pushing).
2. **Assault:** Putting another person in fear of bodily harm.
3. **Theft:** A crime involving stealing.
4. **Possession of marijuana:** Having marijuana on your person or property.
5. **Resisting arrest:** Trying to stop an officer of the law from taking you into custody.
6. **Disorderly conduct:** Failure to obey the orders of an officer of the law.
7. **Felonious restraint:** Knowingly restraining another without the victim's consent.

---

1. All trial participants should treat each other in a professional manner and with respect.

2. The judge controls the court proceedings and should be addressed as "Your Honor."

3. An attorney may object to questions asked by opposing counsel or testimony given by a witness during the trial. When an objection is raised, the judge rules on it. If he or she agrees with the objections, the judge will say "objection sustained" and the question or testimony will not be allowed. If the judge disagrees with the objection, he or she will say "objection overruled," and the question will be allowed.

4. Questioning the witness:
   a. On direct examination, an attorney should not ask questions that lead the witness or put words into the mouth of the witness. In other words, an attorney should not ask his own witness a question that includes a statement of the alleged facts. The witness must state his or her own version of the facts.
   b. On cross examination, an attorney may lead the witness.
   c. An attorney should not ask the witness about irrelevant information (information that has nothing to do with the case).
   d. An attorney should not ask a witness a question that was previously asked and answered.

5. A witness should not testify about what someone else said, heard, or saw. This is called hearsay, and is usually not admissible. The witness should testify only about his or her own first-hand knowledge of facts related to the case.

6. All exhibits must be put into evidence by witnesses who identify the items and have personal knowledge that the item is what it is supposed to be. (This rule applies to all documents, records, and physical evidence.)

7. An expert witness must be qualified as an expert by stating his education, training, and experience in his or her field of expertise.

---

Before the trial begins, the students should have a clear understanding of the duties and responsibilities of each of the participants in the trial.

## BACKGROUND INFORMATION

In a criminal case, the defendant is accused of breaking the law. The prosecutor represents the state in bringing charges against the defendant. The formal charges are sometimes brought by an indictment from a grand jury or by information presented by the prosecutor. The indictment or information specifies the charges against the defendant.

All defendants are entitled to a trial by a jury panel of citizens in criminal cases involving possible incarceration. Sometimes, however, a defendant chooses to waive his or her right to a trial by jury. If the defendant waives the right to a jury trial, then the facts and the law of the case will be decided by a judge.

In the case of Little Red Riding Hood, the criminal charges brought against the wolf may be misdemeanors (less serious crimes) or felonies (more serious crimes) depending upon the jurisdiction. The defendant can elect to be tried by a judge or jury.

All defendants are entitled to be represented by an attorney. If they cannot afford one, the court will appoint an attorney to handle the case. The defendant is presumed innocent unless proven otherwise. The defense attorney prepares for trial by getting as much information as possible from his or her client and determining which witnesses are needed at the trial. The defense attorney wants to present the best possible case for the defendant.

Witnesses with personal knowledge of the facts in the case can be called to testify for either side. In addition, alibi witnesses may be called to explain the whereabouts of the defendant at the time of the alleged crimes, and character witnesses can testify about the defendant's prior experiences that exhibit his good character. Expert witnesses may be called by either side to give the court information of a technical nature such as fingerprint analysis, bloodstain analysis, and medical or psychiatric evaluation of the defendant or the victims.

In cases without juries, the judge listens carefully to both sides of the case, rules on any objections raised by the attorneys, maintains order in the courtroom, and makes a final decision in the case. If there is a jury, the judge instructs the jury on the law in the case and the jury renders a verdict based on the evidence.

The Court Clerk calls the court to order, announces the case, and swears in the witnesses. In addition, the clerk assists the judge in marking the evidence (exhibits), passing the exhibits back and forth between the judge and the attorneys, and sometimes passing physical evidence to jurors.

## PREPARING FOR TRIAL

After the teacher reviews the roles and responsibilities of each of the trial participants, the students select their roles. Depending on the size of the class, there may be more than one trial.

The Defense Team consists of two or three defense attorneys, the defendant (Big Bad Wolf), and three or four additional witnesses—including an alibi witness, a character witness, and an expert witness.

The State's (Prosecution) Team consists of two or three State's attorneys, Little Red Riding Hood, Granny, a police officer, and one or two expert witnesses.

Each of the two trial teams prepares a case. The attorneys interview the witnesses to obtain their versions of the story. These witness statements are like depositions. Each team can decide which witnesses it wants to use, but it is important to make certain that the facts in the case presented by the teacher are not contradicted by the witnesses' stories. The teams also decide what physical evidence and documents they want to use. For example, the State's Team may want to bring in the defendant's pawprints or wolf hairs found at the scene of the crime, Granny's nightgown, Granny's medical report, Granny's bloodstains found on the wolf's clothing, and the police report. The Defense Team may want to bring in a report from the defendant's pawprints to try to prove mistaken identity. After each team determines which witnesses it will call at the trial, the other team is notified. Attorneys review the following Rules of Evidence provided by the teacher and prepare questions for their own witnesses as well as the witnesses on the other side.

## THE TRIAL

The court clerk announces the case and opening statements are presented. The State's attorney states his or her theory of the case and what he or she intends to prove. The Defense attorney states how he or she will prove that the defendant is not guilty as charged, emphasizing the presumption of innocence.

The State's case begins with direct examination. During direct examination, the State's attorneys call witnesses to testify and present evidence to try to prove the defendant's guilt beyond a reasonable doubt. On direct examination, the State questions its witnesses. On cross examination, the Defense attorneys question each of the State's witnesses immediately after the State's attorney finishes questioning the particular witness.

The Defense case begins with direct examination and the Defense attorneys call witnesses to testify and present evidence to try to prove the defendant's innocence. On direct examination, the Defense attorneys question their witnesses. On cross examination. The State's attorneys question each of the Defense witnesses immediately after the Defense attorney finishes questioning the particular witness.

In their closing statements, each side summarizes its case. After the judge has heard from both sides, the Court Clerk calls a short recess so the judge can deliberate and give a decision. If there is a jury, the judge will instruct them on the law in the case before sending them to deliberate.

As the judge or jury announces the verdict in the case, reasons for the decision are explained. Each crime that the defendant has been charged with is considered individually. In most cases, the wolf will likely be found guilty of some crimes but not guilty of others and both sides are, to an extent, winners. If jurors cannot reach a unanimous verdict on a charge, then you may have a hung jury.

When the trial is over, students should have an opportunity to critique their work. They discuss both the strengths and weaknesses in the presentation of each side of the case and make suggestions to improve their trial tactics.

## CLASSROOM VISITORS AND FIELD TRIPS

Classroom visitors and field trips greatly enhance the study of the justice system. Lawyers may come into the classroom to consult with teachers and assist students in preparing for trial. Police detectives and FBI agents can provide insight into gathering information to solve crimes. The canine division of the police department might come into the classroom with police dogs and demonstrate the use of animals in solving crimes. Parole and probation officers can talk to students about their roles in dealing with defendants.

---

### FIGURE 3
### SEQUENCE OF EVENTS IN A CRIMINAL MOCK TRIAL

1. Court Clerk announces the case.
2. Opening Statements
   a. Prosecution: The prosecutor explains to the judge or jury, the evidence to be presented as proof of the charges against the defendant.
   b. Defense: The defense attorney explains the evidence to be presented to deny the allegations made by the prosecution.
3. Prosecution's Case
   a. Direct Examination: The prosecutors question witnesses who testify and present evidence to try to prove the defendant's guilt.
   b. Cross Examination: The defense attorneys ask questions of each prosecution witness to try to break down his or her story or discredit the witness.
4. Defense Case
   a. Direct Examination: The defense attorneys question witnesses who testify and present evidence denying the allegations made by the prosecution.
   b. Cross Examination: The prosecutors ask questions of each defense witness to try to break down his or her story or discredit the witness.
5. Closing Statements
   a. Prosecution: The prosecutor summarizes all the evidence presented and states how the evidence has satisfied the elements of the charges.
   b. Defense: The defense attorney summarizes all the evidence presented and asks for a finding of not guilty.
6. Jury Instructions: In jury trials, the judge gives instruction to the jury on what the law is and the evidence to be applied to the law.
7. Decision
   a. Jury Trial: In most states, a unanimous or nearly unanimous decision is required or a hung jury occurs. In a case where there is a hung jury, the case may be tried again with a new jury.
   b. Judge: If the trial is held without a jury the judge has the duty of determining the facts of the case and rendering a judgment.
8. Court Clerk adjourns the court.

---

After students have participated in the mock trial, they can truly appreciate a visit to court. A trip to a trial court hearing cases involving misdemeanors is ideal because it offers students the opportunity to observe a variety of criminal cases in a few hours. In a morning, you would typically see anywhere from six to ten cases, sometimes more. The cases include many of the same types of crimes that the students have become familiar with in the Big Bad Wolf trial. You should schedule the trip in advance and ask to have the class meet court personnel. On one visit, during the court recess, students were able to meet with the judge, attorneys, and two undercover narcotics agents. You can have students do a creative compare-and-contrast activity of their trial with the court proceeding they observe.

## THE INTERDISCIPLINARY APPROACH

The justice system theme can be integrated into all subject areas throughout the upper elementary school curriculum.

In reading, we use the book *Crime Lab* by George Edward Stanley to work on comprehension and vocabulary skills. This book explores concepts relating to forensic science and deals with various types of evidence found at the scene of a crime. Students answer comprehension questions on selected chapters and use dictionary skills to define vocabulary words taken from the selections. Students also read mysteries that depict the role of detectives, the techniques used in solving crimes, and the importance of evidentiary details in cases.

We analyze the elements of the detective mystery as a literary form during language arts and students write their own mystery stories. In addition, students rewrite familiar fairytales to put some of their favorite fairytale characters on trial. After identifying the elements of the common misdemeanors, students create fairytales in which one or more of the crimes is committed.

Our spelling program is supplemented to include five additional words each week relating to the justice system theme. Words on our list include: attorney, defendant, criminal, justice, misdemeanor, felony, evidence, forensic, testimony, assault, battery, summons, subpoena, jury, and perjury. You may wish to make crossword puzzles, or seek-and-finds, using these vocabulary terms.

Forensic concepts introduced in reading are expanded upon in science by looking at the methods that scientists use to analyze various types of evidence found at the scene of a crime. Students use authentic materials to experiment with the identification and classification of fingerprints. During a trip to the Crime Lab, students can meet with a variety of forensic scientists including serologists, experts in ballistics, and handwriting and fingerprint identification experts. This presents an opportunity to discuss the role of expert witnesses in a trial.

In art, we create props and costumes to be used in the mock trial. Students can create things such as casts made of footprints left at the scene of the crime, objects with fingerprints, bloodstained carpet, wolf hairs, and blood-stained clothing.

In math, students learn to interpret statistics on graphs and charts depicting crime rates in different locations and at different times, and percentages of different types of crimes committed. They also make their own graphs and charts to show crime related data.

As we approach different themes throughout the year, the justice-system concepts continue to resurface and are reinforced. In our unit on endangered species, we explore the case of the snail darter, a small endangered fish, that made it to the Supreme Court. We also do a dramatization of a court case *Humankind vs. the Wolf*. The wolf is brought to trial for murder, harassment, and trespass. This trial is actually a play written and distributed by the Massachusetts Humane Society to raise issues of how humans have caused the wolf to become an endangered species.

We obtain passports and simulate a trip to several different countries, in our Around the World Unit. As we study each country's government, the justice system is explained and compared to our own. Students also investigate the interesting and unusual laws of other nations.

In our Career Unit, students interview lawyers, judges, police officers, FBI agents, detectives, probation officers, and social workers.

We analyze cases and laws related to health and safety in our Health Unit. For example, we discuss why courts have had to become involved in the rights of AIDS patients, and the variety of ways that courts are handling drunk-driving cases.

## CONCLUSION

As the law concepts are woven into other themes and subject areas throughout the school year, the students have an opportunity to reinforce and build onto the foundation of law concepts that has been established in the Justice System Unit. With each additional experience, the quality of the students' responses become more sophisticated.

I have found that in combining a core unit of the justice system that emphasizes the active participation of students with an interdisciplinary approach which extends the law concepts to all other aspects of the curriculum, the result has been that students develop a genuine interest in the subject matter along with a good working knowledge of how the justice system operates.

## RESOURCES ON THE JUSTICE SYSTEM
### BOOKS (STUDENTS)

*A Day in the Life of a Police Detective* by David Paige (Troll Associates, 1981).

*Criminal Justice* (Living Law — The Constitutional Rights Foundation and Scholastic, Inc. Revised 1988).

*Little Red Riding Hood* retold and illustrated by Trina Schart Hyman (Holiday House, 1983).

*The Crime Lab* by George Edward Stanley (Avon Camelot, 1985). Tells how forensic scientists help police solve crimes. Great introduction to types of evidence and expert witnesses.

*Trial by Jury* by Jo Kolanda end Judge Patricia Curley (Franklin Watts, 1988).

*You Be the Jury — Courtroom II* by Marvin Miller (Scholastic Inc., 1989). Courtroom mysteries for students to examine the evidence and decide.

*You Be the Jury — Courtroom III* by Marvin Miller (Scholastic Inc., 1990). Courtroom mysteries for students to examine the evidence and decide.

### BOOKS (TEACHER GUIDES AND REFERENCE)

*Building Bridges to the Law: How to Make Lawyers Judges, Police and Other Members of the Community a Part of Your*

*Law-Related Education Program*, Edited by Charles White (American Bar Association, 1981).

*Criminal Justice Teaching Guide* (Living Law The Constitution Rights Foundation and Scholastic Inc., Revised 1988).

*Teaching About the Law* by Ronald A. Gerlach and Lynne W. Lamprecht (W. H. Anderson Company, 1975).

## ACTIVITY BOOKS

*Create-A-Sleuth* by Eleanor W. Hoomes (Educational Impressions, 1985). Writing detective/mystery stories.

*Everyday Law for Young Citizens* by Greta Barclay Lipson and Eric Barlay Lipson (Good Apple, Inc., 1988). Case studies.

*Real Life Citizenship* by Grethchen DyKstra, Jean Fiedler end John H. Wilson (Scholastic Inc., 1979). Citizens and the Legal System—Rights of Defendants, Witnesses, Jury Duty.

## FILMSTRIP KIT

*Machinery of Justice* (Walt Disney Educational Media Company 1974). Six filmstrips on the following topics: The Jury, Judgment, Police Officers, Attorneys, Trials, Prison, Parole and Probation.

## VIDEO AND INSTRUCTOR'S MANUAL

*Goldilocks Trial*. (1988). Baltimore City Bar Association-Young Lawyers Section.

## ORGANIZATIONS

American Bar Association, Special Committee on Youth Education for Citizenship, 1155 E. 60th Street, Chicago, IL, 60637.

State and Local Bar Associations (Most Bars have extensive mock trial information).

## STATE AND LOCAL LAW ENFORCEMENT AGENCIES

Canine Division: May be willing to come to school and give a demonstration.

Federal Bureau of Investigation, Washington, D.C.

F.B.I.—Local Office

Office of the State's Attorney

Parole and Probation Office

Judith Norton, an attorney/teacher, is teaching fifth grade at Hernwood Elementary School in Baltimore County, Maryland. Ms. Norton previously taught in Baltimore, where she developed law-related education materials for use in grades four through six. [1992 note]

**Mary E. Haas**
**Barbara Hatcher**
**Cynthia Szymanski Sunal**

*What is an "election"?*
   *It's when grown-ups go to school and vote for someone to be President.*
*What do you do when you "vote"?*
   *You pick someone, you say I want this person to be the boss of everybody.*

Like many seven-year-olds, Sheila has some understanding of what voting is, of its role in an election and of what the role of the elected person will be. Such political understandings develop early. (Hess & Torney, 1967; Greenstein, 1969; and Dawson, Prewitt & Dawson, 1969.)

Noted child psychiatrist, Robert Coles (1986), writes: "the attitude that children take toward political authority, toward those who rule them, possess power over them is but one element in their developing lives...a political inclination has a 'developmental history' " (1986, p. 49).

In his work, Coles has observed that children have a great interest in the office and person who is President of the United States. They know about the current President and the things he has done. The President is a fascinating and powerful person who is believed to have super powers to get things done.

The following activities focus on increasing student's awareness of the Office of the President, campaign and election procedures, desirable characteristics an individual should have to serve as President, and the need for citizens to make informed election choices.

Activities below are designed to be usable in a range of elementary grades. Modifications for very young children in the earliest grades are denoted in italics following the description.

## ELEMENTARY AND EARLY CHILDHOOD
*What do polls tell us?*

Conduct a simple class poll. For example, ask children to name their favorite color. Use the findings to determine the most popular colors. Discuss the definition of poll as "asking a few people their opinion on a topic and then predicting the responses of many based upon the results of this poll." Help students generalize their findings about

colors. "Based on your poll, what color do you believe would be the most popular with all second graders in our school? Why?" Ask if students have heard the term "poll" used with the election. Explain that survey is another word for poll and that other kinds of questions are frequently asked. Ask students why presidential candidates would use polls and how this information would be useful.

Have students conduct a poll, organize data, and draw conclusions from data. Appropriate questions in order of complexity include:
a. What kind (characteristics) of a person should be President of the United States? (simplest question)
b. Where do people obtain information about the candidates?
c. What is/are the most important problem(s) facing our next President?
d. How much influence on you does the result of a poll have? (most complex question)

A form can be devised to be used by the students to collect opinions. Such a form can include a list of traits desired in a President, e.g., honest, smart, loyal, rich, hardworking, lawyer, businessman, friendly etc. A chart can be made indicating their opinions ("happy faces" can be used on the chart for younger children). Students could tally the results and responses could be indicated and students asked to suggest reasons for these.

Suggested modification include (a) practicing taking polls in the classroom; and, (b) the teacher gradually relinquishing to children the recordkeeping responsibilities.

Older students can survey and interview voting-age community members using a class-generated survey. Then they can compare their results with polls done by the professionals.

The survey should be analyzed and graphed. Students monitor the candidates' rankings in the professional polls graphing each candidate's ratings. After the election. compare the election results with the predictions of your poll, and those of the pollsters. Discuss the students feelings about polls and particularly the election day polls taken by the media.

*What happens when the majority rules?*

Ask the children what is meant by the term "democracy?" Help them conclude that, in a democracy people decide things for themselves and have an equal say on the choice that the group makes. Decisions are made by voting. The teacher tells the students that they are going to follow majority rule in everything they do for the entire morning. Students vote on everything they do; but before

Reprinted from *Social Studies and the Young Learner*, September/October 1988, Volume 1, Number 1. Copyright 1988 by National Council for the Social Studies.

voting, students discuss what they think they should do. Once the vote is taken, however, the majority decision is binding on everyone.

After lunch the students examine the decisions made and how they feel about them. Questions like these are discussed:

a. How did students feel if they were not a part of the majority group? (simplest question)

b. Did the students who were not in the majority try to influence the group more when the next vote came about?

c. Can you disagree with the majority and still be a part of the class?

d. Did the majority always make the best choice? If they had to make the choice(s) again, would they make the same decisions?

e. What are the advantages of majority rule as we did it in class?

f. What advantages are there to running a nation on majority rule? What disadvantages? (most complex question)

As appropriate, explain the United States has a representative democracy in which elected representatives make political decisions for us during their term in office. The President's job is to make the decisions to keep the country running at all hours every day. The President does have lots of people to help, but if an important problem comes up — even late at night — the President must make the decision. President Truman had a plaque on his desk in the White House that said, "The buck stops here," to remind him that he had to make decisions — even the very difficult ones.

The time frame should be shortened to one hour for very young children. Votes should be tallied on the chalkboard. The decisions should be recorded on chart paper. The simplest questions should be used in the discussion.

*Where do people get their information about the candidates?*

Students brainstorm a list of information sources on a candidate. They then rate each source by asking three questions: 1. Does the speaker or writer have any reason not to tell the complete truth? 2. Can the statement be proven true? 3. Is the writer or speaker saying something they hope is true? Classify each source as a fact, hope, a friendly view, or unfriendly view.

Gather statements made about and by the candidates from various forms of media for several days, each student being assigned a specific source including time and station for broadcast media, or title and section for print media. Among the things that can be recorded are: time, date, speaker's name, location, slogans, and quotes. When students return with their data, it is classified by the number of appearances by candidates on news shows and/or advertisements. Decisions are made on which sources provide the "best" information. Using their data, students list descriptive words, indicating if a particular statement is favorable or unfavorable to the candidate. Ask students to tell why different statements by the candidates might be

made to teachers, the elderly, business owners, or workers. Students can interview a reporter on the role of the press in the election. The students should speculate on what they think is the most difficult part of the reporter's job and how reporters verify their stories. Conclude the lesson by asking the students to complete the following statement. "When listening to or reading about candidates you must_____."

The data gathered should be limited to the number of times a particular candidate appears on a news show and the number of times the person appears in an advertisement. This will necessitate eliminating some of the procedures described.

*What procedures are used for voting?*

In this two-day election simulation, the teacher may select to have several students (1) be the candidates for president or, (2) vote on the candidates of the major political parties or, (3) do both. Research tells us that very young children are able to identify their parents' political preferences.

On the first day, students discuss two important concepts: fair elections (one person — one vote); and, the secret ballot. Children deal with questions like:

a. How can we have a fair election where everyone votes once and only once?

b. Do you have to tell who you vote for or can you keep it secret?

c. Why might some persons want to tell and others keep it secret?

The teacher explains that, in the United States, people vote in their own neighborhoods and a registration of the voters by address is kept in official records. Ask: "For which of these questions is the 'registration procedure' an answer?" The secret ballot is accomplished by having individual paper ballots or a special type of voting machine. A space away from other people's view is provided to the voter for making out the ballot. Students help decide where their class will have its voting simulation and where the voting booth will be placed, discussing the types of locations needed when adults vote on election day.

The teacher arranges for a class registration at a convenient time during the day. Names and addresses are entered into a book, and a place is provided for students to sign beside their name on election day.

On the election day, the students inspect sample ballots that have been correctly and incorrectly marked. They discuss how to mark the ballot accurately with an X so that their ballot will be counted. Classmates are selected as poll workers to see that the students are registered to vote sign the book, receive a ballot. vote in the booth and place their ballots in the box. Several students can be assigned to take turns as poll watchers to insure that poll workers do things correctly At the designated closing time. the ballot box is opened and two students open and read the ballots aloud. They also must agree on disqualifying any improperly marked ballots. Another student records the votes on a tally sheet. Two poll watchers observe to see that the votes are counted and recorded correctly. After the votes are counted, the recorder and watcher sign the sheet verifying the correct record of the vote. The class discusses the voting procedures and the watchers report any problems or concerns they observed. Many schools serve as polling locations and, if available, the students should quietly observe the adults voting.

Very young children can line up and vote at one time. Candidates' names may be identified with different colors so that nonreaders will be able to use the color to identify the appropriate box to mark.

*What is the vocabulary of the elections?*

To understand an election, students should become familiar with the vocabulary unique to the electoral process. New words, acronyms, or figurative expressions need discussion.

The teacher writes on the board "The President stands on a platform." The students tell what they think this term means. The teacher discusses with the children the nature of the platform (it must be strong and connected together). Ask such questions as:

a. Could the President stand on a platform made of chocolate ice cream which is something everyone likes? Pretty marbles?

b. What would be the characteristics of a platform that a person such as the President could stand on?

Teacher draws the analogy that a political platform is a statement that is strong because it speaks to important issues of the country, and it is held together by the support of the people in the political party. They support the ideas and are willing to work to get these things accomplished. Make a bulletin board illustrating the idea that the president stands on a platform.

Words like "ticket," front runner," and "landslide" would be appropriate to include. When possible, concrete references for abstract concepts or analogies such as the platform should be used to help clarify the meanings. Students may make a picture dictionary to reinforce the new terms.

After children have studied words and their meanings, they may enjoy playing the game Election Lingo. Each student makes a card by placing the terms randomly in the individual squares in the manner of a bingo card. The game is played with the same rules for winning as Bingo. However, instead of calling out words, definitions are read and the student marks the correct term.

With very young children, the teacher can ask: "What things should the President do for us after he is elected?" After listing the students' ideas, the teacher tells the children that each candidate tells us ahead of time what he plans to do. These ideas are called his platform. The teacher can indicate whether any of the students' ideas appear in the platform of the current candidates and, if so, in which candidate's platform.

## UPPER ELEMENTARY

*What are the candidates' personal and political profiles?*

Divide the class into groups. Have each group draw the name of a viable candidate. Students prepare a scrapbook or fact sheet on their candidate, including the following information:

- The Candidate and Family (spouse, children, interests, hobbies, pets, etc.)
- Residence or Home State (include a map and mark the location)
- Educational Background
- Work Experiences
- Special Qualifications
- Awards and Honors
- Reasons for Wanting to be President
- Party Affiliation and Experience

Students share what they learn with the class in a talk show or interview format, a well-designed campaign spot for TV or other creative strategies. They conclude with a discussion on the ways candidates are alike and different in their interests and qualifications. They decide which categories of information are the most important for a voter to know before voting.

*Where can you find information about presidential candidates?*

In this activity, students conduct a scavenger hunt to identify sources of information about the candidates. Students may be divided into teams or work independently to locate the following items on a single candidate.

Scavenger List

1  A newspaper advertisement or story discussing the candidates' qualifications or beliefs about an issue.

2. A bumper sticker, sign, button, hat, or similar memorabilia promoting an individual's candidacy.

3. A letter from a candidate urging an individual to vote for him or provide campaign financial support.

4. A paid television or radio spot about the candidate. Document the source, day and time. A news or talk show may also be used in this category.

5. One other source about the candidate, such as an editorial or cartoon.

6. The signature of the candidate.

Examine the collection to identify ways campaign organizers and media inform voters about the candidate's views and qualifications. What are the most effective methods? Why? Which do you believe are most/least expensive? Why? Examine the collected materials for slogans. What makes a good slogan? Try composing slogans for a favorite candidate or research slogans used during the elections campaigns of your favorite presidents.

*Can you detect the propaganda used in the political campaign?*

Propaganda is defined as a deliberate attempt to persuade a person to accept a point of view or take a certain action. Politicians use propaganda to try to convince voters to support them and their ideas.

Discuss with the students the meanings of techniques like: "name calling"; "plain folks"; "transfer"; "testimonials"; "card stacking"; "bandwagon"; and "glittering generalities." Definitions of these terms can be found in most government textbooks. Have students refer to the media to identify the techniques during the campaign. Students collect the information on a standard format showing the techniques used by candidates and the sources of information—television news. newspaper or advertisement. Periodically have the students bring in their forms and share their examples with classmates. This activity will assist the students in identifying facts, opinions, balanced presentation, and biased presentations.

*What can Americans learn about the candidates by listening to them debate?*

During an election year, students have an excellent opportunity to see and/or hear the candidates face one another in debates. In class, prepare the students to listen to the debates. Ask them to write three to five questions they would like to ask the candidates during the debates. As they listen to the debates, the students record if and how the candidates answer their questions. They can also listen for the use of propaganda techniques. Discuss the students' findings and reactions to the debate in class. (A videotape of the program might be of help.) What are the general impressions of the debate? Were the students influenced by anything other than the answers to the questions? Which questions asked by the reporters were particularly good questions? Why? Did the candidates stick to the topic, answer the questions, and use facts to support their statements?

As an extension of this activity, videotape the politicians and professional political observers analyses of the debates. Compare the students' conclusions with the professionals. Did the politicians and observers look at different concerns than the students? Did hearing the professionals' observations cause you to see the debates differently?

## RESOURCES
### CHILDREN'S BOOKS ABOUT THE PRESIDENTS
Sullivan, G. (1984). *Mr. President: A Book of U.S. Presidents.* New York: Dodd, Mead & Company. Contains facts about electing the President. In addition, each President is profiled and important events from his admin-

istration are highlighted.

*Encyclopedia of Presidents Series.* (1986). Chicago: Childrens Press. Attractive individual books on each President from George Washington to Ronald Reagan.

*World Leaders Past and Present Series.* New York: Chelsea House Publishers. This biographical series of 100 leaders from ancient times to the present introduces men and women who have influenced history. A number of American Presidents are included: George Washington, Dwight Eisenhower, Andrew Jackson, Lyndon Johnson, John Kennedy, Abraham Lincoln, Richard Nixon, Franklin Roosevelt, Woodrow Wilson, and Theodore Roosevelt.

## BULLETIN BOARD OR DOOR DECORATION IDEAS
- Presidential Trivia
- Democratic and Republican Candidates (photos, articles, campaign literature)
- Minorities in Politics
- Historical Election Slogans
- Student-Designed Bumper Stickers, Campaign Buttons, or Posters
- Third Parties in American History
- Presidents, Vice-Presidents, and Famous First Ladies
- Political Cartoons
- Propaganda Devices and Examples
- The Campaign Trail—Mapping the Results
- Opinion Polls—Graphic Results (both student made and professional pollsters)

## REFERENCES

Coles, R. (1986). *The Political Life of Children.* Boston: The Atlantic Monthly Press.

Dawson, R., Prewitt, K., & Dawson, K. (1969). *Political Socialization.* (2nd ed.). Boston Little Brown.

Greenstein, F. (1969). *Children and Politics* (rev. ed.). New Haven: Yale University Press.

Hess, R.. and Torney, J. (1967). *The Development of Political Attitudes in Children.* Chicago: Aldine

Newmann, F. M. (1975). *Education for Citizenship Action.* Berkeley: McCutchan.

Mary E. Haas is an Associate Professor of Curriculum and Instruction at West Virginia University in Morgantown. Barbara Hatcher is a Professor of Education at Southwest Texas State University in San Marcos. Cynthia Szymanski Sunal is a Professor of Curriculum and Instruction at West Virginia University in Morgantown. [1988 note]

# Can Controversial Topics Be Taught in the Early Grades?
## *The Answer Is Yes!*

**Robin Haskell McBee**

Should controversial issues become a regular part of the elementary curriculum? Does content that generates polarized points of view have a proper place in the instructional experiences of seven, eight, nine, and ten year-olds?

I am convinced the answer to these questions is yes, and my work in the field of law-related education focuses on developing the capability of teachers to do so. I know that many teachers, principals, curriculum designers, and text book authors (Risinger 1992) would say no to these questions. In their view, controversy is unsettling and requires a sophisticated reasoning ability, which young children do not possess. They believe that students in the early grades need the structure, consistency, and assurance offered by teachers who know the facts and answers, and who provide lessons and textbooks designed to impart these to students. Young students, the argument goes, should concentrate on committing these facts to memory and mastering basic skills in reading, writing, and numerical manipulations that are safely free of political agendas.

Having worked closely with hundreds of elementary school teachers, both in and out of the classroom, I've found that the above philosophy typifies many of their views. My experience and the literature indicate that the intentional introduction of controversy into elementary instructional programs is practically non-existent (Risinger 1992; McAulay 1967). Lower grade teachers often do not feel properly trained or prepared to address such issues, and they are reluctant to engage in teaching subjects that, they feel, will take up valuable instructional time and lead to loss of control over classroom behavior. Some are afraid of repercussions from parents or their administrators while others question their ability to present controversial material from a neutral perspective.

## REAL-LIFE AND CURRICULAR CONNECTIONS

The paradox of this controversy-avoidance syndrome, it seems to me, is the reality that controversy and conflict are everywhere in the lives of young children. Conflicts regularly take place at school among students and between students and teachers over possessions, academic work and performance, put-downs, taking turns, physical aggression (Johnson, Johnson, Dudley, and Burnett 1992), and behavior. They erupt at home between spouses, siblings, or parents and their children over belongings, clothes, money, discipline, child care, chores, competition for attention, and a host of other issues.

Outside of the immediate home and school environments, civil and criminal conflicts and geopolitical controversies are waged regularly in our city streets, town halls, around the world, and on our living room television sets. We are constantly surrounded by and confronted with controversy or conflict of some form or another—regardless of our ages. To pretend this is not so or to avoid dealing with it is to deny students the opportunity to work with relevant, meaningful, high-interest content—a recipe for boredom and lack of motivation (Brophy 1987; Cook 1984).

Beyond the real-life relevance of controversial issues is their curricular relevance. Clearly, students need to acquire the skills of peaceful conflict resolution (Townley 1995; Johnson, Johnson, Dudley, and Burnett 1992). They also need appropriate academic instruction designed to promote the development of what Parker and Kaltsounis (1991) describe as the informed, skilled, and committed "democratic citizen." If the promise of public schools as citizenship training grounds is to be realized, then students—from the very earliest ages—must acquire and practice the following:

1. Skills in interpersonal communication;
2. Tolerance for diverse perspectives;
3. The critical and constructive thinking processes needed to analyze actions and practices in the context of democratic ideals; and
4. The ability to engage in civil public discourse in the face of legitimately diverse claims and interests (Parker and Kaltsounis 1991; Berman 1990; Boyer 1990; Parker 1990).

The very nature and content of history and the social sciences are replete with controversial issues. Every major historic and contemporary encounter between individuals, cultures, peoples, nations, and governments; every human struggle with the land and environment; and every conflict over production, distribution, and consumption of resources is a study in controversy. Downplaying or ignoring controversial topics in the curriculum may be common, but it is illogical and unwise, even at the elementary level:

> [It] is not only a barrier to developing important critical-thinking skills, it also eliminates much of the drama and excitement of studying history and the contemporary human condition. (Risinger 1992, 13)

What's more, it is contrary to the defined purpose of and prescribed curricular approach to social studies by

National Council for the Social Studies (1994).

> The primary purpose of social studies is to help young people develop the ability to make informed and reasoned decisions for the public good as citizens of a culturally diverse, democratic society in an interdependent world. (Ibid., vii)

> A well-designed social studies curriculum will help each learner construct a blend of personal, academic, pluralist, and global views of the human condition … within the framework of civic responsibility … (Ibid., 6-7)

I contend that students will not learn civic responsibility or the skill of informed, reasoned decision making unless they are regularly exposed to diverse viewpoints and the pluralism that characterizes this nation.

## INTRODUCING CONTROVERSIAL TOPICS INTO THE ELEMENTARY CURRICULUM

Given my arguments for introducing controversial topics into the elementary curriculum, the rest of this article is devoted to outlining ways to do it. Luckily, the use of controversial topics in the lower grades is not virgin territory. For example, numerous law-related education (LRE) lessons and activities have been developed for kindergarten through fifth grade classrooms. By law-related education, I mean highly interactive instruction whose content is tied to rules, laws, and the legal system and to rights, roles, and responsibilities in that system—a content that constantly elicits conflicts over what is fundamentally fair to individuals and to society as a whole.

My classroom teacher colleagues, who are experienced in the content and techniques of law-related education, believe that LRE fits logically into their existing curricula and that such typical strategies as "Take A Stand," role-plays, and simulations (e.g., city council hearings, small claims trials, and mediation sessions) provide structured but creative open-ended vehicles for expressing and developing a defense for personal perspectives, for hearing and developing tolerance for diverse viewpoints, and for understanding other, differing views. In other words, law-related education enables these young students to begin to develop the democratic citizen's ability to engage in civil public discourse amidst legitimately diverse claims and interests.

The following brief descriptions of four LRE strategies are easily adaptable to different social studies content at the elementary level. They are accompanied by a more detailed description of a unit on violence that I have taught in part or full to third, fourth, and fifth graders in urban and suburban schools. In the final section, I conclude with advice from experienced practitioners about the best conditions for including controversial topics in the elementary curriculum.

## SOME GENERAL LRE STRATEGIES[1]
### ROLE-PLAY
Students act out loosely defined roles of individuals in law-related scenarios (e.g., contract negotiations, consumer fraud, police arrests, conflict resolution). Scenarios can come from teachers, students, or LRE resource materials, but actual scenes should be improvised rather than scripted. Each session should conclude with a debriefing in which students engage in an open-ended discussion of knowledge gained, procedure, and reactions to the activity.

Elementary teachers frequently mention using this strategy to play the roles of Native Americans and Europeans when they first encounter each other. Other possible applications include exploring conflicts over land use, over resources in early colonial life, between federalists and anti-federalists, and between a husband and wife who have differing views on women's suffrage.

## SIMULATED SMALL CLAIMS COURT
LRE simulations are more sophisticated role-plays in which the players and events are intended to model a simplified version of a particular legal proceeding. In this mini-mock trial, students work in triads as they alternate playing the roles of plaintiff, defendant, and judge. After reading a brief scenario, the plaintiff briefly explains to the judge what has happened and what relief or correction is being sought. The defendant then does the same. The judge may ask clarifying questions before giving a decision.

Teachers are encouraged to have judges share and compare their decisions and reasons for them with the whole class, and to have students briefly discuss how they felt playing their different roles. Repeat the process twice more, using different scenarios and having triad members change roles. Appropriate early grade issues for small claims court simulations include a borrowed item that is returned broken; disagreement over what monetary amount is due for raking leaves, shoveling snow, or babysitting; or a promised act or service that is only partially delivered.[2] The activity should be debriefed at its conclusion as described above.

Elementary teachers use this strategy to model actual small claims court hearings over such typical disagreements as borrowed, exchanged, or sold property or services. They also find the triad structure excellent for illuminating opposing views and decision-making dilemmas in history (e.g., colonists and the king, patriots and Tories, slave owners and abolitionists, confederate and union sympathizers, immigrants and nationalists). Some have also made use of the procedure to resolve minor classroom rules infractions or student disagreements.

## SIMULATED CITY COUNCIL HEARING
The original version of this simulation, called "No Vehicles in the Park," has students play the roles of city council members listening to the testimony of various citizens seeking exceptions to the newly passed law reflected in the title. The law's expressed purpose is to preserve beauty and safety; however, different interest groups want their vehicles exempted (e.g., commuters' automobiles, emergency vehicles, garbage trucks, baby carriages, bicycles, wagons, wheelchairs, parade floats). Teachers often have

students work in small cooperative groups to rate these requests prior to actually conducting the simulated hearing. As in the other strategies, the activity should be debriefed at its conclusion.

Hearings could be held over any major current or historic issue. Typical changes include "no hats in school" (Is a yarmulke, religious turban or scarf, or large bow considered a hat?); "no weapons in school" (Is a boy scout knife, piece of piping, rope, or toy gun considered a weapon?); and "no prayers in school" (Does this include a moment of silence, an after-school Bible study group's prayer, saying grace at lunch, and the coach's prayer before the game?). Debriefing should follow the activity, as in the above examples.

## TAKE A STAND

In this strategy, teachers ask students to show their reactions to emotionally charged statements (usually related to an issue being studied) by literally taking a stand. Teachers make the statement; students decide how they feel and why; then students stand on the agree side of the room, the disagree side of the room, or in the middle if they are undecided. Teachers instruct students not to interrupt, speak out of turn, or make disparaging comments or actions regarding others' opinions. The teacher then begins going back and forth between the "agrees" and disagrees" asking reasons why students believe as they do or have an opposing response to a previous student's reason. (Note that students are allowed to move to another side of the room if they change their minds, but they must do so without causing disruption.) After going back and forth between the agrees and disagrees several times, the teacher then asks for reasons from those who feel undecided. Original statements can then be modified based on student feedback, and students can then be asked to take a new stand.

Elementary teachers frequently use this strategy to encourage students to develop opinions on issues in current events as well as major political controversies in American history. Some teachers have made this a daily or weekly debriefing activity in which students are encouraged to share reactions to what has transpired that day or week.

## UNIT ON VIOLENCE
### OVERVIEW

This five-day unit uses several interactive strategies to help students begin to sort out and discuss the violent events they hear, read, watch (on television or in real life), or experience. It also presents possible legal and personal remedies to violence. Note that the unit is not intended to get students to divulge highly personal and identifiable information (and caution should be taken not to do so). The purpose is to provide a safe environment for students to explore the violence we all experience and possible alternatives to those acts.

### DAY ONE

Introduce the unit with a "Hangman" activity in which the mystery word is v-i-o-l-e-n-c-e. I find that third, fourth, and fifth graders particularly enjoy playing this letter-guessing game as a team or cooperative group competition in which points are earned by teams when a letter is guessed correctly. Once the students have guessed the word, explain the purpose of this unit and the objective for this lesson (to begin exploring individual perspectives on violence).

Have students write down all the single words that come to their minds when they think of violence. Remind them to keep their lists private. Allow at least five minutes to complete lists, and help students having difficulty getting started by coaching them to think of verbs, adverbs, or adjectives that describe what someone does or says when they get violent. Then go around the room, one by one, asking students to share one word from their list and write it on the board. Go around a second time if needed. If a word signifies violence to a child, it should be included regardless of other student or teacher interpretation. Also, students should be allowed to say "Pass" if they prefer not to share a word.

Repeat this whole process a second time, this time instructing students to write down brief sentences or phrases that tell of violent acts that the student has seen or knows have happened to people he or she knows (e.g., a man punching a woman, a woman pulling a little boy by his ear, a street fight between two drunks). Instruct students not to use names or descriptors that tell exactly who was involved (e.g., me, my father, my neighbor's youngest daughter).

Follow up with an assignment to write an imaginary story describing what happened before, during, and after one of the violent acts listed on the board.

### DAY TWO

Begin by asking students whether or not they were able to come up with any good stories. Invite volunteers to share which of the violent acts became the subject of their story. Explain that the objective of today's lesson is to get students to work cooperatively in small groups (or pairs) to come up with a few really good, detailed stories about one of the acts from their earlier list. Using an overhead transparency created with the list of violent phrases from Day One, project it onto a screen. Have students read the list, and conduct a class vote to see which entry the students would most like to have as the focus of their group writing experience. Review the elements of a good story, arrange students into their groups, and instruct them to begin. Have groups exchange completed stories, offer comments on how other groups' stories could be improved stylistically and grammatically, and revise their own stories accordingly. Have one volunteer from each group read the group's finished story to the whole class before handing it in.

## DAY THREE

Using one of the stories as the focal point, ask a local attorney to assist you in identifying possible legal responses to the violent act.[3] Introduce the lesson by explaining its focus on possible punishments for committing violent acts and the lawyer's role in explaining possible sentences for breaking the law.

Read the story aloud, again, to students. Ask if they feel that people who commit that kind of act should be punished and how. Conduct an open-ended discussion encouraging students to share their views and the reasons for their views. Conduct a Take A Stand using a statement that calls for people who commit that kind of violent act to get a particular punishment (one you feel will generate different reactions based on the preceding discussion). Follow this by presenting information to students (or have the attorney present it) on legal remedies for this type of violence.[3] (A possible follow-up might be conducting a mock trial of the civil or criminal case with assistance from the attorney.)

## DAY FOUR

Introduce the lesson by asking students if they've ever lived in an apartment, if they've ever experienced noise coming from another apartment or nearby home, and if the noise has ever been so much that they couldn't sleep. Explain that today they will work with a story in which the main character is having that problem and the objective is to have students learn about and role-play an alternative dispute resolution procedure known as mediation.

Tell students the story of the "Tap Dancer" (Gallagher n.d.). Harry's good friend, Bill, who lives in the apartment above Harry, has recently taken up tap dancing and practices late at night so that he can get good enough to perform. Both Harry and Bill work during the day, so Bill practices at night, which is frustrating Harry, who cannot get to sleep because of it. Harry is angry at Bill for being so inconsiderate, and Bill is hurt that Harry is not more supportive of his tap dancing. Both are sad because their friendship is falling apart.

Have students brainstorm and list on the board what Harry and Bill might do to solve their problem. Tell them that Bill and Harry have agreed to take their problem to a mediator, whose job it is to help Bill and Harry figure out a reasonable "win/win" solution so that both can be happy. Divide students into triads, and have them role-play this mediation session. Debrief the role-plays by discussing the solutions agreed to and the experience of playing the roles of the mediator, Harry, and Bill. Discuss how students might use this type of dispute resolution to avoid violence.

## DAY FIVE

Have students write a one- to three-paragraph essay that answers the question, What do you think we should do to end all the violence in our community?

## CONCLUSION

The above strategies and lessons are easy to use without acquiring major expertise. However, a few cautionary notes are in order. Elementary teachers who regularly work with controversial issues urge teachers to know their students, parents, and community. It is wise to understand which issues are so sensitive that introducing them into instruction will cause more headaches and bad feelings from parents and the community than benefits to students. Establishing and maintaining a good rapport with parents helps them to understand the approach and to be confident in the teacher's objectivity.

The same holds true for teacher relationships with principals. It is equally important to know what the students are capable of understanding, what interests them, and how much open-ended discussion they can handle constructively. Teachers themselves should keep abreast of current issues and diverse perspectives on them by reading at least one major newspaper and news magazine other than the local journal.

Finally, teachers should avoid getting into their personal opinions with students. The teaching role is to facilitate open discussion and to develop student recognition of varying perspectives, not to promote any one point of view. While it is legitimate to have a viewpoint and to share it occasionally with students, care should be taken to do so after students have had a chance to voice their own views and explore those of others. In this way, students will begin to develop the habits of critically thinking, well-informed, active democratic citizens.

## NOTES

[1]  The descriptions of LRE activities offered in this article, as well as additional activity descriptions, can be found in the resource *Living the Law By Learning the Law, A K-12 Law Related Education Curriculum Guide*, published by the Virginia Institute for Law and Citizenship Studies, Virginia Commonwealth University, Richmond (1994).

[2]  For actual scenario descriptions, see the above referenced guide and *Living Together Under the Law*, by Arlene Gallagher, published by the New York State Bar Association's Law, Youth and Citizenship Program, Albany (n.d.). This elementary literature and law-related education guide is also a good resource for more LRE activities and for an annotated bibliography of literature connections.

[3]  Many violent acts violate various state criminal codes and are punishable by fines, incarceration, or mandated community service or victim restitution. Even if there are no criminal codes involved, there may be civil actions (e.g., restraining orders, liability torts) that can be initiated by the victim against the perpetrator or, if the victim is a minor, by the state against the perpetrator (e.g., temporary or permanent removal from custody). A general practice attorney with a few years of experience often has the most versatile experience in

this area and can serve as a good out-of-class or in-class resource. Many attorneys are interested in serving as outside resource people to elementary and secondary teachers and students. Contact local bar associations and LRE organizations for help locating attorneys.

## REFERENCES

Berman, Sheldon. "Educating for Social Responsibility." *Educational Leadership* 48, no. 3 (November 1990): 75-80.

Boyer, Ernest L. "Civic Education for Responsible Citizens." *Educational Leadership* 48, no. 3 (November 1990): 4-7.

Brophy, Jere. "Synthesis of Research on Strategies for Motivating Students to Learn." *Educational Leadership* 45, no. 2 (October 1987): 40-48.

Cook, Kay K. *Controversial Issues: Concerns for Policy Makers.* Boulder: ERIC Digest No. 14, EDRS Document # ED253465 (June 1984).

Gallagher, Arlene. *Living Together Under the Law.* Albany: New York State Bar Association; Law, Youth and Citizenship Program (n.d.).

Johnson, David W., Roger T. Johnson, Bruce Dudley, and Robert Burnett. "Teaching Students to Be Peer Mediators." *Educational Leadership* 50, no. 1 (September 1992): 10-13.

McAulay, J. D. "Controversial Issues in the Social Studies." In *Current Research in Elementary School Social Studies*, edited by Wayne L. Herman, Jr. Toronto: The Macmillan Company, 1967.

National Council for Social Studies. *Expectations of Excellence: Curriculum Standards for Social Studies.* Bulletin 89. Washington, D.C.: National Council for the Social Studies, 1994.

Parker, Walter C. "Assessing Citizenship." *Educational Leadership* 48, no. 3 (November 1990): 17-22.

Parker, Walter C., and Theodore Kaltsounis. "Citizenship and Law-Related Education." In *Elementary School Social Studies: Research as a Guide to Practice*, edited by Virginia A. Atwood. Washington, D.C.: National Council for the Social Studies, 1991.

Risinger, C. Frederick. *Current Directions in Social Studies.* Boston: Houghton Mifflin, 1992.

Townley, Annette. "Changing School Culture." *Educational Leadership* 52, no. 8 (May 1995): 80.

Virginia Institute for Law and Citizenship Studies. *Living the Law By Learning the Law, A K-12 Law-Related Education Curriculum Guide.* Richmond: Virginia Institute for Law and Citizenship Studies, 1994.

Robin Haskell McBee is the Director of the Virginia Institute for Law and Citizenship Studies at Virginia Commonwealth University, Richmond. The author wishes to thank Joanne Funk, second grade teacher and elementary social studies specialist, Norfolk, Virginia; Carolyn Jolly, fifth grade teacher, Charlotte, Virginia; and Bob Wright, fourth grade teacher, Staunton, Virginia, for their contributions to information offered in this article. [1996 note]

# PART 7

## VII PRODUCTION, DISTRIBUTION, AND CONSUMPTION

Economics is the study of how resources are produced and distributed to satisfy unlimited wants. Daily, all of us make choices about how to use our scarce resources. Basic economic questions that need to be addressed by all societies include at least the following: What goods are to be produced? How will they be produced? How will they be distributed? Because we are living in an interdependent world, decisions about trade extend beyond the boundaries of family and household to the nation and the entire world. Elementary students can learn to understand and explain such basic economic concepts as opportunity, cost, scarcity, production, consumption, and interdependence. Typically, economic content is included when topics such as community workers, businesses in our neighborhood, resources of our state and other states, and resources of our nation and other nations are being studied. Within these contexts, young learners examine the consequences of decisions about these and similar questions for themselves and others.

Hartoonian and Laughlin describe the importance of developing decision-making skills necessary for making informed economic decisions. Schug provides examples of both a primary and intermediate grade instructional lesson that teaches about goods and services and how individuals make our economic system work. These lessons and others help young learners develop economic understandings. Schug also provides comments on what, how, and why economics is an appropriate subject for young learners to study. Laney's research-based article reports that young learners can learn to solve economic problems relevant to themselves and offers two practical classroom examples of best practices.

An example of a practical hands-on learning activity that helps young students study and understand economic concepts is presented by Yeargan and Hatcher, who describe the activities of a third grade class that created a corporation and engaged in producing and distributing cupcakes. Maslow describes how her students became active learners as they opened their greeting card business as a way to teach job-related skills, mathematics competencies, economic concepts, and the need to return something to the community.

Murphy and Walsh suggest using economic concepts to help students learn decision-making skills while making linkages between what they learn in schools and their lives outside of school. One type of school-business community partnership activity is identified by Swets, who describes the Junior achievement program she uses with her students in a second grade class. In the five lessons presented by the community business leader, Swets's students were engaged in a variety of learning activities that introduced them to five important economic concepts.

Young learners should learn about our economic system so that they are able to make informed economic decisions concerning their own needs and wants and the needs and wants of others. This will help them to identify their personal roles in the economic life of the country.

## H. Michael Hartoonian
## Margaret A. Laughlin

**The discipline of economics is built upon** the notion that human beings are constantly confronted with making choices concerning the allocation and use of scarce natural. capital, and human resources. Decision making is a fact of life and the form of reasoning underlying this process, whether called "cost benefit analysis," "utility maximization," or simply the "economic way of thinking," provides citizens with a dynamic key to the door of economic understanding.

## ELEMENTS OF DECISION MAKING

We have identified five basic skill categories in the decision-making process. And, while many economic decisions can be made without using all of these skills, the following are included for consideration here: (1) expanding a conceptual framework, (2) understanding sequence, (3) developing alternative sequences, (4) evaluating alternatives, and (5) implementing or carrying out a decision.

By looking at the above skills used in decision making and applying them to a typical situation facing elementary students, teachers will better understand how the process works and how it relates to students' lives.

## USING THE MODEL

The following story, which focuses on an economic problem, is used to illustrate the skills in the decision-making model:

Mary and Mark are twins who are celebrating their ninth birthday. Their grandparents have given them each fifteen dollars as a birthday gift. The grandparents suggest that part of the money should be put in the twins' savings accounts, but the rest may be spent. The decision of how much to save is left to the children. Mark and Mary go off to spend part of their gift money. After visiting several stores, they make a list of possible purchases, and then discuss what to buy. They have found many more items than their money will allow them to purchase.

The task is to help the twins make choices by working through the decision-making process. The skills we've identified can be demonstrated by using the teaching techniques and questions below:

---

Reprinted with permission from the National Council on Economic Education, from *The Elementary Economist*, Fall 1986, Volume 8, Number 1. Copyright 1986 by the National Council on Economic Education, New York, N.Y. 10036.

### 1. Conceptualizing

For elementary students. perhaps the most important skill in the process of decision making is that of conceptualizing, or forming a clear description of the issue or problem at hand. Conceptualizing may be successfully achieved through the development of a story about the economic concept to be learned. This places the problem in a temporal and spatial context. Students could be asked to respond to the story by drawing a picture, acting out the story, or writing about the situation. These activities should stimulate questions regarding facts, definitions, and values which will help students clarify the issue. This in turn leads students to formulate more questions, generate hypotheses, and seek additional information.

Focus questions may include the following: What is the economic problem or issue, and how can it be stated? What are the individual's goals in the situation? In economics it is assumed that individuals seek to optimize their satisfaction; though people share many common goals and values, what satisfies one person, does not necessarily satisfy another. Relative to the story above, students might be asked, "What are Mark's and Mary s goals?" (e.g., getting a specific item now, saving money for future spending) "What are Mark's and Mary's economic and social goals?" If there is a conflict between these goals, students should consider the opportunity costs and renew their priorities. For example, if most of the money is spent now, they won't be able to save very much for future purchases.

### 2. Sequencing

The second skill, sequencing, allows students to note patterns and develop links between elements of the "story." Within this skill category, students learn to ask questions about the cause/effect relationship between events, or the costs and benefits of alternative action. Thinking about consequences—positive and negative, planned and unplanned—is at the heart of this skill.

For our story, students might formulate questions that Mary and Mark need to ask to make a decision, using an "if/then" format. For example, if they put their money together, then they might be able to buy a more expensive gift they could share (e.g., a Trivial Pursuit game). But, if they keep their money separate, then each can make a more personal choice. Students could make a list of the possible choices Mark and Mary might make, and hypothesize about the consequences of those decisions.

### 3. Creating Alternative Sequences

The third skill category addresses the notion of creating alternative sequences in response to "what if" questions (e.g., "What if we spend all of our money and save none?") Frequently, decision makers have more alternatives available to them than are immediately obvious. Generating these alternatives, or possible solutions, requires that the decision maker gather information.

Assign the students the task of discussing several possible solutions that were not initially considered. Focus on questions such as, "What are some other possible solutions to the problem? What criteria should be used?" (When purchasing, e.g., criteria such as cost, durability and preference.) To carry out this task, students will begin to hypothesize about other sequences of events and draw conclusions from the new situations. In our story, students might suggest that Mark and Mary could buy items that could be used to make more money, such as buckets and sponges to start a car washing business. A possible situation might be that Mary will want to buy a blouse instead of a paperback book, which will leave her little to save. Encourage students to describe a number of alternative ways that Mary and Mark might resolve their problem.

### 4. Evaluating Alternatives

The fourth skill is the evaluation of possible consequences or the results of each alternative. To establish and analyze these sequences, the decision maker may engage in predicting, graphing, defining and interpreting. After evaluating the likely consequences of each sequence, the most desirable one is chosen. The decision maker should consider the marginal or incremental benefit that will result from choosing a given alternative over others. Again, a review of priorities will help. This evaluating process is carried out by addressing such questions as, "What alternatives will best meet our goals or values? What alternatives enjoy the most benefits at the least social and personal cost? What are some of the risks involved in each possible solution? What alternatives are most realistic in terms of our present situation (knowledge, resources, and time)?"

Based upon this analysis, the students should decide the best purchase and amount to save for Mark and Mary. Part of the analysis should include a discussion of the goals they believe Mary and Mark have for each birthday gift. For example, "What does Mark hope to achieve by buying the hockey stick?" (practice more, make the team, etc.) "Do the twins plan to meet the expectations of their grandparents?" Tentative solutions may be ranked according to how each one meets their goals.

### 5. Implementing a Decision

Once an alternative is chosen, the next task is to carry it out. Implementing a decision requires management skills. In all probability there will be obstacles to overcome and alterations to be made. Often economic decisions that seem to be a solution to one problem, create others that need resolution. In purchasing an automobile, e.g., an individual must determine how to manage the high monthly payments along with other financial responsibilities. Will s/he learn to economize, work overtime, take a part-time job, or use savings to meet the payments? Management skills are required to implement such decisions successfully.

In Mark and Mary's case, the students should choose the "best" alternative plan, then list the steps they would need to take in order to purchase the items or to save. The students should consider how they would evaluate the decision Mark and Mary made. Was their decision appropriate? Are they and their grandparents satisfied with their decision? Answers to such questions help students evaluate whether the right choice was made.

Similar situations occur daily in our lives and the argument here is that the practice of making economic decisions can help make life a little more rational, and perhaps, more meaningful and rewarding.

We hope this article will be helpful in reflecting on the thought processes typically used in decision making. There are several well-known instructional strategies built upon the conceptual model described in this article. The widely-used Decision Grid is part of a five-step process taught in the Joint Council's "Trade-offs" film/video series.[1] Another instructional device, labeled the Decision Tree by LaRaus and Remy[2] differs from the "Trade-offs" strategy primarily in the method for evaluating alternatives. In the "Trade-offs" model, students generate a set of criteria against which each alternative is measured, while in the Decision-Tree the consideration of positive and negative consequences (with respect to one's goals and values) helps the decision maker evaluate alternatives.

## NOTES

[1] "Trade-offs." Joint Council on Economic Education. Canadian Foundation for Economic Education and Agency for Instructional Technology. 1978.
[2] Citizenship Decision-Making. Roger LaRaus and Richard C. Remy. Addison-Wesley 1978.

H. Michael Hartoonian is an Adjunct Professor at the University of Wisconsin-Madison. Dr. Hartoonian is also the Supervisor of Social Studies Education for the State of Wisconsin and serves on the board of the Wisconsin State Council on Economic Education. Margaret A. Laughlin is an Associate Professor of Education and the Director of the Center for Economic Education at the University of Wisconsin-Green Bay. [1986 note]

# Economics for Kids:
# Ideas for Teaching in the Elementary Grades

## Mark C. Schug

### ECONOMICS, KIDS, AND THE CURRICULUM

Where do you start if you want to teach economics to kids? As you consider introducing your students to economic ideas, one thing seems clear: young people already are active participants in the economy. They are producers; they make contributions through their work: babysitting, delivering newspapers, cutting lawns, carrying out the garbage, washing dishes, running errands, and raking leaves are just a few examples. As you might expect, older children are even more active as workers. Approximately 30 percent of all ninth and tenth graders will be employed during the school year, and more than 80 percent of all students will have been employed before graduating from high school. Adolescents are involved in retail, unskilled labor, and service occupations.

Moreover, kids from birth as well as older children, as every parent knows, are active consumers. This is a fact of life for businesses around the nation and accounts for millions of dollars in sales of clothing, toys and games, records and tapes, snacks, meals out, school supplies, and the like. Young people also are consumers of services. Schooling is the most obvious example; other examples might include mass transportation, health care, and community education programs such as swimming and gymnastics lessons. Moreover, young people have an influence on the economy beyond their own direct spending. They have a powerful voice in family-consuming decisions concerning housing, transportation, and meals.

In teaching, we sometimes tell the students, "You need to know this because someday you will need it." Introducing young people to economics is different. Students already are active contributors to our economic life. Thus, the study of economics should illustrate ideas of immediate interest and value to young people.

### A STARTER KIT

This article is a starter kit and guide for teaching economics to young people. Although it includes specific teaching suggestions designed to initiate instruction in economics, it is not a comprehensive set of teaching activities. The teaching ideas presented are intended to illustrate methods to introduce key economic concepts. Elaboration of these ideas and integration into the existing curriculum are jobs that remain to be done by individual teachers.

### GETTING READY TO TEACH ECONOMICS

There are several issues to consider as you begin teaching economics to your class. Like any new subject, you need to reflect on

- The types of experiences your students bring to this content, including their personal experiences as well as their own thinking about economics.
- Your own understanding of the subject. Many teachers do not have any formal training in economics. If this is a concern for you, there are numerous courses and publications available that stress economic concepts for teachers. The most direct source of information is the Joint Council on Economic Education, 2 Park Avenue, New York, NY 10016. In addition, many colleges and universities offer special teacher workshops on economics, often at reduced tuition fees.
- The types of economic activities you can construct.
- How the activities you select fit into your existing curriculum.

### CAN YOUNG PEOPLE LEARN ECONOMICS?

An overwhelming amount of research, done primarily in the 1960s and 1970s, concludes that elementary and secondary students can learn economic concepts in a regular school setting (Dawson, 1977). Economics, like most other kinds of academic content and skills, can be taught successfully to young people. As you would expect, the level of success varies according to many variables, such as socioeconomic status, academic ability, reading ability, and motivation. Overall, however, it is clear that young people can learn economic ideas.

### HOW DO CHILDREN THINK ABOUT ECONOMIC IDEAS?

As is true with any other subject, you would expect that the way young people think about economic problems varies among the individuals in any particular group of children. Nonetheless, there are some common ways that children think about basic economic concepts. There is evidence that economic reasoning develops in a stagelike manner similar to Piagetian stages of cognitive thinking. Apparently the content of young people's reasoning about economic ideas becomes more abstract, other-directed, and flexible with increasing age.

An illustration might help to clarify what a developmental pattern in economic reasoning might look like. The work of Gustav Jahoda, a professor at the University of Strathclyde, Glasgow, is one example (Jahoda, 1979). He has been interested in how children think about profit—a fundamental idea in a market economy. Based on his extensive work with children, he described children as moving through the following levels:

1. *No grasp of any system:* Children aged six to eight tended to think that purchases in a shop were simple rituals. Many thought, for example, that goods were simply given to the shop. No purchase or profits were involved.

2. *Two unconnected systems:* The children at this level understood that a shop has to pay for the goods it sells. The most common idea was that the shop paid the same amount as the customers for the goods. Moreover, it was not always understood that the money used for buying goods for the shop came from the customers.

3. *Two integrated systems:* Starting at about age ten there is a developing sense of understanding of the relationship between the shop's buying and selling prices. The following is an example from an interview that illustrates how one child thought about profit:

   E: What happens to the money at the end of the day?
   S: I think it gets counted out. I don't think they give it out until the end of the week.
   E: Who do they give it to?
   S: They pay the people who have been serving.
   E: Do they give it all out?
   S: They keep some stuff to buy more for the shop.
   E: Does the shop pay the same for the things?
   S: I think they get them cheaper. If they got them at the same price they wouldn't be making anything.

While research has not identified a detailed pattern of thinking for each economic concept or institution, the existence of these developmental sequences has been substantiated for such concepts as scarcity, price, money, banking, and exchange. The trick in good teaching is to be able to recognize the developmental patterns that exist in children's thinking about economics, and then to design activities that meet the developmental needs of your students. A formal understanding of economic concepts does not emerge fully developed after a couple of economics lessons. Economic thinking—like other types of thinking—develops slowly and changes with age.

## WHAT KIND OF TEACHING ACTIVITIES SHOULD YOU CHOOSE?

In this article, I have included a sample lesson that can be used to develop economic understanding. Some ideas are fairly conventional and will fit easily into standard class activities. Others are more elaborate and require greater teacher preparation. As you select your own teaching activities, the following criteria may be useful.

Economic teaching activities should

1. *Enhance young people's citizenship understanding and skills.* The information being learned should help children make progress toward understanding and making decisions about important social issues.

2. *Provide many opportunities for manipulating data and using concrete examples.* Many economic ideas can be observed in action. Whenever possible, involve students in first-hand experiences with economic concepts. Community-based activities help to meet this criterion

3. *Use formal as well as informal experiences in teaching about economic concepts.* Children often know economic ideas through experience but their understanding is vague and uninformed. Build on informal experience to create clearer understanding.

4. *Tie in to children's own economic experiences.* Don't overlook the fact that children already participate in economic life.

5. *Extend existing content in the elementary curriculum.* The economics activities you select should meet the goals of your school district's elementary curriculum.

## ECONOMIC EDUCATION AND YOUR CURRICULUM

At the secondary level, there is some disagreement about how economics should be included in the curriculum. Some argue that it should be stressed primarily in a capstone economics course, taught by a teacher who is well-trained in understanding and teaching key ideas of the discipline. Others are less sure; they believe that economics can be taught effectively through integration into existing courses such as United States history and government. However, leaders in elementary education are less prone to such debates. The assumption is usually made that economics, if it is to be taught at all, will need to be integrated into other areas of the curriculum.

Social studies and mathematics are the most obvious areas in the curriculum where economic concepts can be stressed. Of these two subjects, the social studies program is the place where economic ideas probably are most useful. The following are examples of questions commonly addressed in the elementary social studies curriculum. These questions represent key points in the curriculum where economic ideas already are stressed.

## SOCIAL STUDIES CURRICULUM: PRIMARY GRADES

- What are needs? Wants?
- What are goods and services?
- Who are workers in my neighborhood?
- What goods and services are produced in my neighborhood?
- What goods and services are provided in my community?
- How does our community pay for government services?
- Why do communities specialize?
- How do communities depend on each other?

## SOCIAL STUDIES CURRICULUM: INTERMEDIATE GRADES

- What is the role of specialization in our state? regions? nation? world?
- How did inventions, technology, and assembly lines change life in our country?
- How were the American colonies specialized?
- How was mass production important for American economic growth?
- How did inventions change American life?
- What were some characteristics of the American entrepreneur?

- What is a market system?
- What is a monopoly? a competitive market?
- What is the role of government in the economy?
- How does the United States today depend on other countries?
- How do people in other parts of the world use their economic resources?

## LESSON: YOUR PART IN OUR ECONOMY

*Goal:* Unfortunately, many Americans do not realize how important they are as individuals in the American economy. The purpose of this activity is to help young people become aware that in many ways they are already important participants in economic life. The important role of individuals in making our economic system work is stressed.

*Level:* Intermediate.

*Teaching Activity:* Class survey and discussion to draw conclusions.

*Procedure:*

1. Explain to the class that when people talk about economics, they are referring to how people are involved in providing for the welfare of their families. Economics involves three main elements. First, it is the study of how people make goods like bread, toys, or cars, and how people provide services like skating lessons, garbage collection, or haircuts. Second, economics involves studying how goods and services are divided among people. Third, economics involves how we use the goods and services we buy. Ask the class
   - Can you think of some ways you are involved in making goods?
   - In what ways are you providing services?
   - What are some goods or services you use?

2. In order to explore the economic activity of students in your class, introduce the "You ARE the Economy!" survey. Distribute the survey to the class. Explain that the information is confidential; students need not put their names on the papers. Students may have questions so be sure to circulate around the class to help.

### YOU ARE THE ECONOMY!

*Survey*

Directions: Read the questions below and answer them as best you can. You may find that for some questions, it will be hard to give an exact answer. If you are uncertain about an answer, it is alright to give your best guess. Your teacher will be coming around to see if you need any help.

a. Make a list of the jobs you do. They can be jobs you do outside your home (like a paper route or looking after a neighbor's pet), or jobs you do around the house (like emptying the garbage or making your bed).

b. How much money do you usually earn each week?

c. About how much of your money, if any, do you spend each week?

d. About how much of your money, if any, do you save each week?

e. If you spend some of your money each week, list below the goods (objects, like a model race car) or the services (when you buy someone else's work, like piano lessons) that you buy. Also name the businesses where you buy goods and services.

f. Think about how your parents spend their money on you. Make a list of some goods or services your parents purchased in the last month that you wanted them to buy. Examples might include toys, clothes, or gymnastics lessons.

g. Name some television advertisements that are meant to attract young people about your age. Hint: Think about the television ads that run on Saturday mornings or after school on weekdays.

3. Collect the completed surveys. With the help of a volunteer, tabulate the results on the chalkboard. Use some of the raw information from the survey to develop classification skills. For example, students list the names of businesses where they spend their money. Individual businesses might be classified into categories like specialty stores and department stores.

Caution: Some of the children's answers on the surveys may contain some sensitive information for the individual child or the family involved. Tabulate the information for the entire class. Avoid associating information with individual students.

4. After the survey data is tabulated, discuss with the class the following questions:
   - What are the most common types of jobs we do?
   - What might happen if kids suddenly stopped working? (Many jobs would not get done, people might have to hire others to do the jobs.)
   - How much money do we spend as an entire class every week? Every month? Every year?
   - What goods and services are most popular in our class?
   - What businesses are most popular in our class?
   - What are the most popular goods or services our class wanted parents to buy?
   - What businesses advertise on television to attract young people to their goods or services?
   - What would happen to all these businesses if kids suddenly decided to stop spending their money? (People might lost their jobs or make less money.)
   - How important do you think young people are in the economy? (Stress the idea that young people are important in the economy as consumers. In addition, people depend on young people to do some jobs and to spend their income for goods and services.)

Mark C. Schug is an Associate Professor of Social Studies in the Department of Curriculum and Instruction at the University of Wisconsin-Milwaukee. Dr. Schug is also Editor of *Economics in the School Curriculum, K-12*, published by the National Education Association. [1986 note]

**Howard Yeargan**
**Barbara Hatcher**

Each spring third graders at Riverside Park Elementary School in San Antonio, Texas, discuss margin of profit, division of labor, and productivity. These are not mere abstractions to these students. Their teacher, Mrs. Frances Rios, captures student interest with a special project designed to make economic concepts comprehensible.

How is this accomplished? By creating their own corporation, these young entrepreneurs learn first-hand about economic principles and the decisions that businesses must make in the market economy. Although company officers are inexperienced in corporate management and employees are struggling to make correct change for a dollar, these third graders do develop an elementary understanding of economics. This is because their teacher designs relevant, participatory experience to illustrate abstract economic concepts.

Mrs. Rios selected the creation of the Cupcake Factory as an appropriate vehicle to generate pupil interest in economics. To prepare for the cupcake venture, class members visited neighborhood bakeries. They noted the products, prices, and services as well as bakery production and marketing strategies. One rule of business is to know what the competition is offering, and these enterprising students learned about the law of supply and demand and competition in the market place.

One of the first tasks facing the young corporation was to determine buyer interest in baked goods. Students approached this problem by conducting a market survey in their school. Survey teams questioned fellow students about preferences for muffins, cookies, and cupcakes. A graph of the results of the study revealed that chocolate cupcakes were in high demand. In addition, the survey teams reported that a cupcake factory on campus could capitalize on location as a prime factor to increase sales. The cafeteria with its high concentration of hungry patrons was designated as the perfect place to market cupcakes. This activity provided opportunities for pupils to organize, analyze, and synthesize information as well as to share their findings in graphic form.

With buyer interest assured and a prime location for the factory established in Room 14, corporate officers and committees were elected to assist in company operations.

Reprinted with permission from the Helen Dwight Reid Educational Foundation, from *The Social Studies*, March/April 1985. Published by Heldref Publications, 1319 Eighteenth Street, NW, Washington, D.C. 20036-1802. Copyright 1985.

Committees for finance, advertisement, production, and purchasing were created. Committees were given detailed job assignments and members of the committees went to work with uncommon enthusiasm. The finance committee solicited operating funds from interested class members. At 10¢ a share, each stockholder received a certificate indicating the shareholder's name, number, and the amount of money invested in the company.

The purchasing committee prudently watched for bargains on cupcake ingredients. Pupils examined grocery ads and compared prices on needed items. Cupcake papers, oil, eggs, cake mix, and frosting prices became the topic of the day. The market survey revealed that 300 cupcakes could easily be sold so the purchasing committee had to determine the amount and best price for raw materials. Making these determinations provided opportunities for students to reinforce reading and computational skills.

Since the sale of company stock did not provide sufficient revenue to cover the cost of the raw materials, the students needed an understanding banker. Now it was the finance committee's turn to secure additional operating capital. For this first experience at borrowing money, the children carefully organized their presentation for the loan officer. They practiced introducing each other, and they discussed the meaning of credit, interest, and contract.

After meeting the bank president and hearing a short credit lesson, the young borrowers signed the terms of agreement and secured a bank note for operating funds for the cupcake venture. Shaking hands with the bank president and conducting business "just like Mom and Dad" was an excellent image enhancer for these pupils.

In the meantime, the advertising committee was enthusiastically preparing a campaign to market cupcakes. Newspaper and magazine ads provided ideas for content, layout, and arrangement. Motivating expressions such as "creamy chocolate," "light and fluffy," "mouth watering," and "finger-licking good" were selected. A flurry of signs appeared in the halls as testimonials for the cupcakes: "Cats like these cupcakes." "Rabbits like these cupcakes." "Even Snoopy endorses Cupcake Factory products!" In addition, students used the public address system in the cafeteria to share the merits of their product and to remind potential buyers of the sale. This activity reinforced both oral and written communication skills of students.

While the purchasing committee was busy selecting cake mix, frosting, and other ingredients at the store, the production committee was planning the most efficient method of factory operation. It was determined that specialization was necessary if 300 cupcakes were to be prepared. Capital goods such as baking pans, oven, and the mixer were assembled. Recipes were studied for the exact proportions of ingredients. Bakers, icers, and clean-up crews were organized. Factory workers realized that too many cooks could spoil the delicate cupcakes, so job descriptions were determined and responsibilities were clearly defined. This experience provided opportunities for pupils not only to experience "division of labor," but also to make decisions and assume responsibilities for assigned tasks.

Finally, the factory was ready for production. Students worried: "Will we make a profit? Will everything be ready on time?" On May fifth, the Cupcake Factory began production. Everyone in Room 14 labored eagerly over their assigned tasks. Large cupcakes with rich, chocolate frosting covered the tables and the aroma of chocolate filled the halls. Customers inquired about the exact time for the sale as cashiers sorted coins in order to have change ready for business.

Sales were brisk and in less than an hour, all cupcakes were sold. As the day's receipts were tallied, bills and coins were separated and counted. The vice president of finance announced a final total of $38.50 for the sale. "This is not profit," he reported. "We will have to pay back the banker and the grocer, but still money will be left over!" But what about the customers? Their chocolate-covered smiles said it all—Uhm-Uhm-Good! How will these young entrepreneurs of the Cupcake Factory be paid for their efforts? They voted for a delicious dividend-in-kind, of course.

The students in Mrs. Rios' class not only talked about margin of profit, division of labor, and productivity, but also experienced these abstract concepts in real-life settings. Children can understand economic principles, and with this teaching process, reading, writing, arithmetic, decision-making skills, and a sense of self-worth can be nurtured. The Cupcake Factory is one example of how enterprising educators can make economics comprehensible and captivating.

BIBLIOGRAPHY

Deery, Ruth. "Classroom Routines: Make Them Pay Off Big!," *Social Education*. (February, 1984), pp. 138-141.

Hatcher, Barbara. "Everyone Talks About The Weather, But No One Does Anything About It," *The Social Studies Teacher*. (April/May, 1983), p. 12.

Kourilsky, Marilyn. *Beyond Simulation: The Mini-Society Approach to Economics and Other Social Sciences*. Los Angeles: Educational Research Associates, 1974.

———. *Mini-Society Experiencing Real World Economics in the Elementary School Classroom*. Reading, Mass: Addison-Wesley, 1983.

———. "The Kinder-Economy: A Case Study of Kindergarten Pupil's Acquisition of Economic Concepts," *Elementary School Journal*. (January, 1977), pp. 182-191.

Kourilsky, M. and Michael Ballard-Campbell. "Mini-Society: An Individualized Social Studies Programs for Children of Low, Middle, and High Ability," *The Social Studies* (September/October, 1984), pp. 224-228.

Kourilsky, Marilyn and J. Hirschleifer. "Mini-Society vs. Token Economy: An Experimental Comparison of the Effects of Learning and Autonomy of Socially Emergent and Imposed Behavior Modification," (July/August, 1976), pp. 376-381.

National Center of Economic Education for Children. *The Elementary Economists*. Volume I and 11. ERIC No. ED 206 545. Cambridge, Mass: The Center, 1981.

Reinke, Diane and Margit McGuire. *The Book Company*. Seattle: Washington State Council on Economic Education, 1980.

Richmond, George. *The Micro-Society School: A Real World in Miniature*. New York: Harper and Row, 1973.

Tieken-Weber, Nancy. "The Cookie Concession: Economics Learning for Fun and 'Prophit,'" *Learning*. (October, 1981), pp. 30-33.

Howard Yeargan is the Director of the Center for Economic Education at Southwest Texas State University in San Marcos. Barbara Hatcher is the Assistant Director of the Center for Economic Education at Southwest Texas State University in San Marcos. [1985 note]

**Roberta E. Maselow**

*Card, Card, Card Connection has low, low, low prices...*
*Come and buy your cards today!*

Drop by a number of New York City elementary schools, and you will hear similar advertising jingles written by children about greeting cards that they design, produce, advertise, and sell. You will see children adding and subtracting fractions to calculate their sales commissions. You will see children writing advertising slogans and making sales pitches. Kids who are motivated and excited—learn!!

*The Card Connection: Business for Children* project gives children an understanding of economics in the early grades. For a long time, it was thought that elementary school children were not capable of learning economic concepts. The evaluative studies of economic education in the primary grades, however, show that children can learn some basic economic concepts and have fun while they learn.[1]

From ages 6 through 8, children think that purchasing an item in a store is a simple ritual. They do not understand that the shopkeeper pays for the item that is sold. Children at this age are not aware of the concept of profit. At the next level, children understand that the goods must be paid for, but they think that the price paid is the same as the selling price. At about 10, children begin to understand the relationship between the purchase price and the sale price.[2]

Teaching youngsters about economics is good news for businesses, which are increasingly having trouble finding entry-level job candidates with basic skills like reading, writing, and mathematics. Many teenagers and young adults have trouble even filling out an employment application form.

## STARTING A BUSINESS

I started Card Connection in my computer/mathematics classroom in Public School 146 in East Harlem. The student body (646 students) is 50 percent African American and 46 percent Latino. Forty percent of our households are classified as living below the poverty line. This greeting card business for children teaches math and communication skills, interview techniques, basic economic concepts (profit, supply and demand, market research, opportunity cost), salesmanship, and more. The project has been replicated in classrooms in the South Bronx, East Harlem, and, most recently, in the Lower East Side of Manhattan.

It's easy to get started. All you need is a minimum initial investment (for paper, envelopes, inks, and a printer), an enthusiastic teacher, a part-time parent volunteer, and the support of community businesses. Students design the greeting cards, which are easily produced in school. For example, you can purchase the Riso Print Gocco Instant Color Printer, an inexpensive silk-screen printer (about $90), at major art-supply stores. Simple enough for a child to operate, the printer uses nontoxic ink and produces professional results.

I introduced my 5th graders to the concept by asking, "How many of you have seen relatives applying for a job?" Many children shared experiences. "Suppose you saw a 'Help Wanted' sign outside your favorite store. How would you apply for the job?" Words such as employment application and interview emerged. Some of the children even had first-hand experience at a family business or a supermarket.

When I asked the children if they would like to work for Card Connection, many hands went up. One child asked, "Are we going to get paid?" Although we cannot legally give children money, we paid them in scrip, which they could exchange for greeting cards. Eventually, local businesses provided gift certificates for the children to compensate them for their work.

The class designed an application form geared to their age level and our business, and we discussed how to complete the form. When we came to a question about experience, one student asked, "How can we have experience if we never had a job? We're just kids!"

"Very simple," I replied, "If you are good at something—that's experience! For example, in order to print cards you should be neat, careful, and able to measure and line up the card with the edge of the machine. What qualities do you need to be in sales? What experience would qualify you to be an accountant?" The children soon found out that they had more experience than they realized.

Next, I invited the children to apply to one of three departments: production, sales, or accounting. The production department prints, folds, and stamps the cards with our company logo, places them in envelopes, and packages and prices them. Other tasks include designing new cards, creating advertising signs posted throughout the school, and maintaining a running inventory to determine which cards to print each week.

The sales department conducts market research; is responsible for advertising (writing jingles and performing them on the public address system, displaying posters, and

Reprinted with permission from the Association for Supervision and Curriculum Development, from *Educational Leadership*, May 1995, Volume 52, Number 8. Copyright 1995 by the Association for Supervision and Curriculum Development.

distributing flyers); sells the cards; writes receipts; counts money; and makes change.

The young accountants check the receipts against the monies collected, maintain books, calculate payroll, write checks for "rent" and other expenses, and set prices that maintain an acceptable profit margin.

A volunteer from the business community interviews students and selects children for each department based on their willingness to work and learn all aspects of the business. All students who apply are hired as long as they are willing to learn their job. Employees are trained in all three departments, so that they can fill in wherever they are needed—just like a real business!

## MAY I TAKE YOUR ORDER?

Card Connection is open two days a week from 11 a.m. to 2 p.m. Typically, the children sell cards during lunch (12-1). The accountants work from 1-2 p.m. A typical day at Card Connection begins with the sales meeting ( 11 a.m. to noon). The salespeople (supervised by a parent or volunteer business executive) count the money in the cash box (about $25) and make sure that they have enough change. Next, comes an inventory to see what cards need to be ordered from the production department. The children arrange the cards in boxes on a rolling cart.

Each salesperson keeps a supply of business cards (low-cost name stamps can be ordered at stationery stores) and wears a name tag (a personalized business card in a clear plastic holder). The sales staff also sign in and out of work on time cards (5x8 index cards). Every day, the business consultant who supervises the program assigns three salespeople to take orders. Each carries a receipt book and a catalog (actually a photo album with clear, plastic pages for changing cards easily when the seasons change). One student is assigned to the cash box to collect money and make change Another student, the supervisor checks the math on the receipts and ensures that customers are treated courteously and receive proper change. An adult supervisor oversees the entire process. Here's a brief scenario.

Wiltaya, a salesperson for Card Connection, knocks on a classroom door and is greeted by a teacher. "Excuse me," she says, "Would you like to buy some cards?" She is invited in. "This is our catalog. We have birthday, thank you, get well soon, holiday, sympathy, and note cards. Our cards are $.65 each, 2 for $1.25, and 3 for $1.75 "

The teacher asks for two birthday cards and one thank you. Wiltaya writes the receipt. "That will be $1.75, please." The teacher gives her a $5 bill. Wiltaya thanks the teacher, and gives the receipt and the bill to Charles, who is in charge of the cash box outside in the hall. He gives her the change due, and Jackie gets the cards from the rolling storage cart. Wiltaya returns with the change and carefully counts it out into the customer's hand: "A quarter makes 60, and one is $3, $4, and $5 Here is your receipt. Thank you very much, and have a nice day."

The children learn that sincerity and politeness go a long way in the business world. Beatrice Badillo, executive assistant of Community School Board #4, said of the Card Connection staff:

> I was quite impressed with their professionalism when they entered my office. Their business approach was remarkable; they even presented a display of their product to me, and after completing our transaction, gave me their personal business cards.

## CREATING COMMUNITY CONNECTIONS

In 1993, the Card Connection project won third place in the National Council on Economic Education's competition for exemplary projects in economics in the classroom. As a result of this award, Peter Bell, executive director of the New York State Council on Economic Education, invited a group of children to present the project to the Board of Directors. At the meeting, Michelle was busy selling cards to members of the board, which included college professors and corporate executives. When asked to introduce herself to the group, she said, "Just as soon as I finish this sale. After all, business is business!"

At a school district meeting, officials watched in amazement as 10-year-old Chavis made a sales pitch to former New York City Mayor David Dinkins. The Mayor bought 14 cards and was photographed with the young tycoon.

The most exciting results of this project are the connections that the children make to their community. Corporate Printing Corporation, for example, became a valuable community partner. Because of the high cost of paper, our profit margin was very low. Most businesses buy raw materials wholesale, but we were paying retail prices. On the back of one of many invitations we received to attend various award ceremonies. I saw the line, "Printed courtesy of Corporate Printing." I decided to call the company. When the secretary asked what company I was from, I answered, "Card Connection."

Joel Glick, executive vice president, picked up the phone. After I explained our situation, he invited me to his office. The next day, I found myself in a conference room at his company, showing samples of the children's work. Before I finished speaking, he said, "I'm going to send you so many cards and envelopes that you are going to beg me to stop!" Glick explained that his taking print shop at a New York City high school had made him decide to become a printer.

Shortly thereafter, I taught the Card Connection kids how to write a business letter. Our first letter went to Joel Glick. I told the children that Mr. Glick had donated the cards and envelopes because he wanted to help others to graduate and to become successful, too. The kids wrote charming letters, one of which said, "Someday I would like us to be in business together."

Glick was so impressed by the children's letters that he came to the school to meet the Card Connection "kidpreneurs." During his visit, he advised the children to get a good education. The children knew that his advice came from the heart. They beamed from ear to ear as they listened to him speak.

Another exciting experience for us was the local ABC affiliate's segment on "Children and Entrepreneurship" for Eyewitness News. Parents signed releases so that the 5th graders could appear on television. The day of filming almost every adult in the school lined up to buy cards. A few days later, the news "teaser" throughout the day said, "See how little tykes become big tycoons on Eyewitness News at 6."

## BUSINESS EDUCATION PAYS OFF

It is my sincere belief that the business community is eager to join hands with educators to give students an understanding of economics and the business world. Our job as educators is to communicate to businesspeople exactly how they can help us. Clearly, children learn much from exposure to the business world, but all their learning isn't about market research and supply and demand. For example, the kids who put in the most hours working for Card Connection became the Board of Directors. When the time came to decide how to spend the profits, they voted to donate the money to Ronald McDonald House, Food for Survival, the AIDS Dance-A-Thon, and the East Harlem Tutorial Program. So, not only do students learn valuable skills for the world of work, but they also learn the importance of giving something back to their community.

## NOTES

1  Mark Schug refers to the work of Gustav Jahoda, a professor at the University of Strathclyde, Glasgow, in describing children's economic development. See M. C. Schug, (1986), *Economics for Kids: Ideas for Teaching in the Elementary Grades*, (Washington, D.C.: National Education Association).

2  R. H. Hendricks, (1989), *Learning Economics Through Children's Stories*, (New York: Joint Council on Economic Education).

Author's note: Although economics is mandated in 16 states and has been infused in the K-12 curriculum of other states, the teaching of economics is still dependent upon the interest and knowledge of individual teachers. There is a need for increased staff development in economic education across the grades.

To further teachers' understanding of economic education, the National Council on Economic Education created the new Economics America program, which has identified six student outcomes in economic education. For more information about the program, contact the National Council on Economic Education, 1140 Avenue of the Americas New York, NY 10036.

Roberta E. Maselow is the Director of Mathematics and Assessment in Community School District One, 80 Montgomery Street, New York, N.Y. Previously, she has worked as an elementary school teacher and supervisor for twenty-three years. [1995 note]

**Sue Murphy**
**Janet Walsh**

The world today is full of opportunities
and exciting information. But it is also complex, technological, and intense. It requires a different set of skills than
was required twenty years ago; or even ten. Today, thinking skills are of prime importance. "Success depends on
the whole society coming to place a much higher value
not just on schooling but on learning. This demands a re-
definition of the purposes of schooling, one that goes way
beyond the inculcation of routine skills and the acquisition of a stock of facts."[1]

Educators, striving to help students become learners and
thinkers, find themselves squeezing critical thinking skills
curricula into an already crowded schedule. We need to find
creative ways and opportunities to incorporate the teaching
of these important skills into the on-going curriculum. The
study of economics offers this opportunity and blends well
into many curriculum areas, especially social studies. Because
economics is founded on everyday behavior, lessons can be
reinforced throughout the school day.

Economics is essentially a study of choices and decision making. Prices are set in the market place based on
what consumers are willing to buy and at the price they
are willing to pay. Prices are based on our choices. But
how many of us feel connected to what goes on in the
market place? Many of us feel victimized and helpless to
affect what goes on around us—in the market place and
in many other realms.

This is also a feeling among many students, especially
those lacking confidence in their abilities. "One characteristic of high-risk individuals is that they do not perceive themselves as having a significant amount of ability
to affect what happens to them in their life. They believe
in fate or luck and frequently experience impotence and
powerlessness in their life."[2] Understanding the basic principles of economics—and their role in everyday life—can
help such students take responsibility for the choices they
make and empower them to direct their lives. If linked to
their work, economics can be especially valuable for students with poor self-concepts and behavior problems.

There is a strong connection between what goes on in
the day-to-day world of economics and what goes on in
our day-to-day living. Yet teaching economics, especially
to young students, can be a disheartening and fruitless

experience unless the students are connected to the material presented. They need to be actively involved. "Good
teachers find ways to activate students, for they know that
learning requires active engagement between the subject
and object matter."[3] Successful teaching of economics to
young students involves helping the students make the
connection between the subject material and their life
material.

## BASIC ECONOMIC CONCEPTS

*Choices:* All people must make choices because we have
   unlimited wants but limited resources.
*Scarcity:* Since limited resources do not allow us to have
   everything we want we must choose the things we want
   most.
*Opportunity Cost:* Choosing one thing also means giving up
   the opportunity to choose something else.
*Indirect Cost:* The activities of some people are harmful to
   others who are not directly involved
*Decision Making:* The process used in making choices.

These basic economic concepts can be presented using examples from students' lives to reinforce the information. Involve them, engage them. Help them apply the
principles in their daily decision making.

## CHOICES

Choices are a large part of the school day. Students can
be shown that they are responsible for their choices and
what happens to them is the result of the choices they
make.

> Student: "He started the fight by calling me a
> name."
> Teacher: "The fight happened when you chose
> to respond when Mark called you a name."
> Student: "I didn't have any problems today."
> Teacher: "You had a great day because you chose
> to ignore things that would affect your day."
> Student: "I didn't do anything!"
> Teacher: "You chose to stand next to Joe and
> laugh when he was name-calling, so you became
> part of the problem. You had a choice."
> Student: "I got pretty far in math today."
> Teacher: "You were successful in math today be-
> cause you chose to work hard."

It is hard to make the connection between personal
choices and what happens to us. Choices are hard to own
because it is easy to claim no responsibility for what happens to us; the victim syndrome is prevalent. A teacher
can reinforce the concept of choices all day, every day.

## OPPORTUNITY COST

"What did that cost you?" is a common question in a classroom that connects economics with life. Choosing one thing also means giving up the opportunity to chose something else.

> Teacher: "You chose to break the rules on the playground and you had to miss recess. Was it worth it to you?"
> Teacher: "You chose not to do your homework last night and it will cost you your break."
> Teacher: "You chose the hamburger so you cannot have the fish sandwich."
> Teacher: "You asked for the jacks so you passed up the opportunity to play checkers with Jason."

Students often do not own their choices and, therefore, do not claim responsibility for the consequences of their choices. Sometimes teachers make too many of the students' choices for them. Instead, teachers should help students take responsibility for their own decisions. Once the concept of "opportunity cost" is introduced, there are many daily ways to reinforce the concept that can enhance the students' ability to make the connection between their actions and the consequences of those actions.

## INDIRECT COSTS

We are social beings who are intricately interwoven with others. We often do not see how our actions or attitudes affect those around us. Yet, the activities of some are harmful to others who are not directly involved. In a classroom, there are many examples of "indirect cost." If one student is angry, it usually brings out anger in others. If a student refuses to share or cooperate, this creates a negative mood in others. If a student holds up the line by not following directions, the whole class is affected. Verbalizing these day-to-day happenings helps the students to realize their connection to the group and the importance of thinking about their actions.

## PERSONAL AND SOCIAL DECISION MAKING

The decision-making process involves five steps:
1. Defining the problem.
2. Listing the alternatives.
3. Stating criteria.
4. Evaluating alternatives.
5. Making a decision.[4]

We have unlimited wants but limited resources; therefore, it is important to be wise choice makers, to be aware that advantages and disadvantages have to be considered to get the maximum benefit.

Students have an opportunity to apply this process daily, and we, as teachers, have the opportunity to let them know that they are making decisions that affect what happens to them.

Examples of opportunities for the decision-making process:

1. One class has a ten-minute break during which the students have an opportunity to choose activities. Since a scarcity exists and not all can play checkers, jacks, etc., students are forced to make a personal decision and at the same time are made aware of how one person s decision affects others (social decision making). If five people wish to play checkers and only two can play, some sort of compromise must be made. Allowing the students to work this arrangement out among themselves teaches the give-and-take that is necessary among young people and helps the students feel some control over the situation. If they own the decision, they are less able to blame the outcome on others.
2. The class could plan a field trip, taking into consideration the criteria of all the students and the alternatives available.
3. Give the class a free hour on a Friday afternoon and allow students to plan that hour during the week.
4. Allow the class to invite a speaker into the classroom, letting students decide who to invite based on the wants and needs of group members.

Given opportunity, guidance, and practice, students can become very responsible decision makers. A teacher's role is to empower the students, to help them take active control, and to help them make important choices. "Good teachers know when to hang back and be silent, when to watch and wonder at what is taking place all around them."[5]

## NOTES

[1] *A Nation Prepared: Teachers for the 21st Century*. (1986) Carnegie Forum on Education and the Economy, p. 21.

[2] Glenn, H.S. ( 1986). *Raising Children for Success*. Sunrise Press, p. 105.

[3] Ayres, W. (1986). *About Teaching and Teachers*. Harvard Educational Review, 56, p. 50.

[4] *Tradeoff*. ( 1978). Agency for Instructional Television, lesson 2

[5] Ayres, W. (1986). *About Teaching and Teachers*. Harvard Educational Review, 56, p. 50.

Sue Murphy teaches children with behavior disorders in the Cincinnati Public Schools. Janet Walsh is a reporter for the *Cincinnati Post* specializing in education issues. The two authors have collaborated on various projects as a result of the Partners in Education Program, which connects area businesses with schools. [1989 note]

# Economics for Elementary School Students
## *Research-Supported Principles of Teaching and Learning that Guide Classroom Practice*

# 48

**James D. Laney**

Many states have recognized the importance of including economic education in the elementary school curriculum. According to Kourilsky (1986), large numbers of today's at-risk elementary school students will never reach high school. Without economics instruction during their elementary school years, these students are not likely to acquire the knowledge and skills necessary for functioning successfully within the American economic system.

Let us assume that economic education for elementary school students is desirable. Is it possible for elementary school students to learn and remember economic concepts? The answer to this question is "yes." As evinced by the findings of empirical investigations, even kindergarten children are capable of mastering economic concepts if the instruction meets standards of focus, concentration, and developmental appropriateness (Kourilsky 1977).

Now, let us go two steps further by attempting to answer the following questions: (1) Which economic concepts should receive primary emphasis during the elementary school years? (2) How can these concepts be taught most effectively?

Any answer to the first question is a subjective one. In my opinion, the most important economic concept for elementary school students to learn is cost-benefit analysis. The development of our children into rational adult decision makers depends greatly on their acquisition of this concept. Cost-benefit analysis is not the only problem-solving model around, but it has been shown to be instrumental in increasing the satisfaction of individuals and families who use it in their everyday decision making (Kourilsky and Murray 1981). If I were allowed to teach only one economic concept to elementary school students, cost-benefit analysis would be my choice.

With respect to the second question, research can serve as a guide to practice. Effective economic education in the elementary school depends upon the application of research-supported principles of learning and instruction. Four such principles, based on my own empirical research, can be summarized as follows:

*Teaching-Learning Principle 1:* Because they are more meaningful and memorable, real-life experiences are superior to vicarious ones in promoting learning and retention of economic concepts. Vicarious experiences are more appropriately used as follow-up activities that reinforce the initial learning and help students transfer the learning to new situations (Laney 1989).

*Teaching-Learning Principle 2:* Experience itself, does not guarantee the acquisition of economic concepts. In order to ensure students' learning, their attention needs to be focused on the economic concepts present within event-based instructional activities. One way this attention focus can be accomplished is through the use of teacher-led, post-experience, inquiry-oriented debriefing sessions, with the classroom organized into an interaction-discussion group (Kourilsky 1983; Laney 1992).

*Teaching-Learning Principle 3:* Invented concept labels enhance students' understanding and retention of economic concepts. Through the invention of such labels, students construct concept meaning for themselves; they make their own sense of the new learning (Laney 1989).

*Teaching-Learning Principle 4:* In accordance with M.C. Wittrock's (1974, 1983, 1987) generative teaching-learning theory, the use of student-and teacher-produced verbal and/or imaginal-related representations of idea; promotes learning and retention of economic concepts. Learning occurs as the student constructs relation' among the parts of the new information to be learned and/or relations between the new information and his or her own knowledge base or past experiences. Because it requires students to use two different types of information processing, the integrated use of verbal and imaginal strategies has the potential to result in greater learning and retention of economic concepts than the use of verbal-only or imagery-only strategies. At about age eight, children develop the ability to generate and profit from images; thus, use of certain imaginal strategies may be more appropriate for intermediate-grade rather than primary-grade students (Laney 1990a; Laney 1990b; Laney and Moseley 1991; Wittrock 1983).

In conjunction with my research in economic education, I have found and developed a number of activities that have been used successfully with elementary school students to teach cost-benefit analysis and the related subconcepts of scarcity, alternatives, and opportunity cost. These activities, described in the paragraphs that follow, illustrate how one or more of the four empirically established principles of teaching and learning described can be applied to economics instruction in the elementary school classroom.

Scarcity refers to a situation in which there is a virtually unlimited number of wants but a limited number of resources to satisfy those wants. This concept can be successfully introduced through real-life experiences. As noted

Reprinted with permission from the H.L. Dwight Reid Educational Foundation, from *The Social Studies*, May/June 1993. Published by Heldref Publications, 1319 Eighteenth Street, NW, Washington, D.C. 20036-1802. Copyright 1993.

by Kourilsky (1983), real-life scarcity situations arise naturally in elementary school settings each day. There is a scarcity of time and space at the learning center; there is a scarcity of playground equipment at recess; there is a scarcity of materials during art class. Occasions such as these provide the teacher with opportunities to hold post-experience classroom debriefings on the concept of scarcity and to let students explore a variety of allocation strategies for resolving the scarcity problem. Kourilsky (1983) suggests that four steps are necessary for conducting a successful debriefing session. These steps, which are printed here along with specific examples of how to apply them when teaching the concept of scarcity, incorporate all four teaching-learning principles in the sample lesson. The lesson features a real-life experience, an inquiry-oriented debriefing session, invented concept label generation, and written and pictorial representations of ideas.

## EXPERIENCE

Students experience an economic event, a real-life occurrence that has value in teaching about economics.

For example, students are confronted with a scarcity situation at school.

▪ *Debriefing Step 1: Describe*
Describe the details of the economic event
For example have students describe the scarcity situation in their own words. Then have students roleplay the situation

▪ *Debriefing Step 2: Identify*
Identify the central issue, problem, or question associated with the event
For example, help students recognize that the existence of scarce resources is a relevant decision-making issue

▪ *Debriefing Step 3: Teach or Review*
Teach or review the economic concept(s) needed for dealing with the central issue, problem, or question.
For example, have students supply their own invented definition and label for the concept of scarcity, such as not-enough or too-few-for-so-many. Then provide students with the conventional concept definition and label.

▪ *Debriefing Step 4: Relate*
Relate the new information to the current rent problem and to the students' knowledge base and past experience.
For example, help students resolve the scarcity problem by having them brainstorm storm possible allocation strategies, discuss and roleplay positive and negative consequences of each strategy, select an allocation strategy, implement the selected allocation strategy, and live with the consequences of their decision. As a follow-up activity, have each student draw a cartoon depicting a scarcity situation she or he has experienced or a scarcity situation from his or her own imagination. Then have each student write a scarcity story to accompany his or her cartoon.

As I have described (Laney 1988a, b), the generation of scarcity cartoons and stories allows students to experience vicariously and apply the concept of scarcity in new, creative ways. Scarcity cartoons are simply pictorial representations of scarcity situations. My elementary school students have created scarcity cartoons that show three circus tents and only two clowns, two mermaid queens and only one throne, three elephants and only one small pond in which to take a bath. Scarcity stories are brief paragraphs that describe scarcity situations. A third-grader wrote this amusing scarcity story: "There were two birds and only one worm. Each bird wanted one worm to eat. They called the problem 'scarcity,' but that did not solve anything. They fought and fought. They thought and thought. And I bet they are still fighting and thinking." As mentioned previously, vicarious experiences with economic concepts, when used as follow-up activities, serve to reinforce students' learning of these concepts and help students transfer these concepts to new situations, real or fanciful.

Opportunity cost refers to one's second choice or one's next best use for a scarce resource. It is the thing one gives up when making a resource allocation decision. I have found that realistic experiences, inquiry-oriented debriefing sessions, and representations of ideas promote children's learning and retention of this concept as it relates to both consumers and producers of goods and services (Laney 1989). The two opportunity cost lessons outlined here incorporate my findings and the four teaching-learning principles.

Opportunity cost for consumers can be taught by having students decide which food item to buy from among three alternatives A suggested sequence for this activity follows:

## EXPERIENCE

Teacher gives students a set amount of money to spend.

Teacher presents students with three food items, each priced at that set amount of money.

▪ *Debriefing Step 1: Describe*
Students describe and roleplay the problem (scarcity of money; only enough money to buy one food item).

▪ *Debriefing Step 2: Identify*
Teacher helps students recognize the central question: What does a consumer give up when he or she makes a decision about how to use a scarce resource?

▪ *Debriefing Step 3: Teach or Review*
Students list alternatives.
Students list and roleplay positive and negative consequences of each alternative.
Students rank alternatives.
Students identify, with teacher guidance, their opportunity cost (second choice).

▪ *Debriefing Step 4: Relate*
Students implement their decision (i.e., eat the food item that was their first choice).
Teacher asks students whether they still like the choice they made.

Teacher asks each student to think of his or her own example of opportunity cost for consumers. Each student writes a story describing his or her example and then illustrates the story by drawing pictures of the alternatives and circling the opportunity cost.

Opportunity cost for producers can be taught by having students decide which art project to undertake from among three alternatives. Teachers can follow this suggested sequence for the activity.

## EXPERIENCE

Teacher presents students with a set of raw materials for making an art project.

Teacher describes three art projects, each requiring the same amount of raw materials.

■ *Debriefing Step 1: Describe*

Students describe and roleplay the problem (scarcity of raw materials or art supplies: only enough raw materials to make one art project).

■ *Debriefing Step 2: Identify*

Teacher helps students recognize the central question: What does a producer give up when she or he makes a decision about how to use a scarce resource?

■ *Debriefing Step 3: Teach or Review*

Students list alternatives.

Students discuss and roleplay the positive and negative consequences of each alternative.

Students rank their alternatives (first, second, third). Students identify, with teacher guidance, their opportunity cost (second choice).

■ *Debriefing Step 4: Relate*

Students implement their decision (i.e., complete the art project that was their first choice).

Teacher asks students whether they still like the choice they made.

Teacher asks each student to think of his or her own example of opportunity cost for producers. Each student writes a story describing his or her example and then illustrates the story by drawing pictures of the alternatives and circling the opportunity cost.

Learning and retention of opportunity cost can also be enhanced through teaching-learning principle 3 by encouraging students to invent their own label for this concept. I have outlined four procedural steps for this purpose (Laney 1989).

## INVENTED CONCEPT LABELING: STEP 1

After studying examples of the concept, students note similarities (critical attributes and summarize them in a single sentence or concept definition.

## INVENTED CONCEPT LABELING: STEP 2

Students, with instructor giving guidance as needed, create a one- or two-word label that captures the essence of the concept.

## INVENTED CONCEPT LABELING: STEP 3

After brainstorming to develop many alternative labels, students decide on a preferred label (e.g., next best for the concept of opportunity cost).

## INVENTED CONCEPT LABELING: STEP 4

Teacher informs or reminds students of the conventional concept label.

Cost-benefit analysis refers to a decision-making process in which one weighs the anticipated costs and benefits of alternative courses of action. This process integrates the concepts of scarcity, alternatives, and opportunity cost. In accordance with teaching-learning principle 4, decision trees and verbal or imagery-related strategies can be used with elementary students to help them internalize the steps of economic decision making and transfer the concept of cost-benefit analysis to their personal decision making. I have found instruction on cost-benefit analysis to be more successful with students in the intermediate as opposed to the primary grades.

In the conventional decision tree activity, students are presented with a hypothetical dilemma. The teacher may ask them to pretend they are at the shopping mall and want to do something that is fun. Assume that it takes two hours to complete one entertainment or recreational activity at the mall. Students pretend to have two hours at the mall before they must go home. The teacher asks the students to decide what to do during that two-hour period.

On a diagram of a tree, students write summary sentences for each step of the cost-benefit analysis process. They write a sentence describing the problem at the base of the tree and a sentence describing their goal above the topmost branches of the tree. On the lowest branches, students write sentences summarizing their alternatives. The middle branches are reserved for sentences describing positive and negative consequences of each alternative. The topmost branches contain a sentence describing the final choice.

An interest-sparking variation of this activity is the use of a diagram of a multi-level shopping mall rather than a diagram of a tree. In yet another variation, students substitute simple stick figures for the summary sentences. The potential for learning is greatly increased when students generate both summary sentences and stick figures Verbal representations such as summary sentences, enhance learning through a familiar information processing mode, whereas imaginal representations such as diagrams and stick figures, are useful as mnemonic devices. All of these representations, whether verbal or imaginal, assist the learner in making connections between the various steps of the cost-benefit analysis model and between the new learning and his or her own knowledge base or past experiences.

All of the aforementioned economic concepts can be taught through experience-based economics programs such as Marilyn Kourilsky's (1977, 1983) Kinder-Economy (for grades K-2) and Mini-Society (for grades 3-6). These programs are organized around the use of real-life experiences and inquiry-oriented debriefing sessions; thus, they incorporate teaching-learning principles 1 and 2.

Kinder-Economy students participate in a set of experience-based situations related to economic decision making in the real world. Experiences with economic concepts, such as classroom scarcity situations, are followed by teacher-led debriefings and reinforcement activities in the form of games, learning centers, worksheets, and filmstrips.

Functioning as producers and consumers in a classroom marketplace, Mini-Society participants experience real-world economics on a scale that is small, manageable, and safe. Learning through experience is not left to chance, for each market day is followed by Kourilsky's (1983) four-step debriefing session as described previously. In each debriefing session, roleplay and guided discussion are employed by the teacher to help students analyze and learn about one or more of the economic concepts that they have encountered in their classroom marketplace. Students experience concept-related economic events on subsequent market days and, over time, integrate the new information acquired during a debriefing with what they already know. Children apply new understandings as they communicate and interact.

As demonstrated by the instructional activities in economics described earlier, research can be used to guide classroom practice. Effective economics instruction requires the application of research-established principles of learning and instruction, such as the four described at the beginning of this article. If the goal of economic literacy is to be reached, researchers, teachers, administrators, and curriculum designers must work together to bridge the gap between research and classroom practice.

## REFERENCES

Kourilsky, M.L. 1977. "The Kindereconomy: A Case Study of Kindergarten Pupils' Acquisition of Economic Concepts." *The Elementary School Journal* 77(3): 182-91.

———. 1983. *Mini-Society: Experiencing Real-World Economics in the Elementary School Classroom*. Menlo Park, Calif.: Addison-Wesley.

———. 1986. "School Reform: The Role of the Economic Educator." *Journal of Economic Education* 17(3): 213-17.

Kourilsky, M.L. and T. Murray. 1981. "The Use of Economic Reasoning to Increase Satisfaction with Family Decision Making." *Journal of Consumer Research* 8(September): 183-88.

Laney, J.D. 1988a. "Can Economic Concepts be Learned and Remembered?: A Comparison of Elementary Students." *The Journal of Educational Research* 82(2): 99-105.

———. 1988b. "A Lesson Plan for Elementary School: Economic Scarcity—Teach It with Cartoons!" *The Social Studies Texan* 4(2): 16-19.

———. 1989. "Experience- and Concept-Based Effects on First-Graders' Learning, Retention of Economic Concepts." *The Journal of Educational Research* 82(4): 231-36.

———. 1990a. "Generative Teaching and Learning of Cost-Benefit Analysis: An Empirical Investigation." *Journal of Research and Development in Education* 23(3): 136-44.

———. 1990b. "Generative Teaching and Learning of Economic Concepts: A Sample Lesson." *Social Studies and the Young Learner* 3(1):17-20.

———. 1992. *Economic Concept Acquisition: Experiential Versus Experience-Based Learning and Instruction*. Research grant report submitted to the Meadows Foundation of Dallas, Texas. Unpublished paper, University of North Texas.

Laney, J.D., and P.A. Moseley. 1991. *The Effect of Economics Instruction on Economic Reasoning: A Comparison of Verbal Imaginal, and Integrated Teaching-Learning Strategies*. Paper presented at the annual meeting of the College and University Faculty Assembly, National Council for the Social Studies. Washington, D.C.

Wittrock, M.C. 1974. "Learning as a Generative Process." *Educational Psychologist* 11 (2):87-95.

———. 1983. "Generative Reading and Comprehension." *Ginn Occasional Papers*. Lexington, Mass.: Ginn.

———. 1987. "Models of Heuristic Teaching." In *International Encyclopedia of Teaching and Teacher Education*, edited by M. J. Dunkin, 65-76. New York: Pergamon.

James D. Laney is an Associate Professor and Assistant Chair in the Department of Elementary, Early Childhood, and Reading Education at North Texas State University, Denton. [1993 note]

# 49

# How Does a Community Work?
# Junior Achievement's New Program for Second Graders

**Judith Lee Swets**

Last year, my principal asked if I was interested in having a new social studies program as a pilot project in my second-grade classroom. This Junior Achievement curriculum would be about work, government, and the interrelationships within communities. The second-grade program, I should note, would be part of a larger K-6 curriculum with similar programs at each grade level.

*How Does a Community Work?*, the program I was about to undertake, includes five lessons, each lasting about thirty minutes. A consultant, recruited by Junior Achievement, would come in to present the lessons. I would be there to assist. A respite from my very active class sounded great. A few weeks later the Junior Achievement consultant, Theresa King, introduced herself to me and my class. She was pleasant, college aged, soft spoken, and well mannered. "Whoa," I thought, "these kids aren't going to listen to her." But I was wrong.

Before the first lesson, I prepped my students. We went over the rules about being courteous and polite, and I bribed them with the promise of a reward if they made me proud of them.

Theresa started the lessons by talking about herself and her job. I could see some of the students getting restless, but when she pulled out a large, colorful drawing of a community and placed it on the wall, they were intrigued. Then she gave the children their own copies; they became more interested and curious. After they got their own colored stickers of different people and jobs, they were completely won over and ready to participate.

Before I go on, I should explain some of the demographics of my classroom population. I teach in an urban school. My class hovered around thirty students. The racial mixture was about 60 percent Hispanic (including Mexican, Puerto Rican, and Cuban), 30 percent white, and 10 percent black. Some of my students spoke only Spanish; some only English; some were bilingual in different stages of learning English; and some were fluent in both English and Spanish. All came from lower-income families. Their reading levels ranged from nonreader to grade-level reader. They were a diverse group, but all seemed to be taken by the program. I believe that what made the program attractive and enjoyable to them was that each was actively involved in the lessons and that the lessons were appropriate for their age.

Reprinted with permission from the Helen Dwight Reid Educational Foundation, from *The Social Studies*, July/August 1992. Published by Heldref Publications, 1319 Eighteenth Street, NW, Washington, D.C. 20036-1802. Copyright 1992.

## HOW DOES A COMMUNITY WORK?

The first lesson's objective was to create an awareness of how people in a community live together and to show that there are many job choices available within it. The consultant led conversations about the different occupations, drawing the students' attention to each job as they put colorful stickers on the community posters

Students had to use their prior knowledge to do this correctly. Their discussions had elaborated upon and expanded their perceptions of job choices in their community.

This exercise provided an easy way for them to learn about something that could be very dry. It also left the students feeling good. The placement of the stickers was something that every student could do; yet the poster was detailed enough to make it challenging for them. The students were ecstatic when they learned that they could keep their posters. They could not wait for Theresa to return.

## THE SWEET-O-FACTORY

The next lesson, The Sweet-O-Factory, was one of my favorites. Its objective was to introduce the children to the concepts of unit and assembly-line production.

The class was divided into two groups, each making the same product -doughnuts. These were "cooked" by putting an "ingredient" sticker on a paper doughnut. After the doughnuts were shaped (punched out of a sheet), they were flavored by coloring the center of each doughnut. Four colors represented the different flavors.

One group of students formed an assembly line, with each line worker making only one part of the doughnut. The other group was set up for unit-production, each student making the entire doughnut.

Before production began, the students were told that a quality-control inspector would check the doughnuts. Only those that passed the quality guidelines would be counted. Each group was then given two minutes to make as many quality-doughnuts as it could.

The students really enjoyed this exercise and, through participation, they came to understand the terms "unit" and "assembly line." They could compare the two processes and analyze which process would be better for making different kinds of products.

## THE ROLE OF GOVERNMENT

Lesson three looked at government, taxes, rights, and responsibilities. A community poster was again used; this was a slightly different version of the one used for occupations, minus government workers. The students were asked to identify the workers who were missing, such as the police officers, park employees, and street sweepers. A discussion ensued about what community life would be like without these employees. A discussion could lead also to the purpose of taxes and government itself.

## WHAT'S THAT BUILDING?
In lesson four, "What's That Building?" the children decided what kind of business should go into a vacant store that was illustrated on the community poster. To continue the visual approach to teaching and learning, a large picture called the "decision tree" was used. The trunk represented the problem, the limbs were the choices, and the branches were all of the positive and the negative results of the choices.

This lesson again encouraged the students' use of high-level thinking skills. They analyzed their choices by weighing the pros and cons in a logical manner. The decision tree made this fairly easy, and it also made it interesting for them. They had to evaluate their choices and make a decision based upon that evaluation. The lesson also showed the students that even when no decision seems absolutely perfect, there usually is one way that appears better than the others.

## MONEY AND BANKING
The fifth lesson introduced the students to the banking system and the exchange of money. Rhymed verse told the story of a quarter—twenty-five cents—from the time it was minted through several transactions. The seemingly difficult-for-children-to-understand concepts were simplified. Why do people need jobs? How are workers paid? What do they do with their paychecks? What are a family's needs and wants? Why do we need to work to satisfy these needs?

## FITTING INTO THE SOCIAL STUDIES CURRICULUM
An advantage of Junior Achievement's second-grade program is that it correlates well with the social studies curriculum presently studied at my school. Our curriculum is called "Our Neighborhoods and Communities."

The first unit in our curriculum focuses on neighborhoods and therefore parallels Junior Achievement's first lesson, "How Does a Community Work?" Both address the concept of a neighborhood community as a place where people live and do many, many kinds of work.

The second and third units of our curriculum, about people working together, why they work, and the need for rules and laws, corresponds with lessons two and five in the project ("The Sweet-O-Factory" and "Money and Banking"). Junior Achievement's third lesson, "The Role of Government" correlates to unit three's section on taxes and the services provided by tax dollars. Lessons four and five of the JA program reinforce and expand upon these concepts.

## IMPLICATIONS
Many of the materials introduced in both my school's social studies text and the Junior Achievement program are abstract, often difficult for some—if not many—young children to comprehend. The student activities in Junior Achievement's program make these difficult concepts more easily understandable because the students are actively engaged in problem solving.

Many of my students are unfamiliar with jobs and work because they are from single-parent families. Often their mothers are on welfare. The children do not have first-hand knowledge about careers, a father working, or how a mother gets money to support the family. They know little or nothing about power or how to have a voice in the government.

In many of the homes in which my children live, the parent is apathetic. At election time, when I have gone out to urge their parents to vote, a common attitude is "What good does that do? My vote doesn't mean a thing."

Because the concepts in the program often are not part of their childhood, it seems important that young students get some start toward awareness, even in second grade. They should understand that they do have a say in how their government works and that they do have choices in how they want their community—if not their larger community, the state itself—to exist and to serve them. All students have merit as individuals; they each are a part of a society, a culture, one that lives and works eventually as a unit.

This program did make the learning enjoyable, even something the students looked forward to doing. They were involved. One remembers what one is involved in.

# PART 8

## Ⅷ SCIENCE, TECHNOLOGY, AND SOCIETY

Science and technology encompass our daily lives in countless ways. Each day, we experience developments in science and technology in the food we eat and water we drink; our transportation from home to work or school and leisure time activities; the media we view, and so forth. New developments in both science and technology require that we as citizens make informed personal and public choices about the uses and abuses of science and technology. As newer technologies develop, new questions arise that require us to grapple socially and intellectually with a range of complex questions. How can science and technology help us to learn about other people and events? How do science and technology affect me and my community? Young children are eager to learn about inventions and inventors and how inventions have changed their lives. They also like to hypothesize about future change and its possible impact on them.

The use of the newer technologies in classrooms helps students to become more motivated and directly involved in their own learning. Remy provides a strong rationale for including the study of science, technology, and society within the social studies program and suggests strategies concerning ways to accomplish this task. Svingen suggests several ways teachers of geography can use electronic technology applications (CD-ROM, video, computers, networks, and tools) to promote active learning through creative teaching. Many of these same teaching and learning applications can also be used when learning other social science disciplines. Wilson and Marsh provide a strong rationale for the use of the Internet as a way to promote interactive student learning by allowing students to access various data bases. They describe several educational networks currently available and suggest ways for teachers to get started using these newer means of communication to promote student learning.

Smith writes that television has both positive and negative influences on students who spend more time watching TV than they spend in the classroom. He argues that teachers can use TV to help young learners develop citizenship competencies and suggests several ways for students to use TV constructively for active learning. Aronson also believes that TV can be used to teach about the world to help learners deal with issues related to multiculturalism and tolerance. He also recommended that teachers help students develop media literacy competencies. Several valuable resources and references are also included in this article.

Finally, Volk discusses the influence that the United States Constitution has on technology and outlines recent court cases related to uses and abuses of technology. Legal questions arising from applications of technology can be used by students to study about the relationships of technology to society.

Science and technology are here to stay. Both influence our personal lives and societal actions and values. Discussions on issues related to science, technology, and society can be addressed effectively by young learners within social studies programs and content.

# The Need for Science/Technology/Society in the Social Studies

# 50

**Richard C. Remy**

Education for good citizenship is the overarching goal of social studies education. Achievement of that goal today has become enormously complicated by rapid advances in science and technology. Daniel Boorstein (1988, 61) eloquently highlighted the challenges posed for citizenship by modem science and technology when he observed that as citizens:

We are baffled and dazzled today by new concepts and "entities" — from double helixes to black holes — that defy common sense, yet we are still expected to have an opinion on what to do about them. Should we legislate against genetic experiments? Dare we venture a defense program in outer space? Is the ozone really threatened? How widespread is the threat of AIDS? Did that doctor really fake this data on a "cure" for arthritis?

This article explores why there is a need to pay attention to content about science/technology/society (STS) in the social studies curriculum, and examines strategies for incorporating STS in the social studies, and expresses some cautions about interdisciplinary approaches to teaching about STS.

## WHY INCLUDE STS CONTENT IN SOCIAL STUDIES?

Given the already overcrowded nature of the social studies curriculum and the continuing efforts of new groups to have their special topics represented in the curriculum, why should social studies teachers devote time to STS? A review of recent education reform reports as well as the growing literature on STS in the curriculum indicates that attention to STS can contribute directly to the core mission of social studies — the preparation of citizens — in several important ways.

## UNDERSTANDING OF SCIENCE IN SOCIETY

Modern societies that aspire to democracy require citizens who are informed about and have some understanding of complex social issues generated by science and technology. In America the public policy agendas of the 1970s and 1980s have been filled with issues generated by advances in science and technology. During the 1980s, for instance, propositions on such issues as returnable bottles and disposable cans, nuclear freeze resolutions, preservation of wilderness areas, and the use of nuclear energy have appeared on the ballots in more than 20 states and 100 cities. By 1982 more than forty million Americans had cast votes for or against the use of nuclear energy, which became the most controversial question appearing on state and local ballots (Naisbitt 1984).

If citizens are to participate intelligently in making decisions related to the uses of science and technology, they must be informed about the major characteristics of such issues. They must understand, for example, that decisions about complex social issues related to STS often require "trade-offs" between conflicting values in which there is no clear right or wrong. The National Academy of Science, for instance, held a meeting of experts on energy to discuss the pros and cons of nuclear power. Their inability to agree led the scientists at the meeting to conclude: "The public will have to choose between energy sources based on individual values and beliefs about social ethics—not on the advice from technical experts" (Naisbitt 1984).

The consequences of public ignorance in a technological society with democratic ideals were stated succinctly by D. Allan Bromley (1982, 1037), a Yale physicist, when he noted that

where the questions of consequence increasingly have scientific and technological aspects, if our public cannot at least appreciate the nature of the issues, quite apart from contributing to their resolution, they inevitably will tend to become alienated from the society. This is a trend that no nation can long endure.

Put another way, ignorant constituents are unable to offer intelligent advice to their representatives in government; and uninformed public officials are unable to represent their constituents wisely. Widespread ignorance of constituents and representatives could make both groups dependent upon a few experts, who could wield disproportionate power that might undermine democratic traditions.

The social studies curriculum is the place where students can learn about the social context and consequences of science and technology. Indeed, a recent study of science educators indicates that the STS issues they identify as most important are of similar interest to social studies educators. These include world-wide hunger, unchecked population growth, depletion of water resources, and the destructive capacity of modern weapons systems (Bybee and Mau 1986).

## CIVIC DECISION MAKING

Making decisions about STS issues is an inescapable part of civic life. As citizens we all make personal decisions that have social consequences. Choosing, for example, to purchase a gas-guzzling car, when aggregated one million times, can have serious effects on both air pollution and petroleum reserves. We also participate in collective decision making about public policies related directly to issues generated by advances in science and technology (Remy 1976, 1989; Remy and Patrick 1985). Should citizens vote to approve construction of a trash-burning power plant? How should citizens vote in a referendum on the construction of a dam?

Decision making about STS issues almost always involves uncertainty about the likely social or environmental consequences of alternative courses of action. Decision theorists call this decision making with risk (Schlaifer 1969; Behn and Vaupel 1982). By "risk" they mean that one only has enough knowledge to assign probabilities to the likelihood of particular consequences for an alternative. Decision making with risk falls between the idealized extremes of decisions under complete certainty (where one can correctly predict the consequences of every alternative) and decisions under conditions of total uncertainty. The number of decisions with risk has increased exponentially as the public policy agenda has become filled with complex issues generated by advances in science and technology.

Decisions about STS issues also involve difficult choices between conflicting values where one can derive no clear view of right and wrong from the facts no matter how much information about the issue is available. Making choices about STS issues requires students to express value judgments when labeling consequences as good or bad. When setting goals decision makers engage in a clarification of values which requires ranking of values. Such thinking about values is at the core of ethical reasoning It means asking—What do I want, and what is right or wrong in this situation?

Because of these characteristics, STS issues present ideal cases for analysis using models like decision trees that can help students acquire basic concepts relevant to improve their understanding of the dynamics of science and technology in modem society (Patrick and Remy 1985). Further, such analysis can help students develop some rudimentary factual knowledge about key, enduring issues such as pollution, energy, and the like.

At the same time, using systematic decision-making procedures to study STS issues in social studies can help students develop intellectual, problem-solving skills and a flexible but organized way of thinking about social decision making. This is important since neither social studies nor science educators can provide students with all the specific knowledge they will need to stay informed about public policy issues likely to arise in their lifetimes.

## MAKING COGNITIVE CONNECTIONS

One of the most important attributes of competent citizens in a complex society is the ability to connect things that seem superficially to be discrete. Such an ability is a clear sign of higher order cognition and learning and is a highly prized goal of social studies education. Mark Van Doren (1982, 384) described the importance of teaching and learning about connections in the general education of citizens when he stated that

the connectedness of things is what the educator contemplates to the limit of his capacity.... The student who can begin early in life to think of things as connected, even if he revises his view with every succeeding year, has begun the life of learning.

When social studies educators have students use systematic procedures to analyze STS issues they are helping students learn how to make connections between diverse fields of knowledge in the sciences and the social studies. Decision making about STS issues connects the social studies and the sciences because the insights and results of both are needed in making such decisions. When dealing with social decisions involving science and technology, the distinct ways of knowing and thinking characteristic of each field are complementary, not mutually exclusive. Each has a necessary but in itself incomplete perspective to contribute to such decisions.

Science, or more precisely the methods and results of the many sciences, contributes vital knowledge about the possible consequences of STS decisions. The social studies contributes ethical and values perspectives to the decision-making process. They shed light on the moral, social, and human values outside the realm of science involved in such choices. They can help decision makers—whether they be individuals or groups—rank and select among preferred outcomes and make value judgments. They can also contribute knowledge about the history of an issue and the public policy processes associated with it.

Appropriate study of decision making can also help build students' skills in analysis and appraisal. Consideration of alternatives, consequences, and goals requires students to learn and apply skills needed to acquire, organize, and appraise information about factual claims. At the same time, it requires students to clarify rank, and judge values in the context of factual claims. These skills are means to independent thinking and learning, which are essential qualities of competent citizenship.

Systematic instruction related to decision making about STS issues could also be well suited to help students develop competence with managing information. Appropriate models such as decision trees can capture key elements of the decision-making process involved in making choices about STS issues. Such models can be a generalizable framework, a conceptual map of social decision making, that citizens—young and old—apply repeatedly to a wide variety of issues and decisions at both the personal and societal levels. Students who acquire such a conceptual "map" of decision making can use it throughout their lives.

## DEVELOPING A COMMON MEMORY

Numerous commissions and task forces have recently made recommendations for improving the civic education of young Americans. Many of these recommendations call for deepening students' understanding and appreciation of their democratic heritage. Social studies educators should realize that attention to STS can contribute directly to achieving this needed reform.

Although the phrase STS describes a contemporary trend in education as well as a host of current issues, it also refers to a more fundamental set of connections among science and the development of Western society. In a recent report on STS for the Social Science Education Consortium (SSEC) Faith Hickman, John Patrick, and Roger Bybee (1987) describe how ideas about science developed during the Age of Enlightenment in the late seventeenth century to the late. eighteenth century came to have a significant influence on the development of American society. During the Enlightenment, scientists came to accept what we know as the scientific method as a way of knowing about the world. At the same time there was a conscious effort to use ideas from the Newtonian synthesis—the idea that there is order in the universe and the order of events can be explained through natural law—as a conceptual framework for the organization of societies.

Philosophers such as Voltaire, Rousseau, and Hume were influenced by Newton's ideas about science and the natural order and devoted aspects of their political philosophies to the search for an ideal society. Although these philosophers' ideals were not to be realized in Europe, colonial America represented an opportunity to apply Enlightenment ideas to the creation of a new social order. Thus it was America that came to realize the Enlightenment by writing its principles into its public documents and by formalizing them into political institutions.

In the Declaration of Independence, for example, Jefferson used words and phrases that reflect Enlightenment ideas such as: "When in the course of human events it becomes necessary," "the powers of the earth," "laws of nature," and "causes which impel." Similarly, the Constitution includes references to science and technology in its provision for a census, the creation of a standard of weights and measures, and the protection of writings and discoveries by copyrights and patents. Moreover, as Hickman, Patrick, and Bybee explain, "Probably the most important connection between science and society is established in the First Amendment" (1987, 2). The protection of "freedom of speech or the press . . . or the right to petition the government for a redress of grievances" have come to be essential to the public distribution and review of discoveries that are the hallmarks of modern science.

In short, science and technology are a key part of our conceptual heritage as found in the documents that gave birth to our country and continue to shape our social development. The SSEC report concludes, "The relationship between science and society could not be more fundamental . . . There is a need to recognize and appreciate the origins of, and justification for, the science, technology, society theme because they relate to the foundation of our culture" (1981, 2-3).

## RESISTING ANTAGONISTS OF SCIENCE

Antagonists of modern science and technology post a critical challenge for social studies educators concerned with education for competent citizenship in our democracy. These antagonists undermine scientific values and attitudes by espousing anti-scientific or pseudo-scientific beliefs. They hope to subvert science and social studies education in schools and want to limit or overturn projects in science or technology that contradict conventional wisdom.

The political pressure exerted by "scientific creationists" to shape the school curriculum in behalf of their doctrine is a prime example of this insidious challenge to educating citizens capable of enlightened participation in civic decisions related to science and technology.

How serious is this challenge? James Michener fears an "anti-science epidemic" threatens the American public (1980, 376). S. E. Luria, a 1969 Nobel Prize winner in medicine, claims: "The failure to understand science leads to such things as the push to give creationism the same standing as the theory of evolution" (1984, 76). Creationists argue for "equal time" in the curriculum to compare their views of human and planetary origins with the standard conceptions of the scientific community.

Leading scientists have strongly disagreed with the "equal time" argument. They explain that the "theory of scientific creationism" is a pseudo-science and therefore not comparable with scientific theories of evolution. The National Academy of Science, along with many prominent scientists, point out that not every idea or hypothesis is considered to be equally worthy and thereby deserving of "equal time" in the classroom. Unlike politics, science is not an exercise in balancing opposing viewpoints to maintain harmony among contending groups. In science, there can be no political compromise in the search to know how our world really works.

The development of anti-scientific or pseudo-scientific beliefs among citizens can greatly reduce the quality of their participation in public policy decisions related to science and technology. To counter such a trend social studies educators have a responsibility to act on the proposition that citizens who know the basic concepts of science and technology, as well as their importance in the American heritage, will be much less inclined to hold beliefs or attitudes, like "scientific creationism," that are hostile to scientific and technological endeavors. The implications of this proposition for social studies educators is clear, we need to find ways to devote some attention in the curriculum to the concepts of science and technology as symbiotic enterprises, their origins and development in Western civilization (and particularly in American history), their functions in contemporary American life, their power and limitations in solving problems, and the benefits and risks associated with their applications to society.

## STRATEGIES FOR INCORPORATING STS IN SOCIAL STUDIES

Phillip Heath (1988) has succinctly presented three alternative strategies for bringing STS content to the social studies curriculum. These are: infusion into existing courses of study, extension of an existing unit of study, and creation of a separate course of study.

## INFUSION INTO EXISTING COURSES

The basic courses of secondary social studies—American history, world history, civics, government, geography, economics—offer entry points for STS content. In world history, for example, the Scientific Revolution in Europe is a good opportunity for lessons on STS, as is the later Industrial Revolution. In U.S. history students might examine such STS topics as the effects on the settlement of the West by developments in transportation and communication. In civics and government they might explore the influence of citizens on national and state policies relevant to science and technology, or congressional support for and regulation of science and technology.

An advantage of the infusion approach is that STS lessons can enhance the integrity and coherence of the existing curriculum and as a result become accepted as an ongoing part of the schools' mission. A disadvantage is that it can be difficult to select what will be omitted from standard courses to make room for STS content. Further, the infusion strategy does not allow for in-depth treatments of STS topics; rather it can lead to spotty and uneven coverage of important topics.

## EXTENSION OF EXISTING UNIT

STS topics and content can be added to the end of a set of lessons or a unit on traditional social studies content. For instance, a government unit on the federal bureaucracy might include a case study of interest group activity aimed at changing some environmental regulations set forth by the Environmental Protection Agency (EPA). Students might role play various officials and interest group leaders and might be asked to make decisions about a controversy that involved a trade-off between jobs and closing a factory that was polluting the environment.

An advantage of this approach is the chance to study an STS topic in depth while retaining a lot of flexibility about how and when to present STS content. A potential disadvantage is the chance that treatment of STS topics could still be somewhat superficial.

## CREATION OF A SEPARATE COURSE

Some schools have created separate courses on STS. The content of such courses tends to be organized around current social issues drawing upon subject matter and concepts from history as well as the various natural and social sciences. Usually these courses are offered as electives for high school students. Such courses are often called "interdisciplinary" or sometimes "multidisciplinary."

A big advantage of this approach is the opportunity to develop an in-depth, sustained, coherent study of the various interrelationships of science, technology and society. Further, as Heath (1988, 2) points out, such courses can give high visibility and legitimacy to this new topic of study. One disadvantage is that unless carefully constructed such a course can take valuable student time away from basic and important social studies concepts, skills and values reamed in the traditional courses. A second potentially important disadvantage relates to the enormous complexity involved in organizing a course that draws content from various academic disciplines.

## CAUTIONS REGARDING INTERDISCIPLINARY APPROACHES

From the 1920s to the 1980s there have been calls, often strident, to develop interdisciplinary curricula based on decision making about social problems and issues (Cremin 1964; Ravitch 1983). We need to be aware of the history of these curriculum reforms to avoid past mistakes and to build upon earlier achievements. Hazel Hertzberg's history of curriculum reform in the social studies discusses attempts to integrate courses both within and between various disciplines or fields of knowledge (1981).

An important part of Hertzberg's history concerns the formidable problem of conceptualization that has hindered interdisciplinary curriculum reform. She notes (1981, 80-81):

> The conceptual problem in combining subjects within the social studies had always been a difficult one that remained largely unresolved....
> When to the usual problems of fusing the social studies were added subjects not so obviously related, the difficulties became even more formidable. The "personal/social needs of adolescents" approach could easily degenerate into . . . a formless curriculum from which students reamed little and which bored them.

There is no broad theory of knowledge that incorporates the sciences and social studies. There is no universal framework, which could be the foundation for a comprehensive interdisciplinary curriculum. Given these conceptual limitations, we should proceed cautiously in attempts to integrate the sciences and social studies. Lessons from history show that it has been much easier to dismantle the curricula of separate subjects than to reassemble them along comprehensive interdisciplinary lines.

Students in poorly organized interdisciplinary courses have often floundered. In a study of courses organized around social problems and decision making, Arno Bellack concludes (1978, 101-102):

> Difficulties in this approach soon became apparent, not the least of which was the students' lack of firsthand acquaintance with the disciplines that were the source of the concepts and ideas essential to structuring problems under study. Without adequate understanding of the various

fields of knowledge, students had no way of knowing which fields were relevant to problems of concern to them.

Similarly, teachers confronted with the demands of an interdisciplinary curriculum have often been overwhelmed. In his prizewinning history of progressive education, Lawrence Cremin concludes (1964, 348):

> Integrated studies required familiarity with a fantastic range of knowledge and teaching materials. In the hands of first-rate instructors, the innovations worked wonders; in the hands of too many average teachers, however, they led to chaos.

One other problem associated with courses based on contemporary social problems and issues, whether in the sciences or the social studies, is lack of historical perspective. Current issues and policies related to science and technology have a past that must be understood if one is to be a capable decision maker about these matters. John Ziman (1976, 6), a British professor of physics, explains that "To make a sense of the present state of science, we need to know how it got like that; we cannot avoid an historical account."

These cautions are not meant to discourage attempts to create interdisciplinary, or perhaps more likely, multidisciplinary approaches to teaching STS. Rather, they serve as a reminder that in attempting to make connections between and within the social studies and the sciences we must learn from past mistakes.

## REFERENCES

Bellack, Arno. "What Knowledge Is of Most Worth?" In *Curriculum Development*. Chicago: Rand McNally Publishing Company, 1978.

Behn, Robert D., and James W. Vaupel. *Quick Analysis for Busy Decision Makers*. New York: Basic Books, 1982.

Boorstin, Daniel G. "The Shadowland of Democracy." *U.S. News & World Report*. 14 November 1988.

Bromley, D. Allan. "The Other Frontiers of Science." *Science* 215 (26 February 1982).

Bybee, Roger, and Teri Maul. "Science and Technology Related Global Problems: An International Survey of Science Educators." *Journal of Research in Science Teaching* 23 (July 1986): 599-618.

Cremin, Lawrence A. *Transformation of the School*. New York: Random House, Vintage Books, 1964.

Heath, Phillip. "Science/Technology/Society in the Social Studies." *ERIC Digest* EOO-S0-88-8. September 1988.

Hertzberg, Hazel W. *Social Studies Reform: 1880-1980*. Boulder, Colo.: Social Science Education Consortium, 1981.

Hickman, Faith M., John J. Patrick, and Roger W. Bybee. *Science/Technology/Society: A Framework for Curriculum Reform in Secondary School Science and Social Studies*. Boulder, Colo.: Social Science Education Consortium, 1987.

Luria, S. E. "Consequences of America's Ignorance of Science." *U.S. News & World Report*. 14 May 1984.

Michener, James A. "The Anti-Science Epidemic." *Social Education* 44 (May 1980).

Naisbitt, John. *Megatrends*. New York: Warner Books, Inc., 1984.

Patrick, John J., and Richard C. Remy. *Connecting Science Technology and Society in the Education of Citizens*. Boulder, Colo.: Social Science Education Consortium, 1985.

Ravitch, Diane. *The Troubled Crusade: American Education 1945-1980*. New York: Basic Books, 1983.

Remy, Richard C. "Making Judging and Influencing Decisions: A Focus for Citizen Education." *Social Education* 40 (October 1976): 360.

———. "Civic Decision Making in an Information Age." In *From Information to Decision Making*, Margaret A. Laughlin, H. Michael Hartoonian, and Norris M. Sanders, eds. Washington, D.C.: National Council for the Social Studies, 1989: 31-39.

Schlaifer, Robert. *Analysis of Decisions Under Uncertainty*. New York: McGraw Hill Book Company, 1969.

Van Doren, Mark. In "Seeing the Connectedness of Things," by Ernest L. Boyer. *Educational Leadership* 39 (May 1982).

Ziman, John. *The Force of Knowledge: The Scientific Dimension of Society*. Cambridge, England: Cambridge University Press, 1976.

Richard C. Remy is the Associate Director of the Mershon Center at Ohio State University in Columbus. [1990 note]

**Bonnie E. Svingen**

Perhaps more than any other component of the public school curriculum, geography instruction can benefit tremendously from technological applications in the classroom. Geography's heavy dependence on map graphics, illustrations, charts, photographs, and video offers teachers rich opportunities to integrate challenging and exciting teaching techniques at all grade levels.

The walls of the classroom are opening wider to the world through a variety of new (and old) technologies. An expanding array of technological innovations is dramatically altering the way geography is being taught in the classroom. To keep up and to become more efficient. teachers are being asked to incorporate CD-ROM, video, computer software, digital cameras, and telecommunications into classroom curriculum and activities. Whether you teach primary, intermediate, middle school or high school, you will enrich yourself and your students by integrating existing and new technology applications into your classroom.

New innovations will add fresh and motivating dimensions to teaching. Start slowly by mastering one simple application or be ambitious and write a grant to fund dramatic and innovative changes. Your students and their parents will appreciate your efforts. As more geography technologies become available, teachers need to keep abreast of them and share their effectiveness with co-workers, at the local school, district-wide, and around the state. Teachers have so many demands on their time that it is difficult to stay current with the growing numbers of programs developed each year, making effective in-servicing on new tools and technologies essential.

Acquiring and applying new technological applications will pay handsome dividends in the classroom. Frequently, students will enjoy themselves to the extent that they will not realize they are studying geography. Students of the 1990s do not have to be coaxed to push buttons or take pictures. They are products of a highly visual environment. Recognizing this, teachers should redirect the Nintendo® generation's interest in technology to a productive, academic format.

This article is an attempt to suggest examples of strategies and classroom activities that can be enhanced by technology that engages and excites students. Furthermore, if you agree that "one of the things that imagery does best is to help us remember" (White 1991), you will probably be able to integrate some of these ideas, examples, and applications into your existing curriculum far more easily than you might think.

Traditional maps come in many shapes, sizes, and projections, and now they have become electronic. Some of the most helpful resources in my classroom are electronic atlases. An urgent need for up-to-date map data became apparent when I began my instruction on the breakup of the former Soviet Union. (And when do we stop calling it that?) Our textbooks, published in 1989, are already out-of-date because they do not include the 15 newly recognized independent republics formed after the Soviet breakup. As a result, a teaching unit was developed based largely on World Atlas® by The Software Toolworks. Our building library owned the CD-ROM version. enabling me to assign students in pairs to a tutorial-type lesson on the 15 independent republics. Rather than send students to the library in twos, I persuaded the librarian to lend me the CD-ROM set-up for a two-week period. This taught me to look at all the resources available in my own building. Many classrooms still lack computers, much less CD-ROMs, but if one is available somewhere in the building, it can be moved easily and safely to your classroom for a short time. To solve the problem of how to work on new equipment with two students at a time, I trained three students to be my "experts." Not only were they able to help the other 28 students in class, they moved the computer to another geography classroom and served as the experts for that teacher. I like to think of that as empowering students.

After I returned the borrowed set-up, I sought an electronic atlas that could be used on the computers in my classroom. Brøderbund Software is a company that produces PC Globe® and Mac Globe® which I purchased through a mini-grant from our parent-teacher organization. These electronic atlases feature maps in four forms: a base map, a cities map, an elevation map, and a geographic features map. They are simple. clear. and functional, and they feature a variety of demographic, political, and cultural information. Students can use the demographics to complete a choropleth of a continent or region. I asked my seventh-grade students what they thought of the resources we had used in our class. "I think it is better than 'old' resources," one responded. "Now we can compare statistics such as life expectancy rate of different countries on a computer or listen to national anthems from a CD-ROM." We recently acquired the National Geographic Picture Atlas of the World® available

Reprinted with permission from Texas A & M, from *Journal of Geography*, July/August 1994, Volume 93, Number 4. Copyright 1994 by Texas A & M.

on CD-ROM in IBM version. The full screen color photographs set this program apart from others.

Another quite different electronic atlas is Small Blue Planet®, the electronic satellite atlas, available on CD-ROM from Now What Software. With it, students can access a variety of maps which include satellite images and chromospheres that show day and night patterns in motion. Included in this article is an example of a tutorial I developed to guide students through a study of the state of Washington. My teaching objectives included completing a state sketch; comparing maps in traditional atlases to satellite maps on a CD-ROM atlas; locating a student's state on a variety of maps; and observing, speculating, analyzing, and evaluating information on land use and population.

Another resource is Arcview®, a geographic information system (GIS) available through Environmental Systems Research Institute Incorporated's Adopt-A-School program. This system enables schools to display information about the city, state, country and world, and it can be used across the curriculum. For future application, students who know how to convert raw data into computerized data with a system such as this will have a great advantage in the information age job market.

Two of my very favorite programs are National Inspirer® and International Inspirer® from Tom Snyder Productions. Both games are designed to be used by a class in the one computer classroom, although they can be used by individuals in a computer lab. The programs have great appeal with students. "I have been learning more about geography than ever before," middle-schooler Melissa Colvig explained. "through teaching materials being used in our classroom. The game International Inspirer has helped me learn things about places I didn't know existed." Heather Neill claims that "These programs help students see what is going on in the world and teaches them more than a bunch of dates and names to memorize." The game is designed with up-to-date materials. Included in the international version are 188 nations and related data. Students collaborate in small groups to plan moves through countries. The computer gives the players bonus points for countries that represent targeted characteristics such as health, economics, the environment, and culture. The resources provided are maps, charts, and graphs with all the information needed for the group to use problem-solving skills. After one round, the students begin to develop more involved strategies to earn more points. For the past three years, I have invited the parents of my students to an evening event we labeled "International Inspirer Night." The students enjoyed showing their parents how they were studying geography, and the parents loved playing the game. One parent responded with a note of thanks which said, "Now that was some way to teach geography to little and to large students, we parents being the latter."

National Inspirer provides the class with a fun and effective way to study the United States in a cooperative learning environment. It is similar to International Inspirer in that students are assigned resources and commodities to look for while learning about locations and characteristics of the United States. Both games are appropriate for grades 4-12. Additional lesson plans and reproducible worksheets are included with the program and teacher's guide. Both games are so well presented in the teacher's guide that the teacher can learn to play it right along with the students. These last two applications would be a great way to introduce yourself and your classroom to geography technology.

The video camera, a standard in most schools, can be put to work in a fun video essay project developed by Kendyl Depoali of Reno, Nevada. Students are asked to develop a photo essay applying the five themes of geography to their home setting. They analyze, organize, and present their surroundings to another group. They are not just learning about geography; they are doing it. My students generally chose Pullman, Washington, as their topic, but some chose their neighborhood, a small rural community, or Washington State University located in Pullman as their focus of study. Depending on what you have available, the film footage can be edited and enhanced. An inexpensive program called VCR Companion by Brøderbund allows students to add a title, animation, and list of credits to their presentations, and music can be added to enhance the final product. This program works well on Apple IIEs and even better on an Apple IIGS.

Our class received a tape prepared by students of Craig Cummings in Belt, Montana. My students loved the portrayal of a small Montana town, especially knowing that it had been prepared by students to be shared with other students. A lively discussion ensued after viewing their tape with questions like "Why did this class use country music?" Central Montana s regional and cultural identity had been captured and depicted more clearly than any book or teacher might have done. When I asked my students if the video made them want to see and learn more about Belt. Montana. the resounding response was "YES!" "We were able to see what Montana looks like," seventh-grader racer Erik Lamb stated, "and they will be able to see what Pullman looks like." My class expressed the hope that, after seeing our tape of Pullman, Washington, students in Belt would feel the same way we had. In addition, teachers in Canada and New Mexico have expressed an interest in exchanging videos. What better way to have students learn about their own part of the country and other regions of North America? The students are the center of activity rather than the teacher. This hands-on model of learning is an effective contrast to the dull image of students lined up in rows with one person at the front lecturing. An internationally recognized definition of media literacy, and one used to mandate media literacy in Canada's public schools, states that it is "the ability to access, analyze, evaluate and produce communication in a variety of forms"(Leveranz and Tyner 1993). This project meets these criteria.

Another simple use of the video camera involves producing a weather report. Lincoln Middle School in Pullman features Channel 1® from Whittle Communications, and each classroom has a centrally linked television monitor, enabling us to show a videotape to every homeroom in our school. When we studied weather, students were required to prepare a daily weather report for the school. It was a terrific way to integrate the skills of geography, script writing, public speaking, graphics, sound production, photography, and technology. By applying academic learning to a real-world activity, students learn to collaborate and to rely on an integrative learning process.

A digital camera is another valuable piece of technology with classroom applications. It is essentially a video still camera whose images are transferred to videotape or viewed directly on a television monitor. Its images can be transferred to the computer with a program called Computer Eye®, one of several digitizing programs. The macro lens feature of the camera allows the student to create a photo essay of a region using pictures from library books and atlases. The advantage of digital pictures is that each reusable disk holds 50 images and poor quality shots can be retaken. The final edited project is played then to classmates or parents on the classroom television. The images may also be imported into a program like Digital Chisel® to be incorporated into multimedia presentations. This may sound complicated, but once you get past the unfamiliar vocabulary, it is quite "doable."

In an age of information, evaluating and applying data are essential skills. Never before has so much information been available to students. For teachers with so many diverse responsibilities, the information overload can be overwhelming. I am just beginning to extend my classroom to the rest of the world through Internet which connects millions of users and institutions worldwide, enabling students to communicate directly with people worldwide. Although Pullman is a small town, it is the home of Washington State University. Mike Kibler, the father of one of my students, invited our class to the electrical engineering and computer science lab on campus. The students were transfixed by the information gathering power of the World Wide Web. Kibler is currently arranging sponsorship of our school in the Global School House Project that allows classrooms to interact with each other by means of video conferences through the Internet.

An easy way to use telecommunications is to use networks as glorified pen pal systems. However, sources such as I*EARN (International Education and Resource Network) are designed specifically to encourage projects among school children that promote international cooperation and understanding. Pullman schoolteacher Kristi Rennebohm-Franz uses this network with first-graders, and she communicates with over 15 locations around the globe. Originally Rennebohm-Franz joined the networks to do a water habitat project, but then Jon Anderson, the Pacific Northwest I*EARN coordinator, paired her with Jane McLane at Kimball Elementary in Seattle to conduct a comparative water habitat project. Rennebohm-Franz and McLane then collaborated by exchanging data

that compared the fresh water habitat of a pond in Pullman with a saltwater habitat in Puget Sound.

The success of the cross-state water habitat project persuaded Rennebohm-Franz to expand her initial project into one with international dimensions. Her class began communicating with other locations around the United States and the globe including Red Lake Falls, Minnesota; Vladivostok, Russia; Puerto Madryan, Argentina; Costa Rica; and Holland. Rennebohm-Franz uses multiple versions of globes and maps in her first-grade classroom to identify the water habitat locations. She explained that primary students need to learn that countries are not always the same color on every map. The variety of resources allows students to look at a country from different perspectives. Wall maps featuring topographic relief enable first graders to literally feel the mountains. In addition, children have individual maps to color, label, and code. As part of their water study, students studied orca whales of Washington, and they asked primary students in Argentina to send information on the southern white whales of Argentina. Rennebohm-Franz's class studied the whales' migration to Baja, Mexico, tracing their path on maps. The class used a software program called Language Explorer( so that the children were introduced to the Spanish language of countries they communicated with. Rennebohm-Franz used a collection of children's literature on the theme of waterways as a way to integrate language arts with geography in the water habitat study. This is an extremely effective way to integrate geography, foreign languages, children's literature, science, and technology in the primary grades.

Pullman's Sunnyside Elementary and Seattle's Kimball Elementary are also doing a project on elders utilizing the I*EARN network which integrates geography with social studies. A family history questionnaire is sent home with each child to be completed by the family. Family members are asked to identify places of birth, to locate where families have lived, and identify the family's country of origin. That data is then recorded on U.S. and world maps. The children exchanged messages that shared favorite family stories, and some first graders wrote to family elders asking them to write back about their childhood memories. Some children and their elders corresponded by fax, showing children yet another way to communicate. Students read stories that focused on the theme of generations within families. A few favorites were: *Molly's Pilgrim* by Barbara Cohen, *Seya's Song* by Ron Herschi, *My Grandmother's Journey* by John Cech, *Dear Annie* by Judith Casely, *Grandfather's Journey* by Allen Say, and *My Great Aunt Arizona* by Gloria Houston. The messages, letters, and maps are being published in an elders' booklet, culminating a project which integrated history and geography with a sense of family and community. The combined classes had connections to six continents of the world with considerable overlap in Europe and Asia. The project has given the children a global connectedness through their families, past and present.

Teachers and school districts should not feel that they need to reinvent the wheel once they have made a commitment to technology. Many excellent materials already exist. For instance, National Geographic Kids Network® "helped students in more than 10,000 elementary school classes plunge into science by conducting experiments and then pooling data with kids doing similar work in other parts of the world" (Corcoran 1993). Two free networks are Fredmail, Free Educational Mail, (619) 475-4852, and FEDOnet, (315) 331-1584, which is a network of over 24,000 bulletin boards (Corcoran 1993).

America Online® is a commercial service that provides the novice with an easy way to access Internet, e-mail, National Geographic Society information, the Smithsonian Institution, Time, and Compton's Encyclopedia. Students can easily exchange information with other students around the world. Likewise, teachers are able to communicate and exchange ideas with other teachers and professionals. For example, the Washington Geographic Alliance has decided to use America Online to facilitate communication among the teacher network in our comparatively large state. WedNet, a state-funded network for teachers and students, is available in many parts of our state and will soon be available here. Other states have established education networks such as California Online Resources for Education (CORE), the Florida Information Resource Network (FIRN), North Dakota's SENDIT K-12, Texas Education Network (TENET), and the Public Education Network (PEN) in Virginia (Dyrli 1993).

When considering the application of technology in the classroom, do not overlook the obvious. My students produce high-quality maps and displays with the help of word processing. Printed labels and titles can transform a well-thought-out but ordinary project into a stimulating and attractive display. For example, I have seen some students incorporate beautifully designed compass roses. Some basic instruction in graphic design helps students prepare their information in a more attractive way. "I think computers are great. Once you get the hang of typing, you can actually type faster than you write! This way we can turn in fast, neat papers without having to worry about messy handwriting," states seventh-grader Alice Lin.

Timeliner® is another program by Tom Snyder Productions which creates a timeline up to 99 pages long. The student types in the dates in any order and the computer sequences and prints them in a scaled, easily read format. I have students draw and design graphics to enhance their timeline, and the new Macintosh® version includes graphics and the ability to import graphics from a variety of paint programs. "When you need to type or print something," middle-schooler Brent Cummings explained, "the computer is right there. The computer helped most by making a timeline for me. All I had to do was type in the dates and it was done."

Several games in the Carmen San Diego® series appeal to students by involving them in exciting detective adventures around the world. After playing Where in the World is Carmen San Diego®, ask your students to write 20 clues that will lead the class to a place or subject of study. This employs higher level thinking and the students love it. Our class has a set of student-written clues for a variety of geography terms and locations which can be used to fill extra minutes at the end of a class period. The clues are read to the students one at a time; the first student to guess the answer gets the point. I maintain a running tally of points earned, and at the end of the year we stage our own "Carmen San Diego Day" with a competition for the highest point earners. Students who are not competing are asked to prepare the clues. This way, everyone is involved in the learning process.

As I find myself incorporating more technology into my teaching, my role in the classroom has evolved into that of a guide or manager rather than the source of all information. It reminds me of the axiom: "Be a guide on the side rather than a sage on the stage." Don't be afraid to share the center stage with your students. The more capable students become with technology, the more anxious they are to display their innovative, technological accomplishments. A student-generated school weather report or an evening event such as an "International Inspirer Night" places student achievements center stage. The smiles of fulfilled students actively involved in doing geography and the proud expressions on their parents' faces will provide you as a teacher all the professional satisfaction you could ever hope for. You will enrich yourself and your students as you expand the walls of your classroom ever wider through the integration of geography and technology applications.

## REFERENCES

Casely, Judith. 1991. *Dear Annie*. New York: Greenwillow Books.

Cech, John. 1991. *My Grandmother's Journey*. New York: Bradbury Press.

Corcoran, Elizabeth. 1993. "Why Kids Love Computer Nets." *Fortune* (September): 103-106.

Cohen, Barbara. 1983. *Molly's Pilgrim*. New York: Lothrop, Lee & Shepard Books.

Dyrli, Odvard Egil. 1993. "The Internet: Bringing Global Resources to the Classroom." *Technology & Learning* (October): 50-58.

Hirschi, Ron. 1992. *Seya's Song*. Seattle: Sasquatch Books.

Houston, Gloria. 1992. *My Great Aunt Arizona*. New York: Harper Collins Publishers.

Leberanz, Deborah, and Kathleen Tyner. 1993. "Inquiring Minds Want to Know: What Is Media Literacy?" *The Independent* (August/September): 21-25.

Say, Allen. 1993. *Grandfather's Journey*. Boston: Houghton Mifflin.

White, Mary Alice. 1991. "Imagery in Multimedia." *The LEARNing POST* (February): 2-3.

Bonnie E. Svingen is a Teacher Consultant for the Washington Geographic Alliance in Pullman, Washington. [1994 note]

**Elizabeth K. Wilson**
**George E. Marsh II**

Significant shifts in theories about curriculum development and teaching methods are presenting dramatic challenges to traditional thinking about teaching social studies. None of these changes poses as great a challenge—or as many opportunities—as the rapid development of computer technology and instant, electronic communication.

In particular, the Internet, an easily accessible means of electronic communication and research, may not only enhance but further revolutionize and even institutionalize these new approaches to teaching.

The Association for Supervision and Curriculum Development, the National Council for Teachers of Mathematics, and the American Association for the Advancement of Science have all advocated turning away from direct instruction toward "active, inventive instruction" (Pechman 1992, 34). This approach is equally applicable to the teaching of social studies from kindergarten through the twelfth grade (Risinger 1992), and, in fact, the National Commission on Social Studies in the Schools endorsed significant changes in curricula and instruction. (The Commission was a collaboration of the Organization of American Historians, the American Historical Association, and National Council for the Social Studies.)

The Commission's Curriculum Task Force has emphasized the need for "exciting" ways to promote the development of critical thinking and problem-solving skills. The Commission's recommendations are similar in some ways to those of other like groups. Almost all have rejected the passive conveyance of facts and direct instruction as acceptable methods of teaching. Instead, they have recommended "active approaches" to replace these time-worn, traditional methods.

The task force has identified many of these active approaches. They include reading, writing, observing, debating, role playing, doing simulations, and manipulating statistical data to foster critical thinking, decision making, and problem solving. In addition, this group has recommended many alternatives to the textbooks that have served as the basis for traditional teaching. These alternatives include such things as original sources, literature, films, television, artifacts, photographs, historical maps, computers, and computer software that assists in learning.

Many professional organizations, the National Commission on Social Studies in the Schools among them, have

called for this type of reform and have urged the adoption of teaching practices that foster improved thinking skills. This new type of learning would replace traditional teaching methods that seem to embrace two primary assumptions. These are (1) that the teacher's primary role in the classroom is to transmit knowledge to learners and (2) that students must directly absorb this information (Rosenshine and Stevens 1986; Good and Brophy 1991).

This traditional reliance on rote learning and memorization is now widely regarded as a serious problem (Lipman 1991). Many educators and lay persons now agree that education's most important goal should be to teach children to solve problems. As a result, many educators have developed new curricula based on learner-centered constructivism to teach their students to function successfully in real-world contexts.

While sound in concept, the need to change the way students think and to promote higher-order thinking skills poses a serious challenge for teachers. According to Walberg (1991), "Students' reasoning is often mistaken but logically consistent, confidently held, and difficult to change" (Walberg 1991, 55). Kamiloff-Smith and Inhelder (1975), Piagetian scholars, reported that children are highly resistant to changing theories once they have formed them, even in the face of overwhelming evidence to the contrary. This implies that new, active teaching methods must emphasize even more strongly than before the relevance of the instructional content. Mere reliance on the use of original sources, artifacts, historical maps, and data sets and the like is not enough. These devices by themselves will by no means guarantee that students will find learning more engaging or relevant than when they were studying ordinary textbooks or being taught in a traditional manner.

As Pechman (1992) notes, "Schools try to teach children to use the formal tools of academic disciplines . . . but many children find few opportunities outside of school to practice what they are taught. The resulting inauthenticity of classroom activity makes it difficult for children to see how school learning applies to their lives" (p. 33).

One solution to this dilemma is close at hand: Use computers in teaching social studies to better engage the interests of students in local, national, and global issues and affairs.

Peck and Dorricott (1994) suggest several reasons why schools should use technology. They include the opportunities that technology creates for students to do meaningful work; the increase in the amount of knowledge that students can absorb and the enhanced quality of thinking and writing that computer technology can foster; and the

Reprinted from *Social Education*, April/May 1995, Volume 59, Number 4.

need for graduates to be globally aware and able to use sources in the "real world," outside the school.

The use of computers, in fact, presents the opportunity to revolutionize the way students work and think. Their use, for example, can stimulate an interest in the written word as students search for documents in remote libraries. Using data bases allows students to independently gather, analyze, interpret, and evaluate their own work. According to Peck and Dorricott (1994), "With few exceptions, children's domains of discovery during the school day are limited to the classroom and the school."

However, today's technology, particularly the vast, electronic Internet communications network, can provide students with easy, inexpensive, and immediate access to the world beyond not just their classrooms but beyond their communities and virtually any other existing boundaries. Thus, while still at school, they can acquire knowledge far beyond the boundaries of their own communities and experiences and gain firsthand knowledge of other cultures. Furthermore, because they are engaging in their own research, the information gained can be personally relevant.

## UNIVERSAL COMMUNICATION AS A TEACHING TOOL

The Internet, also referred to as the "Information Super Highway" or the "National Information Infrastructure," connects millions of computers around the world. It is a global, non-commercial network of networks, some of which focus on education.

The Internet had its origins in the early 1970s as ARPAnet (Advanced Research Projects Agency network). That was an effort by the Department of Defense to link the department's many research and military facilities. Since then, the Internet has evolved into a communications system that links universities, government organizations, corporations, and private citizens.

Any school with a computer and a modem can connect to the Internet through a commercial on-line service or a bulletin board service (a "BBS"). Access is also easily available through many mainframe computers at universities. An estimated 30 million people around the world daily send and receive messages, reports, graphics, and other kinds of information over the Internet, and thousands of separate computer networks connect 1.7 million computers in 125 countries to each other (Stix 1993).

The Internet never rests. Every day millions of people exchange information on an almost infinite number of topics in "forums"; tap into thousands of data bases to conduct research; copy files, documents, even music; participate in live, interactive conferences; and send electronic messages back and forth by "e-mail." Students can exchange views with experts on innumerable topics, download free software, read newspapers published in different places all over the world, obtain the full records of Supreme Court decisions, download speeches made by the President of the United States and other government officials, and take part in numerous other activities that support the goals of a well-founded curriculum in social studies.

Alvin Toffler, the famous futurist, believes that the most important domestic political issue is the wealth produced by information and the media. According to Toffler, "No nation can operate a 21st-century economy without a 21st-century electronic infrastructure" (1991, 368-369). If Toffler is correct, no school can afford to remain unconnected to the electronic infrastructure because, as Toffler puts it, we now live in an age when knowledge is the new capital and electronic technology is the new transportation. The primary access to knowledge, particularly new knowledge, is no longer the library, but the global electronic network that not only includes thousands of libraries but that also presents knowledge that will be outdated and obsolete by the time it is published in books.

The use of technology in the classroom is imperative because graduates will enter a work force that is already inextricably tied into information technologies. Using the Internet to communicate, conduct research, and exchange information prepares students for the technological and information-oriented environment they will face upon graduation. Access to the Internet "breaks through" existing boundaries, including the walls of the classroom, as noted earlier, thus helping students avoid parochialism and isolation. Moreover, the Internet can enhance students' roles as constructivists: Each creates his or her own knowledge as a researcher, communicator, and collaborator on a worldwide network of people and resources.

## TEACHING WITH INTERNET: COUNTING THE WAYS

*Electronic Mail.* Teachers can collaborate with other teachers and professors, and students can write back and forth to "electronic" pen pals by using electronic mail ("e-mail"). Electronic mail is increasingly common, whether on local area networks ("LANS," stored on computer "fileservers") that connect workers in the same building or on the Internet, which allows anyone operating a properly set up computer to communicate with anyone, anywhere in the world who is also hooked up.

*File Transfer.* File transfer, technically called file transfer protocol (FTP), allows students and teachers to transfer files from other computers. For example, a student may locate and transfer the latest U.S. Supreme Court decision, a recent speech made by the President, or the latest maps of Earth's surface from NASA.

*USENET.* Begun in 1979 to link two computers in North Carolina, this is a news and discussion service on almost any imaginable topic. People from all over the world contribute information in response to questions posed by other users.

*Archie.* This is a data base system that regularly "calls" libraries to see what is currently available. It is, in effect, an automatic updating system. Archie currently has catalogs of more than 1,000 file libraries. Like a card catalog, Archie will accept a full or partial file name, and then tell the user where the file is stored.

*Gopher.* Gopher (from "go for") is a huge Internet menu system. Organizations or sometimes individuals from all over the world have set up Gopher "servers" with menus of items. Files and data about almost any topic are stored in thousands of locations. If, for example, a student wants to find information about "NAFTA," the user can instruct a gopher server to search for this topic.

*Veronica.* Veronica is a computer tool that makes gophers easier to use. In many gophers, Veronica will search all of "gopherspace." Veronica can be instructed to search for "museum," and it will find locations of museums available for searching on the Internet.

*WAIS.* The acronym stands for "Wide Area Information Server." There are many WAIS data bases throughout the Internet. One can use gopher to browse for information, just as one would scan a table of contents. WAIS is like an index. Either the gopher or the WAIS will accept a request and then scan the networks to find it.

*ListServs.* This expression is derived from the term "list service." A ListServ is an automatic mailing list for use by members of a special interest group who are interested in the same topic. A student or teacher can "subscribe" to a particular service, and a host computer will send updated information automatically to recipients each day.

There are thousands of ListServs, many of them developed expressly for educational purposes. Students can get information about different countries, or exchange views in English or many other languages.

## ELECTRONIC TEACHING TOOLS FOR SOCIAL STUDIES

The U.S. Department of Education and other federal agencies support computer networks for the benefit of students in grades K through 12. The Department of Education's Office of Educational Research and Improvement (OERI) is creating an electronic information service (SMARTLINE) to provide information about education to educators, parents, and community leaders. Some sources of particular relevance to the social studies curriculum are the following:

*National Geographic Kids Network.* This is a comprehensive international telecommunications-based science and geography curriculum for fourth through sixth graders. Pupils in fifty states and more than twenty countries are assigned to research teams of ten to fifteen different classes. These teams investigate such topics as water supplies, weather, pollution, nutrition, and solar energy.

*Project GeoSim.* The departments of computer science and geography at Virginia Technological University, Blacksburg, have developed "Project GeoSim," which now has two free software programs for education. These are a population module called "HumPop" and a population change simulation program called "IntlPop." They can be accessed by logging onto the archive server on the Internet and downloading the files. To contact Project GeoSim by Internet, its e-mail address is geosim@cs.vt.edu.

*Peabody Museum at Yale University.* Using the Internet, students can obtain information from the Peabody Museum about their states and communities. Several thousand records for each state are available on-line.

*Census-BEA Electronic Forum.* This service of the Department of Commerce provides such government statistics as data about domestic and foreign trade, rankings of states, population, inventories, expenditures on manufacturing, and many other topics.

*Economic Bulletin Board.* Also provided by the Department of Commerce, this service has data on economic analyses such as the census and labor statistics.

*Global Seismology and Geomagnetism.* The U.S. Department of the Interior provides up-to-date information on earthquakes on this network service.

*ERIC.* Most educators are familiar with ERIC, but they may not know that ERIC now provides extensive support on-line for educators at all levels.

## MORE EDUCATIONAL NETWORKS

The U.S. government provides many network services useful to educators, but many other groups also offer useful sources of information. Some are described below.

*Academy One.* Affiliated with the National Public Telecomputing Network (NPTN) and the Cleveland Free-Net, this program provides schools all over the world with access to its community computer systems. Students also have the opportunity to participate in on-line projects, such as group investigation of topics that interest them.

*AT&T Learning Network.* The company provides a curriculum-based telecommunications program for grades K-12 that matches students and teachers in "learning circles" with eight to ten other classes around the world for collaborative learning.

*Consortium for School Networking (CoSN).* CoSN helps educators and students access information and communications resources for learning and collaborative work.

*The EDUCOM K-12 Networking Project.* EDUCOM, principally an organization of university computer personnel, has created this project to link teachers in primary and secondary schools to networks.

*The FrEdMail Network.* FrEdMail is a consortium providing inexpensive telecommunications networks for public agencies and schools, particularly to help teachers and students participate in networking activities. It enables teachers to share experiences, ideas, and materials as well as information for professional development, and provides a gateway to the Internet.

*K12NET.* This network is a system of more than 250 linked bulletin boards that carry thousands of messages each week around the world. Participants access many subject-specific conferences and also collaborate on projects. Developed as a grassroots project, K12Net is a collaborative effort available free to anyone who can access it through a bulletin board.

*KIDSNET.* KIDSNET is a global Internet electronic discussion group for children and their teachers. It deals with computer networks and projects linking children in different schools.

*FidoNet.* FidoNet is one part of the vast computer networks of worldwide bulletin board systems. It is used to send messages and free or inexpensive software to subscribers.

*Global Net.* This network is similar to FidoNet. It covers a wide range of topics including programming, travel information, news, sports, music, and many other topics.

*The Library of Congress.* The Library of Congress plans to announce an ambitious effort to convert into digital form the most important materials in its collection and in the collections of all public and research libraries in the country (Lewis 1994). The project would be a vast "virtual library" of digitized images of books, drawings, manuscripts, and photographs that would look like the "originals" and that could be downloaded over computer networks to students and researchers. The Library eventually intends to provide digitized movies and music, all of which would have historical value for teaching social studies. According to Lewis (1994), "The National Digital Library project would become the most extensive source of content material for the emerging National Information Infrastructure."

## GETTING STARTED

To get started, you will need a computer, a communications modem, communications software, and an account with an Internet service provider. Just about any computer—Macintosh or IBM-compatible—will let you access the Internet from your classroom or your school's media center. Many new computers have modems and communications software already installed.

As noted above, you will need a service provider. In some states, such as North Dakota, Texas, and Virginia, there are statewide education networks that make Internet access easy. In other states, you may need to access the Internet through a local college or university, or subscribe to a commercial service. To get advice about connecting at your school, contact your local media specialist. If you need further information, contact InterNIC at 1-800-444-4345 for a referral to a service provider.

## CONNECTING TO KIDLINK

KIDLINK is an especially useful service for students. KIDLINK has a gopher located at Duquesne University in Pittsburgh. The gopher provides information about KIDLINK projects for students involved in global dialogue via e-mail and other means. For special information, you may contact:

> Mark Hunnibell
> KIDLINK Special Projects
> mark@kids.ccit.duq.edu

To learn about KIDLINK projects, subscribe to the KIDLINK announcement service by sending an e-mail message to listserv@vmi.nodak.edu with the following command in the text of your message: SUB KIDLINK Your-first-name Your-last-name

You can access the KIDLINK gopher in several ways:

1. *Using your own Gopher client:*
   gopher kids.ccit.duq.edu 70
2. *Using telnet:*
   telnet 165.190.8.35  login: gopher
3. *Using a World Wide Web browser:*
   gopher://kids.duq.edu:70/1
   http://kidlink.ccit.duq.edu:70/0/kidlink-general.html
4. *Using e-mail:*
   Send mail to listserv@info.cern.ch. Put the following commands in the body of your mail:
   send gopher://kids.duq.edu:70/1
   help

## CONNECTING TO OTHER GOPHERS

Once you are connected to one gopher, you will have access to other gophers. As a result, you can use many gophers to support your teaching. The next gopher may be in the same state, another state, or another country, all accessed by choosing from a menu. If you want a comprehensive listing of available gophers, check out your local bookstore for books that publish lists of them, or look for them on the Internet.

## OTHER SOURCES [1995 INFORMATION]

For additional information for using Internet or other services that are available, contact the services listed below.

Internet Resource Directory for Educators On-line:
telnet [or ftp] tcet.unt.edu
pub/telecomputing-info/IRD/IRD-telnet-sites.txt, IRD-ftp-archives.txt, IRD-listservs.txt, and IRD-infusion-ideas.txt

NECC and Tel-Ed Conferences
International Society for Technology in Education
1787 Agate Street
Eugene, Oregon 97403-1923
Phone: 503-346-4414 or 1-800-336-5191
Fax: 503-346-5890
Email: iste@oregon.uoregon.edu
(Compuserve: 70014,2117)
(AppleLink: ISTE)

INET
Internet Society
1895 Preston White Drive
Suite 100
Reston, Virginia 22091
Phone: 703-648-9888
Fax: 703-620-0913
Email: isoc@isoc.org

Consndisc (Consortium for School Networking Discussion List):
To subscribe, send a message to
listproc@yukon.cren.org

Ednet:
To subscribe, send a message to
listserv@nic.umass.edu

Kidsphere:
To subscribe, send a message to
kidsphere-request@vms.cis.pitt.edu

KIDS-95/KIDLINK:
Send a message to
listserv@vm1.nodak.edu

Consortium for School Networking Gopher Server:
via gopher: cosn.org (port 70)
via telnet: telnet cosn.org, login: gopher
(no password)

## THE INTERNET AND THE NEXT AMERICAN REVOLUTION

Electronic communication networks are not only changing how work is done but also changing organizational power by circumventing traditional authority in governments and corporations. Due to the easy and frequently instant availability of electronic information, decision making is falling to lower levels in organizations and middle managers are being eliminated.

Students will enter a work force in which they will be expected to handle and interpret electronic information. Learning how to use the Internet can provide students with excellent preparation for their future in the electronic work place.

More important still, the Internet, as a tool for instruction in social studies, is presenting students with an unprecedented opportunity to engage in one of the most "democratizing" movements in the world's history—equal access to unbounded, unlimited information.

## REFERENCES

Bradley Commission on History in Schools. *Building a History Curriculum: Guidelines for Teaching History in Schools*. Washington, DC: Educational Excellence Network, 1992.

Curriculum Task Force of the National Commission on Social Studies in the Schools. (Sandra L. Mullins CIJE Coordinator for ERIC/ChESS). *Charting a Course: Social Studies for the 21st Century*. Washington, DC: National Commission on Social Studies in the Schools, 1989.

Good, T.L., and J.E. Brophy. *Looking in Classrooms*, 5th ed. New York: Harper Collins, 1991.

Kamiloff-Smith, A., and B. Inhelder. "If You Want to Get Ahead, Get a Theory." *Cognition* 3 (1975): 195-212.

Lipman, M. *Thinking in Education*. Cambridge: Cambridge University Press, 1991.

Lewis, P.H. *Library of Congress Offering to Offer Data Superhighway*. New York: N.Y. Times News Service, 1994.

National Commission on Social Studies in the Schools. (Sandra L. Mullins, CIJE Coordinator for ERIC/ChESS). *Social Studies for the 21st Century: Recommendations of the National Commission on Social Studies in the Schools*. ERIC Digest ERIC Clearinghouse for Social Studies/Social Science Education, Bloomington, Indiana; Office of Educational Research and Improvement (ED), Washington, DC, 1988.

Peck, K.L., and D. Dorricott. "Why Use Technology?" *Educational Leadership* 51 (1994): 11-15.

Pechman, E.M. "Child as Meaning Maker: The Organizing Theme for Professional Practice Schools." In *Professional Practice Schools*, edited by M. Levine. New York: Teachers College Press, 1992.

Perelman, L.J. "Restructuring with Technology: A Tour of Schools Where It Is Happening." *Technology and Learning* 2 (1991): 30-37.

Risinger, C. (Sandra L. Mullins, CIJE Coordinator for ERIC/ChESS). *Trends in K-12 Social Studies*. ERIC Clearinghouse for Social Studies/Social Science Education, Bloomington, Indiana; Office of Educational Research and Improvement (ED), Washington, DC, 1992.

Rose, M.T. *The Internet Message*. Englewood Cliffs, New Jersey: Prentice-Hall, 1993. Handbook of Research on Teaching, 3d ed., edited by M.C. Whitrock. New York: Macmillan Publishing Co., 1986.

Stix, G. "Domesticating Cyberspace." *Scientific American* 269 (1993): 100-10.

Toffler, A. *Power Shift*. New York: Bantam Books, 1991.

Thurow, L. *Head-to-Head*. New York: William Morrow and Company, Inc., 1992.

Walberg, H. "Productive Teaching and Instruction: Assessing the Knowledge Base." In *Effective Teaching: Current Research*, edited by H. Waxman and H. Walkey, 33-62. Berkeley, California: McCuthchan Publishing Corporation, 1991.

Elizabeth K. Wilson is an Assistant Professor in the area of teacher education at the University of Alabama, Tuscaloosa. Her interests include social studies education, teacher education, and technology. George E. Marsh II is currently a Professor in the area of teacher education at the University of Alabama, Tuscaloosa. A former secondary social studies teacher, Dr. Marsh specializes in interactive technology. [1995 note]

**Allen Smith**

One of the most important goals of education
today is to equip students with the competencies and skills
needed to be productive and participating citizens in an
increasingly complex society. However, this goal conflicts
sharply with some of the leisurely pursuits and interests
of school children. Television has certainly become one of
the most time consuming and popular of these activities.
However, television viewing, rather than being only a
negative influence in developing and reinforcing important citizenship traits, can be used by educators to promote the important components of citizenship education.
Concrete and practical suggestions are offered on how to
accomplish this difficult yet possible task.

Television, in many ways, is the most important influence in the lives of school children today. Between the
ages of six and eighteen, the average child watches the
equivalent of two and one-half uninterrupted years of television or about forty-five percent more time than he or
she actually spends in a classroom.[1] On the average, a child
spends almost twenty-six hours a week with television as
a companion.[2] Students from low socioeconomic backgrounds spend even more time transfixed by the electronic
images flowing across their television screens.[3]

The problem of the quantity of television is exacer-
bated by the overall quality and kinds of shows watched
by youngsters. Animated cartoons of every conceivable
type, situation comedies, and action-oriented series dominate children's viewing time between the ages of five and
fifteen. Educational programs and documentaries account
for only eleven percent of this viewing time. Public television, other than *Mister Rogers* and *Sesame Street*, seldom, if
ever, captures the attention or interest of children.[4]

In competition with the "magnetic" appeal of television are the goals of education, many of which extend
beyond the confines of the school building. Developing
the important elements necessary to become responsible
and productive citizens is certainly one of the most vital
of these goals. Recently, a number of prominent political
scientists and educators delineated seven comprehensive
competencies which should constitute the minimum training requirements for youngsters in citizenship education.5
These competencies are:

- Acquiring and using information from printed and non-
  printed sources to make informed decisions and judgments

- Assessing involvement in political situations and activities
- Making decisions
- Making judgments
- Communicating ideas to other citizens and political
  leaders
- Cooperating with others to achieve mutual goals
- Protecting and promoting one's interests and values[6]

These seven citizenship competencies are not encouraged or fostered in any deliberate or conscious sense by
commercial television. To be properly practiced and mastered, these citizenship skills require time and patience as
well as such cognitive processes as conceptualization,
analysis, and evaluation on an individual's part before one
possibly acts in some real way based on these delibera-
tions. On the other hand, television, with its overriding
concern to be entertaining and to sustain viewers' interest and attention by incessantly appealing to the visual,
emotional, and listening senses, engenders the very antithesis of the development of these skills and processes.
How could a youngster actively engage in any of these
citizenship skills and cognitive processes by sitting in a
passive, willingly receptive state and responding only to
the constantly changing visual images and sounds bom-
barding and manipulating him or her at rapid speeds from
the screen? Clearly, based on the seemingly total obses-
sion youngsters have in watching countless hours of television, this visual medium is destroying much of the
school's efforts in nurturing and refining these important
citizenship traits.

## RECOMMENDATIONS

Aware of the pervasive influence of television in the lives
of children, educators still have a few feasible options open
to them for teaching and promoting citizenship skills. One
alternative is to exert a wholehearted effort to communicate to youngsters and their parents the deleterious effects of extensive watching of television. In this regard, it
has been disclosed that, to a great degree, it is the parents
and not their children who control what is viewed and the
number of hours the set remains on during the prime time
viewing period.[7] In fact, the ten most popular shows of
adults do not vary significantly from the most popular
programs of youngsters aged twelve to seventeen.[8] Furthermore, due to the increase in the number of two wage-
earning households, many youngsters, for a considerable
number of hours each afternoon and even late at night,
have unsupervised access to television viewing.[9]

The other viable option which seems the more realistic
in light of the seemingly magnetic appeal television has for

youngsters is to devise and implement, within the class-room, activities to utilize pertinent components of television viewing to foster important citizenship competencies. Since television is a natural motivating and interest-capturing medium for schoolchildren, it is an ideal way for educators to engage and interest youngsters in activities that can help them to practice participatory, non-sedentary citizenship skills such as conducting school or community surveys on television-related subjects and promoting their point of view by forming or joining advocacy groups in their school and community. For example, after viewing and discussing the show, *License to Kill*, students may wish to join the fight against drunken driving by becoming involved in an organization such as Students Against Drunk Driving (SADD). Youngsters may decide, after viewing an episode of *Alice* dealing with animal neglect and abuse, to join and plan with others to deal with this problem if it exists in their community. The key is to challenge children to analyze situations, make decisions, and participate actively in different ways in matters that have personal meaning and interest to them. Television, if used eclectically and creatively by educators, provides many opportunities and situations to accomplish these goals.

When making the specific suggestions and strategies that follow, the author recognized that during the viewing of a show, most youngsters desire to be entertained and are not inclined to analyze critically or evaluate what they see. Therefore, teachers may best use the medium by asking students to focus on a few specific questions or areas of concern before seeing a favorite show to alert them to what to observe and analyze. After the show is over, and perhaps with parental guidance, students can write answers to assignment-related questions or elaborate upon issues earlier raised in class.

Most of the specific suggested activities for each of the seven citizenship competencies are geared to the secondary level although many can be adapted and modified for the elementary school level. Adjustments in the complexity of the assignment and the language used will also have to be made occasionally to reflect the particular needs and ability levels of different students. Furthermore, these recommendations are not self-inclusive but rather should be looked upon as starting points, motivational devices, or assignments for lessons and classroom activities at relevant points in the curriculum. The suggestions are phrased in the form of assignments for the students with guidelines for the teacher enclosed in parentheses.

## SUGGESTED STUDENT ACTIVITIES
### ACQUIRING AND USING INFORMATION

1. After watching an historical drama, mini-series, or documentary such as *The Day After*, *Shogun*, *Kennedy*, *King*, or *The Holocaust*, describe in writing important new information or ideas you learned from viewing the program. Use other sources such as texts, encyclopedias, or books to verify the information you learned. (Prime Time Television, 212 West Superior, Chicago, Illinois, often sends to educators materials containing strategies on how students can most benefit from watching these kinds of programs.)

2. Compare two newscasts on different stations concerning a specific news story. The stories might deal with a local pollution problem or an international crisis. In chart form, compare the types of information offered by each station for the event. Add a column from a newspaper report of the same topic.

3. Develop a question about a topic of interest to send into a news program. (A question raised in class or one pertaining to concerns or interests of youngsters such as on space travel, computers, sports, or the nuclear threat are examples.)

4. Compare a product advertised on television with other brands of the same product advertised in newspapers, magazines, or on television. (Some products related to student interests can include video game players, computers, cars, fashions, etc.) Develop a chart comparing the good and bad points for each of the brands of the product.

5. Conduct a class or school survey on the television shows most often watched by students or on the amount of time students watch television. Analyze the results in a report or chart form and report your findings to your class.

6. After watching a show on instructional television in class, what new useful information did you learn about the subject? (Contact Agency for Instructional Television, Box A, Bloomington, IN 47401 on availability in different areas.)

### ASSESSING INVOLVEMENT

1. Describe in writing the action or lack of action taken by one or more characters based on the occurrence of some event or situation. (For example, on such popular shows as *Gimme a Break* and *Alice*, the psychological effects of the danger of a nuclear holocaust on a fourteen year old or the actions of Vera on seeing a pony mistreated in a circus or many other similar situations in other shows could become the focus of an assignment or discussion.)

2. Imagine you were one of the characters on a favorite show who was affected by some outside occurrence or event. Would you have taken the same action or none at all? Discuss in writing. (See previous question.)

3. After watching a newscast, select at least one of the events described. For the event, explain its possible effects on you, your family, your community, or the entire nation. (The events could center on the finding of pesticides in a nearby stream, an oil supply crisis, or a new breakout of hostilities in a part of the world.)

4. Using research, evaluate the effects or relationship between watching television and academic work or criminal behavior. What lessons are to be learned from your findings? Be prepared to defend your position. (The teacher may need to offer some direction in research techniques and the types of sources to use.)

## MAKING DECISIONS

1. List the important decisions that had to be made by a character on a favorite show or program. (Every show has many decisions made by main characters such as on *Family Ties* in which a youngster had to decide whether to disobey a parent and go to a party or on *Masquerade* in which "average" citizens decide to assist the government on some mission. Televised sporting events are ideal since many decisions have to be made by the coaches.)

2. Review at least one important decision described in the previous question. Be prepared to discuss in class who made the decision, why it was made, how it was arrived at, and who was affected by it. Was it a good decision? Why or why not? If you had been the character on the show, would you have made the same decision? Why or why not?

3. Write a short television script or use one provided by the teacher and list the different important decisions that had to be made by the characters portrayed. (The CBS Television Reading Program at 51 West 52nd St., New York, NY 10019, provides to participating schools many scripts on such worthwhile special programs as *The Race to the Pole* and *License to Kill*.)

## MAKING JUDGMENTS

1. List shows where people make many comments or judgments about each other. (*Alice, Jeffersons, Three's Company*, etc.) Do you agree with these judgments? Why or why not? Give examples in your answer.

2. Which shows do you like the best? List the reasons for your opinion.

3. Which character on a favorite show do you admire the most or greatly dislike? (Names such as J.R. on *Dallas*, Fonzie on *Happy Days*, or Alexis on *Dynasty* may be raised.) Offer some reasons for this opinion.

4. Using your favorite show, select characters who would make the best teacher, principal, parent, sibling, or U.S. President. Justify your answer on the basis of the qualities these characters possess for these roles.

## COMMUNICATING IDEAS TO OTHERS

1. Write a letter to a producer or the network of a favorite show explaining why you like the program and requesting pictures of the stars. (CBS: 51 W 52nd St., New York, NY 10019; NBC: 30 Rockefeller Plaza, New York, NY 10020; ABC: 1330 Ave. of Americas, New York, NY 10019)

2. Create a TV guide for upcoming popular shows offering just enough information to interest readers and allow them to make a choice. Include action, comedy, and documentary programs.

3. Explain in writing or orally in class why it is worthwhile to view certain shows and describe the worthwhile features they contain. (A debate may ensue and students should be prepared in its essentials.)

## COOPERATING WITH OTHERS

1. Develop a list of all the shows in which characters regularly cooperate with each other. Explain the ways in which the characters cooperate. (Some shows cited may be the *Smurfs, Simon and Simon, The A Team*, and *Hill Street Blues*.) After creating such a list, attempt to group these cooperative ways into categories. (Such headings as handling emergencies, achieving a goal shared by two or more, etc., can be introduced in class to help students to get started.)

2. List those shows in which the main character usually works alone but does rely in some ways on the assistance of others. Explain why such reliance is needed and offer some examples from shows watched. (*Magnum PI, Fall Guy*, and *Matt Houston* are a few examples.)

3. Develop a list or chart of the advantages and disadvantages of working together to solve problems. Use names and characters from some shows as examples.

## PROMOTING AND PROTECTING ONE'S INTERESTS

1. Write the network about a favorite show which was discontinued. Ask such questions as who made the decision and how it was arrived at. After receiving a response, meet with others who share a similar view and ask whether the decision was fair and how it can be changed. Try to develop a strategy to get the show back on the air.[10] (Network addresses were given in the communicating ideas section. Viewer protests and action did revive the shows *Cagney and Lacy* and *Hill Street Blues*.)

2. Review and list the persuasive techniques (glamour, bandwagon, testimonial, incomplete claims, etc.) developed by advertisers to promote their product. Describe a few recent commercials and the kinds of techniques used. If deceptive or misleading claims were used, decide what action to take, such as contacting the Federal Trade Commission, Washington, D.C. 20280.

3. Create a television commercial promoting a product or service and videotape it. (Ask the class to critique the commercial and the persuasive techniques used to promote the product.)

4. Contact a television advocate organization such as the National Council for Children and Television, 20 Nassau St., Princeton, NJ 08540. Ask what its purposes are and what viewers can do to get more value from television viewing.

## USE TELEVISION TO MOLD GOOD CITIZENS

Television viewing has little likelihood of disappearing from a child's daily menu of leisurely pursuits. Rather it will probably remain, in varying degrees, a permanent fixture in the daily activities of the child's lifetime. Failure of educators to realize the far-reaching negative effects of television viewing on the development and reinforcement of important citizenship skills and traits will only make the task of preparing citizens to participate constructively in the complex democratic system that much more difficult. Therefore, it is incumbent upon educators to make television an instrument in one's pedagogical repertoire to foster many of the important components of citizenship education. This effort, although admittedly a difficult and circuitous one in many instances, must be earnestly made by all educators interested in promoting this important goal.

## NOTES

1   Peter Finn, "Developing Critical Television Skills," *Educational Forum*, 44 (May, 1980): 473.

2   Dorothy G. Singer, Jerome L. Singer, and Diane Zuckerman, *Teaching Television: How to Use TV to Your Child's Advantage* (New York: Dial Press, 1978): 19.

3   Ibid.

4   Ibid., 49.

5   Richard C. Remy, *Handbook of Basic Citizenship Competencies* (Alexandria, Virginia: Association for Supervision and Curriculum Development, 1980).

6   Although other political scientists and educators may have developed their own lists of citizenship competencies, most, if not all, of these concepts can be logically subsumed within the seven citizenship components cited.

7   Barbara Lee and Marsha Rudman, *Mind Over Media* (New York: Seaview Books, 1982): 37.

8   Neil Postman, "The Disappearing Child," *Educational Leadership*, 40 (March, 1983): 13.

9   Neil Postman, "Engaging Students in the Great Conversation," *Phi Delta Kappan*, 64 (January, 1983): 312.

10  Byron Massialas and Joseph B. Hurst, *Social Studies in a New Era: School as a Laboratory* (New York: Longman, 1978): 493.

Allen Smith is a secondary school teacher in the New York City Public School System. [1985 note]

## David Aronson

Sixty years ago, television was a technological curiosity, a laboratory screen of ghostly figures that hardly anyone could imagine would be a force in the society of the future. Today, TV is our constant companion, educating and entertaining us from the nursery school to the nursing home. In the span of a single lifetime, TV has replaced print as the primary medium by which we tell our stories, report our news and decide on our purchases—and our votes.

But as TV has grown in importance, certain of our problems have also mushroomed. Violence, drug abuse, teenage pregnancy, and, in general, a culture that celebrates consumerism and instant gratification while tolerating undercurrents of prejudiced and bigotry—to many people, it makes sense to link these problems to the pervasive influence of television.

Other critics decry the fact that children spend so much of their time in front of the tube. They lament the hours children could spend in more productive pursuits—such as playing or reading—that would foster the children's emotional and intellectual development.

As author Richard Louv has said, "Television hijacks so many of our senses, so many parts of the brain, that it leaves little room for self-generated images and ideas; more important, television is simply a thief of time—of creative time, of family time."

TV's dominance is evident in the statistics: Children spend more hours watching that innocuous-looking box in the living room than they spend in school. They are bombarded by over 100 commercials a day and witness 25,000 TV murders by the age of 18.

The problems associated with television viewing—or at least with heavy viewing—are beyond doubt any longer. Children who watch more than four hours of TV a day tend to get poorer grades, not read as well, have fewer friends and weigh more than their classmates. Most studies show that children who watch an excessive amount of TV violence are less compassionate to others. Such children are also more likely to believe the world is a dangerous place and are readier than other children to resort to aggression.

Yet, until recently, most teachers paid little attention to TV, perhaps because they accepted TV as a given. Now a burgeoning media literacy movement is seeking to change the relationship between the media and educators

and to engage students in a critical analysis of TV's images and messages. So far, it is estimated, 3,500 teachers nationwide have integrated some media literacy into their teaching. (As the term suggests, many in the media literacy movement examine a broad range of popular media, such as rock music, motion pictures and radio, as well as TV. But TV is the dominant medium in most children's lives and is the primary focus of the movement.)

## THE TV AS TEACHER

"It's hard for educators, because we have been charged with carrying on the cultural legacy, the torch of civilization, not to see TV as either trivial or as the enemy," admits Renee Hobbs, a professor of communication at Babson College in Wellesley, Mass., and the director of Harvard's Institute on Media Education. "But TV isn't the enemy, and we've got to stop pretending, ostrich-like, that it's not there. It is, and it's part of our lives." Hobbs ticks off reasons for teachers to include media literacy in the curriculum:

- It involves students with familiar emotionally engaging material.
- It encourages students to evaluate the media—and by extension, their own worldviews—according to the values of honesty, fairness and respect.
- It can help younger students understand the difference between fantasy and reality and encourage older ones to distinguish the glib and glamorous fictions of TV from the more complicated truths they know and experience.

Because students are often more media-savvy than their teachers, media literacy classes are a perfect vehicle for cooperative learning.

For Barbara Totherow, who leads classes in video production and media literacy at Alvirne High School in Alvirne, N.H., there is an even simpler reason for including TV in the curriculum. "Ever since Gutenberg, we have assumed we should teach our kids to deal with the dominant medium of the age," she asserts. For centuries, the dominant medium was print. Now. all of us are getting more and more of our information from the electronic media. It makes sense to teach our kids how to read this medium just as critically as we have traditionally taught them to read print.

## TEACHING THE MEDIA

But what exactly does media literacy entail, and how is it taught?

The central idea behind media literacy is that popular entertainment is one of the most powerful forms of education in society today. Unlike school, the media educate by presenting seductive images that captivate our imagination and manipulate our emotions.

Consider a beer commercial that shows stereotypically beautiful women and powerfully built men partying at a beach house. The commercial reflects several stereotypes— of youth, wealth, beauty and happiness—and offers the unspoken suggestion that these ideals are somehow achieved by drinking beer. Yet the association is made in such a way that viewers are distracted from questioning it.

To watch TV the way many young people watch it— surfing channels, flipping between movies to watch two or three at a time, checking out MTV every few minutes—is to absorb unthinkingly the mixed messages of the medium.

Media literacy encourages students to tease out the messages behind TV's images and to judge those messages by the light of their own intelligence and values. This, in fact, is one of the movement's major virtues. It places the debates about TV squarely in the hands of those presumed to be most susceptible to its influences: the children themselves. As Elizabeth Thoman, the executive director of the Los Angeles-based Center for Media and Literacy, says, "Media literacy is not about finding the right answers, but about asking the right questions."

## THE EVIL FOREIGNER

For teachers who are concerned about multiculturalism and tolerance, asking the right questions can prompt students to develop the critical and imaginative skills to examine what TV tells them about their world. Veteran high school teacher Don Staveley uses a Socratic approach to lead his students to a deeper awareness of the persistence and ubiquity of stereotypes

"I have a section on Western imperialism," says Staveley, who teaches history in Billerica, Mass. "I start by asking my students what they know about the various regions of the world that have been colonized."

The results, says Staveley, fit a distinctive pattern. Most of his students are white and don't want to say anything bad about Africa because they are extremely conscious of the stereotyping of African Americans in this country.

"But they have very strong feelings about Asia and especially about the Islamic countries," Staveley reports. "They believe that women in these places are treated badly, that there's an intolerance for the individual, that in the case of India the customs and religions are based on the worshipping of cows. These are subjects that the students may have already learned more accurate information about academically, but it didn't do any good."

After eliciting the students' comments, Staveley next asks them to try to figure out the source of their ostensible knowledge and how much of it may be based on stereotypes. "They realize that much of what they know comes first from Saturday morning cartoons. and second from advertisements and third from the cinema."

Once Staveley's students discover the source of their stereotypical ideas, they become emotionally as well as intellectually involved in broadening their inquiry. "My job is to make sure that everyone gets a chance to be heard. because many of them start to feel they have been misled, lied to," Staveley says. "They start to wonder just how much of their understanding of the world is being shaped by the media. There are no solid answers, just more or less an investigation that each individual student undertakes in his or her own way."

## FROM STEREOTYPING TO BEHAVIOR

Of course, TV has come a long way from the stereotypes of the *Amos 'n' Andy* era: Gay characters have been sympathetically portrayed on *Roseanne* and *Soap*; on *LA Law* a Hispanic character combined intellect and charm with a dashing corporate career; and African Americans like Bill Cosby, Arsenio Hall and Whoopi Goldberg are enormously popular role models for children of all races.

But if the networks have become more aware of ethnic stereotyping than they once were (the case of Arab Americans being the notable exception), other, more subtle, forms of stereotyping persist: the continuing portrayal of women in terms of their sex appeal; the resort to violence; the division of the world into "good guys" and "bad guys"; the over-representation of glamorous careers.

Because these are such pervasive elements of TV, they become "normalized," passing almost unnoticed into our consciousness. Like the glasses Dorothy wore to enter the Emerald City, TV colors our perception of the world without our being aware of it. Ultimately, these serve to reinforce the idea that certain patterns of behavior are expected and acceptable.

Barry Duncan, the head of Canada's Association for Media Literacy and a long-time schoolteacher himself, says that his primary goal is to instill some skepticism in his students about the world they see on TV. There are goals appropriate to each age group, he says.

"In grade 3, students will have reached the point where they can begin to distinguish the program from the commercials, and, more generally, fantasy from reality. They enjoy learning about how special effects are done, how make-up artists dress up food, for example, to make it look more appetizing than it really is.

"In grade 7, kids are extremely responsive to peer pressure, to fashion, to pop music — and they're starting to date, or aspiring to. A teacher might use a show like *Beverly Hills 90210* to examine gender roles and discuss values. Does the show promote consumerism? Does it encourage conformity? How does the world that the students know correspond to the one on TV, and which, in comparison, seems diminished?

"By grade 12, kids can intelligently dissect political commercials and also discuss the way that politics is reported on. Have we gone from being a nation of citizens, critical participants in the political process, to being a nation of political consumers, whose only role in the process is to select the flavor of the year?"

## TALKING BACK TO THE TV

For many in the media literacy movement, the most exciting portion of their work takes place when kids are given a chance to create their own media by using video equipment lent to them through the schools. The goal is not simply to educate students in the technical aspects of TV production but to encourage them to develop their own work in a medium that is exciting and relevant. Media literacy, say its proponents, involves more than just talking about media. It also involves doing it.

"A lot of kids aren't so much drop-outs as push-outs," contends Renee Hobbs. "By giving kids a chance to work in media, you recognize the cultural knowledge that they bring to school and help them to see that the medium's messages are constructed—that the messages are not value-neutral, natural slices-of-life, but have specific ideological and political consequences."

Hogares Alternative School in Albuquerque, N.M., a residential school for troubled teens, may seem an unlikely home base for an Emmy-nominated news-production team. But last year, under the direction of Caryl Thomas, one of 15 teachers enrolled in a statewide pilot program in media literacy, students there produced a three-part series about graffiti that aired on the CBS-affiliate evening news and almost won the coveted Emmy.

The show was an important experience for her students, says Thomas. "It was such a dramatic opportunity for these kids to all of a sudden have a voice in something as powerful as TV." Many of them have had extremely negative experiences in schools so far, she explains.

"TV requires skills and qualities that these kids generally haven't demonstrated. They have to follow through on something, they have to be consistent, make a commitment and work together to the end, even though the process of putting together a newsclip can sometimes be difficult and frustrating."

This year, Thomas' students are working on a clip about homelessness. Bill, an 11th grade recovering alcoholic and drug addict who was once homeless himself, is one of the leaders of the project. Because he has experienced so many of the things he will be describing in the video, he feels he is especially able to use the media to correct its own stereotypes.

"One of the falsities of homelessness is that it's all old people, all skid-row bums," he says. "That's a tragic misconception. The majority are families. There are infants, toddlers, teenagers, elderly—the complete spectrum. And it's all the races, too. Homelessness is not prejudiced. It can happen to you—no matter what your color."

Bill hopes that his video will help convince kids who are thinking about running away to stay at home and find some way of working out their problems. "The streets are tougher than you are," he advises—a message that he believes rarely comes out in TV's often glamorous portrayal of the underside of city life.

A more lighthearted approach to social issues is being taken by Venita Wolfe, a senior at Zuni High School in Zuni, N.M. Venita's first video project was called "Poor and Worthless," and it was modeled, she says, on TV's *Lifestyles of the Rich and Famous*.

"We got permission to go around filming graffiti, a beat-up old car and motorcycle, and an old sheep camp that we treated as a house." Her goal, she says, was to have fun by turning the premise of the TV show on its head, but she had a more serious aim as well. She wanted to satirize mainstream American stereotypes about life on the reservation. "People think we're all one way, all poor, but we're really more complicated than what you see on the surface."

Wolfe's current documentary is about Zuni clans. It investigates Zuni tradition through interviews with elders and shows clips explaining the function of clan divisions in Zuni life. Through the technology of video, Wolfe says, she is learning about her heritage and helping to preserve it for future generations.

Because media literacy is such a new field, its practitioners are still developing a core curriculum and debating the movement's educational goals and perspectives. But perhaps high school teacher Barbara Totherow put the issue most simply. When asked what she wants her students to gain from her class, she paused, then said, "I want them never to look at TV the same way again."

## RESOURCES [1994 INFORMATION]

*Big World, Small Screen: The Role of Television in American Society* ($14.50) is the report of the American Psychological Association on the relationship between TV and society.
University of Nebraska Press
312 N. 14th St.
Lincoln, NE 68588 (800) 755-1105

The video *In Search of the Edge* offers definitive "proof" that the world is actually flat and employs a host of television techniques to prove its absurd thesis—teaching students not to take everything they see on TV at face value. A teaching guide includes lessons in science, language arts and media studies. (Grades 5 and up. Length: 26 min. Rental $50. Purchase $350)
Bullfrog Films
P.O. Box 149
Oley, PA 19547
(800) 543-3764

*Media & You: An Elementary Media Literacy Curriculum* ($29.95) introduces teachers to the major concepts of media literacy and provides an abundance of activity suggestions designed to increase students' understanding of the media.
Educational Technology Publications
700 Palisade Ave.
Englewood Cliffs, NJ 07632
(800) 952-2665

The Harvard Graduate School of Education sponsors a summer institute on media literacy for teachers and media professionals.
Harvard Graduate School of Education
339 Gutman Library
Cambridge, MA 02138
(617) 495-3572

The Center for Media Literacy is a nonprofit membership organization that promotes media literacy. It publishes a quarterly magazine ($35 membership fee includes an annual subscription) and produces a variety of media literacy workshop kits. Their excellent primer, *TV Alert: A Wake-up Guide for Television Literacy* ($27.95), covers such topics as what TV teaches us about sex and why Dad always controls the remote.
Center for Media Literacy
1962 S. Shenandoah St.
Los Angeles, CA 90034
(800) 226-9494

Children watch more than 30,000 commercials every year and account for almost $80 billion worth of purchases. The videos *Buy Me That!* (28 min.) and *Buy Me That 3!* (30 min.) are entertaining consumer survival guides for kids, introducing them to the techniques and tricks of TV advertisers. Complete with teaching guides. (Grades K-6. Purchase: $79 each)
Public Media Education
5547 N. Ravenswood Ave.
Chicago, IL 60640
(800) 343-4312

*Educating the Consumer of Television* ($15.95) is a workbook with reproducible sheets for students in grades 4-12, designed to help them critically analyze their own viewing habits and develop an understanding of the different genres — from docudramas to MTV — that characterize TV today. (A teaching guide is included for $7.95).
Critical Thinking Press & Software
P.O. Box 448
Pacific Grove, CA 93950
(800) 548-4849

*TV Eye: A Curriculum for the Media Arts* is one of the clearest and best-written guides to the care concepts of media literacy, and it offers a host of stimulating activity suggestions for students in grades 5 and up. (Call for price.)
Boston Film Video Foundation
1126 Boylston St.
Boston, MA 02215
(617)536 1540

*Bright Ideas: Media Education* ($14.95) is a richly illustrated book filled with activity suggestions designed to help younger children understand the effects of the mass media on their everyday lives.
Scholastic, Inc.
P.O. Box 7502
Johnson City, MO 65102
(800) 325-6149

**Kenneth S. Volk**

The United States legal system plays an important historical and contemporary role interpreting the extent of influence between technology and the Constitution. For this reason, Science/Technology/Society curriculum should include activities designed to have students understand this interpretive role. These activities not only serve to broaden students' knowledge and appreciation of associated technological and constitutional issues affecting their lives; but hopefully, a new skill to critically examine and discern the future impacts of technology and the law will be gained. One specific STS activity designed to foster these skills uses actual court cases and a panel of student "judges." Through cases involving such constitutional guarantees as a free press, the right to assemble, and protection from unreasonable searches, students can participate in the legal decision-making process by role playing.

## THE EARLY INFLUENCE OF THE CONSTITUTION ON TECHNOLOGY

The Constitution has strongly influenced technology. This influence can be seen in the framing of the Constitution. In Article 1, Section 8 of the Constitution, it states: Congress shall have the power "to promote the progress of science and the useful arts by securing for limited times to authors and inventors the exclusive right to their respective writings and discoveries." This led to the creation of the United States Patent Office and the licensing of technological innovation.

As noted by Burke,[1] the first regulatory action by the U.S. Congress was in 1852. That year, Congress passed a law setting standards for the design and safety of steamship boilers. In essence, technology was being regulated by Congress. Today, Congress continues to influence technology and other issues. Of the nearly 7,000 bills introduced in each congressional session, many deal with technology in a variety of areas such as medicine, computers, and telecommunications. Although approximately three percent of the bills introduced are eventually passed into law, Congressional influence on technology can be considered significant.

## THE INTERPRETATION OF LAW

In accordance with provisions set up in the Constitution, there are three branches of government. In very general

Reprinted with permission from the Materials Research Laboratory at The Pennsylvania State University, from *Bulletin of Science, Technology & Society*, Volume 14, Number 4. Copyright 1994 by STS Press.

terms, the Legislative branch makes the laws, the Executive branch enforces the laws, and the Judicial branch interprets the laws. Although each branch plays a significant role, it is the Judicial branch which ultimately must define the meaning and scope of the Constitution. It was the case of *Marbury v. Madison* (1Cr. 137.206, 1803) which set the legal precedent for the latter's role and responsibility as being the final interpreter of the Constitution.[2]

Considering the delineated role Congress has in making laws, the responsibility of the Judicial branch in interpreting laws, and the impacts and legality of recent technology, an STS activity can be designed to have these technological issues examined by a court of student "judges."

## "YOU" BE THE JUDGE

An STS activity designed for students to actively discuss legal issues involves the use of student "judges." With selected court cases that deal with the use or application of technology, the judges can then decide the outcome of the case. After the background facts are presented and the student judges make their decision, the actual court outcome is announced. This outcome is then used to clarify the constitutional implications and guarantees derived from the decision. Structured as a one-period lesson, or as a five-minute "quickie" using one select court case at the end of a period, this activity can provide entertaining and thought-provoking discussions on constitutional issues.

To begin this activity, court cases must be collected through various sources. These cases, involving the use of technology might deal with guarantees of free press, the right to assemble, and/or the protection from unreasonable searches. Two excellent sources to collect sample cases are *The Wall Street Journal* and the *Rutgers Computer and Technology Law Journal*.

In the former source, the Law Section often provides very current examples of the application of law and technology. Once a bank of cases have been collected, with summative background information, the "court" can be called into session.

For optimum student involvement, three "judges" are selected from the class. These judges proceed to the front of the class, but before they take their seats, they are asked to put on robes signifying their judicial authority. Graduation robes make very adequate judicial garb to enhance the role playing. Also, before the cases are presented, the opening prologue which starts each session of the Supreme Court is said to those in attendance.

Oyea, oyea, oyea, all persons having business before the honorable, the Supreme Court of the

United States, are admonished to draw near and give their attention, for the Court is now sitting. God save the United States and this honorable court.

A visual display of the court cases plays an important part in having the students understand the technological relevance. Two ways this can be accomplished: with overhead transparencies or computer presentation software.

Through the use of traditional overhead transparencies, a photograph or cartoon can be used to illustrate the case. The legal question is then presented below. At the bottom of the transparency is the answer, as cited in the actual court case. This lower portion remains covered until the judges make their decision.

The use of computer presentation software offers the advantage of introducing sound and video clips, as well as interactiveness into the discussion. Software packages such as Compel work well in this situation. By placing a scanned photograph or cartoon into the presentation slide, YES and NO buttons can be inserted. When the decision is made by the judges, the corresponding button is then selected. The response linked to each button would show the actual court outcome and an amusing sound effect to indicate correct or wrong decisions.

## RECENT TECHNOLOGICAL/CONSTITUTIONAL ISSUES

Over the years, technology has had an impact on our guaranteed rights. Although many of these issues have been "settled" through legislative or judicial actions, the pace of new technological development has created the possibility of new laws and interpretations which were impossible to conceive of only yesterday. These impacts influence our ability to approve, use, accept or reject technology in ways which may restrict, expand, intrude or alter our lives in countless ways. The following examples dealing with the right to privacy, freedom of speech, and right to free assembly will illustrate how recent technology has had an impact on the Constitution. These cases can be used as examples for the courtroom simulation.

Technology often impacts our right to privacy. Although not specifically stated in the Constitution, the right to privacy has been interpreted and implied from the Fourth Amendment which guarantees the right to be secure from unreasonable searches. Since the first case that a court accepted the idea of a "right to privacy," *Pavesich v. New England Life Insurance Company* (122 Ga,190, 50 S.E.68, 1905), judicial acceptance of the interpretation has become more commonplace.[3]

Telecommunications is one new area of technology which has raised issues about our right to privacy. With wiretaps being conducted as early as the 1800s by police conducting investigations and stockbrokers trying to obtain secret information,[4] our right to privacy in communications has been a source of concern. Over the years courts have issued decisions on the legality of wiretaps. In 1928, the Supreme Court ruled wiretapping was not an unauthorized search (*Olmstead v. United States*, 277 U.S. 438),

but later the Court overruled Olmstead in *Silverman v. United States*, (365, U.S.505, 1961). Silverman dealt with the use of bugging devices in a place which the Court determined to be a constitutionally protected area. Legislation also has dealt with issues of wiretaps, with Section 605 of the Federal Communications Act of 1934, and the Omnibus Crime and Safe Streets Act of 1968, as examples.

The recent development of sophisticated communication devices has led to a myriad of new impacts on our right to privacy. For instance, when a person's cordless telephone conversation is listened in on by a neighbor, does this violate their right to privacy? This issues was recently decided in *Tyler v. Berodt*, (877 F.2d 705, 8th Cir., 1989) held before the 8th Circuit Court. This case involved the Berodts who used their own cordless phone to monitor and record the phone conversations of their neighbor. The Court held that the cordless phones were not "wire communications" protected by the Wiretap Act. The Court further found that the speakers had no justifiable expectation of privacy since they were aware their conversation was transmitted by a cordless telephone.

Privacy in the workplace is another issue being challenged by recent developments. There are many types of techniques that are available to employers to monitor and control the workplace. This intrusion into our privacy has been termed by some to be the start of the "electronic sweatshop age."[5] Fish-eye cameras watch for employee theft, computers track their performance and time-on-task, and drug testing checks their physical state. These and other technologies have given employers powerful tools to invade the privacy of their employees, often without their suspecting it. Litigation in this area is also just beginning. For instance, in *Bright v. Northwest Medical Center* (U.S. App., New Orleans, 1991), the employee was found not able to claim overtime pay for being monitored with a beeper and having to remain sober for possible call-in as a condition for his employment. The judge found there was no overtime pay for putting up with oppressive working conditions.[6] Therefore, the nine to five workday is quickly becoming a twenty-four hour responsibility, accountability, and indebtedness to one's employer.

Our right to free speech as guaranteed through the First Amendment has also been impacted by recent technology. One example is the introduction of Caller Identification (ID) services by various telephone companies. This service, now feasible through the use of sophisticated computer software, allows the receiver of telephone calls to identify the caller by a device which displays the caller's telephone number.

Caller ID service impact is being felt. A large percentage of the customers in the Washington, DC area now have this service; the majority of users being businesses and government agencies with a growing number of residential users. The use of Caller ID has been credited with a decline in reported obscene phone calls and a more efficient delivery of pizzas.

Two issues of privacy can be raised: (a) does a person

have a right to know who is calling them; and (b) does a person have a right to freely call another individual, business or government agency without fear of having their number registered and recorded? Both positions are being championed by various groups.

Again, the implementation of this technology has already spawned legislative and judicial action: California Statute c. 483, 1989 requires callers be notified of the possibility of display and that they be able to withhold such display on a case-by-case basis without charge. Pennsylvania's Supreme Court recently held that Caller ID services violated state and federal constitutional privacy protections (*Barasch v. Pennsylvania Utility Commission*, Pa. 576 A 2nd 79. 1990). Given the discrepancy which exists between states' laws, and the desire by telephone companies to expand this particular service, this issue will surely continue to spark debate and must ultimately be decided in higher courts.

The First Amendment to the Constitution also protects the right of people to peacefully assemble. The Fourth Amendment prohibits unreasonable searches and seizures. Through the capability and expansion of surveillance technology by segments of our society, the confidence of going about one's own business without the fear of being watched has changed. Sloan discussed this growth of technology when he stated: "states will have the capabilities to strengthen their coercive capabilities, and instruments of control over their citizens."[8] He continued to caution, "on the other hand, the very same technology may help lessen the importance of the state as the preeminent political actor and enable new non-state actors to challenge the coercive power."[9] Galliti[10] substantiated Sloan's contention by reporting there are more private security employees than there are combined federal, state, and local law enforcement personnel. This has created a situation in which surveillance by security cameras in stores, parking lots, theaters and other public places has affected our right to assemble, in subtle, yet threatening ways. This power of technology has created the need to carefully balance the public's right to peacefully assemble and the public's right to safety.

One court case related to the use of indiscriminate surveillance that stands out is *Katz v. United States*, (389 U.S. 347, 1967). In this case, the Court found that "the Fourth Amendment protects people and not simply areas," and therefore, where a person "justifiably relies" on privacy, it is an unreasonable search for the government to intrude either physically or in any other manner without a warrant. Since that time, the explosion of surveillance techniques has produced different opinions from the courts. In *People v. Henderson* (220 Cal App.3d 1632, 270, 1990), the California Court of Appeals ruled that the Fourth Amendment bars evidence gathered in warrantless videotaping. In a somewhat conflicting decision, the New York Court of Appeals found in 1990 that random videotaping of pedestrians for later identification by an attack victim was admissible evidence. Thus, it seems the legal-

ity of surveillance directed specifically at an individual differs from the broader use of surveillance on groups. Again, these issues will probably continue to be debated in the courts.

Besides these examples of technology and the law, others are noted. Again, it is cautioned that when using cases for the earlier-discussed student activity, sufficient background information be obtained. This information is critical for setting the stage for student debated. The following cases further illustrate recent technological advances and capabilities are being subjected to judicial decisions.

- Can a computer operator claim damages from a public employer for not providing a safe place to work? (carpal tunnel syndrome)

    No, *Haririnia v. Amtrack* 89-1431 DC. (1990). The court determined it was accepted working conditions at the time.

- Can weather modification be done even though it may harm private property?

    Yes, *Slutsky v. City of New York* 197 Misc. 730, 97 NYS 2nd 238 (1950). The public need was found to be more important than private interests.

- Do you have property rights to your body parts, should they be removed during an operation?

    No, *Moore v. The Regents of the University of California* 51 Cal. 3rd (1990). The court determined unless you are informed earlier, body parts may be used for medical research without your approval.

- Can DNA tests be admissible as evidence?

    Yes, *State v. Ford*, 392 SE 2d 781 (1990). Although polygraph tests are not, it was determined DNA testing is statistically reliable.

- Is aerial photography or observation an invasion of privacy?

    No, *California v. Ciraolo*, 476 U.S. 207 (1986). The open sky is not considered private property.

- Do artists such as filmmakers have guarantees against "material alterations" of their work?

    Yes, *Gilliam v. American Broadcasting Co.* 538 F.2d 92 Cir (1976). Material alterations change the original intent or meaning of the work. This goes beyond alterations such as motion picture colorization, which assumes the black and white process was the only available technology at the time.

## ADDITIONAL APPLICATIONS

Although actual court cases have been used in this exercise, it is envisioned new cases, not yet determined by the courts, can be designed for students to answer.

For instance:

- What are the legal ramifications of the Genome Project to genetically "map" individuals?
- What limits of free speech exist with automatic telephone dialing machines?
- How long should medical technology be used to keep people alive?

Hypothetical situations which may be more relevant to students' daily lives might include:

■ Should a student's record located on computer files be available to employers? Specifically, what information should be made available and for how long?

■ If a blood test was developed to check for alcohol, even one month after consumption, should schools conduct random tests on students, as a requirement for graduation?

■ Should students wear ID bracelets in order to be electronically located and monitored in school?

These technologies can be analyzed and debated as to their impacts on the rights of privacy and speech, protections from being a witness against oneself, or protections against cruel and unusual punishments.

## CONCLUSION

This paper presented examples of how the Constitution is continually being interpreted due to new technological developments. These interpretations are made by the judicial system which determines our rights to privacy, speech and assembly. Through the use of a simulated court with "judges", students can actively participate in making decisions about our technological society.

In order for students to understand the personal costs and benefits of technology, educators involved in STS are advised to encourage activities and discussions of a Constitutional nature. With such activities included in STS courses, students will gain a better appreciation of their responsibility to ask questions, critique the issues, and participate in our democratic process.

## NOTES

1. Burke, J.G., "Bursting Boilers and the Federal Power," in *Technology and Change*, J.G. Burke and M.C. Eakin, Editors, Boyd & Fraser, San Francisco, CA., 1979, pp. 356-367.

2. Harrell, M.A. and B. Anderson, *Equal Justice Under the Law*, The Supreme Court Historical Society, Washington, DC, 1988.

3. Goode, S., *The Right to Privacy*, Franklin Watts, New York, NY, 1983.

4. Ibid.

5. Rothfeder, J., M. Galen, and L. Driscoll, "Has Your Boss Been Spying?," *Business Week*, January 15, 1990, p. 74.

6. Moskowitz, D., "Court Decisions Are Mixed on States' Powers Over Waste Management," *The Washington Post, Washington Business*, August 5, 1991, p. 25.

7. Sinclair, M., "Caller ID Service Rings in New Era of Phone Privacy," *The Washington Post*, July 27, 1991, p. B1. Updated statistics: Bell Atlantic, Inc., Washington, DC, 1996

8. Sloan, S., "Technology and Terrorism: Privatizing Public Violence," *IEEE Technology and Society Magazine*, 10(2), 8, (1991).

9. Ibid., p.9.

10. Galliti, R., *Introduction to Private Security*, Prentice Hall, Englewood Cliffs, NJ. 1983.

## OTHER READINGS

Chafee, Z., *Free Speech in the United States*, Anthenum, New York, NY, 1969.

Cullop, F., *The Constitution of The United States*, New American Library. New York, NY, 1984.

Leder, L., *Liberty and Authority: Early American Political Ideology, 1689-1763*, Quadrangle Books, Chicago, IL, 1968.

Urofesky, M.I., *The Continuity of Change: The Supreme Court and Individual Liberties*, Wadsworth, Belmont, CA, 1991.

Wilson, V. (Editor), *The Book on Great American Documents*, American History Research Associates, Brookeville, MD, 1987.

Kenneth S. Volk is an Assistant Professor in the School of Education at East Carolina University, Greenville, North Carolina. [1994 note]

# PART 9

**IX** GLOBAL CONNECTIONS

With a rapidly changing and shrinking world, it is even more essential that students recognize the realities of global interdependence. There are both historical and emerging global tensions that heretofore have defied single nation solutions. For example, global topics of current concern include human rights (including the rights of children), environmental quality, economic development and trade, health care and disease eradication, and political stability, among others. Our survival requires mutual international cooperation; isolation is no longer viable. Questions related to the study of this theme include the following: What are some common issues that affect all human beings? What human factors influence the occurrence of a problem? What events are beyond the control of any single nation? What are some tensions that exist between the notions of nation, nationalism, and multiculturalism? What are some ways that future global issues can be predicted?

Studying patterns, relationships, and interactions enables students to examine important issues that have local, national, and global implications. Most often, young learners study these topics in units that incorporate themes of culture, continuity, and change, and content from geography, economics, or history. Of course, other curriculum areas such as the arts and humanities as well as the sciences can also help students to develop global connections and perspectives.

Hoge and Allen identify topics that should be taught to young learners about other nations. They provide several illustrative examples of the many resources and information available for teachers and children as they study about global connections. Ramler makes a strong argument for global education throughout the school curriculum to encourage students to view the world "through the eyes, the minds, and hearts of others." Angell and Avery's article complements Ramler's suggestions by offering a rationale for teaching about global issues in elementary classrooms. They suggest three instructional approaches that will help students and teachers explore together complex issues related to global understanding. Included is a listing of several organizations that provide valuable resources for teaching about global issues.

The geographic location of a school in Seattle, Washington, enabled first grade students and teachers to implement a global studies program that spread throughout the school and culminated in an exchange visit of first graders with their counterparts of Novosibirsk, Russia. Teachers in other schools and locations may want to consider establishing similar learning opportunities and global connections for students in their school.

Schoolwide art projects such as "See Me, Share My World" are described by Warren. These interdisciplinary curriculum projects allow students to learn more about children in other cultures and settings through drawings, photographs, and other visuals. Finally, Banks urges teachers to recognize the importance of integrating the curriculum with multicultural content, reminding us that the United States is a microcosm of the world. He describes the strengths and weaknesses of four commonly used approaches to multicultural education: The Contributions Approach, the Additive Approach, the Transformation Approach, and the Social Actions Approach.

As we approach the year 2000 and beyond, it is imperative that young learners have numerous opportunities to study people and events in other nations, settings, time periods, and cultures. The survival of our planet depends on both an exchange of information and mutual cooperation.

# Teaching about Our World Community: Guidelines and Resources

**John Douglas Hoge**
**Rodney F. Allen**

The opportunity to teach children about an unfamiliar country arises periodically in almost every elementary teacher's classroom. Such occasions may result from adoption of a new social studies textbook, an international student joining the class, the occurrence of a major world event, or perhaps the teacher's own interest derived from a dream-come-true international vacation.

Elementary school teachers who wish to develop a unit on an unfamiliar country face a variety of concerns and decisions. They are concerned about locating appropriate instructional materials, they feel a legitimate need to develop background knowledge required for accuracy, they must determine what content the students should learn, and they must find ways to overcome the psychological distance felt when dealing with something unfamiliar.

Following is a set of guidelines for teaching about other nations in the elementary school classroom. Suggestions are given for:

1. Determining content and instructional goals.
2. Efficiently building background knowledge.
3. Locating existing commercial and public domain curriculum materials.
4. Beginning, sustaining, and ending the unit in ways that maintain high student interest.

## DETERMINING CONTENT AND INSTRUCTIONAL GOALS

The content and instructional goals for a unit on a "new" country are closely interrelated and may be divided according to knowledge, skills, and attitudes. Instructional goals in these three categories help focus the search for curriculum materials and background information. Instructional goals also help determine the content focus of the unit in that they are statements of what content you want the students to learn as a result of their study. There are many thousands of potential instructional goals for units on other nations and it would be impossible to list them all here. However. three guidelines and a collection of the commonly-asked questions provide help in determining content and instructional goals for units on unfamiliar countries.

■ *Teach memorable facts, concepts and main ideas about the culture and country.*

Reprinted from *Social Studies and the Young Learner*, March/April 1991, Volume 3, Number 4. Copyright 1991 by National Council for the Social Studies.

Since it is impossible to remember everything, it is best to try to focus on a smaller amount of more memorable information and to offer greater depth of instruction centered around this carefully selected collection of facts, concepts, and main ideas. Remember that isolated knowledge means little, so use analogies and other mechanisms to attempt to link the new content to the background and experiences of the children. Following are some hypothetical examples of comparable facts, concepts, and main ideas.

1. The population of the capital city of country X is 225,000 people. The current population of our city is _____.
2. Country X received an average annual rainfall of approximately 50 inches. The average annual rainfall of our community is _____.
3. An extended family structure makes it possible for relatives to help in the daily care of young children. Many young children in our community are taken to day care facilities because grandparents and other relatives live apart from other family members.

It is important that accurate and up-to-date information is conveyed to young students. Remember that even recently produced commercial instructional material is often out of date. In addition, free materials, including materials sent by embassies, are often biased. Recognize, too, that you are dealing with partial pictures of a much fuller cultural and social reality. Help your students avoid common falsehoods and damaging stereotypes by showing your recognition of a more complex and accurate view.

■ *Build learning skills that will serve future learning about the country.*

Children in elementary school need to develop skills for future learning. After all, even the worst student will spend a lifetime learning new things, and many students will go on to occupations that require considerable learning ability. Examples of appropriate skills are:

1. Picture reading/photo interpretation.
2. Map reading and atlas use.
3. Questioning and hypothesizing.
4. Data gathering and analysis.
5. Inferential and critical/evaluative thinking.

Skill learning is an important task: it is essential for the teacher to model good skill learning behaviors and provide competent skill instruction. Remember that skills are learned slowly and must be practiced over time. Like content, it is best to thoroughly teach and practice a smaller number of skills than to speed through several.

■ *Develop positive attitudes toward learning about the country.* One of the most important things an elementary teacher can develop in students is a sense of wonder about the world. Many students know there is an incredibly interesting and diverse world "out there" and all students will appreciate an opportunity to learn about it in a pleasant, active manner. The teacher's leadership is critical to making the unit an experience that will improve students' attitudes toward future study. The greatest mistake an elementary teacher can make in implementing a new country unit is failing to provide the active and interesting instruction needed for her students to develop positive attitudes. Sample attitudinal goals include:

1. Showing an interest in learning about the country.
2. Developing a positive attitude toward the culture(s) of the country.
3. Sharing learning experiences and products with others.

Teachers who emphasize concrete, hands-on learning experiences, and involve the aesthetic as well as the cognitive through the use of song, poetry, movement, and true-to-life simulations will be most successful in developing positive attitudes toward unfamiliar nations.

The content and instructional goals of a unit on another country should also be influenced by what young children typically want to know when given the opportunity to learn about a "new" place. Following is a partial list of questions which children typically ask.

*Geography*

*Where is _____ ?*

a. What is the location of the country?
b. Which direction is it from the United States?
c. How long would it take to get to the country by airplane?

*What is it like there?*

a. What is the climate like?
b. Do they have hot summers and snowy winters?
c. How does this climate compare with ours?
d. What are the other geographic characteristics such as mountains, rivers, plains?
e. What are the major cities, and what are they like (industry, population characteristics, special features)?
f. How do these things affect daily lives of the people?

*Education*

a. At what age does a child begin school?
b. Do working parents use day care for preschool children?
c. Is their school day like ours?
d. Do the children study English or some other foreign language?
e. Are there parochial schools and vocational schools?
f. How does a person become a teacher?
g. Are the teachers mostly men or women?
h. Are teachers well paid and well respected?
i. Do most children stay in school and graduate from high school?

*Religion*

a. What is the religion of the majority of the people?
b. Are there minority faiths, and if so, how are these people treated?
c. Are there special religious holidays and customs?

*Family*

a. What is a typical family like?
b. What is the role of the mother and father?
c. Do women work outside the home?
d. Do grandparents live with the family?
e. Do people get divorced?
f. Are there poor families and rich families?

*Food*

a. What are the favorite foods and most common meals eaten at home?
b. Do people eat out very often?
c. Do people eat "fast foods" like we do here?
d. Is there a MacDonald's?; a Burger King?; a Wendy's?; etc.?
e. Do they have soft drinks/sodas like Coke and Pepsi?
f. How much would a soft drink cost?

*Sports*

a. What is the most popular sport?
b. How many teams are there?
c. Do they play baseball or footfall?
d. Do people watch their favorite sport on television?
e. Are there organized sports for children, like Little League baseball?

*Recreation*

a. What do people do with their leisure time?
b. Do they go on picnics?
c. Are there amusement parks like Disney World?
d. Where do people travel on vacation?

*Television*

a. Are there a lot of stations? Do they have cable?
b. Do they have children's programs? Do they show music videos, quiz shows, nature programs, and sports events?
c. Do they show a lot of commercials?
d. Can most people afford a television?

*Games and Toys*

a. Do they have toy stores like we do?
b. What are the most popular games and toys?
c. What songs and nursery rhymes do children learn?

*Holidays*

a. Do they celebrate Christmas?
b. Is there a holiday like Thanksgiving or the Fourth of July?
c. What other holidays are there?
d. What do people do on these holidays?

*Newspapers*

a. Are there many newspapers?
b. Can the papers print whatever they want?
c. Are there advertisements and funnies?

*Clothes*

a. What do children wear to school? Do they wear uniforms?
b. Do people buy or make their clothes?

c. Do they have lots of clothing stores?

d. How are garments and shoes sized?

e. How much would a new dress or pair of pants cost?

*Money*

a. What type of money is used and what is it called?

b. Do people have credit cards?

c. Are there banks like ours?

e. How much money would a teacher make?

f. How much money would a doctor make?

*Language*

a. What does the language sound like?

b. Are there different regional dialects like we have?

c. What are the phrases for common greetings?

d. What are some unusual sayings or common proverbs?

e. What are some common names for boys and girls?

*Non-Verbal Communication*

a. What is the proper way to greet a new acquaintance, a close friend, or a relative?

b. How much physical distance and contact is there?

c. Is there anything I, as an American, might inadvertently do to offend them?

*Government*

a. What is the government like?

b. Do they have a President?

c. Can all people vote?

d. Who makes decisions about laws?

e. At what age do you get to vote?

*Law and Justice*

a. Do they have police and courts like ours?

b. Can a person sue someone?

c. What are their jails like?

d. Are there prisons and juvenile detention centers?

*National Defense*

a. Do they have an army, air force, or navy?

b. How old do you have to be to become a soldier?

c. Do they have nuclear weapons?

d. Have they ever had a war?

*Societal Problems*

a. Do they have problems with housing for the poor?

b. Are most people able to read and write?

c. Do they have drug dealers and junkies?

By following the three guidelines and remaining aware of the questions young students typically ask, the task of building background information will be more focused.

## BUILDING BACKGROUND INFORMATION

A task central to developing a unit on another country is augmenting your existing background knowledge. This may be done quickly by reviewing the many publications designed to provide adults with concise and up-to-date information and by browsing available curriculum materials. Realize at the onset, however, that you cannot become an overnight expert and accept the fact that your knowledge will increase over time as your unit is taught each year.

Visit the library and check out a recent edition of the *Europa Yearbook* (Europa Publications, 1990) or *Background*

*Notes* (dates vary) from the U.S. Department of State. These sources provide concise, up-to-date, four-to-twenty-page descriptions of the geography, culture, religion, economy, government, and history of countries around the globe and are tailored to the needs of the busy government official or traveler. Major libraries will have both of these resources, and most medium-sized libraries will have one or the other. In addition to these "quick overview" resources, check out recent books on the country and skim them to get an impression of what kind of information they contain. This combination of resources provides a comprehensive mental picture of another country without the burden of days of background reading.

Read a recent encyclopedia article on the country and note important facts and concepts that you can compare to the United States. For speed, you might want to photocopy this article and use a highlighting pen or marginal notes rather than filling out note cards. When available, remember to consult recent yearbooks for the encyclopedia to get a more current perspective on the country.

Call a travel agency and see if they have a collection of brochures, posters, or tourist guides that could be donated to the class. Ask if they know of any local person who has recently visited the country you are planning to study. If the agency will not give out the names of potential contacts, ask if they would make the initial call for you.

Send home a note to parents indicating the need for resource persons who have been to the country. Ask for names and phone numbers of contacts in the community.

Contact your local or state university's office of international students and ask them for the names of resource persons. If they will not provide names, ask them to post a notice concerning your need. Call the international affairs department and see if they have a specialist on your country. Make arrangements for a classroom visit tailored to your needs.

## LOCATING CURRICULUM MATERIALS

Spend time in the children's section of the library investigating what instructional resources are available. Guides such as *The Elementary School Library Collection: A Guide to Books and Other Media* (Winker, 1988); the *Children's Catalog* (Isaacson, Hillegas & Yaakof, 1986), *A to Zoo: Subject Access to Children's Picture Books*, (Lima, 1986); and *The Video Sourcebook* (Weiner, 1990) will provide you with a comprehensive listing of tradebooks and audio-visual materials for children.

Search ERIC, a comprehensive database of journal articles, curriculum materials, and research, using the country name as the search term in the "identifier field." This type of search will locate any materials that focus on the country of interest. Combining this search with a "publication type" of 052 and 051 (the ERIC codes that identify classroom materials) will give you a listing of teacher-created public domain units or lesson plans that are available through the ERIC system as well as identifying published journal articles on the country of interest.

Teachers seeking information from a specific nation might write to the embassy in Washington, D.C. or to its Permanent Mission to the United Nations in New York. While precise addresses will elicit a more prompt reply, teachers can use these general addresses: The Permanent Mission of ____ to the United Nations, United Nations Plaza, New York, NY 10017, and The Embassy of ____ to the United States of America, United States Department of State, 2201 C Street, N.W., Washington, D.C. 20520. Specific addresses for each country's embassy can be found in the Washington Information Directory (see teacher's resource list). When writing, describe your needs and make specific requests for photographs, maps, statistical information, and other material you may need. Allow three to four weeks for a response.

Two additional sources of information and children's materials are the United States Committee for UNICEF and the Peace Corps. The U.S. Committee for UNICEF Information Center on Children's Cultures provides background information kits for teachers that include a bibliography of audio-visual and children's print materials as well as posters, suggested activities, and discussion questions. The Peace Corps's World Wise School Program encourages teachers to use Peace Corps volunteers as a "window for U.S. students to view and experience new countries and cultures." This program facilitates the exchange of letters, artwork, artifacts, and other educational materials. The program also provides elementary and junior high level study guides that contain background information and instructional materials for students.

If you have the money and time, consider taking a vacation study tour to the country. Many national organizations such as Phi Delta Kappa and the Association for Supervision and Curriculum Development offer packaged tours especially for educators. While on tour, collect artifacts and shoot hundreds of interesting photos. (Interesting photos are often not of landscapes or buildings, but those that show people doing things that illustrate the unique nature of the culture. If you must show a landscape or building, be ready to tell an interesting story about it.)

## HIGH INTEREST TEACHING TIPS

The proof of an exciting unit on another country lies in the skillful development of activities that capture students' interest and command their attention. Excellent background preparation and judicious selection of content and goals can only shine through if conveyed by engaging activities. Following is a set of activity ideas for beginning, sustaining, and ending a unit on another country.

## ACTIVITIES TO BEGIN THE UNIT

- Decorate the room after the students leave for the day and greet them in "traditional costume" the next morning. Let the students ask questions to find out as much as possible about the country. Help the students realize that your costume is symbolic, that a variety of dress can be observed depending upon occupation, social status, or customs.

- Create a mystery box filled with trinkets and cultural artifacts that children remove one at a time. Talk about each object and describe what it symbolizes about the culture or country.

- Play popular and traditional music from the country. If possible, translate any words, sing along, and dance.

- Show a travelogue film about the country with the sound turned off. Ask the students to watch silently. Discuss what they have learned just by looking, and list questions they have on chart paper. Show the movie again with the sound on. Debrief the experience by reviewing the list of questions to determine what the students would like to focus on in their study.

- Make up an "amazing facts" pre-test on the country. Let the students discuss their answers and list questions that they would like to have answered. Have the students save their quizzes and questions for comparison with post-tests. Create an attractive display of their learning at the end of the unit.

## ACTIVITIES TO SUSTAIN THE UNIT

- Invite community resource persons identified during your background work.

- Slowly convert your classroom into an environment typical of the country you are studying. Create a sandy beach if the country is in the tropics. Put white paper over all the windows to simulate outdoor snow if the country is in the far north.

- Label objects in the room with the national language and use these items in conversation. Most bookstores sell inexpensive English to foreign language dictionaries. The translations can be used to label objects in the room.

- Spend 10 to 15 minutes each day speaking only the language of the country you are studying. Audio-lingual instructional materials are available for many languages. Consult your local high school language instructors for the most frequently taught languages, or a local college or university for less frequently taught languages. If materials are not available, spend an hour learning common greetings and phrases with a fluent speaker. Take notes, or better yet, record your work.

- Exchange letters or pictures with students of the same grade level. Write a part of each letter in the language of your pen pals.

- Learn folk stories from the country and compare them with our own.

- Locate stories about the country in recent news and post them in categories on a bulletin board. Note the type of news that comes from the country, the use of biased language, and negative or positive images.

- Cook national foods from the country and invite parents and teachers in for a taste test.

- Form small groups and write original tourist guides for the country. Display and share the guides, noting strengths and differences from those that are commercially available. Which is more truthful and informative?

## ACTIVITIES TO CONCLUDE THE UNIT

▉ Hold a festival that showcases your country. Dress in traditional costume, play national music, serve typical foods, deliver short presentations such as a skit, a three minute cultural lecture, a slide show, and a museum tour of collected cultural artifacts. Invite the news media for community-wide coverage.

▉ Send a copy of the children's best work to the embassy that provided materials. Include a thank you letter.

▉ Have the students write thank you cards with simple sentences expressing what was learned during the unit to each of your resource persons.

▉ Hold a "college bowl" type quiz to review all that has been learned.

▉ Give awards for students who made outstanding contributions, the most progress, or spoke the language best.

▉ Compare pre-test and post-test results. Review questions that students generated at the start of the unit.

▉ Make a huge poster showing what your students think "the world should know" about your country. Stress main ideas, concepts, and attitudes.

## CONCLUSION

Every child should experience learning about several countries during their elementary school years. Units on other countries should attempt to provide sufficient depth and accuracy of treatment to avoid blatant stereotyping or dull and superficial learning. Most of all, such units should positively influence the students' attitudes toward learning about other cultures and areas of the world.

Teachers who develop units on other countries need not depart from the established curriculum. Units should emphasize many of the same key social studies concepts and skills regardless of the country or area being studied. Indeed, the content of units on other countries should be directly related back to the students' own lives and to other cultures they have encountered.

Perhaps the best approach to teaching a newly launched unit on another country is for the teacher to act as a resource provider and as a leading co-learner. Taking these roles will help make it clear at the outset that you are not an expert on the country and that you are just as interested as they in gaining more information on this fascinating place. Show your enthusiasm for learning by freely admitting when you do not know an answer and by modeling good answer-seeking behavior when one of these "thoughtful" questions come up.

By providing high quality instruction about other nations, elementary classroom teachers lead children toward the understandings, attitudes, and skills needed to sustain our nation as a leader in our world community.

## TEACHER RESOURCES

Bureau of Public Affairs, United States Department of State. (dates vary). *Background Notes*. Washington, DC: Government Publications Office. This resource provides concise background information on virtually all of the countries around the world. It is continually being updated to reflect changes in political, socio-economic, military, and other aspects of the countries. Each profile contains basic geographic information, maps, tables of socioeconomic information. and historical/cultural background.

Congressional Quarterly, Inc. (1988). *Washington Information Directory 1988-1989*. Washington, DC: Congressional Quarterly Press. This guidebook contains information on all of the embassies of other nations in Washington, D.C. It includes a complete mailing address, phone numbers, and names of key personnel. Teachers should write to the "education and cultural affairs officer" or the "public information officer" to request information.

Educational Resources Information Center (ERIC). Compiles a database of published and unpublished research and curriculum materials. The ERIC database is available from on-line computer service vendors and in CO-ROM formats. ERIC microfiche document collections are available in libraries throughout the nation and world. For more information dial 1-800-USE ERIC.

Europa Publications. (1988). *Europa Yearbook*. Europa, London, UK. Similar to the U.S. Department of State publication, *Background Notes* but produced by a reputable independent publisher.

Isaacson, R.H.; Hillegas, R.E.; end Yaakov, J. (Eds.). (1986). *Children's Catalog* 15th Edition. New York: H. W. Wilson. This is a comprehensive guide to print materials for children. It has a combined author, title, and subject index which may make searching by subject alone more difficult.

Lima, C.W. (1986). *A to Zoo: Subject Access to Children's Picture Books*. Second Edition. New York: R.R. Bowker Company. As the title implies, this resource provides subject access to children's picture books. It contains a "foreign lands" section.

Paxton, J. (Ed.). (1988). *The Statesman's Year Book, 1988-1989*. New York: St. Martin's Press. This reference book, published since 1860, provides basic information about all of the world's countries which any teacher would find useful in planning a unit.

Weiner, D. (1990). *The Video Source Book*. 11th Edition. Detroit, MI: Gale Research, Inc. This comprehensive listing of commercially available videotapes. This resource includes information on documentaries that may be useful in teaching about specific aspects of other nations.

Winkel, L. (Ed.). (1988). *The Elementary School Library Collection: A Guide to Books and Other Media 16th Edition*. Williamsport, PA: Bodart Company. This reference tool is invaluable for locating children's literature and teaching materials on specific countries and topics. For example. if a teacher desired a filmstrip on Mexico, she would enter the country listing section to determine if one existed that was appropriate for her grade level and topic focus. The 16th edition contains citations for 8,374 books, 123 periodicals, and 2,347 audiovisual resources such as filmstrips, recordings, kits, and videocassettes. Each entry contains an estimate of interest and reading level, cost, ordering information, and publication date. Separate author. title, and subject indexes are provided.

World Almanac. (1990). *World Almanac and Book of Facts*. New York: Pharos Books, Scripps-Howard. Published since 1868, this annual reference contains current information on almost every nation on earth. The entries on each nation are brief and to the point, with current embassy addresses in Washington, D.C. and telephone numbers.

## CHILDREN'S RESOURCES [1991 NOTE]

Peace Corps' World Wise Schools Program. For information, call 1-800-424-8580 or write World Wise Schools, 1990 K Street, N.W., Washington, D.C. 20526.

United States Committee for UNICEF Information Center on Children's Cultures. For information call (212) 686-5522 or write to the Information Center on Children's Cultures, U.S. Committee for UNICEF, 331 East 38th Street, New York, NY 10016.

Children's Press publishes an *Enchantment of the World* series that contains 63 individual titles. The series seeks to communicate the unique charm and culture of other parts of the world. Included are geography, history, economics, key attractions, all illustrated with full-color photographs. Each book is approximately 127 pages 8" x 9-1/4" with reference section and index. Intended grade level is five through nine. They also publish the New True Books series of 217 books intended for children in grades K-4. Each 48-page book is designed to help children discover for themselves fascinating facts about the world.

The Steck-Vaughn company publishes the *My World* series that includes several titles for second- and third-grade readers. Also available for children in grades two through five is the *Where We Live* series. Presented as a narrative told by children, each 32-page book describes the culture and geography of a country. Children in grades six and up may benefit from the *World in View* series that presents detailed information.

The Learner Publications Company produces the *Visual Geography* series that currently includes 63 titles for students in grades five and up. Each book is approximately 64 pages 7" x 10". For children in grades two through five, Learner publishes the 34-volume *Families the World Over* series. Learner also publishes the 29-volume *In America* series which details the experiences of the many immigrants who have come to the United States.

Franklin Watts publishes three series about other nations. At grade levels kindergarten through four, this publisher offers a set of books called the *Take a Trip* series. Each book is 32-pages in length. The *We Live in . . .* series consists of 30 titles. Each of these books is 64 pages in length. The third series offered by this publisher is termed the *Countries of the World* series. There are twelve titles in this series for grades five through eight. A fourth series available from this publisher is the *Passport* series. Each of these 48-page books provides a comprehensive introduction to a country and its people.

Silver Burdett Press publishes the *People and Places* series of 24 48-page books for children in grades four through six.

Harper-Collins is the publisher of the *Portraits of the Nations* series for students in grades five and up.

Troll Associates has recently joined the list of publishers of books about other nations for young children with its offering of four 32-page softbound books for children in grades three through five.

John Douglas Hoge is an Assistant Professor of Social Science Education at the University of Georgia, Athens. Dr. Hoge teaches graduate and undergraduate courses designed to improve elementary and early childhood social science education, and maintains a research interest in history, values, and citizenship education. Rodney F. Allen is a Professor of Social Science Education at Florida State University, Tallahassee. As an experienced curriculum designer, Dr. Allen works with teachers and graduate students on ways to improve the teaching of social studies, K-12. [1991 note]

**Siegfried Ramler**

We must prepare our children to deal with the ever-shifting economic and political realities of our shrinking planet.

The changes that took place in Eastern Europe and the Soviet Union late in 1989, the pending economic union of Europe, the unification of East and West Germany, the impact of Japan's economy on the world—these events will profoundly influence the 1990s and will shape the world of the 21st century. Our challenge is to prepare our students for a world where familial geopolitical boundaries and economic assumptions are being replaced by new realities.

These circumstances call for effective global education at all levels and in all disciplines. Global education is not a new concept; global awareness has long been a desirable outcome of student learning in a variety of subjects However, as the old order crumbles the need to provide school experiences with an international and global dimension acquires great urgency.

## REDEFINING OUR POSITION

It should come as no surprise that the United States has not been effective in international education. To begin with, our large population lives in relative isolation on a huge resource rich continent. For this reason, but even more so because of our political and economic dominance during the 20th century, the US has developed a strongly nationalistic character and a correspondingly limited curriculum. For example, many Americans believe that studies of foreign cultures and languages are nonessential— nice to have if you can afford them, but far down the list of priorities. Consequently, only a few thousand students in the U.S. study Russian, while in the Soviet Union, millions study English. The American situation also stands in stark contrast to the small European nations such as the Netherlands, Belgium, and the Scandinavian countries, where many citizens are multilingual. In today's world a provincial approach to curriculum is no longer acceptable.

Now, at the edge of the 21st century, all the countries of the world are interconnected in virtually every aspect of life. World markets have been developed for consumer goods, labor, technology, and energy. The global economy irrevocably ties the economic health of the U.S. to events abroad. Thus, the U.S. must continually redefine its position within the context of global development.

Today the flow of ideas, information, and services is linked globally; and these linkages reach every household and every person. The flow includes the arts, the sciences, sports, medicine, tourism, and entertainment, as well as such unfortunate phenomena as drug traffic, disease, and environmental damage.

In every aspect of life, boundaries between domestic and foreign affairs are disappearing. Planetwide ecological issues include ocean pollution, acid rain, deforestation, toxic waste disposal, and global warming. Solving these problems will require international collaboration and international responsibility.

At the same time that interconnectedness is increasing, we are witnessing remarkable and widespread population migrations, particularly from unstable to stable areas and from Third World to more affluent regions. These migrations are strongly felt in the United States, especially along our coasts, and our population is becoming more multiethnic than ever before. The reality of a classroom of students from various parts of the world, more forcefully than any abstract idea, calls for an international approach to teaching and curriculum.

Finally, in relation to other nations the position of the U.S. has changed from that of dominance to the role of partner, so that our well-being now depends on collaboration and understanding. There is no doubt that gaps in cultural understanding cause some of the current strains in U.S.-Japan relations, for example, and that sensitivity to other cultures is an essential ingredient for success in a global economy.

Economic, scientific, and technological factors now have as great a bearing on international relations as military or strategic considerations, as evidenced by the influence of nations, such as Japan, whose impact is based on economic and scientific strength rather than military power. Individuals now have a greater opportunity for international involvement on a nongovernmental level than ever before, through work with multinational corporations and employment abroad.

All these factors are closely tied to the way we need to prepare our students for the 21st century. But what is global education?

## SEEING THROUGH OTHERS' EYES

According to Hanvey, global education means:
> learning about those issues that cut across national boundaries and about the interconnectedness of

Reprinted with permission from the Association for Supervision and Curriculum Development, from *Educational Leadership*, April 1991, Volume 48, Number 7. Copyright 1991 by the Association for Supervision and Curriculum Development.

systems, ecological, cultural, economic, political, and technological. Global education involves perspective taking, seeing things through the eyes, minds, and hearts of others; and it means the realization that while individuals and groups may view life differently, they also have common needs and wants.[1]

What does it take to bring this about in our schools We must infuse global perspective into all curriculum areas at all levels, including literature, the arts, the sciences, and the extracurricular experiences of students. It's not a matter of simply adding foreign language courses or a unit on international relations, and it doesn't concern only social studies courses. In the past, literature classes in the U.S. and Europe have relied almost exclusively on European literature without paying sufficient attention to the contributions of Africa, Asia, and South America. If our children are to understand other cultures, literature is an ideal medium reflecting universal values and problems. Similarly, we tend to limit ourselves to Western traditions in art and music. Using resources now available in many communities, we can bring non-Western arts into the classroom and enrich our curriculum. Through such experiences, we widen our students' horizons and enable them to extend their perspectives.

Perhaps the most important element required to succeed in global education is what Tye calls the "deep structure" of a school.[2] A school's culture may be closed and ethnocentric or open, cosmopolitan, and international. The faculty and administration, as well as the community surrounding the school can dramatically influence the social environment and climate of the school. To build a cosmopolitan culture within a school, they must provide repeated experiences, beginning in the early grades, that bring the world into the classroom. Together. as a school community, they must take the initiative in inviting artists, lecturers, and discussion leaders to bring international viewpoints to the students. And they must provide textbooks and resource materials that reflect a global perspective.

## BUILDING STRONGER CITIZENS

To build citizens for the 21st century, we must continuously strive to offer instruction that helps students learn to see "through the eyes, minds, and hearts of others." Recently, for example, the National Commission on Social Studies in the Schools recommended that U.S. history, which is usually taught as a separate subject, be combined with world history in a multi-year sequence. The recommendation recognizes that integrating national and world history will allow students to place our national past within its larger international context. The recommendation continues, "The more we understand about the international influences on our past, the more prepared we will be to play a strong role in the global affairs of our future."[3]

To achieve its best effects, global education must go beyond the transmission of information, beyond historical analysis, to what we might call "anticipatory learning." The rapid pace of change and the emergence of new political and economic structures require that we learn to project into the future, taking into account new assumptions and situations. We must move beyond factual learning, even beyond inquiry learning, to problem finding and problem anticipation. Our students must learn to look at issues from different perspectives and then to explore options. Above all, we must lead them to understand and respect cultures other than their own so that they can live and work with people from all around the shrinking globe.

Inviting students from abroad to our schools contributes importantly to the learning environment and opens opportunities for sharing and understanding in formal and informal settings. And it is equally important to encourage our students to participate in study programs abroad. Such opportunities open new perspectives for students and influence the direction of their advanced studies and, eventually, their choice of careers.[4] In a recent survey of several hundred students who participated in such programs, a large percentage specialized in international studies and then chose careers connected with their international interests.[5] Such opportunities will multiply in this decade, and we can prepare now to take advantage of them.

Global education has a strong ethical dimension: a value system that calls us to accept responsibility for the well-being of our planet. This value system requires loyalty that, while in the interests of one's particular nation, is not exclusive to that nation: a loyalty that is a commitment beyond national boundaries. The absence of this extended commitment is at the root of international conflict and tragedy. The record of the 20th century indicates clearly that nationalism without international responsibility leads to disaster. We need only think of Nazi Germany's aggression leading to World War II and of the dictatorial policies of countries in the Middle East and Latin America.

Some Americans fear that global awareness implies abdication of national values, that it accepts ideologies, political beliefs, and practices from other nations without subordinating them to American values. On the contrary, there need never be a contradiction between global understanding and national values and interests. Students must develop an international perspective and international skills if they are to participate as successful and productive citizens on behalf of their separate nations in the global environment.

## GENERAL PRINCIPLES FOR GLOBAL EDUCATION

There is no recipe for a global curriculum to fit any given school or any given region. However, we can agree on general principles for such a curriculum. A committee of the ASCD International/Global Education Commission, under the leadership of Jim Becker of Indiana University, has developed the following working draft of principles.[6]

■ All teachers, as well as all students, should have opportunities to learn about and work with individuals whose ethnic and cultural backgrounds are different from their own.

- International global studies should be viewed as cross-disciplinary, involving the arts, humanities, sciences, and mathematics, as well as foreign languages and social studies. And the global approach should start at the earliest levels of childhood.
- The impact on individuals and on society of the increase in transnational interactions should be included in the curriculum, reflecting interdependence with other nations and the role of the United States in a global economy.
- The changing role of nations in the world system should be explained throughout instructional materials, and the increasing number and importance of international organizations should be highlighted wherever appropriate.
- The changing and evolving role of the United States in world affairs should be included in the study of international trends and developments.

The implementation of these principles presents a challenge to each school and each teacher. One of the aims of ASCD's International/Global Education Commission is to encourage the development of appropriate curriculums and to disseminate successful models and practices. An important step toward this aim was the commissioning under ASCD's aegis of a model curriculum for global education at elementary levels that was piloted and disseminated in 1992.

## MEETING THE CHALLENGE

The children in our schools today will play a part in shaping the world in the 21st century. Our responsibility as teachers and developers of curriculum is to help them become knowledgeable about their planet and about the issues we face for survival and for international harmony. If we succeed in infusing a global perspective into their school experiences, if we can give them and appreciation for cultural diversity, if we can help them understand principles of conflict resolution and of alternative futures in an interconnected world, we will have fulfilled the most important challenge in education of the 21st century.

## NOTES

1. R. Hanvey, (1976), *An Attainable Global Perspective*, (Denver: Center for Teaching International Relations).
2. B. Tye, (1987), "The Deep Structure of Schooling," *Phi Delta Kappan* 69, 4:281-284.
3. National Commission on Social Studies in the Schools, (1989), *Charting a Course: Social Studies for the 21st Century*, (Washington, DC: NCSS).
4. For a comprehensive list of educational travel and exchange programs, consult the "Advisory List of International Travel and Exchange Programs" (1990), published by the Council on Standards for International Educational Travel, 1906 Association Dr., Reston, VA 22091.
5. S. Ramler, (1988), *Another Window* (Honolulu: The Foundation for Study in Hawaii and Abroad).
6. Presented at the meeting of the ASCD Global/International Education Commission, October 4-6, 1990, Alexandria, Virginia, by Jim Becker, University of Indiana; Mary Soley, Foreign Policy Association, Washington, DC; and Jonathan Swift, School of Global Education, Livonia, Michigan.

Siegfried Ramler is the Director of Instructional Services and Coordinator of Curriculum at the Wo International Center, Punahou School, Honolulu, Hawaii. He also serves as Chair of ASCD's Commission for Global International Education. [1991 note]

## Ann V. Angell
## Patricia G. Avery

*You love America—everyone does; or if they don't let them just leave. But if we're going to fight, we have to be sure we can win.... We should say [to the Russians]: "Look, you tell us what you are after, and we'll tell you how we see things, and then we'll find out if there's some way to avoid a war that'll kill us all!" (Coles 1986, p. 256)*

These words of advice come from Gerry, one of the many children interviewed by child psychiatrist Robert Coles (1986) for his book *The Political Life of Children*. An eleven-year-old Bostonian, Gerry displays a strong sense of national loyalty tempered by an awareness of the potential consequences of international conflict. Although his language is simple and straightforward, he sets forth one of the basic principles of conflict resolution: Examine the goals and perspectives of all parties to see if there is room for negotiation.

A growing number of researchers such as Coles are finding that young children know more about social and political issues than was previously thought (Kurth-Schai 1988; Ross 1984; Stevens 1982). Traditional assessment techniques, such as adult-type questionnaires, often portray elementary age students as ignorant and naïve about global issues. Researchers have found that discussions based on students' drawings, open-ended items on written questionnaires, and focus groups give students more opportunities to express their thoughts and concerns in their own language. It seems that when we suspend our preconceptions of what young people should know and how they should demonstrate this knowledge, we find that children can deal with complex issues in surprisingly sophisticated ways. The key to finding out how young people think and learn about socio-political issues, according to Katz (1988), is to provide the "right context" in which they can share their knowledge and concerns about issues.

In this article, we offer a rationale for examining global issues in the elementary classroom and describe ways that teachers can create the "right context" for inquiring about those issues with students. We suggest guidelines for selecting materials that will facilitate inquiry and help students reorganize their thinking about global issues.

## A RATIONALE FOR GLOBAL ISSUES IN THE ELEMENTARY CLASSROOM

Kniep (1989) identifies four major categories of global issues: peace and security, human rights, environmental problems, and national/international development. Why should such issues be an integral part of the elementary school curriculum? We argue that international conflict, human rights issues, environmental degradation, and problems related to international development are already part of young people's lives and that teachers, by making these issues a part of the formal curriculum, can validate and build upon young people's experiences. Helping students make connections between immediate experiences in their own communities and global realities enhances the relevance of civic participation at the local level. Finally, we feel that inquiry into global issues in the elementary grades, when students are most curious about the world around them, lays the foundation for more sophisticated analyses of the issues as students mature.

Most elementary teachers are keenly aware that global issues are already a part of young students' daily experience, both in and outside of school. The equitable distribution of limited resources, consumption and waste management, discrimination, and conflict are regular issues in elementary classrooms, along with problems more often reported in secondary schools such as threats of violence, drugs, and early sexual experience. As Massialas (1989) points out, the school can no longer be regarded as a sanctuary where students are protected from the social ills of the larger society. Educators recognize that the problems students experience in and out of school reflect larger global problems of aggression, overpopulation, resource depletion, pollution, poverty and human rights inequities—issues that students will confront at increasing levels of seriousness and complexity in the future. Exploring these issues within the classroom is a means of recognizing and validating the social, cultural, and political experiences students bring with them to school.

The relationships between local problems and global issues are not often apparent to young people, however. In two recent studies, students tended to associate broad social problems such as pollution and poverty with the national and global spheres but rarely with their local communities (Gamradt and Avery 1990; Katz 1988). When social issues are identified solely with arenas beyond their immediate experience, students lack incentives to become actively involved in examining problems in their schools, neighborhoods, and cities. Making connections between local and global problems may help students recognize ways in which citizens in local communities can play an integral part in effecting positive change across interdependent spheres.

The ability to inquire into global issues and to relate them to local concerns develops gradually, building on prior knowledge and experiences. The elementary school years, therefore, constitute an important time to lay the foundation for the development of these explorations and understandings (Schunke 1984; Stevens 1982). In addition, elementary students exhibit interest in people different from themselves and a growing capacity to appreciate other points of view—orientations that may diminish as they approach adolescence if these are not exercised and encouraged (Torney-Purta 1985)(Advocates for global education emphasize the need to expose young students to multiple perspectives, to give them opportunities to practice taking alternative viewpoints, and to help them reason from those different points of view)(Harvey 1976; Lamy 1990). Curricula organized around global issues offer powerful opportunities for realizing these goals.

## INQUIRING ABOUT GLOBAL ISSUES WITH ELEMENTARY STUDENTS

When selecting approaches and materials for the study of global issues at the elementary level, two considerations seem particularly relevant, in addition to more general guidelines for choosing appropriate strategies and content for young people (for example, an emphasis on concrete, active, and cooperative learning experiences). First, issues should be presented as genuinely problematic. Materials designed for global education at the elementary level are often aimed at building an awareness of global realities rather than engaging students in examining the related causes and consequences of those realities. Although most young children cannot understand all of the variables related to environmental politics, they can begin to recognize that conflicting opinions exist about solutions to environmental problems.

Second, students should be given opportunities for decision making and social action. As young people explore the ways in which global issues affect their lives, they need to feel they can contribute to positive, meaningful change. Within their immediate environment, concern for global hostilities can become an opportunity to examine alternative means of conflict resolution among peers; discussing the depletion of the earth's natural resources can become an opportunity to make class decisions about the use of classroom resources, trash disposal, lunchtime habits, or playground maintenance. Helping students make connections between global issues and classroom contexts reinforces the significance of these personal decisions and actions.

The teacher will often need to go beyond traditional instructional resources for specific social action projects. For example, the "Goat Project" at the International Service Association for Health (INSA) provides materials about development problems in Haiti and invites classes

to adopt a goat that becomes part of an agricultural development program in Haiti. Upper elementary students can receive case histories of political prisoners throughout the world and write letters on their behalf through Amnesty International's Children's Edition of the Urgent Action Network. A recent publication entitled *50 Simple Things Kids Can Do to Save the Earth* (Earthworks Group 1990) offers a wide range of environmental awareness and action projects for young people at all grade levels. Each of these resources serves to extend students' sense of personal efficacy beyond the classroom.

Three instructional strategies or methods seem particularly appropriate for exploring the complexities of global issues and laying the foundation for decision making and social action: small group discussions, roleplay and simulations, and thematic resource folders. In the following sections, we present descriptions of how these strategies promote issues-centered teaching, as well as recommended resource materials that support the three approaches.

## SMALL GROUP DISCUSSIONS —

Two fascinating studies of children's perceptions of social and political issues suggest that opportunities for young people to share their thoughts and concerns with one another constitute a powerful means of exploring global issues (Kurth-Schai 1988; Stevens 1982). Both researchers found that differing peer perspectives are the sources of new information most accessible to students and most likely to prompt them to reorganize their thinking. Stevens suggests that the teacher's role in small group discussions is "not so much a 'drawing-out' of what children know, as an end in itself, as one aimed at helping them to develop skills in recognizing what is relevant to an issue or what questions need to be asked, which is to say, at developing a philosophical capacity" (p. 170).

Children's literature provides an excellent vehicle for initiating small group or whole class discussions. Young students identify with characters in a story and respond with interest and emotion to the experiences and problems they encounter through story events (Levstik 1983). Through their involvement with literature, students can develop an understanding of problems people face in times and places distant from their own reality while, at the same time, they can recognize that they have much in common with those distant others.

Lists of children's literature about global issues have been compiled around a variety of topics. A curriculum offering from UNICEF, *Children's Literature: Springboard to Understanding the Developing World* (Diakiw, Baker, Ledger, Leppington, and Pearce 1989), includes picture storybooks about Africa, global interdependence, Latin American city life, and India; junior/intermediate novels relevant to the themes are also suggested. The National Council for the Social Studies Bulletin *International Human Rights, Society and the School* (Benson and Torney-Purta 1982), suggests criteria for selecting books on human rights and provides an extensive annotated bibliography of children's literature about rights issues, including thirty titles judged appropriate for younger children. Riecken and Miller (1990) offer an annotated list of stories that are suitable for exploring problem solving and decision making with elementary students.

Current events are also recommended as a springboard for small group discussions. Even kindergartners are aware of events that have high visibility in the media, such as the meltdown at Chernobyl or the Persian Gulf conflict (Moore, Lare, and Wagner 1985). Earle (1982) suggests that small group discussions about issues that permeate the public conscience allow the teacher to discover young students' misconceptions and to address their fears. If discussion is based on students' ideas and thoughts, teachers are unlikely to introduce questions that are developmentally inappropriate. Students should be invited to participate voluntarily in a small group discussion; alternative activities should be available for those students who are uninterested or who are not ready to deal with potentially sensitive and difficult issues.

If a more structured discussion format seems appropriate, the decision-making tree (La Raus and Remy 1978) encourages students to identify problems, consider alternative solutions, hypothesize about the short and long-term consequences of alternatives and choose actions based on their Clues. The "tree" helps students to visualize the decision-making process. The "futures wheel" (Pike and Selby 1553) is another model that invites students to consider the consequences of an event. The event or problem is written in the middle of a chalkboard; single lines are drawn to immediate consequences, double lines to second-order consequences, and so on. Strategies such as the decision tree and the futures wheel help students appreciate the problematic nature of global issues and understand that human choices can create alternative futures.

## ROLEPLAY AND SIMULATIONS

Enactments such as roleplay and simulations can help elementary students recognize the complex nature of global issues by inviting them to temporarily adopt alternative realities in which they experience problems from different perspectives and practice making decisions in a nonthreatening context. Because younger children can become deeply involved in roles they assume, their enactments might best be organized around immediate issues of fairness, conflict resolution, and interpersonal relations; intermediate elementary students may enact situations from literature or case studies that more directly portray broader issues. Shaftel and Shaftel (1982) offer particularly useful guidelines for organizing meaningful role play activities in the elementary classroom. Davison (1984) suggests that "freezing the action intermittently to probe students' interpretations, switching roles midway through the action, and repeating scenarios from another point of view during roleplay or simulation activities are strategies that challenge students' thinking about the actions and words being used."

Simulations can be effective vehicles for a broadened understanding of issues if they are carefully constructed and monitored. Through simulations, students may experience the temporary reality of being discriminated against, of being hungry, being a single parent (Davison 1984) or other unfamiliar, controversial, sometimes stressful situations. *Rafa, Rafa*, distributed by Social Studies School Service, is a simulation designed to help students in grades 4-8 explore the dimensions of ethnocentrism. Students divide into two groups and temporarily adopt the communication styles, values, and beliefs of fictitious cultures, the Alphas and the Betas. Participants quickly learn the ways in which stereotypes and misperceptions develop; the debriefing emphasizes methods for improving cross-cultural communication and understanding. In Pereira's (1987) simulation of apartheid, students are divided proportionately to represent "white," "colored," and "black" populations in South Africa, and then informed about the conditions and circumstances of their particular groups. Follow-up discussion encourages students to express their reactions and to explore issues of rights, justice, and fairness of rules from their differing perspectives.

The inequitable distribution and consumption of resources among the first, second, and third worlds is highlighted in a world hunger simulation developed by the American Friends Service Committee, Hunger on Spaceship Earth-Simulation Game. Another spaceship simulation recommended for grades 4-8, *Terra II-A Spaceship Earth Simulation* (Mastrude 1985), deals with the problem of limited resources within a closed system and the interdependence of subsystems. Three software programs from Tom Snyder Productions-*The Environment, Immigration,* and *The Other Side*—provide excellent simulations directly related to global issues. Appropriate for grades 5-12, the simulations require students to make critical decisions regarding land use issues, immigration policies, and international conflict.

## THEMATIC RESOURCE FOLDERS

The thematic resource folder, suggested by Levstik (1983) for involving elementary students in historical issues, is anchored by a focal story that introduces a theme or issue and includes other literary and primary sources that help students investigate the issue. Individual, small group, or class resources folders can be developed as organizers for data that bring students into contact with a variety of sources and viewpoints on a specific global issue, such as hunger, literacy, or women in developing countries. Resource folders might include simple data displays garnered from newspapers or statistical reports from sources such as UNICEF's annual report on The State of the World's Children, the publications of The Worldwatch Institute, or the monthly offerings of World Eagle.

Data generated, collected, and organized by the students themselves may be particularly meaningful. For example, an activity from a 4-H curriculum unit entitled *And My World* . . . suggests that students try to use only 1.5 gallons of water for one day (the amount used by the majority of the people in the world), record how they use the allocated supply, and share the results with the group. A thematic resource folder might include pictures (from newspapers or drawn by students), surveys of family members and friends about their opinions and experiences, or correspondence with students in other schools, towns or countries about the topic. Students' journal entries could be included to document their changing perceptions of the issues.

The introduction of the theme and story early in the school year gives focus to a resource folder, and the folder can become a valuable data bank for exploring the complexities of an issue as it emerges in the news or in other classroom studies. Engle (1989) recommends that a class or grade level conduct an in depth study of one broad social problem over the course of a school year; he suggests that "such study will continually serve to reinforce the importance and relevance of other work in progress in social studies" (p. 190).

By sharing their interpretations of literature, first-hand accounts of others' experiences, and statistical data about world conditions, students discover different viewpoints on the protection of the environment, health care, homelessness, or international conflict. This discovery not only increases students' knowledge and broadens their perspectives, but it also helps them understand that, unlike textbook questions that are typically answered somewhere in the chapter, global issues represent unanswered questions.

## CONCLUSION

Educators know that young students throughout the elementary grades develop tacit understandings, beliefs, and concerns about the world's problems. Children build personal repertoires of problem-solving strategies and decision-making behaviors as they respond to the social dilemmas they experience. Researchers such as Coles (1986), Kurth-Schai (1988), and Stevens (1982) have systematically documented young people's interest in complex social and political issues. Each has concluded that children have the cognitive ability to think about global issues if such issues are referenced in the students' social experience and framed in language that is personally meaningful to them. Without classroom opportunities to examine their existing beliefs and explanations and to think and talk about solving problems and making decisions, students' misconceptions and naive models of complex social phenomena are likely to persist. Thus, the "right contexts" for exploring global issues provide multiple opportunities for the expression of student concerns and beliefs, link the student's immediate world with the wider global community, and offer a caring and supportive environment for intellectual curiosity.

The elementary years represent a critical opportunity for students to develop concepts and skills for reorganizing their thinking about global issues. Encouraging students to appreciate the problematic nature of global issues and inviting students to participate in contexts that allow for decision making and social action may enhance the development of global understanding. Group discussions, roleplay and simulations, and thematic resource folders are three instructional strategies that can help educators to create the "right context" for issues-centered teaching and learning.

## NOTE

The authors would like to extend their appreciation to Mitzi Conway, fifth grade teacher in Gwinnett County, Georgia, for sharing her thoughts and ideas about teaching global issues in the elementary grades.

## REFERENCES

Anderson, L. 1979. *Schooling and Citizenship in a Global Age: An Exploration of the Meaning and Significance of Global Education*. Bloomington, Ind.: Social Studies Development Center.

Becker, J. 1983. *Education for a Global Society*. Bloomington, Ind.: Phi Delta Kappa.

Branson, M. S., and J. Torney-Purta, eds. 1982. *International Human Rights, Society, and the Schools*. Bulletin #68. Washington, DC: National Council for the Social Studies.

Coles, R. 1986. *The Political Life of Children*. Boston: The Atlantic Monthly Press.

Davison, J. G. 1984. *Real Tears: Using Role Plays and Simulations*. Curriculum Review 23(2): 91-94.

Diakiw, J. Y., C. Baker, G. Ledger, S. Lepington, and G. Pearce. 1989. *Children's Literature: Springboard to Understanding the Developing World*. Ontario: UNICEF.

Earle, D. 1982. "Current Events Should be Taught in Primary Classrooms." *Social Education* 46(1): 27-28.

Earthworks Group. 1990. *50 Simple Things Kids Can Do to Save the Earth*. Kansas City: Andrews and McMell.

Engle, S. H. 1989. "Proposals for a Typical Issue-Centered Curriculum." *The Social Studies* 80(5): 187-196.

Gamradt, J. A., and P. G. Avery. 1990. *Capturing the Student's Voice in Educational Research*. Paper presented at the Annual Meeting of the American Educational Research Association, Boston, Mass.

Hanvey, R. 1976. *An Attainable Global Perspective*. Denver, Col.: Center for Teaching International Relations.

Katz, P. A. 1988. "Children and Social Issues." *Journal of Social Issues* 44(1): 193-209.

Kniep, W. M. 1989. "Social Studies Within a Global Education." *Social Education* 53(6): 399-403, 385.

Kurth-Schai, R. 1988. "Collecting the Thoughts of Children: A Delphic Approach." *Journal of Research and Development in Education* 21(3): 53-59.

Lamy, S. L. 1990. "Global Education: A Conflict of Images." In *Global Education: From Thought to Action*, edited by K. A. Tye, 49-63. Alexandria, Va.: Association for Supervision and Curriculum Development.

LaRaus, R., and R. C. Remy. 1978. *Citizenship Decision-making: Skills Activities and Materials*. Reading, Mass.: Addison-Wesley.

Levstik, L. 1983. "A Child's Approach to History." *The*

*Social Studies*, 74(5): 232-236.

Massialas, B. G. 1989. "The Inevitability of Issue-Centered Discourse in the Classroom." *The Social Studies*, 80(5): 173-175.

Mastrude, P. 1985. "Terra II—A Spaceship Earth Simulation." In *Simulations for a Global Perspective*, Intercom #107, (pp. 14-17). New York: Global Perspectives in Education.

Moore, S. W., J. Lare, and K. A. Wagner. 1985. *The Child's Political World*. New York: Praeger Publishers.

Pereira, C. 1987. "Elementary Teaching Strategies." *Social Education*, 51(2): 128-131

Pike, G., and D. Selby. 1988. *Global Teacher, Global Learner*. London: Hodder and Stoughton.

Riecken, T. J., and M. R. Miller. 1990. "Introduce Children to Problem Solving and Decision Making by Using Children's Literature." *The Social Studies*, 81(2): 59 64.

Ross, A. 1984. "Developing Political Concepts and Skills in the Primary School." *Educational Review* 36(2): 131-139.

Schuncke, G. M. 1984. "Global Awareness and Younger Children: Beginning the Process." *The Social Studies*, 75(6), 248-251.

Shaftel F. R., and G. Shaftel. 1982. *Role Playing in the Curriculum* (second edition). Englewood Cliffs, N.J.: Prentice-Hall.

Stevens, O. 1982. *Children Talking Politics*. Oxford: Martin Robertson.

Torney-Purta, J. 1985. "America's Knowledge and Attitudes about the World: Do We Know What We Need to Know?" In *A World of Strangers: International Education in the United States, Russia, Britain, and India*, edited by E. B. Gumbert, 13-31. Atlanta, Ga.: Center for Cross-cultural Education.

## ORGANIZATIONS OFFERING RESOURCES ON TEACHING GLOBAL ISSUES [1992 INFORMATION]

American Friends Service Committee (developers of *Hunger on Spaceship Earth* -Simulation Game). 15 Rutherford Place, New York, N.Y. 10003. (212) 598 0905.

Amnesty International. Urgent Action Network, Children's Edition. Post Office Box 1270, Nederland, CO 80466-1270. (303) 440 0913

International Service Association for Health (INSA). Post Office Box 15086, Atlanta, GA 30333. (404) 634-5748.

National 4-H Council. (*And My World* . . . is distributed by state councils). 7100 Connecticut Avenue, Chevy Chase, MD 20815. (301) 961-2846.

Social Studies School Service (distributor of *Rafa, Rafa*). 10200 Jefferson Boulevard, Post Office Box 802, Culver City, CA 90232-9983. (800) 421-4246.

Tom Snyder Productions (developers of *The Environment, Immigration* and *The Other Side*). 90 Sherman Street, Cambridge, MA 02140. (800) 342-236.

UNICEF (publishes an annual book, *The State of the World's Children*). 866 United Nations Plaza, New York, NY 10017. (212) 326-7000.

World Eagle, Inc. (publishes a monthly social studies resource). 64 Washburn Avenue, Wellesley, MA 02181. (617) 235-1415.

Worldwatch Institute (publishes an annual book, *The State of the World*). 1776 Massachusetts Avenue, NW, Washington, DC 20036. (202) 452-1999.

**Jane McLane**

In Seattle, Washington, an interdisciplinary Soviet-American curriculum exchange—the Kids-to-Kids project—was created by three dedicated teachers who planned and implemented it, and finally visited the Siberian town of Novosibirsk.

"I wonder what kind of rocks they have in Siberia."

"How do you say 'Good morning' in Russian?"

"Do their pop and candy taste the way they do in Seattle?"

These questions—and many others—were asked by 1st graders in Seattle as they shared a cross-cultural curriculum with 1st graders in Novosibirsk, Siberia, USSR.

The project began in the spring of 1989 at Kimball Elementary School with the 1st grade teaching team, Chris Morningstar, Sharon Enga, and me. Our idea was to invite 1st grade Soviet children to visit our school and city, since Seattle was hosting the Goodwill Games in the summer of 1990. We wanted to contact a school in the Soviet Union that had not had many experiences with Americans. We approached Olga Bazanova, a voluntary peace worker in the Families to Families Association in Novosibirsk. Olga's daughter was in the 1st grade at School #25 in Novosibirsk, a school considered progressive for children of parents who work at the nearby University of Novosibirsk. When Olga asked them, the 1st grade teachers at School #25 were excited about the prospect of an exchange with an American school.

## BEGINNING THE PROJECT

Over the summer of 1989, Chris, Sharon, and I brainstormed ideas and activities in music, art, language, literature, science,. and social studies that both schools could share. Our plan was to integrate the subjects through a thematic approach. Later in the summer, Sharon went to the Soviet Union and spent a week at School #25 setting up the exchange agreement.

In 1st grade the major social studies theme is the study of families. Thus, exchanging information about family life in the U.S. and the USSR was a natural starting point for this project. Through this study. the children began to see similarities and differences in the two cultures. The children at Kimball wrote books about themselves and sent drawings of their families' celebrations of winter holidays to their Soviet friends.

Reprinted with permission from the Association for Supervision and Curriculum Development, from *Educational Leadership*, April 1991, Volume 48, Number 7. Copyright 1991 by the Association for Supervision and Curriculum Development.

The study of families branched off into the study of animal families native to the two environments of Washington and Siberia, 'The children made figurines of the various animals wrote reports about them.

The Kimball 1st graders also studied folk and fairy tales common to both Russian and American cultures. They compared five stories from each culture which had similar themes, characters, and settings (for example, Cinderella and Vasilisa).

Art and drama were integrated into this literature unit through two projects. The first was an art activity where—engaging the help of artist-in-residence Stuart Nakamura—the children were able to express these stories visually in the making of silk-screened comparative banners. Later four of the five banners were presented as gifts to School #25, the Families to Families Association and two other schools we visited in Novosibirsk.

The second project drew upon the talents of nearby Cleveland High School drama students. These students volunteered to develop and then to teach drama activities to the 1st graders throughout the school year. When the Soviet visitors came, the Kimball 1st graders presented several short plays based on the folk and fairy tales they studied.

Enthusiasm spread from 1st grade to the rest of the school. A 5th grade class learned some Russian, and many students wrote to pen pals at School #25. During the year, I introduced Russian words and phrases to the entire school during the all-school morning announcement time. Children from different grade levels brought in Soviet-related materials to share with the first graders. And our Kids-to-Kids project became the catalyst for the entire school to develop an interdisciplinary curriculum theme centered on the Pacific Rim.

## THE SPRING EXCHANGE

This year-long project culminated in the long-awaited exchange between the schools. Eight Soviet 1st graders, each escorted by a parent, and four other adults visited us between May and June 12, 1990, staying in Seattle pupils' homes, attending special activities at Kimball Elementary, and sightseeing around Seattle.

The official welcoming event for the Soviets was an all-school assembly with the award-winning children's musical group "Tickle Tune Typhoon," whose music includes the themes we covered in our project friendship, environmental issues, peace, and Soviet-American relationships. It was a very exciting moment for all the school's students, parents, and staff to meet our Soviet visitors.

Few of our Soviet visitors spoke more than a phrase or two of English, and only a couple of Kimball staff knew more than a few words of Russian, but the cordiality and enthusiasm of our meeting was inspiring.

The other all-school event was the Kimball Mini-Goodwill Games. Every student participated in the Opening Ceremony, which included a Parade of Nations (with music and banners) to the playground where a welcoming speech was given in English and Russian—and in seven other languages that represented some of the languages spoken at our school.

Among other special activities was a field trip for Kimball 1st graders and the Soviet visitors to the Suquamish Indian Reservation. The Suquamish Indian children had been learning their language, tribal stories, music, dance, and art in preparation for our visit so they could share their rich culture with the Soviet children and with us. Our experience ended with the sharing of songs, games, and dances from our three cultures.

## THE SUMMER EXCHANGE

On August 25, 1990, eight Kimball 1st graders, each with a parent, traveled with us to Novosibirsk for a two-week visit. There we were greeted warmly by the Soviet friends we had met in Seattle and the new friends we were to visit.

The highlight of our visit was our participation in their first day of school on September 1. It's officially called "The Day of Knowledge," when schools celebrate the opening of the new school year. All the students were gathered outside in front of the school by class groups. The 1st graders were welcomed to the first day in their journey through "The Land of Knowledge" and were given a gift of their first books by the older students. The seniors were also acknowledged for their last year in school. At this ceremony the Kimball 1st graders gave the Soviet 1st graders the silk-screened T-shirts we had made during the school year.

The excitement we had felt in greeting the Soviets in Seattle was reciprocated by the Soviet children, parents, and teachers who greeted us on the first day of school.

Many students wanted to come and stand next to us, say hello, and smile in friendship. Later that day, we teachers had the opportunity to meet and talk with the staff of School #25. The Soviet teachers were eager to meet us and discuss what we taught in school as well as how it was decided. I spoke with one teacher about the educational computer network in which our school participates and discussed the possibility of creating a computer network between our two schools.

## MORE IMPORTANT THAN THE SUMMIT

After we returned home, the staff of School #25 sent Kimball School a letter encouraging the continuation of the exchange of ideas and projects between our two schools. They also invited a group of teachers and students from Kimball to visit their school again in the spring. The host families from both countries are keeping in touch with the students and adults they hosted, by letters, fax, and packages sent by courier. Our staff has investigated the possibility and cost of setting up a computer network between Seattle and Novosibirsk. We are waiting for a response from School #25 to find out if it is possible for them.

When we began, we envisioned the outcomes of this special yearlong curriculum exchange to be an appreciation of our similarities, a celebration of our differences, and the laying of the foundation for lifelong learning as world citizens of the 21st century. We believe we reached those outcomes.

We saw our children easily making friends with the Soviet children they met. We found the Soviet people to be very warm, gracious, and so excited to meet Americans. As Marina Kosinova, a Soviet parent, said in an interview at our school, "This exchange between Soviet and American families is more important than the summit meetings between our two nations' leaders. If our children are friends now, then later as adults they will be friends."

Jane McLane is a first grade teacher at Kimball Elementary School in Seattle, Washington. [1991 note]

**Meg Little Warren**

Art created by their peers in developing countries makes a powerful impression on American kids and teaches them how similar their lives really are.

Room 122 could not accommodate all the parents and grandparents who showed up for the multicultural tasting party at Calcutt Middle School in Central Falls, Rhode Island. More than 120 people crowded the classroom. Tables and chairs spilled out into the hall. The mayor was there, shaking hands and congratulating the 4th grade classes on the wonderful job they had done in organizing the event.

People were waiting in line behind a long table laden with 30 different dishes, labeled with names like baccallau, arroz doce, and Cape Verdean cornbread. The dishes reflected the diverse ethnic makeup of the school. The students had compiled the recipes in a cookbook they were now selling for $2 apiece. They planned to send the proceeds to Sierra Leone, one of the developing countries they had been studying in "See Me, Share My World: Understanding the Third World through Children's Art."

At the start of the "See Me, Share My World" teaching unit, most of the 4th graders at Calcutt had never heard of Sierra Leone. They could neither pronounce the name correctly nor locate this small country on a map, even though several children in their school had recently emigrated from West Africa. But, after two weeks of viewing and discussing the colorful drawings created by their peers in Africa, Asia, and Latin America, the students not only could place Sierra Leone on a map, they knew much about the daily lives of children there—and in five other developing countries—their foods, schooling, health, work, and play. Many students were surprised to find out that three-fourths of the world's people live in developing countries.

The tasting party was a great success, and it was just one of the many multidisciplinary activities that the "See Me, Share My World" teaching unit offered to help children compare experiences and discover connections. The unit's visual and "hands-on" approach helped the students acquire geography skills and familiarity with statistics; more important, they saw the similarities and differences between their lives and the lives of children around the world. They developed both greater knowledge of the global community and empathy for their counterparts in distant villages.

Typically, children summed up their learning like this: "It made me think about what I would be like if I were them" and "Now I care what happens to others."

Calcutt was one of 21 Rhode Island schools chosen to pilot this multidisciplinary global education program, developed in cooperation with local educators by PLAN International USA, formerly the Foster Parents Plan.[1] The idea evolved from Childreach Sponsorship, PLAN's humanitarian assistance program linking caring Americans with needy children and their families overseas through personal sponsorship and communications. Funding to design and pilot a supplementary teaching unit and traveling exhibit of children's artwork came from the U.S. Agency for International Development, with matching grants from local funding organizations.

Over 2,500 3rd through 6th grade students and 115 teachers participated in the pilot phase of the project. The schools ranged from Gilbert Stuart—a large inner-city school with many recent immigrants from Latin America and Southeast Asia—to Clayville, a small rural school near the Connecticut border.

In response to teachers' enthusiasm and recommendations from a pilot evaluation study, PLAN International USA is now disseminating a packaged version of the "See Me, Share My World" program.[2] The new version includes 16 placemat size laminated prints of the best color artwork and black-and-white photographs from the pilot exhibit, a comprehensive teacher guide with 48 reproducible activity sheets, and a teacher training videotape. The exhibit of children's original artwork is also available for rental to schools, libraries, and community organizations.[3]

## THE DAILY LIFE OF A CHILD

"See Me, Share My World" centers around a vibrant collection of drawings and paintings combined with documentary photographs and charts to create a composite portrait of daily life in economically disadvantaged areas in developing countries. The artwork, photographs, and charts introduce American children to their peers in Colombia, Honduras, India, Indonesia, Sierra Leone, and Thailand. The unit is designed to be adaptable to different grade level requirements in grades 3-6 and to students of varied abilities and interests.

Under the umbrella topic "the daily life of a child," the curriculum addresses six universal themes, introduced by motivating questions that provide a focus for viewing and discussing the visual images within a comparative framework. Each theme (question) covers a set of specific objectives, outlined briefly as follows:

1. *Global kinship* (Where do you live?) involves locating the countries where the artwork is from, distinguishing basic differences between developing and developed countries, discussing experiences common to children everywhere, and identifying local/global connections.
2. *Food* (What do you eat?) explores production and distribution of a country's staple foods and investigates the causes of hunger in developing countries.
3. *Education* (Who teaches you?) addresses the issues of access to education, literacy, and learning outside the school classroom.
4. *Health* (What keeps you healthy?) examines the connections between health, environment, and nutrition. It also discusses causes of child mortality in developing countries.
5. *Work* (Why do you work?) examines the role of children's work in rural and urban families in developing countries.
6. *Festivals and Games* (How do you have fun?) enables students to celebrate the universality and diversity of festivals and games worldwide.

## VIEWING THE ARTWORK

The starting point for the teaching unit is to present the children's artwork and elicit students' reactions to the drawings. In these discussions, teachers should take care, as one teacher explained, "not to dwell on facts. This whole project is about feelings from original art and should be fun." Open-ended questions—Which picture did you like best? What do you see? How does it make you feel?—encourage creative and original thinking. Children see different things depending on their own background and experience. There is no one "correct" answer.

When they first see the artwork, many students are surprised. Often the pictures force them to reexamine their television-inspired preconceptions about a country or its people, as illustrated by these remarks such as "I used to think it was all death and sorrow, but it isn't" . . . "even though the kids are poor, they have just as good talents" . . . "They are not as different from me as I thought."

Teachers follow up with the sequenced lessons in the teacher's guide, using hands-on prints of the children's art and a variety of learning activities. For example, in an introductory activity called "World in a Room," students simulate the distribution of wealth in the world by dividing their classroom into world regions and distributing people and pennies proportionately. The "how do you have fun?" section of the teacher's guide provides suggestions for how students can create their own artwork and recreate games and toys used by children in different developing countries.

Activity sheets include maps, charts, reference tables, photographs, and art reproductions. Ten class periods provide adequate time to introduce the unit and spend one or two periods on each of the six thematic sections, although some teachers have extended the "See Me, Share My World" teaching unit throughout the entire year.

### FIGURE 1
### MULTIDISCIPLINARY "SEE ME, SHARE MY WORLD" ACTIVITIES

1. Discuss children's drawings from different countries.
2. Locate the children's countries, and practice other basic map skills.
3. Create artwork comparing your own daily life with that of children from developing countries.
4. Write and perform a dramatic autobiography of what life is like for a child in a developing country.
5. Read folktales from various countries (students choose one to develop into a play or puppet show).
6. Have a storyteller tell African folktales.
7. Invite guest speakers who have lived in or visited developing countries.
8. Bring in everyday products to create a display of our global connections.
9. Analyze import/export links and other economic ties.
10. Make circle and bar graphs using statistics.
11. Play games from different countries.
12. Make various crafts from different countries (students choose the one they want to make).
13. Put together a cookbook containing recipes from various countries.
14. Develop a Children's Bill of Rights.
15. Organize an International Festival with samples of all of these activities to culminate the program.

*Developed by Gloria Monte,*
*Meadowbrook Farms School*
*East Greenwich, Rhode Island*

## EXTENDING LEARNING

The lessons provide an excellent opportunity to integrate geography, social studies, mathematics, language arts, art, music, and health. "It's more than just visuals," says Gloria Monte, a 6th grade teacher at Meadowbrook Farms School in East Greenwich; "it lends itself to great flexibility in incorporating content and higher-order thinking skills into all areas of the curriculum."

For example, Lois Hamel and Denise Garvey, the 4th grade teachers at Calcutt Middle School, were able to meet their health education requirements by discussing staple foods, nutrition, and diets in developing countries. As part of a science and math class, Al Menard, a 4th grade teacher at East Woonsocket Elementary School, experimented with different measurements to mix ORT (Oral Rehydration Therapy—a drink of water, salt, and sugar used in developing countries to treat dehydration). "We tried measuring with grams and liters and found different ways to measure with handfuls and bottle caps."

## THE MAGIC OF ART

Evaluation, based on unit goals, comes from a variety of sources: paper-and-pencil tests administered before and after the unit, student projects and portfolios, classroom observations, and teacher surveys and interviews.

Preliminary analysis of the pre- and post-tests from two Cranston schools shows that before the program, most of the students thought Third World children were very different and disconnected from themselves. After the program students saw more similarities and connections between themselves and their Third World peers. And they began to reconsider their own personal habits and actions. "Now I think when I leave the faucet running" and "we shouldn't waste our resources" were comments from students who started to question practices in their own culture.

Although fundraising and sponsorship are not program objectives, students at more than one-third of the pilot schools have committed themselves to some kind of social action. For example, each month 6th graders at Providence Street School in West Warwick bring $1.50 to class. Half pays for a "Third World lunch" of chili, rice, or beans. The other half goes to Amidu Sesay, the child in Sierra Leone they sponsor through PLAN International USA's Childreach Sponsorship program. Fifth graders at Wheeler School in Providence offered to do extra work at home and saved up their allowances to sponsor a child. Students at Norwood Avenue School in Cranston organized a "goodie" store and voted to send the $120 they earned to Sierra Leone.

Students from five pilot schools testified at the Rhode Island General Assembly in support of the ratification of the Convention on the Rights of the Child. Each school developed its own "Kids' Bill of Rights." Students from Providence Street School collected more than 200 signatures from classmates to demonstrate their support of the convention to Rhode Island legislators.

"See Me, Share My World" is powerful and effective. The drawings and paintings of children in faraway places immediately appeal to American students of all ability levels and backgrounds. These dynamic visual images tap children's natural responsiveness, touching both their hearts and their minds. And it is the engagement of heart and mind that leads them to empathy, caring, and social action—and prepares them to assume the role of global citizens when they grow up.

## NOTES

[1] PLAN International USA (formerly Foster Parents Plan) is part of a worldwide humanitarian organization linking caring sponsors with needy children and their families overseas. Founded in 1937, PLAN is nonprofit, nonsectarian, and nonpartisan. Through its Childreach Sponsorship program, PLAN International USA combines proven tailor-made assistance with complete sponsor accountability and personal communications to help families lift themselves out of poverty. PLAN's development programs are helping 600,000 children and families in 25 countries of Africa, Asia, Latin America, and the Caribbean. Programs overseas are supported by global education and child rights advocacy in the United States. PLAN International USA offers Kids Teach activities about developing countries to U.S. schools that sponsor children. Selected schools also participate in the World Citizen School Sponsorship Program.

[2] The objectives of the pilot evaluation were to determine major patterns, themes, and issues of the project's impact on students and teachers; assess the effectiveness of specific project components; and make recommendations for replication of the project nationally. In the study, children's art emerges as a critical tool for learning important concepts and skills. A full report, including scholars' reviews, is available upon request from PLAN International USA.

[3] Since the pilot phase of the project, more than 100 schools outside Rhode Island, from New Jersey to California, have introduced the new revised teaching unit as part of social studies, language arts, and art curriculums. The exhibit has toured 32 Rhode Island and Massachusetts schools in addition to two libraries and one museum. Children's Television Workshop animated six of the artworks for Sesame Street's 1991 year-long program focus on world cultures.

Meg Little Warren is Project Manager of "See Me, Share My World: Understanding the Third World through Children's Art," PLAN International USA in Warwick, Rhode Island. [1991 note]

**James A. Banks**

## THE WORLD SYSTEM

The torrid weather in the nation's midwestern states during the spring and summer of 1988 and the resulting drought dramatized U.S. links with the world. Some scientists believe that the high temperatures and drought indicated that the greenhouse effect is taking place. The greenhouse effect occurs when pollutants deplete the ozone layer. Some scientists are reluctant to link the high temperatures and destructive drought of 1988 to the greenhouse effect. However, scientists agree that human pollutants, which have global origins, are depleting the stratospheric ozone and that the earth's temperature is rising. Pollutants originating from cities spread from London to Tokyo, Chicago to Sydney, and from Rio de Janeiro to Hong Kong, are damaging the ozone layer and thus possibly contributing to the problems of farmers in Iowa, Illinois, and Nebraska. The depletion of the ozone layer, caused by human pollutants, illustrates that the world is a global system and that all of its inhabitants-wherever they live on spaceship earth-are bound by a common fate and destiny. They share overarching, intractable problems that cannot be solved unless peoples from many different nations, cultures, ethnic groups, and religions work cooperatively. Cooperation by the world's diverse peoples to solve global problems is essential for human survival.

All of the world's citizens have a common destiny. However, the search for solutions to global problems is complicated by the cultural, ethnic, religious, and national boundaries that divide, often sharply, the world's peoples into groups with conflicting interests. These groups consume highly disproportionate shares of the world's resources and exercise sharply different amounts of power in world politics. Two out of three people in the world live in poor and developing nations in continents such as Africa, Asia, and Latin America.[1] Yet, the one out of three people in the world who live in the developed Western nations consume most of the earth's resources and exercise most of the political and economic power in the world. The world is sharply divided between the few who are rich and well-fed in the Western developed nations—who are predominantly White—and the many who are poor and hungry in the developing nations, who are predominantly non-White. These sharp divisions also exist within nations.

Allport's seminal theory teaches us that people from diverse groups can work cooperatively to solve problems only when they function in equal-status situations and when they perceive their fates as shared.[2] We will not be able to substantially reduce international tensions and conflicts until most citizens in the world have a decent standard of living and a modicum of political and economic power. Groups from different nations and cultures who have highly unequal amounts of power, influence, and wealth are rarely able to work cooperatively to solve difficult human problems. A major goal of education for survival in a multicultural global society is to help students acquire the knowledge, attitudes, and skills needed to participate in the reformation of the world's social, political, and economic systems so that peoples from diverse ethnic, cultural, and religious groups will be politically empowered and structurally integrated into their societies. Helping students to acquire the competencies and commitments to participate in effective civic action to create equitable national societies is the most important goal for multicultural/global education in the twenty-first century.

It is necessary but not sufficient for students to acquire interdisciplinary knowledge about diverse groups, a respect for cultural and ethnic diversity, and the skills to function cross-culturally. Such knowledge and skills, while essential, should be used to help students develop the commitment and skills to take actions—in both their present and future lives—to help eliminate structural inequality and personal, cultural, and institutional racism, sexism, and handicapism. Students in the primary and elementary grades cannot remake the world or eliminate racism, sexism, or handicapism in their families, schools, or communities. However, they can become aware of words, phrases, and actions that hurt and of stereotypes that support racial and gender discrimination. They can also make a personal commitment to avoid using such words and phrases and to reject harmful stereotypes. These attitudes and behaviors are the foundation needed to enable children in the primary and elementary grades to become effective and committed civic actors in a larger social and political context when they are adult citizens.

## THE UNITED STATES: A MICROCOSM OF THE WORLD

The salient characteristics of our global society are mirrored in the United States. The United States is a microcosm of the world and contains ethnic, cultural, and religious groups from every corner of the earth. One out of every three Americans will be an ethnic minority by the year 2000. Students can develop the knowledge, attitudes, and skills needed to become effective world citizens by studying the United States and its rich ethnic, cultural, and religious diversity. However, teachers should carefully distinguish teaching about other lands and their interconnectedness (global education)[3] and teaching about ethnic groups in the United States (a component of multicultural education).[4] There are significant differences between teaching about Mexicans in Mexico City and teaching about Chicanos in East Los Angeles. Citizens of Mexico and Mexican-Americans should not be equated, as is sometimes done. Some teachers who have taught a unit on Mexico believe they have taught about Mexican-Americans.

## APPROACHES TO TEACHING MULTICULTURAL CONTENT

Several identifiable approaches to the integration of ethnic content into the curriculum have evolved since the 1960s. The Contributions Approach to integration is one of the most frequently used. This approach is characterized by the addition of ethnic heroes into the curriculum. The mainstream curriculum remains unchanged in terms of its basic structure, goals, and salient characteristics. It is the easiest approach for teachers to use to integrate the curriculum with ethnic content. However, it has several serious limitations. Students do not attain a comprehensive view of the role of ethnic and cultural groups in U.S. society. Rather, they see ethnic issues and events primarily as an addition to the curriculum, and consequently, as an appendage to the main story of the development of the nation.

Content, concepts, themes, and perspectives are added to the curriculum without changing its basic structure, purposes, and characteristics in the Additive Approach. This approach is often accomplished by the addition of a book, a unit, or a course to the curriculum without changing it substantially. The Additive Approach allows the teacher to put ethnic content into the curriculum without restructuring it, which takes substantial time, effort, training, and rethinking of the curriculum and its purposes, nature, and goals.

The Additive Approach can be the first phase in a more radical curriculum reform effort designed to restructure the total curriculum and to integrate it with ethnic content, perspectives, and frames of reference. However, this approach shares several disadvantages with the Contributions Approach. Its most important shortcoming is that it usually results in the viewing of ethnic content from the perspectives of mainstream historians, writers, artists, and scientists because it does not involve a restructuring of the curriculum.

The Transformation Approach differs fundamentally from the Contributions and Additive Approaches. This approach changes the basic assumptions of the curriculum and enables students to view concepts, issues, themes, and problems from several ethnic perspectives and points of view. The key curriculum issue involved in the Transformation Approach is not the addition of a long list of ethnic groups, heroes, and contributions, but the infusion of various perspectives, frames of reference, and content from different groups that will extend students' understandings of the nature, development, and complexity of U.S. society and the world. The Social Action Approach includes all of the elements of the Transformation Approach but adds components that require students to make decisions and to take actions related to the concept, issue, or problem they have studied in the unit.

The four approaches to the integration of ethnic content into the curriculum described above are often mixed and blended in actual teaching situations. The move from the first to the higher levels of ethnic content integration is likely to be gradual and cumulative( The major goal of teaching about racial, cultural, and ethnic diversity should be to empower students with the knowledge, skills, and attitudes needed to help transform our world and enhance the possibility for human survival.)

## RESOURCES

Baker, Gwendolyn. (1983). *Planning and Organizing for Multicultural Instruction*. Reading, MA: Addison-Wesley.

Banks, James A. (1987). *Teaching Strategies for Ethnic Studies* (4th ed.). Boston: Allyn and Bacon.

Banks, James A., and Cherry A. McGee Banks. (Eds.). (1989) *Multicultural Education: Issues and Perspectives*. Boston: Allyn and Bacon.

*Multicultural Leader*. Quarterly newsletter published by the Educational Materials and Services Center, 144 Railroad Avenue, Suite 107, Edmonds, WA, 98020.

Schniedewind, Nancy and Ellen Davidson. (1983). *Open Minds to Equality: A Sourcebook of Learning Activities to Promote Race, Sex, Class, and Age Equity*. Englewood Cliffs, NJ: Prentice-Hall.

## NOTES

1   U.S. Bureau of the Census. (1987). *World Population Profile: 1987*, 3. Washington, DC: U.S. Government Printing Office.

2   Allport, Gordon W. (1979). *The Nature of Prejudice* (25th Anniversary Ed.). Reading, MA: Addison-Wesley.

3   Becker, James M. (Ed.) . (1980). *Schooling for a Global Age*. New York: McGraw-Hill.

4   Banks, James A. (1988). *Multiethnic Education: Theory and Practice* (2nd ed.). Boston: Allyn and Bacon.

James A. Banks is a Professor of Education, Curriculum, and Instruction at the University of Washington, Seattle. A past President of National Council for the Social Studies, Dr. Banks has done extensive work in multicultural education in the United States and has studied and observed it in such nations as Canada, the United Kingdom, Australia, Sweden, and the Netherlands. [1989 note]

# PART 10

## ⊗ CIVIC IDEALS AND PRACTICES

Citizenship education is an overall goal for social studies programs in the United States and elsewhere. It is important that young learners understand the importance of civic ideals and practices necessary to be effective adult citizens, which involves both obligations and privileges. Within the social studies classroom, students need to have numerous opportunities to practice their citizenship roles, rights, and responsibilities. Examples of questions that may be addressed by young learners in citizenship education include at least the following: What is citizenship? How do girls and boys practice citizenship skills in other countries? What can I do to make a positive difference at home and school? How can I influence my government to make my community better? How do laws and rules influence our daily lives?

Passe explains that children have fragmentary information about the world around them. He encourages teachers to help students learn about current events in ways that are meaningful to them so that they can develop an understanding of civic issues. Wade, a strong advocate of community service learning, describes ways teachers can include this learning in several curriculum content areas. She provides a planning checklist for teachers to use when considering community service activities for young learners and a listing of curriculum resources available for such learning opportunities.

McGowan and Godwin address the need to have positive citizenship experiences for children in the early grades that will help them develop skills, responsibilities, and respect as important components in citizenship development. They identify important features of citizenship education programs and offer two learning activities to help teachers accomplish this objective.

Jennings, Crowell, and Fernlund advocate the teaching of social justice through classroom community experiences. They offer five ideas that can be used to help teachers create a positive and transformational learning environment. Nalle describes her third grade classroom practice of teaching fairness and justice by using class meetings to resolve classroom problems and to help students develop genuine respect and real concern for classmates.

Nielsen and Finkelstein express concern about creation of images of our political leaders and ask how teachers can help students form correct perceptions about political leadership. They describe a democratic class interaction model and related classroom activities as examples for students to practice as they gain realistic expectations of leadership qualities and needed skills. Along somewhat similar lines, Parker addresses the need to develop ethical behavior and values by asking the question "Why Ethics?" and suggests three reasons to include a citizenship education program within the school curriculum.

Holidays are a part of any culture, and the celebration of holidays has been a regular part of the traditional elementary curriculum. Naylor and Smith suggest several ways to help teachers consider district or school policies for teaching about holidays and urge that students learn about holidays in a global context.

Citizenship obligations and skills are learned and practiced not only in the classroom but also in a variety of settings. Active citizenship practices extend well beyond the doors of the classroom into the larger local, state, national, and global environments.

**Jeff Passe**

Elementary school children have a keen interest in public affairs. They see news on television, hear adults debating issues, and may even discuss certain topics among themselves. Such major events as presidential elections, hostage crises, assassinations, and natural hazards may provoke interest and enter into the child's world. Yet, most children lack ability to understand the meanings of current events. Most elementary school students are likely to have only fragmentary knowledge about current events with little or no understanding of their larger meanings.

The presidential election provides a case in point. Children can tell you the names of the presidential candidates, but not their political parties. As for the role of the president in the government, the issues involved in the campaign, and the effects of the election on their lives, most elementary children are unable to understand these questions, much less provide any answers. However, a large percentage of elementary children will earnestly tell you whom they would vote for, if given the opportunity.

Children's perceptions of the electoral process are typical of their perceptions of most current events. They pick up phrases and attitudes from adults, older children, and television. Their questions to parents or siblings are likely to receive either simple responses — e.g., "This guy wants to give everything away to the Russians"-or analyses too complex for children to comprehend (e.g., "I like the way our economy has improved"). Neither answer responds to children's need for structures that help them interpret information they have already assimilated such as: What is the economy? How does it affect the American people? What role do presidents play in formulating economic policy? Such understanding is necessary before one can choose among presidential candidates on the issue in question.

The state of current events instruction in the schools is poor (Passe 1988). Current events are rarely discussed in the elementary classroom. When current events are discussed, they are often handled haphazardly with the result that meaningful learning is unlikely to take place. Consider the following common scenarios:

(a) Mrs. S's 3d grade students bring in a newspaper article every Friday. Each child stands before the class and tells about it. The first child reads an article on the Mexican earthquake in a monotone voice, frequently stumbling over the more difficult words. Some of the classmates groan.

Eventually, they become so distracted that Mrs. S orders them to listen. A second child reads fluently an article on a drop in the Gross National Product as the rest of the class stares vacantly. The third child begins to read an article describing a robbery, but Mrs. S interrupts and asks the student simply to tell about it. It is unclear whether the child has previously read the article, but it is evident that the child does not understand what the article describes.

(b) Mr. J provides the *Weekly Reader* for his 4th graders. Each week, students take turns reading articles aloud, paragraph by paragraph. Then they do the puzzles on the back. For follow-up, they answer the summary questions provided in the teacher's edition. No discussion is held.

(c) Ms. W does not have a separate current events period but encourages her 5th graders to discuss the news during sharing time. One student tells about a violent battle shown on the evening news. Ms. W asks the child if he knows who was fighting. When the child doesn't respond, Ms. W writes the words 'Iran' and 'Iraq' on the chalkboard and explains that these are the names of the two warring countries. She then urges the children to watch the news for more information on this matter. The next child stands to tell about her trip to the county fair.

Although these teachers have tried to include current events in the curriculum, their methods are unlikely to improve students' knowledge and skills about them. Teachers might improve their effectiveness if they included some of the following components in current events instruction: (1) a teacher-centered presentation, (2) a factual presentation in terms the students can understand, (3) background data on the students' level, (4) topics relevant to the students' daily lives, (5) student discussion, and (6) follow-up analysis.

*Teacher-centered presentation.* The more complex and difficult the topic, the more likely it is to require a teacher-centered presentation. Current events require background knowledge and skills in interpretation and analysis that are difficult to teach. Effective teachers know how to build carefully from the children's store of knowledge to help them understand the issues involved. On the other hand, children's reading articles aloud to one another is pointless. The child does not present the material in ways that the class will understand. At the same time, the rest of the class will quickly ignore the reader. Oral expression skills may improve, but the children's interest in current events will suffer.

A factual presentation in terms the students can understand. Adults often make references about issues of the day. They may speak of Gorbachev, for instance, without

Reprinted from *Social Education*, November/December 1988, Volume 52, Number 7. Copyright 1988 by National Council for the Social Studies.

identifying him. Or they may refer to SALT without defining the acronym for Strategic Arms Limitation Talks. These references confuse or have little meaning for children.

Successful teachers of current events make every effort to use language that children can understand. To the extent possible, they simplify facts so that children can comprehend the ideas presented. Simplifying information, however, should not render it inaccurate. Choose carefully events that students can understand in their own terms.

*Background data on the student's level.* Understanding current events presupposes a knowledge of history, geography, political science, anthropology, sociology, and economics-in other words, social studies. Comprehending the situation in the Middle East is impossible without knowing the location of the Middle East what countries constitute this region, its cultures, relationships among the Arab nations, among the Arab nations and Israel, and their relationships to the United States, and the political, economic, and geographical implications of those relationships. Effective teachers of current events will determine and provide the background to enable children to understand the contexts of the news.

Providing background information alone, however, is not sufficient; the information must be on the student's level. Consideration of the limitations of elementary students is essential. For instance, when tracing historical antecedents of current events, teachers must be aware of the difficulties young students have with temporal concepts. Similarly, because the student cannot comprehend certain abstractions, such as various economic and governmental concepts (e.g., communism, inflation, nationalism, etc.) attempting to explain them will more likely confuse than clarify. Teachers should provide background data the student can comprehend.

In selecting appropriate current events topics, teachers should build upon concepts that have already been presented to the students. For instance, the study of an election campaign should coincide with or follow a classwide or schoolwide exercise in voting.

Many of the news events that interest students are continuing stories that permit the teacher time to develop appropriate background data. One such item is a presidential visit abroad. Teachers should gather materials to introduce to the class on the culture, history, and geography of the countries in the president's itinerary by using concrete examples such as music, food, slides, and guest speakers. *The Weekly Reader* and other children's news magazines usually provide excellent background material for studying current events. Teachers may use these news magazines effectively to introduce a topic. Many instructors also make use of the teacher's guide to develop follow-up activities that promote application and analysis These mini-units can aid in the student's comprehension of the issues. Teachers should be alert for news items related to people, places, and institutions that the class had studied previously. For instance, after an examination of the Bill of Rights, the class could benefit from news reports on Supreme Court rulings on free speech.

*Topics relevant to children's lives.* If students perceive a topic as irrelevant, they are unlikely to put forth the necessary effort to comprehend the issues involved. A study of the American economy can come alive if a teacher were to show how the state of the economy will determine whether the town's major factory will close. Students prefer to study local affairs (e.g., crime, recreational facilities, transportation, etc.) rather than national and international issues because of their relevance to them.

This is not to say that local events are the only topics that teachers may discuss. National and international issues should also be presented, but teachers must establish the relationship of those issues to the students' lives. For instance, the effects of extreme weather disturbances in another part of the country can be linked to local food prices or to human or environmental costs in a way that impresses the students. Similarly, an examination of a revolution in Central America must include the implications for American interests in the region. If teachers can demonstrate the connections between global events and students' lives, the students begin to pay attention to matters outside their daily experiences.

*Student discussion.* As with any curricular topic, having students participate leads to interest and enjoyment in the lesson. Because the issues of the day may stimulate controversy, students should be encouraged to share their opinions. Once the teacher is assured that the background data are clearly understood, students should be given the opportunity to argue their viewpoints. If guided properly, current events discussions can promote skill in oral expression, critical thinking, problem solving, and listening. The discussion can also encourage learning about tolerance and provide opportunities for analysis and careful thinking. These activities can excite children about the topics discussed and indirectly excite them about school. For many students and teachers, current events can become the highlight of the day.

*Follow-up analysis.* Knowledge and comprehension are low-level thinking tasks. If teachers can show students how to apply high-level thinking to current events, students can begin to apply this to understanding society's problems—one of the basic goals of the social studies. The following models, if applied to the study of current events, will enable students to go beyond knowing and understanding the issues.

▮ *Value Analysis*, developed by Hilda Taba (Walden 1969), provides opportunities for students to compare the values of each side in a dispute. If the *Value Analysis* model were applied to the situation in Beirut when American hostages were held in a TWA aircraft, students would have understood why the terrorists resorted to hijacking to achieve their goals, why then-President Reagan used negotiation instead of force to rescue the hostages, and what they (the students) would have done in the same situation. Using this model, students would develop the ability to consider their own and others' value systems when making decisions.

■ *Decision Making* (Schuncke and Hoffman 1980) allows students to consider solutions, outline possible consequences for each proposed solution, and make a decision based on each individual's value structure. If *Decision Making* were applied to the Beirut hostage situation, students would have weighed the options of negotiating, resorting to military means, retaliating, and using the United Nations to mediate. They would have outlined the consequences of each choice and made personal decisions as to the best option. Students using this model would develop skills in anticipating the consequences of their choices as well as understanding their own value structures.

■ *Taba's Feeling Exploration* (Walden 1969), is similar to Value Analysis in its emphasis on understanding others. In this case, however, the focus is on the feelings of the participants involved. Students explore the feelings of each side in a dispute and then compare how they would have felt in the same situation. If applied to the Beirut hostage situation, students would first put themselves in the positions of the hostages, then the hostages' families, and, finally, the abductors. They would discuss how each group felt and why they felt that way. Then the students would discuss how they would feel in that same situation. Doing so improves the students' abilities to express what they feel as well as their understanding of others.

## CONCLUSIONS

Teachers who are uneasy about teaching current events can diagnose their lessons to see whether they meet the criteria suggested in this paper. When we analyze the three teachers discussed earlier, we can see why their lessons were unsuccessful. Mrs. S's students who read aloud participated in the lesson, but the teacher did not provide the needed direction. Mr. J. through his use of the *Weekly Reader*, provided information on the children's level, but did not permit discussion. Ms. W attempted to give background information by calling attention to the names of the warring nations, but went no further.

It is likely that a child who is knowledgeable and inquisitive about current events will grow into an effective citizen who continues to study social issues and expand knowledge of the world. Development of an effective citizenry is a basic goal of the social studies. Studying current events in the curriculum can improve the quality of our society.

## REFERENCES

Passe, J. 1988 "The Role of Internal Factors in the Teaching of Current Events," *Theory and Research in Social Education* 16, no. 1:83 89.

Schuncke, G. and S Hoffman. 1980. "Developing Problem-solving Readiness in Young Children." *The Social Studies* 71:23-27.

Walden, N.E. 1969. *Final Report: The Taba Curriculum Project in the Social Studies*. Menlo Park California: Addison-Wesley.

Jeff Passe is an Assistant Professor at the College of Education and Allied Professions in the Department of Curriculum and Instruction at the University of North Carolina at Charlotte. [1988 note]

# 63

# Community Service-Learning: Commitment through Active Citizenship

**Rahima C. Wade**

Anita, Marlene, Liza, and David are committed to empowering their students to work for community improvement and social justice through projects that focus on environmental protection, the isolation of senior citizens, the needs of the homeless, and animal rights. Each Friday, David's fourth grade class cares for the animals at the local animal shelter and publicizes animal rights issues in the community. Liza's third graders bake and deliver bread every month to the local soup kitchen. Marlene's fifth graders are creating a Vaudeville Show using songs they are learning from the residents of a local retirement residence. Anita's sixth graders are working to reestablish a prairie in a nearby park. They, like many other teachers from suburbs and cities nationwide, believe that the social studies' professed goal of active citizenship is best developed not just through reading a textbook but also through practical, hands-on experiences in which students identify community needs, develop action plans, and put their ideas into practice. Their students are developing firsthand knowledge about what it means to make a difference; at the same time they are learning valuable personal, social, and academic skills.

While community service is a long standing tradition in American society, the more recent idea of community service-learning — integrating meaningful service to one's school or community with academic learning and structured reflection (Cairn & Kielsmeier, 1991) — has engendered great interest in the educational arena. A number of studies and reports on educational change have called for youth service initiatives (Boyer, 1983; Carnegie Council on Adolescent Development, 1989; Goodlad, 1984; Harrison, 1986). These appeals have been supported by millions of dollars of federal funding for service-learning programs nationwide (Commission on National and Community Service, 1993). Research on community service-learning has revealed many potential benefits for students, including increased self-esteem and self-efficacy, enhanced motivation and interest in school, and greater academic achievement and social responsibility (Conrad & Hedin, 1991; Wade, 1993).

While many educators are recognizing the benefits of community service-learning, both preservice and inservice teachers are concerned about the "how-to's" of planning an effective service-learning project that meets both community needs and curriculum objectives. The following recommendations

Reprinted from *Social Studies and the Young Learner*, January/February 1994, Volume 6, Number 3. Copyright 1994 by National Council for the Social Studies.

are based on service-learning curricula as well as the experiences of over fifty teachers in our local school district's service-learning program.

## GETTING STARTED

In beginning a service-learning project, three tasks are essential: deciding on a community need or problem, choosing a service project, and developing a plan for integrating the service with curricular goals and objectives.

## IDENTIFYING A PROBLEM

The best service-learning projects involve ideas not only from the teacher and students, but input from the local community as well. Here are some of the many ways to identify a community need or problem with students:

- Conduct a survey in the community, local neighborhood, or school.
- Telephone local service providers or invite them to class to speak with students.
- Have students develop a vision of an ideal community or world and then discuss what would need to be changed to make their visions a reality.
- Read the local newspapers and cut out articles on community problems.
- Look through the Yellow Pages for agencies that focus on social and environmental issues.
- Have students attend city council, school board, or United Way meetings and return to class with ideas to discuss.
- Have students identify personal skills, talents, knowledge, or hobbies that might be used to help others.
- Talk to senior citizens or homeless people about both needs and project ideas. If possible, find a way to include service recipients in the project from the beginning to its completion.

## CHOOSING THE PROJECT

After deciding on a problem or need, the next step is to choose a service-learning project. Ideally, service projects will be more than one-time events. Projects that are carried out over a few months or the entire school year are more likely to lead to students' long-term commitment to work for social and environmental change in their communities.

After the class has chosen a need or a problem, brainstorm ideas for projects. If there are specific limits in terms of time, transportation, or funding, specify these at the beginning. Also consider the ages and skills of the students and how much outside help or resources projects will involve. Ideas for many excellent service projects can be found in the curriculum resources listed at the end of this article. Encourage students to work toward consensus on a project idea, or, if need be, to vote on a project to which they can all contribute.

## INTEGRATING SERVICE WITH ACADEMICS

Most elementary teachers teach a variety of subjects. These are just a few of the many ways community service-learning can be integrated within the elementary curriculum.

- *Social Studies*. Discuss with your students the role of civic participation in the social studies. Community activities may involve geography and map skills or learning about local history through interviewing senior citizens, developing a tour guide for historic sites, or renovating an old building.
- *Reading & Language Arts*. Surveys, interviews, and questionnaires involve both writing and communication skills. Students may engage in library research on the service topic or read children's books on the service theme. They may want to share what they have learned and accomplished through writing plays or reports.
- *Math*. If your service project involves fundraising or needed supplies, students can keep a record of monies raised or spent. Building projects can make use of measurement and computational skills. Information students learn about the service theme can be represented in charts and diagrams.
- *Science*. Environmental projects are often compatible with curricular objectives in science. Students can conduct experiments on the quality of local water sources or learn about local birds and trees to create plans for a bird sanctuary. Creating a butterfly garden at a local nursing home or developing a nature trail in an infrequently used park are also opportunities to combine science and service.

## INVITING COLLABORATION

The most effective service-learning projects are usually partnerships between teachers, students, and community members. Students should not be just doing good for others; instead, students should work alongside community members and service recipients for mutual empowerment. Think about who are the best people to involve in the project. Which agencies in the community work on the identified need or problem? Can parents, other teachers, or college practicum students be involved? If additional funding is necessary, local businesses or the school P.T.A. may be sources of support. Contact your state department of education to find out who is your state coordinator for federal community service-funding. Finally, think about ways to involve the recipients of the service project so that they can become more empowered in identifying or meeting their needs.

When working with a number of individuals on a service-learning activity, clarify the responsibilities of all those involved. Who will be responsible for collecting supplies or supervising students on community field trips? Who

will provide orientation for students and others on needed skills and information to complete the service project? How can students be empowered to be responsible for themselves and their learning in connection with the service activities?

## REFLECTING ON SERVICE

As students engage in the service project and related academic tasks, it is important for them to reflect on what they are learning about themselves, others, and the act of serving. Students can engage in reflection through journal writing, drawing, discussion, public speaking, creating a photo essay, or writing a newspaper article on the project. The following questions can be used to foster student reflection.

- How is the service-learning project going?
- What is working? What would you like to change?
- What problems have you encountered and what have you done to try to resolve them?
- What have you learned about others through this project?
- What have you learned about yourself through this project?
- How is this project similar to or different than what you expected?
- What larger social, environmental, or political issues are represented in this project?
- What would you like to share with others about this project?
- What would be an effective way to share what you have learned?

Reflection on the essential components of a service-learning project is also an important task for the teacher.

## CELEBRATING SERVICE

Although the principal intent of a service-learning project is to meet others' needs in the community, it is important to take some time to celebrate the students' collective efforts. Teachers can recognize students' contributions through certificates, ribbons, a popcorn party, pizza, or an extra recess. Celebrating service reinforces to students that in addition to benefiting others, service contributes to personal fulfillment and enjoyment.

## CONCLUSION

Effective service-learning projects involve identifying an appropriate need or problem, choosing a suitable project, integrating the service with academic skills, guiding students in reflection, and celebrating service. While planning service-learning projects takes time and energy, teachers' efforts are rewarded in knowing that they are making a difference for their communities and their students. Students note that "It's fun helping other people" and that "I can enjoy learning more than I think." For teachers who value students' motivation to learn as well as their empowerment and commitment to social change, community service-learning is well worth the effort.

## CURRICULUM RESOURCES ON COMMUNITY SERVICE-LEARNING

Cairn, R. W., & Coble, T. (1993). *Learning by Giving: The K-8 Service Learning Curriculum Guide*. Roseville, MN: National Youth Leadership Council*

Cairn, R. W., & Kielsmeier, J. C. (Eds.). (1991). *Growing Hope: A Sourcebook on Integrating Youth Service into the School Curriculum*. Roseville, MN: National Youth Leadership Council.*

Lewis, B. A. (1991). *The Kid's Guide to Social Action*. Minneapolis, MN: Free Spirit Publishing.

Maryland Student Service Alliance. (1992). *The Courage to Care, The Strength to Serve*. Draft instructional framework in service-learning for elementary schools and middle schools. Baltimore: Author. Available from Maryland Student Service Alliance, 200 West Baltimore Street, Baltimore, MD 21201.

Novelli, J., & Chayet, B. (1991). *The Kids Care Book: 50 Class Projects that Help Kids Help Others*. NY: Scholastic Professional Books.

Springfield Public Schools. (1991). *Whole Learning through Service: A Guide for Integrating Service into the Curriculum Kindergarten through Eighth Grade*. Springfield: Author. Available from the Community Service Learning Center, 258 Washington Blvd. Springfield, MA 01108.

* The National Youth Leadership Council is a national clearinghouse for service-learning in K-12 schooling. You can contact them at: 1910 West Country Road B, St. Paul, MN 55113 or telephone: 612-631-3672.

## REFERENCES

Boyer, E. (1983). *High School: A Report on Secondary Education in America*. NY: Harper & Row.

Cairn, R. W., & Kielsmeier, J. C. (Eds.). (1991). *Growing Hope: A Sourcebook on Integrating Youth Service into the School Curriculum*. Roseville, MN: National Youth Leadership Council.

Carnegie Council on Adolescent Development. (1989). *Turning Points: Preparing American Youth for the 21st Century*. Washington, DC: Carnegie Corporation of New York.

Commission on National and Community Service (1993). "Commission Awards 2nd Round of Grants." *Serve! America: The Newsletter of the Commission on National and Community Service*, 2(4), 8.

Conrad, D., & Hedin, D. (1991). "School-Based Community Service: What We Know from Research and Theory." *Phi Delta Kappan*, 72(10), 754-757.

Goodlad, J. (1984). *A Place Called School*. NY: McGraw-Hill.

Harrison, C. (1986). *Student Service: The New Carnegie Unit*. Lawrenceville: Princeton Univ. Press.

Wade, R. C. (1993). "Social Action: Expanding the Role of Citizenship in the Social Studies Curriculum." *Inquiry in Social Studies: Curriculum, Research and Instruction*, 29(1), 2-18.

Rahima C. Wade is an Assistant Professor of Elementary Social Studies at the University of Iowa, Iowa City. Dr. Wade is also the Coordinator of a Fund for the Improvement of Post-Secondary Education sponsored community service-learning grant. The grant involves preservice training in service-learning in collaboration with the Iowa Department of Education funded Iowa City Community School District Service-Learning Program. [1994 note]

# 64

# Citizenship Education in the Early Grades: A Plan for Action

**Thomas M. McGowan**
**Charles M. Godwin**

America faces many challenges in the final decades of the twentieth century. To resolve the dilemmas that will test the nation, it must receive a healthy infusion of informed citizens from its formative generations. Horace Mann advised more than one hundred years ago that individuals must serve apprenticeships in childhood to be fully prepared for the rigors of self-government (in Massialas 1969, 2). Today's young people must acquire values, skills, and knowledge inherent in the term citizenship. In this view of citizenship education, students learn to make decisions that positively affect the social welfare. In becoming social decision makers, young people gain knowledge about their country's heritage and develop faith in its many strengths. They also learn to test common assumptions and to correct their society's weaknesses. Citizenship training for America's future decision makers, then, should include strong measures of decision making, socialization, and prudence.

Schools provide American children with much of their preparation for effective citizenship. In the school curriculum, social studies commands the center of an interdisciplinary effort to help children learn to make informed social judgments. National Council for the Social Studies (NCSS) bases recent curricular reform efforts on the premise that social studies has a "specific mandate" for citizenship education (NCSS 1984, 250). Thus, a major challenge for social studies teachers is the transmission to young people of the tools for good citizenship.

Yet research suggests that the social studies community neglects an essential audience in its citizenship education efforts—children in the primary grades. National surveys of the state of the art of social studies, such as the National Science Foundation and Project SPAN studies conducted in the late-1970s, indicate that primary teachers spend little class time for activities that foster qualities that the good citizen demonstrates. The few social studies lessons that primary teachers do provide, moreover, typically consist of teacher-dominated paper-and-pencil activities. Social studies instruction in the primary grades rarely engages young children or affords them opportunities to participate in lively, interactive experiences (Morrissett 1982, 78).

## TIME FOR A PRODUCTIVE CITIZENSHIP PROGRAM

This dearth of positive citizenship experiences in early childhood is of particular concern because the primary years seem an ideal time to nurture the basic skills and values so important for productive social decision making. In these first years of school children can readily develop communication skills, rudimentary skills of critical analysis, and citizenship values, such as responsibility and respect for the individual. A major feature of a productive citizenship program for early childhood should be an activist, child-centered learning environment that allows children to investigate and generate ideas rather than simply to listen and then regurgitate information. Dewey insisted that "active participation and involvement" in classroom life foster the responsibility, cooperation, and sense of belonging so essential to citizenship (1916). The NCSS Early Childhood Advisory Board, moreover, encouraged primary school teachers to transform classrooms into laboratories in which children can experience the social decision-making process. Board members asserted that an open, participatory school environment is essential for the real world learning that is necessary for citizenship preparation (NCSS 1983).

Several major schools of learning theory support these calls for instructional strategies that permit young children to learn by doing. Piaget's work in charting the cognitive development of children indicated that children must generate their own knowledge through involvement in active learning experiences. Piaget stated that mastering such basic cognitions as those essential for citizenship is never the result of a "mere impression" made upon the child, but is always due to "active assimilation" on the child's part (Piaget 1971, 107-108). Bruner maintained that learning depends on a child's exploring a number of alternatives. Ideally, the teacher's function is to facilitate children's active exploration of a topic rather than to transmit content to students (Bruner 1964, 309). Rogers focused his model for learning on educational experiences designed to change long-term learner behavior, such as citizenship training. He termed these experiences "significant learning" and theorized that they require personal involvement and self-initiation to achieve lasting results (Rogers 1967, 38). In his "Social Learning Theory," Bandura viewed modeling as a more efficient learning mode than doing. At the same time, he emphasized involvement in and self-direction of the modeling process as factors that influence the degree of learning (Bandura 1977, 24-25). In short, the learning theorists say: Young children cannot absorb citizenship; these qualities must be generated by the children themselves.

A second feature of an effective citizenship program for primary children is the selection of content that is relatively familiar for students. Theorists have cautioned so frequently against basing instruction on subject matter alien to young children that it seems almost a teaching truism to avoid such practice. At the same time, however, researchers have warned that choosing material with which children are totally familiar can restrict their learning. Piaget (1967, 8), for example, noted that the ability to incorporate new knowledge into existing schema greatly facilitates learning; yet he also suggested that children cannot generate new mental structures without exposure to experiences that challenge and sometimes disturb them (103).

These conclusions about appropriate content have implications for designers of primary-level citizenship preparation programs. Youngsters should encounter recognizable situations; at the same time, they should not be totally comfortable in these situations (Jackson et al. 1976). In other words, young children should experience citizenship lessons set in familiar environments-family, classroom, school, neighborhood, playground, and community. These lessons, however, should include elements that lie at the edge of children's cognizance, such as a new twist to a social exchange or an interpersonal conflict or the introduction of people with "different" backgrounds into the familiar setting.

More specifically, norms inherent in the term citizenship are most productively fostered in young children through relatively familiar content. Walsh advises that early childhood is the prime time for nurturing a system of values, attitudes, and feelings that is essential for the practice of good citizenship (Walsh 1980). Teachers must remember, however, that moral growth is not achieved by imprinting rules and shaping children's behavior. Rather, moral development demands the transformation of cognitive structures through positive interaction with a social environment. Logically, constructive interaction cannot occur unless the child has at least a working knowledge of that environment. Young children can best develop such citizenship values as social responsibility, positive social interaction, equal opportunity, lawful behavior, and individual worth through encounters with challenging situations in familiar environments.

An effective citizenship education program for the primary grades should demonstrate a third major feature—a strong skills component. The NCSS Early Childhood Advisory Board insisted that young children develop skills that enhance their ability to learn, make social judgments, and contribute productively to American society in the future. The board cited research skills (collecting and organizing data from a range of sources—photos, interviews, graphs, television, and real-life settings, as well as print materials), map and globe skills (using cardinal directions, understanding basic map/globe terminology), literacy skills, interpersonal skills (seeing various points of view, resolving conflict), and problem-solving skills (considering alternatives and examining consequences) as citizenship competencies that should be included in primary grade citizenship programs (NCSS). Techniques of information processing also deserve particular emphasis in any effort to promote good citizenship in the first years of schooling. Process skills appropriate for young children include classification, seriation, conservation, time-order sequencing, comparing, hypothesizing, drawing conclusions, and making inferences. Cognitively, the primary grades are a transitional time in which most children progress from preoperational to operational forms of thinking (Piaget 1963). To facilitate this process, good teachers provide children with opportunities to apply their developing logic systems to tasks of increasing range and complexity (Jackson et al.).

The final feature that citizenship preparation programs for youngsters should include is the development of thinking skills. Citizenship efforts in the primary years must foster a positive attitude toward learning. These programs can engender a spirit of inquiry in students and encourage them to discover their world. Primary social studies teachers ought to engage students in experiences that encourage their natural curiosity, so that students become active, involved investigators and have opportunities to make decisions about what they have discovered. A citizen, after all, is a lifelong learner who searches for information before making appropriate judgments about the future of his/ her society. The good citizen is an informed citizen. Effective citizenship preparation programs in the primary years encourage children to take their first strides toward a lifetime of knowing about the world around them.

Granted that citizenship training programs should allow children to model qualities that the good citizen demonstrates. Granted also that these programs ought to feature the four characteristics just described. Still, some questions rear their ugly heads at this point. How can such a program be implemented in primary classrooms? What is the best form this approach to citizenship preparation can take? What experiences are appropriate for this type of activist citizenship program for young children?

## GUIDE TO CITIZENSHIP EDUCATION

These questions can be answered by examining a recently developed citizenship education guide, *Teaching About Elections in Indiana* (Engelland et al.). This set of activities, published jointly by the Indiana Department of Education and the Governor's Task Force for Citizenship Education, includes a strong primary level component. The guide was a response to Indiana statutes requiring that schools offer five days of basic training for the state's future voters prior to every general election. The authors of the guide went beyond this mandate, however, and formulated a program of activities offering students the qualities of good citizenship in a more general sense.

The guide contains ten lessons for the primary years. These activities are organized in two mini-units (five lessons for kindergarten and grade one; five for grades two and three). The activities in each of these units are sequentially ordered and share a common scope and theme. They also incorporate subject matter that is relatively familiar for youngsters. For these lessons, the authors selected teaching methods that research suggests are appropriate for young children and also allow students to model citizenship qualities (such as dramatic play, discussion, small group work, games, oral presentation, and role play). These teaching practices involve students and promote interaction. Children solve problems and make decisions in these lessons. Through these methodologies, youngsters become active participants in the citizenship learning process.

The lessons for kindergarten and grade one feature the theme "Freedom and Responsibility." The students learn that Americans are entitled to many rights; with these rights, however, come attendant responsibilities. The activities focus on familiar settings for students—school and family. The lessons build several citizenship skills appropriate for early primary students (listening, oral language, creativity, and positive social interaction). Each activity lasts approximately thirty to forty minutes.

*Teaching About Elections in Indiana* also includes five lessons for grades two and three. These activities share the theme "Rules and the Common Good." Students learn that their society adopted rules to standardize certain aspects of measurement and human behavior. Children learn, moreover, that these standards are not whimsical but provide for the welfare and safety of all citizens. The lessons focus on neighborhood and community settings—familiar ones for late primary students. The experiences build a number of competencies appropriate for this age level such as oral/written language, higher-level thinking (particularly classification and basic problem solving), map and globe skills, and the skills of social interaction. Each lesson lasts approximately one hour.

*Teaching About Elections in Indiana* exemplifies a carefully conceived, field-tested program for citizenship education in the primary grades. The effort necessary to develop such a program, however, might daunt even the most motivated primary teacher. Yet the interested teacher need not neglect citizenship training because of limited time. Social studies activities that offer students opportunities to model the qualities of good citizenship in the classroom abound in periodicals (including *The Social Studies, Learning, Instructor*, and *Social Education*), idea books, basic texts, and teaching guides. These lesson ideas can be integrated individually into a regular social studies curriculum or combined to create more lengthy and meaningful citizenship experiences for young children.

People Puzzles is one example of a social studies activity for primary children with definite citizenship applications. The teacher first finds large pictures of people serving as helpers in school and community settings (police personnel, janitors, technicians, etc.). These pictures are mounted on oaktag, laminated, and cut into jigsaw puzzles (the size and shape of puzzle pieces will depend on the abilities of students). Students work in groups of

---

**Name:** What's Mine and What's Yours?
**Grade Level:** Early primary (kindergarten and grade 1)
**Description of Activity:** This lesson acquaints young children with property rights. Through show and tell, discussion, and an art project, children learn the essentials of ownership and reasons why the rights/responsibilities of ownership deserve their respect.
**Learning Objectives:** As a result of this lesson, students will be able to:

■ Name an item(s) that they own.
■ List several rights of ownership that they can exercise.
■ Differentiate between items that they do and do not own.
■ State reasons why property rights of others should not be violated.

**Learning Activities:** The lesson proceeds as follows:

1. In a class meeting, students share something special that they have brought from home and give reasons why this item is so special.
2. The teacher explains to students that they own these special things and discusses the rights of ownership with them (the right to transport the item, the right to use it whenever appropriate, etc.). The teacher also discusses the responsibilities of ownership with students (the need to protect the item, the need to maintain it properly, etc.). Students offer personal illustrations of how each right and responsibility applies to them.
3. Students offer examples of items that they own and items that they can use, but do not truly own. The teacher helps students differentiate between things they own and things they may use (Can you take it home? Must you take care of it?).
4. Students role play situations showing what might happen if they try to exercise property rights over things they do not truly own.
5. Students draw four items that are their own special property.
6. Students present their drawings to the class and state reasons why these things are their property.

**Evaluation:** The success of this activity can best be measured by examining the appropriateness of items included on student drawings. Observation of class discussions during the activity and student behavior in the long term (has student behavior regarding personal property and the property of others changed?) will also provide data for evaluation.

---

two or three children to assemble the puzzles. The groups then identify their helpers, share them with the other groups, and the entire class discusses the contributions the helpers make to school and community life.

People Puzzles is a fairly simple, hands-on experience for early primary children. Yet it promotes many aspects of good citizenship in youngsters, including introducing the concept of service work and different service occupations and providing opportunities for problem solving as students devise strategies for assembling their puzzles. Above all, this activity encourages positive interaction with others by reinforcing notions of sharing and working together to achieve a goal.

The Holiday Game is another activity that adds a citizenship dimension to primary social studies. In this game, children first discuss the major holidays celebrated throughout the year, then work in small groups to make

---

## ACTIVITY TWO

**Name:** What Would Happen If...?

**Grade Level:** Late primary (grades 2 and 3)

**Learning Objectives:** As a result of this lesson, students will be able to:

■ Demonstrate understanding that laws are necessary for public safety.

■ List a number of laws that contribute to community peace and order.

■ State social consequences if specific laws did not exist.

■ Construct a scenario for a society without a legal system.

**Learning Activities:** The lesson consists of the following activities:

1. The teacher introduces the idea that laws exist to protect public safety and offers examples of statutes intended to promote order and safeguard citizens. Students then brainstorm other similar laws; the teacher lists these examples on the chalkboard.

2. The teacher selects one law from the students' list and guides a discussion of ways in which this law protects the public. Students then describe what might happen if this law did not exist.

3. Working individually, children select a law from the list on the board and write scenarios describing what would happen if the law were eliminated. Students would illustrate their stories with a picture collage (draw a basic outline sketch of the consequences, then add photos from newspapers and magazines to complete the picture).

4. Students share their scenarios and pictures and discuss the many negative consequences that would occur if laws did not exist. To extend the discussion, students can categorize types of dangers that would befall citizens and/or consider life in a society without laws.

**Evaluation:** The stories and picture collages provide useful assessment data. Observation of class discussions, particularly the final session, can also yield data to determine how effectively the four objectives were met.

---

construction paper symbols for each of these major holidays. With clothespins the teacher hangs the symbols onto a long cord strung across the classroom in random order or tapes them to the chalkboard. Students try to identify each holiday symbol and then rearrange the symbols in chronological order. The Holiday Game emphasizes many qualities inherent in good citizenship. Children learn about national holidays and practice time-order sequencing. Perhaps most important, they work cooperatively in small groups to complete a task.

In this article, we have argued that conveying the tools for social decision making to children seems a major challenge facing teachers in the next twenty years. Research indicates, however, that current social studies efforts neglect a promising target for citizenship training: students in the primary grades. If primary teachers are to help meet the citizenship challenge, they must transform social studies in a quantitative and a qualitative sense. Young children need more opportunities to gain the knowledge, practice the rudimentary skills, and formulate the basic values inherent in good citizenship. Primary youngsters also need different types of experiences from those they have now. Primary students need social studies programs that fea-

ture active learning experiences with relatively familiar content. Children should practice skills basic to the exercise of good citizenship. They need social studies activities that nurture their native curiosity and further a love of learning. By adopting such citizenship programs, primary teachers will contribute mightily to efforts to give America the generation of informed social decision makers so necessary as the twenty-first century approaches.

## REFERENCES

Bandura, A. 1977. *Social Learning Theory*. Englewood Cliffs, NJ: Prentice-Hall.

Bruner, J. 1964. "Some Theorems on Instruction Illustrated with Reference to Mathematics." In *Theories of Learning and Instructions Part 1*, The Sixty-third Yearbook of the National Society for The Study of Education. Edited by E. R. Hilgard. Chicago: University of Chicago Press.

Dewey, J. 1916. *Democracy and Education*, New York: Macmillan.

Early Childhood Advisory Board, National Council for the Social Studies. 1983. *Publicizing and Encouraging Elementary Social Studies: Strategies for State and Local Councils*. Washington D.C.: NCSS.

Engelland, C. W., T. M McGowan, and V. Smith. 1984. *Teaching about Elections in Indiana: Kindergarten—Grade 12*. Indianapolis: Indiana Department of Education.

Jackson, N. E., A. H. Robinson. and P. Dale. 1976. *Cognitive Development of Young Children: A Report for Teachers*. Washington: National Institute of Education.

Massialas, B. G. 1969. *Education and the Political System*. Palo Alto, CA: Addison Wesley.

Morrissett, I., ed. 1982. *Social Studies in the 1980s: A Report of Project SPAN*. Alexandria, VA: Association for Supervision and Curriculum Development.

National Council for the Social Studies, 1984. "In Search of a Scope and Sequence for Social Studies." *Social Education*, 44: 250.

Piaget, J. 1971. *Psychology and Epistemology*. New York: Grossman.

———. 1967. *Six Psychological Studies*. New York: Random House.

———. 1963. *The Child's Conception of the World*. Patterson, NJ: Littlefield, Adams

Rogers, C. R. 1967. "The Facilitation of Significant Learning." In *Instruction: Some Contemporary Viewpoints*. Edited by L. Siegel. San Francisco: Chandler.

Walsh, H. M. 1980. *Introducing the Young Children to the Social World*. New York: Macmillan.

Thomas M. McGowan is an Assistant Professor in the Department of Elementary and Early Childhood Education at Indiana State University, Terre Haute. Charles M. Godwin is an Associate Professor in the Center for Curriculum and Instruction at the University of Nebraska, Lincoln. Both authors teach undergraduate and graduate courses in elementary education with elementary social studies as a major emphasis. [1986 note]

**Todd E. Jennings**
**Sam M. Crowell**
**Phyllis F. Fernlund**

One of the unique characteristics of the elementary school classroom is that a teacher and a group of children are together all day for an entire school year. This school experience can provide a long-term, supportive, cohesive environment, and much of social studies can become absorbed into the life of the classroom in a far more powerful way than in a 15-minute time block twice a week devoted to reading and memorizing content. Social studies concepts, values, and democratic principles can become part of the lived experience in the classroom. It is in this context that issues of social justice become significant. This article will examine the concept of social justice in relation to our classroom communities and provide a transformational view of social studies instruction.

## SOCIAL JUSTICE AND COMMUNITY

Classrooms which embody social justice are environments in which individuals and groups have equal access to resources and opportunities. They also entail the discovery and honoring of "voice." Social justice, as a goal of democratic societies, embraces the individual expression of ideas and perspectives as inalienable rights to be protected at all costs. This requires an atmosphere of respect and dialogue that is both encouraging and safeguarding.

When students create environments where they have opportunities to discover and explore questions rooted in their social experiences, they will inevitably raise issues concerning social inequities and problems. These concerns arise from their daily lives in the classroom, the school, and beyond; they may range from student concerns about safety, the environment, and the humane treatment of animals to how disputes are settled during recess, or who gets certain privileges at school. Sometimes these issues are in the form of questions; at other times they come as complaints, conflicts, and acts of resistance. How we deal with them significantly impacts the degree to which a classroom culture is inclusive, students are empowered, and social justice is modeled.

An active learning atmosphere where children participate, create, and interact provides a foundation for a social studies curriculum which embodies justice. Learners need to work with others, to try out new ideas on others,

to receive and give help, to talk about experiences, and to create something new with another. We also know that a child's voice is an important part of learning and builds a sense of efficacy. For example, children who are creating books with their own stories and illustrations have a "voice" in the classroom; they become authors in their own right to be read alongside those adult writers whose books fill the classroom and library. Since classroom participation is strongly associated with learning and achievement (Cohen, 1987), cooperative learning has a strong appeal. We know that learning does not occur in isolation. But even beyond this, social participation is rooted in early community experiences. Children learn how to participate in, benefit from, and contribute to civic and international communities based upon their early experiences in classroom communities.

## THE TRANSMISSION MODEL AND GROUP PROCESS

Although useful in certain instances, didactic, transmissional instruction does not lead to community, expressions of student voice, or opportunities to explore social injustice. Even social studies programs that are more active— incorporating units, simulations, and cooperative grouping, may utilize the transmissional model more than we realize. Transmission models of education focus on the teacher and texts transmitting other people's knowledge, often without sensitivity to the student's own knowledge building. In our rush to cover the district's curriculum guide or the state framework, learners may come to feel that their own views are unimportant or that their own growth is not what school is all about. Often a teacher may only emphasize students' deficits.

Research on the task group level (Cohen, 1987) reveals that low status children often do not participate in the group task. Low status children may be those designated by peers as unpopular, unattractive, of lower social class, or otherwise different from the dominant group's ideal. They may be English language learners, poor readers, or children of non-dominant races, ethnicities, or religious backgrounds. As a result, they are often silent or perhaps excluded, and the participation and achievement is allotted to high status children.

A self-fulfilling prophecy is created within the group context itself, and low status children are silenced and treated as if they have nothing to offer. The point is that status represents a kind of power that is given and taken away by social groups. Hence, cooperative learning groups may, if left unchecked, fail to be cooperative at all and may further reinforce social inequality.

## TRANSFORMATIONAL SOCIAL STUDIES

The transformational model as an alternative to the transmission model does not seek to simply have students mirror the thinking of teachers and texts. Rather, it asserts that the construction of knowledge (particularly knowledge of society and one's role in it) is related to self-concept and develops only within lived social experience. Concerns for social justice follow students' understanding of themselves in relation to societal structures and the groups who make up the society. Consequently, transformational social studies focuses on complex learning experiences and learning communities which impact students' self-understandings relative to society and provides students with opportunities to see themselves as individuals and group members who can make a difference.

How can teachers create transformational learning communities in which social justice is modeled and lived? The teacher must be able to analyze the social context of the classroom. A teacher, who can critically assess what is happening to low and high status children as a result of curricular and classroom management choices, is able to reverse the processes that work against equal access to resources, fair rules, participation opportunities for all, civility, cooperation, individual growth, and feelings of efficacy.

The transformational classroom focuses on the meaningful and purposeful application of learning, not on the demonstration of skills for their own sake. Erich Jantsch (1980) suggests that for too long we have concentrated on "knowing what" and "knowing how" without a deep understanding of ourselves in relation to others and to our environment. A transformational orientation asks: Can the teacher as well as the children in this learning community use their knowledge to create something that changes life for the better? Does the classroom community permit and encourage the teacher and the students to ask what kind of people they want to be and what kind of world they want to live in (Harste, 1994)? These questions form the basis of the transformational model.

## IDEAS FOR IMPLEMENTATION

Transformational classrooms and schools perceive themselves to be micro-reflections of society. They work to counteract the social inequities of contemporary society and to generate a more just and humane vision of the future. Some brief suggestions to consider when implementing a transformational model of education are:

■ *First, elementary social studies for social justice begins by understanding the classroom as a socio-political community:* helping children to understand social relationships, reciprocity, power, and community. As Dewey claimed, "We never educate directly, but indirectly by means of the environment" (1966, p. 19). In this process, teachers need to identify and counteract ways in which classrooms replicate the social injustices (e.g., racism, sexism, classism) present in the larger society. Children need opportunities to engage in social critique, addressing both their classroom and their society.

■ *Second, transformational social studies uses problem-solving situations in which dilemmas of justice are presented in their historical contexts.* For example, students might confront the question of fighting against tyranny versus maintaining loyalty to England that many early pre-American revolutionaries faced. They might consider the case of those who risked their lives to oppose either slavery or aggression against the Native Americans or the plights of workers—particularly child factory laborers—in the 19th and early 20th centuries. These stories not only bring social studies to life, but they allow students to come face-to-face with questions of justice and to engage in social critique. Transformational learning can occur as these situations are expanded to encourage reflection upon the students' own power relationships, lives, and the complex world in which they live.

■ *Third, dialogue and opportunities to interpret text help students to discover their own "voices" and may help them to relate their own experience to what is being studied.* It is important that students have the opportunity for subjective and emotional responses to learning. This is not to ignore rational analysis or conclusion, but rather to understand that social injustice requires a more multi-dimensional response. How can students feel deeply connected to others and show concern and compassion in light of oppression, if we pursue knowledge only with dispassionate objectivity? We may actually encourage students to become dispassionate observers of oppression, apathetic and impotent to redress injustice through an inadequate curriculum.

■ *Fourth, classroom cultures can recognize the importance of rights, respect, and responsibility, and encourage interaction whereby oppression and conflict are dealt with justly and constructively.* These values and constitutional principles provide a process by which pluralism and unity are in dynamic equilibrium. Using these principles in constructive dialogue promotes the value of diverse perspectives and allows for the critical examination of issues affecting us.

■ *Fifth, student involvement in social action projects models active citizenship and creates an experience of solidarity with others who have similar concerns.* Joining with other classes, schools, and community organizations suggests to students that they are a part of something larger than themselves and convinces them of the power inherent within cooperative efforts against injustice.

The social studies for social justice curriculum is multilayered and necessitates a transformational learning process. It is a curriculum of possibilities both for individuals, groups of students, and for the future of society. As Maxine Green so eloquently states, it is a vision of education that brings together the need for wide-awakeness with the hunger for community, the desire to know with the wish to understand, the desire to feel with the passion to see. We may have reached a moment in our history when teaching and learning, if they are to happen meaningfully, must happen on the verge... empowering the young to create and recreate a common world—and, in cherishing it, in renewing it, discover what it signifies to be free. (Green, 1990, p. 23)

## REFERENCES

Cohen, E. (1987). *Groupwork*. New York: Teachers College Press.

Dewey, J. (1966). *Democracy and Education*. New York: The Free Press.

Green, M. (1990). *The Dialectic of Freedom*. New York: Teachers College Press.

Harste, J. (1994). Whole language video conference. Symposium conducted at the School of Education, California State University, San Bernardino.

Jantsch, E. (1980). *The Self-Organizing Universe: Scientific and Human Implications of the Emerging Paradigm of Evolution*. Oxford: Pergamon Press.

Todd E. Jennings is an Assistant Professor in the Department of Elementary and Bilingual Education at California State University, San Bernadino. Dr. Jennings teaches courses in developmental psychology and research methods. His research focuses primarily on the psychological and educational foundations of human rights advocacy. Sam M. Crowell is an Associate Professor of Education at California State University, San Bernadino, and Executive Director of the Center for Research in Integrative Learning and Teaching. He teaches courses in educational foundations, social studies, and curriculum. Dr. Crowell also consults throughout the country on brain-based learning, school restructuring, integrative curricula, and experiential learning. His research involves translating the implications of new paradigms and new ways of thinking into educational practice. Phyllis F. Fernlund is the Chair of the Department of Secondary Education at California State University, San Bernadino. Her research and teaching focus is in social studies education and instructional technology. Dr. Fernlund is the coauthor of a text titled *Civics*, published by Addison-Wesley. [1994 note]

**Kathy Nalle**

My 3rd graders are seated in a circle, discussing classroom rules. "Can we bring our pets to school for sharing?" asks a bright-eyed girl who has a new kitten.

"Please, please!" begs one of the boys. "My dog loves kids. He'd let everyone pet him."

But on the other side of the circle another boy looks concerned. He shares details of his recent birthday party, where a friend had trouble breathing because of the family cat. The children are surprised to hear of such a thing. The circle becomes quiet. Then one boy speaks up: "I really like dogs and cats, but I'm allergic. I can't help it."

Discussing ideas, negotiating rules and solving problems is now an everyday occurrence in Room 15, where I teach a group of mostly middle-class students of widely diverse interests and abilities. But my classroom hasn't always been structured this way. I have spent much of my career as a manager, an arbitrator and, sometimes, a dictator. Then last year, after an eye-opening experience in a university/school collaboration project, I decided to try self-government in my classroom.

I gave my 8- and 9-year-olds responsibility for solving classroom problems. To my amazement, they accepted the challenge with enthusiasm.

An old coffee can at the front of the room functioned as a "community concerns box," and the notes children dropped into it raised all kinds of questions—everything from what to do when a bully attacked them on the playground to whether they could wear hats and chew gum in class. Meetings became the highlight of our day, and eventually we extended their length from 15 to 25 minutes.

Although last year went well, I worried that the democratic classroom idea would not be so easily repeated this year, especially considering the modifications I had decided to make. To the horror of many of my co-workers, I began this school year with only one classroom rule: Act at school the same way you are expected to act at home.

Last year's experience had taught me that voting sometimes caused the group to polarize and feelings to be hurt. This year, I insisted that all decisions would be made by consensus. Since consensus requires unanimous agreement, one dissatisfied group member would have veto power over any decision. I also had the right to contribute suggestions to our community box. As teacher, though, I did not have any special privileges during our decision-making meetings.

Anxiously, I watched and listened to see how this group would react to their new freedom.

The children quickly took the opportunity to speak their minds. While last year's group focused on individual rights and privileges, this group seemed more concerned with feelings. Our first task was to deal with students who were calling out answers and not allowing others to speak. Naturally, everyone agreed that taking turns was important and that people should be able to express their ideas. But how to enforce this principle? As problems and options were discussed, the word "embarrassed" kept surfacing. The children did not want to punish their fellow students in a way that might seem humiliating.

When the students decided that having to stay in from recess would be too embarrassing to deal with, I learned new respect for the feelings of my youngsters. Finally, we determined that the penalty for talking out of turn should be to write 10 times, "I will not shout out in class."

After a week of enforcing the rule, the class decided our mild penalty was so embarrassing that even it should be abolished. Maybe it was just luck, or maybe our discussion had deepened the children's sense of loyalty and concern for each other, but after we eliminated the punishment, the problem disappeared.

We dealt efficiently with most concerns until one day when the issue of bringing pets came up. The pet issue was complicated. Everyone liked pets, but some children had extreme allergies to dogs and cats. How could we all be happy and still respect the rights of others? Children with allergies could not give in, but children without allergies had a hard time appreciating the problem. We were deadlocked. It was obvious that we needed more information before we could decide. At this point we called in the school nurse for advice.

When the nurse arrived the next day, the children had an empty chair in our circle waiting for her. Along with information about allergies and their differing levels of severity she related personal stories about her own children and how allergies had affected them. My students listened wide-eyed, eagerly asking questions. What if the cat only stayed in the room five minutes? What if the allergic person didn't touch the animal? What if the people allergic to the animal left the room while the pet was there?

As the nurse patiently answered each question, the children began to understand that allergies are unique and require individual attention. Forcing a solution upon another person could prove both dangerous and "embarrassing" (that dreaded feeling!).

After the nurse left, we discussed how everyone could make a choice without infringing on the rights of others. Finally, we decided that furry pets could visit as long as they were enjoyed outdoors. People who were allergic could look out the window, and the rest of the class could get close and touch the animal. Of course, pets could be shared in warm weather only, but that was a compromise we could all live with.

Since making the rule, we have had several cats, a dog, a hamster and a guinea pig come to visit. Everyone is happy with the arrangement, and no one feels "embarrassed" to do what is best for his or her needs.

In early December, I asked my students to reflect upon our daily meetings. I asked them four questions: "Are our meetings a good idea? Have you learned anything from our meetings? Should we keep doing this every day? Is it fun to tell your ideas?"

I wanted to find out what they really thought, so I asked that they write their opinions down and turn them in anonymously. The children found the idea of responding this way so exciting that some took out their scissors and literally cut their names out of their papers. This made me worry—what were they writing?

I was relieved to discover that most of the children had extremely positive opinions. Many made a point of saying they had begun to see the benefits of discussing problems with others. Here are some of their responses:
- I think our meetings are a good idea because it helps me figure out problems or concerns that people have.
- Yes, because if we didn't have meetings we might have a fight over something.
- Yes, because if something's wrong, we can fix it.
- I have learned that you can't always have your way.
- I have learned that not everyone is the same.
- I have learned that everyone has a right to their own opinion.

Surprisingly, many of the children who are quietest during the rest of the day, or who have difficulty reading, writing and doing their math lessons, do not miss a chance to voice an opinion during class meetings, and some have emerged as real leaders! The children are beginning to understand that everyone has a special identity. One child expressed this when he wrote, "I think we can learn about classmates by their ideas."

I have also found the tone of our entire day changing. Whereas at the beginning of the school year the children always wanted to know how long they had to complete an assignment, now the question is never asked.

My students have learned that thinking and decision-making are fun, but that they take time. Good answers require reflection. Listening to other points of view can be a lengthy process. Our pace is more relaxed, less competitive. Parents have shared with me that their children have a feeling of self-confidence as well as a new awareness of the feelings and needs of others.

As we work together and share ideas, we all find more creative answers to problems. I, too, am more relaxed and find myself gaining new perspectives. I am not afraid to say, "I've never thought of that. You've shown me a new idea." When the children see that their teacher is willing and even excited to explore new avenues, they find it easier to express themselves.

"Can we work with a friend?" is a constant question. Without thinking, children often leave their seat to complete assignments with others. They are proud of their work, and, best of all, they listen attentively to one another.

I had always valued a quiet classroom. But now I know that meaningful learning—like democracy itself—is sometimes noisy! Our daily discussions have helped me to know my students better. I see worries, frustrations and concerns, as well as demonstrations of empathy and problem-solving, that I would have missed in a regular academic setting.

We still do have our differences of opinion, and not all problems are quickly solved, but everyone agrees that a problem is not solved until we've found an answer acceptable to all. We have learned that every problem has many sides and appears differently to different people.

Most importantly, we are learning to see beyond our differences and identify the feelings—like embarrassment—that we all share. As one little boy in last year's class told his mom, "This year I am learning to read between the lines."

## THE CLASS MEETING

To initiate a democratic classroom, begin by discussing the meaning of the word "community." Lead your students to the realization that each member of a community affects every other member. Then establish the fact that your classroom is a community and that every member has a right to express his or her concerns.

Display a decorated can or box labeled Community Concerns along with a pad of paper. Explain that anyone with a classroom-related problem can make a note and put it in the container. Concerns may be signed or submitted anonymously.

When the first concern appears, schedule a meeting. I have found it wise to set a time limit of about 15 minutes. Short meetings help students to stay focused and generate fresh ideas. Ask the students to arrange themselves in a circle so everyone can see and hear one another. Establish a few ground rules. For example:
- Take turns to speak.
- No idea is too silly to discuss.
- Everyone is equal. The teacher has no more power than anyone else.
- Listen while someone else is speaking.
- There will be no voting. Discussion will continue until a solution is agreed upon or the group decides to disagree and go on to another topic.

Ask a student to reach into the Community Concerns box, pull out a concern and read it aloud to the group. Then, just let the discussion flow. It is helpful for the teacher or a student to list the topics discussed and the pros and cons of each idea so that the discussion stays on track.

In the beginning, the teacher can run the meeting, making sure everyone has a chance to speak, clarifying questions and concerns and asking appropriate questions to encourage consensus. Eventually, the students can take turns running the meeting. In doing so, they will learn leadership skills and feel a sense of empowerment. At this time, the classroom teacher can "melt" into the group—allowing the true meaning of equality to become strikingly apparent.

Kathy Nalle is a third grade teacher at Worthington Estates Elementary School in Worthington, Ohio. She has been teaching for twenty-seven years. [1994 note]

**Lynn E. Nielsen**
**Judith M. Finkelstein**

## What do Gary Hart, Ollie North, and

Joe Biden have in common?

a) Demonstrated national heroism
b) Maintained unusual optimism
c) Possessed gifted leadership
d) Wined, dined and failed.

Decisions recently made by some of our high government officials have created a credibility crisis that has challenged our traditional national image. Throughout the sixties and seventies, we smarted from the embarrassment of defeat in Southeast Asia as well as in the Oval Office. The respectability of the Presidency, traditionally protected from the taint of dishonesty and moral compromise, was called into question.

Various reasons can be cited for the existence of this crisis of confidence, but a major factor has been our ability to closely monitor the private and public lives of our leaders. Items kept in the closet a generation ago are now matters of public record, thanks to technological developments in the mass media. Personal affairs previously protected by the ethics of responsible journalism are now broadcast nationwide, and the President's life is no exception.

With the often well-deserved image bashing of America's leaders came an uncomfortable fault line in the public creed. Though most of us recognize moral fallibility as a common human failing, we simultaneously demand an impossibly high standard of morality for public servants. We generally consider youthful experimentation as an expected, if not desirable, part of social development; but, a young lawyer's aspirations to a seat on the Supreme Court may go up in a puff of smoke if the puff involved marijuana.

Two questions of importance for educators emerge from this situation: To what extent are the schools encouraging ethical double standards and the formation of inaccurate images of political leaders? And How can teachers help children form realistic perceptions of leadership?

To what extent are schools encouraging ethical double standards and the formation of inaccurate images of political leaders?

In dealing with the question of double standards and images, three factors merit consideration: formal and informal teaching; instructional materials; and, school climate.

Though the majority of children receive formal citizenship education via the school curriculum, most of their values, attitudes, and skills related to citizenship derive from their collective informal experiences at school and at home. Expectations for leaders, which children develop early in life, have a lasting impact on their political behavior. Greenstein found that pervading idealistic childhood images of politicians had a profound and enduring effect on the behavior of voting adults.[1]

Siegel found that while the school is one of the most important contributors to the child's image of political authority, textbooks and trade-books are designed to increase pride in leaders and contain material which illuminates the President's positive characteristics only.[2] Similarly, in his assessment of textbook usage in elementary social studies, Polonsky noted that textbooks fail to include controversial or negative characteristics of a national leader, but instead emphasize the heroic side in order to avoid controversy.[3] Regarding the Nixon administration, for instance, one popular, recent American history text mentioned only the President's accomplishments in foreign policy and omitted Watergate and the President's resignation from office. When controversy is avoided in favor of the heroic deeds of leaders, unrealistic expectations may form in young minds.

The results of a study by Ehman and Gillespie underscored the fact that school climate has a significant impact on children's political attitudes.[4] The more participant-oriented the school, that is, the more students played major roles in decision making, the higher the student's political efficacy, trust, and social integration. Conversely, when schools did not encourage cooperative relations, student's attitudes toward leaders became more confrontational and cynical.

Three factors, then, expedite and transmit idealistic and unrealistic images of political authority figures: the child's early informal political experiences in and out of school, textbooks and trade-book materials, and the nature of the school climate.

*How can educators help young learners form realistic perceptions of leadership?*

First, educators need to accept the responsibility for teaching citizenship processes. Given that the teaching of these processes is the generally accepted goal of social studies, it is important to note that values and moral education play an important role in citizenship education. Part of this relates to distinguishing between personal and general values. Whereas personal values vary widely, in a democratic society they are to be tempered by general values that constitute a foundation and framework for democratic social interaction. General values that contribute to our social framework include freedom, justice, equity, responsibility, and privacy. These are frequently cited in the nation's founding documents, and throughout the past two-hundred years, they have been rather consistently defended by the courts.

Second, the learning environment should be restructured to facilitate citizenship participation as an approach to helping our students form realistic perceptions of leadership. Beyond acquisition of knowledge, the school's citizenship program needs to include opportunities to practice citizenship behavior.

Schools that help children acquire knowledge-based citizenship behavior would likely have these characteristics: (a) the student is a participant who plays a major role in decisions; (b) content is based on interesting topics that stimulate thinking, problem solving, and decision making; (c) the teacher is a guide of human interaction with ends clearly in mind, although these are allowed to surface as a result of children's interaction; (d) the curriculum is organized into large time blocks, allowing integration of subjects to occur; (e) students are allowed to work in groups or individually according to the dictates of the situation; (f) cooperative projects with different grade levels are encouraged so children can benefit from working with others at various age levels; (g) basic classroom rules are set early in the year cooperatively by students and teachers and are consistent throughout the school; (h) a developmentally appropriate process (e.g., class meeting, etc.) for dealing with problems in the classroom is established at the beginning of the school year and is used consistently throughout the school; and (i) administrators view teachers as team partners sharing responsibility for creating an optimal school environment for learning.

With these assumptions in place, a school can embark on a citizenship process that engages the following processes of the Democratic Classroom Interaction Model.

## COMMUNICATION

Communication is the base of the citizenship process model. For the teacher, this embodies initiating a problem-solving setting by laying out (with the group's help) a short and positively worded set of rules for interaction. Responsibility for adherence to the rules is a joint undertaking of teacher and students. Infractions are handled in a class meeting. The teacher encourages shared decision making centering on curricular topics carefully chosen by the teaching and administrative team.

Students communicate their perceptions of the problem, thereby developing a sense of ownership of the work, and then proceed to describe possible procedures for solving the problem.

The instructional setting is exactingly planned for optimal interaction.

## PARTICIPATION

In conjunction with others on the instructional team, the teacher, selects units of instruction; serves as discussion leader and guide; and, monitors student participation, to help insure that they remain involved.

Students agree on a plan of action, suggest and select appropriate resources, and decide on the contribution(s) to be made.

## INTERACTION

The teacher mediates and facilitates, perhaps also serving as scribe. It is the teacher who focuses attention on particular aspects of the situation, calling for modification, revision, reinforcement, additional resources, and the like. As teachers, we occasionally may need to distance ourselves so children can make decisions independently.

Perhaps the more effective instructional setting for this phase is small-group pods in an area large enough for separate interactions, but close enough for total group discussions, as needed.

## APPLICATION

The teacher, participating with each group, refocuses attention on the main goal, facilitates process, and above all, listens.

Students share their work with a larger audience through a variety of methods. Modifications of the original plan are made as needed.

The instructional setting is oriented toward independent work at desks or tables, small group work, and large group work (or possibly a combination of all three).

## REFLECTION

Throughout the process, the teacher has been recording students' ability to make appropriate decisions. Now diagnoses are made on how well students have learned effective citizenship skills. Group evaluation also is done at this time.

Students evaluate communication, participation, interaction, and application of knowledge and skills, both as individuals and group members. Strengths and areas needing improvement are identified.

Small, task-oriented groupings, arrangements for large-group discussions, and space for individual work are appropriate for the instructional setting at this point.

## CLASSROOM ACTIVITIES

These activities illustrate how the five processes of the Democratic Classroom Interaction Model can be applied.

*Primary-Grade Activity: A Room Constitution*

*Communication.* At the end of the school year, the children were reflecting on what they had liked and how things could be made even better. They decided that they especially liked the set of room rules they had formulated, and they felt children coming into the room in the fall should know how well these rules worked. Consequently, they decided to list and post them in the room.

*Participation.* Some children, however, felt that the new class might resent their leaving just a set of rules. Others thought that they didn't know what kinds of rules would be needed by the new class. As the discussion developed, the teacher introduced the idea of a set of rules written for everyone in our nation . . . the Constitution.

*Interaction.* The children decided to model their rules on the Constitution. Copies of the document were provided and the meaning of each article and the Preamble were explained. The children rewrote it in terms of functioning in that grade at school. Discussions clarified representatives of the branches of government, their responsibilities, the meaning of the Preamble, etc. The children decided that boys and girls in the new class-were their "posterity."

*Application.* Children from the grade below were invited to a reading of the "Constitution." These children were asked if they thought they could live by it. The children of the new class believed they could, but added that they couldn't be sure until they tried the rules in the fall.

*Reflection.* In the fall, the new class ratified the constitution, and used it to derive their set of room rules. Pictures were made that illustrated the constitution, and in addition, the children wrote notes to the drafters. The constitution and classroom rules were used throughout the following year.

*Upper-Grade Activity: Folk Tales Then and Now*
*Communication.* The teacher began by reading a familiar folk tale to the class, and then asked students to name as many different folk tales as they could remember. They listed several such as *Hansel and Gretel, Cinderella,* and *Beauty and the Beast.* Students were then asked to classify the folk tales according to similarities and differences (many had heroes, some had villains, most contained a moral, etc.). Students were encouraged to write their own "folk tales" using a contemporary political setting, with characters recognizable to everyone, that would lend themselves to character analysis.

*Interaction.* Students shared their tales with the class and discussed how they might share their work with a larger audience. They decided to publish a booklet entitled *A Political Primer.* This would contain all the restructured folk tales authored by class members, as well as blank pages so younger children could make illustrations to accompany each story.

*Application.* The booklet was delivered to classrooms of young children in the school. Time was provided for authors to share their stories and help the children illustrate the texts.

*Reflection.* The teacher lead a discussion on the differences between folk tale characters and the actual persons who play important roles in society and government. Students observed that actual persons are multi-dimensional in their personal makeup, combining a mix of both positive and negative attributes. The lesson concluded with students comparing their own strengths and weaknesses to those of the fictional characters that they created.

## SUMMARY

A credibility crisis in leadership has threatened our national image and spotlighted tatters in the ethical fabric of the land. Despite inconclusive evidence, several aspects of school are suspect as contributors to this crisis, among which are textbooks representing unrealistic moral standards for leaders, and a school climate placing disproportionately high decision-making power in the hands of administrators and teachers to the exclusion of students.

A positive step that can be taken by educators is to structure the school to encourage and reward communication, participation, interaction, application, and reflection. As a result, realistic models of leadership will be observed and applied. Even though this solution will not erase the past, nor most likely provide immediate and dramatic results, it will engender an environment in which decision-making skills will grow and democratic values will flourish.

## NOTES

[1] Greenstein, F. 1. "The Benevolent Leader: Children's Images of Political Authority," *American Political Science Review*, 54, 1960, 934-943.

[2] Sigel, R. S. "An Explanation into Some Aspects of Political Socialization: School Children's Reaction to the Death of a President." In N. Adler and C. Harrington (Eds.), *The Learning of Political Behavior*, Glenview, Florida: Scott Foresman, 1970, 21-37.

[3] Palonsky, S. B. "Political Socialization in Elementary Schools," *Elementary School Journal*, 87, 1987, 493-503.

[4] Ehman, L. H., and G. A. Gillespie. *The School as a Political System.* Final Report of the National Institution of Education, Project No. 3-3067, September 1975.

## REFERENCES

Atwood, V. A. (Ed.) *Elementary School Social Studies: Research as a Guide to Practice*, NCSS Bulletin No. 79, 1986.

Barr, R. D., J. L. Barth, and S. S. Shermis. *Defining the Social Studies*, NCSS Bulletin 51, 1977.

Bragaw, D. H., and H. M. Hartoonian. "Social Studies: The Study of People in Society." In R. Brandt (Ed.), *Content of the Curriculum*, 1988 ASCD Yearbook, 9-30.

Cherryholmes, C. H. "Social Knowledge and Citizenship Education," *Curriculum Inquiry*, 10, 1980, 115-141.

Clements, M. "Dilemmas of the Holmes Report," *Social Education*, 51, 1987, 509-512.

Easton, D., and J. Dennis. *Children in the Political System.* New York: McGraw-Hill, 1969.

Ehman, L. H. "The American School in the Political Socialization Process," *Review of Educational Research*, 50, 1980, 99-119.

Eisner, Elliot W. *The Educational Imagination.* New York: Macmillan Publishing Co., Inc., 1979.

Hepburn, M. A. (Ed.). *Democratic Education in Schools and Classrooms*, NCSS Bulletin 70, 1983.

Hess, R. D., and J. V. Torney. *The Development of Political Attitudes in Children*. Garden City, New York: Doubleday, 1969.

Jacobson, M. G., and S. B. Palonsky. "Effects of a Law-related Education Program," *Elementary School Journal*, 82, 1981, 49-57.

Lyons, S. R. "The Political Socialization of Ghetto Children: Efficacy and Cynicism," *Journal of Politics*, 32, 1970, 288-304.

Marzano, Robert J., Ronald S. Brandt, Carolyn Sue Hughes, Beau Fly Jones, Barbara Z. Presseisen, Stuart C. Rankin, and Charles Suhor. *Dimensions of Thinking: A Framework for Curriculum and Instruction*. ASCD, 1988.

Morrissett, I. (Ed.) *Social Studies in the 1980s: A Report of Project SPAN*. Alexandria, Virginia: ASCD, 1982.

Parker, W., and J. Jarolimek. *Citizenship and the Critical Role of the Social Studies*. NCSS Bulletin 72, 1984.

Patrick, J. J. "Political Socialization and Political Education in Schools." In S. A. Renshon (Ed.), *Handbook of Political Socialization: Theory and Research*. New York: Free Press, 1977, 190-222.

Rosenzweig, L. W. (Ed.). *Developmental Perspectives on the Social Studies*. NCSS Bulletin 66, 1982.

Torney, J. V. "Contemporary Political Socialization in Elementary Schools and Beyond," *The High School Journal*, November 1970, 153-163.

Lynn E. Nielsen teaches third grade at the Malcolm Price Laboratory School of the University of Northern Iowa, Cedar Falls. Author of various publications on Iowa history and primary social studies, Dr. Nielsen received a doctoral degree from the University of Iowa. Judith M. Finkelstein is a first grade teacher at the Malcolm Price Laboratory School. Ms. Finkelstein is the author of a variety of publications on social studies for young learners. [1988 note]

# Why Ethics in Citizenship Education?

**Walter C. Parker**

**eth•ics:** 1. the discipline dealing with what is good and bad or right and wrong or with moral duty or obligation, e.g., A good physician studies not only anatomy, but ethics. 2. A group of moral principles or set of values, e.g., Puritan ethics.

— *Webster's Third International*

This definition points to the two faces of ethics. One is the deliberate examination of values-what they are, how they arise and shape behavior, and what happens when they conflict; the other is devotion to particular values. We will look at both in the course of answering the title's question, and we will do so with the young learner in mind. But first it should be helpful to understand that, for better or worse, elementary schools cannot help but teach values, whether they want to or not.

A ten-year-old named Michael wondered what to do with his life. Seeking advice, he wrote to Buckminster Fuller. An architect, philosopher, cartographer, poet, and inventor, "Bucky" had done much of his thinking outside the mainstream of these fields. Early in his life he had dedicated himself intentionally to serving humanity in the way that an ordinary person might: to seeing and doing what was needed, which if not seen and done would put humanity and its Spaceship Earth at risk. Michael asked about the difference between thinking and doing. Bucky's response was straightforward:

> "Thank you very much for your recent letter . . . the things to do are: the things that need doing; that you see need to be done, and that no one else sees need to be done."

Bucky then tells Michael that doing what he sees is needed will help to bring out his own, unique brilliance — the brilliance that easily gets buried beneath a mass of social conditioning. And, he encourages Michael to "try making experiments of anything you conceive and are intensely interested in. Don't be disappointed," he advises, "if something doesn't work. That is what you want to know—the truth about everything. . . "

The letter's closing is heart-to-heart and captures well Bucky's character:

> "You have what is most important in life—initiative. Because of it, you wrote to me. I am answering to best of my capability. You will find the world responding to your earnest initiative."[1]

Reprinted from *Social Studies and the Young Learner*, September/October 1988, Volume 1, Number 1. Copyright 1988 by National Council for the Social Studies

Bucky died in 1983 at the age of 87. He was an oddity among scientists of his day because he realized that knowing, doing, and valuing are one thing, not three. Bucky learned this in the school of hard knocks. He was thirty-two years old when, standing on the shore of Lake Michigan, disgusted with the way he was using his life and contemplating suicide, he decided that life would be worth living from that moment on if he devoted his heart and mind to activities likely to benefit all humankind. He did just that, proceeding to create homes and modes of transport that were ecologically sane, a map of the earth without the usual distortion of land masses, geodesic domes, and ideas like Spaceship Earth and synergetics. All the while, he described himself as "just an ordinary individual" and "just a good, planetary citizen."

Values are beliefs concerning what is good and bad, right and wrong, worthy and worthless. Human activity is by nature steeped in values in all instances. Bucky's career makes this point obvious. Yet the point is no less true even when less obvious. The act of knowing, whether done formally by a great scientist or informally by a child spinning her first clay pot or a teacher gathering resources for a unit on explorers, proceeds not in a vacuum but in a human being. And this human being is a bundle of priorities, interests, and goals.

So the first answer to "Why Ethics in Citizenship Education?" is that for human beings there is no escape from values. Values are the ground we walk on. They are evident in the attitudes children bring to school from home, as they are in the choices teachers make on which content to emphasize and which behaviors and attitudes to nurture. Values are evident in the kind of citizens that principals and teachers try to help their students become. The first answer is straightforward: There is no human activity and therefore no citizenship education (or language arts or science education) independent of values. Those who argue that schools should not teach values are missing this point. Like it or not, schools do teach values and cannot do otherwise.

## THE IDEAL OF DEMOCRACY

There are two other answers to "Why Ethics?". One is political and is concerned with democracy; the other is social and is concerned with caring. The political answer looks to what a society values, and this society values the ideal of democracy, an ideal making unusually challenging demands of citizens. The ideal of democracy has four aims: first, to rest the rule-making and enforcement of society, as well as conflict resolution procedures, upon the genuine consent of the governed; second, it aims to make public policy formulation, whether on nuclear disarmament or a school closing, the shared task of everyone; third, to protect minorities from unfair incursion by the majority; and fourth, to accomplish change in an orderly enough fashion that democracy itself is not sacrificed to it.[2]

What particular demands are made of citizens in a society organized upon this ideal? In a word, virtue. Virtue can be defined, as Socrates did, as knowing and doing the common good. Thus, virtue is an inseparable blend of knowing, doing, and ethics. James Madison was very clear about this requirement, for even as he helped to frame the democratic plan by which this society would be organized, he fretted that the plan would collapse if the people upon whom it depended lacked virtue. "Is there no virtue among us?" he asked. "If there be not, no form of government can render us secure."[3]

Without virtue, the people at election time cannot discern between candidates who will be despots and those who will be democrats, nor can they supervise them once they have been elected or judge when they should be thrown from office. In short, unless citizens are virtuous, democracy cannot exist. The goal of citizenship education in a society with democracy as its guiding light is the cultivation of virtuous people.

Virtuous people not only know but do. They are informed about history and the social sciences, about what democracies are and how they operate; and, they act. They participate in the political judgments and activities that are democracy. Because their knowing and acting are focused on the common good, they are ethical. Just as knowledge is impotent without action, so also are knowledge and action empty without ethics. We learn this from positive examples, such as Bucky's work, and from negative examples as well. Consider the "inside traders" of Wall Street, or the dishonest car mechanic who knows plenty about automobiles. Or consider the Nazi physicians who mastered the knowledge necessary to perform experimental surgery on prisoners, but who lacked the ethics needed to judge that activity wrong.

The sort of ethics we are now considering incorporates both definitions given by Webster. The first concerned the study of values; the second, commitment to particular values. Not only are virtuous citizens students of values, they share particular values. What set of values do democrats, for all their differences, share and hold dear? Though the question is hotly debated, there is remarkable agreement on a few basic values comprising the democratic ideal. We might call them democratic values. They include devotion to the worth of each individual, to human freedom, to fairness (justice) and the rule of law, to equality, to tolerance of diversity, to self-expression and self-restraint, and to taking responsibility for the common good. For democracy's sake, teachers should try to nurture these values in their students.

But this is just one component of ethics in a democracy. Another has students not merely accept but study these values—analyze their meanings and applications. This is Webster's first definition. More cognitive than affective, this direct study of values encourages children to grapple with the value conflicts in their lives.[4] What is fair? When is it not fair? If a majority votes to go to recess row by row, is that fair to the row furthest from the door? Should enemies be treated the same as friends and family? Is it right to change the rules of a playground game or class meeting after it has begun? Should the Pilgrims have left the Atlantic Coast when they discovered that it was already settled by native groups?

These are all civic problems on which good democrats (even six-year-old democrats) might disagree vehemently. Such disagreement is the basic material of public policy decision making—present, past, and future. For Socrates, this cognitive component of ethics was the most important; with the knowledge gleaned from it students would themselves freely adopt and live according to democratic values.[5]

So, ethics must be incorporated into citizenship education because democracy depends on it. Such an education "is not a boon conferred by democracy, but a condition of its survival and of its being that which it undertakes to be."[6] Democracy depends on everyone for what in other societies is required of only a few. Authoritarian rule is in many respects easier, for citizens have only to obey policy, not make it and judge it. If virtue is democracy's expectation of adults, then adults are foolish not to begin its cultivation early in children's lives.

## CARING AND COMMUNITY

A third answer to the "Why Ethics?" question is more social than political. It is concerned less with reasoning on what is fair and right than with caring—the everyday stuff of human relationships. This third answer is that ethics must be included in citizenship education because there is a crucial realm of citizenship that exists intermediate between individuals and the state or nation. It is the realm of human relating that is relatively unconcerned with general principles and values analysis, but deeply concerned with people whom we know, interact with and perhaps care for.

Here the ethical ideal is not the virtue that supports popular sovereignty but the compassion and responsiveness, the caring and being cared for, that supports daily living together. Nel Noddings calls this the ethic of caring.[7] It is, above all, an ethic that is local and concrete. This is so because our relationships are local and concrete.

This is the everyday realm where children s care of and relatedness to classroom animals, materials, and one another is nurtured. Classroom rules are not merely enforced: rather and much more important than mere enforcement, the roots of these rules in caring are continually examined with children. Violations are opportunities to discuss caring. The teacher is endeavoring to nurture children who examine their actions in light of the feelings, needs, and interests of others rather than in terms of being caught and punished. Of course, a teacher cannot just "talk" this caring into being. She or he must live it and is called upon to be for children a model of a fully caring adult.[8]

This realm of caring is the related world, not the political world. Here, no matter the type of political system, acts of kindness and concern matter very much. Consider the very undemocratic conditions of plantation life for slaves in the last century or of camp life for Japanese-Americans interned in the present century. Even in these settings, acts of everyday caring for one other were not rare. "When we behave ethically as ones caring, we are not obeying moral principles—although certainly they may guide our thinking—but we are meeting the other in genuine encounters of caring and being cared for."[9] This is the realm of moment-to-moment commitment and choice. The commitment is to those to whom we extend our caring, and each choice we make acts to maintain, enhance, or diminish us as ones who care and who are receptive to others.

It is important not to set the ideal of caring against the ideal of democracy. The two are complementary, and they overlap. Nevertheless, we should understand that ethical citizenship is more than maintaining and enhancing government of, by, and for the people; it also is sustaining and enhancing the social fabric of our lives and the caring it requires. Not limited to family members and intimate friends, this caring includes (indeed, must include) the community, our local milieu.

Community caring has not been easy for Americans. Over one hundred years ago, Alexis de Toqueville visited this country and observed the struggle within Americans between individualism and public commitment, between private and public happiness.[10] Recent studies have found a sharp decline in community caring amidst a nearly unrestrained concern for self.[11] The "me first" way of mind is not new, as Toqueville will attest, but it has not always been as extreme or rampant as it is today. Community is in decline, leaving individuals and families to fend for themselves against the impersonal machinery of the mass market, the media, and the state.

And what comes when community goes? The crime, vandalism, drug abuse, fear, and alienation (the list goes on) that are commonplace in our time. In a society that so values privacy and individual freedoms—to sing my own song, to do my own thing, to be left alone—practices of public caring and commitment are put profoundly at risk. These practices, which Toqueville aptly called "habits of the heart," must be nurtured. That nurturing is one of the great purposes of ethics in citizenship education.

## SUMMARY

There are three reasons for including a deliberate program of ethics in an elementary school's citizenship education curriculum. First, school administrators and faculty cannot help but teach values. Therefore, they owe it to the children under their care to consider carefully and choose consciously the values they will encourage and discourage. Second, democracies rely for their very existence upon a virtuous people. In a society organized under the ideal of democracy, the cultivation of virtue, not high SAT scores, is the school's first responsibility. Third, democratic values are not the alpha and omega of living together. Caring, too, is fundamental. Commitment to caring and responsiveness, the glue of families and communities of all sorts—religious, ethnic, professional, neighborhood-is not always convenient, and clearly it must wrestle with the competing desire to be left completely free. However, without commitment to caring for and responding to one another, there is no social fabric, let alone a democratic one.

## NOTES

[1]  R. Buckminster Fuller, *Critical Path* (New York: St. Martin's Press, 1981): xxxviii.

[2]  Israel Scheffler, *Reason and Teaching* (New York: Bobbs-Merrill, 1973): 137.

[3]  Quoted in Theodore Draper, "Hume and Madison: The Secrets of Federalist Paper No. 10," *Encounter* 58 (1982): 47.

[4]  James P. Shaver, "Commitment to Values and the Study of Social Problems in Citizenship Education," *Social Education* 49 (1985): 194-197

[5]  Edith Hamilton and Huntington Cairns, eds., *The Collected Dialogues of Plato* (New York: Bollingen Foundation, 1964).

[6]  Ralph Barton Perry, *Realms of Value* (Cambridge, MA: Harvard University Press, 1954): 431-2.

[7]  Nel Noddings, *Caring: A Feminine Approach to Ethics and Moral Education* (Berkeley University of California Press, 1984).

[8]  Ibid: 178-9.

[9]  Ibid: 175.

[10]  Alexis de Toqueville, *Democracy in America*, J. P. Mayer, ed., and G. Lawrence, trans. (New York: Doubleday, 1969, original work published in 1835 and 1840.)

[11]  See Christopher Lasch, *The Minimal Self* (New York: W. W. Norton, 1984), and Robert N. Bellah, Richard Madsen, William M. Sullivan, Ann Swindler, and Steven M. Tipton, *Habits of the Heart* (New York: Harper & Row, 1985).

Walter C. Parker is an Associate Professor of Social Studies Education at the University of Washington, Seattle. [1988 note]

**David T. Naylor**
**Bruce D. Smith**

Holidays have traditionally been part of the public elementary school experience, so much so that this aspect of school life is often described as "the holiday curriculum." For years holidays have served as occasions for school-wide and classroom specific activities involving plays, musical concerts, decorations, parties, costumes, the making of various artifacts, etc. Many former and present students have fond memories of these times during their childhood years. For them, the holiday curriculum was frequently a source of excitement, joy, and harmony. But that is not true of all students.

In recent years, holiday celebrations in schools have produced community controversies. In response, some schools have virtually abandoned holiday celebrations while some others have doggedly sought to hold onto traditional practices. Most schools, however, find themselves somewhere in-between these polar responses. This article examines the functions of holidays, raises issues about the selection of holidays to celebrate, offers perspectives on holidays as part of the "public culture," and addresses both policy and instructional implications for the holiday curriculum.

## THE NATURE AND ROLE OF HOLIDAYS

The American Heritage Dictionary (1992) defines a holiday as a "religious feast or holy day," and "a day on which custom or the law dictates a halting of general business activity to commemorate or celebrate a particular event." Holidays are cultural events; some are religious, others are secular. Religious holidays commemorate individuals, events, and values which are significant to those who share the beliefs of the group. They differ in regard to the particular individuals, events, and values a religious group chooses to revere. Secular holidays reflect the political, social, racial, and ethnic experiences of a society. They, too, revere particular individuals, events, and values.

Holidays are collective celebrations that serve three important social functions. One is a legitimizing function, sanctioning which people, events, and values merit special attention. Another is a preservation function, ensuring that certain people and events are honored and particular values perpetuated. A third is a cohesive function, binding people together through shared participation in commonly practiced rituals and celebrations. Thinking

Reprinted from *Social Studies and the Young Learner*, November/December 1993, Volume 6, Number 2. Copyright 1993 by National Council for the Social Studies.

about holidays in these ways has implications for developing policy and teaching about holidays in schools.

## HOLIDAYS AND CULTURAL DIVERSITY

Celebrations of holidays in a culturally diverse society can be problematic. Government agencies, especially schools, give preference to the holidays of some groups and not others. For example, contrast how the Fourth of July and Emancipation Day or how Thanksgiving and Kwanza are treated. Note also that Christian holidays often receive more recognition than the holidays of other religions. Another problem occurs when one group publicly misconstrues the meaning of another group's holidays, as when Hanukkah is described such as "the Jewish Christmas." Controversy may also arise because a holiday may be a cause of celebration for some groups while, for others, it may be a cause of sorrow or reflect a different interpretation. For example, Pioneer Day is a day of celebration for Mormons but a day of sorrow for the Native American Utes. October 12, Columbus Day, is viewed differently by various groups including many Hispanic Americans who join with those in Latin and South America to celebrate "the day of the people" (*la raza*), a holiday which honors the common bond shared by all Mexican people of Indian, African, and European ancestry.

## UNDERSTANDING THE "PUBLIC CULTURE"

These perspectives help explain why holidays, like the teaching of history, have become more difficult and controversial in our schools today. As we become increasingly more conscious of our cultural diversity, a need exists to find a framework that ties holidays together as part of a "public culture." Thomas Bender (1989) describes the public culture as the synthesis of the contributions and experiences of various groups that shape our individual, group, and national lives. He suggests that, in a diverse society, public culture needs to be understood as an ongoing contest among social groups and ideas "to define themselves and the nation as a whole" (p. 198).

Bender's perspectives on the nature of the public culture are instructive. Applied to holidays, his views help to explain how holiday curriculum evolved and why there is so much controversy surrounding holidays in our nation's schools. He writes:

> To describe the public culture of a society is to explain how power in all its various forms, including tradition itself, is contested, elaborated, and rendered authoritative. The public world...is not a given. It is historically constructed, the product

of a contest waged, not necessarily fairly, among various social groups and also between inherited conditions and the desire for change. What individuals and groups seek in public life is, as a minimum, legitimacy and justice. At times...one group or another will seek domination by defining the nature of public culture and of American nationality in ways favorable to itself and unfavorable to others...The point is not to homogenize the experiences of various groups, but rather to bring them, with their defining differences, into a pattern of relationships...[that gets] beyond the parts to a sense of the whole. (p.200)

## POLICY IMPLICATIONS

When holidays are understood as part of the public culture, schools are able to deal with them in more appropriate ways. Consideration of the following dimensions of the holiday curriculum promises to yield thoughtful policies for any school or school district:

1. Examine the holidays and the holiday curriculum in the school or school district as a manifestation of the public culture. What do they reveal about our common life as a people and a nation?

2. What balance do the holidays celebrated strike between religious and secular holidays? How representative are the religious preferences of the community, the state, and the nation? What ethnic holidays are included? How representative are they of the ethnic and racial composition of the community, the state, and the nation?

3. Assess the extent to which the district's holiday curriculum fosters legitimacy and justice among diverse groups. Which groups are represented? In what manner? Is the legitimacy of any group denied? Which ones? Why? Are deeply held beliefs of any groups in conflict with the holiday curriculum? Which ones? Why?

4. Identify the process by which the holiday curriculum is established—and changed—in the school or school district. What mechanisms exist for resolving problems surrounding the treatment of holidays in schools? How do groups gain access to the system? How are complaints handled?

5. Emphasize to faculty, administrators, and the community that our public culture is in a state of change. Provide examples of how change in the treatment of holidays has occurred in the school or district. What holidays, if any, are celebrated today that were not celebrated twenty years ago, for instance, Martin Luther King, Jr. Day? How has the manner of celebrating holidays changed over time, Christmas, Halloween, Easter, etc.? What forces have contributed to these changes, federal law, Supreme Court decisions? Which groups in the community may produce changes in the future?

## TEACHING ABOUT HOLIDAYS

When teaching about holidays, it is important to be clear about the learning outcomes to be achieved. Holidays should be regarded as opportunities for children to learn about the nature of our public culture. Children can study the social functions of holidays-legitimacy, preservation, and cohesion and how holidays help us acquire a common identity. For example, children can be asked what ideas are being kept alive and passed on by a particular celebration or what rituals are performed in conjunction with the holiday and how they help us feel that we share something in common. Children can learn to distinguish between types of holidays and investigate why specific holidays have come to be widely celebrated.

There is much to be gained in having children focus on the meaning and significance of specific holidays and how they evolved. When encountering a holiday such as Halloween, children can investigate its historical origins and how it has changed over time. This could help children understand cultural change and appreciate that people may see different meanings in a holiday. Studying the meaning of celebrations and rituals associated with a holiday such as the symbols used to express the seven values of Kwanza leads to important insights and deeper understandings of particular groups.

Children should study holidays in a global context. They should understand that many holidays commonly celebrated in the United States are variants of global patterns. For example, nearly all societies have a major holiday in the fall to give thanks for the harvest and virtually all nations have a political holiday that celebrates their founding or independence. Children should also understand how local customs and practices produce variations in holiday celebrations.

Holidays are a legitimate and important part of the school curriculum. They encompass key ideas from history, geography, anthropology, and the other social sciences. When holidays are dealt with in the manner described in this article, they become vehicles for addressing fundamental social studies goals and objectives, especially the nature and value of living in a culturally diverse society and world.

## REFERENCES

*The American Heritage Dictionary of the English Language* (3rd ed.). (1992). Boston: Houghton Mifflin.

Bender, T. (1989). "Public Culture: Inclusion and Synthesis in American History." In P. Gagnon (Ed.), *Historical Literacy* (pp. 188-202). New York: Macmillan

The extended quotation from *Historical Literacy*, edited by Paul Gagnon and The Bradley Commission on History in Schools (Copyright 1989 by Excellence Network) is reprinted with the permission of Macmillan.

David T. Naylor is a Professor of Education and Bruce D. Smith is an Associate Professor of Education, both in the Department of Curriculum and Instruction, College of Education, University of Cincinnati, Cincinnati, Ohio. Both are specialists in social studies education. [1993 note]

# Classroom Management for Responsible Citizenship: Practical Strategies for Teachers

**Dorene D. Ross**
**Elizabeth Bondy**

Classroom management is a major concern in U.S. public schools (Elam, Rose, and Gallup 1991). Although this concern is well placed, it is important for the public, teachers, and administrators to recognize that inappropriate emphasis on classroom order and control of students can impede the achievement of other important educational aims. In a democratic society, teachers are obligated to work toward developing the capabilities of students, one dimension of which involves responsible citizenship, or the ability and inclination to play an active role in improving society for all people (Ross, Bondy, and Kyle in press). This obligation requires that teachers select classroom management strategies likely to help students develop and use community values and skills including compassion, mutual respect, responsibility, and equality (Goodman 1992). Essential communication and social skills necessary for responsible citizenship include listening, expressing opinions, cooperating, and collaborative problem solving.

Brophy (1985) notes that most research on classroom management focuses on how to control behavior rather than on how to promote the values and skills of responsible citizenship. Most research investigating classroom management has addressed the differences between effective teachers (those who maintain order) and ineffective teachers (those who fail to maintain order). The research, however, has not investigated the characteristics that differentiate effective teachers who emphasize community-related values and social skills from effective teachers who focus exclusively on order. Nevertheless, we must not underestimate teaching practices that promote classroom order. Evertson, Emmer, and their colleagues have provided the most comprehensive classroom management research. Table 1 summarizes four guidelines for effective classroom management derived from their work (Evertson 1989; Evertson and Emmer [1982]; Evertson et al. 1984; Sanford and Emmer 1988).

Teachers who fail to use the guidelines identified in the classroom management research, or who fail to use them consistently, are likely to have chaotic classrooms. Achieving an orderly classroom, however, should not be an end in itself. If teachers hope to develop students' understanding of and commitment to the values and skills of

Reprinted from *Social Education*, October 1993, Volume 57, Number 6. Copyright 1993 by National Council for the Social Studies.

responsible citizenship, they may need to do more than implement the guidelines that have emerged from the classroom management research; strict implementation of the guidelines is likely to achieve order by promoting obedience rather than by teaching students to make socially responsible choices based on internalized community values. To develop community values and the social skills needed for responsible citizenship, teachers must use additional practices to manage their students.

## DEVELOPING THE VALUES AND SKILLS OF RESPONSIBLE CITIZENSHIP: SOCIALIZATION STRATEGIES

■ *Always provide a rationale for rules and routines.* In a review of research on successful socialization practices, Brophy (1985) notes that parents of well-socialized children set standards and expect children to cooperate, but they do not expect immediate and unquestioning obedience. Successful parents recognize that children do not automatically construct internal standards for action by learning to comply with rules established by adults. To help their children construct a moral philosophy, parents share with them the values used to determine rules and routines. Recognizing that rules are based on community values such as caring for others, fairness, honesty, or justice helps children develop criteria for evaluating their behavior and that of others, even in situations where parents or teacher have not specified rules.

At the outset, teachers should state the rationale for rules (i.e., prescriptions for general classroom behavior) and routines (i.e., prescriptions for specific behavior, such as how to set up and clean up science lab materials). The rationale behind rules can also be (and should be) communicated in other ways. Many children's books address values issues. Discussing the underlying values in books and how the values might apply within the classroom helps children understand the classroom values structure. Teachers can use current events activities to help children see that classroom values guide the action of all members of our society. Teachers can also use decision stories (i.e., stories in which two important values conflict) to help children grapple with difficult value decisions. Schuncke and Krogh's *Helping Children Choose* (1983) offers many examples of decision stories appropriate for elementary schoolchildren.

■ *Give students opportunities to make decisions in the classroom.* Pepper and Henry (1985) argue that democracy is based on principles of shared decision making. In a classroom, this means that the teacher shares with students the power to make as many decisions as possible. Benson (1987) echoes the idea that children must learn how to use power. He stresses that involving children in significant decisions communicates a respect for their abilities; an atmosphere of mutual respect, in turn, contributes to children's feelings of belonging. The specific practices described in this section provide opportunities to develop and practice community values and related skills of communication and collaborative problem solving.

■ *Involve students in developing classroom rules.* Cooperatively constructing rules helps students feel a part of the class, creates a sense of ownership of classroom rules that makes cooperation more likely, and provides opportunities to discuss the rationale behind rules so that students will understand the values on which rules are based. Although most rules would be developed before problems occur, teachers should also involve students in analyzing past events and constructing solutions to avoid problems in the future (Goodman 1992).

Involve students in developing and revising classroom routines (e.g., procedures establishing when to sharpen pencils or how students should behave after they have completed seatwork). Teachers should involve children in developing classroom routines for the same reasons children should be involved in developing rules: If children are to believe they have the power to shape their classroom experience, teachers must allow them to raise questions and suggest revisions. For example, students may believe that signing out on the chalkboard to go to the bathroom is too public and embarrassing for them. Through negotiation, the class might develop a more private procedure.

■ *Whenever possible, use classroom routines that provide opportunities to make choices.* Although classroom routines such as when students are allowed to sharpen pencils may seem trivial, they play an important role in the moment-to-moment life of the classroom. These routines are as value-laden as any lesson the teacher teaches. Because students experience these trivial events with such frequency, the values they carry tend to be especially well learned. If teachers want to promote self-discipline and responsibility, options that enable the children to make decisions and exercise responsibility are more desirable than those that deny these opportunities.

■ *View inappropriate behavior as an opportunity for collaborative problem solving.* According to classroom management research, teachers should use inappropriate behavior as an opportunity to teach appropriate behavior. Guidelines for responding to inappropriate behavior range from asking the student to stop the inappropriate behavior to using logical consequences to teach students the relationship between their actions and the results of their actions. In many cases, the latter is exactly what the teacher should do, making sure to stress the rationale behind the classroom rule or procedure and to

remind the student of group agreements where appropriate. At other times, the problem may be disruptive enough to suggest that one or more children have not learned underlying classroom values. Here teachers must stress appropriate behavior at the same time teaching problem-solving strategies and classroom values. Stensrud and Stensrud (1981, 165) state that by giving students the right to participate in the making of decisions that affect their lives, we encourage the learning of self-discipline and cooperation. A central distinction between coercive structures and self-disciplining ones is that the latter is based on cooperative goal structures.

The practices that follow provide students opportunities to develop values of respect, compassion, mutual responsibility, and equality as well as communication and social skills needed for responsible citizenship.

■ *Effective communication provides a basis for collaboration.* Working collaboratively requires that a teacher understand children's perspectives and help each child understand the perspectives of both the teacher and other children. Advocates of a human relations model of discipline (McDaniel 1980) have described specific practices that help people see through the eyes of others. Writers such as Ginott (1971), Gordon (1970), and Dreikurs (1968) have recommended practices that help teachers understand students' perspectives (e.g., active listening, door openers, and "I" messages). Teachers should teach these strategies to students to help them become collaborative, caring classroom members.

■ *Class meetings provide opportunities for collaborative problem solving.* Many problems confronted in classrooms are group problems (e.g., bickering or noisy behavior in communal areas). At the heart of a model for teaching community values and social skills is what Glasser (1965) calls "the classroom meeting," a large group session at which the teacher and students present problems and propose and consider solutions. The classroom meeting is an expression of democracy in action, a cooperative venture that embodies respect, responsibility, and concern for the group. Power and Kohlberg (1986) note that classroom meetings permit students to raise issues important to them, help establish routines and rules that influence their lives, and, therefore, provide instruction about democratic principles and procedures. They stress (1986, 17) that teachers should "be willing to speak up strongly as advocates of justice and community in the democratic meetings."

■ *Collaborative planning and evaluation is the key to solving individual problems.* Although the strategies suggested thus far will help prevent many classroom problems, every teacher faces individual children who have moderate to severe problems functioning within the classroom. Many problems have roots in children's inability to work and play cooperatively. Gaining self-control requires that children learn to resolve conflicts cooperatively by learning to perceive the perspective of other children, to avoid direct confrontation, and to use appropriate social interaction strategies (Ross, Bondy, and Kyle 1993). Children who lack these social skills will be unable to live peacefully with classmates. To help children develop social competence, Rogers and Ross (1986) suggest that teachers provide time for peer interaction, intervene to help children develop social skills, and use structured classroom groups to foster social acceptance and development.

In addition to working on social skills, children should work with the teacher to solve specific problems. In his responsibility training model, Glasser (1965) has described a set of steps for teachers to follow when students behave in ways that cause problems for the group. Glasser's method is designed to help the students accept responsibility for their behavior choices and plan alternative action that takes into account the group's needs. Pepper and Henry (1985) stress that teachers and students should generate alternatives collaboratively and that any new agreements must be acceptable to both. Within such an agreement, teachers and students should specify consequences for future inappropriate behavior and that the teacher is responsible for following through with consequences.

In more serious cases, teachers and students may develop a contract that specifies external reinforcement for positive behavior. Although the use of external reinforcement is not a practice we recommend enthusiastically, a few children have had so little successful experience in a classroom that they do not know how it feels to work cooperatively. External rewards can provide transitional motivation for such children on their way to developing community values and social skills.

▮ *Model the values and skills of responsible citizenship.* Classroom management research discusses the connection between curriculum and management (Brophy 1985); in our view, however, the research underemphasizes the significance of this connection. We have observed serious management problems in classrooms where the curriculum fails to engage students in activity they find meaningful. Furthermore, Wayson (1985) explains that students who do not feel that people within the school accept and care about them are not likely to cooperate with teachers. It is important, then, that teachers consider students' perceptions of the curriculum and the classroom environment as part of their effort to offer them the knowledge, skills, and attitudes necessary for responsible citizenship.

By examining curriculum and classroom environment in an effort to determine the role they play in classroom management problems, and by sharing their reflections with students, teachers create models for their students of the values and skills of responsible citizenship. For instance, teachers who show concern that some students do not find the curriculum meaningful demonstrate their sense of responsibility for the learning of all members of the classroom community. When teachers talk with students to gain understanding of their views of the curriculum, they demonstrate the community values of respect and caring. When teachers share with students their thinking about solving curriculum problems, they again create models for respect, caring, and commitment to the well-being and success of the group. In addition to modeling commitment to community values, teachers model important communication and social skills when they examine their curriculum in this public way.

## CONCLUSION

Decisions about how students should live in a classroom should have foundations in the teacher's educational aims. No one set of most effective techniques for organizing classrooms exists. Decisions about what is best and effective must be based on the teacher's (or school's) vision. We have advocated the aim of responsible citizenship, which entails the development of community values and communication and social skills. Traditionally, classrooms have been organized according to authoritarian power relations. Teachers have laid out their expectations, and students have complied. Students who failed to obey received a predetermined punishment. Under these conditions, students may work quietly and stay in their seats. But what do they learn about themselves, other students, adults, and the society in which they live? Do they learn values of community by participating in this type of stratified system in which they have little power and control?

We are not arguing that teachers and students are equals in the classroom. We believe that teachers have a legitimate authority they should use "to teach [children] how to live according to community values" (Goodman 1992, 104). They do this by creating routines, rules, and practices that help students become responsible for themselves and to others. Although we may see the teacher as having the overall plan that guides classroom activity, students play a central role in the construction of group life through a continuing dialogue with members of the group. In our discussion of classroom practices that promote the development of responsible citizenship we have tried to shift the emphasis away from controlling students' behavior to teaching students how to be responsible members of a community. It is through their relations with others in the classroom that students will learn important lessons about how to live in a community.

## NOTE

The ideas presented in this article are abbreviated and revised from a chapter that appears in Ross, Bondy, and Kyle (1993).

## REFERENCES

Benson, Norman. "Citizenship and Student Power: Some Strategies for the Classroom." *The Social Studies* 78 (1987): 136–39.

Brophy, Jere. "Classroom Management as Instruction: Socializing Self-Guidance in Students." *Theory into Practice* 24, no. 1 (1985): 233–40.

Dreikurs, Rudolf. *Psychology in the Classroom*. 2d ed. New York: Harper and Row, 1968.

Elam, Stanley M., Lowell C. Rose, and Alex M. Gallup. "The 23rd Annual Gallup Poll of the Public's Attitudes toward the Public Schools." *Phi Delta Kappan* 73 (September 1991): 41–56.

Evertson, Carolyn M. *Classroom Management for Elementary Teachers*. 2d ed. Englewood Cliffs, N.J.: Prentice-Hall, 1989.

Evertson, Carolyn M., and Edmund T. Emmer. "Preventive Classroom Management." In *Helping Teachers Manage Classrooms*, edited by D. L. Duke. Alexandria, Va.: Association for Supervision and Curriculum Development, 1982.

Evertson, Carolyn M., Edmund T. Emmer, Barbara S. Clements, Julie P. Sanford, and Murray E. Worsham. *Classroom Management for Elementary Teachers*. Englewood, N.J.: Prentice-Hall, 1984.

Ginott, Haim. *Teacher and Child*. New York: Macmillan, 1971.

Glasser, William. *Schools without Failure*. New York: Harper and Row, 1965.

Goodman, Jesse. *Elementary Schooling for Critical Democracy*. Albany: State University of New York Press, 1992.

Gordon, Thomas. *P.E.T.: Parent Effectiveness Training*. New York: Peter H. Wyden, 1970.

McDaniel, Thomas. "Alternatives to Punishment." *Phi Delta Kappan* 61, no. 7 (1980): 455–58.

Pepper, Floyd C., and Steven L. Henry. "Using Developmental and Democratic Practices to Teach Self-Discipline." *Theory into Practice* 24, no. 1 (1985): 264–70.

Power, Clark, and Lawrence Kohlberg. "Moral Development: Transforming the Hidden Curriculum." *Curriculum Review* 26, no. 1 (1986): 14–17.

Rogers, Dwight L., and Dorene D. Ross. "Encouraging Positive Social Interaction among Young Children." *Young Children* 41 (1986): 12–17.

Ross, Dorene D., Elizabeth Bondy, and Diane W. Kyle. *Reflective Teaching for Student Empowerment*. New York: Macmillan, 1993.

Sanford, Julie P., and Edmund T. Emmer. *Understanding Classroom Management: An Observation Guide*. Englewood Cliffs, N.J.: Prentice-Hall, 1988.

Schuncke, George M., and Suzanne L. Krogh. *Helping Children Choose*. Glenview, Ill.: Scott, Foresman and Co., 1983.

Stensrud, Robert, and Kay Stensrud. "Discipline: An Attitude Not an Outcome." *Educational Forum* 45 (1981): 161–67.

Wayson, William W. "Opening Windows to Teaching: Empowering Educators to Teach Self-Discipline." *Theory into Practice* 24, no. 1 (1985): 227–32.

Dorene D. Ross is a Professor and Elizabeth Bondy is an Assistant Professor of Curriculum and Instruction at the University of Florida in Gainesville. [1993 note]

# PART 11

## CURRICULUM ISSUES

Historically, curriculum development in the social studies has not been an easy task because there is little agreement on the grade level of discipline content focus (scope and sequence) among practitioners and scholars. In the future, social studies curriculum development may be less complex as teachers use the National Council for the Social Studies (NCSS) definition of the social studies and *Expectations of Excellence: Curriculum Standards for Social Studies* in the curriculum development process.

In making curriculum decisions, teachers and curriculum developers need to keep in mind a particular rationale for teaching a specific unit or topic when deciding on one or more instructional practices. The content selection, concepts, and skills to be taught need to be considered in light of the age and maturity level of the learners. Of course, the socioeconomic and demographic make-up of the school and community, as well as a value orientation, all help to shape the curriculum. What, then, is to be taught in a K-6 social studies program? What processes are involved in planning, implementing, and evaluating curriculum?

Authors of the articles selected for this section suggest several approaches to curriculum development and address important issues related to the curriculum. Fraenkel's article on Hilda Taba describes her significant contributions to social studies curriculum development in which she urges teachers to work with concepts and ideas that emphasize a higher level of thinking by students. Next, Alleman and Brophy suggest ways to use literature effectively for instruction within social studies content. They identify several practical problems teachers may encounter when using literature and suggest questions for teachers to consider as they determine whether or not to incorporate literature in the social studies curriculum. In a second article, Brophy and Alleman argue that major social studies goals should be the basis for curriculum development and that instructional practices should match the content.

Krey provides an example of how the first seven curriculum strands can be used to develop a social studies theme using focus questions and classroom learning experiences. She includes a graphic model that shows the relationship of one thematic unit, broad based questions, and related learning experiences that are tied directly to the social studies strands to accomplish civic competence — the major purpose of social studies.

According to Solomon, teachers can develop creative instructional activities to enhance social studies learning by linking facts, ideas, and concepts to help students learn problem-solving and thinking skills. Barr and McGuire report on one such creative strategy. They illustrate how an integrated, structured approach called "the story line" actively involves children in learning social studies content and examining values. This approach, developed and used for twenty years in Scotland, presents real problems as episodes in a story. The students confront and illustrate the episodes as they assume the roles of the characters and develop the story's outcomes.

Basic skills and social studies are important components of instruction in early childhood classrooms, according to Charlesworth and Miller. They suggest many places in the daily routine in which social studies concepts can be taught, as well as important unit topics appropriate in the early grades. Messick and Chapin make a strong case for teachers to incorporate data-gathering skills throughout the social studies curriculum. They advocate gathering data from many sources to help young learners make sense of their world and learn problem solving skills. They illustrate their point by offering examples of several types of learning activities appropriate for young learners.

Curriculum development is a never-ending and ongoing process. As new curriculum efforts and instructional activities become available, teachers are urged to examine them carefully and, if appropriate, incorporate them into effective teaching and learning practices.

**Jack R. Fraenkel**

In 1965, just after she had completed two studies in which she investigated the development and encouragement of student thinking in the elementary social studies curriculum, Hilda Taba received a four-year grant from the U.S. Office of Education to develop a K–8 social studies curriculum (Taba, Levine, and Elzey 1964; Taba 1966). Located at San Francisco State University,[1] the project was entitled "The Development of a Comprehensive Social Studies Program for Grades K–8."[2] The project staff's main task was to develop a series of instructional guides for teachers of grades K–8 that would emphasize the development of student thinking about important social studies ideas.[3]

At that time in her life (she was in her early sixties), Hilda was a nationally recognized authority on curriculum development and design. Constantly in demand as a lecturer and consultant around the country, she was especially interested in social studies, and was a popular speaker at many local, state, and national professional meetings. A full professor of education at SFSU, she taught earlier in her career at the University of Chicago, where she had also worked with Ralph Tyler on several research projects. She was an associate dean for a period of time at SFSU, but found she preferred teaching and writing to administration, and, therefore, had returned to the classroom.

The SFSU project focused on central ideas that Hilda had been advocating for some time, and reflected her basic philosophy about teaching.[4] Those ideas were the outgrowth of much of her lifelong work as a curriculum consultant to a number of school districts throughout the country and abroad, as well as to a variety of other institutions, agencies, and organizations. Many of these ideas were unique in their time, and although they did not necessarily originate with Hilda (many of the leading curriculum theorists of the 1960s—and earlier—propagated ideas similar to hers), she certainly was one of the leaders who had been arguing throughout the 1950s and 1960s for a new approach to curriculum and teaching. She also was one of the leading figures in the new social studies movement that came to fruition in the 1960s.

Hilda was an original thinker par excellence! She had a superb memory and a tremendous capacity for recall. Not always easy to understand, her ideas were sometimes difficult to grasp when she first expressed them; she sometimes

found it difficult to say exactly what she intended (partly because English was not her first language).[5] A continued study of her ideas, however, is well worth the effort.

Many of Hilda's ideas influenced social studies educators considerably. Certainly the opportunity to work with Hilda strongly influenced my own professional development in the early stages of my career. In the remainder of this paper, therefore, I would like to describe briefly a few of the more influential of these ideas, because I think they are as relevant today as they were in 1967 at the time of Hilda's death.[6] Space limitations prevent as thorough a discussion as I would like, but I shall try to provide enough detail to capture the essence of what Hilda had in mind.[7]

## THE IMPORTANCE OF DEVELOPING MULTIPLE OBJECTIVES
Objectives are important for any curriculum developer or teacher. They establish a sense of purpose and provide a basis for deciding what to include, exclude, and emphasize. It is important, said Hilda, whether one is trying to build a total curriculum, prepare an instructional unit, or even write a daily lesson plan, to keep in mind the necessity for developing multiple objectives. Helping students acquire information, for example, is important, but it is never enough. Teachers and curriculum workers also need to think about the formation of attitudes and values, and the development of important ideas, thinking skills, and academic and social skills. This is by no means an easy task, but one that teachers and curriculum developers must undertake if they wish to help students develop to the fullest all of their capacities and talents.

## BREAKING DOWN THE ORGANIZATION OF SUBJECT MATTER INTO THREE LEVELS
Hilda argued repeatedly that three distinct levels of knowledge should be included and developed in a curriculum and that curriculum developers had to treat each level differently. Accordingly, the Taba curriculum[8] organized three blocks of knowledge—key concepts, organizing ideas, and specific facts—in a manner that departed considerably from more traditional arrangements.

## KEY CONCEPTS
Key concepts are words that represent highly abstract generalizations. Examples used in the project materials include (among others) cultural change, interdependence, power, cooperation, conflict, and causality. These key concepts were selected for their power (i.e., their capacity) to organize and synthesize large amounts of information (i.e., specific facts). Because of their power, such concepts can

Reprinted from *Social Education*, March 1992, Volume 56, Number 3. Copyright 1992 by National Council for the Social Studies.

be developed in an increasingly complex and abstract manner throughout a curriculum, and can be illustrated at various levels of abstraction, complexity, and generality. Students can build upon and develop in successive grades their understanding of these key concepts.

For example, teachers can illustrate the concept of interdependence in the 1st grade by discussing the interdependence that exists among the members of the students' families; in the 4th grade, teachers can discuss interdependence among workers in various industries and occupations; in the 7th grade, teachers can discuss interdependence among nations. Key concepts should not be taught to students directly (i.e., by offering them a formal definition), but rather should be illustrated over and over again through a variety of factual examples appropriate to the students' age and grade level.

Such concepts suggest not only organizing ideas that can serve as a focus around which teachers can develop instructional units, but also key questions to ask about such ideas. These key questions in turn help to identify the dimensions of the idea that students need to investigate, and suggest which facts best serve as examples to illustrate and support the organizing ideas.

## ORGANIZING IDEAS

Organizing ideas represent important connections that students should understand after completing a unit of study. They constitute the organizing focus of an instructional unit and are generalizations—usually (although not necessarily) less abstract than key concepts. An example, suggested by the concept of societal control, is the following statement: "To maintain themselves, all societies regulate the actions of their members through some system of laws and customs." Another example, suggested by the concept of culture, is the statement: "In order to preserve their culture, all societies try to inculcate their young into the prevailing way of life."

We should view organizing ideas as hypotheses rather than certainties. They offer insights into the relationships that appear to exist in the world. Hilda argued that when students begin to understand the relationships that the organizing ideas suggest, and when they can support an idea with factual illustrations, they have acquired usable knowledge that will stand them in good stead far longer than will the acquisition of a host of unrelated facts.

Teachers need to repeat organizing ideas at several grade levels, but they should be expressed somewhat differently each time. As we expose students, through their reading (or in other ways), to examples of specific facts that illustrate a particular organizing idea, they likely will express the idea in their own words, which is probably more desirable than if they expressed it exactly as a curriculum developer wrote it. Hilda continually reminded us as we prepared the instructional units that we should view organizing ideas (and urge teachers to view them) as working hypotheses and not as truths to be confirmed. She stressed that teachers should want students to understand and use these ideas, but that they should never insist that they do so.

On the project, we viewed the following five criteria as especially important in selecting organizing ideas:

1. *Significance.* Does the idea represent an important relationship about some aspect (or aspects) of the world?
2. *Explanatory power.* Will the idea help students understand and explain important issues and problems that confront people in today's world?
3. *Appropriateness.* Is the idea suited to the needs, interests, and maturity of the students?
4. *Durability.* Is the idea one of lasting importance?
5. *Balance.* Will the idea promote a breadth and depth of understanding of events, individuals, actions, or occurrences?

## SPECIFIC FACTS

Once teachers have chosen an organizing idea as a focus for study, they can select a variety of specific facts to illustrate and develop the idea. For example, as illustrations of the organizing idea that "to maintain themselves, all societies regulate the actions of their members through some system of laws and customs," ancient Mesopotamia, France during the days of Louis XIV, or contemporary San Francisco could be selected for study as specific examples of the idea. Note that the teacher by no means has to be the one who chooses the facts to be studied; students certainly can suggest examples themselves. It is important to choose a number of contrasting facts because in that way students will come to understand more thoroughly the number and complexity of the relationships that a powerful idea represents.

How does a teacher or curriculum developer decide what subject matter to study? The project staff used the following criteria in preparing their instructional units:

1. How fundamental is the subject matter to be studied?
   - Does it reflect the most up-to-date knowledge available?
   - Does it reflect essential, basic knowledge that has wide application?
   - Does it offer important insights that will help students gain an understanding of themselves and their world?
   - Does it promote a spirit of inquiry?
2. Is the subject matter socially and culturally significant?
   - Is it consistent with the realities of today's world?
   - Does it examine values and value-conflicts?
   - Does it promote an understanding of the phenomenon of change and the problems that change produces?
   - Does it develop minds that can cope with change?
3. Does the subject matter relate to the needs, interests, and developmental level of students?
   - Can it be learned by the students—that is, is it in keeping with the abilities of the students involved?
4. Does the subject matter promote breadth and depth of understanding?
   - Does it develop in students the capacity to apply what they have learned in one situation to a new and different situation?

## SAMPLE RATHER THAN COVER

Hilda continually would say: "You can't cover everything! No matter how many details you know about something, or want to teach to children, there always will be another detail to be learned or, if learned, that you won't remember." "Coverage," she would say, "is an impossibility." It was futile, she thought, even to contemplate trying to cover "all of the facts," since it simply could not be done.

Specific facts rapidly become obsolete. The name of the United States President, for example, changes about every eight (sometimes four) years. The percentage of a given country's oil exports changes from month to month. The temperature in any of a number of cities throughout the world changes daily.

Because it is impossible to teach all the facts about anything, therefore, we can teach only certain facts. Teachers should choose to teach those facts that will enhance understanding of the idea. Because several different facts will promote understanding of an idea equally well, we should not expect all students to study a single set of selected facts. Various students, or the same students at various times, can study alternative data sets. Much will depend on the kinds of instructional materials available, the kinds of students involved, the nature of subject matter the teacher knows well or likes to teach, and the contrasting illustrations the subject matter can provide.

This notion of contrast is important. Students are more likely to obtain a clear understanding of an important idea from a detailed, in-depth study of two or three contrasting samples than from a more inclusive, but necessarily limited, study of several samples.

For example, in teaching U.S. history in the 5th grade, the organizing idea might be that the way of life in the original thirteen colonies was influenced by two factors: (1) who the settlers were and what they brought with them (e.g., ideas, beliefs, skills, and tastes); and (2) whether the characteristics of their landing place (e.g., people, climate, and soil) were hospitable. Students may learn more about this aspect of colonial life by studying two contrasting colonies in detail than by studying all thirteen colonies rapidly and superficially. This does not mean that the other eleven colonies will not be mentioned—rather, it means that the important ideas about colonization will best be conveyed through limited depth studies (Taba, Durkin, Fraenkel, and McNaughton 1971, 31).

In short, facts should be sampled rather than covered. There are far too many facts in the world for anyone to learn all of them in their lifetime. As a result, teachers and curriculum developers have no choice but to select certain facts for students to study. The important question, Hilda would stress, is not how many facts, but which facts we want students to think about.

## ORGANIZING LEARNING ACTIVITIES AROUND CONCEPTS AND IDEAS

Selection and organization of learning activities should proceed simultaneously with content selection and structuring. Learning activities are an important part of the Taba curriculum. They constitute the things students do during their daily work in (and sometimes outside of) the classroom. Watching films, listening to tapes, working in small groups, discussing ideas, taking notes, preparing summaries, analyzing case studies—all are examples of the various kinds of activities included in the instructional guides.

Hilda believed that learning activities should be more than mere busywork. Teachers should design every activity with a definite purpose in mind—one related to helping students understand the organizing idea around which an instructional unit is organized. Furthermore, she believed that different kinds of activities are needed to promote different objectives. Teachers and curriculum developers should not assume that an activity designed to help students understand a particular subject matter, for example, automatically will help them acquire a desired skill or promote a certain attitude toward learning. Activities to promote such non-content-focused objectives must be planned for and appropriately designed. If possible, of course, activities should be designed that contribute to the attainment of multiple objectives (e.g., an activity designed to encourage the mastery of content that also promotes development of a skill).

## LEARNING ACTIVITIES SHOULD BUILD ON WHAT STUDENTS HAVE LEARNED BEFORE

Hilda was convinced that not all students learn things in the same way. She stressed continually, therefore, that teachers must devise various kinds of learning activities if they truly want to help all students learn. She believed that in too many classrooms students were engaged in the same kind of activity every day—mostly listening to teachers talk, reading (or listening to teachers read), or writing (often filling in a worksheet of one sort or another). In Hilda's view, more—much more—variety was needed. As she put it, "different students learn in different ways."

Many students do not learn well at all via talk and the printed word. They need to be more directly or actively involved with the lesson. For this reason, activities such as field trips, role-playing, sociodramas, committee work, drawing, painting, dancing, taking photographs, making maps, working in the community—in short, any and all activities that involve doing things as well as receiving information—are important for students to experience.

Inductively organized learning activity sequences are an integral part of the project's instructional units and the concept of sequencing is a basic part of Hilda's philosophy of learning. In brief, learning activities fall into four (not mutually exclusive) categories: intake activities, the completion of which requires students to take in information in some way (e.g., reading, observing, and listening); organizing activities, which help students organize information they have acquired (e.g., outlining, charting, summarizing, paraphrasing, mapping, and graphing); demonstrative activities, which ask students to use information they have organized (e.g., role-playing, reporting, explaining, generalizing, and making analogies); and creative activities, which ask students to use the information they have learned in a new way (e.g., solving problems, writing essays, forming questions, hypothesizing, and predicting) (Fraenkel 1980, 131–136). Taken together, all four types of activities, organized inductively, make up what are known as "learning activity sequences."

The following is an example of a learning activity sequence designed for 1st graders:

*Concept*: Self-identity.

*Objective*: Children will identify their own and their classmates' voices speaking on a tape recorder.

*Instructional sequence*:

1. Introduce the tape recorder to the children. Show how it operates. Talk into the microphone and record your voice, then play back the recording for the children (intake activity—observing, listening).

2. Let each child record into the tape recorder by making sounds such as clapping, stomping, and whistling. Play back the recording (organizational and demonstrative activities—making own sounds).

3. Let each child hold the microphone and say his or her name into the tape recorder. Play back the recording immediately (demonstrative activity—speaking into the recorder).

4. Explain that there are no right or wrong voices. Point out similarities and differences in the students' voices. Emphasize that each person has a unique voice (intake activity—listening).

5. Replay the tape and have the children point out some similarities and differences in the tone or sound of each other's voices. Record the differences by making a line graph. Using a piece of paper and a crayon, have the children draw in one continuous line, making the line go up if the voice is high and down if the voice is low (organizational activity—charting).

6. Let each child make up a story and record it on the tape without using his or her name. Play back the tape and use these stories to test the children's voice recognition (demonstrative and creative activities—story development and telling). (Fraenkel 1980, 135-136)

A personal note: When I first began work on the 7th grade instructional guide for the project materials, I experienced considerable difficulty in learning how to write a decent learning activity sequence. After a particularly trying day during which I seemed to make no progress, I expressed my frustration to Hilda. She asked me to try to describe why I was having so much trouble. I told her that I thought it was because I wasn't really sure what it meant to teach something inductively.

"What are you working on currently?" she asked.

"I'm trying to work up a comparison of the values inherent in the city-states of Athens and Sparta," I replied.

"How?" asked Hilda.

"By describing and comparing various characteristics of each city-state—family life, social strata, military life, customs, religious preferences, recreational pursuits, etc.

I'm thinking of making a master chart that would present all of this information to the students in a clearly organized way."

"Who is doing the organizing?" she asked.

"I am."

"Aha," she replied, "Could the students do it?"

"Do what?"

"Do the organizing! Sounds like you, and eventually the teacher, are doing all the work. You're giving them a lot of information, but how are you helping them to digest it—to make sense out of it?"

"I'm guess I'm not," I replied. "Can you elaborate on how to do this?"

"Well, could you give the students some information to read or see or listen to about Athens and Sparta, but have them figure out what to do with it? The important thing for you to think about is not how to present the information to the students. There aren't too many ways to present information—text material, movies, filmstrips, recordings, lecture—whatever is the most interesting way for the particular material you're using. Your job is to figure out and design activities that teachers can use to help students to think for themselves, to do the organizing or whatever they need to do to make sense out of the information their teachers ask them to read, listen to, watch..."

"But don't they need information?"

"You bet," said Hilda. "Teachers need to provide students with interesting, relevant, and important information, to be sure. If the students perceive it as interesting and important, they will want to learn it. But the main job for a curriculum developer who wants to get students to do the thinking, as we do, is not to give this meaning to the students directly, but to design activities that allow, encourage, and help students to make sense—their own sense—of the information they come across, whatever the source. Any ideas here?"

"I think I see," I said. "Perhaps they could hold a discussion among themselves about how to organize the data they will be getting. They might want to put it into a chart, but they also might think of another, possibly better, way to organize the information. Perhaps I could have them engage in some role-playing of Greek and Roman citizens discussing the differences between their two city-states. To be able to do this, they would need to find out what life in the city-states was like. Perhaps they could be investigative reporters for a newspaper of the time describing life in the city-state in which they do not live. Maybe they could be 'information specialists,' briefing their fellow 'citizens' about what life is like in the other city-state and comparing it with their own. Perhaps artistically inclined students could illustrate the similarities and differences between Athens and Sparta. Perhaps..."

"Good! You've got the idea," said Hilda. "Just remember, we want teachers to get students to do the organizing, the questioning, the summarizing, the analyzing, etc. Our guides should reflect this. They should not require, request, or instruct teachers to do these things for students."

## TABLE 1: DEVELOPING CONCEPTS
## (LISTING, GROUPING, AND LABELING)

This task requires students to group a number of items on some specified basis. The teaching strategy consists of asking students the following questions, usually in this order.

| Teacher Asks: | Student Responds: | Teacher Follow Through: |
| --- | --- | --- |
| What do you see (notice, find, etc.)? | Gives items | Makes sure items are accessible to each student (on chalkboard, transparency, etc.) |
| Do any of these items seem to belong together? | Finds some similarities as a basis for grouping items | Communicates the grouping that has occurred (e.g., by underlining in colored chalk or marking with symbols) |
| Why would you group these items together?* | Identifies and verbalizes the common characteristics of the items in a group | Seeks clarification of responses (if and when necessary) |
| What would you call these groups that you have formed? | Verbalizes a label (often more than one word) that appropriately encompasses all the items in a group | Records the label |
| Could these items belong in more than one group? | States different grouping possibilities | Records the new or revised groupings |
| Can we put these same items in different groups?** Why would you group them that way? | States additional different groupings | Records new groupings |
| Can someone say in one sentence something about all these groups?*** | Offers a suitable summary sentence | Reminds students, if necessary, to take into consideration all the groups before them |

*The teacher may either ask a student *why* when he or she offers a grouping, or get many groups before considering why things are grouped together.
**Although this step is important because it encourages flexibility, it will not be appropriate in all cases.
***This step is often omitted because as a generalizing activity it may be reserved for the strategy of inferring and generalizing.

We had two important ideas to remember in writing these sequences: (1) never have one intake activity followed by another; and (2) include as much variety as possible in the sorts of activities included. Variety was a characteristic that all effective learning activity sequences had to possess. Nothing, said Hilda, was more detrimental to learning than for an unimaginative teacher to require students to engage in the same activity day after day, no matter how exciting that activity might have been for students initially.

### THE DEVELOPMENT OF INDUCTIVE TEACHING STRATEGIES

I think that Hilda was the first to advocate the development and use of inductively organized teaching strategies. So far as she was concerned, teaching strategies performed the task for teachers that learning activities performed for students. They indicated the actual procedures that a teacher would use to implement certain desired objectives.

Prior to receiving the K–8 curriculum grant, Hilda had developed three such inductive strategies designed to enhance student thinking:[9] developing concepts, inferring and generalizing, and applying generalizations. After her death, the project staff developed four additional strategies—one in the cognitive domain (attaining concepts) (Taba, Durkin, Fraenkel, and McNaughton 1971, 71) and three in the affective domain (exploring feelings, interpersonal problem solving, and analyzing values).[10] Each of these strategies involves a series of basic questions that teachers ask in a given, specified order, and suggests the sorts of responses they might expect from students.

In the strategy entitled "inferring and generalizing," for example, the teacher asks students to make inferences and generalizations about relationships among various kinds of data. In the strategy entitled "applying generalizations," the teacher asks students to apply previously learned generalizations and facts to predict what might logically occur in new situations. In the strategy entitled "attaining concepts," the teacher presents students with a wide variety of examples and nonexamples of a concept and asks them to differentiate between the two.

In the strategy entitled "exploring feelings," the teacher asks students to make inferences about how people feel in an emotional situation and explain why they think they feel that way. In the strategy entitled "interpersonal problem solving," the teacher asks students to propose and evaluate solutions to a problem involving a conflict among individuals or groups of people. In the strategy entitled "analyzing values," the teacher asks students to make inferences about the values that underlie people's actions.

Perhaps the best known, and certainly the most widely cited, of the strategies is "developing concepts." It is reproduced in its entirety in table 1 (Taba, Durkin, Fraenkel, and McNaughton 1971, 67).

Each step of the strategy shown in table 1 is a prerequisite to the steps that follow. This holds true in all of the teaching strategies Hilda and the project staff developed, and is a basic characteristic of their structure. Teachers, however, must not follow a uniform pace in implementing this (or any other) strategy. The pace a teacher employs should always depend on the students and how experienced they are with the strategy. Hilda believed strongly that all of the cognitive and affective strategies were generic strategies—that is, teachers could use them with any kind of subject matter and any type of student, regardless of the student's ability level. The crucial element is that the students, not the teacher, perform the activity called for in the strategy (in this case the grouping and labeling).

It is important that the students perform the operations for themselves, see the relationships between items in their own way, figure out a basis on which to group items, and devise the categories or labels for the groups. The teacher should not do any of these things for them, although on rare occasions the teacher might, if other methods fail, offer an alternative way of grouping items. The important thing to aim for is a climate in which the teacher's suggestion is given no more status than those of the students—that it is offered as simply another alternative for consideration (Taba, Durkin, Fraenkel, and McNaughton 1971, 69).

## EMPHASIZE THINKING

Throughout her professional life, Hilda was extremely interested in helping students understand and use knowledge rather than just remembering it. Accordingly, she wanted teachers to help students think about facts and their significance rather than merely asking them to recall them. Part of her desire in this regard led her to design the three inductive strategies I mentioned earlier. She intended, by developing these strategies, to offer teachers a set of procedures they could use on a regular basis to encourage students to think. A thorough understanding of the strategies, she often said, would provide teachers a vehicle they could use with all kinds of students, regardless of their academic ability. Hilda believed all students, not just the academically talented, were capable of high-level thinking. In fact, she often would provide us with examples of a thoughtful comment that had come from a student who previously had been labeled "below average."

Hilda loved good questions—that is, questions that asked students to do something with data, to look for "a different way to say that," to look for relationships, to seek out similarities and differences, to explain, to compare, to analyze, and to generalize. She continually stressed to everyone with whom she came in contact that all children could think, and that it was the responsibility of everyone who worked in schools to provide them with the skills they needed to do just that.

## AN EMPHASIS ON PEOPLE

Above all, Hilda believed that the social studies should be about people—what people are like, how they are similar and different, what they have accomplished, their problems, their customs, their ways of life, and their cultures. Because of this belief, Hilda felt that the discipline of anthropology was important for curriculum developers to consider as they went about building a social studies curriculum. Insights and concepts from anthropology, she thought, should be explored at all grade levels. Accordingly, the concept of cultural change, for example, was introduced in the 1st grade units by having students discuss changes that take place over time in the composition of families. In the 2nd grade, students would compare the changes that occur in the kinds of jobs people do. In the 3rd grade, students considered the ways that people in different cultures meet their needs and how these ways change over time. Throughout these instructional units and those of the following grades, the activities of people living in various cultures are compared and contrasted.

For example, teachers would ask 3rd graders to compare life in their own culture with life in an Eskimo culture. The teacher first presents a variety of facts about Eskimo life (daily activities, method of hunting, recreation, and family interaction) using stories, films, and filmstrips. Students then engage in activities that help them understand the facts they have acquired. Teachers plan other activities to help students learn some facts about their own culture. At various points teachers encourage them to make (or revise) generalizations about Eskimo culture and about their own culture, and then, eventually, to formulate a synthetic generalization that would apply to both their own and Eskimo culture.

Anthropological ideas seem especially important for students to study for a number of reasons:

- they serve as a counter to ethnocentrism in students;
- they help students understand the influence of cultural factors on people;
- they help students realize the differences in values that exist both within and between societies;
- they help students to perceive both the differences and the similarities among the peoples of the world;
- they help students realize how changes in one part of a society bring about changes in other parts of that society.

Finally, let me present an example of teacher-student dialogue taken from a taped recording of a classroom discussion in which a teacher, trained by Hilda and the project staff, attempts to get students to reason about the relationships that exist between a people and their culture. The dialogue that follows involves a 3rd grade class that had been studying the Zulu as an example of a tribal society in Africa. The teacher was trying to help the class realize that ideas come from people, and do not simply appear out of thin air. Approximately thirty minutes of discussion about change in a tribal society had preceded the following exchange. As a result of this discussion, the teacher had listed the following things on the board:

| Changes | People Who Brought Change |
|---|---|
| Metal tools | Peace Corps |
| Metal pans | Missionaries |
| Medicine | Traders |
| Nurses | Travelers |
| Schools | World Health Organization |
| Books | Soldiers |
| Bicycles | |
| Bigger buildings | |

The following interchange then took place (Fraenkel 1968, 253, 260):

*Teacher:* Do you think these people would have discovered all of these things by themselves someday without the help of all these other groups for teachers?

*Student #1:* No.

*Teacher:* What do you think—how would it be? If these people hadn't come to them?

*Student #1:* Well, they would still be living in their old ways—for instance, their houses—until they just get so old, centuries and centuries. And maybe someday they'd find out about these ways and these things.

*Student #2:* Maybe they would find out about our ideas—like if one African moved to America and traveled around and then came back to his village and traveled all around and spread the idea and told them. Maybe some would not believe it.

*Teacher:* How could this person help them to believe what he saw?

*Student #2:* Tell them, or take a picture of something.

*Student #1:* Or he could do it himself and start building that kind of building.

*Teacher:* Start building better buildings after what—after what he had seen?

*Student #1:* If he wanted to, he could show them how they did it.

*Student #3:* Some people would not believe it unless they went over there, because almost all people believe that they already have everything. I mean, if the African came back and told the people, they probably would not believe it.

*Student #4:* Yes, they would get these things, because they would finally learn. If they could not learn what we have here, how did they learn what they already are doing?

*Teacher:* Say that once more.

*Student #4:* If they can't learn what we learn here, how could they learn what they already had learned there?

This interaction represents an attempt by a teacher not only to help students become aware of an important (anthropological) insight (previously thought about and conceptualized as the focus for an instructional unit) but also to help them gain an understanding of a key concept from anthropology without telling them directly what the concept is.

Many of Hilda's ideas, especially the ones I have described in this article, had a considerable influence during the 1960s and 1970s on inquiry-oriented social studies teachers. The focus on multiple objectives, the spiral curriculum, the emphasis on thinking, the use of inductively organized teaching strategies, the development of teaching and learning units organized around concepts and ideas, and the sequencing of learning activities are as important today as they were twenty-five years ago when they first began to be talked about. It is a rare meeting of Association for Supervision and Curriculum Development, American Association of Colleges for Teacher Education, or National Council for the Social Studies in which her name does not surface when the discussion turns to matters of curriculum design, of "big ideas," of "teaching strategies," or of "teaching students to think." Hilda was one of the major figures in the field of curriculum (and, I would say, in the field of social studies education) during the twentieth century.

We on the project staff (and many others, I believe) consider it a privilege to have worked with Hilda. We miss her. We miss those wonderful staff meetings every week where ideas flourished, and where discussion and debate flowed fast and furious. We miss her ideas, her warmth, her encouragement, and her example. As for me, much of what I learned from Hilda—about teaching, about learning, about curriculum development, and about people—I have tried to incorporate in my own writings and talks with teachers and students. She represented, for me, the best that teaching has to offer.

## NOTES

1. At that time, San Francisco State College.
2. In June 1966, just after I graduated from Stanford University with a Ph.D. in education (with a specialization in social studies education), Hilda hired me to work as a research associate on the project. In September, I joined the project staff. At the same time, I was given a joint appointment as an associate professor in both education and social science.
3. See Jack R. Fraenkel, "A Curriculum Model for the Social Studies," *Social Education* 33 (January 1969), pp. 41–47.
4. For a more complete discussion of Hilda's philosophy as well as her ideas about curriculum, see her 1962 text, which has achieved somewhat the status of a modern classic: Hilda Taba, *Curriculum Development: Theory and Practice* (New York: Harcourt, Brace and World, 1962).
5. Hilda was born in Estonia in 1902 and received her bachelor's degree from the University of Tartu in 1926. She first came to the United States in 1926 as a European Fellow to Bryn Mawr College, where she received

a master's degree. After receiving a Ph.D. from Columbia University, she returned to Estonia in 1930. Returning to the United States in 1933, she taught at several universities before she came to San Francisco State in 1951.

6 Taba's work continues to be referred to in the social studies literature. For a recent example, see Walter C. Parker, "Achieving Thinking and Decision-making Objectives in Social Studies," in *Handbook of Research on Social Studies Teaching and Learning*, edited by James P. Shaver (New York: Macmillan, 1991).

7 For more information and examples, in addition to the references cited above, consult the following sources: Hilda Taba and Enoch I. Sawin, "A Proposed Model for Evaluation," *Educational Leadership* 20, no. 1 (1962), pp. 1–7; Hilda Taba, "Learning by Discovery: Psychological and Educational Rationale," *The Elementary School Journal* 63 (1963), pp. 308–316; Hilda Taba and Freeman Elzey, "Teaching Strategies and Thought Processes," *Teachers College Record* 65 (1964), pp. 524–534; Hilda Taba, "Implementing Thinking as an Objective in Social Studies," in *Effective Thinking in the Social Studies*, 37th yearbook, edited by Jean Fair and Fannie R. Shaftel (Washington, D.C.: National Council for the Social Studies, 1967); Fraenkel (1968); Jack R. Fraenkel, Anthony H. McNaughton, Norman E. Wallen, and Mary C. Durkin, "Improving Elementary-school Social Studies: An Idea-oriented Approach," *The Elementary School Journal* 70 (March 1969), pp. 154–163; Taba, Durkin, Fraenkel, and McNaughton (1971); and Fraenkel (1980).

8 Hilda died two years before the project was completed. The project staff, in her honor, renamed the project "The Taba Curriculum Development Project." For a complete description of the project, see Norman E. Wallen, Mary C. Durkin, Jack R. Fraenkel, Anthony J. McNaughton, and Enoch I. Sawin, *Development of a Comprehensive Curriculum Model for Social Studies for Grades One through Eight, Inclusive of Procedures for Implementation and Dissemination*, Office of Education, U.S. Department of Health, Education and Welfare, Final Report, Project no. 5–1314, Grant no. OE-6-10-182 (San Francisco: San Francisco State College, 1969).

9 For a detailed discussion of the strategies developed, refer to the final report of the project (see note 8 for full citation).

10 See the final report of the project (see note 8 for full citation).

## REFERENCES

Fraenkel, Jack R. "Building Anthropological Content into Elementary School Social Studies." *Social Education* 32 (October 1968): 251–254.

_____. *Helping Students Think and Value: Strategies for Teaching the Social Studies*. 2d ed. Englewood Cliffs, N.J.: Prentice-Hall, 1980.

Taba, Hilda. *Teaching Strategies and Cognitive Functioning in Elementary School Children*. Washington, D.C.: U.S. Department of Health, Education, and Welfare. Final Report, Cooperative Research Project no. 2404, San Francisco State College, February 1966.

Taba, Hilda, Mary C. Durkin, Jack R. Fraenkel, and Anthony H. McNaughton. *A Teachers' Handbook to Elementary Social Studies: An Inductive Approach*. 2d ed. Reading, Mass.: Addison-Wesley, 1971.

Taba, Hilda, Samuel Levine, and Freeman Elzey. *Thinking in Elementary School Children*. Washington, D.C.: U.S. Department of Health, Education, and Welfare. Final Report, Cooperative Research Project no. 1574, San Francisco State College, April 1964.

Jack R. Fraenkel is the Director of the Research and Development Center and Professor of Interdisciplinary Studies in Education in the School of Education at San Francisco State University in San Francisco, California. [1992 note]

# 72

# Trade-Offs Embedded in the Literary Approach to Early Elementary Social Studies

**Janet Alleman**
**Jere E. Brophy**

Recent critics of social studies textbook series have shown consensus around several observations. They have characterized the textbooks of the 1980s as limited in value as learning resources because: topics are covered too broadly without sufficient depth; too many facts are presented in isolation; information about women and minorities is often tacked on rather than integrated in natural ways; excessive space is allocated to pictures and graphics that are unrelated to the text or not accompanied by sufficient explanation; and procedural knowledge is taught essentially separately from propositional knowledge. This separation is accomplished primarily through isolated skill exercises rather than through authentic activities that involve using skills to apply knowledge in natural ways (Elliot & Woodward, 1990; Larkins, Hawkins, & Gilmore, 1987; Tyson-Bernstein, 1988). We share these concerns, but in this article, we focus on a newly emerging problem, namely the inclusion and use of literature selections in K-3 social studies texts.

Over the past five years we have been examining elementary social studies texts in an effort to better understand the enacted curricula that would result if teachers not only used the textbooks but followed the manuals' suggestions concerning discourse, activities, and assessment. The examples used in this article were drawn from the K-3 texts in the 1991 Houghton Mifflin series. This series was selected because it was designed to address some of the criticisms of the 1980s' expanding communities series that had become so similar to one another and because it incorporated children's literature into its texts.

We find that this series offers several advantages over the others, including acceleration of substance (especially in geography and history), good use of maps and pictorial material in developing key ideas, and generally good suggestions for in-class and homework activities. On the other hand, some of its novel elements, especially its literature inserts, have introduced some new problems all their own. Literature selections often run several pages, and exceed the space allocated to covering social studies content. Some units look more like language arts than social studies. Also, many selections focus on trivial and peripheral aspects of social studies. Even when these literary sources provide appeal and interest, they often distract from the main social education

understandings, and in the worst cases they create potential misconceptions or actually contradict social studies goals. We also find examples where the instructional activities accompanying the literary work shift the instruction to language arts. The social studies goals and the major understandings that ostensibly were to be developed get lost in the shuffle.

## EXAMPLES OF LITERATURE USED EFFECTIVELY

Some literary selections are very well suited to the lesson or unit to which they are attached. These selections seem likely to help teachers develop students' knowledge and appreciation of the topics in ways that promote progress toward major social education goals. For example, in a kindergarten unit on community, students are introduced to a poem entitled *The General Store*. They are encouraged to listen to the poem, imagine what the store looks like, and determine if it is old or new. A series of questions that personalize the learning follows. (Examples include: "Would you like to own a store like this one?"; "Would you rather shop in a general store or modern one?" "Why?"). This piece of literature represents a good example of matching the goal and enhancing both the cognitive and affective dimensions of the unit.

*When I was Young in the Mountains* is included as part of a second-grade unit focusing on families. We view this selection as useful for enriching students' understanding and appreciation of life in the past. It fits well with a lesson that addresses life "long ago." Another fine example, included in a third-grade unit entitled "Beyond the Appalachians, is Fresh Water to Drink." This is a chapter from the novel *Little House on the Prarie* that describes the efforts and dangers involved in digging a well for the family. The story is a good one for making the social studies content come to life. It is written from a child's point of view–very engaging to a third grader–presenting a powerful, effective, and cognitive perspective on pioneer life.

## PROBLEMS IN LITERATURE SELECTIONS AND USE

More typically, however, the literature selections focus on aspects of the topic that are relatively trivial or peripheral from the perspective of social studies purposes and goals. For example, a first-grade unit entitled "All Around the Big World," includes an array of inserted literary works: a four-page story, *The Riddle of the Drum*, followed by a song, *Are You Sleeping*, and two poems, *Block City* and *Happy Thought*. None of these selections has much to do with the unit's goals. Such a smattering of unrelated sources from unrelated places leads to little more than confusion. Too often, literature selections are assumed to be good because

Reprinted from *Social Studies and the Young Learner*, January/February 1994, Volume 6, Number 3. Copyright 1994 by National Council for the Social Studies.

they bring "affect" to social studies. Unless they support progress toward social education goals, however, they should not be viewed as effective.

Another general concern about literary selections is their potential for trivializing the content. This especially becomes a problem when folk tales and myths are used in cultural units rooted in history and anthropology. For example, in one third-grade text, several chapters are devoted to The Land and the First Americans. There is some good content about Native American religious beliefs and practices (common themes of reverence to nature and supplication for God's help in providing rain, bountiful harvest, etc.). However, this content is not presented sympathetically. The focus is on tribal myths, folk tales, and ceremonial dances, without mention of modern parallels such as crop blessings, religious rites of passage to adulthood, or marriage and funeral ceremonies. As a result, these Native American beliefs and customs are made to appear primitive or bizarre. Perhaps the publishers are afraid of getting "too close" to modern religions. In any case, part of the problem is the literature emphasis on folk tales and myths. This integration of good stories often leads to bad cultural content choices. The net result is the fostering of stereotypes, rather than understanding, of Native American culture.

Partly because so much space is devoted to literature selections, coverage of basic social knowledge content traditionally taught in the primary grades is very uneven. Also, far too often, instead of enriching the social studies curriculum, these literary selections have the effect of extending the language arts and literature curriculum at the expense of the social studies curriculum (if the latter is defined as learning opportunities that support student progress toward social studies purposes and goals). Some literature choices do not relate well to the social studies unit topic. Others have some relevance but nevertheless reduce the scope and disrupt the flow of the social studies curriculum because they are used as a basis for associated activities that are primarily language arts. A poem entitled *The End* in a lesson entitled "We Grow and Change" spans ages one to six. It begins, "When I was one, I had just begun" and continues through, "But now I'm six, I'm as clever as clever. So I think I'll be six now and forever and ever." Students are to decide why the poem was entitled *The End*, to match the stanzas with the pictures, and for at least one reading, supply the last word of each rhyme. None of these activities, in our opinion, enhance social education understandings.

*Pelle's New Suit* and *The Purse* are two literary works that relate to a second-grade text's theme of Depending on Others. However, the supportive activities focus on language arts. Follow-up to *Pelle's New Suit* begins with review of the steps involved in making Pelle's suit and a discussion of the ways we get new clothes. Then, however, the emphasis shifts to language arts. The children are to answer a series of story comprehension questions, then engage in a letter-writing exercise centered on telling an imaginary friend about the new suit. This experience is followed by a shift to a story entitled *The Purse*. Students are asked to compare how Pelle got his new suit with how Katie got what she wanted in *The Purse*. Katie liked the clinkity-clinkity sound of the money in a Band-Aid box. Students are to name sounds that they especially like and tell how the sounds make them feel. Then each child is to demonstrate a sound or draw a picture of what makes the sound. The lesson concludes with a dramatization of the stories and the suggestion that students create their own dialogue for both stories.

Some literature selections actually contradict the intended goals or create misconceptions. For example, in one kindergarten text that introduces far away places, children are introduced to a poem entitled, *The Edge of the World*. While it is a spirited selection and engenders wonder, its social education value is dubious. Phrases such as "sail over the rim" and "what lies over the rim" create confusion by contradicting what children are taught about the earth's shape and features. A first-grade lesson about friendship includes *The Little Red Hen*. This selection is a poor choice for this topic because it conflates personal friendship with prosocial and Golden Rule behavior. In the story, the Little Red Hen calls her friends together to solicit their help in planting and harvesting a field of wheat. Her friends refuse to help her, so when it is time to eat the fruits of her labor, she refuses to share. The story features characters who are unhelpful and spiteful and carries an undertone suggesting that friendship is conditional. These are not values we wish to instill through our social studies teaching.

Another example that we would label "cute," lacking educational value, and potentially creating misconceptions was found in a second-grade text. The poem, *Truck Song*, included as part of a lesson about transportation, does not present realism about the trucking industry. Instead, it is a romanticized, lighthearted, fanciful version of the trucker's journey. The students are told that the author left out all punctuation so that readers could feel what it was like to drive and drive without stopping, the way a trucker does. Even if this feature has its intended effect, which seems unlikely, the poem misconstrues the real world of regulations to which truckers must adhere. The portrayal of the trip itself is not an accurate portrait of a likely journey or of the life of a long-distance truck driver. Why create misconceptions or unnecessarily shallow interpretations that later have to be unraveled?

## QUESTIONS FOR ASSESSING LITERATURE IN SOCIAL STUDIES

In summary, the literature approach to K-3 social studies has some potential for deepening the cognitive and affective dimensions of content, but it introduces some new problems of its own. Literature selections often:

- focus on trivial aspects of the main topic;
- devote excessive space to literary works at the expense of social knowledge content;

- are too advanced for students to read independently;
- have activities associated with the literature selections which are often more closely aligned with language arts than with social studies; and
- can contradict intended goals or create stereotypes.

In view of these concerns, we suggest that K-3 teachers consider the following questions in order to make thoughtful decisions regarding the inclusion of literature in the social studies curriculum. Does the literary source:

- match the social education goals for the lesson and unit?
- offer sufficient value as a source for social education content and a basis for social education activities to justify the social studies time that will be allocated for it?
- seem to be of appropriate length given the social knowledge that needs to be included for adequate sense-making?
- enhance meaning and not trivialize the content?
- reflect authenticity and promote understanding of the content?
- enrich social studies understandings as well as promote language arts or other subject-matter content or skills?

- avoid potential misconceptions, unnecessarily shallow interpretations, or stereotypes in its depiction of people and events?

## REFERENCES

Elliot, D., & Woodward, A. (Eds.). (1990). *Textbooks and Schooling in the United States*. (89th Yearbook of the National Society for the Study of Education. Part I). Chicago: University of Chicago Press.

Larkins, A., Hawkins, M., & Gilmore, A. (1987). "Trivial and Noninformative Content of Elementary Social Studies: A Review of Primary Texts in Four Series." *Theory and Research in Social Education*, 15, 299-311.

Tyson-Bernstein, H. (1988). *A Conspiracy of Good Intentions: America's Textbook Fiasco*. Washington, DC: Council for Basic Education.

Janet Alleman is a Professor and Jere E. Brophy is a University Distinguished Professor in Teacher Education at Michigan State University, East Lansing. Drs. Alleman and Brophy collaborate on research in the area of elementary social studies. [1994 note]

# 73

**Jere E. Brophy**
**Janet Alleman**

A curriculum is not an end in itself but a means, a tool for accomplishing educational goals. These goals are learner outcomes—the knowledge, skills, attitudes, values, and dispositions to action that one wishes to develop in students. Ideally, curriculum planning and implementation decisions will be driven by these goals, so that all elements selected—the basic content, the ways that this content is represented and explicated to students, the questions that will be asked, the types of teacher-student and student-student discourse that will occur, the activities and assignments, and the methods that will be used to assess progress and grade performance—will be included because they are believed to be necessary for moving students toward accomplishment of the major goals. The goals are the reason for the existence of the curriculum, and beliefs about what is needed to accomplish them should guide each step in curriculum planning and implementation.

Today's social studies textbook series feature broad but shallow coverage of a great range of topics and skills. Lacking coherence, they are experienced as parades of disconnected facts and isolated skills exercises. These problems have evolved as an unintended consequence of publishers' efforts to satisfy state and district curricular guidelines that feature long lists of topics and skills to be covered rather than succinct statements of major goals to be accomplished. If teachers use the textbooks and provided ancillary materials, and if they follow the manuals' lesson development instructions, the result will be a reading/recitation/seatwork curriculum geared toward memorizing disconnected knowledge and practicing isolated skills. Nevertheless, this is what many teachers do, because most elementary teachers and many secondary teachers who are assigned to teach social studies courses have not had enough social studies preparation to allow them to develop a coherent view of what social education is all about, let alone a rich base of social education knowledge and an associated repertoire of pedagogical techniques. Acting on the assumption that the series has been developed by experts far more knowledgeable about social education purposes and goals than they are, such teachers tend to concentrate on the procedural mechanics of implementation when planning lessons and activities, without giving much thought to their purposes or how they might fit into the larger social education program.

The first of these two introductory paragraphs summarizes the classical view of curriculum development widely accepted as fundamental, logical, and even obvious, although not often implemented. The second summarizes major findings of recent research on practice, especially critiques of curriculum materials (Brophy, McMahon, and Prawat 1991; Elliott and Woodward 1990; Tyson-Bernstein 1988) and studies of teachers' curriculum planning and implementation (Clark and Peterson 1986; Thornton 1991). The contrasts between the two paragraphs reflect what we view as troubling about much of contemporary social education.

Some have reacted to these contrasts by suggesting that the classical view is unrealistic and that notions of ideal practice should be developed from descriptions of actual practice—what curriculum developers and teachers are observed to do. We reject this view, because we believe that rather than representing a consensus among informed practitioners, much current practice represents doomed attempts by series publishers to address overly numerous and conflicting goals simultaneously and doomed attempts to use these series by teachers who lack the social education background sufficient to recognize and focus on the most important content and activities. This has contributed to discontent with social education that is indexed by symptoms ranging from student boredom and dislike of social studies to low achievement test scores to civic participation problems such as low voter turnouts and sluggish census returns. We believe that a major reason for such problems is that we have lost the forest for the trees—we have lost sight of the major, long-term goals that reflect the purposes of social education and that should drive the development and enactment of social studies curricula. Consequently, we call for a return to the notion of developing curricula as means to accomplish major goals phrased in terms of intended student outcomes—capabilities and dispositions to be developed in students and used in their lives outside of school, both now and in the future.

## SOCIAL EDUCATION GOALS IN THEORY AND PRACTICE

There is no lack of goals statements in social education policy documents, curriculum guides, and teachers' manuals. These statements tend to emphasize citizen education, referring to providing students with the knowledge, skills, and values they will need to understand modern life and to participate in it effectively as prosocial group members and responsible citizens. Elaborations usually indicate that K–12 social studies courses should prepare students for social and civic participation in modern society, not just teach social science knowledge and procedures. Guidelines published by National Council for the Social Studies (1979), for example, specify that content should be drawn not just from the social science disciplines but from the arts and humanities, current events, and the students' own lives. They also call for integrating this knowledge content with skills and values content in ways that will help students apply what they are learning to their lives outside of school, both now and in the future.

At these lofty levels, social education goals statements make good sense. If they actually drove curriculum development and instructional planning, they probably would yield coherent and effective social studies programs. Unfortunately, however, these major social education goals tend to get lost in the shuffle as policymakers and curriculum planners begin to develop operational plans for implementing them. Typically, these plans involve generation of recommended knowledge topics, skills and subskills, values, attitudes, and participation experiences. These are broken into smaller and smaller subunits as the curriculum guidelines become differentiated across and within grade levels. Gradually, the big picture gets lost and, thus, the ostensibly fundamental purposes and goals do not functionally guide curriculum development and instructional planning.

Curriculum developers and teachers typically do not proceed by asking themselves what students should be able to do as a result of each lesson or unit. If they did, they would focus on those aspects of each topic that their students most need to know about and appreciate the significance of in order to apply what they learn to their social and civic lives outside of school. Instruction would focus on these important ideas and related values and skills, developing them in depth with emphasis on understanding, appreciation, and life application. Within and across units, the curriculum would reveal coherence and functional utility as a method of moving students toward the guiding social education goals.

Instead, however, too many curriculum developers and teachers appear to proceed by asking what knowledge, skills, and values are emphasized in the state and district guidelines for the grade level and then covering them, especially those that are likely to be tested. With attention focused on coverage of particular topics and subskills, the larger social education purposes and goals that are supposed to guide the entire process begin to fade into the background, as do many of the originally recognized connections and intended life applications. There is a general failure to tie things together. Knowledge content becomes fragmented into disconnected bits that can be memorized but not easily learned with understanding of their meaning or appreciation of their potential significance. Skills are taught and practiced in isolation from one another and from the knowledge content, and not as tools for using the knowledge content in authentic life applications. The social studies curriculum becomes a collection of miscel-laneous definitions, facts, and generalizations to be memorized for tests, instead of a vehicle for helping students understand and participate effectively in the world.

## LOSING SIGHT OF MAJOR SOCIAL EDUCATION GOALS

To the extent that content coverage lists, rather than major social education goals, drive the curriculum, not only the content but even the goals of many of the units and individual lessons become disconnected and trite, often to the extent that they lack life-application potential and thus have little social education value. For example, Naylor and Diem (1987) cite the following hierarchy of curriculum goals as typical for social studies:

*District-wide goal (taken from the NCSS guidelines):* to prepare young people to become humane, rational, participating citizens in a world that is becoming increasingly interdependent.

*Program-area goal for social studies, K–12:* to enable students to recognize and appreciate that people living in different cultures and subcultures are likely to share some common values with other cultures and subcultures and to hold other different values that are rooted in experience and legitimate in terms of their own culture or subculture.

*Grade-level goal for social studies, Grade 1:* to understand and appreciate that the roles and values of family members may differ according to the structure of the family, its circumstances, and its cultural setting.

*Unit-level goal for social studies, Grade 1:* to understand that families differ in size and composition. (51)

The last (unit-level) goal is phrased in purely descriptive, knowledge-level language, and it is trite for a unit goal even at the 1st grade level. It makes no reference to the anthropological and sociological concepts (e.g., cultures and roles) or to the values and dispositions (e.g., multicultural appreciation and citizen participation) referred to in the higher-level goals. Unless the teacher has a coherent view of the purposes and nature of social education, or unless the manual does an unusually good job of keeping the teacher aware of how particular lessons fit within the big picture, the result is likely to be a version of social studies that is long on isolated practice of facts or skills and short on integration and application of social learning.

Typically, manuals do little or nothing to help the teacher put these low-level goals into perspective as elements in a larger plan to move students toward major social education goals. Most of the time, they do not do so because they cannot do so: The curricula that they represent were not developed systematically to accomplish major social education goals. Instead, they were developed to "cover" long lists of disconnected knowledge topics and isolated skills. The students will learn little or nothing about family values and roles in different cultures; they will only learn that families differ in size and composition, that they grow and change, and that their members work and play together. In short, they will learn a few obvious generalities about families, but not much about variations in family roles across time and culture, the reasons for these variations, or the life-style trade-offs that they offer. There is little here to advance students' knowledge of the human condition, to help them put the familiar into a broader perspective, or even to stimulate their thinking about family as a concept.

Several consequences, most of them undesirable, exist when the focus of a unit goal is restricted to family size and composition. The "composition" part at least has potential: If developed properly, it could lead to informative and thought-provoking lessons on family composition and roles as they have evolved through time and as they exist today in different societies. To have much value as social education, however, such lessons would have to emphasize not merely that such differences exist, but why. The students might learn, for example, that a major social effect of industrialization is the reduction of the extended family's role as a functional economic unit, which precipitates a shift from an extended family to a nuclear family as the typical household unit. Instead of living and working together as a large extended family, following industrialization small nuclear families live in separate households and spend most of their time with nonrelatives. Their members may pursue a greater range of occupational and life-style options than exist in nonindustrialized societies, but they usually must do so without the continuing involvement and support of a large extended family.

Teaching students such conceptually based content about families will help them to locate the familiar in a larger perspective. Developed effectively through discussion and activities, such content will help students to understand and appreciate the trade-offs involved in various economic systems and associated life-styles and, perhaps, to function more effectively as family members within society at large. Unfortunately, however, the teachers' manuals that accompany contemporary elementary social studies series rarely even mention such substantive aspects of the topic of family composition, let alone provide teachers with suggestions for developing them effectively.

## TRITE GOALS MAKE FOR TRITE CONTENT

Missed opportunities to develop substantive content are just part of the problem. Too often, the content developed is inherently trite or is developed in ways that do not promote progress toward significant social education goals. Triteness is often embodied in the goals themselves, as exemplified here in the focus on family size. First graders are already well aware that families differ in size, so what is the point of making this a major goal? Even worse, what is the point of following up such instruction with exercises requiring students to classify families as either "big" or "small"?

Such lessons or activities lack substantive social education value. They do not appear in these series because major social education goals suggest the need for them. Instead, according to Tyson-Bernstein (1988), they appear there because publishers, working from lists of topics and skills to cover, have discovered that a focus on family size provides them an entry point for inserting certain generic skills exercises into the social studies curriculum (e.g., counting the members in depicted families and comparing and contrasting big and small families). Other such exercises call for students to infer whether depicted families are "working" or "playing" or to inspect drawings of families depicted before and after an addition has occurred and to circle the family member who represents the addition.

This is not an isolated example. Contemporary social studies series are riddled with units and lessons that feature trite goals and isolated skills exercises rather than development of important social education ideas taught for understanding, appreciation, and application to life outside of school.

Units on shelter convey the fact that people live in a great variety of homes, but usually say very little about the reasons why they live in these different kinds of homes and nothing at all about advances in construction materials and techniques, weatherproofing, insulation, or temperature control that have made possible the features of modern housing that most children in the United States take for granted. Units on government mention a few titles (president, governor, mayor), places (Washington, state capitals), and symbols (flag, ballot box), but precious little else. In particular, they say little about the functions and services performed at various levels of government. Thus, students learn that the positions of mayor, governor, and president exist, but not what these people or their governments do. In higher grades, students are exposed to reams of geographical and historical facts without enough concentration on major themes and generalizations, cause-and-effect relationships, linkage to local examples and current events, or other instructional framing and scaffolding to help them appreciate the significance of the information and consider how it applies to their lives outside of school.

## ALIGNING SOCIAL STUDIES INSTRUCTION WITH MAJOR SOCIAL EDUCATION GOALS

To bring social studies curriculum and instruction into better alignment with major social education goals, we will need to honor those goals not just in theory but in practice. Instead of merely listing them as lofty but nonfunctional statements of ideals, we will need to reaffirm major social education goals as the reasons for the existence of social studies curricula and begin to use them as the functional bases for curriculum planning. Guided by these goals, we need to ask ourselves what outcomes (capabilities and dispositions) we want students to acquire from a particular curriculum unit, and then plan the unit accordingly. We offer two examples of what this might mean in practice.

## A UNIT ON SHELTER

Social studies teaching in the primary grades emphasizes universal human characteristics, needs, and experiences (food, clothing, shelter, transportation, communication, occupations, social rules, government and laws) addressed within the contexts of family, neighborhood, and community. We believe that an important social education goal for each of these topics is to build initial understandings that will enable students to grasp the basics of how that aspect of the social world functions, not only in the local community and in the contemporary United States generally, but also in the past and in other cultures today. Our suggested instruction would be designed to expand the students' limited purviews on the human condition and especially to help them put the familiar into historical, geographical, and cultural perspective, thus increasing their understanding and appreciation of social phenomena that most of them have so far taken for granted.

Thus, rather than simply teaching that shelter is a basic human need and that different forms of shelter exist, our suggested instruction would be designed to help students learn to understand and appreciate the reasons for different forms of shelter. Students would learn that people's shelter needs are determined in large part by local climate and geographical features and that most housing is constructed using materials adapted from natural resources plentiful in the area. They would learn that certain forms of housing reflect cultural, economic, or geographic conditions (e.g., tepees and tents as easily movable shelters used by nomadic societies, stilt houses as adaptation to periodic flooding, and high rises as adaptation to land scarcity in urban areas).

Students would learn that inventions, discoveries, and gradual improvements in construction knowledge and materials have enabled many people today to live in housing that offers better durability, weatherproofing, insulation, and temperature control, with fewer requirements for maintenance and labor (e.g., cutting wood for a fireplace or shoveling coal for a furnace), than anything that was available to even the richest of their ancestors. They also would learn that modern industries and transportation make it possible to construct almost any kind of shelter almost anywhere on earth, so that those who can afford it can live comfortably in exceedingly hot or exceedingly cold climates.

These and related ideas would be taught with appeal to the students' sense of imagination and wonder, with emphasis on values as well as knowledge (e.g., consciousness-raising and age-suitable activities relating to the energy efficiency of homes or the plight of the homeless). Development and application activities might include such things as a tour of the neighborhood (in which different types of housing would be identified and discussed) or an assignment calling for students to take home an energy-efficiency inventory to fill out and discuss with their parent(s). Students would begin to see the function and significance of elements of their physical and social environment that they were not aware of before, and to appreciate current and future opportunities to make decisions about and exercise some control over aspects of their lives related to their shelter needs.

## A U.S. HISTORY UNIT

In teaching a history unit on the American Revolution (e.g., to 5th graders), our goals would emphasize developing student understanding and appreciation of the origins of U.S. political values and policies. Consequently, our treatment of the Revolution and its aftermath would emphasize the historical events and political philosophies that shaped the thinking of the writers of the Declaration of Independence and the Constitution. Content coverage, questions, and activities would focus on the issues that developed between England and the colonies and on the ideals, principles, and compromises that went into the construction of the Constitution (especially the Bill of Rights). Thus, students would learn not only about "no taxation without representation," but also about the colonists' experiences that led them to want to limit governmental powers, protect against unwarranted search and seizure, guarantee free speech, and separate church and state.

Assignments calling for research, critical thinking, or decision making would focus on topics such as the various forms of oppression that different colonial groups experienced (and how that oppression influenced their thinking about government), as well as the ideas of Jefferson and other key framers of the Constitution. Thus, there might be critical discussion or research on the methods that the framers developed to limit governmental powers and protect minority rights, the grievances that King George and the American rebels had against each other, the merits of the Boston Tea Party as a revolutionary act, or how things might have developed differently if the American Revolution had never occurred or had been suppressed by the British.

We would place less emphasis on Paul Revere and other Revolutionary figures who are not known primarily for their contributions to U.S. political values and policies and less on the details of each of the economic restrictions that England imposed on the colonies. We would place no emphasis at all on the details of particular battles and would not require activities such as time-consuming construction of dioramas depicting those battles.

## TEACHERS SET GOALS, THEN ALIGN INSTRUCTION ACCORDINGLY

In presenting these examples on shelter and on the American Revolution, we do not mean to suggest that the illustrated goals, content emphases, and instructional approaches are the only, or even necessarily the best, ones to adopt in addressing these two topics. Instead, we offer the examples as illustrations of how clarity about primary goals helps one to fashion units and lessons likely to cohere and function as tools for accomplishing those goals and to result in instruction that students find meaningful, relevant, and applicable to their lives outside of school. The particular goals emphasized will vary with the teacher's social education philosophy, the ages and needs of the students, and the purposes of the course. Teachers of military history in the service academies, for example, would have different goals and thus would approach the unit on the American Revolution with content emphases different than those in our example.

## WHAT TEACHERS CAN DO

In response to widespread concern about the shallowness and disconnectedness of contemporary social education series, a few states and districts have begun to pull back from their long lists of content coverage requirements and to place greater emphasis on shorter and more coherent statements of major social education goals and intended outcomes. We hope this trend continues and creates market conditions that will encourage publishers to develop series more coherent and effective as tools for teaching social studies for understanding, appreciation, and life application.

In the meantime, teachers who desire a more coherent social education curriculum can take certain steps to overcome some of the limitations of materials that feature trite goals, parade-of-facts content, and parade-of-skills-exercises activities. First, they can think through their social education goals, identifying the capabilities and dispositions they want to develop in their students throughout the year as a whole and in each of their individual units. Then they can examine their curriculum materials in light of these goals. Taking the viewpoint of the students, they can first read the student text (i.e., not the teacher's manual, which contains more guidance and information) to see what information is included and emphasized and what information is not, noting places where additional structuring or input will be necessary to focus students' learning on important ideas. Then they can study the teacher's manual, assessing the suggested questions, activities, and evaluation devices to determine the degree to which they will be useful as tools for helping students accomplish their primary social education goals. After examining their instructional materials in light of their goals, teachers will be in a better position to help their students focus on important aspects of the content (augmenting with additional input if necessary), skip pointless questions and activities, and substitute other questions and activities that support progress toward the goals they wish to emphasize.

Recent research on effective subject-matter teaching has identified several key characteristics of instruction that emphasize understanding, appreciation, and application to life outside of school (Brophy 1989, 1990; Prawat, 1989). These characteristics include: (1) development of a limited number of important ideas in depth rather than superficial coverage of breadth; (2) organization of content into networks structured around these important ideas and taught with an emphasis on the connections between them; (3) teacher-student discourse that features reflective discussion and dialogue focused on these key ideas rather than a simple recitation of specific facts; (4) activities that provide students with opportunities for authentic applications of what they are learning; and (5) evaluation mechanisms that focus on important understandings, appreciations, and applications rather than on isolated facts or skills.

To create such teaching, one must begin by clarifying one's major social education goals and then considering their implications not only for the kinds of questions and activities that should be included but also for the selection of content to be introduced in the first place and the key ideas around which to structure one's teaching of this content. To the extent that this is accomplished, social studies curricula (whether developed by publishers or by individual teachers) would have the following desirable characteristics.

1. The curriculum would be goals-driven. Everything in it, the content as well as the questions, activities, and evaluation devices, would be included because it is expected to function as a means of promoting progress toward the major social education goals that have been identified for emphasis. Whatever secondary goals it might serve (e.g., allowing for cooperative learning experiences or providing practice in research and writing skills), each content element, question, and activity within each lesson would have a primary purpose linked directly to accomplishment of major social education goals expressed in terms of intended student outcomes (capabilities, dispositions). These purposes would be made clear to the students, so that they could participate in lessons and activities with metacognitive awareness of their goals and metacognitive control of their learning strategies. In teaching an American Revolution unit with emphasis on events that shaped the political philosophies of the framers of the Constitution, for example, the teacher would make clear to students that (1) the Revolution was important not just as a war but as the culmination of a series of events that led to the establishment of the United States as an independent nation and (2) the military aspects of the Revolution settled the issue of who would govern the new nation, but its philosophical and political aspects determine how the new nation would be governed.

2. Knowledge content would be selected for its importance and potential for life applications, and it would be developed and applied accordingly. Cultural literacy would be one relevant criterion here, but by itself it would not be considered sufficient reason to include particular content. Certain highly specific content, such as Franklin's observation that "If we don't hang together, we will surely hang separately" or Lincoln's Gettysburg Address, is worth retaining because of its connection to ideas of enduring importance. Other such content ("Don't shoot until you see the whites of their eyes," "Shoot if you must this old gray head ..."), however, is more difficult to justify as needed to promote accomplishment of important social education goals.

3. Skills would be selected and used as tools for applying knowledge in ways that promote progress toward the major goals. Skills would be included in the curriculum in places where they were needed for this purpose and thus could be used in natural, authentic applications. Development of knowledge content would not be distorted to create opportunities for isolated skills exercises; nor would the content flow be interrupted for unrelated skills practice. Skills would be taught when introduced and used thereafter, but only in the context of applying knowledge for authentic social education purposes. Skills that were not needed for these purposes would not be taught as part of the social studies curriculum. Thus, in the unit on shelter, primary grade students might chart or compare and contrast the tradeoffs involved in urban versus rural living or predict the types of shelter likely to be found in a place with a given climate and specified natural resources. They would not, however, be asked to count or graph the numbers of houses of various types shown in an illustration or to identify the main ideas in paragraphs about the White House. Similarly, 5th graders might be asked to research or debate aspects of the American Revolution, but not to find the geographical coordinates of battle sites or circle the compound verbs in the Declaration of Independence.

4. Appreciations, values, attitudes, citizen action dispositions, and social and citizen participation skills similarly would be developed in natural and authentic ways suited to the knowledge addressed in the unit. Across units, the curriculum would be an integrated whole rather than a collection of isolated strands. Furthermore, the knowledge, skill, value, and dispositional aspects would be developed within authentic or holistic application contexts and not addressed in isolation. Thus, students would not just learn facts about shelter or the American Revolution; they also would learn about the trade-offs offered by different forms of shelter or government and be encouraged to think about their own personal preferences and about current policy issues in these areas.

5. Questions and activities would be included because they were seen as needed for learning key ideas or for using the content in ways that promote progress toward major goals. Student interest would be desirable but would not by itself constitute a sufficient reason for inclusion. Questions and activities would create important learning experiences, not just entertaining discussions or enjoyable tasks. Thus, questions and activities would focus on developing understanding and appreciation of cause-and-effect relationships and on encouraging critical thinking and thoughtful decision making about applications of the content to quality of life and civic policy issues. Students would not be asked to recite miscellaneous facts (especially facts that were not going to be used in application activities), to draw or color houses or Revolutionary War scenes (for no particular purpose), or to play games or engage in competitions that relate to unit topics in a general thematic way but do not develop or provide opportunities to apply key ideas.

6. Evaluation, both of the class as a whole and of individual students, also would be geared to the major goals. Thus, emphasis would be placed on questions and assignments calling for communication of major understandings and for critical thinking, decision making, values analysis, and other higher-order applications rather than on low-level memory items.

7. In general, planning and teaching would be structured around coherent curriculum units designed to accomplish major social education goals. There would be no intrusion of unrelated content or skills, no artificial division of material to suit a two-page lesson format, and no activities that ostensibly extend lessons or allow for subject-matter integration but actually have little social education value.

We believe that the key to implementing these suggestions is the individual teacher's understanding of social education—not just as social studies content to be covered but as a coherent citizen education effort driven by major social education goals and associated intended outcomes. Even if they are required to use inadequate materials, teachers who have clear conceptions of what they want their students to be able and disposed to do following each of their social studies units should be able to plan their units accordingly and thus improve the quality of their social studies teaching considerably. Teachers who do not yet possess a sufficiently well-delineated and functional conception of social education purposes and goals can develop one by reading several social education curriculum and instruction textbooks and studying the curriculum guidelines and related policy statements issued periodically by NCSS. For more of the authors' ideas about what is involved in teaching social studies for understanding, appreciation, and higher-order applications, see Brophy (1990) and Brophy and Alleman (1991).

## REFERENCES

Brophy, Jere E., ed. *Advances in Research on Teaching*. Vol. 1. Greenwich, Conn.: JAI Press, 1989.

———. "Teaching Social Studies for Understanding and Higher Order Applications." *Elementary School Journal* 90 (1990): 351–417.

Brophy, Jere E., and Janet Alleman. "Activities as Instructional Tools: A Framework for Analysis and Evaluation." *Educational Researcher* 20, no. 4 (1991): 9–23.

Brophy, Jere E., Susan I. McMahon, and Richard S. Prawat. "Elementary Social Studies Series: Critique of a Representative Example by Six Experts." *Social Education* 55 (March 1991): 155–160.

Clark, Christopher M., and Penelope L. Peterson. "Teachers' Thought Processes." In *Handbook of Research on Teaching*, edited by Merlin C. Wittrock. 3d ed. New York: Macmillan, 1986.

Elliott, David L., and Arthur Woodward, eds. *Textbooks and Schooling in the United States*. 89th yearbook of the National Society for the Study of Education. Part I. Chicago: University of Chicago Press, 1990.

National Council for the Social Studies. "Revision of the NCSS Social Studies Curriculum Guidelines." *Social Education* 43 (April 1979): 261–278.

Naylor, David T., and Richard A. Diem. *Elementary and Middle School Social Studies*. New York: Random House, 1987.

Prawat, Richard S. "Teaching for Understanding: Three Key Attributes." *Teaching and Teacher Education* 5 (1989): 315–328.

Thornton, Stephen J. "Teacher as Curricular Gatekeeper in Social Studies." In *Handbook of Research on Social Studies Teaching and Learning*, edited by James P. Shaver. New York: Macmillan, 1991.

Tyson-Bernstein, Harriet. *A Conspiracy of Good Intentions: America's Textbook Fiasco*. Washington, D.C.: Council for Basic Education, 1988.

Jere E. Brophy is a University Distinguished Professor of Teacher Education at Michigan State University, East Lansing, and Codirector of the Center for the Learning and Teaching of Elementary Subjects. Janet Alleman is a Professor of Teacher Education at Michigan State University in East Lansing. [1993 note]

# Social Studies and Basic Skills in the Early Childhood Classroom

# 74

**Rosalind Charlesworth**
**Nancy L. Miller**

Social studies should be everywhere in the early childhood classroom. However, in these days of minimal competency testing and pressures to push formal reading, writing, and arithmetic down into the kindergarten, and even into the preschool curriculum, social studies is often left out. Paper and pencil tasks are used to teach basic skills which could be taught through more appropriate, concrete activities and real experiences. Social studies content can support these kinds of experiences. Early childhood teachers need to be reminded that social studies should run as a thread through the entire school day for preschool and kindergarten children. "Social studies is the glue that bonds together the elements of the curriculum for young children."[1] History, geography, economics, political science, ecology, multicultural education, career education, social living, values education, moral education, and current events can be integrated throughout the classroom for young children. Children can acquire basic skills through social studies content using the traditional early childhood learning center environmental organization. Social studies instruction can also be implemented using unit approaches and daily routines and activities.

## ENVIRONMENTAL ORGANIZATION

The learning center organization which is common in early childhood classrooms lends itself to promoting social education. This type of environment can be set up to be attractive and inviting with materials that provide opportunities for exploration and discovery. Children can feel free to move at their own pace, make mistakes, and solve or adjust to possible problems which result from their mistakes.[2] It is also essential that children have the opportunity to work cooperatively in order to develop social studies skills and concepts. Cooperative work is promoted through organizing the environment around learning centers.[3]

## THE CENTERS

Social studies can be taught through the block, dramatic play, art, sand and water, library, and discovery/exploration centers. In each center, concepts and skills basic to reading, language, math, and writing can be learned simultaneously with social studies concepts.

Reprinted with permission from the Helen Dwight Reid Educational Foundation, from *The Social Studies*, January/February 1985. Published by Heldref Publications, 1319 Eighteenth Street, NW, Washington, D.C. 20036-1802. Copyright 1985.

The block center fosters the development of social skills in relating to others, cooperating within a group, developing self-esteem, and sharing. Cognitive skills such as classifying, comparing and contrasting, and problem solving which are basic to math, science, and social studies are an integral part of block play. The students' concepts of their community and its geography are reflected in the buildings and roads which they construct. In order to make a building that will stand and roads on which cars can travel smoothly, the children must use basic concepts of measurement and proportion to pick out the correct size blocks and organize them. Use of positional words (such as up and next to) while building with blocks will help develop concepts which need to be understood for dealing later with maps and with following instructions for completing worksheets and tests. The concept of people's dependence on one another will be fostered through the children's learning to return things to their proper places in order to leave the area ready for others to use.

The dramatic play area supports the development of all social skills: sharing, cooperation, taking turns, planning, etc. It also affords an opportunity for the representational activity which must precede the use of written symbols. When playing another role or using water as coffee or small blocks to represent food, children learn that something can represent something else. Role playing in this area reinforces social studies concepts presented in units or observed in the community, on TV, or in films and allows children to act out roles such as those related to various types of jobs and careers. Through working and playing with others, the children reinforce values such as respect and affection. This center can not only be a home but also can be modified to include a store, beauty shop/barber shop, repair shop, television studio, or other businesses as the need or desire arises. When businesses are set up, children develop economic concepts through the exchange of goods and services for play money.

Role playing can also be used to assist children in viewing situations from another perspective.[4] Children's stories allow students to try out roles in which they portray characters with a viewpoint other than their own. Role playing also may be used to assist children in solving social problems in a nonthreatening situation. Through the use of appropriate stories, children can learn that others have to deal with some of the same problems, emotions, and feelings with which they must deal.

In the art center, children use various media to make items which reinforce social studies learning taking place in units of study. Social skills develop as several children work together, share, and converse. Art materials can be used to express representations of the students' knowledge of the social world. Concepts such as soft, hard, rough, and smooth are developed and can be applied in geography when related to knowledge of the earth's surface. Careful use of materials in order to have an adequate supply over a period of time teaches conservation concepts. Students develop a positive self-image through recognition of accomplishments by teacher and peers. At the same time perceptual and motor skills needed for handwriting improve as children draw, cut, paste, paint, and use clay and playdough for their projects. Telling about what they have made and having their ideas put on paper supports language development and prepares the way for learning to read.

Many geographic concepts are developed in the sand and water area. Children build various land forms, see how erosion takes place, and try out miniature types of transportation vehicles. They can also use the sandbox to create three-dimensional maps of the school and community. Career education can be taught through considerations of the types of workers needed to dig sand, haul sand, build roads, etc. Noting that changes take place as they work with sand and water will assist children in the development of the concept that change is a constant thing that takes place in many ways. As in other centers, social skills continue to develop here. Simultaneously, math concepts related to volume, size, and space are learned as the children build, haul sand, and fill and empty containers.

Planned and spontaneous use of the library/reading centers relates to every discipline of social studies. Maps, books about the earth and universe, and books showing or telling about various regions of the world can be used to develop geography concepts. Values, feelings, and attitudes develop through use of stories. Newspaper clippings and children's magazines can be used to present current topics. Historical concepts can be learned through pictures and stories. The use of books and pictures is an invaluable aid when teaching multicultural concepts such as understanding and appreciation of different cultures and the similarities basic to all mankind. At the same time, children are learning the concept of print and what it represents, concepts of sequence, and the critical aspects of books and other print materials which support understanding and motivation for reading.

The discovery/exploration center contains changing sets of materials which follow the children's interests and the units of study. These might be items indigenous to a particular culture being studied, a geography game such as classifying pictures of things that are found "on land" or "in water," live plants and animals to aid in the teaching of environmental education concepts. These materials can also spark children's imagination and language ability resulting in experience stories which also serve as precursors to formal reading.

## UNITS

Social studies units can be introduced as determined by students' needs and interests. For example, one of the first units usually introduced in the early childhood classroom is "All about Me." Such a unit is basic for young children who are at a critical stage in the development of their self-concepts. If a child's self-image is the foundation on which he will build his future relationships with others and his world, then fostering self-esteem becomes the first task of social studies. The more adequate a child feels about himself, the more likely he is to feel confident to learn about other people and the world around him.[5]

In the Me unit, the child can develop geography concepts of direction as well as spatial arrangements and interactions through body awareness and movement. Each child's home can be identified on a map of the area. History concepts of time and change can be taught through the making of a personal booklet which is developed throughout the year and shows how changes in knowledge and physical appearance take place as time passes. In the area of multicultural education, this unit reinforces the concept that all people are dependent on one another as each child sees himself as an important, contributing member of a group. By seeing others progress through the year and learning about them, each child can develop an understanding and appreciation of the different people who make up his world and can see the differences and similarities in people. Concepts in ecology develop as the child observes the environment and accepts responsibility for its care. Thinking skills develop when the child compares himself to others and notes the likenesses and differences. Social skills, values, feelings, and attitudes may be enhanced by this important, continuous study. The teaching of units integrates music, art, role playing, a variety of language and reading experiences, math, science, and field trips.

## DAILY ROUTINES AND ACTIVITIES

Many social studies skills and concepts can be taught through daily routine activities and everyday living in the classroom. Following are some examples of how social studies concepts can be taught:

*History*—The concept of time (which is also a basic math concept) may be taught daily through the use of time words. A time line calendar can be displayed and used to help the children visualize the passage of time. An illustrated daily schedule placed in a prominent place can be referred to regularly when determining what comes next, when we go to lunch, etc. Time can also be taught through trying to beat the clock or timing ourselves with a stop watch when cleaning up or getting ready for a different activity. Changes in routine, classroom arrangement, work displays, and nature may be noted to develop the concept that change is a constant thing to which we must adjust.

*Economics*—The concept of scarcity can be reinforced through the need to use time wisely in order to have time for special activities. Children may also have opportunities to select a snack, surprise, or book in order to learn to make decisions and live with them. Again, the concept of time and the skills needed to decide how much of the available materials or snack foods each child should receive are also basic math concepts and skills.

*Political Science* — Concepts basic to living in a democratic society are developed through following rules as well as through group cooperation and interaction.

*Ecology* — Caring for and observing living things in the classroom helps children see that various forms of life are interdependent. Children develop awareness of the appreciation for their own environment by keeping their classroom in order and by displaying items of beauty such as a flower or work of art. Social consciousness develops as children accept their share of responsibility for care of their environment by turning off unnecessary lights, keeping their classroom and schoolyard neat, and using paper towels, water, and other materials conservatively.

*Current Events* — During sharing time, the children share news items (personal or otherwise) which are of importance to them. A classroom newspaper can be made by writing the news item on a large piece of newsprint. Each child can illustrate his own news item. Each page is then added to the others to make a student newspaper which can be placed in the reading center. Newspaper clippings of interest may also be discussed and displayed. All these activities support the development of language and other skills basic to reading.

*Career Education* — Children develop attitudes and values important to the world of work through daily responsibilities of feeding fish, taking the lunch report, wiping tables, etc.

*Social Skills* — Almost every moment of every day these skills are being developed through relating to others, living as a part of a group, sharing, and cooperating within a group.

*Attitudes and Values* — Consciously and incidentally values and attitudes are taught on a daily basis. The teacher needs to be a model for the values of courtesy, caring, learning, leadership, responsibility, honesty, fair play, and happiness. Observation and imitation are important means through which attitudes and values are learned by young children. Other values can be taught more directly. For example, respect for and understanding of our flag can be taught directly so that the Pledge becomes a meaningful rather than an empty routine.[6]

The development of appropriate social skills and positive attitudes and values are, of course, basic to constructive classroom behavior. Early education lays the groundwork for attitudes and school behavior which support children's dealing with the expectations of the later grades.

## SOCIAL STUDIES AS GLUE

A strong social studies program can support the total early childhood curriculum. Early childhood teachers cannot validly state that the push for basic skills instruction leaves no time for social studies. Social studies can support the basic education program through motivating learning and supplying a vehicle for application of basic skills and concepts as it permeates the entire curriculum.

## NOTES

[1] Betty L. Broman, *The Early Years in Childhood Education* (Chicago: Rand McNally College Publishing Company, 1982): 203.

[2] *Curriculum Guide for Kindergarten Teachers*. (Baton Rouge, Louisiana: East Baton Rouge Parish Public Schools, 1980): 7.

[3] Tom Davidson, et al, *The Learning Center Book: An Integrating Approach* (Santa Monica, California: Goodyear Publishing company, 1976): 177.

[4] Jacques S. Benninga and Ruth Ann Crum, "Acting Out for Social Understanding," *Childhood Education*, 58 (January/February, 1982): 145.

[5] Carol Seefeldt, *Social Studies for Preschool-Primary Child* (Columbus, Ohio: Charles E. Merrill Publishing Company, 1977): 213.

[6] Carol Seefeldt, "I Pledge . . . ", *Childhood Education*, 58 (May/June, 1982): 309.

Rosalind Charlesworth is the Coordinator of Elementary School Programs in the College of Education at Louisiana State University, Batan Rouge. Nancy L. Miller is a kindergarten teacher in the East Baton Rouge parish public school. [1985 note]

# 75

# Operationalizing the Thematic Strands of Social Studies for Young Learners

**DeAn M. Krey**

The advent of the ten thematic social studies strands identified by National Council for the Social Studies (NCSS) marks a fresh era of thought about the teaching of social studies. Spawned from a definition that describes the social studies as the integrated study of the social sciences and humanities to promote civic competence (National Council for the Social Studies, 1994, p. 3), the thematic strands point to a core of fundamental knowledge drawn from many academic disciplines. In particular these comprehensive thematic strands draw most heavily on the social science disciplines of anthropology, archaeology, economics, geography, history, law, philosophy, political science, psychology, religion and sociology, as well as appropriate content from the humanities, mathematics, and natural sciences. (Ibid)

## THE TEN THEMATIC STRANDS

Each of the 10 thematic strands encompasses meanings from one or more of the disciplines. The thematic strands which have been identified by NCSS follow:

- **I** Culture
- **II** Time, Continuity, and Change
- **III** People, Places, and Environments
- **IV** Individual Development and Identity
- **V** Individuals, Groups, and Institutions
- **VI** Power, Authority, and Governance
- **VII** Production, Distribution, and Consumption
- **VIII** Science, Technology, and Society
- **IX** Global Connections
- **X** Civic Ideals and Practices

(NCSS, 1994, pp. x-xii)

The power of the 10 thematic strands lies in their potential to serve as a framework for social studies curricula and stimulate visions of effective classroom learning experiences.

This article presents a new thematic model for operationalizing the thematic strands of social studies during the learning experiences of young students. It includes a visual representation of the relationships between a thematic teaching unit, focus questions, classroom learning experiences, the 10 thematic strands of social studies identified by NCSS and civic competence. The general thematic model and a specific model are both included.

Reprinted from *Social Studies and the Young Learner*, September/October 1995, Volume 8, Number 1. Copyright 1995 by National Council for the Social Studies.

## THEMATIC STRANDS AND FOCUS QUESTIONS

Whether the approved social studies curriculum of a school calls for teaching units of study with traditional foci such as *Families* or *The Westward Movement*, or innovative foci like *Quilts* (McCall, 1994) or *Pockets* (Field & Labbo, 1994), an initial step is to itemize the basic knowledge to be drawn from the social science disciplines. For example, consider a unit of study with a focal point of *The Places We Call Home*, written for children ranging in age from 6-9 years old.

Brainstorming what to teach about *The Places We Call Home* could result in the following systematic itemization of knowledge in the form of sets of focus questions. (It should be noted that the focus questions listed here are a suggested partial listing of those that could appear in each set. Only Thematic Strands I to VII are included due to space limitations.

## SET I–CULTURE

- What leisure activities take place in my home(s)?
- What is the ethnic background of those who live in my home(s)?
- What traditions are observed by the people in my home(s)?
- What religious beliefs are held by people in my home(s)?
- What language(s) is (are) spoken in my home(s)?

## SET II–TIME, CONTINUITY, & CHANGE

- How has (have) my home(s) changed?
- When was (were) my present home(s) created?
- Has my family always lived here?
- Who else has lived here?
- What stories exist about events that have occurred in my home(s)?

## SET III–PEOPLE, PLACES, & ENVIRONMENTS

- What does (do) my home(s) look like? Inside? Outside?
- What is the location of my present home(s)? Why?
- What are the physical and the human characteristics of the place(s) I call home?
- Where else has my family lived?

## SET IV–INDIVIDUAL DEVELOPMENT & IDENTITY

- What is special to me about my home(s)?
- What special events have I experienced in my home(s)?
- What is my favorite space within my home(s)?

## SET V–INDIVIDUALS, GROUPS, & INSTITUTIONS

- What family members live in my home(s)? (Each child should be invited to include all persons in the settings they call home.)

FIGURE 1: GENERAL THEMATIC MODEL FOR TEACHING SOCIAL STUDIES

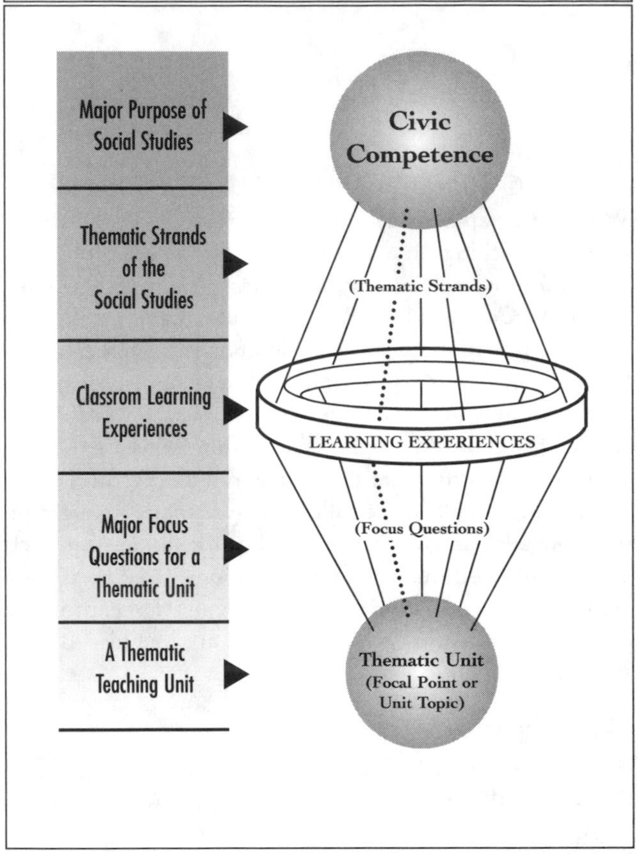


FIGURE 2: THEMATIC MODEL FOR TEACHING A THEMATIC UNIT WITH THE FOCUS ON *THE PLACES WE CALL HOME*

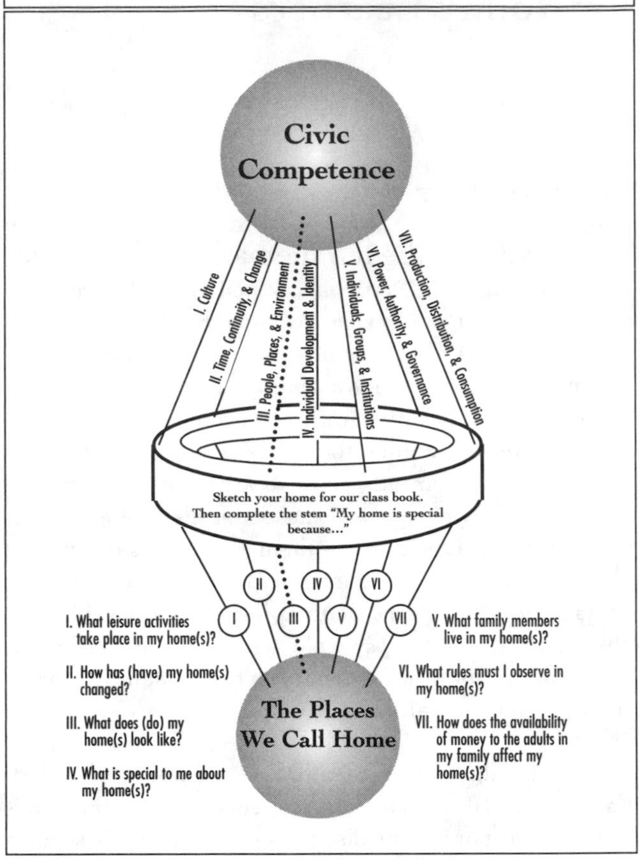


- Who are our neighbors? How are we alike/different?
- In what groups do my family members and I participate?

## SET VI–POWER, AUTHORITY, & GOVERNANCE

- What rules must I observe in my home(s)? Why?
- Are there rules I must follow in my yard(s) or neighborhood(s)? Why?
- Who enforces rules and laws in my neighborhood?
- How can I get help if I need it?

## SET VII–PRODUCTION, DISTRIBUTION, & CONSUMPTION

- How does the availability of money to the adults in my family affect my home(s)?
- What does it cost to live in different types of homes?
- What personal possessions do I keep in my home(s)?

Having itemized the knowledge about *The Places We Call Home*, one can easily see that the groupings of focus questions are directly related to one or more of the ten thematic strands of social studies. For example, Set Three of the question groupings given above, which begins with the question, What does (do) my home(s) look like? develops the meanings contained in Thematic Strand III, People, Places and Environments. The remaining sets of questions which maintain home(s) as a focal point emerge from the other thematic strands creating the "integrated study of the social sciences" called for in the National Council for Social Studies definition of social studies (NCSS, 1994, p. 3).

## A THEMATIC MODEL FOR TEACHING

The next phase in the teaching process, after brainstorming focus questions for a thematic unit, is to choose learning experiences which enable children to answer the focus questions. The learning experiences might involve a children's book, a role play, a learning game, an interview, a computer simulation or an infinite variety of other activities. As children are engaged in these experiences, the teacher's role is to guide the children toward building the conceptual knowledge (or meanings) of the appropriate thematic strands of the social studies. Finally, as children begin to demonstrate acquisition of knowledge related to one or more of the thematic strands, they grow toward civic competence. To summarize the entire teaching process, Figure 1 details the thematic model for teaching social studies. The phases address (a) a thematic teaching unit, (b) focus questions, (c) classroom learning experiences, (d) thematic strands of social studies, and (e) the major purpose of social studies, which is civic competence.

## AN APPLIED EXAMPLE OF THE THEMATIC MODEL

Figure 2 provides an example of a specific learning experience from a unit focused on *The Places We Call Home*. Starting at the bottom of the model and following Spoke III which has the focus question, What does (do) my home(s) look like?, a teacher could choose the learning experience of making a class book. Children would then be asked to make sketches of their present home(s), ei-

## CONSTRUCTING A THEMATIC UNIT: *THE PLACES WE CALL HOME*
## WITH EMPHASIS ON STRAND ⬤ PEOPLE, PLACES, AND ENVIRONMENTS

The unit is for children ranging in age from 6-11 years old. It includes historical fiction, biography, autobiography, journals and poetry. The books lend themselves to being read aloud by the teacher and contain supporting illustrations. Any of the books cited could be placed at the center of the Thematic Model shown in Figure 1. Seven of the NCSS Thematic Strands are matched with Focus Questions and text information below:

### CULTURE/WHAT LEISURE ACTIVITIES TAKE PLACE IN MY HOME(S)?

Chall, M. W. (1992). *Up North at the Cabin*. New York: Lothrop, Lee & Shepard. A cabin in Northern Minnesota is the setting for this historical fiction. Based on the author's own traditional vacations, the young girl in the story has memorable experiences with other family members and nature.

Keegan, M. (1990). *Pueblo Boy*. New York: Cobblehill Books. This is a biography of a child growing up in the San Ildefonso Pueblo in New Mexico.

### TIME, CONTINUITY, AND CHANGE/HOW HAS (HAVE) MY HOME(S) CHANGED?

Dragonwagon, C. (1990). *Home Place*. New York: Macmillan. In this book of historical fiction a family, hiking in a wooded area, discovers artifacts at an old homesite, leading them to imagine the way of life of the family who called this place home in another time.

Knight, A. S. (1992). *The Way West*. New York: Simon & Schuster. This is an authentic journal account of a nine-member family and their wagon train trek from their home in Iowa to Oregon Territory in 1853.

### PEOPLE, PLACES AND ENVIRONMENTS/WHAT DOES (DO) MY HOME(S) LOOK LIKE?

Houston, G. (1992). *My Great Aunt Arizona*. New York: HarperCollins. This biography tells the story of the author's great aunt who was born in Appalachia and became a teacher. Arizona Houston-Huges influenced generations of children who attended school in the Blue Ridge Mountains.

Siebert, D. (1989). *Heartland*. New York: HarperTrophy (div. of HarperCollins). In this book of poetry the Midwest people and farmlands of today are described and illustrated.

### INDIVIDUAL DEVELOPMENT AND IDENTITY/WHAT IS SPECIAL TO ME ABOUT MY HOME(S)?

Shannon, G. (1993). *Climbing Kansas Mountains*. New York: Bradbury Press. This book of historical fiction presents a boy and his father who share a special hometown experience by driving across their town and climbing a local grain elevator. The boy treasures the time spent with his father and the adventure of seeing his home and its surroundings from the top of a "Kansas mountain".

Rosen, M. J. (Ed.). (1992). *Home*. New York: HarperCollins. In this book thirty authors and illustrators give personalized answers to the question, "What does home mean?" (Their time and talent were donated so that proceeds from the book could be used to aid the homeless.)

### INDIVIDUALS, GROUPS AND INSTITUTIONS/WHAT FAMILY MEMBER(S) LIVE IN MY HOME(S)?

Cooper F. (1994). *Coming Home: from the Life of Langston Hughes*. New York: Philomel Books. This biography explains the many life experiences that helped Langston Hughes define home. From hearing Grandma Mary's stories in Kansas to living and writing poetry and stories in Harlem, New York, he came to see that home was within himself.

Bedard, M. (1992). *Emily*. New York: Bantam Doubleday Dell Pub. This book of historical fiction is based on evidence about the poet Emily Dickenson at home in her Amherst, Massachusetts neighborhood.

### POWER, AUTHORITY AND GOVERNMENT/WHAT RULES MUST I OBSERVE IN MY HOME(S)?

Yolen, J. (1992). *Letting Swift River Go*. New York: The Trumpet Club. A father and daughter recall the characteristics of their Swift River hometown in New England. They visit the reservoir that covered with water the homes of the people who used to live there. This historical fiction recounts an event that has occurred in many locations in the world where large cities must have water.

McLerran, A. (1992). *Roxaboxen*. New York: Puffin Books. Based on historical evidence, this book tells the story of a young girl, her sisters and friends who were careful to observe the rules of their invented home town at the edge of the Arizona desert.

### PRODUCTION, DISTRIBUTION AND CONSUMPTION/ HOW DOES THE AVAILABILITY OF MONEY TO THE ADULTS IN MY FAMILY AFFECT MY HOME(S)?

Hendershot, J. (1987). *In Coal Country*. New York: Alfred A. Knopf. In this autobiography, the life of each member of a miner's family living in Willow Grove, Ohio on Company Row is seen through the eyes of his daughter.

Cross, V. (1992). *Great-Grandma Tells of Threshing Day*. Morton Grove, IL: Albert Whitman & Co. This historical fiction presents a story about two children on a Missouri farm in the early 1900's as they experience the work and excitement of threshing day.

ther the inside or the outside. While the children sketch, the teacher would circulate and discuss with children the physical and human characteristics of the place(s) shown in their drawings. In addition, each child would be asked to complete the sentence stem, My home is special because … and write it on their sketch.

For closure, the children would be invited to share their sketches with the class and the teacher would question further about the physical and human characteristics shown in the sketches prepared for the class book.

It can be seen that the example learning experience shown in Figure 2 puts emphasis on Thematic Strand **Ⅲ**, People, Places, and Environments (the geography spoke). That is, as children make sketches that show the physical and human characteristics of the place(s) they call home, they are focusing on a place and describingthe environment in which they and their significant others interact. However, when the teacher asks the children to complete the sentence stem about why their home is special, the thematic strand that becomes important is Strand **Ⅳ**, Individual Development and Identity (the psychology spoke).

Figure 2 shows that it is also the case that several other thematic strands such as Individuals, Groups, and Institutions will emerge during lessons like the one described above. Having the focus question of, What family members live in my home(s)?, it follows that this strand will logically be included in classroom discussions about the sketches of homes completed for the class book. This demonstrates the integrated nature of social studies learning experiences for young children. It is a reminder that all of the social sciences have a contribution to make when teaching social studies to young learners.

## REFERENCES

Field, S. L., & Labbo, L. A. (1994). "A Pocketful of History." *Social Studies and the Young Learner*, 7(2), 4-7.

McCall, Ava L. (1994). "Including Quilters' Voices in the Social Studies Curriculum." *Social Studies and the Young Learner*, 7(1), 10-14.

National Council for the Social Studies. (1994). *Expectations of Excellence: Curriculum Standards for Social Studies*, Bulletin 89, Washington, DC: Author.

DeAn M. Krey is a Professor in the Department of Elementary Education at the University of Wisconsin, River Falls. Dr. Krey teaches in an integrated elementary methods block, which includes social studies, language arts, and science. [1995 note]

**Warren Solomon**

Today's front-page education news is dominated by stories of negative outcomes: about how the nation's schools are producing incompetents in many fields including history, literature, geography, and economics; about how many of today's students will be unprepared to serve in tomorrow's high-tech work force; and about how the nation is falling behind economically and politically.

With such news, creativity in teaching seems to capture little attention. Yet the argument can be made that creative teaching is needed to help with the above problems, and this discussion, which supports that argument, addresses three questions related to creative teaching in social studies:

1. What does creative teaching look like in social studies?
2. How may social studies teachers become more creative?
3. Why is creative teaching in social studies important?

## WHAT DOES CREATIVE TEACHING LOOK LIKE IN SOCIAL STUDIES?

To help re-examine my thoughts on creative teaching in social studies, I conducted an informal survey of twelve elementary teachers and supervisors who were members of a select Missouri social studies committee. These individuals responded thoughtfully to two questions: "What do you associate with teaching social studies creatively in the elementary school?" and "What do you associate with social studies teaching that is clearly not creative in the elementary school?" Following is a summary of their ideas:

## THE "NON-CREATIVE" CLASSROOM

In these classrooms, wrote one of the teachers surveyed, the "teaching [is] only from the textbook. . . . Students answer questions from the textbook or . . . [do] nothing but worksheets, worksheets, worksheets." Another responded, the teacher is "following each page and paragraph within a textbook-giving the same emphasis to every paragraph and calling for rote learning." All twelve respondents had the same message: Teachers in these classrooms allow one textbook to determine what they teach, with students simply expected to learn the material in it. Their approach is one of management and routine, much like that found in reading programs based on basal readers.[1]

Reprinted from *Social Studies and the Young Learner*, September/October 1989, Volume 2, Number 1. Copyright 1989 by National Council for the Social Studies.

## THE "CREATIVE CLASSROOM"

The resources used in "creative" classrooms are far richer than those listed above. Teachers in these classrooms go beyond single textbooks and use a variety of media including literature, music, and the visual arts. They also draw upon the community and its people and use the ideas and experiences of the students themselves as important inputs for learning.[2]

The contrast between the two classrooms extends beyond the resources to the learning goals. Creative teachers, not content with the learning of facts from a single source, want their students to become competent in solving problems, making decisions, communicating effectively, and collaborating with others. As people who synthesize ideas from many sources to create their instructional plans, these teachers expect their students to use many sources to construct their understanding of the world.

The consensus among educators surveyed in describing social studies in "creative" classrooms was that these are classrooms of student engagement in a variety of learning experiences (art projects, cooperative learning, role plays, simulations, debates, projects of all sorts, and field trips).

## HOW MAY SOCIAL STUDIES TEACHERS BECOME MORE CREATIVE?

To teach social studies creatively requires both the will and the ability to do so.

We cannot expect teachers who regard social studies to be unimportant or who are content to let others decide what is to be taught in their classrooms to have the will to plan creatively for social studies. Teachers with the will to be creative, on the other hand, are people who see themselves as decision makers. They elect to prioritize objectives and select or make quality materials for accomplishing them. They are not content with workbook pages and commercial tests unless, upon examination, those are determined to be sound means to their objectives. Moreover, when they use textbooks, they choose how to do so deliberately, because they know that they, more than textbook authors and editors, know their specific objectives and children.

The ability to teach social studies creatively involves making connections, three types of which follow:

*1. Connections between major ideas in social studies fields of study and the lives and interests of students.* Whereas one teacher told this writer that third graders cannot understand the concept of profit, a more creative teacher helped her third graders grasp the concept's meaning by having them form a "corporation," make and sell products, and calculate their profit by subtracting their expenses from their revenues. They even factored into their expenses a classroom overhead cost with help from their principal. The creative teacher, in a word, can make connections between ideas from social studies fields and the experiences of students, to "humanize knowledge," to use an expression of Goodlad.[3] Success in making those connections depends upon teachers informing themselves both about their students' ideas and interests and about major ideas from history and the social sciences. Fortunately, recent studies in history,[4] in geography,[5] and in economic education[6] are helpful for teachers to become informed about key ideas from those disciplines. In addition, the bicentennial of the U.S. Constitution has facilitated the explication of fundamental ideas related to our political system.[7]

*2. Connections between content being studied and other content areas.* Creative teachers find ways to connect learnings in social studies to those in other subject areas. Here are a few examples: One teacher challenges her students to communicate their learning in graphic, mathematical ways. Some teachers are making connections to science through the science, technology, and society movement.[8] Many teachers are emphasizing writing across the curriculum.[9] Some teachers enrich their students' understandings of history and other cultures through works of art, music, and literature from other times and places.

Teachers can make connections among fields of study by using illustrations in textbooks relating art to history and cultural studies, by keeping on the lookout for relevant workshops—some from art museums and science centers—and by reading in the area.

*3. Connections between study skills and theories of learning and content being taught.* As content is taught, opportunities abound to advance students' study and research skills. Some creative teachers work to expand their repertoires for teaching strategies for learning. They try, as proponents of "metacognition"[10] advocate, to help students become conscious of their own thinking processes and be experimental in ways of tackling assignments, to help students approach thinking as a problem-solving effort in which they become explicit about the task at hand, plan strategies for addressing the task, monitor their progress, and make modifications as needed.[11]

## WHY IS CREATIVE TEACHING IN SOCIAL STUDIES IMPORTANT?

We have discussed the essence of creative teaching and how teachers may teach more creatively. The question now is whether it is worth the effort to plan for more creative teaching in social studies. It is indeed possible, we must concede, for creative teachers to design units directed to trivial objectives or to no objectives at all. In such cases, time of both teachers and students is probably being wasted. If, on the other hand, teachers, through creative planning, have made connections among objectives per-

taining to important social studies content and skills, students' learnings from other subjects, and students' life experiences, the means are present to achieve significant learning, even to turn around the problems described at the beginning of this article.

First, the content taught in classrooms of creative teachers, as discussed above, would not be in the form of isolated facts, but taught as ideas linked to each other and to students' experiences. Research indicates that comprehending a subject is more than accumulating bits of information; it involves connecting new knowledge to prior knowledge.[12]

Second, creative teachers, themselves people who value solving problems and using ideas, are more likely, we might hypothesize, to value and promote such thinking among their students. In a word, they are teachers likely to help their students develop competence as students and independent thinkers and to gain possession of skills needed for the culture of a political democracy.

Third, creative teachers, by engaging students actively in their own learning, are likely to have students who "buy into the enterprise of becoming educated people" and who are more likely to help students want to stay in school. A by-product of their teaching may well be the addressing of the social problem of American students leaving school before graduation without skills needed to participate actively in the economic and political life of this nation.

In conclusion, if we value having students who understand the subjects they study, who learn how to investigate topics and social issues, and who will want to remain in school and further their education, we need to find ways to make our schools an environment in which creativity in teaching is valued and can thrive.

## NOTES

[1] Winograd, R. & S. G. Paris. (Dec 1988-Jan 1989). "A Cognitive and Motivational Agenda for Reading Instruction." *Educational Leadership*, 46, 30-36.

[2] For a discussion of the types of resources creative social studies teachers may draw upon, see Missouri Department of Elementary and Secondary Education. *A Guide to Social Studies Curriculum Development for Missouri Educators*. (1980). Jefferson City Missouri: Missouri Department of Elementary and Secondary Education, 12-17.

[3] Goodlad, John. (1984). *A Place Called School: Prospects for the Future*, p. 125. New York: McGraw-Hill.

[4] Bradley Commission on History in Schools. (1988). *Building A History Curriculum: Guidelines for Teaching History in Schools*. North Olmsted, Ohio: Bradley Commission on History in Schools.

[5] Association of American Geographers and National Council for Geographic Education. (1984). *Guidelines for Geographic Education in the Elementary Secondary Schools*. Washington DC: Association of American Geographers.

[8] Gilhard, June, et al. (1988). *Economics. What and When*

*Scope and Sequence Guidelines K-12*. New York: Joint Council on Economic Education.

7   See, for example, the elementary student text of the Center for Civic Education, *We the People...* (1988). Calabasas, CA: Center for Civic Education.

8   For information about this movement, see the newsletter, *STS Reporter*, Pennsylvania State University, 117 Willard Building, University Park, PA 16802.

9   Nelms, B. E (1987). Response and Responsibility: Reading, Writing, and Social Studies. *Elementary School Journal*, 87, 571-89. For examples of strategies that may be used to promote the development of writing skills in social studies, see Missouri Department of Elementary and Secondary Education. *The Social Studies Basic Skills Connection: Practical Strategies for Teaching Basic Skills in Conjunction with Social Studies Content.* (1982). Jefferson City, Missouri: Missouri Department of Elementary and Secondary Education, 41-46, 52-53, 57-60.

10  Metacognition is "... being conscious of our own thinking and problem solving while thinking ..." Costa, Arthur L. (1985). *Teaching For, Of, and About Thinking. Developing Minds*, p. 21. Arlington, VA Association for Supervision and Curriculum Development. A person engaged in metacognition while making an economic decision, for example, would not only be thinking about the choices and alternatives involved related to the decision, but also about his strategies in making the decision, how adequate they are, how well they are working, and whether they need to be revised.

11  Solomon, W. (1987). Improving Students Thinking Skills Through Elementary Social Studies. *Elementary School Journal*, 87, 557-570.

12  Brandt, R. (Dee 1988-Jan 1989). On Learning Research: A Conversation with Lauren Resnick. *Educational Leadership*, 46, 12-16.

Warren Solomon is Curriculum Consultant for Social Studies in the Missouri Department of Elementary and Secondary Education. He has chaired the NCSS Advisory Committee on Curriculum and was recently elected president-elect of the Council of State Social Studies Specialists. [1989 note]

**Ian M. Barr**
**Margit E. McGuire**

## TEACHING AND LEARNING IN THE SOCIAL STUDIES

The long-term aims of social studies for learners are to establish understanding of the ways in which our society works and to prepare them to participate fully and with confidence as responsible members of that society. Broadly interpreted this requires that learners develop the knowledge, skills, values, and dispositions to function effectively in a democratic society. Thus, the role of social studies is critically important in today's schools as young people must gain the depth of knowledge and the ability to apply a wide array of skills if they are to participate as citizens in a pluralistic and interdependent world.

The National Council for the Social Studies Task Force on Teaching and Learning[1] has outlined key components of instruction in the social studies. The document states that ". . . social studies teaching and learning become more powerful when they are meaningful, integrative, value-based, challenging and active." These five themes for effective instruction require careful planning and thoughtfulness on the part of the teacher when designing learning opportunities. The very nature of social studies calls for an integrative approach to learning as the study of any topic draws on the knowledge base that informs that topic. Additionally, the skills employed to understand and synthesize a topic of study utilize other areas of the curriculum such as reading, writing, and mathematics. Learning must be meaningful to the lives of young people and engaging to them in active, challenging, and important ways. Of course, teaching and learning are value-laden activities and the social studies must give due account to the values that are implicitly or explicitly embedded in any teaching program. These five themes serve as a foundation for examining strategies that foster social studies understanding.

## FROM THEORY INTO PRACTICE

While such statements provide the necessary foundations on which an effective social studies curriculum should be built, we know from experience that the translation of such principles from theory into effective practice is not easy. Too often teachers regard such statements as little more than rhetoric. Too often policy statements are not supported with practical advice on how to turn the high-sounding principles into effective classroom practice. This article aims to provide a practical means of binding together an appropriate view of social studies and an effective strategy for learning and teaching.

## STORYLINE

In a 1991 article,[2] McGuire suggested that the storyline method was a valuable way of integrating the curriculum. Since then, considerable interest has been expressed in the ideas contained therein. Indeed, it would seem that the storyline method is potentially more than simply a means to curriculum integration. It can serve as a humanizing core for the whole curriculum. Keiron Egan[3] has argued that Dewey's ideal of all studies being tied to the living social experience of the child is not being met in today's schools. Storyline is one strategy that can assist in moving toward that ideal; it makes the curriculum become real and relevant in social terms. In Scotland, Denmark, Germany, Iceland, and The Netherlands, this method has proved to be an approach to teaching and learning that is not only well founded in social terms but also very motivating.[4] This long-term interest in Europe and more recently in the United States suggests that storyline is a powerful strategy for curriculum integration as well as motivating social studies teachers.

## WHAT IS STORYLINE?

Storyline is a structured approach to learning and teaching developed in Scotland over the last 20 years and is particularly suited for elementary and middle school applications. It builds on the key principle that learning, to be meaningful, must be memorable and that by using learners' enthusiasm for story-making, the classroom, the teacher's role, and learning itself can be transformed. As well as providing contexts for active learning, it develops in learners a powerful sense of ownership of their learning and often a renewed enthusiasm on the part of teachers for teaching.

## PRIMARY FEATURES OF STORYLINE

The primary features of storyline:
- Concerns itself with places, people, and events; in other words, the social world.
- Contextualizes learning.
- Naturally integrates curriculum areas.
- Builds on the learner's prior experience.
- Develops a range of important concepts.
- Develops skills within motivating contexts.
- Provides meaningful opportunities for content assimilation.
- Promotes a range of key social values. (It is principally

Reprinted from *Social Studies and the Young Learner*, January/February 1993, Volume 5, Number 3. Copyright 1993 by National Council for the Social Studies.

concerned with providing learners a conceptual understanding of the social world as well as a range of content, skills, values, and attitudes that will equip them to participate effectively in that world.)

## CHALLENGES IN TEACHING

Disaffection and lack of motivation are, of course, not problems exclusive to the social studies; most of what schools offer is profoundly demotivating for many young learners. Nevertheless, it is a fact that social studies is an aspect of the curriculum that students like least. That is an uncomfortable truth for social studies educators; however, most of the school curriculum seems remote from the preoccupations and interests of the learners. It seems remote because many important and enduring concerns are dressed up in a language and register that is difficult for many young and lively learners to relate to and therefore to understand. Storyline can be a means of providing contexts and metaphors that can bring to life these important issues for young learners.

## LEARNERS' PRIOR EXPERIENCE

There has been, in recent times, an increased recognition of the importance of the learning and experience children bring to school. Child-centered Piagetian approaches to learning and teaching are now recognized increasingly to have probably neglected certain key factors—most crucially the role of discourse and the importance of social interaction as important bases for learning. The work of Vygotsky[5] has been most influential in developing an awareness that the child's understanding is shaped not only through encounters with the physical world but through interactions with people and in culturally meaningful situations.[6] These encounters are made significant principally through language. Such a view of learning is absolutely consistent with the storyline approach which utilizes both the prior learning and experience of the child and engages the learner in active dialogue. To be effective, such approaches require a teacher orientation that is essentially facilitative. No longer can teachers regard themselves as the purveyors of knowledge and truth. They never were, but if we are to recognize the importance of what Bruner[7] calls "folk psychology" as a system by which "people organize their experience in, knowledge about, and transactions with the social world" and narrative as the process by which much "meaning-making" is achieved, then as educators we must utilize the powerful learning resource that resides inside the heads of all learners. But breaking out to a view of the teacher as a facilitator and enabler, as an orchestrater of learning, can be challenging. What storyline provides is a structure within which both the learner and the teacher can feel secure. Using the storyline method can be in one respect a first step towards a broader and more socially responsible conceptualization of the teaching/learning process.

## STORYLINE AS AN ACTIVE METHODOLOGY

One consequence of the move to a greater recognition of the learner's contribution to classroom interactions is a greater degree of classroom activity. But let's be clear: although storyline is essentially an active methodology, it must not be misunderstood as always physically active, always doing, always engaged in the manipulation of materials. Thinking is activity! Storyline provides an ideal setting in which to develop critical thinking skills, problem-tackling activities, interpersonal skills, positive attitudes and, at the same time, develop knowledge and understanding.

## ESTABLISHING A CONTEXT

An introduction to a storyline often begins with the teacher explaining that as a class they are going to create a story together. The place, time, and characters are developed with students as the teacher considers the objectives that are to be taught through the storyline. For example, the place and time might be established for a storyline by reading something like the following description which creates a picture in learners' minds:

As the two-lane road drops down into this seemingly quiet valley, one is struck by the quaintness of the scene especially since it is located so close to an urban area. The lush hillsides are dense with evergreen trees which surround the valley. Homes are tucked into the hillside but the evergreens are so thick one hardly knows they are there. Beyond the hills is the Cascade Range and on a sunny days the snow sparkles like diamonds in the sunshine. One is often struck by the beauty of the valley with its contrasts in colors and its backdrop of the mountain range.

Driving into the valley, rich farmland can be seen on either side of the road. For most of this century small dairy farms have existed along with other farms which grow berries and other crops that need a rich soil and adequate rainfall. At one end of the valley a small town which has existed since the early 1900s, sleepily goes about its daily rituals. The storefronts are mostly made of wood and brick and the main street serves as the commercial part of town. Off the main street are homes with big grassy yards and tree-lined sidewalks. The railroad intersects with the main street and once served as the primary means for transporting goods from Eastern Washington to Seattle. Now the railroad sits rusting as trucks have assumed that role. This is Cedar Valley.

This fictitious place can be created as a class mural to which each student contributes. The image of Cedar Valley is shaped by each student's vision of the valley and the making of the mural provides a visual foundation for the emerging storyline. Once the place and time have been established, the characters need to be created for the story. For this particular time and place a discussion as to who might live in this valley will help establish the characters.

A next step is to organize students in small groups to create families who live in Cedar Valley. Family groups will take many forms as students bring their own knowledge and backgrounds to this experience. Students make their family members like paper dolls and write information telling names, ages, physical characteristics, special interests, personality traits, and other interesting aspects about each of their family members. The introduction of the families to the class provides valuable opportunity for language work; developing vocabulary, oral communication skills; and group cooperation.

## THE EPISODIC STRUCTURE

The children are engaged in "collaborative storymaking"[8] which will lead them through a number of episodes in an unfolding narrative. The teacher's plan is constructed around these episodes within which the key ideas and curriculum content is delivered as the class becomes involved in the storymaking. All this takes place within a cycle of LOOK/LISTEN-ACT-REFLECT/DEVELOP, an interesting variant on the PLAN-ACT-REFLECT cycle in that it starts with action and not planning.

For this particular storyline, the key ideas to be developed might be a deeper understanding of community and land-use issues. One of the primary episodes is the construction of a shopping mall in this serene valley. Before this land-use issue can be explored, however, it is essential that the storyline develops in such a way that the students see and care about Cedar Valley as a tight-knit community rich in small-town traditions where people have a sense of pride and belonging. This can evolve by having students write about their setting and describe imagined historical events of the past in their community. Further, events and relationships among families in the community can provide opportunities for role play by students to deepen understanding of relationships within Cedar Valley.

Key questions can help shape the events in the storyline such as: What jobs might exist in this community? What might be some of the traditions in this community? What is everyday life like in Cedar Valley? Why do you think people like to live here? What historical events have happened to make Cedar Valley the community it is today?

When the shopping mall is proposed, questions would focus around land-use issues and amenities. What are the advantages and disadvantages of a shopping mall in Cedar Valley? How do communities decide how land can be used? What if the community decided it didn't want the mall, what could be done? These kinds of questions provide opportunities for learning about local government, due process, and the role of the citizen in a participatory democracy. Research skills, writing persuasive arguments, making oral arguments and the like could all be developed through this storyline.

## MULTIPLE OBJECTIVES

The strategy provides teachers with the opportunity to achieve multiple teaching objectives because of the way in which a plethora of learning outcomes are addressed by the learners. Most obviously there will be a range of objectives specific to the social studies content, but there also will be opportunities to set objectives in other aspects of the curriculum such as language, mathematics, and expressive arts. This is because the learning/teaching context is integrated and rich in opportunities. Social and personal development objectives can also be set within the interactive context of the storyline classroom. In fact, a difficulty can be to resist the temptation to overload the storyline with too many objectives.

As in the example in this article, the storyline briefly described could be developed in many ways. Attention could be focused on community life, jobs in the community, family interactions, land-use issues, dealing with change, or a variety of other topics. It is important for the teacher to determine the focus of the storyline and then develop it accordingly with the active participation of the learners.

## NOTES

1    NCSS Task Force on Teaching and Learning. (1994). "A Vision of Powerful Teaching and Learning in the Social Studies: Building Social Understanding and Civic Efficacy." In *Expectations of Excellence: Curriculum Standards for Social Studies*. Washington, DC: NCSS: 158.

2    McGuire, M. E. (January/February 1991). "Conceptual Learning in the Primary Grades, The Storyline Strategy." *Social Studies and the Young Learner*, 3 (3), 6-9.

3    Egan, K. (1988). *Primary Understanding*. New York: Routledge; and *Teaching as Storytelling*. Chicago: University of Chicago Press, (1989).

4    Barr, I.M. (1986). *Die Methode Glasgow*. Glasgow: Evaluation Advisory Service; and Letschert, J. (1991). *Topic Work: A Storyline Approach*. Enschede, The Netherlands: Institute for Curriculum Development Publications.

5    Vygotsky, L.S. (1962). *Thought and Language*. Cambridge, MA: Massachusetts Institute of Technology Press.

6    Edwards, D. and Mercer, N. (1987). *Common Knowledge*. New York: Methuen.

7    Bruner, J.S. (1990). *Acts of Meaning*. Harvard: Harvard University Press.

8    Scottish Consultative Council on the Curriculum. (1989). *Some Aspects of Thematic Work in Primary Schools*. Dundee: Scottish Consultative Council on the Curriculum Publication.

Ian M. Barr is the Director of Curriculum Development and Evaluation with the Scottish Consultative Council on the Curriculum, the national curriculum development agency in Scotland. He taught in elementary and high schools before becoming an evaluation specialist. His particular interests are holistic approaches to learning and the elementary school curriculum. He is also a Co-Director of the Dillingen Symposium in Germany, an international forum for the study of international and multicultural issues in education. Margit E. McGuire, immediate Past President of NCSS, is Professor and Chair of Teacher Education at Seattle University. Dr. McGuire has been the consultant and author of integrative curricula for elementary schools. [1993 note]

# Using Data in Elementary Social Studies Programs

# 78

**Rosemary G. Messick**
**June R. Chapin**

Students, as active learners, are busily
engaged in perceiving and interpreting data, which leads
to their construction and reconstruction of social reality.
Whether this social reality includes the knowledge and
skills of civic decision making depends on the kinds of
experiences children have. For young children, school is
the first civic arena. Both intentional and unintended experiences are crucial to their development as rational, civi-
cally conscious problem solvers.

Teachers have two broad, related guidelines to follow
in facilitating children's development of social reality. The
first is to recognize the cognitive, psychological, and social characteristics that impinge on children's ability to
relate to data. The second is to develop the art of selecting
and arranging appropriate settings in which children become ever more conscious of their use and creation of data.
These acts lend more or less power to their thinking.

## FITTING THE TASK TO THE CHILD

Recognizing these developmental contingencies is the first
step for structuring appropriate experiences in civic decision making. The second step is determining how to structure the curriculum to focus on civic decision making. Two
layers of the curriculum need to be considered in this step.
The most basic layer is the civic culture of the classroom
society. The topics we choose to study constitute the second layer. Let us look briefly at developmental contingencies that guide our curriculum thinking and at two layers of curriculum organization the civic culture of the
classroom and topics of study.

*Characteristics of Young Children.* The developmental
tasks typical for primary grade children (K—4 ) must
guide the structuring of situations that lead to data generation, interpretation, and decision making. Young children are engaged in expanding their egocentric view of
the world. They learn, often reluctantly, to take the perspectives of other persons. In the process of decentering,
they perceive that one person can incorporate several roles.
They begin to group or classify phenomena by characteristics, e.g., size, shape, or age. Psychologically, they are
less introspective and more able at physical than verbal
expression of feelings. For children of this age, competition and group work are new and often stultifying. They

are only beginning to become interested in the product as
well as the process of their learning.

Children in the intermediate grades (5-8) are more able
to deal cognitively with what is unfamiliar than children in
primary grades. They can see themselves in the context of
time as well as space. Psychologically, most middle graders
enjoy individual challenges and team activities. They spend
extended periods working on projects and making products. Socially, middle-grade children are keenly aware of
fairness and enforced rules. They assume reciprocity in
friendship and see that their acts have social consequences.

*Classroom Culture.* Living and working together in a
classroom setting can become an experience in civic decision making. The classroom that reflects habits of democratic ideals of individual rights and concomitant responsibilities, equality of opportunity, due process, and consent
of the governed in the conduct of daily living helps teach
young children these ideals. Too often, however, classroom
management "systems" deny children opportunities to
observe their own and others' behavior and make conclusions or rules about how good relations and learning can
best be promoted. Finding ways to infuse classroom management with opportunities for children to participate
meaningfully requires that teachers think about the larger
goal of civic education. Asking first graders, for example,
to vote on an issue of classroom procedure such as lining
up to go out for recess or electing the "citizen of the week"
may not be meaningful to the children or useful to classroom efficiency as a decision-making exercise. On the
other hand, discussing the good examples of cleaning up
before leaving for recess and keeping individual check-
off charts that give access to the class "good citizenship
club" are positive and developmentally meaningful to
young children. Classroom routines and information sharing based on visual representations of "class data" instruct
young children about the habit of measuring and counting representations of the real world. Ongoing activities
that chart classroom events such as losing teeth, having
birthdays, reading books, growing seeds, and feeding animals provide ways of representing events that lend children a heightened sense of history and time. Compiling
an ongoing classroom diary, journal, or time line that
stretches around the classroom walls allows young children to look back at their shared yesterdays and connect
them to today's events. Rather than using data to make
group decisions, as is appropriate for older students, the
focus for young children is on using data that assists them
individually to construct and reconstruct their worlds.

Although using data to make group decisions is not
necessarily part of young children's repertoire, middle

Reprinted from *From Information to Decision Making: New Challenges for Effective Citizenship*, NCSS Bulletin Number 83, pp. 11-18. Copyright 1989 by National Council for the Social Studies.

graders take delight in it. Scheduled times for student-led class meetings reinforce the meaningfulness of the decision-making process. If the power of class meetings as an exercise in decision making is to be realized, students need to tackle issues close to their lives and make real decisions to carry out. Teachers can promote these activities by the questions and problems they pose about classroom procedures for children to investigate. Organizing teams to collect data, for example, on what happens to the playground equipment after recess or how long it takes to handle announcements or check papers will involve coaching children on how to record what they count, time, or observe. Once data from a series of events or days are collected and organized, children have some tangible information to reflect upon. They can discuss the reliability of the data, and suggest ways to change or improve the situation based on reasons or criteria for the change. If they record these reasons, the new routine can be evaluated to see whether it does respond to the class-created criteria or standards.

## TOPICS FOR STUDY

Finding the fit between the developmental stages and topics of study that involve the civic decision-making cycle continues to be a challenge. Finding avenues that open personal engagement with larger issues to children is essential for capturing interest. Extending the possibility through the accumulation of data about the issue and viewing the issue from more than one perspective is the instructional obligation.

Conventional wisdom confines primary-grade children to topics consistent with the tangibles of their daily lives. Thus analyzing how the work of the world gets done begins with the family unit and moves on to the school and neighborhood. Changes in the context of young children's daily lives suggest that we need to see these conventional topics in a global context. Veteran kindergarten teacher Barbara Schubert's experience illustrates the significance of contextual change. Schubert incorporated the use of a globe with toy sharing. Whenever a kindergartner brought a toy to sharing time, Schubert helped the child find out where the toy had been manufactured. Red adhesive dots were placed on the globe to identify the toy's point of origin. Over time the stickers began to accumulate in certain areas—Taiwan, Hong Kong, and Japan. Schubert led the class to talk about trade. They became curious about the sources of their clothing and food and about what their local area produced for the rest of the world. She was amazed that the children were persistent in their interest and able to verbalize thoughts about such abstract and wide-ranging topics. Children brought their parents into the classroom to show them the globe and were able to tell them about the location of the dots as well as what they meant. The topic was informal and ongoing and, as Schubert discovered, developmentally appropriate. In part, this topic was possible to teach because of changes in children's lives caused by expanded world trade, tele-vision, family mobility, and immigration. Of equal importance, we would argue, to unlocking this kind of a topic for young children was the impetus Schubert used: Toys are personal and prized.

Issue-oriented topics that concern natural resources can engage middle-grade students. Their almost universal love of animals makes research on endangered species an attractive theme upon which to build integrated science and social science experiences. Data collection on the habitats, habits, population, reasons for decline, and measures to protect and rescue individual species is an essential beginning to exploring what can and should be done to maintain the world's biological variability. Other topical possibilities that could also incorporate a complex cycle of civic decision making are local and regional land use and planning.

Organizing an issue-oriented unit assumes that elements of history and geography will be naturally infused into the research. For example, to understand the current transportation in a given locale, it is important to uncover reasons for building or pulling out rail or trolley lines or constructing canals and locks. Were there spring floods and summer drought seasons to overcome? Did the rivers run contrary to where goods needed to go? Did private individuals or public monies build the lines? Did freeways connect new population centers or follow old routes? Which came first, roads or population centers? Most textbooks do not, indeed could not, provide the amount and variety of data required to entertain issue-oriented topics. To engage students in research of this sort, teachers need to prepare an array of source materials. To undertake topics that involve students in the complete cycle of civic decision making requires team efforts and locally oriented curriculum work undertaken over time.

## DATA-GENERATING STRATEGIES

Elements of the processes and skills involved in civic decision making can be incorporated in all social studies topics. Reviewing some of the data-generating strategies highlights several possibilities and materials.

*Historical Newspapers, Diaries, and Letters.* Organizing a set of locally and regionally pertinent copies of historical newspapers for distribution to teachers facilitates relating the past to the present. All newspapers keep archives. Most would gladly contribute a sample that focused on reproducing the local version of major events such as the explosion of the atomic bomb or that included a sample copy of the newspaper from each decade since publication began. The comparisons that could be made depend on the topic under study, but could range from prices of items on sale advertised at local retail outlets to styles of dress and major public policy issues.

Any historical topic is enriched by reading diaries and letters written by people of the period. Excerpts from diaries that are related to issues or events can bring data about a period to life for children. Two examples that could enrich the human side of national issues are the collection of famous speeches by noted Indian chieftains: Indian Oratory (Vanderwerth 1971) and first person narratives of escapes to freedom in the North in The Underground Railroad (Blockson 1987).

More recent events such as the Vietnam War or the effects of the Peace Corps can be illuminated by family letters. Middle-grade students should be alerted to asking parents and grandparents about letters saved from wartime or immigration experiences. Reading such letters opens up the complexity of issues as well as the reality of daily living in the past and their families' connection to it.

*Oral History.* Collecting oral histories can be a powerful means of sensitizing children to the importance of process in reconstructing the past. Interviewing senior citizens and grandparents in their communities gives children greater appreciation of the worth of seniors and can strengthen the bonds between the generations.

A fertile initial oral history topic is interviewing senior citizens about what elementary school was like when they attended. Children are fascinated by knowledge about their grade level. Questions about what subjects were taught, number of hours in school, games played, transportation to school, and what discipline the teacher used have high interest.

Questions for the interview should be short and simple. They need to practice the etiquette of asking their respondents' permission to use their information for a class project. Each student needs to prepare a written copy of the questions. Before going to their sources, children need to practice interview techniques in class. They should anticipate how they will record answers to their questions. They need practice in note-taking if that is the mode of collection chosen. If they plan to tape the interview, they need to practice taking notes from the tape.

Data from oral interviews are excellent vehicles for practicing the historian's craft. Students can examine whether respondents embellished the truth. Did they really walk two miles to school in three feet of snow? Does the person only remember the pleasant things about school? Students need to discuss what causes people to have selective memories about past events. By comparing different interviews on the same topic, students can plot areas of agreement about what life was like in elementary school. To support their hunches about these similarities and differences, they should go back to their data and compare the ages of their respondents or the places they went to school. For further corroboration, teachers can call upon the resources of the local historical society. Oral history projects move students from the passive role of reading about history to an active role of collecting and analyzing data about the past.

*Time-Lapse Map Study.* Using a series of maps or pictures that portray local and regional development over time helps students make spatial connections to the past. To make a visual composite of city or regional growth, students can colorcode a current map according to periods portrayed on the various historical maps of the same

area. Tracing names of neighborhoods, streets, and other prominent points of interest over time can uncover the changes in ethnic or tribal settlement patterns.

Students can trace the study of growth, transportation, and trade through a series of historical maps. Frequently, highways were built over native trails. Settlements often grew or stopped growing depending upon whether a railroad, canal, or paved road was built nearby. Middle-grade students can connect products to kinds of transportation. For example, mining centers are linked to manufacturing centers by rail or waterways. Historical map series show that cities and agriculture in the Southwest grew with the development of reservoir and canal systems.

Using a series of historical maps can be overwhelming to middle grade children. They need to narrow the data array and focus on telling the story of just one name, trail, river, or block on the various maps. They will find that to confirm guesses about their topic, they need to locate other resources. Although maps alone do not tell all the details students need to flesh out the story of their place, they are a good beginning.

*Data Bases.* Included in all the strategies for generating data, of course, are data bases. The hypothesis-testing kinds of thinking that can be promoted with data bases make them absolute musts for issue-oriented topics that require comparison and analysis. Traditionally, teachers have organized parallel groups to gather data and fill in the cells of a wall-sized retrieval chart. Horizontally, the cells typically listed common cultural characteristics such as food sources, shelter type, religious beliefs, clothing styles, recreation, family education, profession, location, contributions, and famous quotations. Vertically, the group topics such as Native American groups or famous people of the Revolutionary War were listed. After the class heard general group presentations, they could compare and contrast the groups and generalize about the broader topic based on the data contained in the chart constructed by the class group study.

Now electronic retrieval charts provide a technologically assisted way to stimulate drawing comparisons and testing hypotheses. Continuing to input classroom data gives repeated opportunity to interact with the mechanics and play with the power of rearranging the data. Data collections can be built on topics tailored to the interests of students: books read by individuals, movies seen, personal surveys of experiences, preferences in food, music, television shows, tracking weather and climate in world cities from daily newspapers, team and individual sports statistics, and individual daily calorie intake. The personal nature of the data and the electronic ability to display rearrangements of it can encourage students to call up comparisons.

More premade data base microcomputer programs are coming onto the market. Many require students to use them as electronic references. These come with teacher instructions to get students started in posing questions that probe and re-sort data according to different categories.

Some premade data bases are embedded in simulation-type

formats. *The Oregon Trail* (1985) is probably the one known best. Students are placed in roles that require decision making based on data as the trip from Missouri to Oregon unfolds. The *Carmen Sandiego* (1985) series has forced more students to become familiar with the *World Almanac* than generations of teachers combined! Geographical data and note-taking must be used successfully to trace the elusive Carmen. Other programs that involve the use of data are available. For example, *The Sea Voyagers* (1985) provides students a biographical profile of explorers from 1400 to 1800 and then provides data on maps, charts, models, graphs, tables, pictures, and cartoons that students must interpret to "play the game." Such programs can be used to link the traditionally reading-based social studies curriculum to an interactive setting that gives students practice in using data to make decisions.

## SUMMARY

What general guidelines for the elementary teacher emerge from the several data-generation strategies outlined? First, skills should not be taught in isolation from interesting and relevant content. This means that the development of data-generation skills cannot be separated from either the content or the values that govern their use. If the content inspiring data generation is linked to children's interests, they will enjoy the process. Second, the stages of problem solving — identifying a problem, formulating a tentative hypothesis, data gathering, and accepting or rejecting the original hypothesis — need to be incorporated into any data-gathering strategy and explicitly highlighted. Third, the primacy of group discussion throughout the data-gathering process is essential. Students should constantly be working in small groups and brought back to the whole group when they are engaged in understanding the meaning of the processes and the data. When the give-and-take of group discussion is based on data gathered about a topic of student concern, we can be assured that the thinking skills necessary for personal competency and effective citizenship are being developed.

## REFERENCES

Blockson, C. *The Underground Railroad*. Englewood Cliffs, New Jersey: Prentice-Hall, 1987.

*Carmen Sandiego*. San Rafael, California: Brøderbund, 1985.

"City Blocks," in *Microzine*. Jefferson City, Missouri: Scholastic, 1987.

Diem, R.C. *Computers in the Classroom*. How-to-Do-It Series 2, No. 4, Washington, D.C.: National Council for the Social Studies, 1981.

*The Oregon Trail*. St. Paul, Minnesota: Minnesota Educational Computer Consortium, 1985.

*The Sea Voyagers*. Greenwich, Connecticut: CBA, 1985.

Truett, C. "The Search for Quality Microprograms: Software and Review Sources." *School Library Journal* (January 1984): 35-37.

Vanderwerth, W.C. *Indian Oratory*. Norman, Oklahoma: University of Oklahoma Press, 1971.

White, C.S., and A.D. Glenn. "Computers in the Curriculum: Social Studies." *Electronic Learning* (September 1984): 54-64.

Rosemary G. Messick is a Professor of Education at San Jose State University in California, where her interests are in elementary and early childhood education and the use of computers. Dr. Messick has traveled widely and has taught and conducted research in Brazil. She is active in the California Council for the Social Studies, where she has presented a variety of programs of interest to social studies teachers. June R. Chapin is a Professor of Education at the College of Notre Dame in Belmont, California. Over the years, Dr. Chapin has written several textbooks for students and has published widely in professional social studies journals. She has been active in the California Council for the Social Studies and the National Council for the Social Studies, as well as in the College and University Faculty Association of NCSS. Dr. Chapin makes frequent presentations at various social studies programs. [1989 note]

# PART 12

## INTEGRATION AND THE SOCIAL STUDIES

"Social studies is the integrated study of the social sciences and humanities to promote civic competence," begins the NCSS adopted formal definition of social studies (1992). Using the concepts, information, theories, and methodologies from the various social sciences to examine a range of social problems and issues facing citizens is essential. Integrated learning as a tool in developing curriculum seeks to blend school subjects when creating and implementing social studies thematic units. Often, the themes selected for instruction are social studies issues or problems.

Advocates of integrated or thematic units believe that learning is best done when it is applied to real, practical situations rather than learning facts and skills in isolation. In creating and implementing social studies thematic units, students and teachers will find it valuable to seek information from the arts and humanities, because the works of visual and performing artists, musicians, and authors offer valuable insights into society and culture. Examining questions related to the environment cannot be accomplished without a knowledge of science while mathematics helps to organize numeric data and predict probabilities.

An integration of social science disciplines is often required when teaching social studies. Curriculum and content integration has long been an established practice by many elementary teachers of social studies when teaching about a person, place, or event. In planning and developing curriculum for instruction, teachers should ask themselves the following questions: How do I define integration? Is it always a good practice for me to integrate social studies instruction with other subjects? When do I integrate social studies and to what extent is the integrity of social studies content being maintained?

Mansfield describes, in some detail, a teacher who developed an integrated unit about Egyptian life. She includes many responses by the teacher and fifth and sixth grade students to this curriculum unit and identifies four characteristics for successful teaching of integrated instructional units. Alleman and Brophy examine how integration is being applied in textbooks and classrooms and suggest five guiding principles to help distinguish productive from counterproductive attempts at content integration. Heath describes an eight-step planning strategy to use in developing and teaching integrated units that relate content and skill learning across several content areas. He also discusses many of the concerns expressed by teachers related to integrated learning.

The section concludes with samples of integrated units that are strong in social studies concepts, attitudes, and skills. Atwood, McGuire, and Nickell illustrate how soup can be used as an organizing theme to examine cultures through an integration of concepts from the social sciences and inquiry skills through varied teaching strategies. Braun, Kotar, and Irick present a cross-discipline example of integration that stresses the development of attitudes and ethics toward hard work and compassion through the development of a school garden. Stanley takes students out of the classroom on walks along a nearby river and builds models that combine science, geography, and history into the study of a local river and a changing environment. Because the preservation of rain forests seems to be of great interest to young people, Rosenbusch describes an approach to studying this environment, which emphasizes social studies, second language, and culture.

Elementary curriculum is most powerful when it integrates traditional school subjects into units of study that explore themes and topics in depth and through perspectives provided by science and the humanities. Integrated learning seems to be effective in helping young learners make important connections across the curriculum and into the real world. It is important that integration complement and enhance social studies instruction and that social studies learning be maintained while engaging in the use of integrated curriculum content.

# 79

# Students' Perceptions of an Integrated Unit
## A Case Study

**Barbara Mansfield**

Social studies is a subject area that can act as a vehicle for presenting the skills and concepts that permeate the whole curriculum (Charlesworth and Miller 1985). Within the primary division (K-3), the program is frequently presented in this fashion, using social studies as an umbrella under which a variety of subject perspectives and skills can be brought to bear on a specific topic or theme. At the junior level (4-6), this integrated approach is rarely used because teachers tend to present a subject-based program. A provincial review conducted by the Ontario Ministry of Education (1985) reported that of the forty-two schools reviewed, only a "few" (1-25%) junior-level classrooms were consistently integrated. In this case, an integrated curriculum was defined as "learning which is synthesized across traditional subject lines, and learning experiences which are arranged in order to be mutually reinforcing."

While critics of the thematic way of organizing social studies programs have said that this approach lacks vigor and continuity, theme-based units can have a number of strengths. They may be relevant to the students' interests and experiences, have the capacity to deal with emerging issues, and ensure that specific topics are covered (Wood 1987). They also present a framework upon which the integrated approach can be developed.

The term "integrated studies" is interpreted in several ways and is applied to practice in varying degrees. Integration occurs when the boundaries between the content of various subjects are weak or blurred. In other words, the content of each subject is subordinate to some idea that reduces its isolation from the others (Bernstein 1975). The curriculum involved may be teacher developed and controlled or predominantly child initiated. If it is the latter, many topics may be dealt with at the same time within a classroom because each child may be working in his or her own area of interest. When the theme is teacher developed, it tends to take the form of a unit of work that cuts across the traditional subject lines. The manner in which learning is encouraged can range from formal class lessons to group activities to independent research.

Integration also occurs along a continuum from a partial to a total inclusion of the program subjects (UNESCO 1982), and many teachers integrate only part of their program. For instance, they may cut across the disciplines of language arts, social studies, and science to present a theme about "The Community." Those subject areas that are not included within the theme are dealt with in the usual manner. In some schools, integrated studies involve not only the cooperative use of the various disciplines' skills and information but also cooperation among teachers to develop and present the different aspects of the theme in a coherent and meaningful way (Schools Council Integrated Studies 1972).

Although several studies have examined and described the organizational factors and the processes involved within particular integrated approaches to organizing curriculum (UNESCO 1982; Ladenberg and Silfern 1983; Boehnlein and Ritty 1977; Cameron 1986), little has been said about how children perceive these practices. Do nine-to-twelve-year-olds understand the implications of integrated studies as compared with the traditional subject-oriented program? Have they a preference for one over the other, and if so, why?

The descriptive case study presented in this article examines how a class of grade 5/6 students reacted to, and what ideas the students had about, an integrated unit in which they participated. It looks at the way in which the children associated many of the process changes with integrated studies.

## METHODOLOGY

Participant observation and open-ended interviews with the students and the teacher were the two principal forms of data collection. During the five-week period in which the integrated unit was in progress, I spent three days a week observing in the classroom. Both individual and small group interviews were conducted with seventy-five percent of the students whose names have been changed. This involved all students for whom I had parental permission to interview formally. I used a constant comparative methodology (Glaser and Strauss 1967; Glaser 1978) to analyze the collected data and record emergent categories.

## THE SETTING

Maple Hill School, located in a middle-class suburban area of a small Ontario city, is a pleasant modern building housing approximately 350 kindergarten to grade 6 students. Teaching methods and program approaches vary with the teachers, but the tendency has been for classes to be more activity oriented in the primary grades (K-3) while the junior division (4-6) presents a subject-oriented and more traditional program.

The grade 5/6 class that is the focus of this study was composed of seventeen grade 5 and ten grade 6 students.

In addition to their classroom teacher, Mrs. Ball, there were also specialists responsible for teaching music, French, and physical education. The manner in which program responsibilities were broken down promoted a very fragmented approach to curriculum.

## THE INTEGRATED UNIT

Mrs. Ball decided to use the social studies theme of "Life in Egypt" as the basis for developing a five-week integrated unit with her class. Almost all the time spent in the regular classroom was devoted to activities surrounding the theme. In this way, the teacher used social studies as "the glue that bonds together the elements of the curriculum for young children" (Broman 1982, 203).

The unit was teacher developed and controlled to a great extent. Three strands made up its framework.

a. Activity cards for which students had both compulsory and choice selections were developed by the teacher. These cards were divided into categories such as information, creative writing, word study, research, art, and problems.

b. Teacher-initiated formal lessons were taught and followed by activities that supported the lesson focus.

c. Other activities, which included creating a large mural, seeing films and slides, preparing for Egyptian Day, writing in journals, reading stories, and working on child-initiated projects were also part of the program.

The students were given notebooks in which they were to keep notes, pictures, and any written work that their activities involved. Tracking sheets were pasted on the front and back covers of the notebooks. These sheets listed all of the activity card titles with the compulsories underlined. Columns entitled "date completed" and "comments" were filled in by the teacher as the students completed each activity. When the unit was finished, the students had a complete record of what they had accomplished.

Mrs. Ball worried about the lack of math included in the unit's activities so she took time out during the first few weeks to teach formal math lessons. As time passed, the class got more deeply involved in the Egyptian theme, and Mrs. Ball resigned herself to giving up the lessons until the end of the unit.

## STUDENTS' PERCEPTIONS

As the student interviews progressed, two points became evident. The children tended to view the integrated unit in two ways. Some equated doing activity cards with integration while others suggested that integration involved focusing upon a topic and learning a lot about that topic. In some cases, students combined both views.

During the unit, many procedural changes did take place, which influenced the classroom interactions. Although students valued these changes and attributed them to the integrated approach, many of them were not necessarily inherent to this particular approach. Approaches that give students the opportunity to make choices, promote informal communication within the class, and use an activity-based approach to learning are common to several programming styles. But it is important to note that most of the students had definite opinions to express about what they thought integrated studies involved and how this approach differed from the more subject-based one they normally experienced.

## THE TENSION BETWEEN AUTONOMY AND CONTROL

Children felt that they had much more freedom and choice during this unit than they had within the regular program. Much of this feeling was derived from the activity-card portion of the unit when the students were allowed to choose their own activities. They had few time limitations placed upon them and were given more freedom to interact with other students. At the same time, the children clearly realized that this freedom was limited. They knew that the teacher retained control of the program, but they accepted this without question because the limited freedom of choice was much more than they usually had. Andy and Charlie's conversation exemplifies this understanding.

A: Well, like you can choose any topic at all and like, sometimes the teacher just says, "You do this and you do that." But you can choose what you want to do.

B: [B is the interviewer] So choice has a lot to do with it?

C: Yeah.

D: Because you have freedom. She tells you what to do, and this time she can tell you what to do but there's more things to do. Like, she tells you to do cards, and there's so many different topics with the cards. Not just one thing to do.

Another more subtle control on the children's behavior was the culminating activity, "Egyptian Day." The students knew that on the final day of the unit they would be making several presentations to their parents and other students within the school. Mrs. Ball introduced potential plans for Egyptian Day on the first day of the unit, saying: "Before we get to Egyptian Day, you're going to have to work hard learning things about Egypt." The importance of this celebration and its influence on the children is evident from the following remarks.

H: And then they [the students] think, well, if there is the Egyptian Day at the end, we'll work hard because I might get the part I want.

K: And everything is going to be hanging up on the walls.

H: And if they do good on one part, like they wrote funny poems and they might be the jester—not the jester but the person who announces it.

I: Well, people are trying hard for things to be neat because people are going to be coming and looking in their notebooks and looking at their art work and what they've done.

## COMMITMENT

During the five weeks of the unit, the level of student commitment to the activities involved was high. Indicators of this commitment included positive changes in behavior, pride in work, completion of tasks, high level of interest, and perception of time.

Several individuals discussed how their behavior, as well as that of their fellow students, had changed and the reasons responsible for those changes. They believed that the students were more involved in their work and much happier in class. The major reason for this change was a lessening of teacher talk and teacher direction, which allowed for more student choice and active participation in classroom activities. This lessened the chance of being bored and thus getting into trouble. Connie presented this point of view when she stated:

> Yeah, kids don't seem to be goofing off as much. They don't seem to be yelling out and that's because the teacher isn't talking too much. So they're really doing basically their own things. As I said, the teacher's not really telling them what activity they should be doing. I think they goof off a lot because they wanted to do their own thing really. So the teacher really just tells you what part of the unit you're going to be doing today.

The belief that this unit was more fun than the normal program appears to have strongly influenced the children's attitudes and behavior. Was the work fun because it was easier (as some believed) or was it easier because it was fun? In either case, activities that are enjoyable tend to gain our interest and commitment. Also, because the students took ownership of their activities, they worked harder to complete them properly.

It is interesting to note that Mrs. Ball's opinions on behavior during the unit were very similar to those of her students.

> They're actually working.... [During the usual program George and Ronnie] would just sit there. They'd be quiet, or they'd try to get somebody's attention in the room, or they'd throw an eraser to get somebody. Like, they weren't really keen on what they were doing.... They've been working just fine. You know, [Bill's] the only one that really at times has still goofed off a bit, but that's only been after he's usually worked for a good half-hour block, which is far more than he worked before. . . . [Y]esterday afternoon, you could have heard a pin drop in there, and they were all so enthused about making their names in hieroglyphics and hanging them over their own heads.

The students appeared to be very proud of their work. Several children indicated pride in the art and research work. Also, having a special notebook just for the unit was a strong factor in the promotion of this pride. Edith and Emily stated outright that they were proud of their notebooks, whereas Sally liked hers because she felt that it would hold good memories for her of what she had done during the unit. The students also felt good about the positive comments that the teacher had written on their tracking pages. Marty and Alice presented another reason for liking their special notebooks:

M: Well, I like mine. I think it's neat too. . . . You get your own book to have it all in instead of looking all over all these books, one for art and one for math and everything.

A: It's neat; it teaches a topic. You just don't scribble it or something. You just make it neat . . ., [as if] it's one of your best notebooks.

There was a concerted effort on the part of the majority of students from the start of the unit to complete their assigned activities. Students frequently worked on these tasks when there was no pressure to do so. The following excerpt from my field notes presents an example of this phenomenon.

> I arrived just before recess was over. It was raining, so students had stayed in. Many of them had already started working on a card, and Mrs. Ball was busy discussing things with individual students.

Why did the children put in so much extra time and effort on their activities? Emily suggested, "Just to get them finished, and we enjoy doing them, I guess."

Completing activity cards became a strong personal and social goal in the class. Children were often overheard comparing the number of cards they had finished. In one case, Susan spent five minutes drifting from one person to the next, asking how many cards each had done. Amy completed thirty-nine out of a possible forty-two activities and became the class heroine for this feat. Her classmates kept a close watch on her progress throughout the unit. The one major exception to this race was Cornelius, who, by the end of the unit, had completed few of his obligatory assignments. He seemed to have trouble finding information and was easily distracted from his tasks. Much of his time was spent in watching others complete their work.

The level of interest remained high throughout the unit. The variety of activities available appeared to promote this feeling. When asked why she thought that activities were interesting or fun, Sylvia replied,

S: Well, usually the work, it gets long and boring. You have to do so much written work. I like art a lot, and so you get to do art and stuff, play games, and you learn a lot from these things too. And the research cards are lots of fun 'cause most of them are easy and they're neat to find out facts about.

The content of the unit was also innately interesting to the children. When I asked the students to write down their favorite thing about the unit, a third of them focused upon the information they had learned rather than the processes in which they had been involved. These students said that they liked things such as King Tut, pyramids, mummification, gods and goddesses.

The high level of interest prompted the children to discuss the unit at home with their parents. Several students brought things from home to share with the class-for example, hieroglyphic charts, Egyptian photographs, pictures, and money. Helen brought in a wooden model of a pyramid, which she and her father had constructed at home.

The old saying of "Time passes quickly when you're having fun" seems to have been borne out here. The following comment, which Heather made about wasting time, exemplifies the level of commitment that many students had toward their work.

H: It wastes time too.

B: How does it waste time?

H: Well, you think while you're writing you've been there for half an hour, but actually it's been about an hour that you've been working on one [activity].

B: Why do you think that happens?

H: Because you work on it so hard and then you don't know how fast the time went by.

## INTERACTION

One of the goals most teachers have is to promote positive interaction and helping behaviors among their students. The Egyptian unit's structure appeared to encourage this. Children were allowed to "visit" with each other freely, and frequently they helped one another to find needed resources or information. In many situations, they shared ideas and reacted to each other's completed work. At times, they shared the same activity, working either in a parallel fashion or together.

When the children chatted with others, the majority of their talk focused upon the Egyptian theme, with both content and process being discussed. Among the several reasons that students went visiting were: looking for new ideas, getting information on a specific topic or about the way in which to do an activity, trying to locate a card or resource material, being curious about what others had done, and discussing social items that had little to do with school work. The following excerpt from a group interview indicates that the students were aware of the different reasons for visiting.

B: I've noticed that while they're doing their work. some people get up and wander around and visit for a while. Do you know what sorts of things these children tend to talk about?

K: Well, some people want to know questions.

S: And some just want to read their things.

H: I like going around because if I can't think of anything then I just go around and look at what the other people are doing to get some ideas.

S: You ask some people when you need to know something, like something on Anubis and somebody was doing an activity card on Anubis. You could just ask them.

The classroom environment became a very supportive one during the progress of the unit. The helping behaviors observed were spontaneous in nature, arising from the natural interaction among the children rather than being superimposed by a formal group structure that the teacher controlled. This type of behavior was quite evident during a class assignment in which each child took on the persona of an ancient Egyptian god, goddess, or pharaoh. In preparation for doing this, each student had to research his or her character. Throughout the initial period of time allotted to this task, there were many incidents of students' finding and sharing information about each other's characters. This activity engendered an excitement about and interest in helping others to locate needed information. The children identified strongly with their chosen characters. This response was very similar to that which McCarthy and Braffman (1985) reported when they observed children in the process of assuming Victorian identities as part of a history project.

The children suggested that interaction patterns with the teacher had changed too. Hilda's comment that "she [the teacher] can wander as much as she wants now instead of having to stay by the board when she has to teach a lesson" suggests that this approach to teaching-learning might promote greater teacher-student interaction. Several comments made by the students support this view. These students also felt that the integrated approach was more difficult for the teacher because she now had to deal with the many topics dictated by the activity cards. They felt that it must be hard for the teacher continually to change focus as she moved around the room to help different students deal with a variety of topics.

## FRAGMENTATION/CONTINUITY OF THE PROGRAM

During their interviews, the students were asked whether or not they saw a difference between the unit and their ordinary school program. The answers given by some students indicate their awareness of how fragmented the regular program was and how the integrated approach promoted a more holistic learning process.

K: Well, I like doing subjects and that, but I like doing Egypt. It's really interesting, and I think I like working on a topic better because it's more . . . one topic, you don't have to switch from one subject to the next. Otherwise, the next day you carry on from the last subject, and you've done so many after that or if it's at the end of the day, you've done so many like the next day you just forget. Like, I like doing the integrated unit 'cause you don't have to change.

C: I thought it was kind of better because, well, usually you keep changing subjects, and this time you just centered yourself on usually one thing, and you can do that all day or keep going.

Mrs. Ball's comments on this topic tended to support the idea presented by the children. At one point, she discussed her science program. In her opinion, because of the lack of time and the spacing between lessons, the carry-over was not good and the program had no clear focus. When comparing this view with her feelings about the components of the regular program, Mrs. Ball saw many positive aspects in the integrated unit. She compared her sense of direction in the Egyptian unit to what happened during a science unit, which she had taught at an earlier date:

We didn't do anything. I just felt like, well, the whole month had gone by and we had one note in our notebook. There was nothing to mark.

There was nothing to evaluate. I don't think the kids particularly got a lot out of it. I didn't feel like I got a lot out of it. This way there is a sense of knowing where you're going and what you're doing, and you're immersed in it.

## EVALUATION OF THE INTEGRATED UNIT

By changing the mode of program organization and presentation, the teacher affected a multitude of classroom behaviors. The way in which she interacted with the children within pedagogical situations became more individualized and less formal. Students were permitted to socialize with each other more frequently, which, in turn, often led to peer teaching situations. Evaluation became an ongoing, integral part of the program rather than the final step. Finally, children and teacher began to view subject content as being somewhat overlapping rather than being molecular or separate in nature. As mentioned earlier, all of these elements are not necessarily the outcomes of an integrated program, but they were significant changes in the minds of both the students and the teacher.

Participating in the integrated unit was a positive experience for all the students who were interviewed. Throughout the duration of the unit, a highly supportive environment was created, one in which individuals had more autonomy in choosing their activities and how they went about completing them. They also were able to socialize with others in a variety of ways not usually permitted within the normal program.

The fact that each student was working on his or her own activity much of the time may have contributed to this positive attitude in another way. The constant comparison that students make about each other's progress and level of competency when completing either group or class tasks was missing in this situation. (Although the students often talked about their work to each other, they were usually involved with different activities, so the discussion was descriptive or helping in tone rather than comparative.) Therefore, individuals could work at their own speed and level of ability without the pressure of being judged constantly against their peers. This also encouraged the teacher to look at each child's work within that child's own framework of ability.

The high level of student commitment to the unit's activities appears to have been promoted by several factors. The first has already been discussed: autonomy. The holistic approach to studying a topic was a second significant factor. Both the students and the teacher enjoyed the lack of fragmentation within the Egyptian unit. Both felt that not having to change their focus from subject to subject was a relief and allowed them to learn in more depth and scope.

Finally, the children's commitment was secured by the variety of processes in which they were involved and the fact that much of the topic's information was innately interesting. Several students discussed how much they liked being able to paint, build models, write poetry and stories, and watch films rather than always having to make notes in their notebooks as they usually did during regular classes. They also found the Egyptian topics fascinating and were often encouraged to read further to find out more information about a specific topic.

Teachers who are interested in attempting the integrated studies approach for the first time might consider (a) potential student interest in the theme, (b) a variety of activity processes, (c) some degree of student autonomy to be built into the unit, and (d) ways in which social interaction could be encouraged. This study describes a program that was only partially integrated, because a few subjects were held separate. For the teacher who is a novice in this area, this approach may be a first step on the path toward complete integration.

## REFERENCES

Bernstein, B. 1975. *Class, Codes and Control* (Vol. 3). London: Routledge and Kegan Paul.

Boehnlein, M., and J. Ritty. 1977. "Integration of the Communication Arts Curriculum: A Review." *Language Arts* 54(4): 372-77.

Broman, B. 1982. *The Early Years in Childhood Education*. Chicago: Rand McNally. Cameron, B. 1986.

Cameron, B. 1986. *You Are There: Reading, Feeling, Thinking History*. North Dakota University, Grand Forks: (ERIC Document #ED278590).

Charlesworth, R., and N. Miller. 1985. "Social Studies and Basic Skills in the Early Childhood Classroom." *The Social Studies* 76(1): 34-37.

Glaser, B. 1978. *Theoretical Sensitivity*. Mill Valley, CA: Sociology Press.

Glaser, B., and A. Strauss. 1967. *The Discovery of Grounded Theory*. Chicago: Aldine Publishing Company.

Ladenberg, V., and M. Silfern. 1983. "A Year as Woodland Indians: The Social Studies Core of the Third Grade." *Moral Education Forum* 8(2): 24-30.

McCarthy, L., and E. Braffman. 1985. "Creating Victorian Philadelphia: Children Reading and Writing the World." *Curriculum Inquiry* 15(2): 121-51.

Ontario Ministry of Education. 1985. *Education in the Junior Division: A Look at Forty-Two Schools*. (Provincial Review Report No. 5).

Schools Council Integrated Studies. 1972. *Exploration Man: An Introduction to Integrated Studies*. Oxford: Oxford University Press.

United Nations Educational, Scientific, Cultural Organization. 1981. *Integrating Subject Areas in Primary Education*. Bangkok, Thailand: (ERIC Document Reproduction Service No. ED 238 536).

Wood, F. 1987. *The Social Education Framework: P-10*. Ministry of Education, Schools' Division, Victoria, Australia.

Barbara Mansfield is a member of the Faculty of Education at Queens University in Kingston, Ontario, Canada. [1999 note]

# Is Curriculum Integration a Boon or a Threat to Social Studies?

# 80

**Janet Alleman**
**Jere E. Brophy**

Curriculum integration is one of those ideas that is obviously good. Articles and in-service speakers extol its potential for enhancing the meaning of what is taught, saving teachers time by reducing the need to make as many preparations, reducing the need to rush to try to get everything covered, and making it possible to teach knowledge and skills simultaneously. For social studies and other content area subjects that suffered reduced time allocations as a result of the back-to-basics movement, integration is often pictured as a way to restore necessary content emphases. In general, integration is pictured as a viable response to problems of content balance and as a way to save time and make for natural, holistic learning.

These seemingly compelling arguments have predisposed most educators to view integration as a desirable curriculum feature. Indeed, the implicit maxim is "the more integration, the better." A few years ago, we shared this predisposition. Even now, we find it difficult to resist the notion of integration as a good idea in the abstract. In recent years, however, we have been carefully examining the best-selling elementary social studies series, looking not only at the student texts but at the questions, activities, and evaluation methods provided as ancillary materials or suggested in the accompanying teachers' manuals. We also have been observing classrooms and talking to teachers about integration practices. We have found some positive features of the integration activities suggested in textbook series or described by teachers; we have also found some undesirable ones. Too often, activities described as ways to integrate social studies with other subjects either lacked educational value in any subject or promoted progress toward significant goals in other subjects but not in social studies.

Rather than expanding the scope and enhancing the meaning and importance of the social education curriculum, these so-called integration activities disrupt its coherence. In effect, they amount to intrusion of language arts or other skills practice exercises into social studies time and, thus, are better described as invasion of social studies than integration with social studies.

Focusing on instructional activities, we will provide examples of what we consider inappropriate integration attempts drawn from curriculum materials, classroom observations, and teacher interviews. Then we will suggest guiding principles that can serve as criteria for distinguishing

Reprinted from *Social Education*, October 1993, Volume 57, Number 6. Copyright 1993 by National Council for the Social Studies.

productive from counterproductive integration attempts, and we will present a checklist that can be used as a self-monitoring tool.

## FORMS OF INTEGRATION

Worthwhile integration implies that a single activity accomplishes significant curricular goals in two or more subjects simultaneously. Integration comes in many forms. Sometimes the nature of the topic makes integration natural or even necessary. Some topics inherently cut across subjects (to teach about ecology, for example, one must draw content from both science and social studies). Other topics are primarily identified with one subject but require applications of another to be learned meaningfully (e.g., map and globe studies are part of geography and consumer education is part of economics, but both of these topics require applications of mathematical knowledge and skills). Problems with so-called integration activities usually do not occur with these more natural forms of integration, although we have seen map and globe skills exercises and consumer economics exercises that were more artificial mathematics skills practice than authentic social education activities.

Most of the problems occur with forms of integration that are not inherent in the topic and thus involve integration for integration's sake. Teachers can use these forms productively, however. For example, adding content drawn from a secondary subject can enrich the content in the primary subject (e.g., reading about and displaying the works of an artist as a means of enhancing the study of a historical period). And combining knowledge from a content-area subject such as social studies with processes from a skills subject such a language arts can be effective.

In the latter forms of integration, the focus of the instruction and the accountability pressures placed on students may be on the knowledge, the processes, or both. If students were asked to write to their political representatives about their legislative roles or policy positions, the assignment would be primarily a social education activity although it would include application of writing skills. In contrast, students might be asked to write about an imaginary visit to the White House as an exercise in descriptive writing. If the emphasis in structuring and grading were placed on the technical aspects of composition and form, the assignment would be mostly a language arts activity, not a social studies activity. Finally, students who were studying book reporting skills in language arts and the American Revolution in social studies might be asked to read and report on biographies of key Revolutionary figures. Such an assignment might promote progress toward important goals in both subjects, especially if the goals were made clear to the students and the reports were graded separately for technical features and for historical content.

Social studies series frequently seek to integrate subject matter by adding content drawn from other subjects (artistic or literary works or biographical inserts, for example) or by calling for use of language arts or other skills to manipulate social studies content. These so-called integration activities may or may not have educational value, depending on the nature of their primary goals. If an activity's primary goal is not an educationally significant one, the activity does not belong anywhere in the curriculum. If its primary goal is educationally significant but is not a social education goal, the activity may belong in the curriculum but should not be scheduled during social studies time. For an activity to be considered part of the social studies curriculum, its primary focus should be one of the social education goals that have been established for the social studies unit—a goal that would be pursued whether or not this particular activity were included.

## ACTIVITIES THAT LACK OR MASK SOCIAL EDUCATION GOALS

Unfortunately, many of the activities we have observed in social studies classes or discussed with teachers, as well as many of the activities suggested in or supplied with the manuals that accompany current social studies series, lack significant social education value. Some of these lack educational value in any subject and are just pointless busy work (alphabetizing the state capitals, for example, or counting the number of states included in each of several geographical regions). Others may have value as language arts activities but do not belong in the social studies curriculum, for example, exercises that make use of social studies content but focus on pluralizing singular nouns, finding the main idea in a paragraph, matching synonyms, or using the dictionary. Other activities are potentially useful as vehicles for pursuing significant social education goals but are structured with so much emphasis on language arts that the social education purpose is unclear.

For example, a 4th grade manual we reviewed suggests assigning students to write research papers on coal. Instructions emphasize teaching the mechanics of investigating the topic and writing the paper. The manual makes little mention of social education goals or major social studies understanding. It does not note that humans have unlimited wants and limited resources; nor does it discuss issues such as conservation of natural resources or the development of energy alternatives. With the task narrowly conceived and the focus on research and report writing, it is unlikely that the resulting individual reports would yield enough variety to allow students to benefit from one another's work. Consequently, the social education value of this assignment will be minimal and its cost-effectiveness will be diluted further because of the considerable time required to obtain and read content sources for content's sake, copy or paraphrase data, and make presentations to the class.

We observed similar masking of social education goals in a unit on families in which teachers ask students to recreate their families by portraying each member using a paper plate decorated with construction paper, crayons, and yarn. The plates were to be used to introduce family members to the class and then combined to create mobiles. This is another time-consuming activity, and the teacher structured it to emphasize the artistic dimensions rather than the social education dimensions. If it really served significant social education purposes to have students introduce their families to classmates (and we doubt that it does), they could do so more effectively through photographs than through paper-plate representations. We would prefer that the class spend the time learning about the nature of and reasons for variations in family configurations and roles in various cultures during various historical periods.

We observed a comparable example in a 4th grade unit on tropical regions in which students were asked to construct examples of homes in tropical parts of the world. Again, such an activity would take a great deal of time, especially if authentic building materials were used and the instructions emphasized artistic construction activities rather than social education concepts and principles. To address effectively social education content such as the influence of climate and local physical geography on living conditions, the teacher would do better to lead discussion of a collection of pictures selected to illustrate variations in shelters and ways that local conditions affect them rather than having students construct models.

## COST-EFFECTIVENESS PROBLEMS

Time-consuming art and construction projects are often labeled ways to extend or integrate social learning, but they often fail to focus on significant social understandings. Some of these projects develop (or at least allow) opportunities to use social studies knowledge or skills (for example, constructing models or maps of the home or school), but others simply lack social education value (for example, carving pumpkins to look like U.S. presidents).

Besides artistic construction, role-play is another frequent basis for activities that are either inherently limited in social education value or too time consuming to be cost-effective. For example, one unit on families we came across called for students to dress in costumes, play musical instruments, and participate in a parade as a means of illustrating how families celebrate. On the following day, they were to write about the event. This series of activities offers tie-ins with humanities and physical education and provides a stimulus for language arts work, but it lacks significant social education content. The emphasis will likely be on the doing rather than the knowing and understanding. Using pictures with structured discourse would provide a more cost-effective and focused learning experience.

Another activity, suggested as a follow-up to a lesson on jobs in the family, calls for the teacher to divide the class into groups of four and assign roles of mother, father, brother, and sister. Each age group acts out the following situations: a child wants to learn to ride a bicycle, a child wants to make a Halloween costume, or the children in the family want to do something special for a parent's birthday. Again, these activities appear to lack social education value, and no information is directed toward the teacher about structuring the activities beforehand or about leading debriefing discussions afterward to focus students' attention on important social education ideas.

Cost-effectiveness problems are also presented by collage and scrapbook activities that call for cutting and pasting many pictures, but not for thinking or writing about ideas linked to major social education goals. Instructions for such activities are often offered in ways that focus students on the processes involved in carrying out the activities rather than on the ideas that the activities should develop, and teachers often evaluate the final products on the basis of criteria such as artistic appeal. As a result, students may spend a great deal of time on such hands-on activities, yet fail to accomplish significant social education goals.

If activities are worthwhile at all, it is because they fulfill important curricular, and in this case social studies, purposes—not because they cut across subject-matter lines. We believe that the time teachers spend on activities that cut across subject-matter lines should be assessed against the time quotas allocated for those subjects in ways that reflect the cost-effectiveness of the activities as means of accomplishing each subject's major goals. Teachers should not divert classroom time allocated for social studies to activities that lack significant social education value. Thus, a teacher might justify a project for which students make puppets to depict U.S. presidents if the activity is planned primarily as an art project and assessed against art time. We do not believe, however, that this activity can be justified as a social education activity unless the students also spend time investigating and synthesizing biographical data. Even then, the teacher should ask "Does the constructing take precedence over the understanding?" and "Is this activity the best choice given the limited time allocated for social studies instruction?" Cognitive and affective engagement need not, and in some cases should not, be hands-on.

## CONTENT DISTORTION

Attempts at integration sometimes distort the ways teachers represent or develop social studies content. For example, a unit on clothing included a lesson on uniforms that called for a follow-up activity in which students would make puppets of people dressed in uniforms. The teacher set up situations in which two puppets meet and tell each other about the uniforms they are wearing. This activity was problematic because it was time consuming, because it emphasized art activities over social education content, and because it called for knowledge that was not developed in the lesson (which provided only brief information about the uniforms worn by fire fighters and astronauts). Most fundamentally, however, it was problematic

because it resulted in a great deal of social studies time being spent on uniforms, a topic which at best deserves only passing mention in a good unit on clothing as a basic human need.

We also observed content distortion in a unit on pioneer life that included a sequencing skills exercise built around an illustration of the five-step process of building log cabins. The last three steps in the described sequence were arbitrarily imposed rather than logically necessary and did not correspond to the illustration. It appeared that the authors wanted to include an exercise in sequential ordering somewhere in the curriculum and chose this lesson as the place to include it, rather than seeing this exercise as important for developing key knowledge about pioneer life.

Developers often insert unnecessary counting and sequencing activities into social studies materials as a way to incorporate mathematics skills. Another lesson example called for students to read statements about various constitutional amendments and to identify the amendments by number. This already dubious assignment was complicated further by directions calling for the amendment numbers to be placed in the proper squares of a three-by-three-inch matrix which, if filled out correctly, would yield the same "magic number" as the sum for each row and column. As if this were not convoluted enough, the instructions called for the students to "put the number of the amendment in the box with the same letter as the sentence that describes it." This illustrates what can happen when integration is sought as an end in itself by materials developers or teachers who are focused on covering topics and skills rather than on accomplishing social education goals.

## DIFFICULT OR IMPOSSIBLE TASKS

Ill-conceived integration attempts sometimes require students to attempt to do things that are difficult, if not impossible, to accomplish. A 5th grade lesson on the English colonies called for students to demonstrate their understanding of the joint stock company by diagramming its structure to show relationships and flow among the company, stocks, stockholders, and profits. Besides being a distraction from the main ideas in the unit, this activity seems inappropriate because the operations of a joint stock company, although relatively easy to explain verbally, are difficult to depict unambiguously in a diagram. Again, it appeared that this instructional activity existed because the curriculum developers felt the need to include a "making-a-diagram" exercise somewhere, and not because they saw it as a natural and appropriate way to develop understanding of key content.

Another activity, questionable for similar reasons, called for students to construct battle maps illustrating strategy and key events in a Revolutionary War battle. Another called for students to use pantomime to communicate one of the six reasons for the Constitution as stated in the Preamble. Even if one believes that exercises in pantomime belong in the social education curriculum (we do not), this is about as farfetched and inappropriate an application of pantomime as we can imagine. Finally, a lesson on feelings included an assignment calling for students to draw happy, sad, and hungry faces. In the absence of familiar and commonly shared cultural expectations concerning the facial manifestations of hunger, how are students supposed to go about the task of depicting a hungry face?

Activities should develop the key ideas in a unit and be difficult enough to be challenging and to extend learning, but not so difficult as to leave students confused or frustrated. Too often, activity suggestions call for students to display or use knowledge they have not been taught in the curriculum and they are not likely to have acquired elsewhere (e.g., having 1st graders role-play scenes from Mexico when all they have learned about Mexico is its location on a map, or having 4th graders debate state-level budgetary cuts when the only background information they have been exposed to is a single textbook page describing the roles of legislators).

## FEASIBILITY PROBLEMS

Activities also must be feasible for implementation within the constraints under which the teacher must work. Certain activities are not feasible because they are too expensive, require space or equipment that is unavailable, involve unacceptably noisy construction work, or pose risks to the physical safety or emotional security of the students. For example, a suggested follow-up to a lesson on following directions called for the teacher to post the four cardinal directions in their proper locations around the classroom, then to have the students line up and march around the room to music as the teacher called out directions ("March north. March east.") This attempted integration of social studies with physical education would not have much social education value even if it were conducted in the gym, but at least it could be implemented there. To undertake this activity in a classroom crowded with desks and other furniture is to invite chaos and injury.

Failure to be realistic about constraints led to rejection of an integration activity proposed by a teacher we know. She planned to take her class to see a small exhibition of art by Monet to illustrate how his work was influenced by the geographical features of France. This activity involved a two-hundred-mile round-trip, so the plan was rejected. A more viable alternative would be to acquire prints of the artist's work and bring them to class for observation and discussion.

## ACCOMPLISHING INTEGRATION WHILE MAINTAINING THE COHERENCE AND THRUST OF SOCIAL STUDIES

Teachers cannot depend on the manuals accompanying contemporary social studies series to focus their efforts on activities that call for appropriate use of integration. In the name of integration, these manuals suggest a great many art projects, isolated skills exercises, and other activities that have minimal social education value and little or no connection to the main ideas developed in the units. The most recently published series have downplayed the insertion of isolated basic skills exercises into social studies units, but they have begun to emphasize new features such as literary selections and cooperative learning activities. Sometimes these new features are selected and used in ways that are well suited to development of unit topics, but sometimes they are not. Some of the activities that are based on the inserted literary selections are essentially language arts activities with little or no social education value, and some of the suggested cooperative learning activities involve artificially forcing the cooperative format into learning situations to which it is not well suited. Although its particular manifestations evolve, the problems of so-called integration activities that diminish the coherence and thrust of the social education curriculum persists.

The following guiding principles will help you determine if an individual instructional activity is appropriate for an integrated learning experience in social studies.

■ Each integration activity must be a useful means of accomplishing a worthwhile social studies goal.

■ The activity must represent social education content appropriately and not distort the integrity of the subject matter.

■ The activity's benefits to social education must justify its costs (for both teacher and students) in time and trouble.

■ The activity must be geared to the appropriate level of difficulty.

■ The activity must be feasible for implementation within the constraints under which the teacher must work (e.g., space and equipment, time, and types of students).

These notions about assessing activities that integrate across subjects for their educational value in general, and their social education value in particular, involve applications of a larger set of principles that we have developed for assessing, selecting, and designing learning activities that enable school subjects to be taught for understanding, appreciation, and application (Brophy and Alleman 1991). The most basic of the principles is goal relevance: each activity should have at least one primary goal that, if achieved, will represent progress toward one of the major social education goals that underlie and justify the social studies curriculum. This principle applies just as much to activities that integrate across subjects as to activities that focus exclusively on social education. Teachers who value social education and want to enact a coherent social studies curriculum will need to bear this in mind and make sure that the thrust of that curriculum is not blunted by significant time spent in activities with only marginal social education value.

In view of the kinds of problems noted here, we believe that it is important for teachers to stop thinking about curricular integration as necessarily a good thing and begin to think about it as something that is feasible and desirable in some situations but not in others.

Teachers will have to learn to assess activities not just for whether their students are likely to enjoy the activities and will be able to complete them successfully, but also for whether the activities offer sufficient educational value to merit inclusion in the curriculum. We offer a set of principles and guidelines for making such decisions in Brophy and Alleman (1991). For judging activities that purport to integrate across subjects, we suggest that social studies teachers also consider the following questions:

▐ Does the activity have a significant social education goal as its primary focus?
▐ Would this be a desirable activity for the social studies unit even if it did not feature across-subjects integration?
▐ Would an outsider clearly recognize the activity as social studies?
▐ Does the activity allow students to develop meaningfully or apply authentically important social education content?
▐ Does it involve authentic application of skills from other disciplines?

▐ If the activity is structured properly, will students understand and be able to explain its social education purposes?
▐ If students engage in the activity with those purposes in mind, will they be likely to accomplish the purposes as a result?

## REFERENCE

Brophy, Jere, and Janet Alleman. "Activities as Instructional Tools: A Framework for Analysis and Evaluation." *Educational Researcher* 20, no. 4 (May 1991): 9–23.

Janet Alleman is a Professor of Teacher Education at Michigan State University in East Lansing and a Senior Researcher with the Classroom Strategy Research Project. Jere E. Brophy, University Distinguished Professor at Michigan State University, East Lansing, is Coordinator of the Classroom Strategy Research Project and Codirector of the Institute for Research and Teaching. [1993 note]

**Phillip A. Heath**

Citizens of a midwestern town have won their battle to prevent location of a waste disposal facility near their town, where it could have jeopardized the safety of the local water supply.

After months of collecting information, meeting in community groups, communicating with environmental agencies, and debating with officials of the national landfill company seeking to develop the facility, a legal decision was reached preventing the use of the controversial site for waste disposal purposes.

At the same time, other debates were taking place regarding the rising costs of waste disposal in the community, other possible locations for landfills, and alternate means of waste disposal.

In a local elementary classroom, young learners made a six-week study of some of the same issues adults were considering. Simulations were developed and information was collected from printed sources, interviews with experts, and guest speakers. Hypothetical alternative sites and disposal techniques were investigated and proposed, and their consequences were debated. In a mock city council meeting, testimonies were presented and after debate and consideration of the alternatives and consequences, a vote was taken by members of the council.

This fourth-grade social studies unit focused on citizenship, decision making, and environmental issues. At first impression such units often seem exclusively within the domain of social studies; but in reality, to be effective they need to be interdisciplinary. Not only do they require the computational and measurement skills of mathematics, the knowledge and skills of science, but also an ability to put these into a social context.

Three points from these events set the tone for the remainder of this discussion. First, public issues can have an impact on classroom instruction directly and indirectly. Second, good units of instruction can be developed around issue themes that effectively integrate student learning from several disciplines. Third, integrated instruction and learning, including the use of units with current issues as their themes, can enhance the knowledge and skill development normally associated with each of the disciplines involved.

The purpose of this discussion is to examine some basic considerations in planning instruction that connect social studies, science, and mathematics. An exemplary unit is used to illustrate a possible approach.

Reprinted from *Social Studies and the Young Learner*, January/February 1989, Volume 1, Number 3. Copyright 1989 by National Council for the Social Studies.

## PLANNING STRATEGY

An eight-step strategy was designed for developing and teaching the integrated units. Note that with the exception of the first two steps, students were directly involved in the process.

1. *Select a unit with potential to integrate math, science, and social studies and to consider important issues and problems.* The broad unit "community planning" was chosen because it was consistent with local curriculum goals, permitted a study of decision making at the local city council level, and had potential for social action projects.

2. *Identify major outcomes.* Some of the major goals, concepts, and skills of the unit included helping students understand:

   a. The meaning of citizen participation in decision making.

   b. Group decision making and being able to relate a current community issue and local government to this process.

   c. The interrelationship of science, math, and social studies in the investigation and resolution of public issues.

   d. The concept of trade-offs.

   e. To be able to use skills and tools of mathematics in collecting and reporting data. These include presenting information in table, chart, and graph forms; comparing and contrasting ideas; representing various sizes and measurements; translating measurements from maps and legends; and, applying costs versus benefits.

   f. The various occupations of individuals in the community. It should be noted that it was soon found that to effectively integrate instruction and learning, the content of the unit had to be expanded beyond the content of classroom textbooks. It is suggested that this would probably happen in the majority of effective integrated multidisciplinary units.

3. *Select an important issue or problem.* Students examined a variety of current community issues and problems, and with the guidance of the classroom teacher, selected "landfills." It should be noted that a subsequent unit related bicycle safety, changes in transportation needs due to changing technology, and formation of rules and laws. Another considered fossil fuels, community planning, and energy consumption.

4. *Select major themes or strands.* In a series of teacher-led discussions, which resembled "show and tell" or "webbing" as used in reading and language arts classes, several

major themes or strands were identified that provided a "clothesline" or gave direction and continuity to the unit and also applied major skills and knowledge from math and science. The teacher provided considerable guidance in recommending skill applications from mathematics. While the major strands remained essentially the same throughout the unit, many additional categories were added and their "cells" were filled with major skills and concepts from each of the disciplines.

5. *Developing an Instructional Strategy.* A number of instructional techniques such as reading for information, using printed and pictorial resources, guest speakers, interviews, classroom discussions, and constructing bulletin boards were used. The most exciting technique was the use of simulations in the action outcome part of the unit. Through simulations, students debated issues, alternatives, and consequences of proposed courses of action. Leading up to a presentation in an actual city council chamber, students collected information, prepared presentations, investigated roles of city council members, studied the procedures of city councils, and notified the local press of the activities of the class. In the presentation, class members assumed the roles of city council members and citizens. The activity gave new meaning to instruction dealing with decision making and citizen participation in local government. Students experienced the outcomes of almost real decisions in a realistic social context.

6. *Developing Scope and Sequence.* The major purpose of this very brief outline of the instructional plan was to ensure sufficient time for the unit, proper timing for the introduction and development of skills with appropriate activities, and a quick check to ascertain if major concepts and skills were included.

7. *Instruction.* Actual instruction evolved from the interaction of the teacher and students. Considerable emphasis was given to student decision making throughout the unit. This ranged from decisions regarding whole class activities to individual decisions about what kind of material to give in a class presentation.

8. *Assessment and Evaluation.* The assessment of learning involved both formal and informal techniques. Teacher observation of students in decision-making situations, assessment of presentations according to predetermined criteria, conferences with students, and formal quizzes were used. The criteria used in development, assessment, and evaluation were: (a) a clear set of expectations understood by each student prior to the unit, (b) sufficient opportunity for each student to demonstrate knowledge and skill learning in a variety of ways, (c) an accurate written procedure for recording and reporting information, and (d) student involvement in developing the criteria. An underlying agreement between the teacher and students was that the teacher would be "transparent" as to expectations and criteria for assessment and evaluation.

This planning format was used with equal success in grades two through seven. Teachers and students agreed that the units were exciting, relevant, and added "life" to teaching and learning. The teachers agreed that while workload increased, the time was well spent. They contended that they were the "real" learners.

## DISCUSSION

While the teachers involved in these multidisciplinary units reported success in student learning, there are many educators who question the need for, and value of, a multidisciplinary approach.

One concern relates to the meaning of integration. The term "integration" as it is being used here refers to instructional approaches relating content and skill learning, and applications within and across content areas. Understanding the concept of integration is helped by viewing it as a continuum with a separate subjects approach at one end and a single interdisciplinary subject at the other.

Integration using a separate subjects approach is usually a result of realigning or timing the content of existing disciplines in order that similar concepts and skills in each area can be developed at the same time. For example, an energy unit in science would parallel a community unit in social studies.

A comprehensive unit at the other end of the continuum is an example of a total interdisciplinary approach. Developed at the start of this century, the approach gave rise to units of work that were thematic in nature, involved almost total daily immersion of teacher and student, and lasted for several weeks. Subject matter divisions were blurred, if not impossible to detect.

Newly integrated subjects (or courses) focusing on science-technology-society, that have been developed recently in junior and senior high schools are related to the total interdisciplinary approach. While these subjects/courses have earned mixed reviews, their rationale, framework, and teaching materials are potentially useful to educators who wish to integrate these subjects in the elementary school.

Especially valuable is the work at Pennsylvania State University in the S-T-S Project, and the materials produced by the Social Science Education Consortium, including their "Framework for Curriculum Reform in Secondary School Science and Social Studies" (Bybee, Hickman, and Patrick, 1987).

Many teachers find themselves between the two extremes represented on the one hand by the separate-subjects approach, and on the other hand by the interdisciplinary approach. Probably the most favored approach occurs in integrating subjects within a single social studies or science unit.

Despite the favor it has found with many, the idea of integrating subjects is open to question in the minds of many teachers. Often, their reluctance is based on one or more of these three assumptions. First, mathematics is one of the most important and functional school subjects, while social studies is the least (Goodlad, 1983). Second, integration reduces the level of knowledge and skill learning within the disciplines involved. Third, developing and organizing materials and strategies for integrated teaching puts an extra burden on the teacher.

While there is some truth to the last item, there are sound counter arguments to the first two. A substantial percentage of classroom time is spent in teaching and learning about facts with limited opportunities for application of learning. Through integration and inclusion of meaningful problems and issues, students can be expected to raise their level of cognitive abilities and learn how to use content and skills in problem solving and decision making.

Present compartmentalization of teaching and learning does not facilitate application of skill and knowledge across disciplines or the application of these to "real-life" issues. Admittedly, some classroom time normally devoted to introduction and reinforcement of facts and skills will be lost when additional activities and content are added. However, the increased potential for developing higher levels of cognitive abilities is a good trade-off. Instructional strategies which integrate instruction in math, science, and social studies can complement and reinforce learning in each discipline and, through application of material learned to current issues and problems, increase both the quality and quantity of learning.

Educators continue to rate citizenship education as the primary purpose of education (Hahn, 1985). As knowledge and related technologies, issues, and problems continue to grow at a rapid rate, education for effective citizenship will also become increasingly difficult to achieve. Citizenship education is multifaceted and contains competencies that can only be achieved through the "linking" of learning from many disciplines. Clearly to "do" good social studies requires the inclusion of vital and current issues and problems that are examined and debated from a multidisciplinary perspective. The need for this perspective, particularly in math, science, and social studies, is summarized quite well in a statement made by Milson and Ball (1986). Integration is "...effective because the learning of concepts will be enhanced by approaches from different points of view. Realistic, because students will encounter an integrated problem-solving situation consistent with the demands of present day living."

## REFERENCES

Ron Brandt. "On Science and Curriculum: A Conversation with James Rutherford," *Educational Leadership*, December 1983/January 1984.

Cohen, Herbert and Frederick Staley "Integrating With Science: One Way to Bring Science Back into the Elementary School Day," *School Science and Mathematics*, November 1982.

Goodlad, John I. "What Some Schools and Classrooms Teach," *Educational Leadership*, April 1983.

Hahn, Carole L. "The Status of the Social Studies in the Public Schools of the United States: Another Look," *Social Education*, March 1985.

Hickman, Faith M. and John J Patrick, and Roger Bybee. *Science, Technology, Society: A Framework for Curriculum Reform in Secondary School Science and Social Studies*. Boulder, Colorado: Social Science Educational Consortium, Inc. 1987

Milson, James L. and Stanley Ball. "Enhancement of Learning Through Integrating Science and Mathematics," *School Science and Mathematics*, October 1986.

Selby, Cecily Cannan. "Integrated Mathematics, Science and Technology Education Opening Doors and Opening Minds," *The Technology Teacher*, February 1988.

Smith, Allen "Promoting Reasoning Skills: An Interdisciplinary Approach," *The Social Studies*, November/December 1985.

Phillip A. Heath is an Associate Professor of Education and the Associate Dean at the Ohio State University, Lima. Dr. Heath is a member and former Chair of the Science and Society Advisory Committee, NCSS, and has authored articles on children's decision making, integration of instruction and learning, and science and technology in the social studies. [1989 note]

# In the Soup: An Integrative Unit

# 82

**Virginia A. Atwood**
**Margit E. McGuire**
**Pat Nickell**

*"Emphasis on specific disciplines obscures the unifying
questions of [humans'] experiences."*

*Peter Dow*

## Integration of elementary school curricula

is coming on strong—again. There is a difference this time,
though. Rather than forcing all the curriculum into the mold
of a unit's topic, teachers are seeking the natural connections—the goal is substance, not show. The watchwords
are relevance, motivation, and investigation.

Teachers recognize that young children view their
world holistically. At the same time, they know that children today are, generally, more knowledgeable and cosmopolitan than their counterparts forty years ago when
curriculum integration was "in." Today's children live in a
media-stimulated environment and are easily bored and
turned off by the textbook mimeograph sheet routine
which passes for social studies in many elementary school
classrooms. Curriculum integration is pedagogically sound
but it must be carefully and logically planned. One way
to meet the needs of these citizens of the 21st Century is
to select unique organizing themes that motivate students
to investigate interesting phenomena. The central theme
or idea becomes the catalyst for developing the concepts,
generalizations, skills, and attitudes which are the goals
of elementary school social studies.

This article demonstrates two important aspects of integration: integrating the social sciences within social studies
and integrating or correlating social studies with other subject areas of the curriculum. The activities are samples from
a unit using soup as the organizing theme to develop the
concepts of culture and needs as they relate to customs, time,
and geographic location. Soup was chosen because of its
universality In some form, it has been a part of all cultures
for thousands of years. All children are familiar with soup; it
is part of their diet. Materials are readily available and lend
themselves to teaching concepts, skills, processes and generalizations from social studies, language arts, health, science,
fine arts, and math. The goals of the unit are:

1. To introduce or reinforce student understanding of the
   concept of culture.
2. To teach children that people around the world share
   the same basic needs and meet those needs in some of
   the same ways.

Reprinted from *Social Studies and the Young Learner*, September/October
1989 and November/December 1989, Volume 2, Numbers 1 and 2.
Copyright 1989 by National Council for the Social Studies.

3. To teach children that people meet their needs using
   available resources.
4. To teach children that the manner in which those needs
   are met may vary over time and across cultures.

## INTEGRATING THE SOCIAL SCIENCES

A major goal of elementary school social studies is helping students learn about other cultures, other places, and
other times, as well as understanding their own culture
and time. This means understanding people: how and why
they interact with each other individually and in groups;
how they meet their physical, social. and intellectual needs;
and how these relate to the place and time in which they
live. The knowledge base for social studies is drawn primarily from history and the social sciences—all of the social sciences, each making a unique and important contribution. To have a more thorough and balanced view of
ourselves and others, we must develop the concepts, generalizations. and data gathering and analysis skills particular to geography, economics, anthropology, sociology,
political science, psychology, and history.

From the multitude of possible choices, topics and
problems must be chosen which utilize the knowledge base
of all the social sciences, are relevant to the lives of children, can be taught through direct experience or building
on prior experiences, and which have a high potential to
motivate. The following are sample lessons that demonstrate the thematic approach for integrating the social sciences into a viable social studies unit. Specific content and
goals are provided with each lesson: obviously, these can
be adapted to meet the needs of individual classrooms.

## "PLACE" SETTINGS

*Goals*

■ To have students examine soup "place" settings and
draw conclusions about the culture and history these
settings portray.
■ To have students identify food as a basic need and give
examples illustrating the universality of soup.

*Materials (Select from the following)*

■ Worker's lunch setting: (old) thermos bottle; (old metal)
lunchbox; stew-type soup; sandwich (e.g., bologna).
■ Child's lunch setting: child's place-mat; glass of milk;
child's bowl of alphabet soup; peanut butter sandwich
(half).
■ Japanese setting: bento box; chopsticks; rice; green
salad; miso, or other Japanese soup; Japanese-type
teacup with green tea (greenish liquid).
■ Mexico or Southwest U.S. setting: woven straw mat;
colorful ceramic bowl; chili; heavy glass goblet; burrito
or taco.

■ Louisiana setting: oilcloth table covering; chicory coffee; bowl of gumbo; oyster crackers; filé; Louisiana Red Hot or Tabasco Sauce.

## TEACHING STRATEGIES

1. Arrange place settings on tables about the classroom and have students visit each table.
2. With students seated, direct a discussion around the following questions:
   ■ What can you conclude about the people who might sit at each setting?
   ■ What is your evidence?
   ■ Where might each setting be found?
   ■ What does each setting have in common? (SOUP)
   ■ What might we conclude about soup? (For example, it is found everywhere; it is a basic part of the diet for rich and poor; it has been around since early in history, perhaps since prehistory; it is common to all cultures.)
   ■ What are the probable differences between soups of the rich and poor; those of other periods in history; those of various parts of the world?

## EXTENSIONS

1. Place settings which include a representative centerpiece depicting other foods, flowers, animals, clothing, or products will enhance learning about the era or area. Students might be asked to research the country, region, or era the place setting represents to create these centerpieces.
2. Have students draw or create place settings for other groups based upon knowledge or research. See if classmates can then identify the various places or time periods depicted in each setting.
3. Have students write a dialogue which might occur at one of the place settings among the people who might be seated there.
4. On a map, have students locate places where the place settings might be found.

## "GEOGRAPHY IN SOUP"
*Goal*
■ To develop an understanding of differences among regions by examining soups traditional to various regions.

*Materials (for each small group of students)*
■ Recipe books, encyclopedias, blank outline maps of the U.S. and the world.

## TEACHING STRATEGIES

1. Divide students into small groups and provide each group with recipe and reference books, and maps.
2. Assign one of the following soups to each group: gumbo, clam chowder, (french) onion soup, vegetable soup, gazpacho, potato soup, chili.
3. Ask students to make judgments about where they think these soups probably originated and why.

4. Have students research to find the ingredients for the soup assigned. Have them list the ingredients and determine where each food item is commonly grown or produced in the United States or world. Have groups indicate on the maps where selected ingredients are commonly found, using symbols of their choosing.
5. Students may also wish to research the geographic and historical origins of some of the ingredients, tracing their migration routes to the U.S. A good source for this is "Eating Your Way Into Geography: Linkages, Migration and Cultural Diffusion," a handout provided by the National Geographic Society at summer institutes and workshops.

## EXTENSIONS

Provide, or have students bring in, regional recipe books from various parts of the country. Based on examination of recipes in the regional cookbooks, what conclusions can be drawn about the meat and vegetable products indigenous to the regions?

## "MINI-MARKET ANALYSIS"
*Goal*
■ To develop skills for gathering, organizing and interpreting data.

*Materials*
■ Paper and pencil.

## TEACHING STRATEGIES

1. Have students predict the five or six soups they think might be the most popular among students at their school.
2. Have small groups or pairs of students go to each classroom in the school and poll students as to their favorite soups.
3. Based upon the results, ask students to draw conclusions using the following questions to direct discussion:
   ■ Do results have anything to say to parents? the school cafeteria cooks? soup companies? television advertisers?
   ■ What ingredients or textures seem to make certain soups more popular than others?
4. Inform students that they have participated in what business and industry call a "market analysis." Discuss why market analyses are useful. Have students brainstorm what types of companies might use market analyses, and how they might be accomplished. How are results used? Ask students if they can think of any products which have come on the market and then been dropped. Discuss market analyses relative to television shows and sponsorship of television shows, especially events such as the Olympics.

## EXTENSION

If you live near a soup company (e.g., Campbell's or Lipton), have a speaker in from the company or take a field trip to watch soup being made and discuss the uses of market analyses.

## INTEGRATION AND CORRELATION

The concepts of interaction, change, and environment are "claimed" by both science and social studies. Observing, inferring, classifying, serial ordering, and gathering, organizing and interpreting data are skills used in social studies, science, language arts, math, and the fine arts. Clearly, there are many natural connections among the various curriculum areas. When these connections are recognized and teaching is structured to acknowledge and reinforce them, integration or correlation may occur. For our purposes, integration and correlation are defined as teaching strategies in which concepts and skills from several curriculum areas are taught simultaneously while studying a particular theme or topic.

In integration there are no content boundaries. Students are unable to discern when social studies ends and science or language arts begin. In fact, there are no such beginnings and endings as students investigate a topic from various perspectives. When subject areas remain discrete, but a common theme serves as the organizer for developing instruction in each, then correlation is occurring.

It is likely there are more natural connections between social studies and language arts, science, or the fine arts, although all areas of the curriculum connect at some point. However, there are unique concerns in each of the curriculum areas which may be overlooked or ignored unless taught specifically and from the perspective of that subject area. An often repeated caveat must be restated: Good teachers look for natural connections rather than forcing integration at the expense of sound pedagogy. To insist on a totally integrated, or even correlated, curriculum is unrealistic.

## THEMES

Interesting themes develop naturally out of social studies, and the more unique they are the more motivating they will be. In selecting a theme, consider the extent to which it relates to a number of areas of the curriculum. For example, "In the Soup" is a theme which lends itself to a variety of curriculum areas and learning activities and, at the same time, provides opportunities to link subjects and motivate students. They have time to explore a question or phenomenon from a variety of angles rather than simply covering one unrelated topic after another as they move from subject to subject through the school day.

The following lessons are offered to stimulate thinking about integration and correlation. Each can be taught at various grade levels with adaptations.

## MAKING SOUP

*Goals*
- To develop process skills for gathering and interpreting data.
- To develop concepts of life cycle and food sources.
- To learn about the availability of particular soups and soup ingredients to specific groups of people.

*Materials*
- Soup ingredients, hand lens, utensils for cooking, heat source.

## TEACHING STRATEGIES

1. Choose a vegetable soup recipe that includes vegetables from roots, stems, fruit, and seeds. Divide the class into groups so that each group can make soup. Assemble the necessary ingredients and utensils.
2. As students begin to make their soup, have them make observations about the ingredients. For example, describe how potatoes look, feel, and smell prior to peeling or cutting. Use the hand lens to make observations, especially of onion skin and spices that are used in the soup.
3. Provide opportunities for students to infer or predict the number, size, and location of seeds. For example do larger vegetables or fruits have larger or more seeds than smaller ones?
4. Have students classify ingredients according to the part of the plant (i.e., root, stem, seed, or fruit), food group, or where that food is grown.
5. Have students discuss or write about questions such as: Did the Pilgrims (Colonials, 49ers, Caddo Indians, Longhunters in Kentucky, etc.) have access to these ingredients? Why or why not? What kind of soup did they eat? What is your evidence?

## EXTENSIONS

Students may wish to write a poem or story describing their experience making soup. This is an opportune time to discuss words which describe tastes, textures, and smells.

Discuss the production of ingredients such as flour, chili powder, or filé.

## THE BEST SOUP BOWL

*Goals*
- To develop concepts of change, interaction, energy transfer, and variables.
- To develop processes of observing, inferring, hypothesizing, measuring, and designing and conducting experiments.

*Materials*
- Bowls of various shapes, sizes, and materials; heat source; thermometers; liquids (water or soup).

## TEACHING STRATEGIES

1. Ask students what attributes make a good soup bowl and why. Possible responses include: material, thickness of the walls of the bowl, shape and size of the bowl. Most students hypothesize that these attributes help keep soup hot. Ask whether containers that retain heat also keep liquids cold. If experimentation determines that they do, other experiments can be conducted with cold liquids, which are obviously safer.
2. Help the class design experiments. For example, to determine which containers keep soups hottest, styrofoam, paper, plastic, and glass containers might be compared; controlling variables such as size, shape, and the amount of liquid in each container. Based on

their results, students can design and or construct the best soup bowl.

## EXTENSION
Students could design and conduct experiments to test the effects of several variables on the rate of cooling of liquids. A common practice is to cool soup by stirring and blowing on it. Conduct experiments to determine the fastest way to cool soup. Once again remember to hold other variables constant.

## MEASURING SOUP

*Goals*
- To practice multiplication and division of numbers.
- To work with fractions.
- To develop measuring skills.

*Materials*
- A soup recipe with suitable measurements to convert.

## TEACHING STRATEGY
Review measurement. Distribute the recipe and note how many people the recipe will serve. Have students increase or decrease the amounts in the recipe depending on the number of people to be served or on which fractions are being taught. Have students practice measuring, then organize them into small groups and have each group make the soup based on the new measurements.

## DRAMATIZING SOUP

*Goals*
- To reinforce skills of listening, talking, reading, and writing.
- To work cooperatively in a group.

*Materials*
- Stories about soup, such as *Soup with Rice, Mouse Soup, Stone Soup, Tawny Scrawny Lion*, or *Wombat Stew*, and appropriate props or materials for making puppets.

## TEACHING STRATEGY
1. Divide the class into groups and assign each a story to role play. Have students determine props they will need or have them make puppets of the characters. Remind students that it is not necessary to remember the exact words of the story; they can paraphrase. Practice the story so they become familiar with their roles and the story line; role play the story.
2. After students have performed their role plays, discuss similarities in the stories. Focus on how and why soup figured into each story. If the stories reflect different cultures, focus on cultural similarities and differences among the stories.

## EXTENSION
Choral reading activities provide a vehicle for appreciating the richness of some stories. *Wombat Stew* is an excellent story for choral reading activities.

## SOUP INVENTORS

*Goals*
- To work cooperatively in a group.
- To develop writing skills.

*Materials*
- Sample recipes of soups, ingredients, utensils for making soup.

## TEACHING STRATEGY
1. Arrange students in groups and distribute soup recipes. Have them examine the recipes for types and quantities of ingredients, noticing particularly the way instructions are written. Instruct groups to create and write their own recipes. Identify "experts": that is, good cooks or, perhaps, local chefs, to evaluate and make suggestions about their recipes. Students then may modify their recipes as necessary. Focus on writing instructions clearly and concisely.
2. Have students write about their roles as soup inventors. They might also write thank-you letters to the "experts" or write a soup company and send copies of their recipes.

## EXTENSIONS
Have students make grocery lists of ingredients they will need and establish budgets for purchasing ingredients. If possible, plan a field trip to a grocery store to purchase ingredients. Make the soups. Then devise a taste test of the soups and graph individual preferences on a bar or picture graph.

Have groups create advertisements and invitations to family members for a "Soup Party."

## REFERENCE
Atwood, V A.. McGuire. M.. & Nickell, M. P. (September/October 1989). "In the Soup: An Integrative Unit Part 1." *Social Studies and the Young Learner*, 2, (1).

Virginia A. Atwood is a Professor of Elementary Education in the Department of Curriculum and Instruction at the University of Kentucky, Lexington. Dr. Atwood edited the NCSS Bulletin *Elementary School Social Studies: Research as a Guide to Practice.* Margit E. McGuire is a Professor and Chair of Teacher Education at Seattle University, Seattle, Washington. Dr. McGuire has been the consultant and author of integrative curricula for elementary schools. Pat Nickell is Social Studies Coordinator for Fayette County (Kentucky) Schools. A former classroom teacher, Dr. Nickell coauthored "Global Perspectives Through Children's Games," part of the NCSS How-To-Do-It Series. [1989 note]

# 83

# Cultivating an Integrated Curriculum
## *The School Garden*

**Joseph A. Braun, Jr.**
**Michael Kotar**
**James Irick**

*As there was not always quite enough to eat, Benjamin used to borrow cabbages from Flopsy's brother, Peter Rabbit, who kept a nursery garden . . .*

*Potter, 1909, p. 13*

The above quote from a classic in children's literature brings to mind some questions about the role gardening can play in integrating the school curriculum. Shouldn't part of the school curriculum be about teaching children with the skill of caring for the earth through gardening and the value of sharing with others the products that are produced? Can gardening become a basis for instilling an ethic Noddings (1984) calls caring? How can gardening serve as an integrating theme for the curriculum to help students learn some of the skills and concepts that are typically covered in the elementary years? This article proposes answers to these questions.

In the following sections, we identify some developmental perspectives that teachers may keep in mind in their work with children. Also described are specific gardening activities that teachers can incorporate into their curriculum to promote cognitive and social growth in their students.

## ATTITUDES AND ETHICS TOWARD WORK AND CARING

Elementary social studies should serve to initiate children into the culture. This means that, in addition to knowing information about their culture, students also must develop appropriate attitudes and appreciation for the world of work as well as for other members of the society. As Menninger (1970) notes, "We only know that most children are so clumsily taught that they seem to have learned more about how not to work than about how to work. Not methods so much as attitudes need to be taught" (p. 166). Jarolimek (1982) writes that affective outcomes dealing with attitudes, appreciations, and feelings are sought in career education.

Caring for a garden can help children and adults achieve Jarolimek's affective career outcomes. Menninger reminds us that notables such as the theologian Tertullian, the historian Carlyle, and the poet Emerson were not compelled to spade up gardens, dig ditches, or lift stones, but did these

Reprinted from *Social Studies and the Young Learner*, January/February 1989, Volume 1, Number 3. Copyright 1989 by National Council for the Social Studies.

things out of enjoyment (1970). The point that Menninger makes is that the motive power for work and play come from the same source, and that given the correct external and internal conditions, work can be pleasurable. The external conditions he describes as favorable sound exactly like those a school garden would promote, "... comfortable group feeling, absence of intense discomfort or fatigue, a realization of pride in the product, and a conviction that the work is useful and appreciated" (p. 166). Like Menninger, we believe children should acquire an understanding of the enjoyment of work and how each person's work contributes to the life and health of the larger society. In addition to an ethic of work, we shall now consider how a school garden can help students develop health attitudes and relationships with others in our society.

Boyer points out that schools fail to help students make connections with the real world (1987). One of the connections that Boyer laments as missing is intergenerational. In our modern society, children are often separated from any significant contact with the elders of our culture. To overcome this, we contend that gardening is an experience that the old and young can share together. For example, students could work in conjunction with senior citizens to maintain school-yard gardens. During the summer, the garden could be cared for by interested students, scout troops, or other youth organizations in cooperation with senior citizens. These arrangements could easily be worked out through different community agencies. As the garden nears harvest, students would be encouraged to share the bounty with these senior citizens or the needy, just as Peter Rabbit loaned cabbages to Benjamin Bunny "when there was not always enough to eat."

Such an arrangement serves to develop an ethic Noddings calls "caring" (1984). She explains, "ideally, caring will extend well beyond the circle of teachers and students to embrace all those interested enough to make themselves known and available in the school . . ." (p. 198). Noddings argues that the development of this ethic should be nurtured and fostered just as teachers promote cognitive development. Interestingly, she extends her discussion of the developmental nature of human caring to include the topic of plants. She observes that while a true caring relationship between humans and plants will always be one-sided, the relationship can sustain one as caring, but plants can't reciprocate. Or can they? Consider that plants provide the following: food and fiber, oxygen, pharmaceuticals, building materials, and fuel. Of course, in Noddings' schema this does not constitute caring, but the point is by our caring, plants return products that we cannot live without.

## FIGURE 1: CONCEPTS AND SKILLS LEARNED THROUGH A GARDENING EXPERIENCE

| SUBJECT | SKILLS AND CONCEPTS | ACTIVITIES |
|---|---|---|
| **Social Studies** | Caring | Caring for plants, classmates, and community members. |
| | Cooperation | Successful cooperation in large and small groups. |
| | History | Role of agriculture in human civilization (e.g., victory gardens, invention of the cotton gin, etc.). |
| | Geography | Mapping the garden. Geographical origins of fruits and vegetables. |
| | Sociology | Studying the role and status of farmers in different societies. |
| | Anthropology | Examining the different tools used by farmers all over the world. |
| | Political Science | Legislation and support programs that exist for farmers, and the development of the farm labor union movement. |
| | Economics | Methods of distributing the products from the farm and prices are determined by the Board of Trade. |
| | Multicultural | Cultural use of plants. |
| **Science** | Science Processes | Observing, measuring, classifying, inferring, and experimenting. |
| | Soil | Identify soil organisms, types and amendments. |
| | Botany | Study seed genetics, germination, and rates of plant growth. Map food chain. |
| | Nutrition | Learn about nutritional value of fruits and vegetables. |
| | Weather | Study relationships of weather to plant growth. |
| **Mathematics** | Measuring | Measuring garden areas. Weighing of seeds, fertilizer, and produce. Division of produce. |
| **Fine Arts** | Drawing | Plants. Research plants and gardens in art history. Compare aesthetic layouts of gardens. |
| | Printmaking | Making leaf prints and prints from other parts of plants. |
| | Music | Learn songs about plants and gardening. |
| **Language Arts** | Reading | Read stories from children's literature and poetry about plants and gardens. |
| | Writing | Creative stories about gardening. Diaries of garden experiences could be kept. Letters to volunteers. |
| **Physical Education/ Industrial Arts** | Tool Use | Direct use of hand tools in garden digging, raking, and planting. |

A garden becomes a natural laboratory where students can observe a second connection that Boyer argues education should help students make. Specifically, he argues that the inexorable connection between producing, consuming, and discarding needs to be understood by students who are to be the citizens of the twenty-first century (1987). A school garden becomes a living laboratory where students observe and experience the essence of integration: nothing happens in nature that is not in relation to the whole. Gardening can teach these as well as economic concepts such as goods and services, division of labor, and interdependence.

Gardening is a pleasurable human activity that can help young learners develop positive attitudes towards social studies topics such as the world of work, caring for the environment, and developing relationships with the elderly. Additionally, the garden, and associated activities, can be an integrating focus that facilitates the acquisition of concepts and skills across the disciplines. Here's how.

## THE FATHER OF KINDERGARTEN

Friedrich Froebel, German pioneer of the kindergarten movement, was one of the first to advocate gardens in schools. In fact, the etymology of the word kindergarten is "garden of children." This reflects Froebel's great love of nature and his view that education should be closely linked to it. He viewed nature as complete: a holistic and single system. Furthermore, he maintained that education should likewise be whole: inclusive of all the child's activities.

Blankenburg, a town in the Thuringian Forest of Prussia, was the sight of his first kindergarten in 1837. In Froebel's kindergarten everything was linked to nature, and he organized his curriculum so that a considerable part of the children's time was spent on gardening (Downs, 1978). Each child was allocated a small bed for individual gardening. In addition, there were two large beds common to all, one for flowers and the other for vegetables. Froebel's goal was to have children garden for their own enjoyment; but at the same time he helped his students learn about geometric shapes, botany, biology, music, art, and oral language development through the thematic integration of the garden. An overriding concern was that each child be responsible for a portion of the two larger gardens by keeping the section well cultivated, realizing that they were working for the good of all.

In many ways, Froebel was a man ahead of his time. He was unable, however, to foresee the effects of development psychology on curriculum, and our understanding of how teachers can help children learn. Nonetheless, his holistic approach to curriculum, and use of gardens to integrate subject matter are just as timely now as when he proposed them.

## SOCIAL STUDIES LESSONS FROM THE SCHOOL GARDEN

If Froebel were alive today, he would undoubtedly use the garden as a vehicle for teaching many of the concepts and ideas that can be drawn from social studies. One of the five themes of geography is concerned with human-environmental interactions. Gardening is an excellent example of how people have modified their need to produce food to match their environment. The Chinese use a terrace system because of their mountainous terrain. We in America, on the other hand, have large open spaces in the plains and our system of farming reflects this. The French developed a unique, and particularly bountiful, method of farming due to the small amount of land available to the Parisians in the late nineteenth century.

Economics is another social science discipline that could use the garden as a springboard for lessons. Certainly, the great drought that parched Midwestern farmlands last year has affected food prices. Similarly, we have developed a rather complex system for delivering farm produce that students can study while they grapple with the problem of distributing their produce from the school garden. The sale of wheat to the Soviets and combating world hunger are value-related issues that children might consider. Students also could learn about what is rapidly becoming a major ecological problem in Third World countries, as tropical forests are being turned into pasture lands for cattle grazing, or to create profits from the sale of lumber harvested with cheap labor (Brown, Flavin, Wolf, 1988).

A gardening curriculum can be easily adapted to any grade level by varying skill level and concept complexity. For example, mapping the design of the garden would be a social studies activity adaptable to any grade. Kindergarten students can work on skills like counting seeds or measuring plant growth. Sixth graders can be engaged in the more complex task of compost production or studying the life cycle of annuals. With global education objectives in mind, plants from other cultures, such as Chinese or Japanese vegetables, could be grown and their use in those cultures studied. The age of discovery had its origins in the rising trade of spices and herbs from East to West. Along with growing spices and herbs, upper-grade students could study the history and geography associated with this period of civilization. Primary aged children might extend their reading skills through children's literature selections such as *Rabbit Hill*, *Johnny Appleseed*, *Peter Rabbit*, or *McBroom Tells a Lie*. A number of disciplines, including social studies, science, math, fine arts, language arts, and physical education can be integrated into a curriculum designed around a class garden. Lessons presented by the inventive teachers are limited only by one's imagination.

## IMPLEMENTING A SCHOOL GARDEN

The results of a recent National Gardening Association survey show that 78 percent of elementary teachers already garden at home. More than half indicated a strong interest in using garden activities to enrich the elementary curriculum (Gwynn, 1988). Thus, teachers can readily take an area from their personal life and combine it with their professional expertise to help students acquire skills in classifying, observing, measuring, and communicating which have been related to gardening by Pugh and Dukes-Bevans (1987).

Schools that have undertaken gardening projects report valuable integration and academic achievement (Berghorn, 1988; Nelson, 1988; Stetson, 1988). Nelson describes how a school-yard garden helped tie subjects together in the students' mind (1988). Prior to using a school-yard garden she notes, "They are unable to apply practically what they have learned in one subject to another. Students' learning becomes pigeonholed...it can stifle the desire for additional education since, in the student's mind, none of it relates to real life." (p. 23). In an inner-city, a school-wide greenhouse had noticeable effects on student enthusiasm for schoolwork and science scores (Stetson, 1988).

Creating and maintaining a school garden might not be as difficult a task as one would think. To protect the beds, it is best to have them in an enclosed area. Perhaps a parent's organization might help finance the purchase of materials for a chain link fence. During school vacations and holidays, provisions must be made to insure the plants are properly cared for. When elementary students work with senior citizens, or other community groups interested in helping schools succeed, it seems likely that they will learn valuable social studies lessons: cooperation, intergenerational communication, the ethic of caring, and the value and pleasure of hard work in producing food.

The allocation of school property for gardening purposes does not require large amounts of acreage. In fact, very fecund gardens can result in surprisingly small areas if the biodynamic, organic method of French intensive gardening is used. Up to four times the normal yield can result and the method has proved successful in varied climates and soils throughout the United States (Jeavons, 1979). The parsimonious use of land, and emphasis on organic materials, make this technique ideal for use by schools. The French intensive method provides students the opportunity to study the interaction of a balanced natural ecosystem and accompanying insect life.

The kinds of problems that would be encountered in constructing and protecting a school-yard garden are not insurmountable. Witness the number of low-income gardens that can be found among inner-city vacant lots. With a commitment of time and energy by interested faculty and students, school-yard gardens can flourish as part of a curriculum that Froebel would have been proud to see operational: a curriculum that is holistic and involves learners in a variety of occupations and activities.

## REFERENCES

Berghorn, G. "Tending Their Own Gardens." *Indiana Alumni*, June 1988, 18-21.

Boyer, E. L. "Connections: A Journal Through the Human Learning Process." California State University Centennial Address, Chico, CA., October 17, 1987.

Brown, Les R., Flavin, C. and E. C. Wolf. "Earth's Vital Signs." *The Futurist*, July/August 1988.

Downs, R.B. *Friedrich Froebel*. Boston: Twayne Publishers, 1978.

Gwynn. M. L. "A Growing Phenomenon." *Science and Children*, 25, April 1988, 25-26.

Jarolimek, John. *Social Studies in Elementary Education*. New York: Macmillian, 1982.

Jeavons, John. *How to Grow More Vegetables*. Berkeley: Ten Speed Press, 1974.

Menninger, Karl. *Love Against Hate*. New York: Harcourt, Brace, & World, 1970.

Nelson, C. J. "Harvesting a Curriculum." *Science and Children*, 25, April 1988, 22-24.

Noddings, *Nell Caring: A Feminine Approach to Ethics and Moral Education*. Berkeley: University of California Press, 1984.

Potter, Beatrix. *The Tale of the Flopsy Bunnies*. New York: Penguin Books, 1909.

Pugh, Ava F. and Lenell Dukes-Bevens. "Planting Seeds in Young Minds." *Science and Children*, 25, November/December 1987, 19-21.

Joseph A. Braun, Jr., is an Associate Professor of Elementary Social Studies on the Faculty of Curriculum and Instruction at Illinois State University, Normal. Michael Kotar is an Associate Professor of Elementary Science and the head of the Oroville Teaching Center for the Department of Education at the California State University, Chico. James Irick is a recent graduate of the Multiple Subjects Credential Program at California State University, Chico. [1989 note]

# 84

# A River Runs Through Science Learning
## Tap Community Resources to Create an Integrated Science and Social Studies Unit

**Lois R. Stanley**

It's raining hard now, but no one seems to notice. Wearing slickers, rain hats, and boots, fifth-grade students look at a white enamel pan in which a rock, cold and wet from the river, is beginning to show signs of movement. Squeals of "Gross!" are interspersed with shouts of "Awesome!" as students observe dragonfly and caddis fly larvae move down the rock and back toward the water. The parent-volunteer is as curious as the children, alternately thrilled and startled as another part of the rock seems to move. This is river science at its best.

Does that sound like a typical day at your school? With a little planning and community support, it could be. You can transform your schoolyard and its vicinity into an arena in which students explore the history of the community and learn about their local environment and ecosystem management. We did, and a study of rivers is now an important part of our school's curriculum.

## THE SOURCE

The river program in our area—Wilton, Connecticut—grew out of a project begun by the Junior League in the early 1970s. This group saw the need for a school program highlighting the importance of clean, fresh water and recognized the importance of letting students learn through an integrated, hands-on approach. As a volunteer organization, the league also recognized the potential of involving community members in the program as river guides, thus providing additional "teachers" and more one-on-one time with students. To develop the program, league members researched the scientific and historical background of the area and published *The River Book* as a handbook for volunteer river guides in local schools. The book includes a list of suggested concepts for fall and spring walks, a sample trail map, and an identification key for native plants and animals.

The Junior League's efforts 20 years ago created a framework for the popular outdoor program that continues in area schools today. Recently, I met with a committee of interested teachers and parents associated with Cider Mill School to take a fresh look at the river study. Together, we devised an updated approach, and now the revamped program is in place. Designed for students in fourth and fifth grades, it focuses on the history and natural environment of our area; includes firsthand interaction with a local

river, the Norwalk; and emphasizes parent-volunteers (four per class) who donate more than three hours time in the classroom and also lead small groups (five or six students each) on two 90-minute river walks, one in the fall and one in the spring. The volunteers also work with students to build a representation of the Norwalk River's watershed. As the science resource teacher, I trained the volunteers and scheduled the walks and watershed presentations.

Here is how we worked together to update the existing program.

## FIRST THINGS FIRST

To begin, we analyzed the schoolyard and community resources with the school's science and social studies curricula in mind. We discussed ways that we might use our surroundings to simulate a time or place that the children study. At our school, students in the fourth and fifth grades study American history, and their science lessons include units on communities (interdependencies between plants and animals) and energy sources. Our location is rich in early American history, and we are close to a river that empties into the Long Island Sound. The surrounding environment holds evidence of river formation, the passage of glaciers, and the presence of Native American and colonial settlements. We decided that our outdoor learning program should encompass all of these elements.

Once we decided on the elements, we needed to choose the major topics to be included. We wanted the topics to be

- closely tied to the science and social studies curricula;
- helpful in showing the connections between the two disciplines;
- better understood through outdoor activities than through indoor ones;
- directly related to our local environment;
- easily illustrated by props or natural phenomena in our schoolyard or nearby river site;
- and related to current environmental issues.

After much brainstorming, debate, and discussion, my colleagues and I chose the following topics:

- river formation and glaciation;
- the components of a river system, including the elements of flood plains, marshes, aquifers, and the estuary link to the sea;
- the water cycle and its connection to the river system;
- ways that humans, through time, have used and misused the river;
- and ways that plants and animals depend on the river system and interact in the river community.

Reprinted with permission from the National Science Teachers Association, from *Science and Children*, January 1995, Volume 32, Number 4. Copyright 1995 by the National Science Teachers Association, 1840 Wilson Boulevard, Arlington, Virginia 22201-3000.

Our next step was to select activities to illustrate the concepts, such as making glaciers and modeling their movement over land and rock; testing different soils to see how well each type filters water and then comparing the soils tested to samples from the marsh and floodplain; and locating watersheds on which students live and identifying the aquifers closest to them on maps from our town hall.

Parent-volunteers were a big help during this phase of the program. Because they were so involved with this unit and its content, the parent-volunteers began to leave relevant magazine articles, books, and videotapes on my desk on a regular basis. My job was to sort through the material, choose what to use, and distribute those items to my colleagues.

After the activities were chosen, we mapped out the area we wanted to use for our outdoor classroom. We drew a one-page map of the river trail and carefully marked the specific sites for each activity. Then, on separate pages, we outlined the concepts to be discussed and the activities to be completed at each site.

## INDOORS AND OUT

Another key component of our river unit was conducting classroom activities that supported the outdoor learning. For example, students created model watersheds from sand and a water-drip system to discover how rivers form and the effects of flooding. In addition, they studied glaciers and built models of them from sand, pebbles, and water frozen in paper milk cartons. Students also studied the water cycle, completing a number of activities from the book *Water Precious Water* (Hillen, Weibe, and Youngs, 1988).

For the culminating indoor activity, students gathered around the model watershed to reenact the history and formation of the Norwalk River. (For instructions on how to build a watershed model, see *The River Book* [Willis, Norton, Foster, and Forrester, 1977].) This volunteer-led discussion prepared students for the river walk and introduced humans and history into the geophysical study of rivers.

First, students observed a Wisconsin glacier move toward Long Island Sound, transforming a V-shaped valley into a U-shaped one. Then, with clay, students constructed a river winding through the valley and discussed the terms source, flood plain, meanders, and estuaries.

Next, they covered the board with forest and had the first inhabitants of Connecticut, the Native Americans, arrive. Students discussed Native Americans' use of the river, choice of village sites, and impact on the ecosystem. As colonists and then modern populations moved onto the model watershed, we discussed the same points. "Why did the colonists build where they did? How did they use the river? What effects did the building of dams and mills, large-scale farming, domesticated animals, and increased human population have on the ecosystem?"

As roads, schools, office buildings, and parking lots covered the model's forests and farmlands, children recognized the need for even more space. They drained swamps and straightened the river to make more room.

They placed businesses and homes on the flood plain and discussed how that action would affect the river's ability to clean water, feed aquifers, and regulate floods.

But the students did not leave feeling discouraged about the demands on our resources. As we discussed state and local laws concerning wetlands, students recognized the need for regulations concerning building sites, water purification, waste processing, and other issues that impact wetlands and water quality.

After our classroom activities, students were ready to investigate the real thing—the Norwalk River.

## ON THE TRAIL

Our first outdoor activity was a walk from the school to the river. During the walk, parent-volunteers explained how Native Americans, and later colonists, used plants for survival, as they pointed out vegetation that possessed nutritional or medicinal qualities. A woodchuck conveniently had made a mound on a spot along the trail, so students and volunteers also discussed hibernation.

Where the trail meets the river, students ground corn on the rocks as the Native Americans had, and then discovered that the rocks they were using were the remains of a stone dam and water-powered mill. Students discussed methods of grinding corn, comparing the Native Americans' way to the colonists' use of the wheel to harness the river's power.

The water moves fast at this spot, bubbling over rocks, so here the children discussed another way animals survive winter—diapause. The volunteer asked, "Why are insect nymphs found on these rocks and not in the slower-moving water ahead?" Then the group discussed how the faster moving water provided oxygen and food for the insects, and they talked about how this water will not freeze because it is moving rapidly.

We walked along the river to the place where it widens and the water becomes calm and sluggish. Here, students compared the fast-moving water at the old mill site and the slower moving water here. We asked them, "Where was there more evidence of erosion? Is there a difference in the substrate of the river, in the number and kinds of trees along the banks? What about changes in elevation?"

At a footbridge crossing to a small island, we paused to contemplate the human influence on the balance of nature in this river community. We discussed mink and muskrats, for example, and the effects of trapping. The mink is the muskrat's natural predator, so when the mink population decreases in size because of trapping, the muskrat population increases in size. In fact, the burrowing of an overpopulation of muskrats led to the collapse of a dam in our area; we talked about a recent newspaper article reporting that event.

The island was our final stop on the outdoor trail. Ducks often migrate to this part of the river, so the group discussed migration as a means of winter survival and the need for wetlands along waterbirds' migration routes. Then a volunteer presented students with the following scenario:

> It is late fall and winter snows will soon cover the ground. You have just landed on this island after months at sea. What do you see in the way of materials, plants, and evidence of animals that might help you to survive until spring?

Students responded by offering information about plants' nutritional and medicinal values, and they suggested creative ways to capture some of the native animals they learned about during their walk.

## ASSESSMENT MEASURES

After the walk, each parent-volunteer and student completed an evaluation form. In addition, students were tested on content.

To assess the program's overall effectiveness, we considered the following questions:

▮ Were concepts from science and social studies integrated successfully? Could students, for example, verbalize or give examples of the connections between human history and the river?

▮ How well did the outdoor segment clarify and/or expand concepts? Could students, for example, understand the colonists' need for water power? Could students identify the plants and animals they observed during the walk? Could they name ways in which these plants and animals depend on the river? Did they recognize that weeds and insects sometimes thought of as pests have a purpose in the river ecosystem?

▮ Were the students involved and interested in the program?

▮ Did students gain a different perspective because of the integrated, outdoor approach?

Volunteers are an important component of this program. They are invaluable in gathering materials and ideas, making props, and leading children through the program. The fact that the volunteers are also parents adds validity to the program and sends the message, "This is important. My parent has taken time from other obligations to be here."

The volunteers are all willing learners and their enthusiasm adds to the children's excitement. Through participation in the program, many parent-volunteers become advocates for the school and for the goals of the study. As one parent said, "We were fighting the town for the right to fill a marsh in order to subdivide our property. After participating in the river unit, we could not with clear conscience continue the appeal."

In fact, after this program, neither parent nor child will ever view a river in quite the same way. This river study left students, teachers, and parents with a better understanding of and sense of responsibility for their local environment, particularly the river.

## RESOURCES

Children's Television Workshop, *3-2-1 Contact*. (1991). *Down the Drain* [videotape]. Berkeley, CA: Author.

EME Corporation. (1989). *Glaciers* [videotape]. Danbury CT: Author.

Friedman, A. (1991). "A Big Lesson in a Small Pond." *Science and Children*, 28(5), 27-29.

Hillen, J., Weibe, A., and Youngs, D. (Eds.). (1988). *Water Precious Water: A Collection of Elementary Water Activities* (Book A). Fresno, CA: AIMS Education Foundation.

Kaufmann, J.S., Knott, R.C., and Bergman, L. ( 1989). *River Cutters*. Berkeley, CA: Lawrence Hall.

National Geographic Kids Network. (1989). *Acid Rain* [kit]. Washington, DC: Author.

———. (1991). *What's in Our Water?* [kit]. Washington, DC: Author.

Thier, H.D., Karplus, R., Lawson, C.H., Knott, R., and Montgomery, M. (1978). *The Rand McNally SCIIS Program*. Chicago: Rand McNally.

Vandas, S. (1992). "Wetlands: Water, Wildlife, Plants, and People." [article and foldout] *Science and Children*, 30(1), 39-41.

Voorhis, K. (1993). "Taking a Course in Nature." *Science and Children*, 31(3), 23-26.

Willis, L.. Norton, B., Foster, S., and Forrester, J. (1977). *The River Book*. Wilton, CT: Six Town River Board. (Available from Barbara Findley, President-elect. Six Town River Board, 82 Middlebrook Farm Rd., Wilton, CT 06897-2016).

Lois R. Stanley is a K-6 science resource teacher at Cider Mill School in Wilton, Connecticut. [1995 note]

# 85

# Preserve the Rain Forests
## Integrating the Social Studies and a Foreign Language into Thematic Instruction for Young Students

**Marcia H. Rosenbusch**

A national trend in elementary school education is the movement toward an integrated curriculum (Gonser 1992). In such a curriculum, traditional subject categories (math, science, social studies, and English language arts) are no longer taught as separate entities. Instead, the content areas are taught in the context of central, broad themes in what is termed thematic instruction. Gonser notes that science and social studies are the two curricular areas most conducive to building thematic instruction because they are so rich in content and provide many opportunities for organizing skills and experiences.

The integration of curricular content with the foreign language curriculum has received a great deal of attention in the field of elementary school foreign languages. Immersion and partial-immersion programs, the most intensive foreign language programs, teach the curricular content areas in the foreign language. Met (1992) encourages teachers of less-intensive foreign language programs to include content themes in their programs through thematic instruction. Pesola (1992) also supports thematic instruction by proposing a "thematic center" as the starting point for curriculum development in elementary school foreign language programs.

In this article, I explore the process used in planning and evaluating the teaching of a theme from the social studies as the basis for thematic instruction in the elementary school foreign language classroom.

## THE SOCIAL STUDIES THEME

Traditionally, the social studies prepares students to be responsible citizens of the nation in which they live. More recently, in response to a trend toward greater global awareness, this focus has broadened to that of preparing responsible world citizens (Evans 1987). Gibbons and Neuman (1985-1986) clarify the responsibilities global citizens have to help solve the problems of the world, to understand and care for others, to protect and use wisely our natural resources, and to promote an attitude of peaceful cooperation in the resolution of global issues.

The appropriateness of beginning the development of global citizens at the elementary school level has been effectively argued by Evans (1987, 548) who reviewed the research and concluded that the "research indicates that elementary students are not only developmentally ready but that this might be an especially important age to include global concepts in the curriculum." Evans also notes that "if children are to develop a global perspective, schools must provide them with the skills to analyze and evaluate information so that they will be able to participate as citizens in an evershrinking world." National Council for the Social Studies (NCSS) expands this idea and suggests that four goal areas should guide the development of student skills (Chapman et al. 1982):

- Knowledge should be reliable, accurate, carefully researched and rationally-based and should represent all viewpoints
- Skills to live effectively in the future should be developed, including higher-order thinking skills, communication and interpersonal skills, and self-confidence
- Values representing differing cultures should be compared, and value conflicts should be examined in a supportive atmosphere
- Social participation should be encouraged as an option after thoroughly researching issues and carefully formulating decisions.

Evans (1987, 553) notes that "the content used must help build global understanding and must be presented in a manner that is appropriate for students' development." Kniep (1989) proposes a framework for content that includes global issues and problems such as poverty, pollution, energy, hunger, disease, and the use of natural resources.

I have found (Rosenbusch 1992) that the global problem of poverty can be effectively introduced to elementary school children. When a theme on one aspect of poverty—housing—was taught in a foreign language program for kindergarten and first grade children, the evaluations completed by the children's parents and the observing teachers confirmed that the children had gained a new perspective on the housing problems of the poor. Baugher supported this finding when this same housing unit was taught to second graders in the foreign language classroom (personal communication, April 20, 1990). Borich replicated this finding with fourth graders (personal communication, April 10, 1992).

The theme developed for the project described in this article is based on natural resources, one of the global issues for the social studies proposed by Kniep (1989) and Gibbons and Neuman (1985-1986). The rain forests of Costa Rica were selected for the focus of the theme on natural resources because students would have an opportunity to learn about a Spanish-speaking country and because sources of information about the Costa Rican rain forests were abundant.

## THEME DEVELOPMENT

An invaluable guide to the development of the theme of the Costa Rican rain forests were the four goal areas defined by NCSS—knowledge, skills, values, and social participation.

## KNOWLEDGE

Researching the knowledge to be presented was an important early step in the development of the themes. Every effort was made to provide knowledge that was both reliable and accurate, as emphasized by the NCSS guidelines (Chapman et. al. 1982). Print, film, and videotape sources were explored as well as personal experience. Both public and university libraries are excellent sources of information on rain forests. The various types of information examined are:

- General information on rain forests to help gain an overall perspective on the topic
- Specific and accurate information on rain forests in Costa Rica to help determine the exact focus and to be sure of the correctness of the information
- Children's stories and teacher's guides to explore how information on this topic has been presented previously to children
- Accounts of personal experience to identify anecdotes about the rain forests that would be of interest to children and that would help make their study "come alive."

On the basis of the subject content identified, and in consideration of the developmental level of the children to whom the unit was to be taught (first grade), their experience with Spanish (beginners), and the intensity of the program (one-half hour a day for two weeks), goals for the subject matter content of the theme were established. The teachers planned to have the children

1. Locate Costa Rica and the United States on a map.
2. Identify and describe typical plants, animals, and birds of the Costa Rican rain forest.
3. Identify the general characteristics of the rain forest.
4. Compare the physical features, climate, and plant and animal life of their won state with the Costa Rican rain forest.
5. Identify five food products from the rain forest that enrich their lives.
6. Describe threats to the rain forests.
7. Describe ways that people are working to protect the rain forests.
8. Explain how children can help to preserve a Costa Rican rain forest.
9. Participate actively in the preservation of one acre of the Children's International Rainforest in Costa Rica. (Goals 6,7, and 8 were completed in English; all the others were completed in Spanish.)

## SKILLS

The student skills that received specific focus in the planning of the classroom activities were higher-order thinking skills and communication skills. Although the format of the classes was also designed to enhance interpersonal skills and self-confidence, the fact that the program in which the theme was used was of only two-weeks duration did not allow for observation of significant growth in these areas.

The enhancement of thinking skills above the level of knowledge on Bloom's taxonomy (1956) was the basis for the organization of various activities. In one of the activities involving the skill of analysis, the teacher asked the children to determine a classification for visuals depicting previously learned life forms. They could classify the various schemes by size or color of the life form or by type of life form (plants, animals, and birds).

After the teacher informed the children about the levels of the rain forest, the children applied this information in hypothesizing differences in the microclimate at the highest level of the rain forest (emergent) and the lowest level (floor) for the amount of sunshine, rainfall, and wind.

At the end of the unit, after a presentation of slides showing destruction of the rain forest, children demonstrated their comprehension of the information by summarizing and interpreting the information in English. The teacher asked them to imagine the future for the life forms of the rain forest if the destruction were to continue.

The enhancement of communication skills was a natural focus because most of the activities were taught entirely in Spanish. English was used only when the intellectual tasks and the verbal responses required from the children exceeded their ability to communicate in Spanish. For example, they used English to describe their suppositions about the continued destruction of the rain forest.

Throughout the class activities, the teacher encouraged the children to listen and observe carefully to find clues that would help them determine the meaning of the Spanish message. The teachers urged them to make intelligent guesses about meaning based on what they saw and heard. The teacher used the Natural Approach (Krashen and Terrel 1983) to help make meaning clear and to elicit the children's verbal responses so that the response progresses gradually from physical response to yes-no answers and to one word and short phrase answers

## VALUES

Because of the age level of the children in the program, a comparison of cultural values and an examination of value conflict was not possible. With older children, a teacher would be able to examine differing values and points of view, for example, the views of those who want to make a living from the rain forest in ways that destroy it and of those who want to preserve the rain forest and avoid all destructive practices.

From this unit, the children gained an appreciation of the life forms of the rain forest. The teacher avoided playing on the children's emotions and did not simplify the situation into "bad" versus "good." Instead, the teacher presented the reality of destruction as a challenge that needed a creative solution.

## SOCIAL PARTICIPATION

Providing students, especially young children, with opportunities for active social participation must be handled very carefully because they have limited capability for researching issues and formulating decisions by themselves. Teachers must be aware of the powerful and potentially controversial role they play in this aspect of teaching about global issues (O'Neal 1989).

Children's social participation should be invited, and each child's decision on whether or not to participate should be respected. The social participation proposed by the teacher for young children should be carefully considered in light of parent and community values.

Children need an opportunity for action in order to enhance their understanding of their responsibilities as global citizens (Gibbons and Neuman 1985-1986). Children enjoy satisfaction from knowing that their action can help, even in a small way, in resolving a global problem. Older children who can research all viewpoints on issues and carefully formulate their own decisions need to take an active role in deciding the action that they will take to help resolve a global problem.

Children studying the Costa Rican rain forests participated in a project to help expand the International Children's Rainforest in the Monteverde region of Costa Rica. This project to save the rain forest was begun by a determined 9-year-old, Roland Tiensuu of Sweden. Roland and his classmates raised enough money to purchase fifteen acres of virgin rain forest in Costa Rica. In the United States, three organizations coordinate donations from children for the rain forest: The Children's Rainforest, The Nature Conservancy, and The World Wildlife Fund's International Children's Rainforest Program.

Because the children in Spanish group had just finished learning about recycling, they were invited to gather soda cans, which are redeemable in Iowa for five cents. Working with their teachers, the children earned the fifty dollars needed to purchase one-half acre of rain forest and received a certificate of acknowledgment from the Monteverde Conservation League that coordinates the rain forest project in Costa Rica.

## ACTIVITIES DEVELOPMENT

Throughout the unit the children participated in hands-on activities. These activities were ideal for teaching in Spanish because the context clarified the meaning of the words. Children were able to understand the context-rich statements and the questions used by the teacher and to demonstrate their comprehension through physical action (pointing, sorting, grouping, placing) and by short oral responses.

Ideas found in the resource materials were frequently adapted to meet the goals of the program. One such adaptation occurred during the making of a Morpho butterfly, a beautiful iridescent blue butterfly typical of the Costa Rican rain forests. A pattern for the butterfly was found in *Naturescope* (1989). Although directions indicated that the pattern was to be colored with crayons, the teacher decided to explore different materials to achieve a more realistic product that was visually pleasing.

The teacher chose mylar in a brilliant, shiny blue, which can be purchased at party supply shops or stationery stores. Because the underside of the Morpho butterfly is not colorful, beige tissue paper was cut to the shape of the butterfly and glued to the mylar. Because mylar is difficult for young children to cut with scissors, the mylar was pre-cut in the butterfly shape.

The children glued together the mylar and tissue paper and, when dry, trimmed off the excess tissue paper. Next, they punched a hole on either side of the body at the midsection with a paper punch. A brown pipe-stem cleaner was twisted once around the child's middle finger, then slipped off the finger. The ends of the pipe-stem cleaner were placed through the two holes punched in the butterfly, twisted together, and left standing up as the antennae of the butterfly. The butterfly could then be placed back on the finger like a ring and made to fly, with wings fluttering realistically as the child moved his or her hand.

Photographs of the Morpho butterfly were placed in the classroom for children to examine as they worked to help clarify further the characteristics of this beautiful creature of the rain forest. After participating in this activity, children had no difficulty identifying and describing the characteristics of the Morpho butterfly.

## EVALUATION OF UNIT

Several evaluation techniques were used to determine the children's responses to the classroom experiences and the effectiveness of the theme in developing a global perspective in children.

After one activity of the Costa Rican rain forests unit, the teacher asked the children's parents to write down their children's responses to the directive, "Tell me about your Spanish class today," as had been suggested by Rogers (1989). That day in class the children had used construction paper and a juice can to make a model of a bromeliad, a flowering rain forest plant that gathers rain water in its center (Naturescope 1989). The children's responses clearly demonstrated the enthusiasm they felt for their classroom experience and their understanding of what a bromeliad is. Their responses included these statements:

> We made a plant that lives in the rain forest and we are going to be studying about the rain forest. We made a plant for a rain forest and we pretended it might bloom. We made it out of construction paper and a can.

> It was good. And fun. I like doing the actions the people do. I like the things we do at the table. We made a plant with agua (water) in the middle that comes from the rain forest. I like the teachers. I like everyone there. I like when we talk in Spanish because I learn new words.

At the end of the classes, parents were asked to evaluate the unit by filling out a short questionnaire. All of the parents responded affirmatively to the question, Did your child enjoy the Spanish program? Parents were also asked if their children had demonstrated greater global awareness. Typical responses follow:

> Before this program our daughter was not aware of the rain forest.

> Yes. Awareness and interest in learning the location of countries and more about the rain forest. She has enjoyed the new information about the rain forest. She has expressed concern for helping save them.

> Talked about the rain forest. Wanted to save cans to buy a piece of the rain forest.

The teachers who observed and did practice teaching in the children's class as part of their elementary school foreign language teacher preparation program evaluated the curriculum at the end of the experience. In response to the directive, Please evaluate the content of the global unit that was planned for your group, the teachers reacted very positively. Their only concern was for a need for more time to teach the concepts. They reported:

> Results in their comprehension show that the concepts were within their grasp. The unit could certainly be expanded for older ages. The topic with its animals and weather seemed to have high interest level for the five- to seven-year-old.

> The rain forest unit was an interest-holder for the children because of their love of animals. This unit can be expanded quite a bit, but I think that we covered the activities and objectives quite well. More time is needed!

## CONCLUSIONS

The social studies and foreign languages enrich the elementary school curriculum when they are integrated in thematic instruction. Themes from the social studies that enhance children's perceptions of themselves as global citizens provide exciting curriculum opportunities for the elementary school foreign language program. In this project, the design of a unit on the rain forests of Costa Rica was based on four goal areas defined by the National Council for the Social Studies. The results of the evaluation of this unit suggest that thematic instruction can effectively encourage a global perception in even the youngest children in an elementary school foreign language program.

## REFERENCES

Bloom, B. S., ed. 1956. *Taxonomy of Educational Objectives, Handbook 1: Cognitive Domain*. New York: David McKay.

Chapman, J., J. Becker, M. E. Gilliom, and J. Tucker. 1982. "NCSS Position Statement on Global Education." *Social Education* 46:36-38.

Evans, C. S. 1987. "Teaching a Global Perspective in Elementary Classrooms." *The Elementary School Journal* 87:544-55.

Gibbons, M., and M. Neuman. 1985-1986. "Creating a Curriculum for the Global Future." *Educational Leadership* 43: 72-75.

Gonser, C. 1992. "Components of the Elementary School Curriculum." In *Colloquium on Foreign Languages in the Elementary School Curriculum. Proceedings*, September 1991, edited by M. Rosenbusch. Munich, Germany: Goethe Institut Munchen.

Kniep, W. M. 1989. "Social Studies within a Global Education." *Social Education* 53:399 403.

Krashen, S. D., and T. Terrell. 1983. *The Natural Approach: Language Acquisition in the Classroom*. Hayward, Calif.: Alemany Press.

Met, M. 1992. "The Place of Foreign Languages in the Elementary Curriculum." In *Colloquium on Foreign Languages in the Elementary School Curriculum. Proceedings*, September 1991, edited by M. Rosenbusch. Munich, Germany: Goethe Institut Munchen.

Naturescope. 1989. *Rain Forests: Tropical Treasures*. Washington, D.C.: National Wildlife Association.

O'Neil, J. 1989. *Global Education: Controversy Remains, but Support Growing*. ASCD Curriculum Update, Association for Supervision and Curriculum Development: 1-8.

Pesola, C. A. 1992. "In Search of a Framework for Curriculum Development." In *Colloquium on Foreign Languages in the Elementary School Curriculum. Proceedings*, September 1991, edited by M. Rosenbusch. Munich, Germany: Goethe Institut Munchen.

Rogers, V. 1989. "Assessing the Curriculum Experienced by Children." *Phi Delta Kappan*: 714-17.

Rosenbusch, M. H. 1992. "Is Knowledge of Cultural Diversity Enough? Global Education in the Elementary School Foreign Language Program." *Foreign Language Annals* 25: 129-36.

Marcia H. Rosenbusch is a faculty member of Iowa State University in the Department of Foreign Languages and Literatures, where she has established a program for elementary school foreign language teachers. [1994 note]

# PART 13

# USING LITERATURE TO SUPPORT SOCIAL STUDIES LEARNING

The printing press and moveable type have had a great impact on the depth of information people can obtain about their world. For example, a Sunday *New York Times* newspaper contains more information than a person living in the Middle Ages acquired during his or her entire lifetime. An undergraduate degree becomes obsolete within three years because of the rapid creation of new knowledge. Today we are in the midst of an electronic information revolution that provides almost instant access to information from around the world. Although reading is not the only way for children to learn about the world, it remains the primary source of data and commentary needed for social learning. Social studies textbooks have an enormous impact on curriculum because of their frequent use by teachers. About 90 percent of teachers rely on a textbook as their primary source for teaching social studies content.

In recent years, many educators have advocated supporting or replacing textbooks with trade books and other literature when teaching social studies. Well-written trade books provide a more detained treatment of topic, give another perspective of the subject, and have the potential to be more exciting and challenging because of their writing styles and greater use of illustrations. The ongoing debate about the superiority of textbooks or trade books for teaching social studies should not be an issue in itself. Rather, teachers of social studies should be concerned with the several reading, comprehension, and interpretation skills students need to develop in order to be effective readers and strategic learners of social studies. An important question to ask is, How can biographies and other trade books be used to promote greater understanding of people, places, and events in social studies? As young learners gain new information through reading, they move toward becoming active citizens who think critically and make competent decisions.

Hickey describes reading skills needed by children to become critical readers. She also advocates using a wide variety of resources, including charts and graphs, newspapers, magazines, and books, to help students make intelligent decisions as they strive to achieve their personal goals. McGowan, Erickson, and Neufeld address the arguments for literature-based teaching and match them with the present research. They caution against embracing a literature-social studies connection without hesitation, because present research concentrates on the acquisition of knowledge and fails to address specific issues in the learning of social studies skills and attitudes. They provide a compelling case for a change in the emphasis of research on the topic of social studies and literature, as well as a good bibliography from which to begin a research study.

Because studying the lives of people helps students learn such social studies concepts as culture, environment, time periods, and human characteristics, traits, beliefs, and values, biographies and autobiographies provide rich resources for social studies interaction. Zarnowski reports on how students in New York City reexamined their ideas about the world after reading and responding to biographies of contemporary women and reflecting on the contributions of these women. She recommends that teachers assist students with the reading of biographies by providing them with a focus for their work. Kazemek discusses the use of biographies with children and young adults, pointing out the important responsibilities in selecting appropriate reading material. To illustrate problems often encountered in juvenile biographies, she discusses in some detail the strengths and weaknesses of several biographies of Dr. Martin Luther King, Jr. Similar problems may be applicable to other biographies as well. In addition, biographies and autobiographies can be used effectively throughout the year as spring boards for mini-units and other active learning opportunities.

Allen and Hoge explore how teachers can use literature to teach geographic understanding, reasoning, and other skills, which, in turn, help children develop geographic literacy. Hicks provides three sample lessons for use in the early grades in which children's books are used to help teach both social studies concepts and skills related to civic competence. Her lessons illustrate how being aware of the social studies standards, and using them to focus instruction, helps the story book become a more meaningful element in improving social studies instruction. Clearly, social studies teachers need to encourage students to read widely in order to obtain new information and gain various perspectives on problems. They also need to assist students in linking their reading to important social studies concepts and skills through planning and instruction. Through such activities, literature supports important social studies goals and complements other ways of gathering and processing social studies knowledge.

## M. Gail Hickey

Writers in the field of social studies have helped increase educators' awareness of the importance of teaching for critical thinking. *Bloom's Taxonomy* and its implications for a hierarchical order of thinking skills is now commonly used to plan instruction for addressing upper levels of cognition. Reading, like thinking, also involves a hierarchy of skills. At the lower level, comprehension skills are literal, and involve recall of details, sequence of events, and recognition of main ideas. At higher levels, reading comprehension skills include recognizing cause and effect, distinguishing fact from opinion, identifying propaganda techniques, recognizing purpose, distinguishing relevant from irrelevant information, recognizing bias, noticing emotionally-charged words, and comparing and contrasting sources. Collectively, the higher order skills represent a process known as "critical reading."

### CRITICAL READING

Turner (1988) defines critical reading as "analytic thinking for the purpose of evaluating what is read." Its emphasis carries over into other subjects, with particularly strong implications for the social studies. Although basal readers now address some higher order skills in an isolated fashion, for the most part these skills are not taught as having applicability in other parts of the curriculum. In spite of this, teachers have a responsibility to teach critical reading as a content skill in social studies for the middle grades.

Students in the middle grades should be able to demonstrate certain critical reading skills related to the social studies (Forgan and Mangrum 1985). Among these are the ability to

- recognize cause and effect relationships
- read to distinguish fact from opinion
- read critically to identify propaganda techniques.

### UNDERSTANDING CAUSE AND EFFECT RELATIONSHIPS

An understanding of cause-effect patterns in social studies is based on prior knowledge and the ability to make inferences (Irwin 1986). Students frequently draw erroneous conclusions about cause-effect from social studies materials because they have not been taught that the order of wording does not necessarily provide clues about which part of the sentence is the cause and which is the effect.

What can teachers do to help students recognize cause and effect?

- Present real-life examples: i.e., ordering a meal at a favorite fast-food restaurant. Ask students what they did, and why.
- Call attention to signal words in expository writing, such as because, therefore, so, and then, so what, in order to; have students find examples of signal words in their social studies text that indicate a cause-effect relationship.
- Elaborate on cause-effect situations during the school day. "If you forget to return your homework, what might happen? Why do you think so? What experiences have you had in the past that lead you to that conclusion?

### DISTINGUISHING FACT FROM OPINION

Alexander and Heathington (1988) state emphatically that "... no other thinking skill in social studies is more important than the ability to distinguish fact from opinion." Facts are statements that are objectively verifiable; opinions express someone's preferences, feelings, or personal opinion.

What experiences can teachers provide to help students begin to distinguish fact from opinion?

- Television commercials and newspaper articles supply a wide range of examples for the study of fact versus opinion. Urge students to question the statements presented through these media formats, and decide whether the information is verifiable.
- Have students rewrite or restate factual information as opinion, and vice versa.
- Divide the class into pairs, and provide the partners with a list of names, events, and terminology related to a current social studies topic. One partner will compile a collection of facts, while the other compiles a collection of opinions. Have students then get into groups of four. Each pair will quiz the other by reading a statement from their collection and asking, "Fact or opinion?"

### IDENTIFYING PROPAGANDA TECHNIQUES

Durkin (1989) suggests that effective instruction about propaganda enables students to make distinctions between material which "(a) deliberately distorts and even lies in order to promote something that may be mentally or physically harmful, (b) attempts to get people to do or believe something that has a recognized worth, and (c) is persuasive but harmless." In order to gain competency in this skill, students must become aware of propaganda devices and be able to recognize examples of these.

How may teachers help students develop this awareness? One way is to prepare and display a chart listing

Reprinted from *Social Education*, March 1990, Volume 54, Number 3. Copyright 1990 by National Council for the Social Studies.

and explaining propaganda devices and have students find examples in their reading.

When students have been introduced to the process of critical reading in the social studies with these kinds of activities, teachers should give attention to the more complex comprehension skills. These include recognizing purpose, distinguishing relevant from irrelevant information, recognizing bias, recognizing emotionally charged words, and comparing and contrasting reports.

## RECOGNIZING PURPOSE

Teachers should encourage students to ask, "Why did the author write this? What are the author's reasons for including this information? What am I to learn by reading it?" When students see that authors usually have a definite purpose for writing something, they can begin to define this purpose with the following questions:
- What is the obvious (public) purpose?
- What may be the author's "hidden" purpose?
- What is my purpose for reading this piece?

## DISTINGUISHING RELEVANT FROM IRRELEVANT INFORMATION

Once students have learned to recognize the author's purpose, they can begin to distinguish between ideas and information that support the purpose (and are relevant), and irrelevant information or statements that may distract from the purpose, or even mislead the reader.

## RECOGNIZING BIAS

When students understand authors' purposes and know how to separate irrelevant information from that which is relevant, they are ready to decide whether an author has revealed his or her personal biases. Writers often reveal their biases through their choice of language as in the example shown here:

Writer # 1: The First Lady has spared no expense to turn the White House into a veritable tourists' showcase.

Writer #2: White House officials report that the First Lady has commissioned a refurbishing of several rooms which are open to the public.

## RECOGNIZING EMOTIONALLY CHARGED WORDS

When students realize that words have connotations which may reveal emotional overtones, or bias, they need to be shown that writing is not always straightforward communication. Some writers try to arouse the emotions of readers through deliberate use of emotionally charged language. Have students list all the synonyms they can think of for a certain word, such as "woman," then categorize these under headings of "Positive," "Negative," or "Neutral." Discuss the emotional significance inherent in various synonyms listed, and have students search for examples in their reading.

## COMPARING AND CONTRASTING REPORTS

Provide students with two or more accounts of a particular historic event. Have them compare and contrast authors' points of view, accuracy in reporting, and use of persuasive language.

Use newspaper accounts to compare and contrast reports of a particular current event. Collect these articles over a period of a week or more to enhance analysis.

As an additional aid, a checklist of critical reading questions can be duplicated and given to each student, who will then refer to it while reading social studies-related materials.

## THE CRITICAL CONNECTION IN REVIEW

What should the teacher of social studies know about planning to teach critical reading skills at the middle school level? Spache (1977) and Durkin (1989), in a comprehensive review of research on teaching critical reading in the content areas, note several significant implications for instructional planning. Indications from this research for instructional planning might be summarized as follows:
- Students cannot be expected to demonstrate critical reading with material that has not been introduced properly. Prior knowledge of content is essential to synthesis and analysis of material.
- Direct training in study skills for handling information found in charts, graphs, and maps is essential to students' critical appraisal of this information.
- Comprehension beyond the literal may be limited by below-average reasoning ability.
- Readers who react while reading and demonstrate associative thinking abilities will more quickly grasp the fundamentals of critical reading than those who do not.
- Students need frequent opportunities to read and discuss contradictory viewpoints. This practice will help them learn to suspend judgment until accounts by several sources have been read.
- Teachers should make every effort to help students clarify purposes for reading assigned materials. Students should be guided to react to assigned reading with original objectives in mind.

In summary, Samuel Taylor Coleridge (Atkinson and Longman, 1985) once said there are four kinds of readers. He described the first as being like the hourglass—their reading, like sand, runs in and out, leaving nothing behind. The second is like a sponge—soaking up everything, and releasing it in nearly the same state, only a little less clean. The third is like a strainer all that is good flows through and the refuse remains. The fourth is like the worker in a diamond mine—throwing away what is worthless and keeping only the purest gems.

As teachers of the social studies, we must encourage our students to become; like the worker in the diamond mine capable of detecting information of worth as they read, able to distinguish the important from the unimportant. We must equip them with the skills required for critical reading: wisdom, reflective thought, and logic. If we

## FIGURE 1: PROPAGANDA DEVICES

| DEVICE | DEFINITION | EXAMPLE |
|---|---|---|
| *Bandwagon* | The "everybody's-doing-it" approach; if they are, then you should too. | "Nine out of ten people surveyed prefer Ninja tennis shoes." |
| *Card Stacking* | Presents only one side of an issue, using carefully selected facts or opinions to make the best (or worst) case possible. | "As our lieutenant governor, Candidate Jones consistently supported higher taxes, government interference in trade, and raises for public officials" (with no mention of the candidate's stand on positive issues). |
| *Glittering Generality* | Sweeping generalizations associated with certain virtues (e.g., motherhood, freedom) in an attempt to discourage examination of critical ideas. | "If I'm elected, I promise world peace will be achieved." |
| *Name Calling* | The use of negative labels in order to evoke an emotional response and draw attention away from the real issue. | Calling a local politician a "communist." |
| *Plain Folks* | Making an appeal by associating an idea or product with the common people, or "plain folks." | Family of five convenes at breakfast table, and everyone drinks "Tropic-Sun" juice. |
| *Testimonial* | Association of a concept or product with a highly respected individual in an attempt to persuade others to accept it. | A well-known athlete states that he uses a certain deodorant every day. |

are to prepare our students to make intelligent decisions about products, entertainment, and politics, then we must teach them to read newspapers and magazines with an intellectual eyebrow cocked. To equip children for leading us into tomorrow, we must help them become thinking readers today.

## REFERENCES

Alexander, J.E., and B.S. Heathington. *Assessing and Correcting Classroom Reading Problems*. Glenview, Ill.: Scott, Foresman/Little Brown College Division, 1988.

Atkinson, R., and D. Longman. *Reading Enhancement and Development*. St. Paul, Minn.: West Publishing Company, 1985.

Bums, P., B. Roe, and B. Ross. *Teaching Reading in Today's Elementary Schools*. 3d ed. Boston: Houghton Mifflin Company, 1984.

Daines, D. *Reading in the Content Areas*. Glenview, Ill.: Scott, Foresman and Company, 1982.

Devine, T. *Teaching Reading Comprehension*. Boston: Allyn and Bacon, 1986.

Durkin, D. *Teaching Them to Read* 5th ed. Boston: Allyn and Bacon, Inc., 1989.

Fraser, D., and E. West. *Social Studies in Secondary Schools*. New York: Ronald Press, 1961.

Forgan, H., and C. Mangrum. *Teaching Content Area Reading Skills*. Columbus, Ohio: Charles Merrill Publications, 1985.

Irwin, J. W. *Teaching Reading Comprehension Processes*. Englewood Cliffs, N.J.: Prentice-Hall, Inc., 1986.

Spache, G., and E. Spache. *Reading in the Elementary School*. 4th ed. Boston: Allyn and Bacon, 1977.

Turner, T. N. "Higher Levels of Comprehension: Inference, Critical Reading, and Creative Reading." In J. E. Alexander's *Teaching Reading*. 3d ed. Glenview, Ill.: Scott, Foresman/Little, Brown College Division, 1988.

---

## FIGURE 2:
## QUESTIONS TO GUIDE THE CRITICAL READER

- Why did the author write about this topic?

- Do the authors know what they are writing about? Is the author likely to be biased? Why?

- Is the information current?

- Does this account hold your interest? What about it kept you interested?

- Is the author's perspective logical or emotional? Does the author use emotional words?

- Is the author employing any undesirable propaganda techniques? Which ones? How does the author use them?

- Is the author implying things not directly stated? What are these? What does the author say that leads you to believe this?

M. Gail Hickey is an Assistant Professor of Education at Indiana University, Purdue University in Fort Wayne, Indiana. [1990 note]

# 87

# With Reason and Rhetoric
## Building the Case for the Literature-Social Studies Connection

**Thomas M. McGowan**
**Lynnette Erickson**
**Judith A. Neufeld**

Literature and social studies teaching have demonstrated a persistent, attractive connection. Educators have long argued that many features of trade books, particularly their detailed descriptions, complex characters, and melodic passages, allow young readers to construct understandings in powerful ways. The potential that these books hold for promoting citizenship learning has made literature-based instruction an appealing option for many social educators.

Advocates past and present have championed trade books as a resource for social studies instruction. More than 150 years ago, Johann Friedrich Herbart proposed conducting the study of history with literary sources to instill desirable social attitudes in children (see Rippa 1988). For the past forty years, educators have repeatedly proclaimed literature's instructional benefits. Proponents have argued, for example, that fiction brings historical figures alive for children (Dahmus 1956; Dawson 1965; Huus 1961). They have proposed that literary works contain the threads that can bind seemingly disparate content areas into an integrated curriculum (Norton 1988). Currently, literature-based teaching attracts interest from many social educators. The NCSS Annual Conference program of 1995 featured roughly fifty sessions advancing the instructional possibilities of trade books (NCSS 1995).

Adherents of the literature-social studies connection often cite the perceived shortcomings of traditional textbooks to justify their advocacy. For example, some proponents have insisted that trade books provide more current information in a more engaging manner (Holmes and Ammon 1985) and nurture children's imaginations more readily (McClure and Zitlow 1991) than do textbooks. Others characterize textbooks as limited in scope, sacrificing deep analysis for extensive coverage and contributing to students' inability to transcend factual recall for reflective thinking (Brophy, McMahon, and Prawat 1991; Brozo and Tomlinson 1986; Guzzetti, Kowalinski, and McGowan 1992; Sewall 1988; Tyson and Woodward 1989). Still others have urged teachers to rely almost exclusively on trade books as resources for social studies lessons, relegating the textbook to a supplementary role (Ceprano and English 1990; Graves 1989; Johnson 1989; Zack 1991).

Although the literature-social studies connection has attracted many vocal patrons, some educators have questioned whether it constitutes a miracle cure for the much-publicized ills that beset social studies teaching and learning. A number of educators have cautioned that literature-based teaching seems vague and ill-defined, raising doubts about the precision and effectiveness of this instructional approach. They have noted that advocates use the terms literature, trade book, story, story book, and children's literature synonymously to identify any written account that is not a text book, whether the work is poetry, fiction, biography, or nonfiction (McGowan and Sutton 1988). Taking a different critical perspective, Hellenbrand (1988) expressed strong reservations about recommendations that teachers use trade books to liven and integrate social studies courses. His opposition stemmed from a concern that literature cannot be "used" without demeaning or trivializing an artistic work. Conversely, Alleman and Brophy (1994) have raised the issue that literature-based teaching demeans and trivializes the purposes and content of social studies. Their case studies of elementary classrooms revealed that teachers rarely make literature selections with social studies goals and concepts in mind. They choose books for their literary quality and appeal. Consequently, literature-based teaching too often misses significant aspects of a topic that are essential for promoting civic competence.

In view of its widespread advocacy, these concerns about the literature—social studies connection seem to merit further investigation. Yet these concerns remain the exception, beyond an educational mainstream that increasingly calls for social studies teaching based on literary sources. Many state guidelines for social studies curriculum, in fact, have mandated the adoption of literature-based teaching to integrate the content areas and promote citizenship learning (Arizona State Board of Education 1988; Crabtree and Ravitch 1988; New York 1982; Wisconsin Department of Public Instruction 1983).

## THE CASE EXAMINED

Proponents of the literature-social studies connection make their case reasonably, persuasively, and often emotionally. They offer powerful and compelling arguments for using trade books to promote civic competence. Curiously, most advocates do not support their claims for the effectiveness of literature-based social studies teaching with research findings. From 1929-1988, various educational journals included 164 articles exploring the association between trade books and social studies teaching (McGowan and Sutton 1988).

Yet only 4 percent of these citations were data-based examinations of the nature and/or effectiveness of literature-based teaching. The remainder consisted of bibliographic essays, rationales for literature-based teaching, and strategies for implementing this instructional approach. Although research studies have appeared more frequently in recent years, reading theorists and constructivist psychologists, not social educators, conducted most of these investigations; they typically examined the effects of literature-based teaching on students' literacy rather than their civic competence (Fielding, Wilson, and Anderson 1984; Smith 1993).

At this point, we might ask why the trade book-social studies connection has attracted such a vocal following. Literature-based teaching must exert a persuasive power indeed for so many social educators to endorse it so enthusiastically, without much proof of its effectiveness. What forces generate this appeal? Although this question seems intriguing, we pursue a line of inquiry that seems more productive and practical. Can literature-based instruction contribute to the teaching and learning of social studies content? In what ways? To what extent? Stated more directly, is the case for the trade book-social studies connection built with reason or rhetoric?

*Defining Our Terms.* Before addressing these questions, we need to define how we view the key elements of literature-based social studies teaching. By literature based, we mean instruction using trade books rather than basal textbooks as the major information source for social studies lessons. Although unpublished materials such as diaries, letters, and documents may promote student learning, we do not include these sources in our conception of literature.

By social studies, we mean "the integrated study of the social sciences and humanities to promote civic competence" (NCSS 1994, 3). We adopt this definition for purposes of clarity. Educators have engaged in a seemingly endless effort to conceptualize the social studies, debating numerous interpretations of the field. Although these definitions vary widely in their specifics, they have agreed on a central mission for social studies—promoting civic competence (Brophy 1990). Our adopted definition not only emphasizes this common purpose, it carries the endorsement of the field's principal professional organization, National Council for the Social Studies.

*The Essentials of Civic Competence.* Because we live in a world characterized by diversity and change, civic competence may seem an elusive and complex notion, more an ideal construct than a set of real qualities that students might learn to demonstrate. The curriculum standards for social studies, however, clearly mark civic competence as an attainable and necessary purpose for social education, a prerequisite for assuming what Jefferson termed "the office of citizen" (NCSS 1994, 3). The developers of these standards identify three essential elements which constitute civic competence: knowledge about the community, nation, and world; skills of data collection and analysis, decision making, problem solving, and collaboration; and a commitment to the values of our democratic republic.

Logically, these essential elements should guide our line of inquiry about the viability of the trade book-social studies connection. To address our series of questions, we reviewed a cross-section of articles advocating the uses and researching the effects of literature-based social studies teaching. We analyzed the arguments and assessed the evidence regarding how literature-based instruction can contribute to promoting the knowledge, skills, and values that constitute civic competence. Our review allows us to describe the complex, convincing case that advocates have made for the trade book-social studies connection and to determine that it has been built with a mixture of reasonable evidence and persuasive rhetoric.

## ACQUIRING KNOWLEDGE FOR CIVIC COMPETENCE

The social studies curriculum standards strongly assert that young citizens must acquire factual information and construct deeper meanings about the local, state, national, and global communities in which they live (NCSS 1994). Civic competence requires knowledge drawn from various disciplines that transcends any single field. Civic competence demands that students not only know the facts, concepts, and ideas necessary to participate in civic affairs, but that they understand the processes through which they came to know these things and why a citizen should know them. Ultimately, students must demonstrate that they can hold the office of citizen by translating their knowledge into plans for civic action.

*The Argument.* Advocates of literature-based teaching believe that trade books help young citizens gain a range of understandings that seems both comprehensive and complex. Literary works provide students with a more complete grasp of a wider range of topics than do more traditional sources of social studies information (Brozo and Tomlinson 1986; Davis and Palmer 1992; McClure and Zitlow 1991). Their rich detail "fleshes-out" the skeleton of basic information presented in most text books (Ceprano and English 1990; Larrick 1955; Huus 1961). Trade literature, particularly picture books, offers young readers "vicarious visual images that make the long ago and the far away more concrete" (Harms and Lettow 1993, 364).

According to its advocates, literature-based teaching allows students to link their knowledge of the past to the social issues of the present (Danielson 1989; Fuhler 1991; Norton 1990; Zarrillo 1989) and extend their understanding of the ways in which people and places change over time (Harms and Lettow 1993). Children extend their grasp of the personalities and events that have shaped our world as they read engaging literary accounts presented from multiple perspectives (Garcia, Hadaway, and Beal 1988; Harms and Lettow 1993; Wheeler 1971). Young readers comprehend key geographic concepts (Lorrie 1993). They not only absorb great quantities of detail, they also make meaning in personal and satisfying ways (Wheeler 1971).

*The Reasonable Evidence.* The element of civic competence most often investigated by researchers is the extent to which students acquire social studies knowledge through literature-based instruction. Although study findings do not substantiate every assertion made by trade book advocates, the research supports these claims to some degree. Levstik (1986, 1989, 1990), for example, confirmed that students, particularly early adolescents, associate with the characters they "meet" in historical literature. Young citizens form the strongest relationships with people facing daunting challenges, such as Helen Keller or a Holocaust survivor. Bonding with story characters often motivates learners to uncover more information about the circumstances surrounding a heroic struggle, positively influencing their historical understanding in the process.

Other researchers have explored how literature "fills in the gaps" left by incomplete textbook explanations of historical events. Beck and McKeown (1991), examining the historical understanding of upper elementary students, found that quality trade books supply sufficient detail for learners to make the causal connections to sequence important ideas. Class activities that draw on richly descriptive trade book passages allow young readers to link the past with the present and to recognize how things change over time.

Similarly, the work of Monson, Howe, and Greenlee (1989) revealed that novels more fully answered young children's questions about how people live in other countries than did textbooks. Smith (1993) compared the conceptual understanding of students exposed only to social studies textbooks with children who read selected works of historical fiction rather than basal readers. Students in the experimental, literature-based classrooms could recall about 60 percent more information than could children in the control classrooms. Morrow, O'Connor, and Smith (1990) concluded that kindergartners exposed to literacy instruction based on trade books could recall more information and show increased understanding of concepts than could young children receiving a more traditional teaching approach. Offering "some empirical support" for literature-based social studies instruction, Guzzetti, Kowalinski, and McGowan (1992, 121) concluded that "students can acquire more concepts and a greater understanding of those concepts through literature ... than through a traditional approach."

## PROMOTING SKILLS FOR CIVIC COMPETENCE

The social studies standards document lists skill categories that excellent social studies programs should promote (NCSS 1994). Students must gain the capacity to acquire information and manipulate data; develop and present policies, arguments, and stories; construct new knowledge; and participate in groups. Young citizens should not practice each skill in isolation; they should engage in integrative experiences in which the skills enrich one another.

*The Argument.* Advocates contend that instruction based on trade books provides opportunities for children to develop a range of skills central to gaining and exercising civic competence. Moreover, the experiential and integrative

nature of this approach allows children to combine related skills and apply these competencies to solve "real-world" problems. In particular, proponents argue that involvement with quality trade books can encourage students to think critically and reflectively (Brozo and Tomlinson 1986; Davis and Palmer 1992; Farris and Fuhler 1994; Usery 1966).

As they experience literature-based activities, students integrate information from multiple disciplines to ready themselves for social action (Harms and Lettow 1993). They comprehend material from various genres and can read these sources in a critical way (Wheeler 1971; Zack 1991). Reading and conversing about good literature "can enable a child to think about something important with an adult (and to talk about it or not) in a comfortable atmosphere" (Fassler and Janis 1985, 496).

*The Reasonable Evidence.* Although advocates argue persuasively that literature-based teaching builds a range of student competencies, the research supporting these claims, when viewed as a body of work, seems relatively "thin" and occasionally contradictory. Beck and McKeown (1991) offered one of the few examples of research examining the impact of this approach on student skills. Investigating student knowledge acquisition, they assumed that students could not think critically about topics they did not comprehend, because they require "sufficient quantity and quality of information to allow critical consideration" (489). The researchers noted that trade books seem to generate sufficient understandings when used productively with young readers. Levstik's naturalistic study (1986), however, revealed that sixth grade students identified so strongly with story characters that critical questioning of their behaviors became problematic.

Ellis (1990) found more positive indicators of student performance in action research examining the uses of literature-based instruction at the secondary level. He formed reading teams so that young people could engage in dialogue about the issues presented in literary sources in a positive and nonthreatening environment. In these settings, students interacted productively and made constructive decisions about what they should learn.

## NURTURING VALUES FOR CIVIC COMPETENCE

Certain values, such as respect for a person's fundamental rights and basic freedoms, underlie our democratic way of life and ensure our belief in a common good (NCSS 1994). Any systematic program of social studies teaching must develop students' commitment to these ideals. Instruction should include activities that encourage the formation of these values and allow children to weigh their priorities, as well as experiences in which young citizens examine how values are formed and how they influence human behavior.

*The Argument.* Many advocates insist that teaching with trade books can promote multiple aspects of children's affective growth. Literature-based teaching stimulates children's interests (Fassler and Janis 1985; Huus 1961) and invites children to appreciate and enjoy the learning process (Davis and Palmer 1992). Children experiencing multicultural literature emerge with a heightened social sensitivity to the needs of others and the recognition that people have similarities as well as differences (Norton 1990). Literary encounters help "children ... feel what others feel. This heightens their sensitivity to people and expands their awareness of human options" (Barnes 1991, 18). Young citizens first identify, internalize, and empathize with main characters, then with "real people" as they try to cope with or resolve problems forced on them (Ceprano and English 1990).

Some advocates propose that this approach can shape core values and increase students' commitment to participate in public affairs. By "injecting a study of social ethics" into the reading curriculum, for example, teachers can boost the likelihood that children will practice ethical behaviors such as appreciating the dignity of labor and gaining a "sympathetic attitude toward the joys and cares of others" (Tuttle 1954, 19). Other proponents have added conflict resolution, compassion, humanism, tolerance, and world understanding to this list of ethical behaviors (Fassler and Janis 1985; Gallagher 1988; Sowers 1947).

Moreover, by interacting with trade books, children "can come to sense what it means ... to be kind, honest, or fair. The extensive use of 'real' stories provides an opportunity for integrating values education" (Gibbs and Earley 1994, 11). Because quality literature engages so many personal dimensions simultaneously, children make personal meaning from the complexities, joys, and wonders of the human experience and become motivated to act on their world (Graves 1989). Encounters with literature may cause students and teachers to explore and act on their cultural values and beliefs (Rasinski and Padak 1990).

*The Reasonable Evidence.* Confirmation that literature-based teaching nurtures values that contribute to civic competence seems lacking. Some research suggests that this approach can influence young citizens' affective growth, but this evidence seems limited and often inferential. Levstik (1990), for example, found that elementary children consider literary texts more authoritative than basal texts. They believe trade book accounts over text book versions, largely because literature makes such an affective impression on them. Guzzetti, Kowalinski, and McGowan (1992) compared the conceptual learning and attitudes toward social studies of two sixth grade classrooms; one experienced literature-based teaching while the other received a traditional, textbook approach. The literature group demonstrated significantly better understanding of key concepts and more positive views of social studies, although the attitudinal changes could not be considered significant.

Benner (1991) investigated how nursing students form appropriate professional values. She concluded that dictating behavioral guidelines or principles has a limited effect. Instead, ethical development must be informed by a community of practitioners who engage in dialogue about stories in which particular characters and situations exemplify moral values. To apply Benner's findings to a secondary school population demands something resembling a "leap of faith." Still, her research suggests that values cannot be shaped by presenting students with static universals, but by illustrating appropriate behavior in stories that expand their ethical views.

## THE CASE ASSESSED

The number of convincing arguments for social studies instruction based on literary sources far outweighs the amount of published research documenting the extent to which literature-based teaching promotes the knowledge, skills, and values that constitute civic competence. Evidence seems limited, inconclusive, and concentrated on how trade books enhance students' knowledge acquisition. Before embracing the literature-social studies connection without hesitation, educators need expanded research about the effects of this approach, particularly its impact on skill development and values formation. Eeds and Wells (1991) urge us in a sensible direction. They give social studies researchers a task: "to examine what happens when children are allowed to read interesting content and then discuss their reading freely and openly ... with their peers and teacher" (Eeds and Wells 1991, 137).

Because they lack adequate research support, we might accuse proponents of overstating the case for literature-based instruction. We might dismiss their claims as the rhetoric of a passionate interest group. At the same time, methods and materials for using trade books to promote civic competence are readily available (Kiefer 1988; Tiedt 1989). Advocacy pieces proclaiming the benefits of the literature-social studies connection are strikingly plentiful. One of the few points on which social educators generally agree is that trade books have the potential to enhance the social studies curriculum.

A case so compelling must be more than rhetorical. Whether based on research or the personal experiences of trade book advocates, the case must rely on reason as well. We join educators who have advanced the literature-social studies connection and recommend that teachers adopt this potentially productive instructional approach. We also recommend that researchers assemble more evidence so that the effects of literature-based teaching become common knowledge and reason exceeds rhetoric. We feel strongly that their investigations will reveal an important truth. To paraphrase Robert Coles (1989), stories call to all who hold the office of citizen, inspiring us to attain civic competence, so that we can tackle the issues that test our nation's resolve.

## REFERENCES

Alleman, J., and J. Brophy. "Trade-offs Embedded in the Literary Approach to Early Elementary Social Studies." *Social Studies and the Young Learner* 6, no. 3 (1994): 6-8.

Arizona State Board of Education. *Arizona Social Studies Essential Skills.* Phoenix: Arizona Department of Education, 1988.

Barnes, B. R. "Using Children's Literature in the Early Anthropology Curriculum." *Social Education* 55 (1991): 17-18.

Beck, I. L., and M. G. McKeown. "Social Studies Texts Are Hard to Understand: Mediating Some of the Difficulties." *Language Arts* 68 (1991): 482-90.

Benner, P. "The Role of Experience, Narrative, and Community in Skilled Ethical Comportment." *Advances in Nursing Science* 14, no. 2 (1991): 1-21.

Brophy, J. "Teaching Social Studies for Understanding and Higher Order Applications." *The Elementary School Journal* 90 (1990): 351-417.

Brophy, J., S. McMahon, and R. Prawat. "Elementary Social Studies Series: Critique of a Representative Example by Six Experts." *Social Education* 55 (1991): 155-60.

Brozo, W. G., and C. M. Tomlinson. "Literature: The Key to Lively Content Courses." *Reading Teacher* 40 (1986): 288-93.

Ceprano, M., and E. B. English. "Fact and Fiction: Personalizing Social Studies through the Textbook-Tradebook Connection." *Reading Horizons* 30 (1990): 66-77.

Coles, R. *The Call of Stories*. Boston: Houghton Mifflin, 1989.

Crabtree, C., and D. Ravitch. *History-Social Science Framework for California Public Schools, Kindergarten through Grade Twelve*. Sacramento: California State Department of Education, 1988.

Dahmus, J. H. "A Godsend to Ancient and Medieval History." *The Social Studies* 47 (1956): 224-28.

Danielson, K. E. "Helping History Come Alive with Literature." *The Social Studies* 80 (1989): 65-68.

Davis, J. C., III, and J. Palmer. "A Strategy for Using Children's Literature to Extend the Social Studies Curriculum." *The Social Studies* 83, no. 3 (1992): 125-28.

Dawson, M. A. "Literature Enlivens the Social Studies." *Education* 85 (1965): 294-97.

Eeds, M., and D. Wells. "Talking, Thinking, and Cooperative Learning: Lessons Learned from Listening to Children Talk about Books." *Social Education* 55 (1991): 134-37.

Ellis, D. "Creating a Literature Focus in the History Classroom." *Australian Journal of Reading* 13 (1990): 242-52.

Farris, P. J., and C. J. Fuhler. "Developing Social Studies Concepts through Picture Books." *The Reading Teacher* 47 (1994): 380-87.

Fassler, J., and M. G. Janis. "Books, Children and Peace." *Social Education* 49 (1985): 493-97.

Fielding, L., P. Wilson, and R. Anderson. "A New Focus on Free Reading: The Role of Trade Books in Reading Instruction." In *The Contexts of School Based Literacy*, edited by T. E. Raphael, 149-160. New York: Random House, 1984.

Fuhler, C. J. "Add Spark and Sizzle to Middle School Social Studies." *The Social Studies* 82 (1991): 234-37.

Gallagher, A. "Children's Literature and the Ethics Dimension." *Social Studies and the Young Learner* 6, no. 1 (1988): 25-27.

Garcia, J., N. L. Hadaway, and G. Beal. "Cultural Pluralism in Recent Nonfiction Tradebooks for Children." *The Social Studies* 79 (1988): 252-55.

Gibbs, L. J., and E. J. Earley. *Using Children's Literature to Develop Core Values*. PDK Fastback 362. Bloomington, Ind.: Phi Delta Kappa Foundation, 1994.

Graves, D. "Research Currents: When Children Respond to Fiction." *Language Arts* 66, no. 7 (1989): 776-83.

Guzzetti, B. J., B. J. Kowalinski, and T. McGowan. "Using a Literature-Based Approach to Teaching Social Studies." *Journal of Reading* 36, no. 2 (1992): 114-22.

Harms, J. M., and L. J. Lettow. "Bridging Time and Space: Picture Books with Historical Settings." *Social Education* 57 (1993): 364-67.

Hellenbrand, H. "American History and Literature, an Essential Dialogue: Putting Together What the Disciplines Have Taken Apart." *Social Studies Review* 28 (1988): 64-70.

Holmes, B. C., and R. I. Ammon. "Teaching Content with Trade Books: A Strategy." *Childhood Education* 61 (1985): 366-70.

Huus, H. "Children's Books Can Dramatize Social Studies." *NEA Journal* 50 (1961): 44-45.

Johnson, J. "Literature-Based Curriculum Replaces Textbooks." *Curriculum Review* 28 (1989): 8-10.

Kiefer, B. "Picture Books as Contexts for Literary, Aesthetic, and Real World Understandings." *Language Arts* 65 (1988): 260-71.

Larrick, N. "Children's Books in the Teaching of Social Studies." *The Instructor* 64 (1955): 15.

Levstik, L. S. "The Relationship between Historical Response and Narrative in a Sixth-Grade Classroom." *Theory and Research in Social Education* 21 (1986): 1-15.

———."Historical Narrative and the Young Reader." *Theory Into Practice* 28 (1989): 114-19.

———."Mediating Content through Literary Texts." *Language Arts* 67 (1990): 848-53.

Lorrie, B. Y. "Using Literature to Teach Location." *Social Studies and the Young Learner* 5, no. 3 (1993): 17-18, 22.

McClure, A., and C. Zitlow. "Not Just the Facts." *Language Arts* 68 (1991): 27-33.

McGowan, T. M., and A. M. Sutton. "Exploring a Persistent Association: Trade Books and Social Studies Teaching." *Journal of Social Studies Research* 12, no. 1 (1988): 8-16.

Monson, D. L., K. Howe, and A. Greenlee. "Helping Children Develop Cross-Cultural Understanding with Children's Books." *Early Child Development and Care* 48 (1989): 3-8.

Morrow, L. M., E. O'Connor, and J. K. Smith. "The Effects of a Storybook Reading Program on Literacy Development of At-Risk Kindergarten Children." Paper presented at the annual meeting of the American Educational Research Association, Boston, April 1990.

National Council for the Social Studies (NCSS). *Expectations of Excellence: Curriculum Standards for Social Studies*.

Washington, D.C.: NCSS, 1994.

———. The 75th NCSS Annual Conference, Chicago, 1995. Washington, D.C.: NCSS, 1995.

New York, The University of the State of, State Education Department, and Bureau of General Education Curriculum Development. *K-6 Social Studies Program.* Albany: State Education Department, 1982.

Norton, D. E. "Teaching Multicultural Literature in the Reading Curriculum." *The Reading Teacher* 44, no. 1 (1990): 28-40.

Norton, R. "Similarities between the History-Social Science Framework and English-Language Arts Framework: What It Means for Elementary Teachers." *Social Studies Review* 28 (1988): 48-52.

Rasinski, T. V., and N. D. Padak. "Multicultural Learning through Children's Literature." *Language Arts* 67 (1990): 576-80.

Rippa, S. A. *Education in a Free Society: An American History.* 6th ed. New York: Longman, 1988.

Sewall, G. T. "American History Textbooks: Where Do We Go from Here?" *Phi Delta Kappan* 69 (1988): 552-58.

Smith, J. "Content Learning: A Third Reason for Using Literature in Teaching Reading." *Reading Research and Instruction* 32, no. 3 (1993): 64-71.

Sowers, F. R. "Trade Books." In *Proceedings of the Annual Conference on Reading*, edited by William S. Gray, 207-214. Chicago: The University of Chicago Press, 1947.

Tiedt, I. *Reading/Thinking/Writing: A Holistic Language and Literacy Program for the K-8 Classroom.* Boston: Allyn and Bacon, 1989.

Tuttle, F. P. "Social Ethics through Literature." *American Childhood* 39 (1954): 19-20.

Tyson, H., and A. Woodward. "Why Students Aren't Learning Very Much from Textbooks." *Educational Leadership* 47, no. 3 (1989): 14-17.

Usery, M. L. "Critical Thinking through Children's Literature." *Elementary English* 43 (1966): 115-18.

Wheeler, A. H. "Individualizing Instruction in Social Studies through the Use of Children's Literature." *The Social Studies* 62 (1971): 166-71.

Wisconsin Department of Public Instruction. *Program Improvement Guide for Social Studies Education in Wisconsin.* Madison: Department of Public Instruction, 1983.

Zack, V. "'It Was the Worst of Times': Learning about the Holocaust through Literature." *Language Arts* 68 (1991): 42-48.

Zarrillo, J. "History and Library Books." *Social Studies and the Young Learner* 2, no. 2 (1989): 17-19.

Thomas M. McGowan is an Associate Professor of Education at Arizona State University, Tempe. Dr. McGowan teaches social studies methods courses and serves as Coordinator of Scales Professional Development School in Tempe, Arizona. Lynnette Erickson teaches social studies methods courses at Arizona State University, Tempe, and is completing dissertation research, a case study of a literature-based approach to teaching social studies. Judith A. Neufeld teaches social studies methods courses at Arizona State University, Tempe, and is completing a dissertation examining how teachers in a professional development school conceptualize their craft. [1990 note]

# 88

# Learning about Contemporary Women
## *Sharing Biographies with Children*

**Myra Zarnowski**

*During a spring 1976 program of* Meet the Press, *when she was asked if the country was ready for a woman, particularly a black woman, as a vice-presidential candidate, she smiled and answered, "The country is not ready, but it's getting ready, and I'll try to help it!" (Haskins 1977, 196)*

The woman who gave that response is former Congresswoman Barbara Jordan. Before her death, she was one of many contemporary women who are active in fields such as politics, literature, education, and entertainment. Teachers have no difficulty finding other examples of women who are shaping our times—women such as Margaret Thatcher, Winnie Mandela, Sandra Day O'Connor, and Mother Teresa. Teachers do have problems teaching about these women in a way that dramatically captures the essence of their lives and accomplishments without making them seem too good to be true.

We can show children that women are making important choices right now—choices that affect their lives and often the lives of others. Not only can children understand decisions made by other people, but they can also begin to evaluate them. Since children will ultimately become decision makers themselves, it is enlightening for them to see how successful decision makers do it. As Kieran Egan (1986) has pointed out, elementary school children are interested in learning about how real people (as opposed to superheroes) successfully deal with real problems. What are their strategies? What accounts for their successes? Children can find the answers by reading and discussing biographies of women who are successful.

## WHY BIOGRAPHIES?

Biographies are useful resources for teaching about contemporary women because they can feed a student's curiosity about the personal and professional lives of individual women. At the same time, biographies teach the student about the social conditions under which these women lived. Barbara Tuchman (1979) has referred to the biography as "a prism of history" because it offers a human focus for understanding the larger events of history. Biographies let readers see how individuals shape their times and are, in turn, shaped by them.

Biographies that are written expressly for children have two important features (De Luca & Natov 1980): They are relatively short, and they provide enough background information to enable a child to make sense of the events described. Writers of children's biographies do not assume that children are familiar with events that occurred before they were born; instead, they fill in the missing information.

Besides the appeal and accessibility of biographies, they are also written in a form that is logical for introducing children to history in general and to women's history in particular. This is because biographies resemble the fictional stories with which children are already familiar. Like fiction, the biography describes a series of events that occurred over time. Yet, unlike fiction, particularly historical fiction, biography does not present a confusing mixture of fact and fancy (Downey 1986). Moreover, biography that is well written is not only good history but also good literature.

Biography fills a need in social studies programs for a more detailed treatment of the lives of women. Commenting on current social studies textbooks, the National Women's History Project (1985) reported that while women have long constituted over fifty percent of America's population, the standard social studies texts fail to reflect this reality and view women from an incomplete perspective as passive nonparticipants in the nation's events. In contrast to this, biographies of women, show them in active roles.

## READING BIOGRAPHIES OF CONTEMPORARY WOMEN WITH URBAN STUDENTS

In order to learn more about the effectiveness of using biographies with elementary school children, several fifth graders joined me in reading biographies of contemporary women. These children from an urban public school in New York City were selected because they were average or above average readers who would benefit from reading and responding to literature. The group of five girls and three boys represented different ethnic and racial backgrounds: Three were Hispanic, two Indian, one black, and two Caucasian.

These children spent a three-week period reading a number of biographies, writing daily journal entries, and sharing their thoughts about their reading.

## THE BIOGRAPHIES

Of the sources available for locating biographies of contemporary women, a most useful one is Mary-Ellen Siegel's book *Her Way* (1984). It provides an annotated list of more

Reprinted with permission from the Helen Dwight Reid Educational Foundation, from *The Social Studies*, March/April 1988. Published by Heldref Publications, 1319 Eighteenth Street, NW, Washington, D.C. 20036-1802. Copyright 1988.

than 1,700 biographies of notable women written for readers from kindergarten through high school levels. Other useful and widely available sources include *Adventuring with Books* (Monson 1985) and *The Best of Children's Books* (Sutherland 1986).

Well-written biographies of contemporary women, particularly those written for children, portray their subjects honestly, citing both weaknesses and strengths. The books also show evidence that the authors did some careful research, using primary source material when available. When teachers select biographies of contemporary women, they should include books that describe women who are highly motivated in a number of different areas in order to show the wide range of opportunities for personal development. For example, in this study, fifth graders read about Margaret Thatcher, Mother Teresa, Dolly Parton, Golda Meir, Diana Ross, Dorothea Lange, and Betty Friedan.

## RESPONSES TO BIOGRAPHIES OF CONTEMPORARY WOMEN

After the children had read a few of the biographies, they were asked to respond to the following question in writing: What are biographies like? Responses from the children indicated that the children understood that a biography gives facts about the person's life and focuses on an individual's development in roughly chronological order. The children's journals provided information about the impact their reading was having on their thinking about contemporary women. Their responses echoed the message, frequently found in children's biographies, that through hard work and determination, women could achieve.

In their later journal responses, the children attempted to assimilate the information they learned from reading a number of books with the information they knew from personal experience. In addition, the children began dealing with these significant questions: Do contemporary women pursue the same career goals as contemporary men? Do women generally cook, clean, and care for their families? Do contemporary women feel that they must have careers?

Among the group, there was clearly an issue of confusion about what women of our time prefer. The children's journals pointed out contradictions between what they read and what they knew from experience. For instance, one child wrote of women and men as "almost equal," and another youngster stated that women are mostly athletes, singers, and politicians. Several sentences later, this same child noted that most women stayed home all day. As the role of contemporary women developed into a burning question, one child strongly suggested, "Let's talk!" The group discussed people we knew as well as people we read about and talked about the variety of things women of today do.

For teachers, the most significant point here is the children's sharing their thoughts in speech and in writing so that teachers can begin to understand their thinking.

In class discussions, children often point the way to topics to pursue. Vivian Gussin Paley (1986) makes this point in her classroom investigations of the dialogue of kindergarten and nursery school students. According to Paley, "someone must be there to listen, respond, and add a dab of glue to the important words that burst forth" (p. 127). Her message is appropriate for teachers at all levels.

Discussions of the biographies of contemporary women yielded a number of interesting topics, with one related to the issue of whether biographies of successful women inspired children or overwhelmed them with levels of success they could not hope to achieve. The children suggested that both possibilities were tenable. One child wrote that readers "might get upset" if they failed at a career they had learned about through books; another child, in contrast, stated that a biography could inspire a person to "a dream that might come true."

A number of children found biographies inspiring, and even asked to write biographies of friends, relatives, or people they had read about. Overall, the children seemed enthusiastic and willing to explore the material as well as their thoughts about it.

The students, in addition, often asked about and shared their knowledge of new words and concepts. For instance, after reading about Margaret Thatcher, one youngster told the others about the Shadow Parliament. Another child, after reading about Mother Teresa, wanted to know more about leprosy. Other topics surfaced too: the Great Depression of 1929, the evacuation and incarceration of Japanese-Americans during World War II, anti-Semitism, and Zionism. What the children learned from their reading fueled our discussions of history and the world around us. Surprisingly, it was not until the students had been meeting with me daily for two-and-a-half weeks that one youngster asked why all the biographies were about women and none were about men.

## EXTENDING CHILDREN'S UNDERSTANDING OF CONTEMPORARY WOMEN

The choices of biography stimulated interest in learning about the lives of contemporary women. The books engaged children in sustained independent reading and fueled group discussions and journal writing. Most important, they led the children to reexamine their ideas about the world.

In addition to this method of reading and responding, there are a number of alternative strategies for guiding children's reading of biographies about contemporary women. The following suggestions focus on particular aspects of reading and writing biography.

*Focus on a single life.* Instead of reading about different women, children can read several biographies of one woman. Through their discussions, they can determine how the biographies are similar and how they are different. Children will realize that biography is an interpretation of facts and that several biographies about the same woman can be written, with each presenting something unique.

*Focus on lives of accessible subjects.* A live subject can answer questions and supply information for a biographer. If students write biographies of women in their community, they will have access to much data and will have to organize it in a meaningful way.

*Focus on events.* Students might select those events they see as turning points in a woman's career, and these events could be dramatized in order to share them with a larger audience.

*Focus on primary source material.* Children could be encouraged to find primary source material that supplements a biography they are reading and create a display of such material.

*Focus on time.* One way to focus attention on time is to have children construct a time line of events in history that occurred during the lifetime of a particular woman. Students can consider the effect of these events on the woman's life.

Biographies of contemporary women provide a stimulating focus for units, mini-units, and lessons. Material that is current, attractive, and accessible is available now; it just needs to be shared with children.

## REFERENCES

DeLuca, G., and R. Natov 1980. "An Interview with Milton Meltzer." *The Lion and the Unicorn*, 4 (1): 95-107.

Downey, M. T. 1986. "Teaching the History of Childhood." *Social Education*, 50: 262-267.

Egan, K. 1986. "Individual Development in Literacy." In S. de Castell, A. Luke, and K. Egan (eds.), *Literacy, Society, and Schooling: A Reader*. Cambridge: Cambridge University Press.

Haskins, J. 1977. *Barbara Jordan*. New York: Dial.

Monson, D. L. (ed.) 1985. *Adventuring with Books*. Urbana: National Council of Teachers of English.

Paley, V. G. 1986. "On Listening to What the Children Say." *Harvard Educational Review*, 56: 122-131.

Siegel, M. 1984. *Her Way*. Chicago: American Library Association.

Sutherland, Z. 1986. *The Best in Children's Books*. Chicago: University of Chicago Press.

Tuchman, B. W. 1979. "Biography as a Prism of History." In M. Pachter (ed.), *Telling Lives: The Biographer's Art*. Washington, DC: New Republic Books.

*Women as Members of Communities*. 1985. Santa Rosa, CA: National Women's History Project. (ERIC Document Reproduction Service No. ED 260 998).

Myra Zarnowski teaches in the School of Education at Queens College of the City University of New York. [1988 note]

## Francis E. Kazemek

Try this brief quiz, and see how well you do.

1. Who authorized wiretaps on Martin Luther King, Jr.?
2. Who called King the "most notorious liar in the country, a communist, and a moral degenerate"?
3. When did King initiate sit-ins at lunch counters and other public places throughout the South?
4. What group of people helped King in 1963 save the "Birmingham Campaign" from failure?

   (*The correct answers to the quiz are: 1. the Attorney General of the United States, Robert Kennedy; 2. the Director of the FBI, J. Edgar Hoover; 3. King did not initiate the sit-ins, college students throughout the South did; 4. elementary and secondary school students.*)

If you are like most of the inservice and preservice teachers and librarians to whom I have given this short quiz, you will have answered one or more of these questions incorrectly. Martin Luther King, Jr., and the civil rights movement of the 1950s and 1960s are history not only to elementary and secondary students but also to a great many teachers as well; a thirty-two-year-old teacher was not even born during the Montgomery bus boycott of 1955-56 in which King first gained national prominence.

Elsewhere I have explored and highlighted the superficial, partial, and, ultimately, inconsequential nature of classroom materials and methods devoted to the study of King and his times (Kazemek 1988). One of the truly great persons of the twentieth century, this person for whom we have dedicated a national holiday is often reduced to little more than another worksheet exercise or a handful of trivialities about his childhood—and this is usually done for only a few days of a couple of weeks a year.

I believe that the primary reason for many of the reductive and totally inadequate approaches to what King meant, and continues to mean, for our country is teachers' unfamiliarity with King's life and the era in which he and other civil rights activists struggled for equal rights for all people. With few exceptions, the average thirty-year-old teacher learned little, if anything, about King in the social studies and history textbooks she or he used while in elementary and secondary schools. Even today, for the most part, such textbooks are inadequate for helping students explore the dimensions and meanings of King's life. Thus, unless the teacher had concentrated on contemporary American history in college or has a personal interest in King and the civil rights movement of the 1950s and 1960s, her or his knowledge of King and his times is probably fuzzy, at best. It is little wonder then that teachers often rely upon commercial packets and worksheets that simplify (if not trivialize) King's life to dates, apocryphal stories, the "I Have a Dream" speech, and sententiousness.

My primary purpose is to present briefly some resources that teachers can use with their students so that both teacher and students learn more about King and, more important, act in some way upon his vision of America. After a general discussion of important criteria for selecting biographies for children and young adults, I wish to explore various problems in biographies of King that have been written for elementary and secondary students and examples of some good biographies of King. Some activities that would provide teachers and students with a general orientation for celebrating King's life and vision are also presented.

### BIOGRAPHIES FOR CHILDREN AND YOUNG ADULTS

Huck (1987) says that we can look at biographies for children and young adults as being either "authentic" or "fictionalized." An authentic biography, like most biographies written for adults, is well researched, focuses on events and facts of the person's life, and is supported by evidence and documentation. A fictionalized biography is also grounded in thorough research; however, it does not use the expository style of authentic biography. Rather, the author dramatizes events and personalizes the subject by using a narrative mode. Huck says that because students, especially elementary students, tend to read biographies as they read fiction, that is, for the plot, dialogue, and action, they usually prefer fictionalized biographies over authentic ones. Such biographies allow students to learn much more than a collection of facts about a subject; instead, they allow students to enter into the life of the person, to learn about the person as a human being, and to understand how the person helped shape her or his own life and how that life was also shaped by other people, times, and events.

Whether teachers use authentic or fictionalized biographies with children, Huck maintains that they should select those books according to certain criteria. First, is the biography accurate? Is it well researched, and does it contain facts? If it is a fictionalized biography, is the invented dialogue realistic and plausible? More important than what the biography contains is what the biography leaves out concerning the person's life. Huck contends, and I agree absolutely, that it is better not to use biographies with children than to present them with a distorted image of a person based on conscious omission of unflattering information about that person's life. Second, how does the author deal with characterization? Is the subject of the biography presented as a real human being with both virtues and faults? Is the author true to the complexities of the person's life, neither demeaning nor eulogizing her or him? Too often biographer's for children and young adults present the person as being too good to be real. Third, what is the author's theme? Is her or his interpretation of the subject's life balanced and fair, or does the author manipulate facts and events to fit a chosen theme and desired vision of the person's life?

## PROBLEMS FOUND IN JUVENILE BIOGRAPHIES OF KING

Using these criteria, one can easily find various misconceptions, misrepresentations, and even distortions in various biographies about King. After reading and studying most of the biographies (either in or out of print) currently available in libraries, I have grouped these misrepresentations and problems into five categories.

## DISTORTIONS AND PIOUS GENERALITIES

It is not hard to find in various biographies the easy generalities concerning King's personal life that we expect to find in textbook-type materials. These are the kinds of statements that one finds in books about Washington, Lincoln, and other American heroes. For example, we read that learning was always easy for Martin and that he was a good student. The fact of the matter is that he was a slightly better-than-average student in high school and struggled during his first year at Morehouse College because of his poor reading skills. Similarly, we read about what a happy husband and good father King was. Again, such statements belie the facts. King was seldom home after the Montgomery bus boycott; he was constantly on the road preaching and organizing. His married life with Coretta was a troublesome one, and he was racked with guilt over not being home enough with his children.

These personal misrepresentations are relatively benign compared with the more political ones. King and the civil rights movement of the 1950s and 1960s were political and unsettling to the status quo. If we are truly to study King's life and what it might mean for us today, then we cannot exclude politics and controversy from the classroom. Unfortunately, this is what some of the biographies, like typical sanitized and neutered textbooks, do. Thus, for example, building on yet another distortion, that of the Kennedys and their "Camelot," we read either explicitly or implicitly that John and Robert Kennedy unequivocally supported King and the civil rights movement and that they were partners with King in his efforts to gain equal rights for blacks. From historical documents we can learn that the Kennedys' support of the movement and of King was lukewarm, at

best. King was disappointed and often depressed over their lack of commitment. He constantly had to challenge and force them to act. Moreover, and to me, this is the most disturbing, we often get a portrait of King in some of these biographies as a passive (in the pejorative sense) man. In reality, King was an active, nonviolent, political resister who struggled against an economic system that generated poverty and inequality, local and state governments in the North and South that repressed blacks in one way or another, and a federal government that was waging war in Southeast Asia. Hosea Williams, one of King's co-workers in the civil rights movement, observed that there is "a definite effort on the part of America to change Martin Luther King, Jr., from what he was really all about-to make him the Uncle Tom of the century. In my mind, he was the militant of the century" (Garrow, 1986, p. 625).

## LACK OF ACKNOWLEDGMENT OF KING'S SHORTCOMINGS

Biographies for children and young adults, I believe, need not, perhaps should not, show the individual with "warts and all." We want to hold up to our students models of how to be human, courageous, and compassionate in an often-times inhuman world. This does not mean, however, that we simply ignore the weaknesses and human frailties of an individual. As Huck (1987) contends, a biography for children should not present an individual as being too good to be true.

Many of the biographies of King do present him as a too-good-to-be-true type. They do not present him as a complex human being with both great strengths and weaknesses; rather, they present him as a kind of superman, an almost mythic figure, who can then all-too-easily be relegated to a difficult and turbulent past when such larger-than-life figures were among us. Once a person is seen in mythic or superhuman terms, she or he ceases to have practical relevancy for ordinary children and adults. Thus, while we might honor the person in a variety of ways, for example, with a national holiday, we effectively ignore the deeper and broader meanings of her or his life by perceiving it in a historical rather than present tense.

Some biographies of King ignore such things as his own doubts and misgivings about his role in the civil rights movement. They pay little, if any, attention to the constant infighting among the various civil rights organizations, for example, Kings' Southern Christian Leadership Council (SCLC) and Wilkin's National Association for the Advancement of Colored People (NAACP). King's personal weaknesses, especially during the last few years of his life, not usually mentioned.

I am not maintaining that all of these issues should be presented in biographies for children and young adults. I do contend, however, that attention needs to be given, in an appropriate manner for a particular age range, to the fact that King's accomplishments were achieved while he wrestled with a variety of personal, social, and political problems.

## KING AND THE CIVIL RIGHTS MOVEMENT

Various biographies for children and young adults imply, directly or indirectly, that it was King who initiated the civil rights activities throughout the South during the late 1950s and early 1960s. We know, however, from detailed and scholarly research (Branch 1988; Garrow 1986) that King was almost reluctantly swept up by a movement that was much greater than he. The events of the time helped to make and transform King; he, likewise, helped to make and transform them. The important point is that the civil rights movement was not King's movement. It was the movement of many brave and selfless people: children, men, and, especially, women. The Southern Christian Leadership Conference's "mother conscience" and director of the famous Citizenship Schools throughout the South, Septima Clark, observed shortly before her death:

> In stories about the civil rights movement you hear mostly about the black ministers. But if you talk to the women who were there, you'll hear another story. I think the civil rights movement would never have taken off if some women hadn't started to speak up. A lot more are just getting to the place now where they can speak out. (Clark 1986, p. 83)

## LACK OF BALANCE

A serious shortcoming of various juvenile biographies is the lack of balance in attention paid to the different periods of King's life. These books do not present King's whole life from 1929 to 1968. Generally, they overemphasize his early years and contain the usual vignettes and apocryphal stories associated with historical figures. Instead of George Washington and the cherry tree and Abe Lincoln studying by firelight, we now have little Martin being rejected by the mother of his former white playmates. For example, one biography for primary grade children devotes eighteen pages to King's life through the Montgomery boycott and eleven pages to the rest of his life. A book for intermediate grade children has sixty-six pages dealing with his life up to Montgomery and twenty-four pages for Montgomery and beyond. A biography for secondary students spends one hundred pages presenting King's life up to 1959 but only forty-two pages to the rest of his life. Because King is known and honored for the real work and struggle in which he engaged from 1956 to 1968 and not for his rather typical and secure childhood and young adulthood, this unbalance, I believe, actually serves to lessen the importance of his life.

## FALSE IMPRESSIONS ABOUT THE ACCOMPLISHMENTS OF THE CIVIL RIGHTS MOVEMENT

Perhaps the most serious problem with many biographies of King for children and young adults is the implicit, and in some cases even explicit, assumption that King and the civil rights movement solved the many problems that blacks and other minorities in the United States have experienced — racial prejudice, segregation, and poverty. A young reader can leave such biographies with the belief that there really is no need for continued struggle in civil rights because King and others fixed everything in the past. This is especially true for those children (and their teachers) who happen to live in rural or homogeneous communities such as mine in the Pacific Northwest. Minorities are few in numbers, and the difficulties attendant upon life within major metropolitan areas or within isolated and poverty-stricken rural areas are not experienced and are merely something one sees on television or reads in the newspaper.

We know that King did not fix everything. In fact, in many ways, things have gotten worse for blacks and other minorities since King's death. For example, Edelman (1987) has observed that of the four- and five-year-old children in the United States today, one in four is poor; one in three is nonwhite or Hispanic; one in six has no health insurance; one in six lives in a family where neither parent has a job; one in two has a mother working outside the home and only a minority of those receive quality child care. Edelman (1987, p. 3) documents this:

> During the 1950-1955 period, the United States ranked sixth in the infant mortality among twenty industrialized countries and Japan tied for seventeenth place. By the 1980-1985 period, Japan ranked first and the United States tied for last place among the same groups of countries.
> A black baby born within the shadow of the White House and U.S. Capitol is less likely to survive the first year of life than a black baby born in Third World Trinidad and Tobago.

Thus the danger of such simplistic and reductively melioristic biographies of King is that children (and their teachers) will overlook or ignore the reality described above and in a real sense negate King's life and work by failing to carry on where he left off.

## EXAMPLES OF GOOD BIOGRAPHIES FOR ADULTS AND CHILDREN
### BOOKS FOR TEACHERS

The last five years or so have seen the publication of detailed, insightful, and critically acclaimed books dealing with King and his era. Taylor Branch (1988) won the Pulitzer Prize for his *Parting the Waters; America in the King Years 1954-1963*. This mammoth study, over a thousand pages long, explores in great detail the first part of King's public career. *Bearing the Cross: Martin Luther King, Jr., and the Southern Christian Leadership Conference* by David J. Garrow (1986) is still the most complete biography of King's whole life. Stephen B. Oates's *Let the Trumpet Sound: The Life of Martin Luther King, Jr.* (1982) is a less comprehensive and critical biography than either Branch's or Garrow's book, but it is highly readable, accurate, and not nearly as long as the other two. Any of these three books will provide the interested teacher with a solid background into King's life and times. Last, teachers might want to read some of King's own writing. *Strength to Love* (1963), a collection of his important sermons, reveals his range, beliefs, convictions, and religious grounding. *Why*

*We Can't Wait* (1964) is King's account of the Birmingham campaign and includes his famous "Letter from Birmingham Jail."

## BOOKS FOR CHILDREN AND YOUNG ADULTS

The biographies and books described briefly in this section are simply examples of the kinds of materials we should use with our students. I am not attempting to be exhaustive in my discussion.

*The Life and Death of Martin Luther King, Jr.* (Haskins 1977), *Martin Luther King, Jr.* (Harris 1983), and *Martin Luther King, Jr.* (Faber and Faber, 1986) are three excellent biographers for upper-elementary students and adolescent readers. They are also fine background reading for the busy teacher who does not have time to read the three adult biographies described earlier. Haskins' book is a biography for junior and senior high students. It is detailed, candid, and admirable for the way it presents the complexity of King's life: for example, "Martin still had grave misgivings about the boycott" (p. 45); "Because of his busy schedule, Dr. King had little time to spend with his family" (p. 86); "[A]lthough the contents of the tape have never been disclosed, it presumably had to do with embarrassing extramarital activities on King's part" (p. 144). This book, with black-and-white photographs, also contains a section on the aftermath of King's death. Harris's readable and thought-provoking biography for junior and senior high students contains black-and-white photographs and is shorter than Haskins's. Harris deals honestly with the aftermath of King's death. For example, he cites the gains made by blacks since 1968 but also discusses the worsening conditions of poverty, unemployment, a lack of housing, and the effects of ghetto life on the underclass. "In the seventies, the Vietnam War, recession, inflation, and oil-price increases began to sap the nation's dollar resources, cutting short the promise of King's triumphs" (Harris 1983, p. 108). Finally, Faber and Faber's fictionalized biography for upper elementary and junior high students is less candid, critical, and insightful than either Haskin's or Harris's book. Nonetheless, it is accurate and readable for the younger student. It is 125 pages long and also contains black-and-white photographs.

*The Life and Words of Martin Luther King, Jr.* by Ira Peck (1968) is an inexpensive paperback biography for intermediate and junior high students. Peck effectively structures the biography around King's own words and supports the brief text with many black-and-white photographs. *King Remembered*, by Schulke and McPhee (1986), is a highly readable account of King's life and times as told through interviews with his friends and associates and over one hundred black-and-white photographs. Important features of the book include the complete text of the "Letter from Birmingham Jail" and a succinct chronology of the key events in King's life and the nonviolent civil rights movement. This book would be especially appropriate for readers from middle-junior high through adult levels. Similarly, Rowe's *An Album of Martin Luther King, Jr.* (1970) is a seventy-two-page collection of photographs of King throughout his career. The brief texts accompanying the photographs make this book appropriate for all readers, elementary through adult. Last, Eve Merriam's passionate poem, *I Am a Man: Ode to Martin Luther King, Jr.* (1971), captures for any reader, elementary through adult, the spins, courage, and dedication that made King the extraordinary human being he was.

Although there are many other biographies and books for children and young adults dealing with King's life and times, some well-written and commendable and some poorly written and/or inaccurate and trivial, a reader cognizant of the criteria I discussed above and familiar with some of the books briefly described in this section will be able to separate easily the wheat from the chaff.

## USING BIOGRAPHIES OF KING

In an article published in the *Journal of Education* (Kazemek 1988), I described the importance of teachers' and students' emulating and acting in some way upon King's ideals and vision of America. Studying about King for one week a-year, generally through worksheets and with a focus upon isolated and remote facts and dates related to King's life, seemed sorely inadequate. Rather, I discussed how teachers and students could celebrate King's life all year long by focusing upon what King was about. I proposed such activities as studying racism and prejudice, exploring violence and war and their alternatives, confronting personally and collectively in various ways the scandal of homelessness and poverty in our country, visiting the old, sick, and lonely, and investigating the effects of sexism in our classrooms, communities and society at large.

I believe that well-written and critical biographies, especially those described here, can help prepare students for these activities. By better understanding who King was, what he stood for, and how he dedicated his life to justice and brother/sisterhood-by entering into his life through reading—students and teachers can then begin to engage in educational activities that not only transform the individual but also contribute to the transformation and shaping of a more just and humane society. If education does not do that, if it is concerned primarily with the transmission of information, if reading and writing are perceived as neutral skills instead of a means of empowerment, then education is sterile:

> Human progress never rolls in on wheels heels of inevitability; it comes through the tireless efforts of men [women] willing to be co-workers with God, and without this hard work, time itself becomes an ally of the forces of stagnation. We must use time creatively, in the knowledge that the time is always ripe to do right. Now is the time to make real the promise of democracy and transform our pending national elegy into a creative psalm of brotherhood [sisterhood]. (King, cited in Schulke and McPhee 1986, p. 280)

## REFERENCES

Branch, T. 1988. *Parting the Waters: America in the King Years, 1954-63*. New York: Simon and Schuster.

Clark, S. 1986. *Ready from Within: Septima Clark and the Civil Rights Movement*. C. S. Brown, ed. Navarro, Calif.: Wild Tree Press.

Edelman, M. W. 1987. *The Children's Time*. Washington, D.C.: Children's Defense Fund.

Faber, D., and H. Faber. 1986. *Martin Luther King, Jr*. New York: Julain Messner.

Garrow, D.. J. 1986. *Bearing the Cross: Martin Luther King, Jr. and the Southern Christian Leadership Conference*. New York: William Morrow.

Harris, J. L. 1983. *Martin Luther King Jr*. New York: Franklin Watts.

Haskins, J. 1977. *The Life and Death of Martin Luther King, Jr*. New York: Lothrop, Lee, and Shepard.

Huck, C. 1987. *Children's Literature in the Elementary School*. New York: Holt, Rinehart, and Winston.

Kazemek, F. E. 1988. "The Fierce Urgency of Now: Honoring the Life of Martin Luther King, Jr. In and Out of the Classroom." *Journal of Education* 170: 66-76.

King, M. L., Jr. 1986. "Letter from Birmingham Jail." In *King Remembered* by F. Schulke and P. McPhee. New York: Pocket Books.

King, M. L., Jr. 1963. *Strength to Love*. Philadelphia: Fortress Press.

King, M. L., Jr. 1964. *Why We Can't Wait*. New York: Harper.

Merriam, E. 1971. *I Am a Man: Ode to Martin Luther King, Jr*. Garden City, N.Y.: Doubleday.

Oates, S. B. 1982. *Let the Trumpet Sound: The Life of Martin Luther King, Jr*. New York: New American Library.

Peck, I. 1968. *The Life and Words of Martin Luther King, Jr*. New York: Scholastic.

Rowe, J. A. 1970. *An Album of Martin Luther King, Jr*. New York: Franklin Watts.

Schulke, F., and P. McPhee. 1986. *King Remembered*. New York: Pocket Books.

Francis E. Kazemek teaches in the Department of Education at Eastern Washington University in Cheney, Washington. [1990 note]

**Rodney F. Allen**
**John Douglas Hoge**

Public concern about geographic illiteracy has given rise to calls for renewed emphasis upon geography instruction (Koener. 1987; Libbee & Stoltman, 1988: Winston, 1986). But elementary school educators may find it difficult to add still more instruction to an already overcrowded day. Many elementary educators might, however, consider the case for emphasizing geographic literacy within the study of children's literature.

A vast range of exciting children's literature is available that includes not only stories from many places around the United States but also translations of stories from many lands and cultures (see Resources). The interaction of characters in such stories follows a plot that is developed within a place or setting. In addition, authors use the language of geography and images of the natural and human-made landscape in setting the stage for their stories. They depict geographic relationships within and among places as a necessary element of their story and they establish emotive tones for places as a part of the storytelling craft.

Children's stories, well told. promote high interest and form a fine base for increasing geographic literacy. Our argument for the use of literature to teach for geographic literacy is based on the belief that geographic literacy is more than mere memorization of place names and the recall of isolated facts about people and places. Geographic literacy goes beyond the recall of information to the development of key geographic understandings about the environment (Backler & Stoltman. 1986: GENIP, 1987: Stoltman & Libbee, 1988).

## FEATURES OF GEOGRAPHIC LITERACY

Within the context of elementary education, geographic literacy might be seen as having three interrelated features. First, geography, like any discipline, has its own specialized vocabulary and concepts. To participate in geographic discourse, students need to know—and use correctly—the terms and concepts involved. Terms for places, the concepts of directions and seasons, and features of the natural landscape are a part of this language of geography which children must master to be geographically literate.

Second, geographic literacy involves the learning of generalizations regarding relationships among people,

Reprinted from *Social Studies and the Young Learner,* March/April 1990, Volume 2, Number 4. Copyright 1990 by National Council for the Social Studies.

places, and other phenomena. For example, generalizations about the influence of weather on agriculture, or farmers' attempts to modify natural growing conditions, are fundamental and comprehensible to children. Generalizations about the relationship of the topography, latitude, and elevation of a region and its climate are also fundamental and accessible to upper elementary students.

Third, geographic literacy involves the use of information about a place to reveal its "hidden" geographic relationships, a feature the English have called "reading the landscape." Being able to determine the web of geographic interactions that occur within a region and inferring aspects of the development of a place over time are examples of this form of geographic literacy.

## A CASE IN POINT

These three features of geographic literacy can be developed using children's literature as a vehicle. The following illustrates this using an abbreviated version of Hao Jan's delightful story, *Making Snowmen* (see Appendix).

Instruction would begin with a prereading activity, focusing students' attention on why they are reading the story. A discussion of the construction and characteristics of snowmen, the ways people learn to help others in a community, and the pattern of living in a small village are potential springboards for reading this story.

After the initial reading, the teacher may go beyond the prereading springboard discussions to the fundamentals of geography which are essential to comprehending this story. Divided according to the three areas of geographic literacy outlined above, the following illustrates how this might be done.

*Geographic Vocabulary and Concepts.* First the story offers many opportunities to teach basic geographic vocabulary and concepts. Some of the key terms which appear in *Making Snowmen* are:

1. *Cardinal Directions:* Eastern and northern are used in the story. North, east, south. and west are the cardinal directions.
2. *Seasons:* The four seasons (winter, autumn spring. and summer) are named and used in the story.
3. *Climate/Weather:* The author uses the climate and weather terms snow, clouds, wind, breeze, and rain.
4. *Natural and Human Landscape Features:* Natural and human-made landscape terms as hillside, slope. field, road, ditch, village, and path appear in the story.
5. *Spatial Interaction:* The story links the village and town with roads; the field and gardens with paths. Children should be asked to reflect upon the specialized uses of

such passageways. the products, people, and ideas which are exchanged via these routes, and what life might be like without them.

6. *Area Differentiation:* The story implies differences in places. For example. the teacher might ask how towns are different from villages in this story, or how gardens are different from courtyards.

7. *Resources:* The story offers many examples of resources used in productive activity including land, labor, rice straw, and donkey droppings!

*Geographic Reasoning*: Second, the story offers teachers the opportunity to engage students in geographic reasoning which may lead to an understanding of basic geographic generalizations. For example:

1. In paragraph number four, human behavior is presented in a geographic context that raises the question, "Why?" The teacher may ask students to explain why people are carrying snow to the fields and what these villagers hope to gain through such behavior. With the students' ideas on the chalkboard, the class might read on to where the storyteller offers reasons. The reasons may be explained by the teacher in terms of cause and effect, checking back with students to their initial ideas. Such directed story analysis might lead to the following generalizations: Variations in weather patterns may disrupt normal farming operations causing crop losses. People have tried many methods of irrigation and planting to help modify the effects of variable weather.

2. Later in the story, children read that snow for making snowmen is taken only from the paths and the ditches. The teacher might pause to write the children's explanations of this behavior. After reading continues, the reasons for this hard work are revealed. The increased snow in the garden provides additional water in the spring. protects the soil during the winter, and reduces the number of insects. Students might weigh these reasons against theirs while considering the connections between snow, insect numbers, and moisture for crops. The generalizations yielded from this study might be: In order for water to be useful for agriculture, it must he distributed evenly near the roots of crops. Snow is a significant source of water in mountainous areas which are located in the middle latitudes far from large bodies of water.

3. For older students, the teacher might encourage the use of climatic and physical maps of China to try to locate possible sites for this village. Surely this village, located in a hilly region, was serious about its water needs. Its crops and farming style suggest some regions in China rather than others. While the story provides no right answer, clues are present for geographic reasoning. Potential generalizations for this activity are: The physical geography of specific regions of countries located in different areas of the world may be highly similar. Maps may be used to locate the potential site of a place within a country if information is known about its weather and topography.

*Reading Geographic Landscapes*. Third, literature offers an opportunity to help students develop their geographic imagination by "reading the landscape" of the village. For example, students could be encouraged to picture the relationships among the people, gardens, fields, and slopes. Using the cues in the story, simple paper cut-outs of the mountains, fields, gardens, people, paths, roads, and houses could be arranged on a flannel board to demonstrate the possible positions of elements within the village. Once some agreement is reached regarding the layout, students could draw a mural of the village with all its geographic features labeled. As a final experience, students might try to map the village they have constructed in the mural, using symbols and other map elements to show the gardens, fields, houses, paths, mountains, and roads. The flannel board activity, mural, and map will truly reflect students' comprehension of the geography of this special village in China.

## CONCLUSION

This article demonstrates what a creative teacher might do with children's literature to teach for increased geographic literacy: The emphasis upon the geographic concepts, generalizations, and imagination is but an extension of the teacher's concern for literal, applied. and interpretative comprehension of any reading material. In many stories, the full understanding of the characters' actions requires careful thought about geography. Similar geography-focused story analysis procedures may be used with a broad range of children's literature including such as award-winning children's books as *Owl Moon*, and *Where the Buffaloes Begin*.

By engaging students in geographic discussions and activities such as those described, the teacher becomes an adult model for children-one reflecting the intrinsic value of learning about the interactions of people with their environment. If we remain alert to the potential of literature to involve children in geographic thinking, geographic literacy may well become a more frequent outcome of elementary schooling.

## RESOURCES

Chinese children's literature (People's Republic of China) may be ordered in the United States from: China Books and Periodicals, Inc.. 2929 Twenty-fourth Street, San Francisco, CA 94110, (415) 282-2994.

Notable children's trade books in the field of social studies are reviewed by a committee of the National Council for the Social Studies. An annual list appears in the April/May issue of *Social Education*.

## REFERENCES

Backler, A. & Stoltman. J. (1986). "The Nature of Geographic Literacy." *ERIC Digest No. 35*. Bloomington, IN: ERIC Clearinghouse for Social Studies/Social Science Education.

Baker, O. (1981). *Where the Buffaloes Begin*. New York: Frederick Warner

The wind died down and the snow stopped flying. The red rays of the sun began to peep out from behind the clouds in the eastern sky.

Just then, the sound of a whistle came from the road that ran through the village.

Yu-ling hurriedly changed into a pair of old padded shoes and tied a string round her trouser legs at the ankles. Yu-ling was only 11. But when she dressed like this she looked like a grown-up commune member.

Yu-ling was getting ready to help her father and mother carry snow to the fields.

Little Tsai, Yu-ling's younger brother, was only in the first grade in school. Since he wasn't going to work himself, he tugged at his sister's hand and begged her to stay behind and help him make a snowman.

Yu-ling got a bit worried. Now that a chance had come to help the commune members carry snow, she didn't want anything to spoil it.

"Listen, little brother;" she coaxed. "You wait at home and when I get back from work I'll make a big snowman with you. Won't that be wonderful?"

"No, no! The snow will melt before you come back," Little Tsai protested, shaking his head.

"This job of carrying snow is really important," Yu-ling explained. "Didn't you hear what Papa said about it? There wasn't much rain in our village last autumn. Now we're carrying snow from the hillside to the wheat fields to cover them with a white blanket. When it melts it will be just like giving the winter wheat a slow watering. Next spring the wheat will grow strong and we'll have plenty of delicious buns to eat. Think how nice that'll be!"

"No, no," Little Tsai sobbed.

Soon the children's parents appeared, with baskets and shoulder-poles, preparing to set out for the northern slope.

Some children stuck their heads in the door of Yu-ling's house. "Yu-ling, will you stay and take us out to play?" they asked her.

"We're going to make snowmen, aren't we?"

"Yes, yes," Little Tsai hastened to reply for his sister.

Yu-ling hardly knew what to say. Her big dark eyes were on the glistening white snow in the courtyard. She was a girl who liked to think things through and often she had many good ideas. Now, as she looked at the snow, one flashed into her mind.

"Fine, let's make a snowman," she cried out to her playmates at the door. "Each of you find at least two friends to join in. The more the better."

The village road soon rang with the children's shrill voices as they called together their friends. There were at least 25 of them.

Yu-ling said, "Let's break up into threes. Each group of three can make one snowman. Do you agree?"

"We'll set two snowmen in front of every house, like sentries," Chen-tzu suggested.

"I agree to make a lot of snowmen, too," Yu-ling said. "But the snow on the road is so trampled and dirty they won't look good. Besides. the road is narrow There won't be room for all of us!"

"Where, then?" the children asked.

"The vegetable garden's a better place. The snow is clean and white, and it's big enough..." said Yu-ling.

The youngsters marched off to the vegetable garden. At their head was Little Tsai, singing as he walked, quite the little hero.

The garden was flat and covered with thick snow. Not a footprint or a speck of dirt on it. White as newly milled flour. Light as newly fluffed cotton.

It made Yu-ling happy to see this. And in her mind she pictured how it would look in the spring, greener than any other place, vegetables growing up crop after crop. Then she thought of how it would be in the summer, too, with countless bright red tomatoes, and of how vivid they would look at picking time, heaped up under the sun. And she thought of the autumn, when the big cabbages, half as tall as a man, would be loaded on the trucks and carts to go to town. But now it was still winter . . .

The children had scattered and started building their snowmen.

"Wait a minute!" Yu-ling called. "We'd better not use the snow in the garden. Let's get the snow from the path and the ditches alongside and carry it over. There's plenty there!"

Shouting their approval the children flew to the path and ditches like a flock of birds.

The snowmen went up one by one. Little Chubby's was the biggest of all. Little Tsai helped him make two large eyes for it out of donkey droppings, and stuck rice straw in its chin for a great beard which blew in the breeze. No one who saw it could help laughing.

Chen-tzu made a woman commune member of snow. He did a splendid job, giving her a round face and bobbed hair, and pressing a corn stalk into her hand. Little Tsai mounded a plump baby and put it on her back.

The clouds dispersed and floated away, clearing the sky for the sun to shed its dazzling rays on the snow. This made the garden twice as beautiful as before. The children joined hands and danced round the many snowmen they had made. How happy they were!

Suddenly Little Tsai glimpsed Grandpa Wang approaching from the village. Grandpa Wang minded the vegetable garden and the sight of him gave Little Tsai a scare because the old man was ever so strict.

"Run! Grandpa Wang s coming!" Little Tsai shouted over his shoulder.

But before the children could scatter, Grandpa Wang was already there, saying "Don't run off! I have something to tell you."

Grandpa Wang went into the garden and had a look at the snowmen. He gave a happy laugh. "Thank you, children," he said. "This time you deserve a pat on the back."

The children looked at each other puzzled.

"You've piled all that snow onto our vegetable garden. It'll keep down insects and protect the soil. You've done a good job," said Grandpa Wang.

Hearing his words, the children understood everything. Their joyful laughter was so loud the snow tumbled down from the trees.

Billig, E. (1977). "Children's Literature as a Springboard to Content Areas." *The Reading Teacher* 30. 855-859.

Geographic Education National Implementation Project (GENIP). (1987). *K-6 Geography: Themes Key Ideas and Learning Opportunities*. Western Illinois University, Macomb IL: National Council for Geographic Education.

Hao Jan. (1974). *The Call of the Fledgling and Other Children's Stories*. Beijing: Foreign Language Press. No copyright.

Koerner, T.E. (1987). "How Well Do Americans Know Geography?" *National Association of Secondary School Principals Bulletin*, 71 (499), 58-70.

Levstik, L. S (1985). "Literary Geography and Mapping." *Social Education*, 49, (1). 38-43.

Libbee, M. & Stoltman, J. (1988). "Geography Within the Social Studies Curriculum." In Natoli, S. J. (Ed.), *Strengthening Geography in the Social Studies* (pp. 22-41). Washington DC: National Council for the Social Studies.

McGowan T.M. (1987). "Children's Fiction as a Source for Social Studies Skill Building." *ERIC Digest Number 37*. Bloomington, IN: ERIC Clearinghouse for Social Studies/Social Science Education.

Stoltman, J. and Libbee, M. (1988). "Geography in the Social Studies: Scope and Sequence." In Natoli, S.J. (Ed.), *Strengthening Geography in the Social Studies* (pp. 42-50). Washington, DC: National Council for the Social Studies.

Winston, B.J. (1986). "Teaching and Learning in Geography." In S.P. Wronski and D.H. Bragaw (Eds.), *Social Studies and the Social Sciences: A Fifty-Year Perspective* (pp. 43-58). Washington, DC: National Council for the Social Studies.

Yolen, J. (1987). *Owl Moon*. New York: Philomel Books.

Rodney F. Allen is a Professor of Social Science Education at Florida State University, Tallahassee, and a member of the Florida Geographic Alliance. Dr. Allan works with K-8 school teachers to develop methods and materials to promote geographic literacy. John Douglas Hoge is an Assistant Professor of Social Science Education at the University of Georgia, Athens. Dr. Hoge works with K-6 teachers to improve the teaching of social studies. [1990 note]

**Sandy Jean Hicks**

Not too long ago, I had the opportunity to introduce the new social studies curriculum standards (National Council for the Social Studies 1994) to a curriculum committee with which I am working. It should not surprise anyone to learn that when I introduced the standards, I received what could best be described as "blank stares" from the teachers sitting around the table. Many of these teachers asked, "How do you teach all that you are required to teach and, on top of that, deal with these new standards?" Although the committee agreed to use the social studies standards as a focus for our further discussions, I realized that the concerns expressed around our small table reflected the concerns and attitudes of many teaching professionals at the elementary level.

## SO MANY SUBJECTS, SO LITTLE TIME

Time is an issue for every educator. With the push toward excellence in mathematics and science, we all too often fail to provide our students with the necessary experiences and skills to function in a democratic society. Because of very real time constraints, social studies is at times given short shrift. In particular, we fail to capitalize on a learning opportunity for young children, ages six to nine, who are beginning to form concepts and generalizations about the way the world works (National Commission on Social Studies in the Schools 1989). We should dedicate large segments of instructional time in the primary grades to teaching key social studies concepts, laying the foundation for civic competence, which is essential for the functioning of a democratic society.

To develop civic competence, students need to appreciate the values on which this country was founded, acquire and apply information about the world in order to make decisions, and gain the skills necessary to take action as citizens (NCSS 1994). Practicing citizenship requires students to have a sense of duty to themselves and others. Because such responsibilities impel children to become active citizens, these responsibilities must be considered foundational understandings that need to be developed early. Although young children are studying about the heady responsibilities of citizenship, they are also learning basic competencies in literacy and mathematics. It is no wonder my enthusiasm for the standards was met with stares from my colleagues on the curriculum committee. Where can a teacher find the time in a school day to teach so much important content?

Reprinted from *Social Education*, April/May 1996, Volume 60, Number 4. Copyright 1996 by National Council for the Social Studies.

## INTEGRATING THE CURRICULUM

The answer to the dilemma of finding time to adequately address all the elementary curriculum areas seems to be a theme-based, integrated curriculum. Such a curriculum provides a series of structured, multidisciplinary, and multidimensional learning experiences that are responsive to the needs of students and more realistically represent the world in which they live. Children's literature is a perfect conduit through which learning can occur in such an interdisciplinary context (Fredericks, Meinbach, and Rothlein 1993).

Integrating the curriculum happened to be one of the first suggestions made by teachers on the social studies curriculum committee with whom I work, because members already engage in this instructional approach. In addition, although the social studies standards initially received a lukewarm reception, committee members soon realized that they should take the developers of the standards at their word. The document really is a practical, theme-based guide for developing K-12 social studies programs that emphasize and encourage educators to adopt integrative teaching approaches (NCSS 1994).

As the standards' developers and my committee colleagues agree, children's literature is a natural means for exploring social studies issues in an integrated context (NCSS 1994). Many trade books tell stories that children find meaningful and engage their imaginations. Some districts, in fact, have abandoned basal readers at the primary level, substituting children's trade books to provide instructional focus. If teachers adopt a theme-based curriculum with literature as the foundation for each unit (as the social studies standards suggest), the issue of time management does not seem such a daunting task.

## INSTRUCTIONAL STRATEGIES AND SAMPLE ACTIVITIES

What follows are three lessons in which children's books are used to teach social studies concepts and skills related to civic competence. For each teaching strategy, I have indicated which of the ten themes that structure the social studies standards will receive particular emphasis. Additionally, the core skills (as presented in the standards document) that each lesson promotes are identified by number:

1. Acquiring information and manipulating data
2. Developing and presenting policies, arguments, and stories
3. Constructing new knowledge
4. Participating in groups

Although I have constructed each lesson for a particular grade level, these teaching ideas can be modified and used appropriately at other developmental levels as well. Unfortunately, the scope of this article limits discussion of the process of developing an integrated instructional unit, the organizational context in which these sample lessons would naturally be placed. In presenting these lessons, I have assumed that the instructional content of any thematic unit and the lessons within it should integrate multiple curriculum areas. Additionally, all sample lessons reflect a literature-based approach to social studies teaching. They present ways in which selected works of children's literature might be used to promote civic competence in an integrated manner. Many of these recommended trade books have been identified as "Notable Children's Trade Books in the Field of Social Studies." The year in which each selection was named a "Notable Trade Book" is indicated in the lesson plans that follow.

## LESSON 1: PERSONAL RESPONSIBILITY
*Grade Levels: Pre K–Kindergarten*
*Children's Literature:* The Day of Ahmed's Secret *(Heide 1990, reviewed 1991).*
*Standards Themes:* **❶ ⓘⓥ ⓥⓘⓘ ⓧ**

### Accessing Prior Knowledge
This lesson involves *The Day of Ahmed's Secret* (Heide 1990), a story about a young boy who delivers fuel in Cairo, Egypt, and looks forward to surprising his family with the news that he can write his name. Before reading the book aloud, the teacher shares that when she was the student's age, she helped her mother set the table—that was her responsibility. She then asks the students if any of them have jobs or chores that they are responsible for at home. As the students respond, the teacher organizes their ideas in a web on the board. She asks three or four children to talk about why they do their jobs [probable response: "to help our family"]. She repeats the process by asking students what responsibilities they have in school. Two webs representing two different settings are now on the board. Promotes Core Skill One.

### Prereading Activity: Setting the Purpose
The teacher then shows the book to the students and reads the title to them. She thumbs through the illustrations, and she asks students to predict (using the title and pictures) what they think the story might be. She lists their responses so that they can refer to them after sharing the story. Promotes Core Skill One.

### Reading the Story
The teacher reads the story aloud, pausing frequently to check for understanding and to confirm students' predictions about the story. She also underscores the idea of responsibility by referring to the examples of people taking responsibility that permeate the book. After reading the book, the teacher reviews the sequence of the story, asking for volunteers to indicate what events came first, second,

third, and so on. As the students order events, the teacher will post sentence strips that summarize these events in the appropriate sequence on the board. After the sequence of events has been illustrated, the class can choral read the simple sequence statements. Promotes Core Skill One.

The teacher then leads a discussion on the subject of responsibility, asking students to define the term (using the prereading activity and the review of events to provide terminology and ideas). The class then lists the different responsibilities and responsible parties in the book, and responds to the following questions: What would happen if someone did not act in a responsible way? and What might happen to the responsible person and other people? Promotes Core Skills Two and Three.

### Take Action
At this point, the teacher initiates a discussion of different class responsibilities that students can assume and develops procedures with the students for assigning those responsibilities. As a closing activity, children can create a class book with pictures and captions depicting how young citizens can take on responsibility. Promotes Core Skills One through Four.

### Additional Related Literature
Here are a number of "Notable" children's books with accompanying activities that teachers can use to extend treatment of responsibility beyond the lesson generated from *Ahmed's Secret*.
1. *Family Farm* (Locker 1988, reviewed in 1989) depicts the many responsibilities involved for an entire family running and maintaining a family farm. After the book has been shared, children can do the following:
   a. Identify the responsibilities that each individual had on the farm. Promotes Core Skill One.
   b. Write a class letter to the family in the story that explores the responsibilities each family member had. Promotes Core Skill Two.
   c. In small groups, decide what other crops can be grown on the family farm and what each family member's responsibility would be in growing them. Report back to the class or construct a poster illustrating what the group has decided. Promotes Core Skills Three and Four.
2. *Eskimo Boy: Life in an Inupiaq Eskimo Village* (Kendall 1992, reviewed in 1993) and Arctic Hunter (Hoyt-Goldsmith 1992, reviewed in 1993) provide different examples of the life of two Inupiaq Eskimo boys and their responsibilities both in traditional and modern life. With an understanding of the story, students can do the following:
   a. Compare the responsibilities of Norman (*Eskimo Boy*) and Reggie (*Arctic Hunter*), using a Venn Diagram. Promotes Core Skill One.
   b. Compare Norman's responsibilities for basic needs to those of class members using a graphic organizer. Promotes Core Skills Two and Three.

c. In small groups, generate questions that could be asked of Norman and Reggie regarding the nature of their responsibilities. Then, groups exchange questions and answer them. Promotes Core Skill Four.

## LESSON 2: A CITIZEN'S RESPONSIBILITY TO THE COMMUNITY

*Grade Levels: One and Two*
*Children's Literature:* Kate Shelley and the Midnight Express *(Wetterer 1990, reviewed in 1991).*
*Standards Themes:* I III IV V X

*Accessing Prior Knowledge*
*Kate Shelley and the Midnight Express* is the true story of a young woman who saves the lives of hundreds of train passengers at the risk of her own life. Before a read-aloud session, pair students and have them share a time in which they helped someone. Make sure that students answer the following questions in their descriptions:

1. Whom did you help?
2. How did you help them?
3. Where did the event take place?
4. When did the event take place?
5. How did the person whom you helped feel afterward?

Each student will report the event described by his/her partner in a whole-class sharing session. Promotes Core Skill Four.

*Prereading Activity: Setting the Purpose*
The teacher introduces the story and tells the students that Kate helps someone in the story just as they have helped people. The teacher reads the author's note aloud. He points out Ireland on the world map or globe (Kate was born in Ireland) and then locates Moingona, Iowa (Kate's family settled in Moingona when they moved to the United States). He then engages students in a discussion about whether they have ever moved, asking them to compare how Kate felt with how they felt when they moved. The teacher finishes reading the author's note, and asks students what responsibilities they have around the house. He lists them on the board, then focuses students' attention on Kate's responsibilities and how she had helped others. Promotes Core Skill One.

*Reading the Story*
The teacher reads the story to the students, pausing periodically to focus on four key events: Kate going out into the storm to move the farm animals to safety, Kate helping when the train falls into the river, Kate going to Moingona station to warn railroad personnel that the bridge was out, and Kate leading the rescue party to the bridge. After the story has been shared, the teacher asks students how they would feel if they were in Kate's situation, and guides them to realize that Kate met her responsibility to her community (her "duty" as she refers to it). Promotes Core Skill Three.

*Take Action*
Have students list people or organizations in their community that might require help (e.g., local homeless shelters, food and clothing banks, elder hostels, animal shelters). In small groups, students can research how they can help an organization of their choice and develop an action plan to present to the class. After each group presents, the class votes on which organization they will support (this selection does not preclude helping other groups at a later time). Help students find the human and material resources to implement the class action plan. Promotes Core Skills One through Four.

*Additional Related Literature*
Here are a number of "Notable" children's books with accompanying activities that teachers can use to extend treatment of community responsibility beyond the lesson generated from Kate Shelley and the Midnight Express.

1. *Teammates* (Goldenbock 1990, reviewed in 1991). After hearing this story of how one of Jackie Robinson's teammates, Pee Wee Reese, stands up for Robinson's right to play baseball, children can do the following:
   a. Define the term "racism," providing examples from the story that illustrate the term. Promotes Core Skill One.
   b. Develop a written description of how students would have felt being Jackie Robinson or Pee Wee Reese. Would they have taken the same action? Promotes Core Skills Two and Three.
   c. In small groups, list ways in which Robinson and Reese took responsibility to fight racism in their community. Promotes Core Skill Four.
2. *Sweet Clara and the Freedom Quilt* (Hopkinson 1993, reviewed in 1994). Sweet Clara designs a quilt that contains a map showing the route to freedom. To examine how *Sweet Clara* assumes community responsibility, students can do the following:
   a. Describe the actions that Clara takes to act responsibly toward members of her community. Promotes Core Skill Two.
   b. In small groups, children brainstorm other ways people could have helped slaves escape to freedom. Promotes Core Skills Three and Four.

## LESSON 3: RESPONSIBILITY FOR THE ENVIRONMENT

*Grade Levels: Three and Four*
*Children's Literature:* Just a Dream *(Van Allsburg 1990, reviewed in 1991).*
*Standards Themes:* I II III IV VIII X

*Activating Prior Knowledge*
Before having students read *Just a Dream*, the teacher asks the students to quickly write what they know about environmental problems. They should include any work they have done to help the environment. After writing, volunteers can share their responses with the class. Promotes Core Skills One and Two.

*Prereading and Reading Activities: Setting the Purpose and Sharing the Story*

Students should read *Just a Dream* in pairs. Before they begin, students will examine the pictures and title to get a sense of what the story will be about and record their predictions. As students finish the story, they should discuss what they learned with their partners and consider how humans have affected the environment from the events in Walter's dream. Have students summarize the story's message and propose what they could do to help the environment. List their responses on the board or overhead. Promotes Core Skills Three and Four.

*Take Action*

In small groups, students will identify different areas of the school, evaluate which area most needs attention, and design a project that will help clean it. *Going Green: A Kid's Handbook to Saving the Planet* (Elkington, Hailes, Hill, and Makower 1990, reviewed in 1991) would be a useful resource, because it describes social action projects involving the environment that students can do in their own homes, schools, and local communities. Each group will be responsible for implementing its plan and presenting progress reports to the class. Promotes Core Skills One through Four.

*Additional Related Literature*

Here are a number of "Notable" children's books with accompanying activities that teachers can use to extend treatment of environmental responsibility:

1. *Come Back, Salmon: How a Group of Dedicated Kids Adopted Pigeon Creek and Brought It Back to Life* (Cone 1992, reviewed in 1993). Elementary school students help save a creek, restock it with salmon, and wait to see if the salmon will return to the creek to spawn. After reading the book, students can do the following:
   a. Write and ask for a progress report on Pigeon Creek. Promotes Core Skills One and Two.
   b. Research other similar renovation projects and present findings to the class. Promotes Core Skill Three.
2. *The Old Ladies Who Liked Cats* (Greene 1991, reviewed in 1992). This ecological folktale demonstrates the importance of taking action to solve problems. This book introduces activities in which students can do the following:
   a. List the causes of the ecological imbalances described in the story, emphasizing their interconnectedness. Promotes Core Skill One.
   b. Research a true story of ecological balance and restoration (such as *Come Back, Salmon*), then write a fictional retelling of the true story (modeled after *The Old Ladies Who Liked Cats*). Promotes Core Skills Two and Three.

## CONCLUSION

This article argues three important instructional points:
1. The necessity to instruct students in civic competence
2. The use of the social studies curriculum standards (NCSS 1994) to help teachers help students become citizens
3. The need to integrate, with special focus on using trade books to provide more realistic opportunities for children to acquire citizenship learning.

These sample lessons suggested ways that children's literature can be used to introduce and help students acquire social studies skills and knowledge. The literature-based strategies suggested in this article are by no means the final word. The joy of using children's literature stems from the versatility of quality books—one book can be used in multiple ways, and multiple titles can reinforce a key idea. Only the imagination and creativity of the teacher limit the possibilities for social studies teaching and learning.

## BIBLIOGRAPHY OF SELECTED CHILDREN'S BOOKS

Cone, M. *Come Back, Salmon: How a Group of Dedicated Kids Adopted Pigeon Creek and Brought It Back to Life*. San Francisco: Sierra Club, 1992.

Elkington, J., J. Hailes, D. Hill, and J. Makower. *Going Green: A Kid's Handbook to Saving the Planet*. New York: Puffin, 1990.

Goldenbock, P. *Teammates*. San Diego: Harcourt Brace Jovanovich, 1990.

Greene, C. *The Old Ladies Who Liked Cats*. New York: Harper Collins, 1991.

Heide, F. P. *The Day of Ahmed's Secret*. New York: Lothrop, 1990.

Hopkinson, D. *Sweet Clara and the Freedom Quilt*. New York: Knopf, 1993.

Hoyt-Goldsmith, D. *Arctic Hunter*. New York: Holiday House, 1992.

Kendall, R. *Eskimo Boy: Life in an Inupiaq Eskimo Village*. New York: Scholastic, 1992.

Locker, T. *Family Farm*. New York: Dial, 1988.

Van Allsburg, C. *Just a Dream*. Boston: Houghton Mifflin, 1990.

Wetterer, M. *Kate Shelley and the Midnight Express*. Minneapolis: First Avenue Editions, 1990.

## REFERENCES

Fredericks, A., A. M. Meinbach, and L. Rothlein. *Thematic Units: An Integrated Approach to Teaching Science and Social Studies*. New York: Harper Collins, 1993.

National Commission on Social Studies in the Schools. *Charting a Course: Social Studies for the 21st Century*. Washington D.C.: National Council for the Social Studies, 1989.

National Council for the Social Studies. *Expectations of Excellence: Curriculum Standards for Social Studies*. Washington, D.C.: National Council for the Social Studies, 1994.

Sandy Jean Hicks is an Assistant Professor of Elementary Education at the University of Rhode Island, Kingston. [1996 note]

# PART 14

## COOPERATIVE LEARNING

Cooperative learning has many approaches and is often used in elementary classrooms to allow students to work together, share success, and experience the joy of learning. Cooperative learning emphasizes student cooperation, rather than competition, and stresses interdependence, shared leadership, group problem-solving, individual accountability, and the development of communication and social interaction skills within a group setting. Many learning activities in the social studies classroom lend themselves to cooperative group work; as such, teachers often use these groups on a regular basis. Questions that teachers may consider include the following: What is cooperative learning? Which cooperative learning model is best for me and my students? How can I meet the needs of individual students within a group setting? What are some concerns or problems that I might encounter using cooperative group learning? What are some additional teaching approaches that I could use?

Colomb's article, written with Chilcoat and N. N. Stahl, offers practical advice as the authors describe Colomb's experiences in establishing and using cooperative learning practices in his classroom. R. J. Stahl and VanSickle offer ten important ideas to help teachers build a conceptual framework related to cooperative learning as they develop instructional activities. The authors suggest several possible results for students who engage in cooperative group learning experiences.

Baloche recommends integrating creative questioning to encourage creative thinking and to help students develop cooperation skills when working with classmates. Several sample questions that may be used to promote the development of critical thinking skills are included in this article.

Barnes and O'Farrell identify the essentials of cooperative learning activities and provide examples of cooperative activities such as "Jigsaw" and "Co-op Co-op."

Cooperative learning is a theory, philosophy, and practice that requires time, effort, energy, and a reevaluation of previously held ideas and practices. Cooperative learning is just one teaching/learning method. Teachers are encouraged to experiment with a variety of teaching strategies and grouping practices in their social studies classes.

# Elementary Students Can Learn to Cooperate and Cooperate for Learning

**Robert J. Colomb**
**George W. Chilcoat**
**Nancy N. Stahl**

Elementary social studies teachers expect their students to learn to interact with their classmates, get along with others, and take responsibility for themselves. This expectation, however, is not always followed up with instruction on how to accomplish these goals. A classic example is a silent primary or elementary classroom. Many teachers in these classrooms sincerely believe that silence is golden. But is it? Does silence allow for proper communication between the teacher and students or between students? Do periods of silence result in improved thinking, high achievement, and acceptance of personal responsibility? We think not.

One problem with such ideas about silence is that we do not live in a silent society. We live in a society where mass communication demands that we be interdependent. In fact, no single group can exist without the active and continuous interaction of its members. If teachers must prepare students for the world outside the classroom, they must help them to succeed in a world that communicates, that cooperates, and that views responsibility in the context of social meanings. If students are to do this beyond the classroom, teachers then have an obligation to make sure students learn how to interact, to cooperate, to succeed, and to be responsible in the classroom.

Although we expect students to speak, we often forget that many need to learn how to speak. They need to learn such things as how to articulate their thoughts, when to speak, how to control the level of their speech, and what kinds of language are appropriate and inappropriate in particular situations. Many students learn these things through trial-and-error experiences, but many are unsuccessful. These unsuccessful students either avoid speaking or often speak in ways that are inappropriate. In the classroom, we need to help students learn the art and skills of speaking, especially of academic, interpersonal, and cooperative speech.

We must not automatically assume, however, that when students are talking and working in groups in the classroom, they are meeting the teacher's expectations. Students may be speaking with no one listening. They may be sharing ideas and information with no one learning. They may be working alongside others in a group without working as a group. These students may be interacting but not becoming skilled at interacting. They may assume responsibility for getting their portion of a project completed without learning to be responsible outside such projects.

As these possible results suggest, talking and silence in the classroom are not either-or choices. What is occurring during the silence and during the talking is important.

Using cooperative learning techniques, elementary teachers rely heavily upon student speech and student silences to help large numbers of students meet the teacher's achievement and affective expectations. When used appropriately, cooperative learning theory and strategies can be powerful tools for teaching social studies.

## THE EVOLVING COOPERATIVE LEARNING EXPERIENCE IN ONE ELEMENTARY CLASSROOM

This section emphasizes the perspective and experiences of Bob Colomb, currently a 2d grade teacher at Sunset View Elementary School. Written in the first person, this section creates a personal sense of the nature of cooperative learning from one elementary teacher's perspective.

My elementary teaching experience has consisted of involvement in various grade levels from 1st through 6th. For years I had used student groups for all kinds of reasons. I never really felt as though I had used groups very well, but students did seem to enjoy being in them and groups did change the routine of the class activities. In other words, I had used groups to do things but had not paid much attention to their structure and organization. During this time I also felt that the sense of cohesion and teamwork I always thought would evolve from students working in groups never emerged. Students formed groups, did their group work, and left their group as though the group had never existed. What I felt was missing was a way to organize the students and groups so they could accomplish what I thought they could.

For years I tried various kinds of group activities, even using commercially produced materials and those given out by presenters at conferences to enhance the quality of my students' group work and the benefits that I thought should result. Although these provided a greater variety of group tasks and activities, they still fell short of what I wanted and what my students needed.

When I first heard about cooperative learning I was both excited and wary. The initial information sounded too good to be true. Could groups really accomplish all that I heard and read they could accomplish? Was it really that easy to transform my class into a cooperative learning environment? Could something that effective be that simple to learn to use? My caution was partially an outgrowth of the attitudes of so many elementary teachers that cooperative learning was only a theory that wouldn't work in their classrooms. Some of my colleagues suspected that this was another theory from university professors who hadn't been in real elementary or secondary classrooms for decades. There were also concerns that cooperative learning was a new fad that would come and go like so many others in recent years.

I was curious and concerned about how I could improve my teaching. I also felt that, as a professional, the least I should do was find out more about cooperative learning to determine whether I should use it in my classroom.

## HOW I BECAME INVOLVED

When an opportunity arose, I volunteered to travel from Utah to Southern California to see cooperative learning in action. I wanted to find out whether the rumors about its effectiveness were true.

I visited the ABC School District (not its real name) where Spencer Kagan's cooperative learning methods were being implemented. I observed 1st, 3d, 4th, and 6th grade classes. In every classroom, students were using their peers in various ways to teach themselves. At first I was not impressed and was not sold on what I saw. I had expected to visit classrooms in which students had had extensive experience using cooperative learning, were almost "super learners," and had teachers who were veteran users of these strategies. Instead I found teachers and students who were just past the starting line themselves.1 These teachers were in the early stages of becoming better implementors of cooperative learning teams.

With this perspective, my interpretations of what I was watching changed. Coming to understand that these students were just getting started, I became impressed with what they were learning, how well they stayed on task in their small groups, and how well they interacted with one another. If I could get my students to do many of these things by the end of the year, I would be pleased. If this is what students could accomplish early in their use of cooperative learning, I started to imagine what they could do when they really became experienced using these strategies. This visit whetted my appetite enough to investigate and read all I could find about cooperative learning.

## WHAT I FOUND IN THE THEORY, RESEARCH, AND LITERATURE

What proof was there that cooperative learning did what people claimed it could do? More than 530 classroom studies on cooperative learning have been reported (e.g., Johnson and Johnson 1989; Slavin 1990, 1991). These research studies reveal that structured cooperation with others consistently produced higher achievement and productivity than when individualistic or competitive structures were used. Furthermore, students did better in many affective areas (such as getting along with both peers and the teacher), in the quality of their talking with one an-

other, and in the time they spent voluntarily on task (Johnson and Johnson 1987, 1989). In short, these research studies reveal that cooperative learning done well improved the whole child in nearly all the areas of concern to elementary teachers.

What also impressed me was that what I found in the professional journals and textbooks was not just theory and theory research: I found countless studies done in classrooms like mine where teachers were using cooperative learning with their own students. I found that cooperative learning could work in my classroom if I wanted to put in the time and effort necessary to implement it as it should be implemented.

The philosophy of cooperative learning promotes cooperation and collaboration so that students' energy can be channeled by specific instructional strategies to promote positive academic, affective, and social interaction goals. I learned that appropriate cooperative learning apparently would enable my pupils to achieve higher academic results and productivity.

This was what I was after!

The closer I looked at cooperative learning and its basic elements, the more convinced I became that this could be an effective way to teach social studies. I had to try it in my own classroom. I felt that at last I had something I could adapt and use to enhance student learning of academic and social skills. I decided I would put this new philosophy of cooperation and interaction to the test.

## EARLY FRUSTRATIONS LED TO FURTHER EXPLORATION AND ADDITIONAL STRATEGIES

Well into my second year of using cooperative learning I remained frustrated with the lack of whole-group inclusion activities. Up to that time I had applied nearly all the basic elements of cooperative learning and was using them to the best of my ability. Still something was lacking. A colleague and I decided that we needed more whole-group inclusion before we formed our students into small groups. We eventually labeled the element missing in the original list of basic elements "diversity of grouping procedures." I believe this element is critical if the elementary classroom is to evolve into an effective cooperative learning environment.

This diversity, one of the most important elements of cooperative learning, is often ignored. Many educators begin cooperative learning in small-group learning situations, forming their classes into small groups before cooperative skills are practiced by students. In the whole-class group activities I started using, my students learned and improved individual cooperative skills that enabled them to work together in small groups like well-oiled machines. If students fail to achieve acceptable levels of cohesion and skill before placing them into small groups, one major result of using cooperative learning groups will be frustration for the students and teacher alike. When students acquire the skills and get the practice they need, however, frustration is rare.

To ensure quality team achievement, I first created a cooperative atmosphere within my primary level classroom through whole-group inclusion or class-building activities. I find that during the class inclusion activities the cooperative philosophy is modeled for all students. Teacher and students alike are able to see the philosophy and theory behind cooperative learning in actual practice. They also observe the guidelines, expectations, rules for behavior, and attitudes demonstrated and reinforced. Various rewards are used to praise appropriate behaviors and attitudes.

I advise teachers just getting started with cooperative learning in their classrooms to start here. Based on my experience, I believe elementary students will achieve their potential fully only after whole-group inclusion is attained.

After I came to realize how important class-building activities were to maintaining a cooperative atmosphere, I continued to use these activities all year long, using a different social goal, content area goal, or academic skill as the focus of each new activity. For instance, I might use math, science, literature, or reading tasks in addition to my social studies topics. Many of my colleagues here at Sunset View agree on the importance of the skills and attitudes that result from these class-building tasks. By continuing cooperative efforts in the class throughout the year, our students reach levels of learning never achieved in my pre–cooperative learning classroom.

Cooperative learning is not a panacea for the problems in education. It is, however, a philosophy and an approach to teaching in which I fully believe.

## COOPERATIVE LEARNING AS A PHILOSOPHY

Cooperative learning is first and foremost a philosophy. Of course, a philosophy without effective implementation strategies has no power—just as a set of strategies with no philosophical context will have little effect. They are interdependent. The philosophy of cooperative learning through the theory was appealing to me and led me to investigate and then to use many strategies. While using these strategies, I never lost sight of the philosophy-theory behind them. I have observed many teachers use these strategies unsuccessfully because they expect the strategies to work with any philosophy they choose. These strategies work to the extent that their practice is guided by consistent theory and philosophy. I encourage all teachers to spend at least as much time studying and learning to use the philosophy-theory of cooperative learning as they do learning the strategies. Neither will work well without the other.

How do elementary teachers use this philosophy in their classrooms? They must learn the theory, structure the class tasks, get students talking and working together, play down competition, and increase students' positive interdependence. In other words, elementary teachers must use cooperative learning.

Students love to talk. They get excited about moving about in the classroom. They get excited about finding out what others think. They want to share what they know.

They are interested in hearing about and studying new things. They tend to get turned off in classrooms where the activities result in one student after another saying the same thing as the teacher goes around the room or circle for each student to say something. In addition, many students have learned that if they get too excited while talking about what they are studying or learning, the teacher will insist that they be quiet to cut down the noise level.

I have found that students have not been taught how to be quiet and how to talk within extended interaction situations. They are directed to be quiet but not taught how to be quiet.

In my classroom, I hear structured noise or on-task noise generated from on-task conversation that allows other students and me to listen to the learning that is occurring at that moment. For students to achieve quality structured noise, I teach them how to come face-to-face with one another so that all they need are their twelve-inch voices rather than their typical twenty-four-inch voices.

Elementary students also need to learn how to be quiet and how to be good listeners when they are quiet. In other words, they need to learn that being quiet means they have a number of jobs to do that do not require talking—that being quiet means far more than merely shutting up.

## MY CLASSROOM TODAY

Many of my classroom activities start out with whole-group inclusion activities before we move to specific small-group work and then finally to individual work. When the individual work is completed, the product is brought back to the small-group level again and then to the whole group for presentation and interaction. I consider this type of cooperative learning an advanced form. Ideally, for me, a teacher would want to take a class from whole group to team, from small-group team to individual or competitive, then back to the small group, and finally from the small-group learning teams to the whole group. This shift must be made slowly at first.

On a typical day, the first thing we do in the morning is form a big circle on the floor so everyone faces each other. After some initial conversation and sharing, student groups begin to complete their assigned tasks. One group may work on the calendar for the month, another the science bulletin board, another the social studies project display, and so forth. Each group knows they are responsible for one of these classroom routines each month. Their particular routine changes each month. Early in the year we spend time in our whole-class group learning what it means to be responsible and learning how to carry out each routine so that it is acceptable.

Instead of having a room with fancy, commercially produced bulletin board materials or materials that I spend hours cutting and pasting and my students essentially ignored, my room now has relevant and fact-filled boards that get attention from nearly every student on a daily basis. Students now observe what other groups put on their boards and they seem to learn a lot from what is posted.

As the months go by, the student groups get better at completing these routines and improving the quality of their projects.

In that first week we also spend time learning how to interact and work in groups and how to work as a group. The various roles students may need to carry out are explained along with examples. We talk about why these roles are important and what might happen if a role is not carried out. We also share some of our feelings about these roles and why those in the class need to do their jobs in the groups. Some time is spent helping students to feel they are important to the success of the group they are in. We even talk about the ways students can use the groups to learn the material. After the first few weeks, my students have a good sense of what they are to do in their learning groups. We review and continue to work on all these things throughout the year.

Early on, I assign specific roles to specific students in each group. This assignment ensures that the same students are not in the same role all the time. Later, students are allowed to pick the major roles they will play, once again with the restriction that they cannot play the same role all the time.

Helping students think about guidelines for their attitudes and behaviors in these groups takes a lot of time at the beginning. What is gained in student achievement, on-task behavior, and improved social skills, however, more than makes up for the time spent helping them become good cooperative group members.

Usually by the end of the first month of the year, I have determined the membership of the base groups where each student will remain throughout the year. Except in rare situations, this is each student's permanent group. Because these are permanent, I am very careful in my selection of which students should be together for this length of time. From time to time, however, new but temporary groups are formed. These groups are used for different reasons, one of which is to ensure that students work with more of their peers of different gender, race, or ethnic backgrounds.

Small groups with the same and different student membership are used in math, science, reading, language arts, and social studies. Students may remain in their base groups or be reassigned to new groups for one day or several weeks. They may be in one, two, or three different groups on some days depending on what we are studying in the different subject areas. We are not in cooperative learning groups all the time.

I also use various group strategies. Using Jigsaw, for example, students placed in teams may choose to study a particular time period of history but different incidents within this period. Two girls and two boys in a group together once decided to study and learn about the Vietnam War era. The girls did not want to write or study about the war itself, but were interested instead in the hippie movement. They each took a different approach to the hippie movement. The boys investigated two different aspects of the war. One looked at the military situation; the other at the political. The four students then met together and brought back all that they had learned to the group, put it together as a group, and presented a fantastic informational project to the class.

In this same class, each group was also responsible for completing a large section on a historical time line that covered all the walls of the room. This complete project took us about two months and encompassed research, presentations, writing, art, science, reading, and cooperative skills. As students found specific information, they placed it in their section of the time line once their group had confirmed its relevance, importance, and accuracy. At the end of the unit, students shared with the class what they had learned in their particular section of investigation.

I have found that students need not always complete all of the assignments each day just to have it done. For instance, if they are given fifteen questions to answer as part of their social studies group task, I would much rather they answered ten correctly for the day's work, and that they all really knew the correct answers to those ten questions, than have partially correct answers for all fifteen. In part, this decision reflects my acceptance of my role as facilitating optimal student learning as opposed to having students merely finish assignments regardless of what they learn or do not learn.

To ensure that students are working on task and are helped in their learning efforts, the class has adopted the use of the raised hand which is the universal sign in cooperative learning that it is time for everyone to be quiet. This quiet time functions as a time-out during which new directions can be given, points of uncertainty can be clarified, and specific questions can be answered. Students learn early that once the hand is raised, everyone is to take time out in their group work and stop in silence. I am still amazed at how well this signal works and how fast students catch on to the meaning of the raised hand.

One day I received a phone call from a parent informing me that the phone at his house had rung at 6:30 that morning. The call, made by a student in my classroom, was for his child. The parent was concerned that his child had been awakened too early in the morning and that the caller was a student in the class. I investigated the matter.

I already knew that many of the students in their small groups had exchanged phone numbers to make sure that students had done their parts of one or more assignments outside of class. After a while, it was not uncommon for them to call each other at home in the evening and on weekends. They shared information and made sure that their groupmates had the assignment when they were not in class for one reason or another. On more than one occasion, two or three members of a group have called a fourth who had missed several classes to tell him or her that they were concerned about the student's absence and about the student generally. They also told the absent groupmate that he or she was part of a team and the team couldn't succeed when not all its members were there in class working together.

When some of these students did arrive back in class they often reported that the members of their groups had called many times to see how they were doing. I now find fewer students voluntarily missing class as the year goes by and students are better informed about what they missed while they were absent.

Getting back to the parent's call, I found out that this particular student's group was working on a major part of their project and needed everyone in class on that day. The student had missed the day before and his group was concerned he would not be there on that day. So one member of the group volunteered to call the absent student that morning to urge completion of the assignment and attendance at school. The student was in class and was prepared. I find it hard to express my reaction to finding out that the cohesion and mutual concern fostered in this cooperative learning environment would result in 2d graders actually calling each other at 6:30 in the morning to encourage attendance, to lend personal support, and to insist upon completion of the homework assignment. What is more remarkable is that these are not overachievers; they are children of varied socioeconomic and ethnic backgrounds who have emerged as students within this cooperative and learning environment.

## OVERCOMING CONCERNS: TWO CASES

Implementing effective cooperative learning has implications beyond the classroom walls. A number of situations have arisen that generated concern by people other than the teachers and their students. These situations were handled in ways that promoted the preservation and growth of the cooperative learning environment. The two cases below illustrate how particular concerns were successfully managed.

One problem that emerged from the use of cooperative learning concerned substitute teachers who came into my classroom. These teachers usually expect to have a quiet classroom and maintain total control. In part, they tend to view a quiet classroom as one that meets the absent teacher's expectations. In addition, they don't want anyone to have the impression that they have no control over the students. With cooperative learning, you give the power of learning to the students and they help with the teaching. Over time the cooperative teams produce many higher-level thinkers and active learners. Students become accustomed to interacting to help each other learn. Consequently, some of these students will have a difficult time making the transition back to the old way of life, B.T. (i.e., before talking was acceptable). To head this problem off, the same substitute teachers are assigned to cooperative learning classrooms. To further relieve this problem, inservice training sessions in the cooperative learning model should be required of all substitute teachers assigned to these classrooms.

Another problem encountered was that of parents who, for many reasons, did not understand what I was doing with their children in my classroom. This problem was re-solved by having a back-to-school night. Parents were given a two-hour training session on the cooperative model and how it was being used in the school. The session included discussion of the research findings along with activities so the parents could have practical experience with cooperative learning. The parents were also given some guidelines and ideas they could apply in their own homes. Many parents requested that follow-up parent training classes be provided so they could be better users of the cooperative models at home. These training sessions have been held. Many parents in our district are now familiar with the cooperative learning philosophy and its basic elements.

## FINAL POINTS

Appropriate cooperative learning is not easy to start and not easy to achieve. I have trained with Spencer Kagan and with Roger and David Johnson. David once told me that when he came to visit, he would ask me how my cooperative learning model was going. He said he would not ask how his cooperative learning model was working in my class. Because cooperative learning is a philosophy, theory, and set of practical strategies, an elementary teachers must take and use what really works for them. The most difficult part of putting cooperative learning into practice is just to begin. After students begin working for themselves and using their energy for educational purposes, being in a cooperative learning classroom becomes fun. I have more fun and more success with each new month of the school year.

When I travel, presenting cooperative learning workshops, I constantly run into teachers who have been using parts of cooperative learning for their entire careers. What they lacked, however, was a guide to direct them with structured yet flexible methods that would help their students achieve the affective, social, and cognitive learning they desired. Cooperative learning gives names to many of the things teachers do or need to do. The strategies provide concrete ways of refining many existing things they do and guidance for new group structures and tasks. I remind them that they need to develop a philosophy of cooperation and cooperative learning and to use the how-to guidelines to provide structure and organization to this philosophy.

I also point out that even though their students were in groups doing group projects of one kind or another, they may have been using ideas and guidelines that actually prevented or impaired appropriate cooperative learning from occurring. They realize that even though they would like to believe it, they may not be using cooperative learning in their classrooms.

## CONCLUSIONS AND EPILOGUE

Bob's experiences are those of one elementary teacher. Each teacher's experiences will be different in many ways from those in this Provo, Utah, classroom. We want to point out, however, that there will be many similarities. To make cooperative learning work in any classroom, teachers will need to read the theory, research, and practical how-to literature on cooperative learning, accept the research findings that cooperative learning can generate the numerous positive results claimed, use the guidelines and organizational plans for cooperative groups, and develop a philosophy of cooperative learning that will guide decisions and behaviors in the classroom. In forming a personal conception and philosophy of cooperative learning aligned with the theory and research, teachers will evolve their own personalized versions of cooperative learning. Consequently, they will apply their own cooperative learning philosophies, and not Kagan's (1989; Brandt 1990), Johnson and Johnson's (e.g., 1987, 1989), or Slavin's (e.g., 1990).

We caution that these individualized philosophies must remain aligned with major features of those that have proven themselves on countless occasions in classroom settings. For instance, a cooperative learning philosophy should not allow the teacher to have a half-hour cooperative learning activity three or four times a week as though cooperative learning was a subject like math, science, or language arts. Cooperative learning is a way of teaching and learning, not a subject to teach or activity to complete. A cooperative learning philosophy should not allow just any group work to be accepted as bona fide cooperative learning in practice. Although many teachers do some things consistently with cooperative learning, many group activities we have observed in classrooms are not compatible with appropriate cooperative learning theory or practice.

Social studies is the most natural subject to be learned in a cooperative mode because social studies, when taught properly, requires active discussion and discovery. The very name, social studies, should be a clue to what our students need to be doing every day in our classrooms. This name also should be a clue to teachers for ensuring students are doing social studies.

Cooperative learning done well will create a mood of cooperation in your classroom and among your students that will most likely lead to at least four things: students will enjoy social studies more than under conventional teaching strategies; their retention of knowledge will increase; their social and interpersonal skills will improve; and their relationships with students different from themselves will improve. Finally, social studies education should provide experiences that encourage students to want to learn and to achieve their maximum potential. Cooperative learning is a proven way to accomplish these goals.

## NOTE

[1] As I reflected upon that first experience in these classrooms I came to realize that to do cooperative learning well requires study, comprehension, acceptance of a number of new ideas, breaking of old notions and habits, effort, and time. The teachers I observed during their early stages of using cooperative learning are to be commended for their work and for their courage in opening up their classrooms to cooperative learning in the infancy of their development.

## REFERENCES

Brandt, Ronald. "On Cooperative Learning: A Conversation with Spencer Kagan." *Educational Leadership* 47 (January 1990): 8–11.

Johnson, David W., and Roger T. Johnson. *Learning Together and Alone: Cooperative, Competitive, and Individualistic Learning*. 2d ed. Englewood Cliffs, N.J.: Prentice-Hall, 1987.

_____. *Cooperation and Competition: Theory and Research*. Edina, Minn.: Interaction Book Company, 1989.

Kagan, Spencer. *Cooperative Learning Resources for Teachers*. San Juan Capistrano, Calif.: Resources for Teachers, 1989.

Slavin, Robert E. *Cooperative Learning: Theory, Research, and Practice*. Englewood Cliffs, N.J.: Prentice-Hall, 1990.

_____. "Synthesis of Research on Cooperative Learning." *Educational Leadership* 48 (February 1991): 71–82.

Robert J. Colomb works at Sunset View Elementary School, Provo, Utah. George W. Chilcoat works at Brigham Young University, Provo, Utah. Nancy N. Stahl works with the Arizona Department of Education, Phoenix. [1992 note]

# Cooperative Learning as Effective Social Study within the Social Studies Classroom: Introduction and an Invitation

**Robert J. Stahl**
**Ronald L. VanSickle**

*Nothing is so practical as a good theory.*
*—Kurt Lewin*

One of the strongest illusions that influences many educators' and parents' notions of the nature of schooling elevates and sometimes glorifies noncooperative attitudes and behaviors. "Only the strongest survive," "It's a dog-eat-dog world," and "Competition makes the world go around" are frequently heard expressions of this illusion about preparing students for the real, competitive world that exists out there beyond the school yard and the school years. We tend to forget that the real world exists for students every moment they are outside school and, for many, inside their school as well.

A complementary illusion is that of the rugged individual—the strong, self-sufficient, and independent individual coping in the real world and achieving great things alone against great odds. Charles Lindbergh, Jane Addams, Martin Luther King, Jr., and George Washington are lauded for their personal accomplishments as though they had no colleagues or support groups that worked cooperatively to help them achieve their dreams and hopes. Focusing on what individuals have done as though they were alone in their endeavors is to overlook and misrepresent how these individuals worked toward their goals. As students find answers to questions such as "How was it possible for Charles Lindbergh to fly nonstop across the Atlantic?" and "What factors contributed to the success of Jane Addams's Hull House in Chicago?" they discover the network of cooperative support that contributed to the successes associated with each individual.

Social studies educators strive to enable their students to become educated and competent so that they will be successful in the world. Students should study individual and group actions, thoughts, and artifacts in ways that will both facilitate their achievement of selected social studies knowledge and abilities and enable them to function well inside and outside the social studies classroom. Our task as professional educators is not to establish a mini real world in the classroom where students are left to sink or swim on their own as though the purpose of school is to provide survival experiences. Rather, we need to continue to work in our classrooms so that whenever and

wherever students hit the water, they will be able to swim well both on their own and with others from then on.

The purpose of this volume is to reflect upon what students and social studies educators can gain by rejecting the competitive, rugged-individual illusions and choosing to develop a cooperative perspective on learning. What can we gain by having students work cooperatively in small groups rather than spending much of their time doing their academic work alone? What evidence is available that social studies students achieve more by working together cooperatively than by working alone or by competing for a limited number of rewards? What instructional alternatives might enable more of our students to achieve the attitudinal social studies goals we set? What might a teacher gain by using cooperative learning groups as an alternative to conventional individualistic and competitive instructional strategies?

We will attempt to provide answers to such questions throughout the chapters that follow. The answers strongly indicate that appropriate cooperative learning groups can result in large numbers of students achieving our expectations for them both inside and beyond the social studies classroom.

This chapter will attempt to build a conceptual framework for understanding cooperative learning as an alternative instructional approach. We encourage further exploration and use of cooperative learning structures and strategies in the classroom. First, however, we will introduce the cooperative learning approach to social studies by examining a number of assumptions about students as learners and about social studies educators' commitments to achieving the maximum learning for their students.

## ASSUMPTIONS

We assume that students enter the social studies classroom wanting to succeed and not merely to survive. Students want their studies to make sense and to mean something from their own perspectives. They want to leave school with new knowledge, abilities, and orientations that will enable them to function well in the world as well as within the school and the social studies classroom.

We assume that virtually all students can learn nearly every set of knowledge, abilities, and perspectives that social studies educators expect them to learn. We are optimistic about what students can learn within appropriate instructional conditions. This view of learners suggests that we can provide learning environments in schools that will help improve students' learning and thus motivate them about social studies topics, content, and abilities.

Furthermore, this view reinforces the belief that every student should attain social studies goals and abilities. Finally, this view values each student as an individual capable of achieving success in the classroom regardless of conditions outside that classroom.

We assume that academic success eventually leads students to engage actively in activities likely to continue that success. Students who do well in particular areas of the social studies tend to be interested in other topics and data they perceive as related. Students who do well in the prerequisite knowledge and abilities are more likely to be successful and interested in complex and challenging topics, knowledges, and abilities. Conversely, students who do not have the prerequisites or prior successes are not likely to become or remain interested in social studies topics without them. Social studies teachers must not assume that topics, activities, and teacher personality will automatically motivate students who lack the prerequisites to become highly involved, interested, and studious. Therefore, teachers who are concerned about the levels of their students' interest and achievement need to consider using strategies that facilitate student success. These teachers will find that as they use these strategies appropriately, their students will tend to improve their learning and their interest and involvement in social study.

We assume students expect their teachers to do what is necessary to facilitate successful attainment and maintenance of the targeted knowledge, abilities, and orientations. They hope that their teachers are committed to taking them from where they are to as high a level as they are able to achieve. They hope their teachers do not intend to teach only as much as is convenient for the entire class to cover. These expectations and hopes are consistent with an essential reason for providing social studies education — to prepare young people to be humane, civil, rational, participating citizens in a world that is increasingly interdependent, pluralistic, and changing (NCSS 1979).

We assume that social studies educators are committed to providing students with quality curriculum and instructional opportunities that facilitate their attainment of valued social education goals.

We assume that social studies educators, because they are professionals, will seek out, seriously consider, and, where appropriate, learn to use alternative curriculum and instructional strategies to help each student achieve maximum success. Consequently, we assume that in situations where students are not learning the academic content, are not using appropriate social interaction abilities, or are not attaining the positive self-conceptions teachers expect, teachers will seriously consider an instructional approach that offers considerable promise for changing the situation in their classrooms. Cooperative learning is one approach that, from theory through actual classroom practice, works in helping students become successful learners.

We assume that even teachers who have students who are achieving at acceptable levels and who do use many appropriate social interaction behaviors continue to search for and use instructional strategies that may increase the positive results of their present strategies. In other words, we assume that social studies educators have a continual desire to improve their teaching.

Finally, we assume that to be effective in a school setting requires a considerable amount of cooperative effort and support from one's colleagues to ensure that appropriate social study occurs within the social studies classroom.

## SOCIAL STUDY IN THE SOCIAL STUDIES CLASSROOM: "GETTING BETTER TOGETHER"

Social studies classroom instruction has always included individual and group work. Thinking about what constitutes effective social studies instruction has generally focused on specific subject matter and citizenship knowledge, abilities, and perspectives. Consequently, teachers who emphasize the learning of these knowledge bases, abilities, and perspectives are teaching social studies. Group activities are often integral parts of classroom instruction. Students participate in groups within which they are to acquire and practice abilities associated with effective citizenship. Teachers expect students to communicate clearly, use social and group interaction abilities, and work together to complete assigned group tasks.

Effective social studies teaching also involves appropriate social study.

In this context, the word "socia"l reminds us that the words and language rules we use in the classroom and resources are part and parcel of culture. We think and speak using terms, symbols, grammar, and meanings that are integral parts of the language that we share within our society. Although students construct and ultimately must make knowledge their own, they do so in one or more societies or subgroups that influence, share, and interact using language. In addition, students use, share, negotiate, and revise meanings according to the verbal and nonverbal language others use in their social world.

"Social" also refers to the need to engage in worthwhile, goal-oriented tasks within supportive interpersonal environments. These social tasks and environments need to be relatively frequent and endure over extended periods of time. Within such environments individuals must become active, contributing, and integral parts of the social community that benefits from their participation. To be effective within this social environment, students must learn and practice the knowledge, abilities, and attitudes necessary to function effectively within the social group and as part of the social community that is formed. Individuals must have a sense of belonging to, participating in, and contributing to one or more groups as a viable, personally meaningful, social community.

According to this view of the term social, it is not enough to be in a classroom of students who may on occasion interact or do things together in small groups or as a class. Individuals in a class must come to sense that they constitute a meaningful social community in which certain actions and attitudes are acceptable and others are unacceptable. They must come to value what the community and the required social interaction mean and can do for them. If we generate such environments in the classroom, students will not see themselves as individuals in a class, but rather as members of a social community that happens to meet in a social studies classroom.

This view of social is consistent with the essence of effective citizenship within any community. If individuals are to participate and contribute, they must have a sense that the community is worthwhile and that their involvement will have both personal and social meaning. Individuals must be an integral part of the group rather than merely working alongside others in the group. They must come to believe that their voices can help to change society and that their votes count to change and improve society. Individuals must sense a personal power within the social group and believe that the group will benefit from their contributions. Likewise, students must perceive and receive benefits from active participation within their community (the classroom).

By study we mean the systematic and focused pursuit of knowledge and the ability to apply that knowledge when needed. Students should engage in inquiry, apply appropriate study skills, or use other strategies for acquiring knowledge and abilities; they should not merely complete projects either by themselves or in groups. Consequently, when students finish their study, we and they should expect that they are able to do things they could not do prior to this effort.

If social study is to become a component of social studies classrooms, teachers must find ways to enable students to form viable social communities that work cooperatively and systematically to acquire new knowledge and abilities as a group. Members must see these groups as beneficial both for themselves and for the group. That is, each individual must be a successful learner and the achievement of the group as a group must be relatively high. Teachers need to structure classroom activities, rewards, and student roles such that students establish a social community and participate as effective members of this community at the same time focusing on achieving the shared learning goals.

Cooperative learning strategies are a means by which social studies teachers can arrange for, promote, and reward social study in their classroom. As students engage in completing appropriate social study activities, they are likely to benefit in a wide variety of ways beyond academic achievement and become skilled at using social interaction behaviors.

One way to envision cooperative learning group participation and benefits is captured in the expression "Getting Better Together."[1] By working with one another in appropriate ways, students enhance each other's knowledge and abilities as well as their own. Essentially, by working together to facilitate each other's learning, students "get better" individually and "get better together" as a team focused on team success.

These strategies, however, are not likely to be used appropriately unless the teacher has an adequate conceptual view of cooperation and cooperative learning.

## BUILDING A CONCEPTUAL FRAMEWORK ABOUT COOPERATING TO LEARN AND COOPERATIVE LEARNING GROUPS

The notion that teachers can achieve positive results consistent with social studies education goals through the use of cooperative groups is not new to the social studies. Social studies teachers have always expected—and continue to expect—that cooperative groups must be more than collections of students who sit together, complete essentially independent tasks, and fit their individual parts together so that they have a single product as proof of their cooperative effort. Students are expected to work as groups and not merely in groups. They are to work with one another as a team of learners and as full partners in each other's learning efforts and success. When such group cooperation exists over a sufficient period of time, both the quantity and the quality of interaction are high and student achievement for all is optimal for the time spent.

Slavin (1983) delineated cooperative learning as a distinct instructional model with particular criteria that separates it from typical group work and group activities. For Slavin, teachers need to establish heterogeneous groups of four to six members who are mutually responsible for each other's success relative to the same knowledge and abilities. Group members earn recognition, rewards, and sometimes grades based upon the academic achievement of their respective groups. This does not mean that all cooperative learning model-builders share all of these criteria and set the same expectations, goals, and guidelines. Sufficient overlap and consistency across many of these models, however, maintain their integrity as examples of the cooperative learning model.[2]

Teachers are most likely to use cooperative learning strategies correctly once they build an adequate conceptual framework that provides the perspective needed to carry out the strategies on a moment-by-moment and day-by-day basis (Johnson, Johnson, and Holubec 1990). This framework should work to modify present misconceptions about cooperating to learn and cooperative learning groups and prevent future misconceptions from arising. Below are a number of ideas that should become permanent fixtures in conceptions of cooperative learning.

Not all cooperative groups are instructionally effective (Slavin). Leaders in this field continually caution teachers, supervisors, and administrators against believing that cooperative learning strategies simply involve students jointly working to complete group projects or worksheets. Students working in groups do not necessarily constitute cooperative learning groups, and all the positive effects of cooperative learning will not automatically result. In short, all cooperating groups are not equal; only those that meet the guidelines and standards for cooperative learning warrant this label.

Cooperative learning is not against all competition. Advocates of cooperative learning are not opposed to all competition; rather, they oppose inappropriate competition (Johnson and Johnson 1991). Indeed, one cooperative learning model, Teams-Games-Tournament, builds in a competitive phase as part of the instructional strategy. Proponents believe that cooperative groups in and of themselves do not guarantee quality, positive interaction, group success, and individual achievement. Cooperation is not envisioned as a miraculous activity that works merely because one engages in or is expected to use it. Sports enthusiasts are well aware that some basketball teams operate as five individuals on the court who just happen to wear the same colored uniforms. Although these individuals may play alongside one another, the extent of their cooperation in this situation is minimal. For cooperative learning groups to be effective, students must come to envision their group as a team whose members have two mutual goals in mind: the group's success as a group and the highest possible individual achievement of every group member. Students must also accept their peers as academic and social teammates who share equally in the team's ultimate success or lack thereof.

Cooperative learning strategies should not replace all other teaching strategies in the social studies classroom. Cooperative learning is intended to be an alternative approach to structuring teaching and learning tasks. Consequently, teachers may continue to use instructional models and activities that effectively help students attain the many positive goals they set. Students need to learn how to succeed as individuals in individually important activities such as exploring personally interesting topics or becoming proficient at individual abilities. They also need to engage in competitive situations so that they learn to handle both the challenges of competition and the fun involved in pursuit and rivalry (Johnson et al. 1984). Using cooperative learning techniques, social studies teachers should modify, not replace, their current teaching styles and methods. Cooperative learning groups can take on many forms, all of which require that students work interdependently in small groups to help each other acquire and retain the academic content, knowledge, and abilities set for them.

Cooperative learning approaches are instructional guides, not curriculum guides. Cooperative learning models are strategies for structuring the learning environment within classrooms. These models cannot substitute for, make obsolete, or make up for poor curriculum decisions (Stahl 1990). They cannot improve curriculum decisions already made. These models are tools that facilitate student progress toward achieving the cognitive, affective, and social outcomes set within the curriculum used. These strategies are what teachers use after the curriculum decisions have been made. In other words, one does not start with cooperative learning and then plan the curriculum. Rather, one makes the curriculum decisions and selects the cooperative learning strategies that are most appropriate for the students involved and the learning they need to accomplish.

Cooperative learning models are independent of the outcomes selected and the materials used during the group tasks (Stahl 1990). Teachers may use many cooperative learning strategies in connection with textbooks, content-filled handouts, or other printed resources—nearly any resource aligned with what students are to learn. If a teacher uses a strategy only in reference to a textbook, however, it is the teacher's decision and not the strategy that is responsible for this textbook dependency. If a teacher uses a particular cooperative learning strategy only to help students memorize and recall basic facts and low-level skills, this also reflects a decision the teacher has made. Every cooperative learning model, when used appropriately, can enable students to move beyond the text, memorization of basic facts, and learning lower-level skills. They can serve to help students become proficient transferers of academic and social knowledge and abilities.

Cooperative learning techniques or strategies are structured ways of operating within a classroom. One key for ensuring that cooperative learning models work is to envision each model as describing a particular way to structure the learning, the learning task, and the learners' roles (Kagan 1989, 1989–90). Such structures are content-free ways of organizing social interaction aimed toward enabling all students to be successful. Structures provide steps, guidelines, and requirements that, when met, will allow students to achieve their maximum potential in alignment with clear outcomes. Teachers may use structures such as Jigsaw, Coop-Coop, and Teams-Games-Tournament over and over across an extremely wide range of topics, content, grade levels, and outcomes (Kagan 1989, 1989–90). These structures differ according to their cognitive processing, academic, affective, and interpersonal emphasis, length of time for completion, required teacher and student roles, usefulness for selected content, and degree of complexity.

Each cooperative learning strategy should not be viewed as a structured way of operating within the classroom—as an activity. The distinction between a learning structure and an activity is important. Activities like those found in many books and articles describe what a teacher might ask a group to complete within a single lesson or unit. Students might complete the activity, however, without students or the teacher ensuring that they are meeting requirements for appropriate cooperative learning group work. Merely because one labels an activity a cooperative learning activity or strategy does not make it so. What counts is that the learning task(s) and environment are structured such that the requirements are met. When students can complete appropriate cooperative learning tasks, teachers should expect all students to leave the group task and the course with high levels of success for the outcomes set for them.

Each group member need not learn appropriate cooperative learning group behaviors. Students must acquire, practice, and refine the variety of positive group behaviors necessary for them to work as a group so that they become skilled users of these abilities and accompanying attitudes. We cannot expect students to bring all the appropriate abilities and attitudes with them to these groups or to develop them simply by being told to work as a group. In many instances, teachers will need to take time before they form the groups, during the group interactions, and after the groups have finished to describe particular productive and dysfunctional group behaviors and attitudes. These are as much a part of the group learning process as the academic content and abilities. Proponents of cooperative learning emphasize the need to help students learn what is necessary to contribute to the group's goal-directed efforts.

Appropriate cooperative learning structures and guidelines are neither simple nor easy to implement (Johnson et al. 1984). Even for teachers who have used groups in the past, learning concepts and procedures of cooperative learning strategies and properly implementing them in the classroom requires time, effort, and adherence to the criteria provided. Although the concept of cooperation is simple and appealing, teachers should not assume that achieving high levels of cooperation for learning will be easy. Cooperative learning as an approach to teaching generally, and the various cooperative strategies in particular, are complex ways of operating in the classroom. They require the typical teacher to use a number of new behaviors that will take time to perfect. Old notions that run contrary to effective cooperative learning are likely to persist. These notions and accompanying behaviors represent habits that teachers and supervisors will need to unlearn while learning the ways of appropriate cooperative learning. Old habits are hard to break—much less forget; teachers wanting to use cooperative learning need to accept at the start that creating effective cooperative learning classrooms will be challenging work. They will find, however, that the positive results for both students and themselves make the effort and time spent worthwhile (Johnson et al. 1984).

Cooperative learning will work even if only one teacher in the school or department is using it. Sometimes teachers have a sense that if they are the only one using cooperative learning their students will not gain much by its use. Consequently, they may try a few cooperative learning activities waiting for the day every teacher uses them. Cooperative learning has been effective in achieving many of the valued goals of social studies education, and social studies teachers should consider its use solely on this basis. We would encourage teachers to become the first cooperative learning teacher in their department or school. With the success that is likely to follow, colleagues will join this movement toward expanding the cooperative learning concept to more students and into more classrooms.

In this section we addressed a number of fundamental features of appropriate cooperative learning along with a sample of misconceptions to overcome. We need to include these ideas in a large, comprehensive, conceptual framework for cooperative learning. Social studies educators may read these and other materials on cooperative learning and believe that they are already engaged in cooperative learning in their school or classroom. The section that follows should help teachers begin a systematic assessment of current group instructional practices to determine the extent to which they are already practicing cooperative learning.

## AM I ENGAGED IN COOPERATIVE LEARNING?

Teachers who use groups and supervisors who promote group work might perceive that they are already engaged in cooperative learning in the classroom. Numerous criteria and guidelines are available to verify whether what occurs within these groups meets the requirements for appropriate cooperative learning groups (e.g., Aronson et al. 1978; Cohen 1986; Johnson and Johnson 1991; Johnson et al. 1984; Kagan; Slavin, 1990; Stahl 1992). One way to determine if cooperative learning is occurring is to observe how closely students follow these structures and requirements. To the extent that all group members meet these requirements, appropriate cooperative learning group activity is occurring.

Another way to determine whether group activities and assignments are consistent with appropriate cooperative learning is by collecting systematic, objective data about the effects of cooperative learning on the majority of students compared to expected student outcomes of cooperative learning. For instance, most students involved in cooperative group tasks over an extended period should

- improve scores on academic tests
- voluntarily increase their personal contact with other students in a variety of contexts
- have strong feelings of group membership
- work cooperatively in small group settings toward attaining a common goal
- have many of the positive attitudes necessary for working effectively with others
- feel positively about others in their groups
- be willing to share and interact positively within group settings
- integrate their academic learning and social and intergroup relations
- improve relations with individuals from ethnic or racial groups other than their own
- be willing to express and discuss their own ideas in public
- improve their opinions about and relationships with handicapped students
- see their peers in a positive light
- increase the number of friendships based on human qualities
- have enhanced positive self-concept and self-esteem
- be positively adjusted psychologically
- have high levels of intrinsic motivation to learn
- accept their peers as knowledgeable agents in learning, i.e., as learning resources

- have proficiency in critical reasoning abilities and strategies
- seldom be disruptive and engage in increased on-task behaviors
- increase the amount of time they spend on-task
- have positive attitudes toward teachers, principals, and other school personnel
- have positive attitudes toward learning, school, and the subject matter content

Not all cooperative learning groups, whether lasting one class period, one week, or one month, will generate all of these results every time. Rather, these are results that are likely to occur when such learning groups function over an extended period of time. If the group structure and activities being used are not making noticeable progress along many of these lines by the end of the first semester, for instance, then teachers should reassess the extent to which they are already engaged in cooperative learning.

The list is also relevant for teachers not using groups or using groups only sparingly over the course of a school year. If teachers and their students are not achieving the results listed above from the strategies, resources, and activities they are using, they should consider seriously cooperative learning group strategies.

## AN INVITATION

We invite social studies educators to study and reflect upon the information here. We invite them to acquire a conception of appropriate cooperative learning and to envision how they might use these strategies and guidelines in their classrooms. We invite educators to arrange for face-to-face communication with colleagues in their department, district, conference session, or college classroom to review this information and develop this vision cooperatively. Taking such steps should encourage social studies educators to work collaboratively and cooperatively to increase the effectiveness of cooperative learning groups in their classrooms. Finally, we invite social studies educators to ensure their social studies classroom activities facilitate successful social study via appropriate cooperative learning structures. When these are done, the evidence suggests that students can and will "get better together."

## NOTES

[1] The motto "Getting Better Together" is attributed to Jim Weyand, former principal of Bill Reed Junior High School in Loveland, Colorado. A most remarkable educator, Jim invented and used many of the concepts and principles of cooperative learning with his faculty and staff beginning in the early 1970s to build and maintain cooperatively one of the most powerful, effective, and collegial instructional staffs one author, Bob Stahl, has personally encountered. Jim's genuine concern for students and student success evolved into a collegial team whose members, by working as a staff development cooperative learning team, "got better together" to enable students to achieve remarkable levels of academic, affective, and social abilities.

[2] Introductory descriptions of a number of cooperative learning models are available in the works referenced.

## REFERENCES

Aronson, Elliot, Nancy T. Blaney, Cookie Stephan, Jev Sikes, and Matthew Snapp. *The Jigsaw Classroom*. Beverly Hills, Calif.: Sage, 1978.

Cohen, Elizabeth. *Designing Groupwork: Strategies for Heterogeneous Classrooms*. New York: Teachers College Press, 1986.

Johnson, David W., and Roger T. Johnson. *Learning Together and Alone: Cooperative, Competitive, and Individualistic Learning*. 3d ed. Englewood Cliffs, N.J.: Prentice Hall, 1991.

Johnson, David W., Roger T. Johnson, and Edythe J. Holubec. *Circles of Learning: Cooperation in the Classroom*. Alexandria, Va.: Association for Supervision and Curriculum Development, 1984; Reprint. 3d ed. Edina, Minn.: Interaction Book Company, 1990.

Johnson, David W., Roger T. Johnson, Edythe J. Holubec, and Patricia Roy. *Circles of Learning: Cooperation in the Classroom*. Alexandria, Va.: Association for Supervision and Curriculum Development, 1984.

Kagan, Spencer. "The Structural Approach to Cooperative Learning." *Educational Leadership* 47 (December/January 1989–90): 12–15.

_____. *Cooperative Learning Resources for Teachers*. San Juan Capistrano, Calif.: Resources for Teachers, [1989].

Lewin, Kurt. *Field Theory in Social Science: Selected Theoretical Papers by Kurt Lewin*. Edited by D. Cartwright, 169. London: Tavistock, 1952.

National Council for the Social Studies. "Revision of the NCSS Social Studies Curriculum Guidelines." *Social Education* 43 (April 1979): 261–66.

Slavin, Robert E. *Introduction to Cooperative Learning*. New York: Longman, 1983.

_____. *Cooperative Learning: Theory, Research, and Practice*. Englewood Cliffs, N.J.: Prentice-Hall, 1990.

_____. *When and Why Does Cooperative Learning Increase Achievement? Theoretical and Empirical Perspectives*. Baltimore: Johns Hopkins University, Center for Research on Elementary and Middle Schools, OERI no. G86-00061986, 1989.

Stahl, Robert J., ed. *Cooperative Learning: Making It Work in the Social Studies Classroom*. Menlo Park, Calif.: Addison-Wesley, 1992.

Stahl, Robert J. "Essentials of Cooperative Learning: Key Concepts, Requirements, and Guidelines for Implementation." Presentation at the annual meeting of Arizona Council for the Social Studies, Mesa, Arizona, October 1990.

## ADDITIONAL SOURCES

Johnson, David W., Geoffrey Mariyama, Roger T. Johnson, Deborah Nelson, and Linda Skon. "The Effects of Cooperative, Competitive and Individualistic Goal Structures on Achievement: A Meta-analysis." *Psychological Bulletin* 89 (1981): 47–62.

Newmann, Fred M., and Judith A. Thompson. *Effects of Cooperative Learning on Achievement in Secondary Schools: A Summary of Research*. Madison: National Center on Effective Secondary Schools, University of Wisconsin, 1987.

Schmuck, Robert A., and Patricia A. Schmuck. *Group Processes in the Classroom*. 6th ed. Dubuque, Iowa: William C. Brown, 1992.

Robert J. Stahl works at Arizona State University, Tempe. Ronald L. VanSickle works at the University of Georgia, Athens. [1992 date]

# Breaking Down the Walls
## Integrating Creative Questioning and Cooperative Learning into the Social Studies

**Lynda Baloche**

## What are all the possible reasons people might have to build walls?

The children are in groups of three, seated around large sheets of newsprint when the teacher begins by asking this intriguing question. Each group gets to work—all group members are working at the same time on the same large sheet of paper, using pictures and words to represent ideas. As they work, the children quietly coach each other with encouraging comments, such as "keep going" and "write some more." After about five minutes, the children stop, discuss their ideas, and circle four ideas to share with the whole class. During this phase of the activity, each child has used a different colored marker, and the groups are asked to circle at least one idea from each color on the paper. One member in each group is asked to report what that group has circled, and the papers are then hung up around the room.

Next, the children gather in a come-together spot where each child sits with a story buddy. The teacher then introduces the book *Talking Walls* by Margy Burns Knight. Stopping at the words "these walls tell many fascinating stories," the teacher asks each pair of story buddies to join up with another pair to create a foursome. Announcing to the class that "I'm going to come around and ask each group to think about our classroom in a different way and from a different point of view," the teacher travels to each group and asks questions: How might our classroom look from the point of view of the back wall? How might our classroom look from the perspective of the window wall? The teacher reminds the children to be sensitive to the ideas of every member in their group and reminds them to acknowledge the ideas of their group's members by using the special phrase "I like your idea because...." As the children work, the teacher circulates among the groups, listening and modeling the use of the phrase, I like your idea because.

The children have counted off from one to four in their groups, and the teacher uses numbers to choose a representative in each group to talk. Individual children share their perspectives with the class amidst smiling, laughter, and encouragement. The children are given a few extra minutes to turn back into their foursomes to discuss not just the different perspectives that they have heard but

also how well they remembered to listen and acknowledge each other's ideas.

Bringing the focus back to *Talking Walls*, the teacher begins to read—about the Great Wall of China, the Aborigine wall paintings in Australia, the Painted Caves at Lascaux, the Wailing Wall in Jerusalem, the carved cliffs near the Bay of Bengal, the Ka'aba in Mecca, the mysterious green granite walls of Great Zimbabwe, the giant stones in the Inca city of Cuzco, the five-story "apartments" in Taos Pueblo, the vivid murals of Diego Rivera, the Museum of Civilization in Canada, the Vietnam Veterans Memorial in Washington, D.C., the prison walls in South Africa, and the construction and destruction of the Berlin Wall. Using questions such as "Suppose you discovered a painted cave deep in the forest, what might you do?" "Imagine you painted a mural about your life, what might you include?" and "What might you do if you wanted to move giant stones?" the teacher stops at several points and asks the children to close their eyes and imagine. After each quiet moment, the children are given an opportunity to share what they thought about with their story buddies and finally with the entire class. Partner sharing is reflective because the children are reminded to practice good listening and to repeat their partner's ideas before sharing their own.

The teacher finishes reading and the pace changes. The children are divided into groups of three and asked the question "How is a wall like a story?" Within each group, the children have been assigned the roles of "noise monitor" and "idea encourager" to help insure that work time is productive. The students have five minutes to discuss their ideas. After five minutes, they are told to make a plan for how they are going to represent their ideas to the class. One child in each group records the plan, and then the groups begin to transfer their ideas onto big sheets of paper. Once again, each child in the group has a different colored marker, and this helps the teacher to monitor the children's work.

When the groups are finished, the sheets of newsprint are hung, and the walls of the classroom are quickly transformed into an art gallery. The class embarks on a gallery tour as each group of children moves about the room discussing the work of other groups. The tour concludes, and the groups discuss what they have seen and add new ideas to their own work. The children are also given a moment to evaluate the plans that they recorded earlier.

The next day, the teacher introduces the lesson with the question "If you were a wall, how might you feel?" After a moment of reflection, the children are invited to use their bodies to create statues that show how they might feel. They then move into triads and, after sharing their feelings, begin the main tasks of the day. The teacher has prepared packets of information about several of the settings represented in *Talking Walls*—including China, Jerusalem, India, Mecca, and the Peruvian Andes—and each group quickly begins to learn about the people, climate, and customs of one of these settings so that they might begin to answer the question: How might the world look from the point of view of the wall? Groups use a variety of strategies, including scripted dialogues, Venn diagrams, stories, and murals, to explore their questions and organize their information. The teacher constantly monitors, encouraging children to share ideas, make plans, and seek understanding—both of each other and of the cultural settings that they are studying. The children are involved in their investigations and plans, so involved that they do not even notice when the teacher writes a new question on the board: How might the world be transformed if all walls were beautiful?

Teamwork is something most of us value and, according to recent studies, is the number one skill that employers want but often find lacking in their employees (Erdman 1992). Those of us who work with children know that merely putting children together in groups does not insure teamwork, and, as Goodlad (1983, 240) observed, schools provide students with little opportunity to develop "satisfying relations with others based on respect, trust, cooperation, and caring." The cooperative learning literature that has proliferated in the past decade or so can help us move from mere group work into the types of caring teamwork and cooperation that Goodlad often found lacking. In this article, we will focus primarily on the cooperative learning model of David and Roger Johnson in our attempt to understand how cooperative group work can be structured in the classroom and, specifically, how cooperative groups were structured in the opening scenario.

## USING COOPERATIVE LEARNING TO DEVELOP COOPERATION

According to the Johnsons (1991), a lesson should include five basic elements to be truly cooperative. These five elements are positive interdependence, face-to-face promotive interactions, individual accountability, interpersonal and small group skills, and group processing.

## POSITIVE INTERDEPENDENCE

The Johnsons and Holubec (1991, 4:6) define positive interdependence as "the perception that (a) you are linked with others in a way so that you cannot succeed unless they do (and vice versa), and/or (b) their work benefits you and your work benefits them. It promotes a situation in which individuals work together in small groups to maximize the learning of all members." There are nine basic types of positive interdependence: goal, celebration or reward, resource, role, task, fantasy, outside enemy, environmental, and identity.

In the opening scenario in this article, the teacher used at least four different types of positive interdependence to structure the various cooperative activities. Groups shared goals, resources such as newsprint and markers, and roles such as recorder, reporter, noise monitor, and idea encourager. They shared their environments as they sat next to their story buddies at the come-together spot and as they put their heads together over small work areas delineated by sheets of shared newsprint.

## FACE-TO-FACE PROMOTIVE INTERACTION

According to Johnson, Johnson, and Holubec (1:11), "cooperative learning requires face-to-face interaction among children within which they promote each other's learning and success. There is no magic in positive interdependence in and of itself. It is the interaction patterns and verbal interchange among children promoted by the positive interdependence that affect education outcomes." When structuring a lesson cooperatively, teachers make many decisions that influence the quality of the face-to-face interaction, including critical decisions about group size, group composition, and group duration.

In the opening scenario, the teacher used groups of three different sizes. During the story, pre-established story buddies were used to help students reflect on what they were hearing. Pairs of buddies were combined to create short-term foursomes, whereas other work was accomplished in triads that remained constant. In general, it is wise to keep groups small—twos for sharing, triads for diversity and variety, and foursomes, often created by linking pairs, to challenge collaborative skills and encourage complexity. Teachers frequently find that groups larger than four are cumbersome, noisy, and time-consuming and that some members feel left out of discussions and decisions.

During the opening example, children worked in teacher-selected groups of various duration and size. Impromptu, short-term foursomes help insure that children have an opportunity to work frequently with everyone in the class. Triads, which remain constant for a unit or marking period, give children the opportunity to work together long enough to learn to appreciate each other and to experience academic and interpersonal growth and success. Long-term story buddies help provide children with safe sharing opportunities and also make it easier for teachers to have children move, group, and share quickly and frequently. In general, teachers form groups with heterogeneity in mind—not just heterogeneity by ability but heterogeneity by gender, social status, ethnic or economic background, learning styles, and content preferences.

During the *Talking Walls* segment, the teacher used several techniques or structures, including "think-pair-share," "numbered heads together," and "gallery tour," to facilitate face-to-face interaction (Kagan 1992). When children were asked to imagine or suppose, they were asked to think first by themselves, then to pair, and, finally, to share some of their ideas with the entire class. This structure helps insure that children will hear a variety of ideas without sacrificing either individual reflection or the opportunity to explore their own and their partner's ideas. When the teacher wanted to call on one person in a group of four, the children numbered off in their groups, put their heads together to share their ideas, and then responded as individuals when the teacher called on them by number. This structure helps to insure that children feel both equal responsibility for, and equal opportunity in, the work of the group; it also helps teachers break down their own unconscious response patterns. When it was time for the children to find out what other groups thought, the groups took a tour about the room to discuss what had been hung on the walls. This activity tends to make for a lively discussion, quite unlike what might happen if group reporters just stand and describe what their groups have done.

In general, teachers also encourage promotive face-to-face interaction by their own behavior. The teacher's actions—moving from group-to-group, monitoring both the content of the activity and the process, asking children to repeat ideas and to encourage each other, modeling these behaviors, and sharing observations with the class—help give children the message that working together to promote the learning and interaction of all group members is valued.

## INDIVIDUAL ACCOUNTABILITY
Within the cooperative structure, it is important for teachers to structure individual accountability, both to insure that individuals contribute to and understand the group's work and to insure that each child can individually apply some procedure or knowledge learned in a group.

In the opening scenario, several techniques were used to insure individual accountability. When children worked together over large sheets of newsprint, each child used a different colored marker so that, at a glance, the teacher would know that each child was contributing and could also assess the quality of those contributions. When children worked in foursomes to discuss their story from different perspectives, she used "numbered heads together" to insure that students would be called on individually to respond. As the children work together to investigate the settings for their walls, she might require them to list the jobs and responsibilities of each group member to help insure that their work goes smoothly and that no one hitchhikes on the work of others.

## INTERPERSONAL AND SMALL GROUP SKILLS
As all teachers know, placing children in a group and telling them to cooperate does not necessarily mean that they can and will do so. The skills of collaboration do not magically appear when they are needed but, in fact, must be taught and practiced as a part of the cooperative lesson. Role plays, simulations, examples from literature or film, studies of family groups, and studies of different cultures can all be used to illustrate good or poor collaborative skills.

Several collaborative skills were targeted in the opening scenario. Each and every time children gathered in groups, they were given not only specific goals to accomplish but also reminded of specific collaborative behaviors. These behaviors included offering encouragement, repeating an idea (a simple form of paraphrasing), making a plan, and "I like your idea because ___." In general, the first skills many teachers choose to target include skills such as getting to one's group quickly and quietly, using quiet voices, staying with the group, and avoiding putdowns. More complex skills include repeating an idea (a simple form of paraphrasing), making a plan, criticizing ideas—not people, and asking for justification.

## GROUP PROCESSING
When children work together in groups, it is essential that they evaluate both how well they are completing tasks to achieve their academic goals and how well they are working to build and maintain their working relationships.

In the opening scenario, the children repeatedly processed their work together. They reflected on their work when they circled four items from their opening listing activity. In their foursomes, they talked about the different perspectives that they had heard. After the gallery tour, they evaluated their plans and added ideas that they had gathered from other groups. In addition, they frequently reflected on how they worked together to help build and maintain effective cooperative relationships.

## NURTURING CREATIVITY
The World Future Society, when asked to rank the skills and talents that leaders of the future would need in order to be effective, ranked creativity first (Bleedorn 1986). Just as teamwork has become a workplace basic, the American Society for Training and Development reported that, during 1990, more than one-third of the Fortune 500 companies sponsored training in creative thinking (Gundy 1991).

Although teachers frequently report that they value creativity in the children they work with (Baloche 1984), Goodlad (1983, 241) observed there is often a "gap between the rhetoric of individual flexibility, originality, and creativity . . . and the cultivation of these in our schools." As teachers know, merely telling children to be creative does not insure creativity—just as telling children to work in a team does not insure teamwork. Fortunately, just as the cooperative learning literature can help teachers structure true teamwork in their classrooms, the creativity literature can help teachers nurture creativity as well.

What is probably most important, from the point of view of the classroom teacher, is the concept of a creative classroom climate. Happily, the kind of classroom climate that cooperative learning has the potential to create—one characterized by a sense of safety, acceptance, support, and belongingness (Johnson 1980)-is essential to the development of both creativity and psychological health (Maslow 1970, 1976; Rogers 1961).

Equally important, although perhaps less immediately obvious, is the concept of intrinsic motivation, or internal locus of evaluation, which is, it appears, a basic characteristic of the creative person (Amabile 1983; Getzels and

Jackson 1962; Maslow 1970, 1976; Perkins 1984; Rogers 1961; Torrance 1962). Group processing can be used to structure frequent opportunities for children to evaluate their own work and processes in ways that encourage the kind of internal locus of evaluation and intrinsic motivation that are needed for continued work and productive creativity.

Children (and adults) also need creativity skills or techniques to help them to think creatively (Amabile 1983; Guilford 1962; Stein 1974-1975; Torrance 1965). In the opening scenario, these techniques were introduced and developed through the use of frequent and well-planned questioning.

## TRANSFORMING QUESTIONS TO NURTURE CREATIVITY
The Transforming Questions model (Baloche and Platt 1992) was developed to encourage teachers to ask questions that encourage creative thinking. The model contains six different levels of questioning—listing, imagining, perspective taking, being, relating, and transforming—and incorporates several well-established creativity techniques that are compatible with cooperative group activity. The model is not strictly hierarchical, but because some of the questions are more complex and abstract than others, teachers often use several levels of questioning to help children warm up to creative thinking. The questions tend to use conditional verbs, such as might and could, that seem to give both children and adults more permission to imagine and be creative (Larger 1989).

Listing questions suggest the possibility of multiple answers. Sentence stems such as "List all the potential . . ." "What are all the possible . . . ?" "In what ways might we . . . ?" and "How might we . . . ?" are useful ways to let children know that multiple answers, not just one correct answer, are being sought.

In the opening scenario, listing was used as a kind of warm up for the activity that followed. When the children encourage each other with such phrases as "keep going" and "write some more," they help establish the expectation that multiple ideas are desirable. The large format of the newsprint encourages children to view ideas as group rather than individual property (Thelen 1981) and also helps to encourage "piggy-backing" of ideas, an activity fundamental to the listing process (Koberg and Bagnell 1981). Having children list, before they stop to discuss, also encourages deferred judgment.

Imagining questions invite children to enter into a fantasy, make suppositions, and predict possible consequences. The use of guided imagery or sentence stems beginning with suppose, what might, imagine, what might happen if, what could, and what if are useful ways to begin imagining. In the scenario opening this article, imagining is used to help insure that the children stay with the story and have the opportunity to imagine themselves in various settings.

Perspective-taking questions encourage children to think flexibly and view a problem situation or issue from a variety of viewpoints. Flexible thinking is considered by some as fundamental to creative thinking (Guilford 1962; Torrance 1990). Perspective-taking ability has been closely linked to the development of empathy, altruism, and role-taking ability (Kohlberg 1976; Kohn 1990) and seems particularly well suited for explorations in the social studies.

Perspective taking is often initiated with teachers' questions that begin thus: "How might these events look to _____ ?" " Can you tell the story from _____ perspective?" and "What other perspective might _____ ?" Points of view and perspectives might include animate or inanimate, human or nonhuman, part or whole, famous or unknown.

In the opening scenario, the teacher chose: the inanimate perspectives of walls, both the familiar walls of the classroom and the more exotic walls of *Talking Walls*. It is exciting to think what kinds of cultural details children might learn as they work together to describe what they see from the perspective of a wall in a far-off land.

Being questions invite children to move beyond taking a perspective and into total involvement, identification, and empathy. When using being questions, it is common to ask "If you were _____, how might you feel?" In our opening example, the teacher allows both quiet reflection time and sharing time when using a being question. Being questions tend to be emotionally complex, and "body statues" were used to allow children to express feelings in a way that did not require talking.

Relating questions invite children to consider the relationships between different people, places, and things by making comparisons, associations, analogies, and metaphors. These questions tend to help children break away from habitual patterns of perception and thinking, an ability known in the creativity literature as "breaking-set" (Amabile 1983). When formulating relating questions, it is useful to compare dissimilar elements such as concrete objects and abstract concepts, living and nonliving things, and the nonhuman and the human (Gordon 1961). Relating questions are often structured like this: "How is a _____ like a _____ ?"

In the opening example, the children relate a wall to a story. This helps them to explore the idea that walls have stories to tell. The large sheets of newsprint encourage both group ownership of ideas and intergroup sharing, and asking children to add new ideas to their work, based on what they have seen in other groups, helps them to develop an ability to value differences.

Transforming questions invite children to investigate change and explore patterns. Transforming questions often begin with the phrases: "How might _____ change if _____ ?" and "How might _____ be transformed if _____ ?"

SCAMPER (Eberle 1981) is a useful tool because it reminds one to ask: How might you Substitute, Combine, Adapt/Adopt, Modify/Magnify/Minimize, Put to other uses, Elaborate/ Eliminate, or Rearrange/Reverse/Recycle? The Transforming Questions model has the potential to provide teachers and children with the kinds of opportunities for meaningful cooperation and creative thinking that are likely to change their experiences with the social studies, their thinking, and their relationships.

As teachers explore the social studies with their students, they might want to ask these questions:

■ What are the creative, cooperative ways that you might use to incorporate the social studies into your daily classroom life?

■ How might your classroom look and sound and feel if children learned to imagine a world without walls that hurt?

■ How might your creative, cooperative classroom look from the point of view of your classroom walls?

■ If you were a creative, cooperative classroom, how might you feel and what might you say?

■ How is teaching, using the Transforming Questions model, like the breaking-down-walls activity?

■ How might your classroom, your community, and our world change if children learn how to transform walls?

## REFERENCES

Amabile, T. M. 1983. *The Social Psychology of Creativity*. New York: Springer-Verlag.

Baloche, L. A. 1984. *Facilitating Creativity and Group Cooperative Skills in the Elementary Music Classroom: A Model, a Curriculum, and a Study*. Ph.D. diss., Temple University, Dissertation Abstracts International 46:06, 1549A.

Baloche, L. A., and T. J. Platt. 1992. *Converging to Diverge: Creative Thinking in the Cooperative Classroom*. Paper presented at the meeting of the International Association for the Study of Cooperation in Education, Utrecht, Netherlands.

Bleedorn, B. D. 1986. "Creativity: Number One Leadership Talent for Global Futures." *Journal of Creative Behavior* 20(4):276.

Eberle, B. 1971. *Scamper*. Buffalo, N.Y.: DOK Publishers.

Erdman, A. 1992. "What's Wrong with Workers?" *Fortune*, August 10, p. 18.

Getzels, J. W., and P. W. Jackson. 1962. *Creativity and Intelligence: Explorations with Gifted Students*. New York: Wiley.

Goodlad, J. I. 1983. *A Place Called School*. New York: McGraw-Hill.

Gordon, W. J. J. 1961. *Synectics*. New York: Harper and Row.

Guilford, J. P. 1962. "Factors that Aid and Hinder Creativity." *Teachers College Record* 65:380-92.

Gundy, W. 1991. *Creativity Training Growing*. Creativity in Action, Creative Education Foundation.

Johnson, D. W. 1980. "Constructive Peer Relationships, Social Development, and Cooperative Learning Experiences: Implications for the Prevention of Drug Abuse." *Journal of Drug Education* 10:7-24.

Johnson, D. W., R. T. Johnson, and E. J. Holubec. 1991. *Cooperation in the Classroom*. Edina, Minn.: Interaction Books.

Kagan, S. 1992. *Cooperative Learning*. Laguna Niguel, Calif.: Resources for Teachers.

Knight, M. B. 1992. *Talking Walls*. Gardiner, Me.: Tilbury House.

Koberg, D., and J. Bagnall. 1981. *The Revised All New Universal Traveler*. Los Altos, Calif.: William Kaufmann.

Kohlberg, L. 1976. "Moral Stages and Moralization: The Cognitive-Developmental Approach." In *Moral Development and Behavior: Theory, Research, and Social Issues*, edited by T. Lickona. New York: Holt, Rinehart and Winston.

Kohn, A. 1990. *The Brighter Side of Human Nature: Altruism and Empathy in Everyday Life*. New York: Basic Books.

Langer, E. J. 1989. *Mindfulness*. Reading, Mass.: Addison-Wesley.

Maslow, A. H. 1970. *Motivation and Personality*. 2nd ed. New York: Harper and Row.

———. 1976. *The Farther Reaches of Human Nature*. New York: Penguin.

Perkins, D. N. 1984. "Creativity by Design." *Educational Leadership* 42(1): 18-25.

Rogers, C. R. 1961. *On Becoming a Person: A Therapist's View of Psychotherapy*. Boston: Houghton Mifflin.

Stein, M. I. 1974-1975. *Stimulating Creativity* (Vols. 1-2). New York: Academic Press.

Thelen, H. A. 1981. *The Classroom Society*. New York: John Wiley and Sons.

Torrance, E. P. 1962. "Non-Test Ways of Identifying the Creatively Gifted." *Teachers College Record* 65: 220-26.

———. 1965. *Rewarding Creative Behavior*. Englewood Cliffs, N.J.: Prentice-Hall.

Torrance, E. P., and H. T. Safter. 1990. *The Incubation Model of Teaching: Getting Beyond the Aha!* Buffalo, N.Y.: Bearly.

Lynda Baloche is an Assistant Professor in the Department of Childhood Studies and Reading at West Chester University, West Chester, Pennsylvania. [1994 note]

**Buckley Barnes**
**Gail O'Farrell**

More than just having students work together, cooperative learning is a set of instructional strategies that include cooperative student-to-student-interaction based on subject matter as an integral part of the learning process. (Kagan 1988). Practices vary greatly. They may be as simple as having students in pairs briefly discuss a lesson, or as complex as team assignments occurring over a period of weeks.

Cooperative learning differs from traditional group work in that it includes structuring of learning tasks and evaluation to ensure positive interdependence and individual accountability. Slavin (1987) concurs that individual accountability is important and adds group rewards and equal opportunities for success as key elements. Johnson, Johnson, Holubec, and Roy (1984) elaborate on the elements necessary for group work to be considered truly cooperative.

Cooperative learning is not having students work individually in close proximity to others. It is not having more able students help the less able, nor is it allowing one student to do most of the group's work while the rest do little or nothing.

## ESSENTIALS OF COOPERATIVE LEARNING

If cooperative learning is to be effective, the following guidelines need to be kept in mind.

1. Each student in the group is dependent upon all other group members in order for the group goal to be reached.
2. Tasks are divided among group members.
3. Materials, resources, and information are shared by group members.
4. Each student in the class is dependent upon all members of all groups for learning.
5. Students must interact directly with one another.
6. Each student must be held accountable for mastering all of the material assigned to all groups.
7. Students must be taught the skills necessary for group functioning. These include listening, taking turns. offering ideas, asking questions, and compromising.

Reprinted from *Social Studies and the Young Learner*, January/February 1990, Volume 2, Number 3. Copyright 1990 by National Council for the Social Studies.

## SOME PROMISING BENEFITS

Johnson, Johnson, Holubec, & Ray (1984) compared the effects of cooperative, competitive, and individualistic strategies of instruction for 122 studies using meta-analysis. In no case did cooperative learning result in lower achievement than competitive or individual methods, and in most situations the result of cooperative learning was greater than for the other two strategies. This advantage was true regardless of grade level, subject area, or type of learning (concept attainment, problem solving, retention and memory, and rote decoding).

In addition to achievement advantages, Johnson and his colleagues (1984) reported that cooperative learning compares favorably in the development of critical thinking, attitudes toward subject areas, and self esteem. Students also expand their interpersonal skills and liking for classmates especially across gender, ethnic, ability, and social lines.

## TYPES OF COOPERATIVE LEARNING STRATEGIES

Numerous types of cooperative learning strategies have been developed. Some are designed for mastery of basic skills and information, while others are oriented toward complex group projects requiring higher level thinking skills. Although specifically designed curriculum materials are available for cooperative learning, there are models which provide frameworks for applying cooperative learning in any subject area and grade level using regular materials found in classrooms and schools. Two of the most popular strategies are Jigsaw and Co-op Co-op.

*Jigsaw*. In Jigsaw, a group of students teach one another factual content. Each child is assigned to both a study group and a learning team. First, study groups meet and by studying together become expert on their assigned topics. Next, students go to their learning teams to teach teammates the content they have learned in the study group. Finally, all students in the class are tested and held individually accountable for knowing the content presented by all learning team members.

*Co-op Co-op*. In this activity, small groups work together to further their understanding of a topic, which they then share with the entire class. The name Co-op Co-op is derived from this design; the students are cooperating in small groups in order to cooperate with the whole class.

## WORKING WITH TEAMS

Two essential activities in working with cooperative learning teams are team formation and building team spirit.

## JIGSAW

### Overview

The purpose of Jigsaw is to have a group of students teach each other factual content.

Each child is assigned to both a study group and a learning team. First, study groups meet and by studying together become expert on their assigned topic. Next, students go to their learning teams to teach teammates the content they have learned in the study group.

Finally, all students in the class are tested and held individually accountable for knowing the content presented by all learning team members.

### Steps

1. Obtain or prepare curriculum materials so that each study group member has specific information to learn and teach to his learning team.
2. Form teams in accordance with the guidelines.
3. Conduct team building exercises as suggested.
4. Select and prepare study group leaders to keep their groups on task, resolve differences, and serve as contact persons with the teacher.
5. Assign each team member a number.
6. Have students report to their study groups according to their number. All of the "1's" will get together, etc.
7. Distribute materials to students. All of the "1's" receive the same materials. The "2's" receive identical materials different from those given to the "1's", etc.
8. Instruct each group to become expert in the content it has been given. Each study group teaches and tests each member until all members thoroughly understand the assigned content.
9. When the study group content has been mastered, students rejoin their learning teams. Each team member teaches his assigned content to the rest of the group, and learns from the others the content they were assigned to teach. Learning teams teach and test members until maximum learning is achieved within the time limit.
10. Test all members of the class on all of the content.
11. Assign grades consisting of the average of each student's individual score and the team mean. For example, if Joe's individual score is 88 and the team mean is 84, then Joe receives test score of 86.
12. Inform students at the beginning of the activity that their grades will be partially dependent on the team mean. Realizing that their grades will be affected by the achievement of their teammates encourages students to stay on-task and minimizes socializing in the teams.

---

*Forming Teams*

These procedures have been found to be effective in establishing teams.

1. Rank order students according to achievement from highest to lowest.
2. Assign the top, bottom, and two middle achievers to team one.
3. Using the remaining students on the achievement list, repeat this process until all teams are formed. Heterogeneous teams are essential to the success of cooperative learning.
4. Revise teams if:

   a. members are all of the same sex.

   b. Teams do not proportionately reflect the ethnic makeup of the class.

## CO-OP CO-OP

### Overview

Co-op Co-op is a very broad framework useful with a wide variety of content. It is designed for small groups working together to further their understanding, and then share with the whole class. The name Co-op Co-op is derived from this design; the students are cooperating (in small groups) in order to cooperate (with the entire class).

The duration of Co-op Co-op units can vary from one-day miniprojects to units lasting several weeks. This approach can be used concurrently with a traditional class structure. In this example, students work one or two days a week on their Co-op Co-op projects.

### Steps

1. Teams are formed.
2. Team building exercises are conducted as suggested.
3. The class is led in a student-centered discussion of the unit to be studied. The purpose of this discussion is to determine what the students want to learn during the unit, not to lead them to identify specific topics at this early stage of the unit.
4. Each team then selects a unit-related topic. In a unit on the Middle East, for example, one team might select Egyptian inventions, another imports/exports, etc.
5. Teams subdivide their topic among team members. Individual student choice is of high priority, but teacher approval is required.
6. Students research their subtopics using not only their texts, but all other available information and materials.
7. Each student presents what was learned to the team. Team feedback is provided to each presenter and suggestions made regarding the preparation of a presentation to the entire class.
8. Team members refine their presentations.
9. Team presentations are made to the entire class. Innovative formats (skits, AV, debates, and demonstrations) are encouraged by the teacher.
10. Evaluation consists of: individual self-evaluations; team self-evaluations; class evaluations of the group presentation; and teacher evaluation of individual and group work and presentations. (See sample evaluation forms.)

---

   c. Best friends are on the same team.

   d. Students who have serious difficulty getting along are on the same team.

*Teambuilding Exercises*

Teambuilding is a key element of cooperative learning. It is important for members of a team to develop respect and trust for each other to provide a setting in which learning can be maximized. If teambuilding is neglected. the group members may be too competitive or too social.

Teams must develop a feeling of interdependency so that each person's gain is everyone's gain. Occasional competition between teams is fine, but the goal should be to develop a cooperative classroom where all students view themselves as being on the same side, encouraging each other to do their best. An important advantage of teambuilding is that these skills can be transferred to other activities.

*Procedures*

1. Ask each team to choose a name, pennant, motto, or other identification symbol. Emphasize that all team members must be listened to. Decisions must be by

consensus, not by majority vote, and no member is permitted to vote for something with which he seriously disagrees. These rules provide guides for future interactions which require participation, consensus, and respect for individual rights.

2. Have teams play activities such as "Roundtable." This usually consists of having one piece of paper and one pen for each team. One student makes a written contribution and then passes the paper to the next team member. The teacher asks a question with many possible correct answers, such as, name all the states you can or all the equivalent fractions for one-half. Roundtable can he used as a race or with little or no time pressure.

3. Have teams participate in trust building exercises such as:

a. Team members catch one trencher who falls backward. Emphasize safety procedures.

b. Team members guide a blindfolded member around obstacles in the room.

c. Teams put together a simple puzzle which requires each member to contribute. Each member may be given several pieces of the puzzle to foster participation and interdependence.

## CONCLUSION

Cooperative learning is an alternate strategy of teaching. It is not intended to be the only method used in a classroom. A variety of methods is desirable, including more traditional individualistic and competitive teaching as well as cooperative ones. For teachers willing to expand their repertoire to include cooperative learning, both they and their students will be pleased with the outcome in terms of student interest and achievement.

Teachers need not feel discouraged if their first attempts are imperfect. With practice, both teachers and students will develop the necessary skills. Kagan (1988) suggests implementing cooperative learning in a limited way at first. After teachers develop confidence in using one method, they probably will be eager to try others.

Among the most exciting aspects of cooperative learning is that students become responsible for learning and sharing what they have learned. A cooperative classroom provides an atmosphere which encourages students to develop their natural tendencies for curiosity, creativity, and expression.

## REFERENCES

Gwilliam, J., Hughes. G.. Jenkins. D., Koczka, W. & Nicholls, L. ( 1983). *Working Together, Learning Together: The Cooperatively Structured Classroom*. Regina: Department of Cooperation and Cooperative Development- Education Unit, Saskatchewan Co-operation and Co-operative Development.

Johnson, D., Johnson. R., Holubec, E & Roy, P. ( 1984). *Circles of Learning: Cooperation in the Classroom*. Washington: Association for Supervision and Curriculum Development.

Kagan, S. (1988). *Cooperative Learning: Resources for Teachers*. Riverside: University of California, Riverside.

Slavin, R. (1987). *Cooperative learning: Student Teams*. Washington: National Education Association.

Buckley Barnes is a Professor of Curriculum and Instruction at Georgia State University, Atlanta. Gail O'Farrell teaches social studies at Richard Middle School in Gwinnett County, Georgia. [1990 note]

# PART 15

## ASSESSING SOCIAL STUDIES LEARNING

Assessing student learning in social studies is a difficult, and often ineffective, task. All too often, teachers, administrators, and politicians have relied on data generated from standardized test results as a means of determining what students do or do not know. Quite often, the questions included on such tests do not reflect the curriculum content being taught at a particular grade level. Sometimes, the tests are given at an inappropriate time of year (e.g., early fall, prior to the time for student study of the content). Content knowledge is important—as well as integral—to social studies learning, as are the processes of acquiring, organizing, interpreting, and communicating data as meaningful concepts and generalizations. As the general public, school boards, and many educators become more vocal about poor test results, attention is being given to the development of new ways of assessing important social studies curriculum in order to decrease the strong reliance on testing for isolated facts and minimum comprehension.

Alternative ways of assessing student learning in various content areas are underway by individual teachers in many states and districts. Although the goals of the more authentic assessments are worthy, they are difficult to attain and require educators to rethink many of their former beliefs about testing procedures and their meaning. The time and effort given to the development of quality assessment tools is time well spent. Teachers should ask themselves questions such as the following: What is assessment? What do I want my students to learn? How will I know if my objectives have been met? How can this information be communicated to the students and others? How can I use assessment data in my curriculum plans in selecting instructional activities?

Wiggins, whose career has focused on tasks of assessment, responds to several questions about this topic, which have been posed by Nickell, a district social studies coordinator and currently NCSS president-elect. In the interview, Wiggins addresses issues such as fairness, skills, content, test bias, and scoring. He summarizes the goals of authentic assessment by recommending that what is valued in the instruction is the goal toward which one needs to strive in assessing student learning. Adams and Hamm explain how student portfolios can serve as devices to link learning and assessment. They offer practical suggestions for solving frequently asked questions concerning content and ways of encouraging student participation in the preparation and evaluation of portfolios. For Parker, the major problem of performance assessment is the need to correlate student tasks to the social studies curriculum when devising scoring rubrics. He identifies the exemplary efforts of the schools in Oakland County, Michigan, which have developed rubrics for assessing civil discourse. Nickell draws on a research base to help prepare appropriate performance assessment tasks and evaluation criteria. She illustrates, through several social studies examples, the four principles designed for elementary teachers to use with their students.

Assessment information is an important ingredient when revising the curriculum. Whereas tests of the traditional type may not completely disappear from the schools, the use of multiple methods of assessment may become the norm. Whatever the outcome, one thing remains true: Assessment will not be meaningful if it does not match the social studies curriculum objectives.

**Pat Nickell**

Grant Wiggins (Nickell, 1992) defines "performance assessment" as "students performing with knowledge...to do something, fashion something, construct something, speak, write, turn the stuff of content into some product or performance." This form of student evaluation requires more than simple recall of facts or information or replication of a skill; it asks students to apply knowledge and skill for a purpose. "Authenticity" in performance assessment emphasizes having students carry out or closely replicate a task or process that is required in the real world. While we generally think of performance assessment as assuming an active format—manipulation of reality, acting, debate, demonstration, and the like—it may also rely solely on pencil and paper. As long as the student is generating a response to a prompt in which he or she must apply learned skills and knowledge to real-world tasks, the event may be termed "performance assessment" or "authentic assessment."

In a number of states, performance assessment is either recently adopted or currently under consideration as a possible replacement for or enhancement of traditional forms of large-scale standardized testing. Rather than focusing on state-level testing, however, this author has chosen to give emphasis to classroom-level assessment, with ideas set forth to guide classroom teachers as they go about the business of developing appropriate means of assessing student learning in particular classes about specific material.

Four principles will be offered which have emerged from the literature on performance assessment, and examples will be provided to enable teachers to recognize how these principles might guide the development of performance events or tasks for use in the classroom. Tips are also included to assist teachers in evaluating student products and responses.

*1. Performance events or tasks are virtually indistinguishable from authentic, activity-based instruction.*

For years, we treated instruction and assessment as separate entities. We taught and then we tested; or we pretested, then taught, then posttested. The test has long been a discrete component of classroom activity. On the other hand, performance assessment for classroom purposes virtually erases the distinct line between instruction and assessment. In practice, a good performance task for assessment will look just like what has long been recognized as a good activity designed to help students expand and apply what is being learned.

Ms. Martino has been teaching her fifth grade social studies class to interpret data from a variety of sources—maps, charts, graphs, etc. For assessment purposes, she incorporates an activity (Figure 1) which asks that the students pretend they are reporters who must create an article explaining factual information, such as comparative prices of food in three major cities. Only the students know that this is their "test"; an outsider might wonder why she is remaining curiously aloof from the students as they are completing the task.

---

### FIGURE 1: COMPARING FOOD PRICES

In our nation's capital, Washington, D.C., the average price of a dozen eggs is $.99. In Tokyo, those eggs would cost $1.95 and in Paris you would pay $2.75. A quart of milk in Washington averages $.58, in Paris, $.87 and in Tokyo, $1.31. One would think that rice would be cheaper in Japan than in France or the U.S., but surprisingly, Washingtonians pay only $.49 per kilogram, while Parisians pay $.59 and those in Tokyo pay the most at $1.20! The most expensive item in anyone's grocery cart, however, is steak. A pound of boneless sirloin in the D.C. area averages $5.28. In Paris it runs $6.68, but in Tokyo? TWENTY-THREE DOLLARS AND NINETY-SEVEN CENTS!

*You work for USA Today. Your editor wants you to present this information clearly and accurately in a visual way so readers can understand it more easily and quickly than by reading the text as shown above. Use the space below to show how you might do this.*

*Just in case your editor doesn't like the one you developed above, think of another way to present the information. It should also be quicker and easier to read and understand than the original paragraph, but somewhat different from your first idea.*

---

A concern with this form of assessment is the degree to which teacher evaluation can be objective and fair. Thus, Ms. Martino has designed a scoring rubric (Figure 2) to enable her to grade student responses and report outcomes both to students and parents. She has previously discussed her expectations with students and thus they are not at all surprised at the grades they receive.

*2. Performance assessment is a better gauge of whether students know and can do what is important.*

This principle arises from all the arguments against traditional fixed-response testing. Central among these is that simply the accumulation of knowledge may lead to astuteness in trivia games, but cannot guarantee astuteness in solving problems, making wise choices and decisions, figuring out the best means to an end, or evaluating information and occurrences.

Anna Orenstein teaches her fourth graders about the regions of their state, Kentucky. (Figure 3) They explore various aspects of each region, including attributes of the land and how they differ from region to region. As a culminating assessment, Anna gives students a hypothetical scenario in which they are given an occupation dependent on geographical features (for example, cattle farming) and must apply their understanding of Kentucky's regions to determine the best location.

Fixed-response test types—multiple-choice, matching, fill-in-the-blanks—rarely tell us whether students are able to sort through and interpret information for important purposes, and simply cannot gauge whether students are able to generate appropriately constructed responses, express in writing their evaluation of actions and situations, and justify opinions. Yet these are some of the things we must all be able to do in order to function well in our everyday lives.

*3. Performance assessment is a better match with real-world tasks.*

This principle is related to Principle 2, above, yet deserves special consideration as teachers attempt to design assessment tasks. Simply stated, no task is worth designing if it isn't worth doing. The test of a good task is whether it calls upon students to do something worthwhile and similar to something that, if done well, would make their lives easier in the real world.

Karen Avery teaches seven and eight-year olds in a primary setting. She believes that children need many and early experiences through which they learn about diversity among cultures to enable them to appreciate differences and relate effectively with individuals from varied backgrounds. Her unit on Africa is an example, having cross-cultural understanding as one of it objectives. Her opening activity (Figure 4) is a task designed to encourage students to begin thinking about the similarities as well as differences between life in Africa and the United States. Her students read a book about growing up in another culture, then they must compare and contrast the experiences not only of the boys in the book, but also of the book's characters and themselves. The task also provides Karen with good baseline information about students' perceptions and attitudes about cultural differences.

## FIGURE 2: SCORING RUBRIC

**Superior performance:**
- Both presentations give information in very effective VISUAL ways (charts, diagrams, graphs, etc.);
- Both presentations include all information accurately;
- Provides two distinctly different ways to present information;
- Both presentations are clear and easy to understand.

**Acceptable performance:**
- Both presentations are rendered as visuals;
- The information presented may include minor inaccuracies;
- The information included is, or is very nearly, complete;
- The two presentations are different from one another;
- The presentations are easier to derive meaning from than the text.

**Novice performance:**
- Presentation is not visual, or a visual presentation is described in text form;
- There is an attempt to provide information, but it is inaccurate and/or incomplete;
- There is only one presentation or two that are basically the same;
- Meaning is lost due to presentations being no easier to interpret than the text, or due to inaccuracies or missing information.

**Unacceptable performance:**
- No attempt

In the process of task design, it is most important to be sure that what has been taught has real-world application and that those applications are what guide the design process.

To put this principle into practice, readers may wish to try the following:

1. Think of what it is you are currently doing with your students. What is your topic? What are your objectives?
2. Why is this material important? When have you used it in your own life in the past year, outside the classroom and beyond your personal reading? (If you haven't, are you able to justify its importance?) What did you use it for?
3. How will students use it and for what purpose (other than within your classroom)?

   You are now ready to design an assessment task.
4. Create a situation which calls for your students to use the material you are presenting. Write it up in an interesting and authentic fashion. Be specific about what is expected of their response or product. This is a performance task.
5. You need to be fair about grading their work and you want to be able to do it quickly. Therefore, decide what criteria are important for evaluating their success. What do you think they should demonstrate for you? Is it clear what you expect in the way the task is presented? If not, either edit the task or change your criteria. Describe what you think an outstanding response would look like; a good response; an average response; a barely acceptable response; and an unacceptable response. You now have a scoring rubric.

## FIGURE 3: YOU, THE CATTLE FARMER!

Imagine that you spent most of your summers as a young person with your aunt and uncle who had a cattle farm in Minnesota. You really enjoyed your months working with your uncle on the farm and you decided a long time ago that you would like to become a cattle farmer. You have now worked for several years in a plant in Lexington, trying to save enough money to buy a small herd and begin farming. Today you were informed that your uncle, who recently died, left you 50 head of cattle to help you fulfill your dream. Because you love Kentucky, you want to bring the cattle here, but you need to decide upon the best region of the state for cattle farming.

Using what you have learned about the various regions of Kentucky, make a determination as to an area you think is most suitable. Write a letter to your best friend (who doesn't want you to leave Lexington!) explaining where you will locate and what factors you used to make your decision. You should not only consider where cattle farming can be successful and why, but also your personal needs and preferences regarding proximity to cities, recreation facilities, bodies of water, etc. Be sure to use correct letter form and include as much information as possible so that he/she will understand and support your decision.

---

While this is a simplified and sketchy model, it should allow the teacher to recognize some of the critical differences between performance task and fixed-response test types, and to begin the process of task design.

*4. Performance assessment should drive changes in instruction as well as testing even for lower performing students.*

It is now considered a given that teachers "teach to the test." Shepard (1989), Wiggins (1989) and others claim that the trick is not to get teachers to quit doing so, but to make the test more worthwhile. Performance assessment, these theorists claim, is a more worthwhile instrument toward which to gear instruction. It requires higher-order thinking, generative responses, and can be formatted for assessing students independently or in groups. We cannot, however, reserve this type of instruction only for advanced learners. All students must learn to solve problems, make decisions, and discern the most appropriate ways to achieve an end. Critics of traditional testing argue that typical multiple-choice approaches serve to "dumb down" curriculum and instruction. "Conceiving instruction in the format of multiple-choice items . . . leads to endless drill and practice on decontextualized skills" (Shepard, 1989, p. 5). This, it is argued, is especially true of instruction for lower functioning students where test-taking preparation—raising scores—has been given central attention in the schooling process.

Mr. Spooner teaches a heterogeneous group of sixth graders. His most recent geography unit on Latin America also involved the development of an improved geographic vocabulary. Ongoing efforts have included assisting students in developing a mental map of the United States and providing multiple opportunities for students to make

## FIGURE 4: FAR AWAY AND CLOSE TO HOME

Read *A Country Far Away*. Use your own words to tell three ways the boys' lives are different from each other. Then tell three ways their lives are alike. Last, tell which boy's life is most like your own and tell why. Use sentences and your very best words.

*Reference: A Country Far Away, by Nigel Gray. New York: Orchard Books. 1988.*

---

independent judgments and provide logical explanations for them in writing. All of these efforts appear in the assessment task he uses to evaluate their progress and the scoring rubric he has developed to assist him in grading student responses.(Figure 5)

Student responses to this task may look very different depending upon the students' educational background and prior knowledge. However, the skills required are ones that all students should have in order to read and understand a newspaper, participate in normal conversations referencing places in the U.S., posit an idea and provide an explanation, and communicate in writing. If all our students are raised on challenging tasks from early childhood, then by the time they are in middle school, even our students "at risk" will have little difficulty addressing tasks such as those offered here.

## CONCLUSION

The principles presented here are designed to provide rationale and guidance for the development of performance tasks for classroom use. It is hoped that teachers will give these ideas serious thought, especially in terms of what we know is best for children: that they deserve not only interesting and high-quality instruction, but equally interesting and high-quality evaluation instruments; that they deserve to have us care about what they really know and can do; that they deserve practice in dealing with real-world challenges; and that all students deserve these things—not just those thought to have special gifts and promise.

## REFERENCES

Nickell, P. (1992). "Doing the Stuff of Social Studies: A Conversation with Grant Wiggins." *Social Education*, 56(2), 91-94.

Nickell, P. and Wilson, A. (1994). *Creative Teaching Strategies in Social Studies: Alternative Assessment*. Boston: McDougall Little/Houghton Mifflin.

Shepard, L. A. (1989). "Why We Need Better Assessments." *Educational Leadership*, 46(7), 4-9.

Wiggins, G. (1989). "Teaching to the (Authentic) Test." *Educational Leadership*, 46(7), 4147.

Pat Nickell, President of NCSS, is an eighteen-year veteran elementary teacher. Dr. Nickell is currently the Director of Instructional Improvement for the Fayette County Public Schools in Lexington, Kentucky. [1996 note]

## FIGURE 5: LANDLOCKED!

The Random House Dictionary of the English Language defines "land-locked" as "shut in completely, or almost completely by land; not having access to the sea." Look at our map of South America. Using your interpretation of the definition of "landlocked," would you say there are any landlocked countries in South America? If so, name them. Explain your answer.

*Picture a map of the United States in your mind. Is Indiana land-locked? Some people would say "yes," others "no." State YOUR opinion and support why you think as you do:*

*If a country is landlocked, what are several things it might do to gain access to the sea? Explain each idea:*

## FIGURE 6: SCORING RUBRIC FOR "LANDLOCKED!"

### Distinguished Level
- Responses are clear, accurate, and well-structured
- Responses supported by related and reasoned information
- Parts 1 & 2 consistent or differences fully justified
- Part 3 reasonable and fully explained, demonstrating under-standing of political implications of sea access

### Proficient Level
- Responses are clear, accurate, and readable
- Responses are supported by related information
- Parts 1 & 2 are consistent or differences justified
- Part 3 offers one or more suggestions, explained, but may not exhibit understanding of political importance of sea access

### Apprentice Level
- Responses readable and acceptably structured, but may include minor inaccuracies
- Responses to parts 1 & 2 may be inconsistent, but both are supported
- Response to part 3 provides one or more underdeveloped or weak ideas, perhaps unreasonable
- Part 3 indicates little understanding of the importance of sea access, other than for saltwater resources or recreation

### Novice Level
- Responses to parts 1 & 2 inaccurate and/or unsupported by related information
- Responses are poorly structured
- Parts 1 & 2 are inconsistent; one or both unsupported
- Part 3 poorly developed, unrelated, or shows no understand-ing of the need for access
- No attempt or responses irrational or unrelated to the task

**Walter C. Parker**

The trend to complement paper-and-pencil assessments with performance assessments continues at full speed in social studies. Paper-and-pencil tests remain valuable, of course: even advocates of newer approaches recognize that these have their place in a student's portfolio. Such tests can help teachers gather data on how well students understand important concepts and their ability to recall key information. To most teachers and parents, this kind of assessment matters.

Performance assessments serve a different purpose: They help teachers find out whether and how well students can translate this knowledge into action (Airasian 1994). Here, students are asked to carry out a real task—for example, to map the playground, or to present a closing statement in a trial. In doing so, they use and apply information, understandings, and abilities in a specific context—for example, deciding where to locate a swing set, or persuading jurors to acquit Socrates.

In combination, paper-and-pencil tests and performance assessments can provide rich information about student learning.

## DEVISING CRITERIA AND STANDARDS

Social studies teachers who are developing performance assessments face two vexing problems: (1) the need to correlate assessment tasks with the curriculum, and (2) the need to devise scoring rubrics to determine how well students have performed.

The challenge in correlating the tasks with the curriculum is to make sure the assessment is not designed for its own sake, irrespective of the curriculum, but to help students and their teachers find out how well students have learned, or are learning, essential subject matter. This problem also arises with paper-and-pencil tests, of course; indeed, they are notorious for having little to do with valued curriculum objectives.

As for devising scoring rubrics, the problem is to decide on both the criteria and the standards to be used in assessing student performance. Bear in mind that a rubric is "a predetermined set of criteria that will be used to score a student's performance" (McCollum 1994). The criteria, which correspond to performance standards, are the specific aspects of a task—the specific behaviors—

Reprinted with permission from the Association for Supervision and Curriculum Development, from *Educational Leadership*, May 1995, Volume 52, Number 8. Copyright 1995 by the Association for Supervision and Curriculum Development.

that are most important to its successful completion. Standards are gradations of performance based on that criteria. On a rating scale, each criterion in the set will be worth three, four, or five points.

## OAKLAND COUNTY'S APPROACH

Among the most valued outcomes of social studies curriculums is the students' ability to understand—and practice—democracy. To assess a student's grasp of the concept of democracy—its history, variants, and the conditions that support it and undermine it—teachers can use traditional paper-and-pencil tests.

But how can teachers evaluate students' ability to put democratic principles into action? In particular, to discuss public issues in small heterogeneous groups in a reasonable, informed, and civilized way—in other words, to engage in civic discourse? This is where performance assessments come in.

Some of the best work in using performance assessments to see how good students are at civic discourse is being done in Oakland County, Michigan. County social studies specialists David Harris and Michael Yocum identified 14 performance criteria (see Figure 1) on which to assess students, 6 of which are substantive and 8, procedural. They then developed a four-point rating scale, which provided clear descriptions of exemplary, adequate, minimal, and unacceptable actions. Students are given one score for the substantive criteria and another for the procedural criteria.

Teachers may assess students' performance based on these criteria by directly observing a small group discussion, or by videotaping the discussion for later viewing. Based on field tests Harris and Yocum conducted, they recommend a group of five or six students and a discussion that lasts 15-20 minutes.

Before assessment can be meaningful, the learning target—civic discourse—must be clarified for both teachers and students. To help teachers use the rubric, inservice education is needed. Teachers then need to introduce the rubric to students.

Sixth grade teachers in Oakland County are using Harris and Yocum's scoring rubric to assess their students' achievement of 1 of the 13 curriculum objectives for that grade:

> Students will participate constructively in substantive discussions of contemporary public issues faced by people living in Canada and Latin America.

Eighth and eleventh grade American history teachers can use the same rubric for improving their students' ability to

## FIGURE 1:
## PERFORMANCE CRITERIA FOR CIVIC DISCOURSE

**Substantive**

- States and identifies issues
- Uses foundational knowledge
- Stipulates claims or definitions
- Elaborates statements with explanations, reasons, or evidence
- Recognizes values or value conflict
- Argues by analogy

**Procedural**

*Positive*

- Acknowledges the statements of others
- Challenges the accuracy, logic, relevance, or clarity of statements
- Summarizes points of agreement and disagreement
- Invites contributions from others

*Negative*

- Makes irrelevant, distracting statements
- Interrupts
- Monopolizes the conversation
- Engages in personal attack

discuss public issues. It should also be a good resource for helping students think and talk about current events.

A detailed description of this rubric appears in the *Handbook on Teaching Social Issues*, published by National Council for the Social Studies in 1996.

## REFERENCES

Airasian, P. W. ( 1994). *Classroom Assessment*, 2nd ed. New York: McGraw-Hill.

McCollum, S. L. (1994). *Performance Assessment in the Social Studies Classroom*. Joplin, Miss.: Chalk Dust Press, p. 14.

Walter C. Parker is an Associate Professor of Curriculum and Instruction in the College of Education at the University of Washington, Seattle. [1995 note]

## FIGURE 2:
## SCORING RUBRIC FOR ASSESSING CIVIC DISCOURSE

| | EXEMPLARY (3) | ADEQUATE (2) | MINIMAL (1) | UNACCEPTABLE (0) |
|---|---|---|---|---|
| **SUBSTANTIVE** | Weighs multiple perspectives on a policy issue and considers the public good, or uses relevant knowledge to analyze an issue, or employs a higher order discussion strategy, such as argument by analogy, stipulation, or resolution of a value conflict. | Demonstrates knowledge of important ideas related to the issue, or explicitly states an issue for the group to consider, or presents more than one viewpoint, or supports a position with reasons or evidence. | Makes statements about the issue that express only personal attitudes, or mentions a potentially important idea but does not pursue it in a way that advances the group's understanding. | Remains silent, or contributes no thoughts of his or her own, or makes only irrelevant comments. |
| **PROCEDURAL** | Engages in more than one sustained interchange, or summarizes and assesses the progress of the discussion. Makes no comments that inhibit others' contributions, and intervenes if others do this. | Engages in an extended interchange with at least one other person, or paraphrases important statements as a transition or summary, or asks another person for an explanation or clarification germane to the discussion. Does not inhibit others' contributions. | Invites contributions implicitly or explicitly, or responds constructively to ideas expressed by at least one other person. Tends not to make negative statements. | Makes no comments that facilitate dialogue, or makes statements that are primarily negative in character. |

# "Doing the Stuff of Social Studies": A Conversation with Grant Wiggins

# 98

## Pat Nickell

*Dr. Grant Wiggins is Executive Director of Consultants on Learning Assessment and School Structure and has done extensive writing and consulting in performance assessment and authenticity in testing. Guest editor Pat Nickell interviewed Wiggins to bring his perspective to a special section of* Social Education. *In this interview, Wiggins provides insight not only into the area of testing, but also to a number of other issues in social studies instruction.*

*Nickell*: Dr. Wiggins, when I first spoke with you about doing this interview for *Social Education*, you mentioned that at one time you were a social studies teacher. Would you provide us a bit of background on that?

*Wiggins*: Actually, my first few years of teaching I taught your basic soup-to-nuts world history course for 9th graders. After teaching that course for a couple of years, I taught psychology for a while, which I enjoyed a lot. Actually, my background is in philosophy and for some years I developed courses in philosophy for the high school level.

*Nickell*: Today you are considered one of our gurus on assessment. What sparked your interest in this particular area of education?

*Wiggins*: I think what got me into it and what has people who are willing to listen to me listening to me, is that I come at this not as an assessment expert, but as somebody who cares deeply about curriculum and instruction and who saw the strangleholds that bad assessment had on teaching.

When I was working with Ted Sizer as one of the original staff members of the Coalition of the Central Schools, my charge was to work on the ideas of "student as worker/teacher as coach" and "diploma by exhibition of mastery" which were two of the nine coalition principles. One of the things that became clear was that though everybody had a pretty decent idea of what the phrase "student as worker/teacher as coach" might mean, very few people understood how to rethink the diploma to make it an "exhibition of mastery," or what others call "outcomes-based." In particular, very few schools knew how to get beyond traditional testing, and that was holding them back in terms of integrating curricula and developing student inquiry. So it just became natural that I would work on that.

*Nickell*: You used the term exhibition of mastery. We more frequently hear this referred to as performance assessment. Could you give us a definition here?

*Wiggins*: I think the simplest way to do that is to contrast "students performing with knowledge" versus what happens on a traditional short-answer or multiple-choice test. With regard to the latter, a student doesn't perform with knowledge or use it or produce a document or artifact or performance, the student just points to an answer. Performance assessment, on the other hand, says the students have to do something, fashion something, construct something, speak, write, turn the stuff of content and problems into some product or performance. It implies that there's much more to success than just being good at drills; students must try to get good at integrated performances. We know that all of the drills in basketball are not the same as the game for which one does the drills. But most tests are just collections of drills, if you follow the analogy.

We have a number of interesting performance assessments now, for instance, that ask the student to construct a museum exhibit, to do an oral history, or to be in a mock trial in a historical setting. Many of our students rarely get exposed to the fun challenges that are actually involved in "doing" the subject. We have typically said you can't "do" the subject until you master a whole lot of facts and subskills. My view says that's a mistake. It doesn't work in basketball and it doesn't work in history.

*Nickell*: What you are saying relates to another term that we associate with writing and thinking and that is the term authentic. Could you talk a little bit about what you mean by "authentic" assessment?

*Wiggins*: What the term has come to mean for me and others relates to the analogy that I just described. Most tests, most forms of assessment, are not authentic representations of subject matter challenges. They are more like checkup tests and quizzes and drills. An "authentic" assessment is one that would be much more a simulation or representation or replication of the kinds of challenges that face professionals or citizens when they need to do something with their knowledge. Most people, once they leave school, never have anything to do with multiple-choice tests in history. Their use of history has to do with doing research and making a presentation to the board or the Rotary or their firm. The whole idea of secret, secure tests in which you try to figure out what's going to be on the test and then you hope you guess right—all of that is quite inauthentic. We've come to use tests simply as an expedient to check up on whether kids mastered some facts, but it has nothing to do with the authentic act of mastering historical analysis and information.

*Nickell*: Students need to know what is expected of them, what they will need to do, and then be able to do that. In that way, it seems much more fair as well.

*Wiggins*: Yes, fairness is an idea that is really embedded in the idea of authenticity. An assessment in which you don't know either the task or the standards against which you will be judged is not only unfair, it's downright foolish if our aim is to get people good at important tasks.

*Nickell*: Social studies provides a wealth of opportunities for problem-solving tasks and other critical-thinking activities, but it also frequently requires students to imagine other times and places that can be "experienced" only through contrived means such as video and audio re-creations and simulations. When we talk about the need for assessment tasks to be authentic, how can we manage that when history and geography often are so abstract, so distant from the students' real world?

*Wiggins*: Well, let me give you an example—the re-creation of the trial of Socrates. I used to do it as just a teaching exercise; later in my career, I turned it into an assessment activity. Re-creating the trial using the documents that we have available to us—most notably, Plato's "Apology"—and getting students to look at why the artists and craftsmen and priests were all upset; getting them deeper into the tensions of the time and getting them to question whether this was really a democracy, etc., all helped students "get into" the historical characters and the historical complexities of the time. In addition, they realized how similar and how different the times are then and now. Best of all, there was room for plenty of independent interpretation—a skill I wanted them to have. Students were assessed on the accuracy of their arguments and the effectiveness of their case.

*Nickell*: This next question can be a bit sticky, I suppose. Performance or task assessment focuses primarily on skills—what students can do. Of the four basic subject areas, social studies is the more content-centered or knowledge-based. I know that we want the skills of using that knowledge to be developed. We want students to be able to take that knowledge and reconstruct it for a variety of purposes. But, I'm afraid as assessment tasks are designed and people are focusing on the "doing" processes—the skills—that we are going to get away once more from placing real importance on good, sound knowledge. How do you feel about that?

*Wiggins*: I think your caution is a wise one. We have a perpetual tendency in this field to wave back and forth between extremes. I, for the life of me, don't understand how there can be knowledge without skill that develops it and presents it, nor how there can be skill without knowledge which causes you to want to develop skill. Let me give you a couple of examples of why I think this betrays a lack of understanding on people's part about their own field. Here is a question that occurred on the 1990 freshman European history exam at Harvard. "Imagine yourself Jean Jacques Rousseau, but living in the early twentieth century. Write a brief review of Freud's work in light

of your own theories." Now, what I think is worth noting is that this is considered a kind of standard essay exam question—that if you want to do well at places like Harvard, you have to be able to be both imaginative and knowledgeable. We are just talking about a failure to demand well-designed tasks that require both knowledge and skill when we get into this debate. We can't design tasks so that the student is judged only on the criterion of whether they put together a nice presentation. We must design the criteria and the nature of the challenge so that the student couldn't possibly do it well without digging deeply into the content and using it effectively.

*Nickell*: What about the relationship—or worse, the nonrelationship—between state and district assessment programs? Don't you agree that if a state is going to go with performance assessment that the classroom assessment program must comply?

*Wiggins*: Not only do I think it must comply, I think it must come from a groundswell of interest at the classroom level. I think these things go hand in hand. Where there is little or no compliance, it will be very difficult as an individual teacher to adopt a full-fledged performance assessment strategy. It requires leadership at the local building level to make the restructuring happen. But yes, of course, the idea will succeed or fail depending upon the extent to which classroom teachers want to do it and are doing it on a regular basis.

*Nickell*: From the teacher's point of view, I would like for you to address another issue: I know that when I give students twenty-five multiple-choice items, each having one correct answer, and the same items are given in fifty other locations across the country, the responses of all the students tested can be scored identically. In performance-based assessment, we have no such assurances that the scoring is going to be identical and it would seem that this raises a fairness issue. How do you address this question for parents, students, and teachers?

*Wiggins*: That is indeed an issue that has to be faced. It is probably worthwhile to look at the areas where human judgment has been a long-standing tradition. You look, for instance, in athletics, music, art; you look at the professional certification processes, board certification in medicine, and things of that sort. We know a few things about performance assessment. When you use multiple judges, when you have clear scoring criteria, when you have an oversight process to make sure that you acknowledge and adjudicate differences of opinion (and which, for instance, anybody who's ever been an advanced placement reader has done and knows works quite well), the issue sort of fades away as a controversy. You can get very, very good scorer reliability by the process that I just described. The APs have been doing it for thirty years.

I find that of all the commercially available multiple-choice tests, the ones that are absolutely without justification and foundation are the social studies ones. They are a bunch of glib, trite, decontextualized, common-sense, civic-type questions. And that is inevitable because we don't have a national syllabus and national textbook. To have a social studies test that is linked to no text and no syllabus is madness. We may have a reliable score, but we don't know what the heck it means.

*Nickell*: Let's turn to a different kind of an issue for a minute. We have long had to contend with problems of gender and cultural bias in testing. As we move more toward performance assessment, are we likely to take steps backward on the issue of gender and cultural bias, or are these tests somehow a better way to get around such problems?

*Wiggins*: I think there are two answers to the question. One is, gender and cultural bias have nothing to do with the form of the tests. If people are culturally and gender biased, then it will be reflected in the tests and test procedures that are used. "Secure" multiple-choice tests are not very easily subject to scrutiny for such things as bias because of the proprietary and secrecy-for-validity issues that make it very difficult to get inside these tests. If, on the other hand, we were using more performance-based forms of assessment in which many of the tasks and criteria were known in advance and judged by wise people in the field to be worthy tasks and worthy criteria, then that is a step forward. That doesn't change the fact that the judging might be biased. But, again, I don't think that has anything to do with the test procedure per se—that has to do with just making sure that you deal with bias in the scoring of the response, which leads right into my second answer. At the district and classroom level, people need to get in the habit of reading student work "blind," not knowing who the author is. That is the fastest way to get rid of a lot of bias in the scoring. We, of course, do this routinely on a large scale. When we score state and national exams we don't know whose papers we are reading. If we are very clear about the criteria, and if tests are subject to public scrutiny and oversight, the problem is minimized.

*Nickell*: The reference to classroom-level testing brings me to the following: I maintain that testing is an extraordinarily powerful tool with which a teacher can either make or break a student. I don't think it's conscious and I don't intend to sound accusatory with this question, but I think that sometimes teachers may not fully recognize how powerful that tool is. They have the ability to make sure that a student gets an A or an F by simply manipulating the design of the test. Designing performance tasks at the classroom level, rather than "objective" tests, would seem to increase rather than decrease this capability. Do you see this as an issue?

*Wiggins*: To that question I would wonder just what is the point of the test. Is it to catch people learning or catch people not studying? Whether teachers admit it or not, we grade on curves. The best students in our class get A's, the worst students get D's, and the ones who don't show up get F's. Everyone is delighted if everybody in a school gets 5's on the history advanced placement test. Everybody is not delighted if everybody gets A's in U.S. history. The vocational teacher and the athletic coach want everybody to do well. Many teachers take pride in the fact that it doesn't happen in their classroom. It shows they have "high standards." That makes no sense to me. You can have high standards and help everyone succeed.

Colin Powell in a speech to New York City teachers said, "Look, we operate under the assumption that everyone will succeed in a mission. We have to. We do our training to make it possible. Why isn't that the view the teachers have of their work—that they are not done until everyone succeeds?" Some people will instantly say that is impossible. I'm convinced that is not such an intelligent reaction. It has everything to do with what you see your mission as a teacher and a tester to be.

*Nickell*: Several states are looking at performance assessment to replace the traditional forms of standardized testing statewide. I know you have worked with a number of these programs. Do you feel this is a major trend that is going to become institutionalized as the way of assessing students in the future?

*Wiggins*: I am not convinced that's the case because of the considerable cost in money and time. Again, we are right back to the basic issue of purpose. The state is rarely in business to chart a course and set standards. The state's business is to make sure that people are getting a minimal education according to their constitutional right. Many teachers are utterly confused about the relationship between state tests and their teaching. A state test is merely a checkup. It's an indicator; it's an audit. The view that it is something that everybody should teach to is really quite wrongheaded. If everybody in the district were really holding people to the highest possible standards in social studies, the state test scores would zoom up.

Several states are developing performance assessments. I think that will continue. Certainly writing assessments have been fairly successful around the country. I think it is not at all likely that we will do what is common in Europe which is to rely more heavily on oral exams and simulations.

*Nickell*: What about the growing interest in portfolio assessments?

*Wiggins*: I think portfolios are probably more likely to take root because they are manageable from a time and cost perspective. And there's plenty of tradition of coming together to review student work in other countries and in professional disciplines in this country. By letting us sample more tasks, over time, we get more reliable—and authentic—evidence.

*Nickell*: We are beginning to hear more and more people talk about putting students in groups, having them perform a task, and then assessing their performance as a member of a group.

*Wiggins*: That goes back to the basic premise of the relationship between outcomes, assessment, and curriculum and instruction. This is an if/then statement: If you value the outcome that students will be able to collaborate effectively on complex tasks, then you ought to assess it. We have historically assessed only what is easy to test, not what's important or part of our stated outcomes. It is difficult, however, to test all our valued outcomes, and we shouldn't be naive about this. It's vital that any test meet all standards of validity and reliability, and with some collaborative forms of testing that is very difficult. So, it is a design challenge. Remember that in many instances it has been done for years and years. In vocational education they have collaborative competitions involving auto mechanics, finding the common defect in a car. I have seen a number of business class presentations that involve collaborative group efforts where student teams are devising a product or doing a market plan. I think what's instructive in those instances, by the way, is that there is a product that we can analyze, and through it we can analyze the contributions of the individual participants.

*Nickell*: It often seems as if group assessment is not as outcome-based as it is process-based.

*Wiggins*: It certainly shouldn't be. I don't want to see four students get A's for being collaborative if they produce a piece of junk. I think it is very useful to take the term performance assessment—collaborative or otherwise—quite literally. You aren't done until you do it right. And we look at the product to determine if the group was effective. Of course some people will say, "Well, gee, what if one good person does two-thirds of the work?" To which I say, more power to them. That's called smart behavior in the real world. After all, are we assessing group performance or are we assessing individual performance? Don't we want people to figure out intelligent ways to divide up the labor? Just because it doesn't suit your scoring system, you can't force people to work a certain way that is not natural if they have figured out a logical or comfortable way to do the task that you assign them. I would say, make it what I call "intellectual outward bound." Make it impossible for the group to succeed at the task unless the group acts like a good group. That's the design challenge.

*Nickell*: Dr. Wiggins, let's summarize for social studies teachers, administrators, and teacher educators. These are the people who are going to be looking at assessment over the next few years deciding what is best in their situation.

*Wiggins*: I would summarize by saying, let's begin with some of the national reports in social studies. Let's look, for instance, at the Bradley Commission report and see these really nice outcomes like "developed historical empathy" and "come to understand that times and places vary," and all the other things that are in that report. We must then ask the question, what does it mean to assess richly and deeply whether students have mastered these desired outcomes of social studies? What does it mean to do justice to the subject in terms of teaching the student? Assessment should be built out of the answers to those questions. It's a common-sense case that says if we value it, we should assess it. If we value research and presentation, we should assess it, because the opposite is also true. If we don't assess it, we won't get it, and we know that happens. The argument for authentic assessment is really just an argument for the articulation of assessment with curriculum and our objectives.

*Nickell*: On behalf of National Council for the Social Studies and all readers of this special section on testing, thank you so much for your important contribution. Best wishes as you continue your efforts to reform one of education's "precious antiques."

Pat Nickell, President of NCSS, is an eighteen-year veteran elementary teacher. Dr. Nickell is currently the Director of Instructional Improvement for the Fayette County Public Schools in Lexington, Kentucky. [1996 note]

# Portfolio Assessment and Social Studies: Collecting, Selecting, and Reflecting on What Is Significant

**Dennis M. Adams**
**Mary E. Hamm**

Educators generally agree that methods for assessing educational growth have not kept pace with the changing curriculum (Quinta and McKenna 1991). Traditional assessment generally ignores performance or process measures. Interest is growing in authentic (meaningful) assessment which allows students to select, collect, and reflect on their learning and gives them an opportunity to use critical-thinking skills as they select the academic efforts that might best represent them. The process itself is a powerful educational experience.

Although gaining popularity in art, writing, and reading classes, the concept of portfolio assessment has yet to span the entire curriculum. Teachers in mathematics, science, and social studies are just beginning to examine the possibility of using these processes to collect, organize, reflect on, and display selected work samples.

Various reading and writing projects have used portfolios for several years (Graves 1986). Harvard University has had a successful arts program for over five years that uses portfolios for instruction and evaluation (Mitchell 1989). In addition, the National Assessment of Educational Progress has recently suggested using portfolios to assess students' writing and reading abilities. With increasing frequency, colleges and universities are asking students to submit portfolios as part of their entrance requirements (Farr 1990). Schools are even beginning to evaluate faculty through teaching portfolios.

Assessment portfolios can assist teachers in monitoring and evaluating students' performance. The information accumulated in a portfolio assists teachers in diagnosing learners' strengths and weaknesses. Teachers can also use the information to gain an understanding of student achievement, knowledge, and attitudes. Portfolios allow the individuals represented to become aware of their own learning history and to become directly involved in assessing their progress. Thus, the barrier between the learner and the assessment of the learner starts to crumble and assessment can become a form of personal development and instruction.

## THE PORTFOLIO AS AN ASSESSMENT TOOL

A portfolio contains evidence of an individual's skills and dispositions. More than a "folder" of work, a portfolio represents a deliberate, specific collection of a student's accomplishments.

---

Reprinted from *Social Education*, February 1992, Volume 56, Number 2. Copyright 1992 by National Council for the Social Studies.

---

| WHAT MIGHT BE INCLUDED IN A TEACHING PORTFOLIO |
| --- |

1. Instructor's personal assessment of students, colleagues, school, and self-appraisal of performance.
2. Detailed representative course outline or lesson plan.
3. Description of steps taken to evaluate or improve one's teaching (self-evaluation, attending workshops, obtaining instructional development grants).
4. Student evaluation data from several courses.
5. Current research, publication, and community and professional service efforts.
6. Principal or supervisor's assessment.
7. Assessment of student progress during a course of study.
8. Any wrong turns?
9. Statement from colleagues who have observed the instructor teaching.
10. Statement from colleagues who have observed the instructor's materials, lesson plans, student work, and creative accomplishments.
11. Videotape of the instructor teaching a class.
12. Personal statement by the instructor describing future teaching goals. With this kind of reflection teachers can see their professional growth over time. The goal is to open people's minds to positive change.

---

The student and the teacher select the items carefully to represent a cross section of the student's creative efforts. Portfolios can be used as a tool in the classroom to bring students together, to discuss ideas, and to provide evidence of understanding and the ability to apply it. Through critical analysis of their work—and the work of peers—students gain insight into other ways of looking at a problem. They develop new understandings of their thinking as they become accomplished at evaluating their own work.

Teachers are using portfolios to document students' development and focus on their growth over time, emphasizing performance and application, rather than knowledge. Portfolios can assist teachers in diagnosing and understanding student learning difficulties including problems with growth in ability, attitudes, skill development, expression, and the ability to collaborate with others. Because they assess student progress over time, they can help students improve their learning and teachers improve their teaching.

## THE PURPOSE AND DESIGN OF A PORTFOLIO

A one-time collection of examples cannot build an adequate picture of students' understanding. Portfolios provide a means of gathering representative material over time. Teachers should give careful attention to:

■ what is assessed
■ the portfolio's design
■ the appropriateness of the contents to what is assessed
■ the intended audience

The purpose of the portfolio should determine its design. The teacher, the student, or the nature of the portfolio's contents can determine its range and depth. Teachers could ask students to select examples of their work that fit into categories such as:

■ a sample that reflects a problem that was difficult for you
■ work that shows where you started to figure it out
■ a sample that shows you reached a solution
■ a sample that shows you learned something new
■ a sample of work in which you need to keep searching for ideas
■ two items of which you are proud
■ one example of a comical disaster

Involving students in the selection process allows them to participate directly in their learning and evaluation, thus promoting intellectual autonomy and self-respect. Learners, teachers, and parents can improve their understanding of the student both in and out of school because portfolio contents can reveal a surprising depth of thinking and provide insights into personal issues. Collecting, organizing, and reflecting on their school experience and that of their peers allows students to communicate who they are and how they view themselves in relation to others. According to Mumme (1990) portfolios may include such things as:

■ group assignments and team ideas
■ teacher comments and assessments
■ student writings
■ student reflections, journal entries, reactions, and feelings
■ collected data entries, logs, and research
■ problems and investigations
■ individual and group projects
■ creative expressions (art, audio- and videotapes, and photographs)
■ rough drafts and polished products

Items selected should be dated and accompanied by a caption or description. A cover letter by the author, a table of contents, and a description of the assignment or task are other ways to assist the reader. As the portfolio develops, students can add, delete, improve, revise, edit, or discard some of its contents. Each element can represent a different form of expression and means of representing the knowledge and skills acquired.

## PRACTICAL QUESTIONS TEACHERS FREQUENTLY ASK

What type of physical container would hold representative pieces?

■ For older students a three-ring binder is most frequently used for items such as oral history interviews, copies of historical documents, photos of community service activities, worksheets, and class notes. Handouts can be three-hole punched and added to journal entries, written comments, quizzes, and other documents. Students may wish to purchase three-ring separators with folder compartments to insert items such as maps, magazines, or software disks. More elaborate kinds of three-ring notebook containers may include plastic casings in which students can insert pictures, articles, and posters.

■ An artist's folder (portfolio container) is useful for gathering things like video cassettes and three-dimensional projects. The cardboard folder has a string closure to prevent things from falling out. They are fairly inexpensive and come in a variety of sizes from three by five inches for index cards to three by three feet for larger projects. Photographs can be taken of large projects and videotapes made of others.

■ Elementary teachers often use large boxes. Students place their written work in folders by subject and place the folder in a decorated box labeled with the student's name. Other items are also included in the box. The items may change from month to month, but the boxes are kept for the entire year. Selected "treasures" remain. Boxes are stacked for easy access and neatness.

■ A combination of containers may be the best approach depending on the contents and nature of the assessment.

## WHO USES PORTFOLIOS?

Portfolio assessment is not just for younger students. Students from kindergarten through graduate school can benefit from using assessment portfolios.

## HOW ARE PORTFOLIOS EVALUATED?

Suggested criteria for evaluating student portfolios follow.

*Evidence of critical and creative thinking.* Does the student's work show that he or she has:

■ demonstrated an understanding of the responsibilities of citizenship?
■ organized and displayed data?
■ conjectured, explored, analyzed, or looked for patterns in assignments?
■ made use of the intellectual tools of analog and inquiry?
■ evidenced an understanding of democratic values and social responsibility?
■ used concrete materials (or drawings or sketches) as an aid for interpreting and analyzing problems or issues?
■ used technology (video excerpts, computers, graphics, or calculators) to suggest solutions to problems?
■ searched for information, and explored and critically examined research data?

*Quality of activities and investigations.* Will the student's activities or investigations help him or her develop an understanding of significant social studies concepts? Do the activities cut across several social science disciplines?

*Variety of approaches and investigations.* Does the portfolio provide evidence that the student used a variety of approaches? Does the portfolio include a variety of resources and provide research to support opinions and differing approaches to solving a problem? Does the portfolio include a variety of activities or investigations?

*Demonstrate understanding and skill in situations that parallel previous classroom experience.* The portfolio should provide evidence that the student understands the reason for using certain procedures, what they are looking for, and what the data mean.

*Assessment should be integrative.* Is assessment oriented toward critical thinking and solving problems, not simply based upon recall? Some other integrative assessments that can be added to the portfolio include:

- observational notes by the teacher
- student self-assessment
- progress notes written by the teacher and student— often these are written collaboratively

Portfolios are nothing more than a technique. If we put standardized test scores in we are missing the point. Portfolios, if used correctly, provide teachers with the opportunity to stress what they value as important in the learning process.

## PORTFOLIO ASSESSMENT AND THE CURRICULUM OF THE 1990s

The great moral attribute of self-government (popular sovereignty) cannot be born and matured in a day; and if children are not trained to it, we only prepare ourselves for disappointment if we expect it from grown men....As the fitting apprenticeship for despotism consists in being trained to despotism, so the fitting apprenticeship for self government consists in being trained to self-government.

—*Horace Mann*

Learning requires communication—with self, peers, and knowledgeable authorities. It also requires effort and meaningful assessments of these efforts. Since students need to be involved actively in evaluating and providing examples of their own learning, they must document the probing questions they are asking, identify what they are thinking, and reflect on their understandings. In this way students can create, evaluate, and act upon material that they and others value. Assuming active roles in the learning process and taking responsibility for what students are learning goes beyond simply recognizing that they have made a mistake to imagining why, getting feedback from others, and finding practical ways to do something about it.

Portfolios provide a powerful way to link learning with assessment. They can provide evidence of performance that goes far beyond factual knowledge and offers a clear and understandable picture of student achievement. They also provide opportunities for improved student self-image and self-worth. They can enhance self-esteem by having students take active roles in selecting and evaluating what they have learned.

Selections, journal entries, and organizational style reveal important information about their own attitudes. Portfolios provide a chance to look at what and how students are learning while paying attention to their own ideas and thinking processes. This can help both teachers and parents. As children express ideas and reveal their thinking, teachers gain insights into how to design instruction to match students' demonstrated needs. Thus, portfolios are an ongoing conversation between student and student, student and teacher, and student and self.

To function in the future, students need to become actively involved in evaluating their own learning. Constructing portfolios can contribute to helping schoolwork promote an attitude of efficacy, wonder, and curiosity that stirs an appetite for lifelong learning. As students learn to work cooperatively in small groups, write about and discuss their ideas, keep journals, brainstorm, share, and construct portfolios, they expand their knowledge, horizons, and possibilities. Through such collaboration in a caring community, students construct meaning as they document and build their knowledge of themselves and the world.

## REFERENCES

Adams, Dennis, and Mary Hamm. *Cooperative Learning: Critical Thinking and Collaboration across the Curriculum.* Springfield, Ill.: Thomas, 1990.

Farr, R. "Trends, Setting Directions for Language Arts Portfolios." *Educational Leadership* 48 (1990): 103.

Frederiksen, N. "The Real Test Bias: Influence of Testing on Teaching and Learning." *American Psychologist* 39, no. 3 (1981): 193-202.

Graves, D. Writing: *Teachers and Children at Work.* Portsmouth, N.H.: Heinemann Educational Books, 1983.

Hamm, Mary, and Dennis Adams. *The Collaborative Dimensions of Learning.* Norwood, N.J.: Ablex, forthcoming.

Mitchell, R. *Portfolio Newsletter of Arts PROPEL.* Cambridge, Mass.: Harvard University Press, 1989.

Montey Neill, D., and N. Medina. "Standardized Testing: Harmful to Educational Health." *Phi Delta Kappan* 70 (May 1989): 688–697.

Mumme, J. *Portfolio Assessment in Mathematics.* California Mathematics Project. Santa Barbara: University of California, 1990.

National Commission on Testing and Public Policy. *From Gatekeeper to Gateway: Transforming Testing in America.* Chestnut Hill, Mass.: National Commission on Testing and Public Policy, 1990.

Quinta, F., and B. McKenna. *Alternatives to Standardized Testing.* Washington, D.C.: National Education Association, 1991.

Resnick, L. *Education and Learning to Think*. Washington, D.C.: National Academy Press, 1987.

White, E. M. *Teaching and Assessing Writing*. San Francisco: Jossey-Bass, 1985.

Wiggins, G. "A True Test: Toward More Equitable Assessment." *Phi Delta Kappan* 70 (September 1989): 703–713.

Dennis M. Adams is a Professor in the Education Department at Green Mountain College in Poultney, Vermont. Mary E. Hamm is an Associate Professor of Elementary Education at San Francisco State University in San Francisco, California. Both have coauthored a number of books and articles on education including *Cooperative Learning* (Charles Thomas, 1990), *Cooperative Learning and Educational Media* (Educational Technology Publications, 1990), and *The Collaborative Dimensions of Learning* (Ablex Corporation, in press). They are currently collaborating on a new book: *New Instructional Developments for Teaching and Learning for the 21st Century* (Jossey-Bass). [1992 note]

# APPENDIX

## ADDITIONAL RESOURCES FOR CURRICULUM DEVELOPMENT AND UNIT AND LESSON IDEAS

Social studies teachers are eager to find additional sources for information about a particular topic as they begin to develop curriculum and plan instructional strategies. The following list of professional organizations offers a variety of teacher and/or student materials useful in teaching social studies. Readers of this publication are urged to contact them for additional assistance.

**American Bar Association**
Youth Education Publications
ABA Division for Public Education
541 North Fairbanks Court
Chicago, IL 60611-3314

**Center for Civic Education**
5146 Douglas Fir Road
Calabasas, CA 91302-1467

**Educators for Social Responsibility**
23 Garden Street
Cambridge, MA 02138

**ERIC Clearinghouse for Social Studies/Social Science Education (ERIC ChESS)**
2805 East Tenth Street, Suite 120
Indiana University
Bloomington, IN 47408

**National Center for History in the Schools**
University of California, Los Angeles
10880 Wilshire Blvd., Suite 761
Los Angeles, CA 90024-4108

**National Council on Economic Education**
1140 Avenue of the Americas
New York, NY 10036

**National Council for Geographic Education**
Indiana University of Pennsylvania
Indiana, PA 15705

**National Council for History Education (NCHE)**
26915 Westwood Road
Suite B-2
Westlake, OH 44145-4656

**National Council for the Social Studies**
3501 Newark Street, NW
Washington, DC 20016-3167
http://www.ncss.org

**National Geographic Society**
1145 17th Street, NW
Washington, DC 20036-4688

**Social Studies Education Consortium (SSEC)**
P.O. Box 21270
Boulder, CO 80308-4270

*Teaching Tolerance* is available to educators free of charge (when requested on letterhead) from:
**Southern Poverty Law Center**
400 Washington Avenue
Montgomery, AL 36104

For detailed copies of the various standards available, readers should contact these sources:

*Expectations of Excellence: Curriculum Standards for Social Studies* — National Council for the Social Studies

*National Standards for Civics and Government* — Center for Civic Education

*National Geography Standards* — National Council for Geographic Education

*National Standards for United States History* — National Center for History in the Schools

*National Standards for World History* — National Center for History in the Schools

*National Standards for Economic Education* — National Council on Economic Education

Several states are in the process of adopting social studies standards, revising curriculum, selecting textbooks, and developing assessment tools. The editors recommend that teachers contact the state social studies consultant at the state education agency, social studies professors of education at a nearby college or university, and/or social studies district coordinators for assistance in using the NCSS standards. In addition, these educational leaders should be able to inform teachers about social studies and social studies-related activities, such as the state geographic alliance workshops and meetings of the state and/or local social studies councils within their state. The editors urge teachers to be active in their schools, districts, and states, as well as in NCSS, as a part of their citizenship responsibilities to colleagues, students, and the larger community.